AF473726

TIME TO ACT

FOR THE ACTORS

Many sessions have taken place in addition to the ones represented in this book. It is an on-going project and the actors who have not been selected so far will appear in subsequent volumes, which will focus on other themes. My sincere thanks to them.

TIME TO ACT

SIMON ANNAND

Foreword
CATE BLANCHETT

Introduction
VICTORIA BROACKES

Design
LOUISE BRODY

TERRA

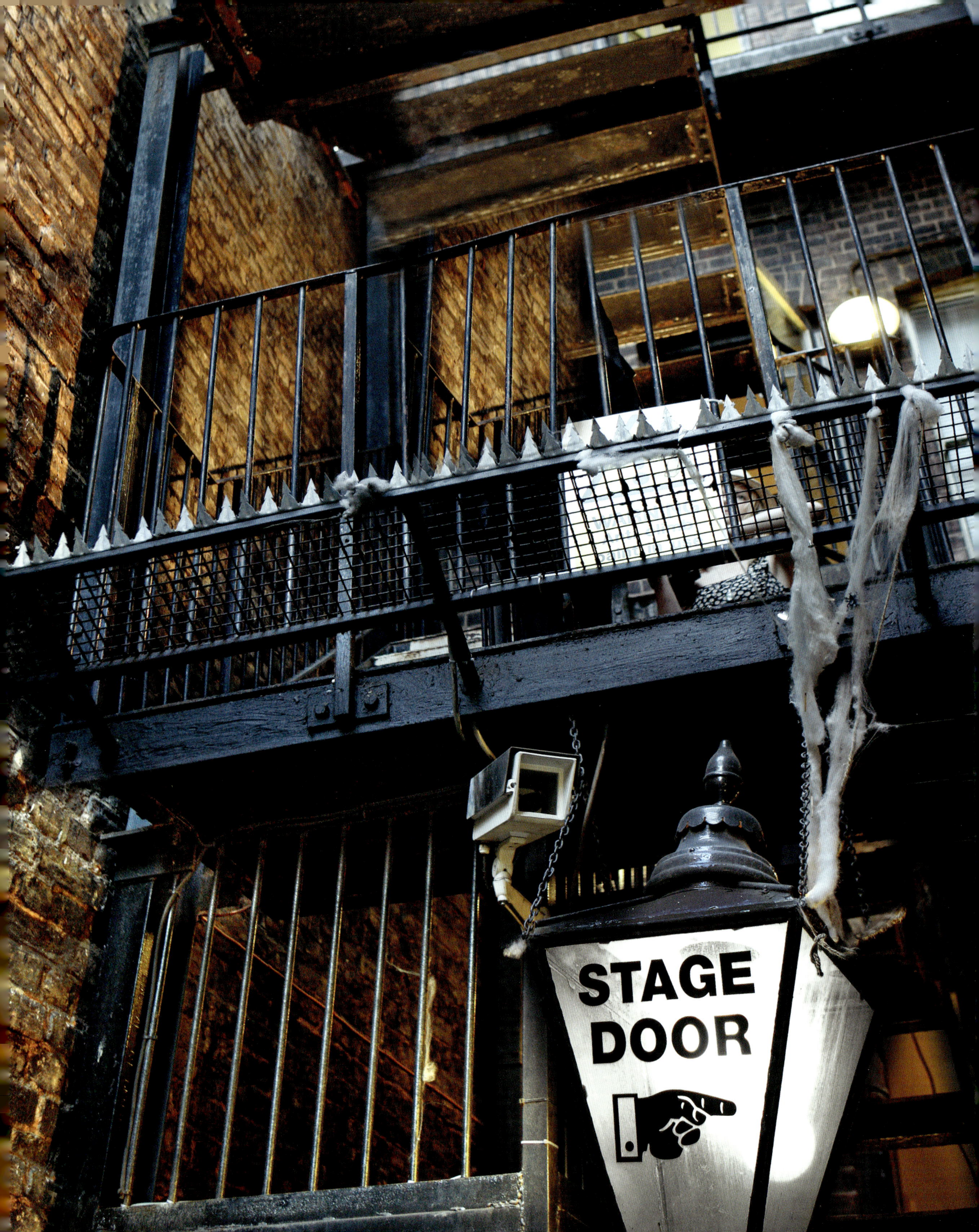
STAGE
DOOR

I love actors. It's a weakness in a producer, but it explains why I jumped at the chance to be involved with the book you're now holding.

The vulnerability of actors is extreme. Their power is also extreme.

I find it impossible not to love the people who create this world of such extreme highs and lows. And you can see how Simon also loves them, how he documents the way they travel from living as themselves to inhabiting someone else, how he frames them in situ, in cramped dressing rooms and crowded corridors, or peering into their mirrors as if they are trying to identify the people they're about to become.

When Simon and I first discussed this book we saw it as an extension to *The Half*, his first essay in demonstrating the passage of the actor from street to stage. We couldn't have known how his photographs would also be permanent records of a world that may, I fear, never again exist so exuberantly.

Treasure this trove, please.

PETER WILSON
Producer, *The Woman in Black, An Inspector Calls*

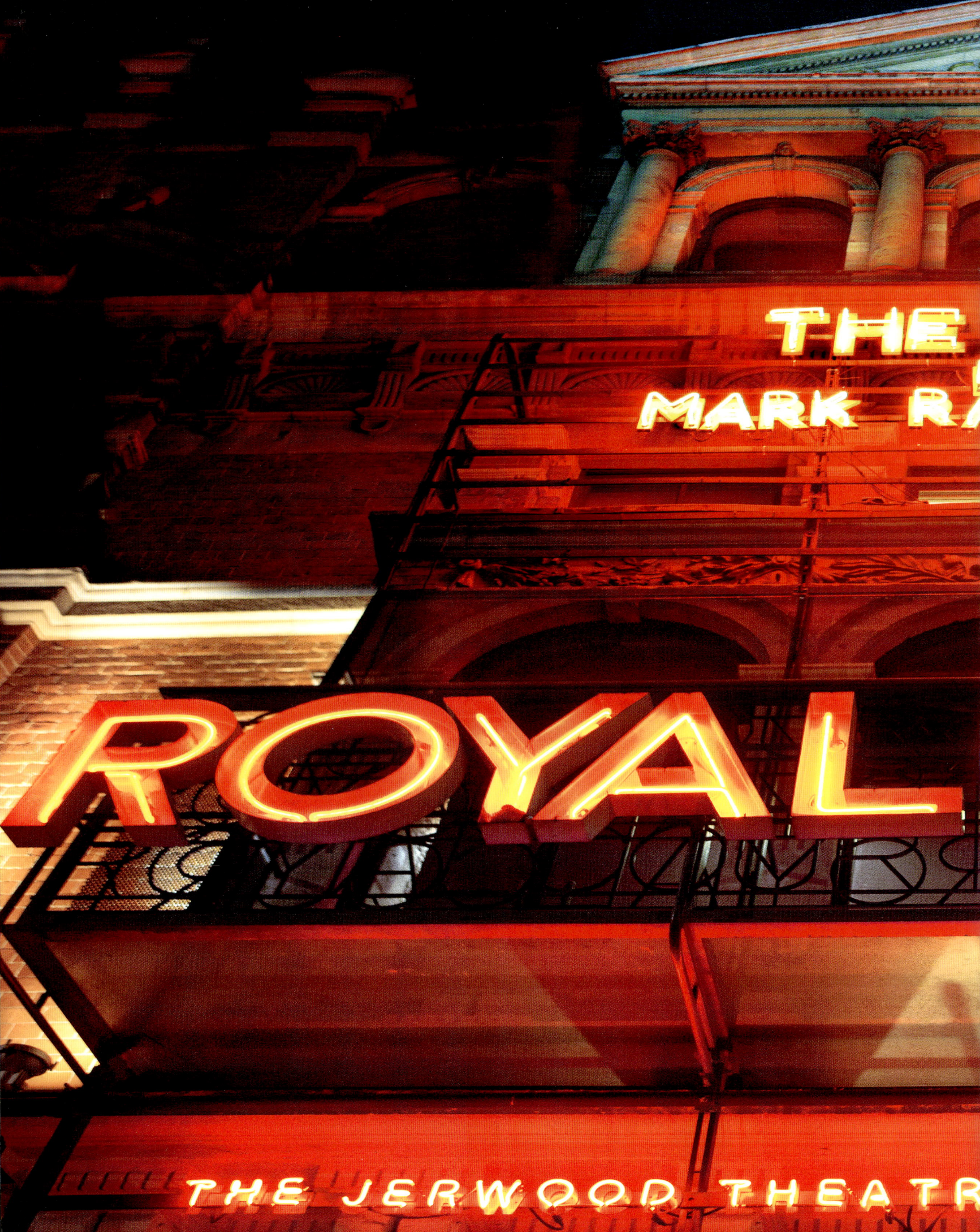
THE
MARK
ROYAL
THE JERWOOD

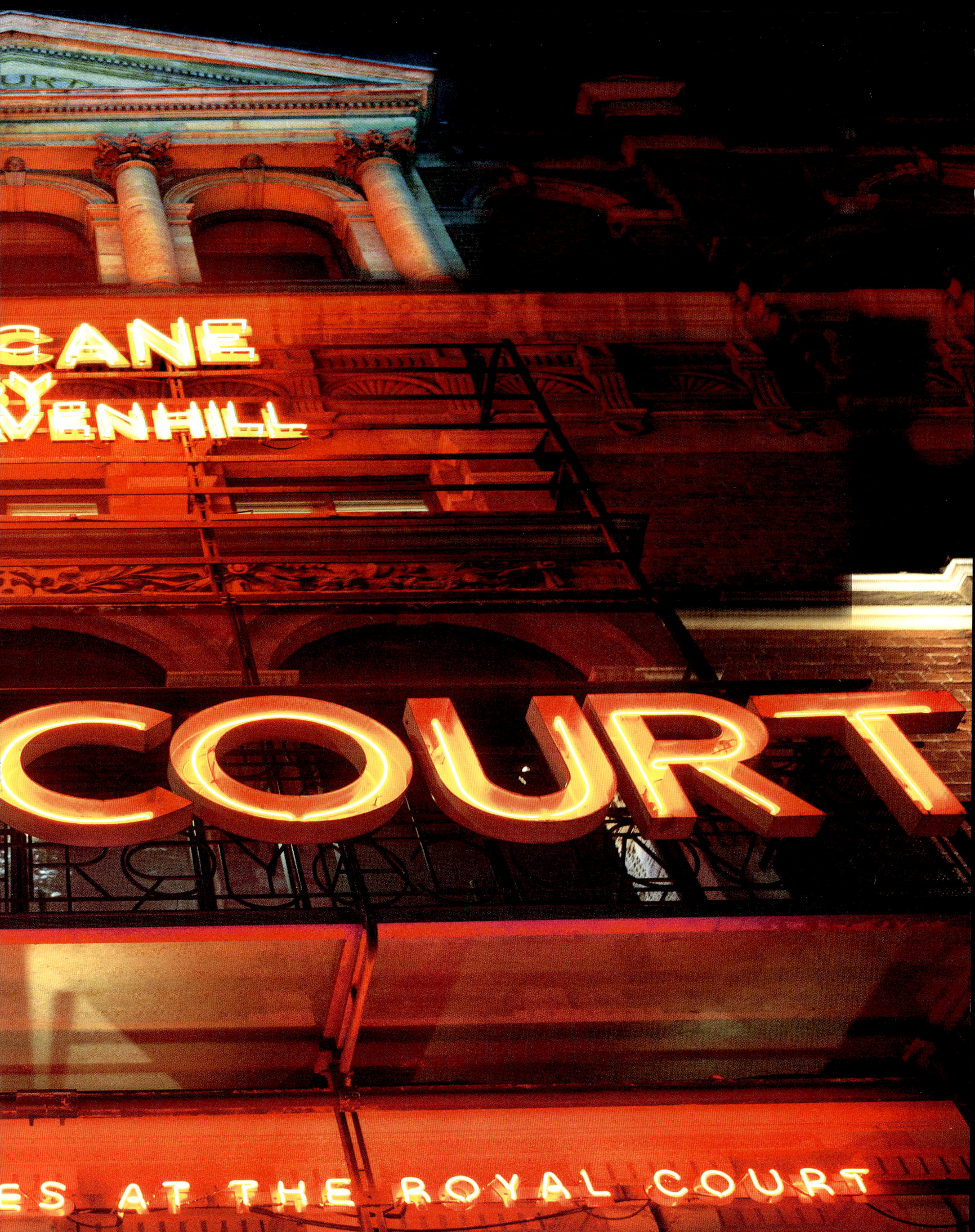
CANE
VENHILL
COURT
ES AT THE ROYAL COURT

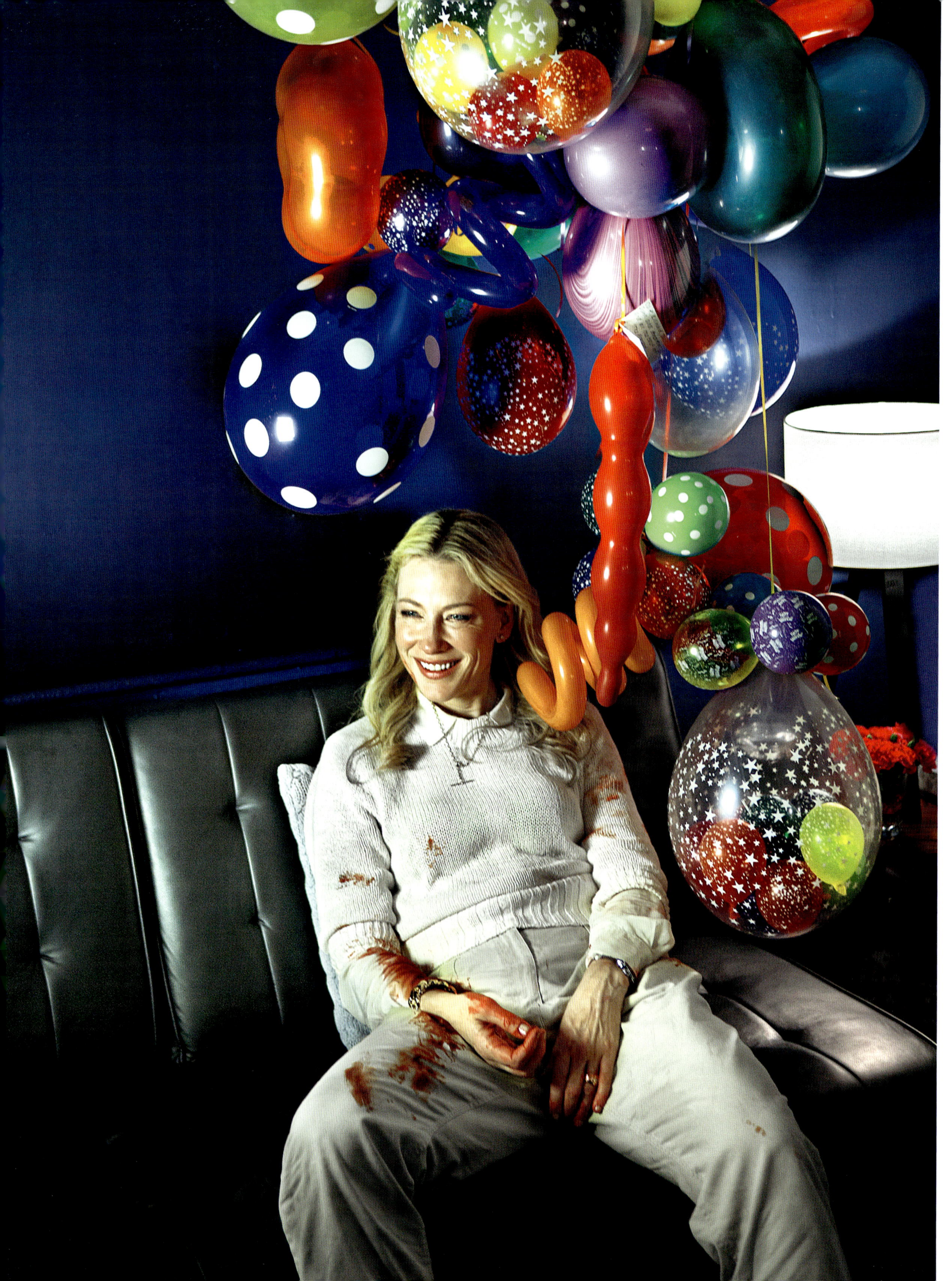

FOREWORD

The dressing room is a strange space. Intensely private, full of superstitions, whirling with thoughts and emotions, yet simultaneously intensely public – people running in and out, mic checks. An intimacy of dressers. Last-minute notes being given. Jokes cracked. 'The front curtain isn't operational tonight, so we need to gather in five to re-block the opening...'

A flurry of ablutions, hilarious observations shared from the journey in from the so-called 'real' world to this, our deeply unreal reality of the half hour until act one beginners, when we throw ourselves into the ring and see what happens. Will it happen tonight?

Into this swirl, for the last thirty-seven years, Simon Annand has been quietly welcomed. Only he, who has spent so long inside rehearsal rooms capturing the dynamic and expressing the movement of performers in action – the muscular conversation that is putting on a theatrical production – would be able to enter the backstage area, camera in hand, and cause nary a ripple...

It is as difficult to capture actors and creative teams in unselfconscious action as it is to arrest birds in flight. His aim is to illuminate the process (and in the case of Annand's book *The Half*, to present prelude and aftermath) in a way that invites an understanding in the viewer. And now, in *Time to Act*, he deepens this exploration further.

But there lies Simon's skill. He is inside this process with his subjects. His sensitivity to atmosphere is, quite simply, astonishing. His decades-long examination of lives lived in the theatre is an invitation into very private worlds, at the second before they become public.

It is an opportunity, in a world obsessed with outcomes, to understand procedure – the constant, restless process of actors searching for becoming, for danger, for risk, for the journey itself, without expectation that a definitive destination will ever be reached.

The readiness is all.

'Act one beginners – stand by, lighting, hair, wardrobe, wigs and make-up!'

CATE BLANCHETT

CATE BLANCHETT, ETHEL BARRYMORE THEATER, 2017

FOLLOWING PAGES: The Harold Pinter Theatre and their display in the stage-door area where the actors sign in. It is interesting to see the kinds of images used to promote actors in different eras, and how many distinguished actors have worked at this theatre.

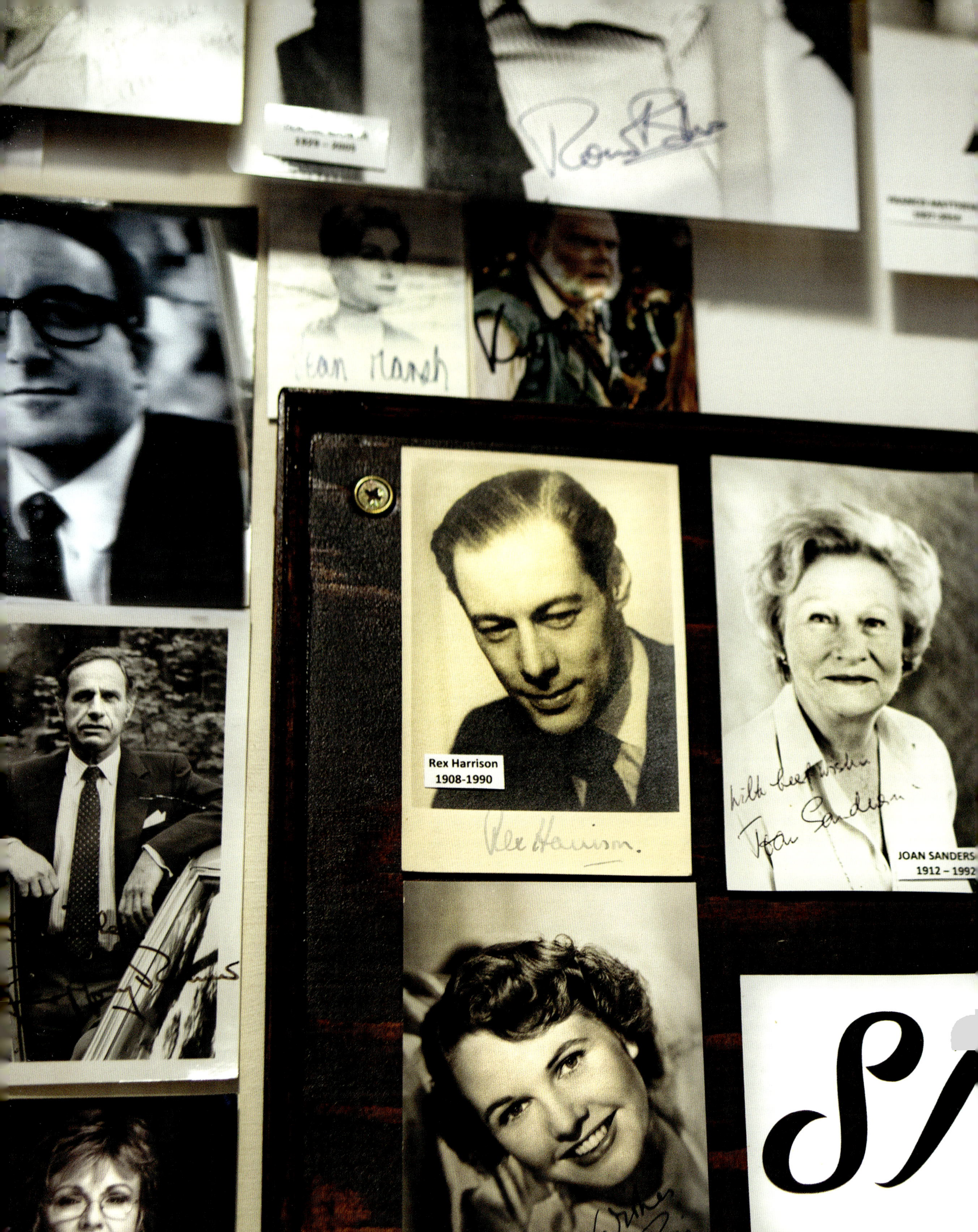
Rex Harrison
1908-1990
JOAN SANDERS
1912 – 1992

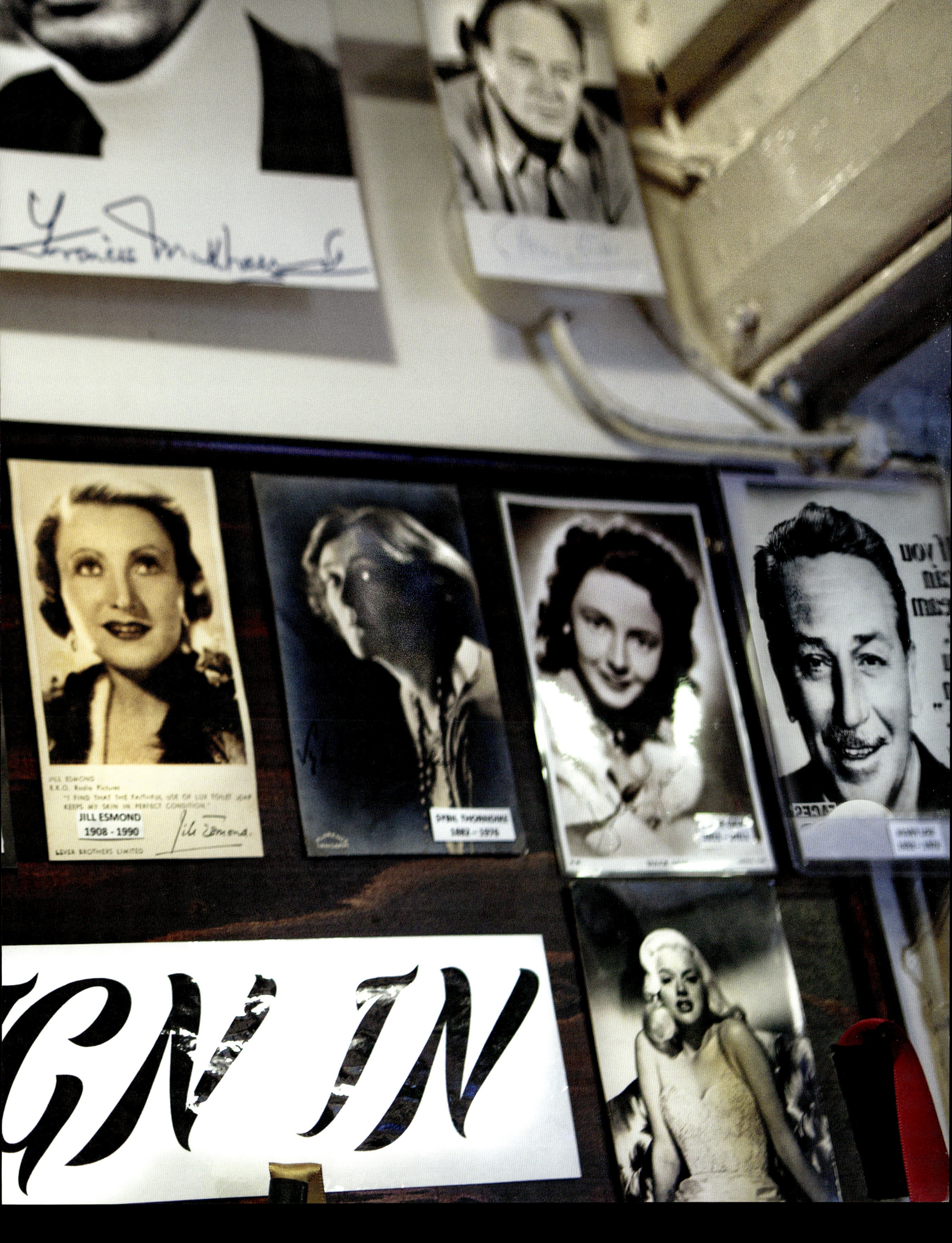
JILL ESMOND
1908 - 1990
GN IN

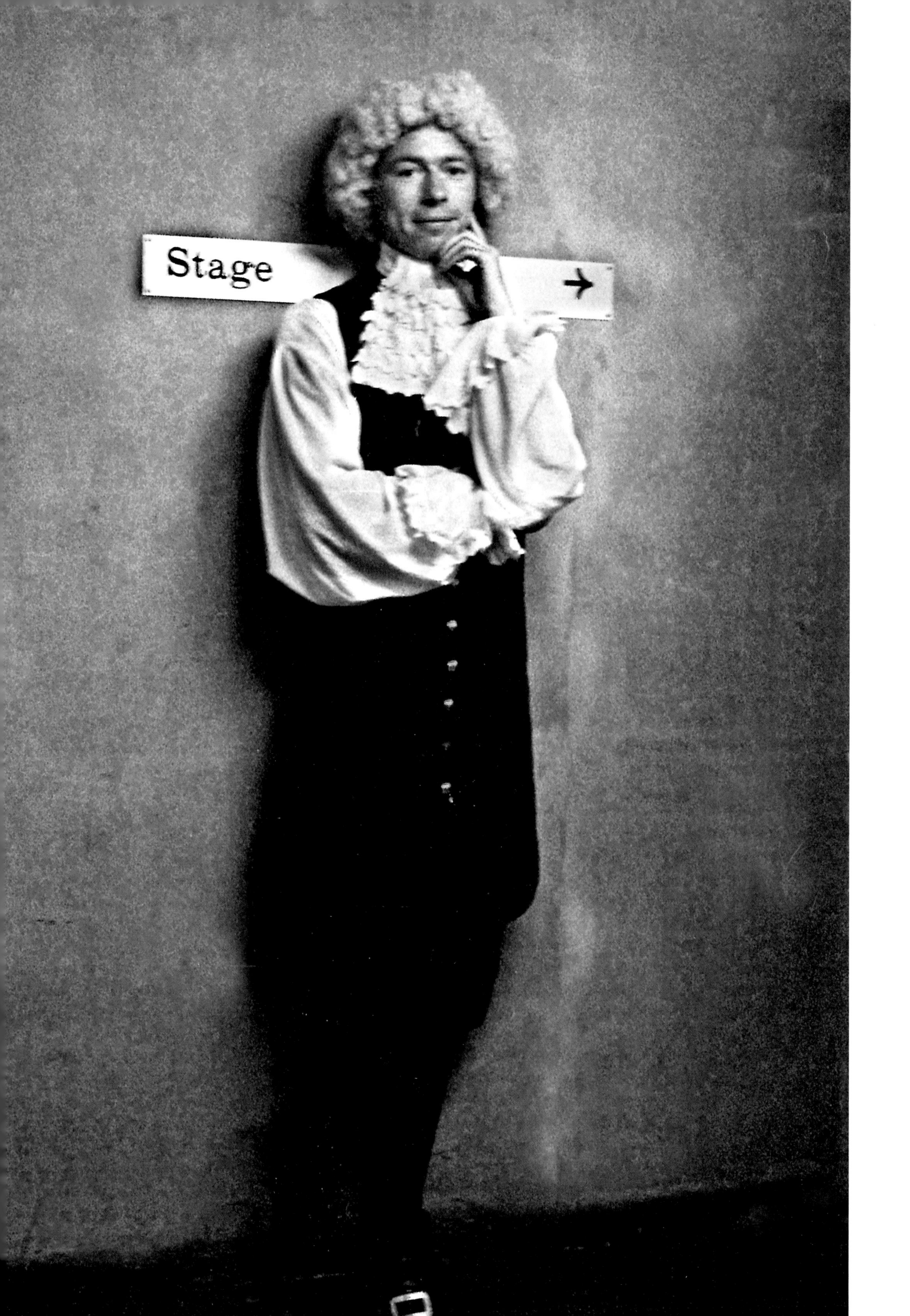
Stage

SIMON ANNAND'S WORLD

I cannot precisely remember when I first encountered Simon Annand. But around 2004 I do remember a meeting to view his work in the (now closed) V&A Theatre Museum in Covent Garden, and finding it immediately fascinating. One does not need to be an actor or theatre professional to feel the compelling power of Simon's photographs – images of an actor in the final moments before he or she steps onto the stage in front of an audience. One does not even need to know the actor or the character they are about to play. Even without these, the photographs elicit a pure human empathy for the act of preparation, the glimpse into a private moment when the actor must leave all thoughts and concerns of the day behind and transform him or herself into whoever he is to play that night. It is both imaginable and unimaginable.

It has been my pleasure to have known Simon Annand since then. This early meeting led to the first of several iterations of an exhibition created at the V&A with Simon, which in various forms toured the UK and the continent over several years. For this first exhibition in 2005, we named the show *The Dressing Room*, in part because we were unsure whether the general public understood the term 'the half' and its significance, in part because we conceived the idea of exhibiting the photographs in the actual dressing rooms of the small studio theatre at the heart of the V&A Theatre Museum. Along with the psychological insights the photographs revealed, their window into the dressing rooms of major stars and West End theatres was itself fascinating.

An early photo, about to go on stage as a servant at the Lyric Theatre Hammersmith in Bill Gaskill's production of *The Relapse*, 1983. For two years I had been serving at the bar, eager to experience what it was like to actually be on the stage, with a live audience staring back at you. The servant had no lines and his main function was to accompany the lead actor Simon Callow, who played Lord Foppington, at one point carrying him around in a Sedan chair.

Contrary to the glamorous image of theatre dressing rooms that we might imagine, most people would be surprised to see the cramped conditions in many British theatres today. Particularly in older theatres, where there is no space to expand backstage, facilities can be scruffy, and even modern ones can be functional and confined – they are rarely luxurious. Even so, modern dressing rooms are generally an improvement on those of the past. In Elizabethan Britain, actors dressed in communal changing rooms in the 'tiring house' (the attiring house) behind the stage. When, from 1660, women were also allowed to act on the public stage, separate dressing areas were provided for them in the larger theatres. Then, as now, the stars were given private rooms in which to prepare, whilst the rest of the company shared. In smaller theatres, facilities were often communal, and touring companies had to make do with any available space.

Although leading actors may have had their own rooms, privacy was not a priority – anyone could visit the 'tiring rooms' to see the actors and glimpse backstage life. Thankfully for actors, this has changed – 'the half' is recognised as a precious and necessary half-hour of calm and privacy. But thankfully for us, Simon's photographs take us into this unseen world, to capture these moments of intense concentration, transformation and nerves that have been hidden from public view for centuries. Alongside revealing so

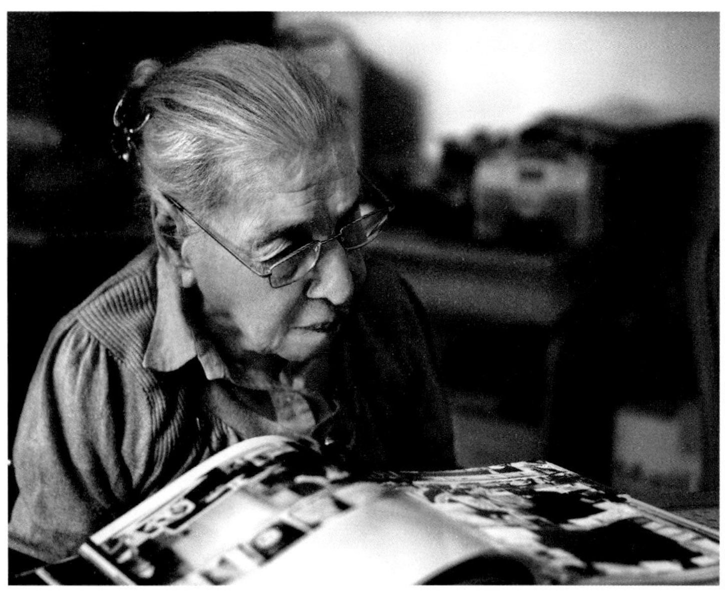

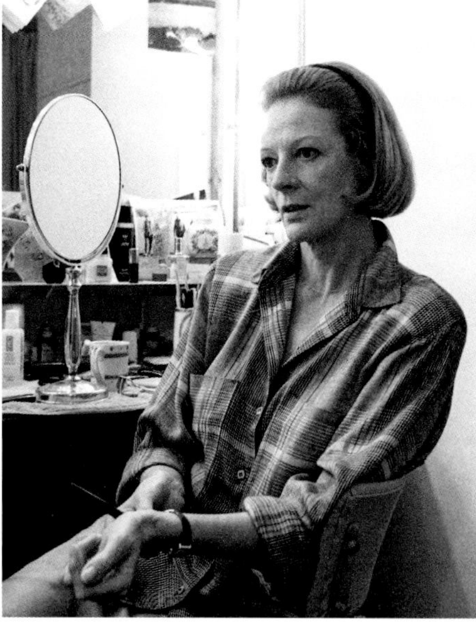

much of the real person transforming into their character, they also highlight how modern performers – even the stars – often have to make do with the facilities used by their Victorian predecessors. This also speaks volumes about the profession and the commitment of those that work in it.

In curating *The Dressing Room* at the Theatre Museum, we went all out to evoke both the atmosphere and the psychology of 'the half'. With Simon's photographs as the centrepiece of every room, we furnished the dressing rooms as if they were in use, with notes and flowers, used ashtrays, make-up and hair accoutrements. We even created a soundtrack in this private space in the countdown to performance; a mixture of Tannoy announcements, from 'This is your quarter hour call. Fifteen minutes to Act I. Your quarter hour call. Thank you'; to semi-private announcements, 'Can whoever owns the red Beetle parked in Bay B please move it'; to the actors' imagined own reflections, 'I wonder if that newspaper's theatre critic will be in tonight'; and even unwanted thoughts that could crowd into an unquiet mind: 'Did I remember to turn the oven off?'

Simon started this body of work thirty-seven years ago, and the continuously expanding collection has gone from strength to strength and been seen around the world. Since opening at the Theatre Museum in 2005, *The Dressing Room* became *The Half*, and travelled to nineteen venues over thirteen years, including the National Theatre in London, the Wales Millennium Centre in Cardiff, the Arles Photography Festival in France, the V&A in London, the Royal Shakespeare Company in Stratford upon Avon, the Bakhrushin State Theatre Museum in Moscow and the Player's Club in New York.

In recent years, social media has given us an insight into the 'backstage' world (in all its forms) of the famous, but the images people choose to share of their own lives are different, rarely capturing them at their most private and vulnerable, as Simon's photographs do. However 'natural' they seem, we know there is an element of staging that comes with projecting an image of oneself online. To be able to capture actors in moments of natural, unposed concentration demands a very strange dual skillset: having the confidence to be the only other presence in the room, snapping away at such a personal, high-stakes and intimate moment, whilst also being able to become somewhat invisible and allowing the actor to undergo their necessary and usually solitary preparation.

ABOVE LEFT: Eve Arnold looking at my book, *The Half* in 2008. I was fortunate to get to know Eve in her later years. Given her deep knowledge of both photography and actors, when she confided in me 'if only I had thought of this idea', the encouragement gave me a moment of infinite clarity and affirmation.

ABOVE RIGHT: Maggie Smith, *Interpreters*, Queen's Theatre, 1985. She was extremely generous with her time. We spent two unforgettable hours chatting before taking a single photo.

OPPOSITE: Anthony Hopkins, *Pravda*, National Theatre, 1986. In those days, interviews were part of the session and Tony explained at length why he had returned from America. His portrayal of Lambert LeRoux was the strongest performance of power I ever saw.

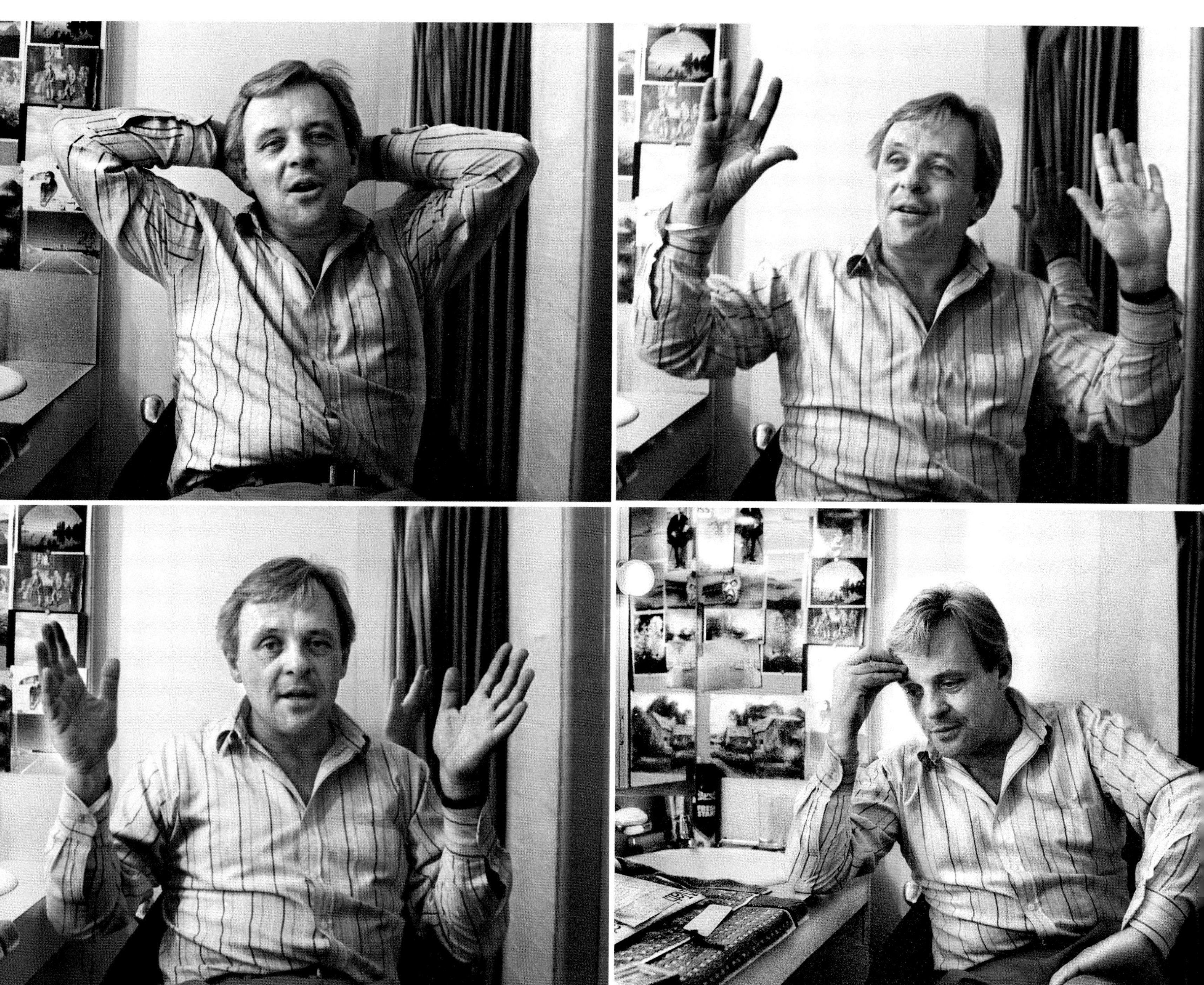

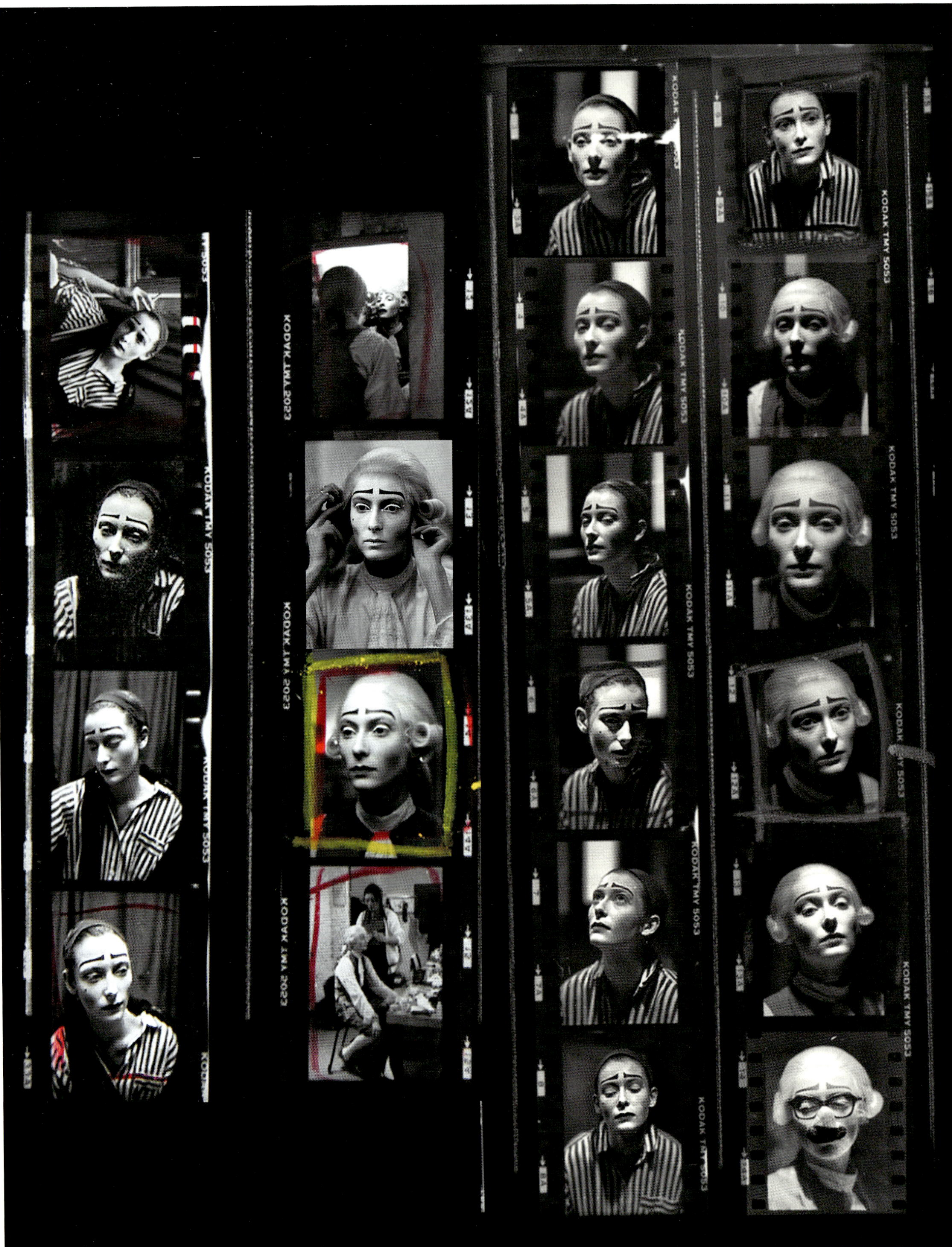
KODAK TMY 5053

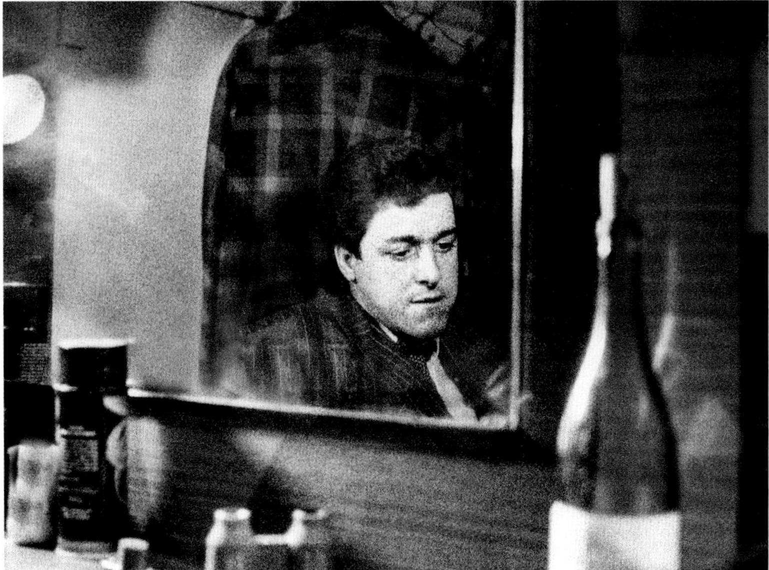

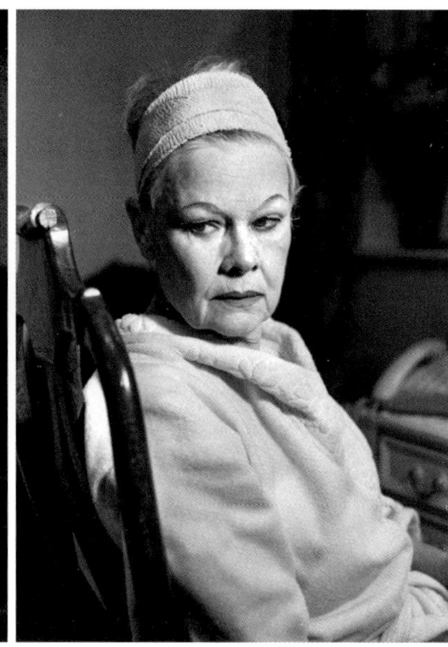

Simon has always attested that the photographs are not an attempt to chronicle a certain period in London theatre, or to suggest that the productions chosen are better than others which may not have been included. It is all about the actors – who have always been personally selected by Simon, rather than commissioned for a magazine or newspaper.

So who is this man behind the camera? Quietly spoken and thoughtful, Simon's personality lends itself perfectly to his line of work. He possesses great knowledge and appreciation of theatre, and of the art and practice of photography, allied with precision and determination to achieve only the best. Simon's enthusiasm for the theatre began as a pupil in the 1960s at a school with its own Victorian replica of a Greek theatre. But the first time he was paid to shoot a major production came in the 1980s at London's Old Vic theatre, when Jonathan Miller became artistic director. Since then, Simon has taken production photographs and been fortunate to work on a number of important productions (including *War Horse* and *Jerusalem*) and for other great directors. These experiences gave Simon the opportunity to work on a wealth of different shows, from the modern classics of Ibsen, Chekhov, Strindberg, and Pinter, to Shakespeare in many forms, as well as musicals, pantomime, opera, experimental and physical theatre, international circus and even burlesque. This book brings these strands together, avoiding any hierarchy. Simon, looking back across all these styles and forms, says: 'Each one has its own complexity and each one is as difficult to perform as another.'

Some of the images are intended to be 'fly-on-the-wall' in their approach and others are not. What links them is an aesthetic which is essentially humanist, rather than predatory. The actors are seen as workers, not celebrities. His photographs reveal a fragility and humanness, without undermining the courage that comes with being a performer. They also give an insight into the intimacy of the actor's dressing rooms and the various ways they mentally prepare: a calming cigarette; a final bit of chat with co-stars; the finishing touches of make-up; or perfecting the body language of their character… Simon is on the actor's side and his camera respects all facets of their preparation before going live on stage.

Victoria Broackes, Senior Curator, V&A Department of Theatre and Performance

OPPOSITE: Tilda Swinton, *Mozart and Salieri*, Almeida, 1989. Tilda is photogenic doing just about anything.

ABOVE LEFT: Griff Rhys Jones, *Charley's Aunt*, Lyric Theatre Hammersmith, 1983. The first dressing-room photograph I ever took. Griff was playing an ebullient character, which contrasted with the melancholic atmosphere in his room. It was this that gave me the idea for a book on 'the half', a project which continues to this day.

ABOVE RIGHT: Judi Dench, *The Royal Family*, Theatre Royal Haymarket, 2001. Judi has been very supportive of *The Half* project, ever since the early 1980s. For this I am eternally grateful. She is universally loved for her work, her sense of humour and her kindness.

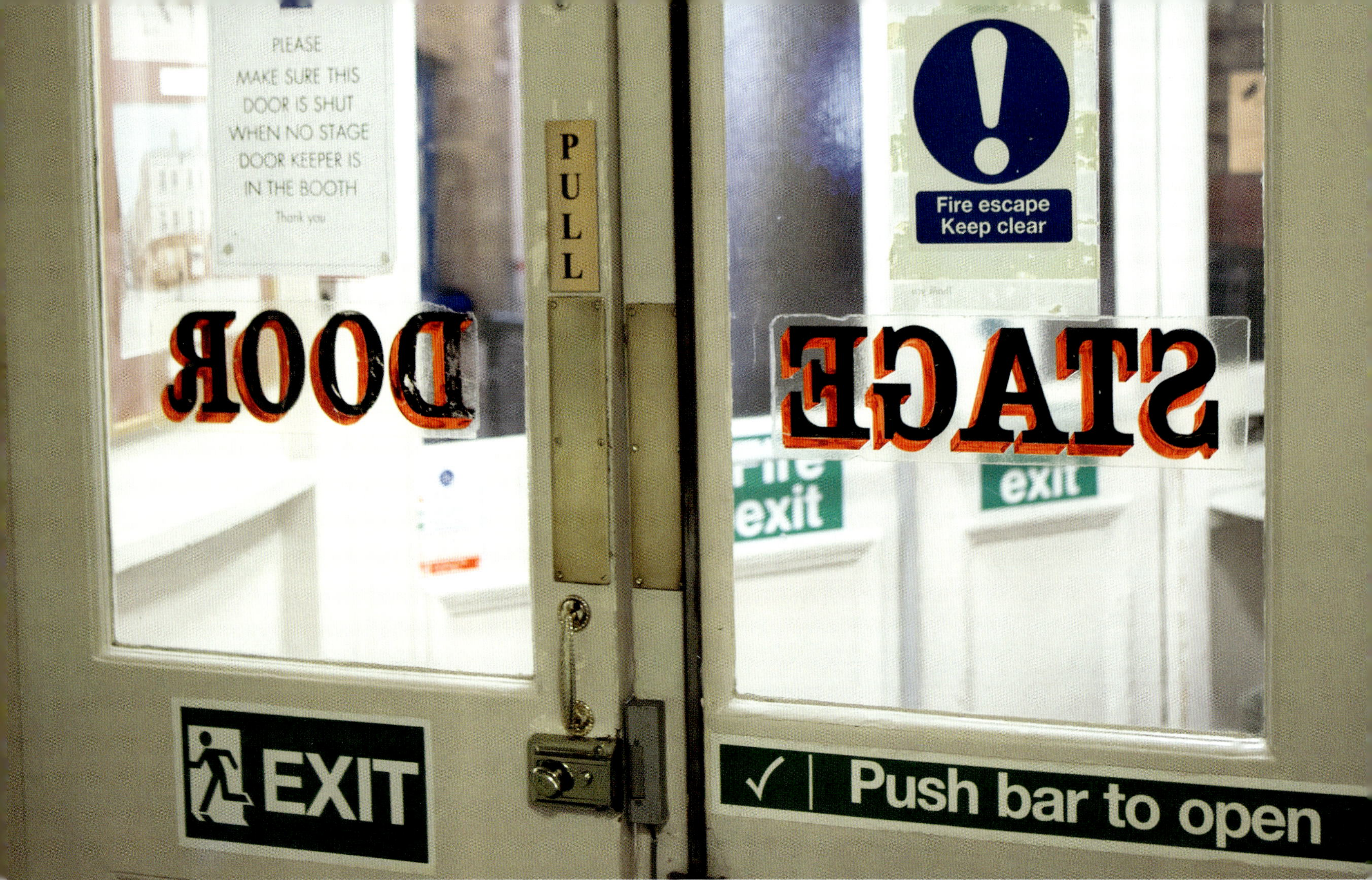

PLEASE
MAKE SURE THIS
DOOR IS SHUT
WHEN NO STAGE
DOOR KEEPER IS
IN THE BOOTH
Thank you
PULL
Fire escape
Keep clear
DOOR
STAGE
EXIT
Push bar to open

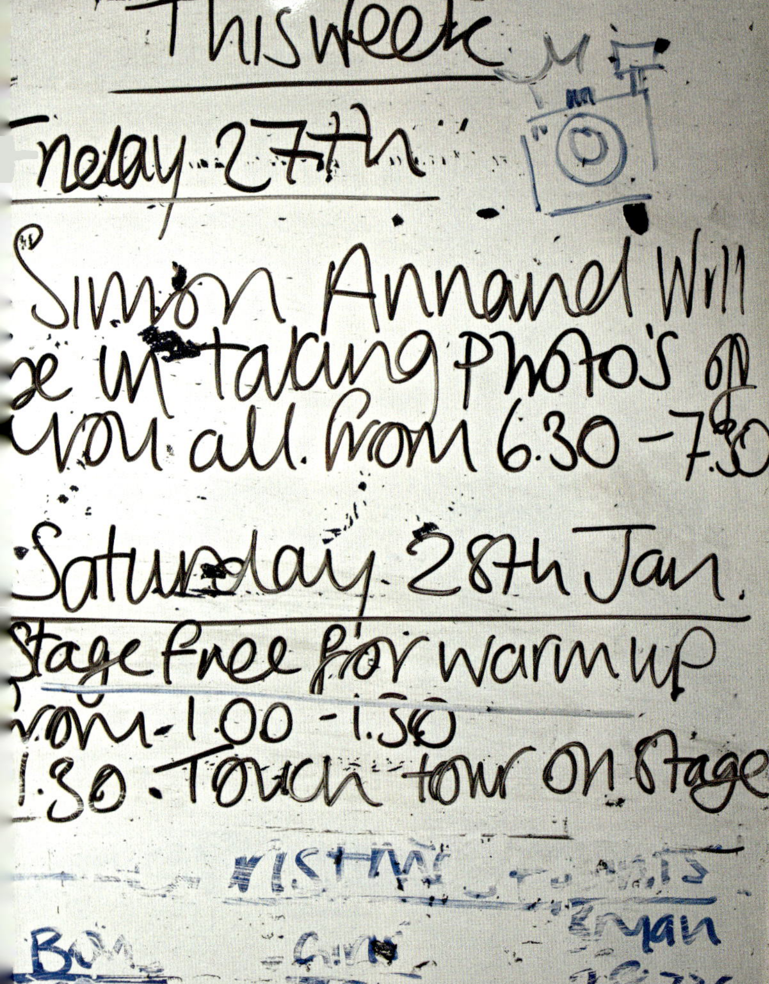
This week
Friday 27th
Simon Annand will
e in taking photo's of
you all from 6.30 - 7.30
Saturday 28th Jan
Stage free for warm up
from 1.00 - 1.30
1.30 Touch tour on stage

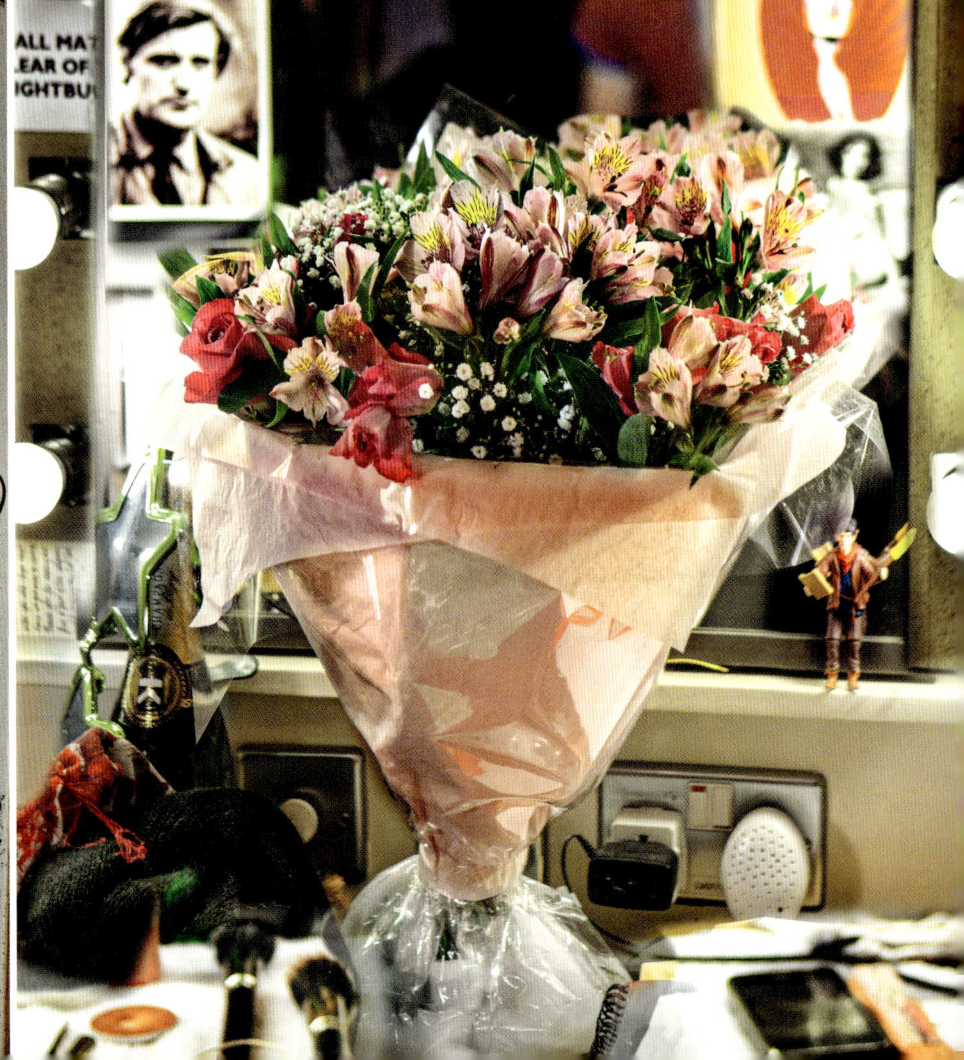

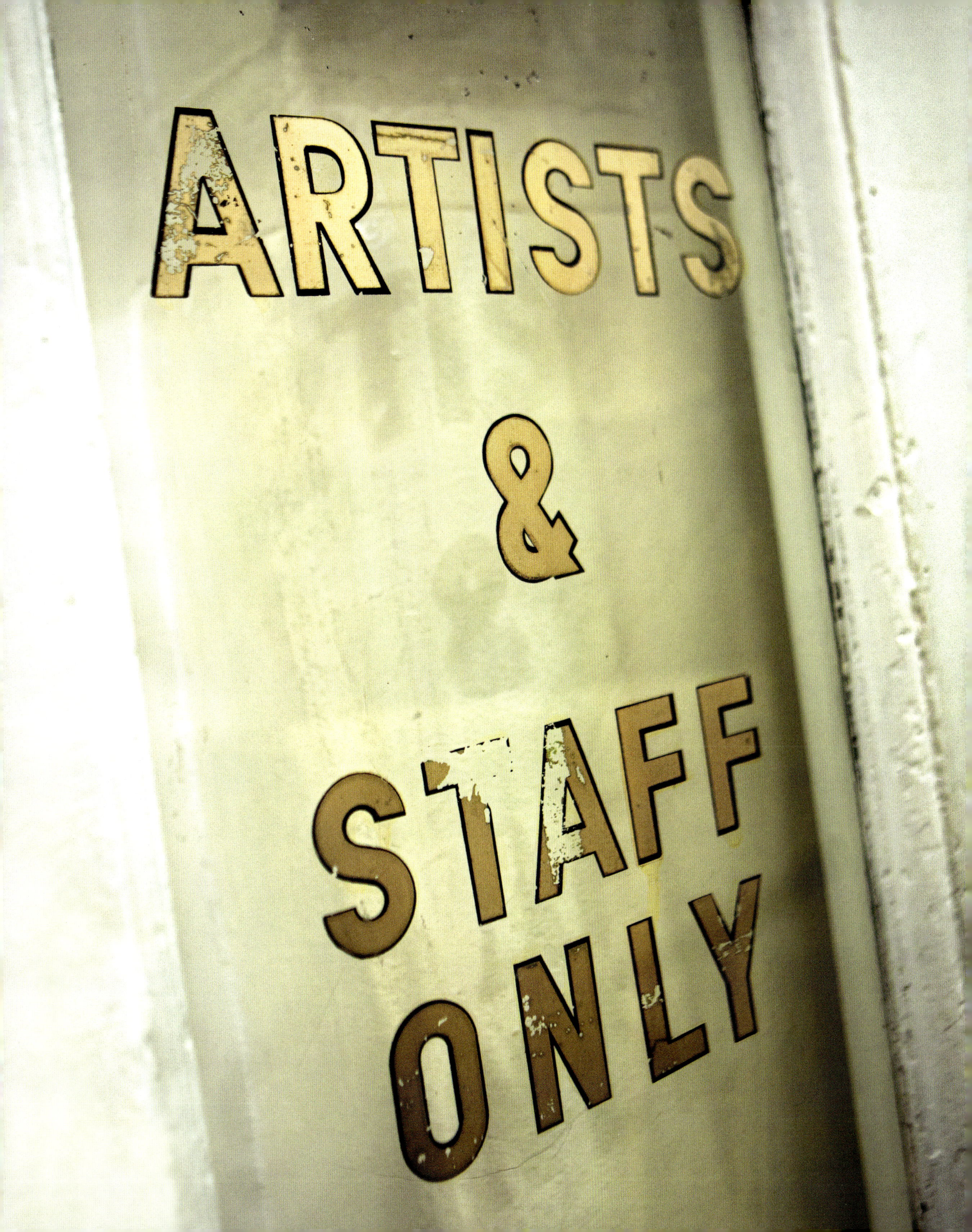

ARTISTS

&

STAFF
ONLY

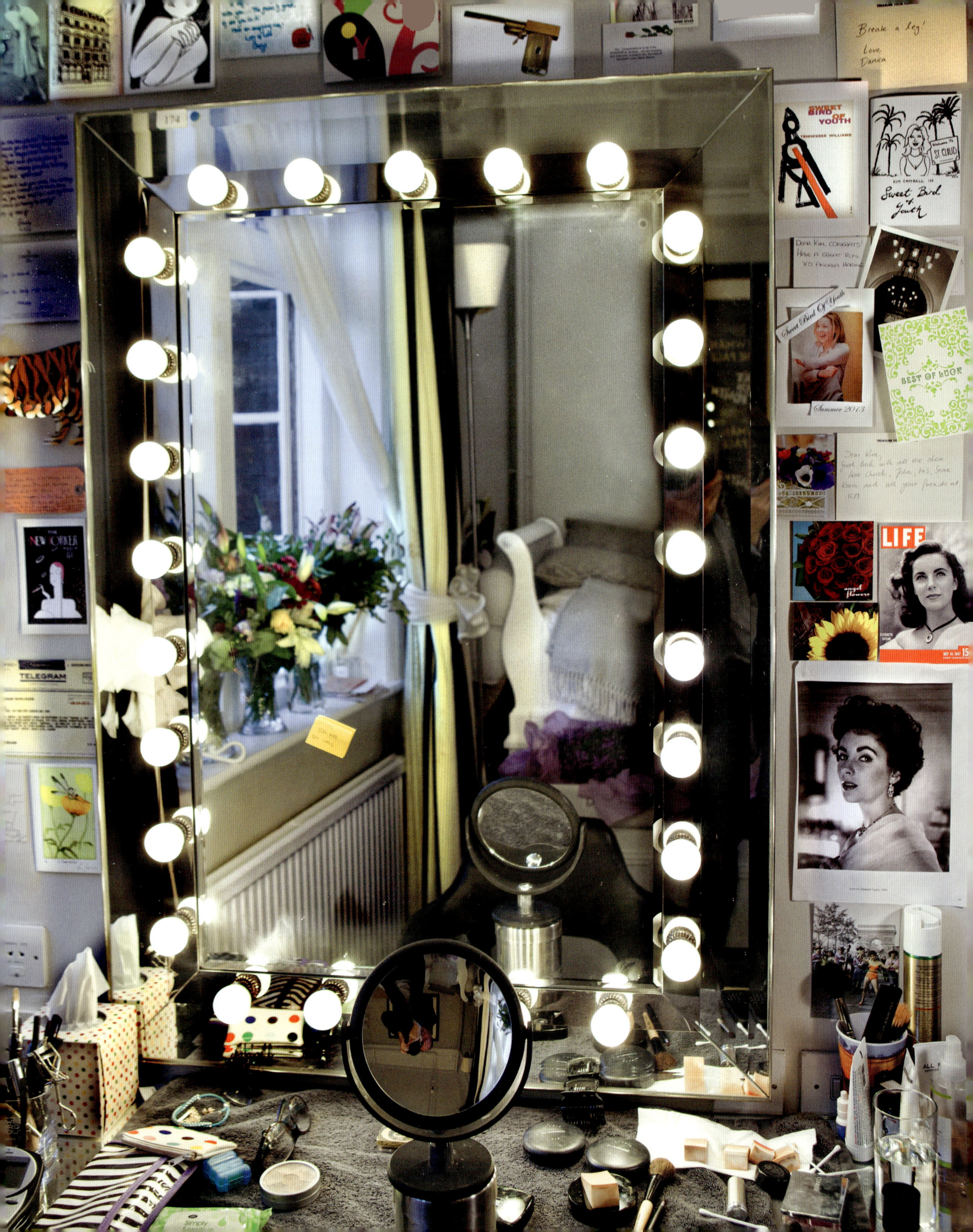
Break a leg!
Love,
Danica
SWEET BIRD OF YOUTH
TENNESSEE WILLIAMS
Sweet Bird of Youth
ST CLOUD
Sweet Bird Of Youth
Summer 2013
BEST OF LUCK
LIFE
TELEGRAM

PROLOGUE

In *Time to Act* the actors have given their permission for a photographer to be present and want the process to be seen. Each actor has their own way of spending the thirty minutes before curtain-up. The spectrum varies from a Method approach, which is inhabiting the character at all times, to the opposite, holding the fictional character back and only releasing it at the last minute before entering the stage. A Method actor might request complete silence during the session.

There have been a few thousand sessions for this monograph. The purpose of every session is to add a fresh story to the existing narrative. It is a challenge to find something new each time. The only way to achieve this is to be open to the 'rhythm of the room' when you first enter and to resist any temptation to control it.

A photographer must trust his subject. It is the relationship a person has with themself, inside their own head, that makes them photogenic. With an actor who is about to go on stage, there is also their relationship with a fictional character, which makes the psychological exchange between them particularly interesting. It is for this reason that I often ask an actor to arrange a session late in the run, when the fictional character they are playing has been completely absorbed and the photographer's presence is less likely to distract.

The actor's residence in a room is temporary and the length of stay depends on the success of a show. The incoming actor will decorate a dressing room in his or her own way. The older the building, the more it is part of history, which always helps to create an atmosphere.

KIM CATTRALL'S DRESSING TABLE, OLD VIC THEATRE, 2013
Many leading actors across the generations have looked into this mirror.

People have often asked about rituals. There are many and they are varied, but it is for each actor to reveal this for him- or herself. Another frequent question is whether the actors are nervous. Nerves can come from different sources, including from an actor's private life. Each evening they have a choice, either to use what has happened to them during the day, or to contain their feelings if they are unhelpful for the performance.

One of the central principles in *Time to Act* has been to avoid the tendency to make an actor look like 'an actor' wherever possible. The subject has always been regarded as a man or a woman first, famous, or not, and as an actor second. It is the journey that actors embark on that is fascinating, not the fact they are actors.

Due to the millions of images taken across the world on mobile phones there has been much talk of the 'death of photography'. In spite of the proliferation of imagery, it is just as difficult to take an informed or iconic photograph as it ever was. When the pen was invented, which was a revolutionary tool that democratised the ability to record information, it did not at the same time create an excess of poets.

Nearly all of the images in this book are shutter driven rather than lens powered. The decisions of when to press the shutter are based on complicity with the subject, as opposed to making the subject look 'more interesting' by using an extreme lens or composition. 1/125th of a second is all it takes to make an image. It is the perfect short story.

SIMON ANNAND

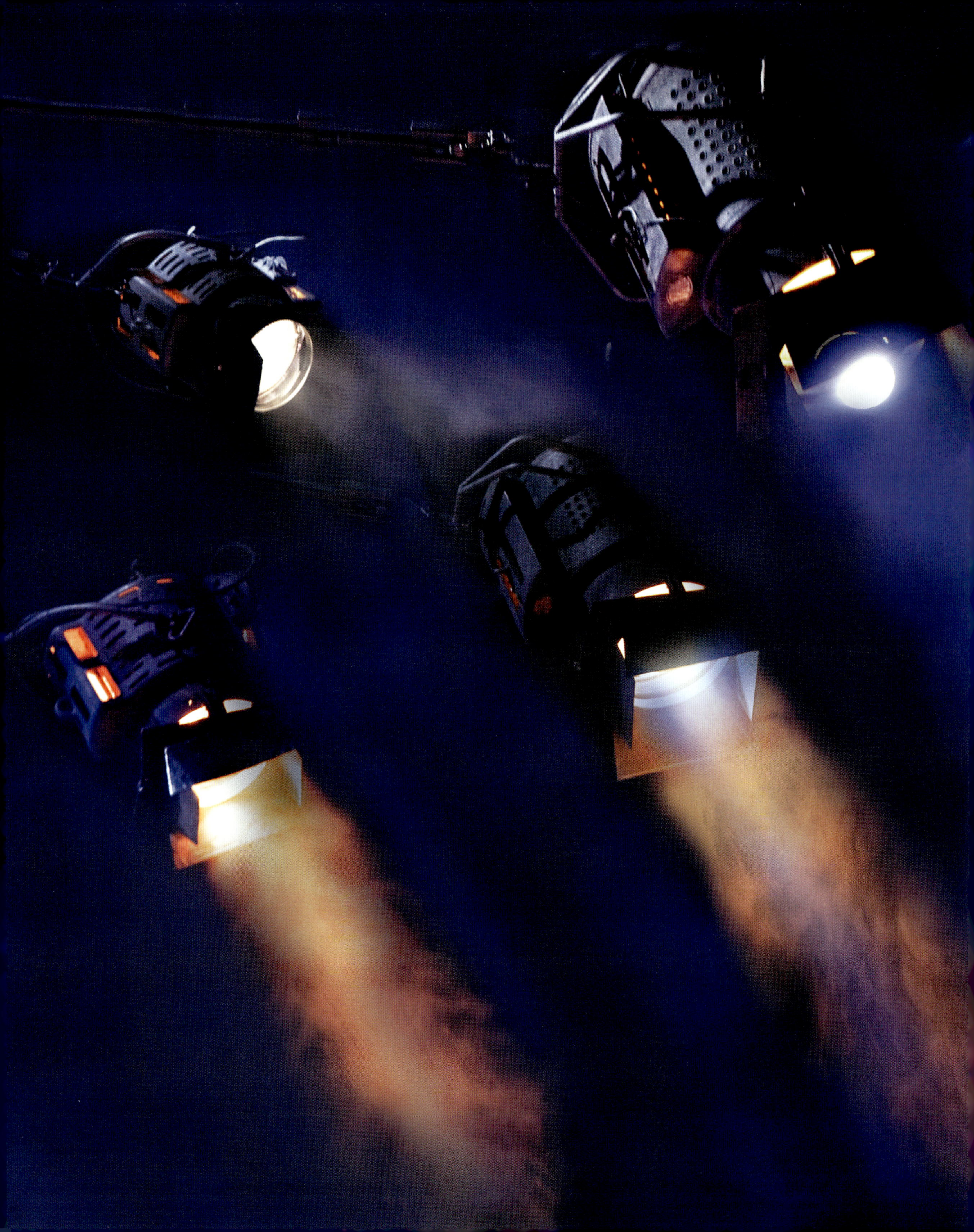

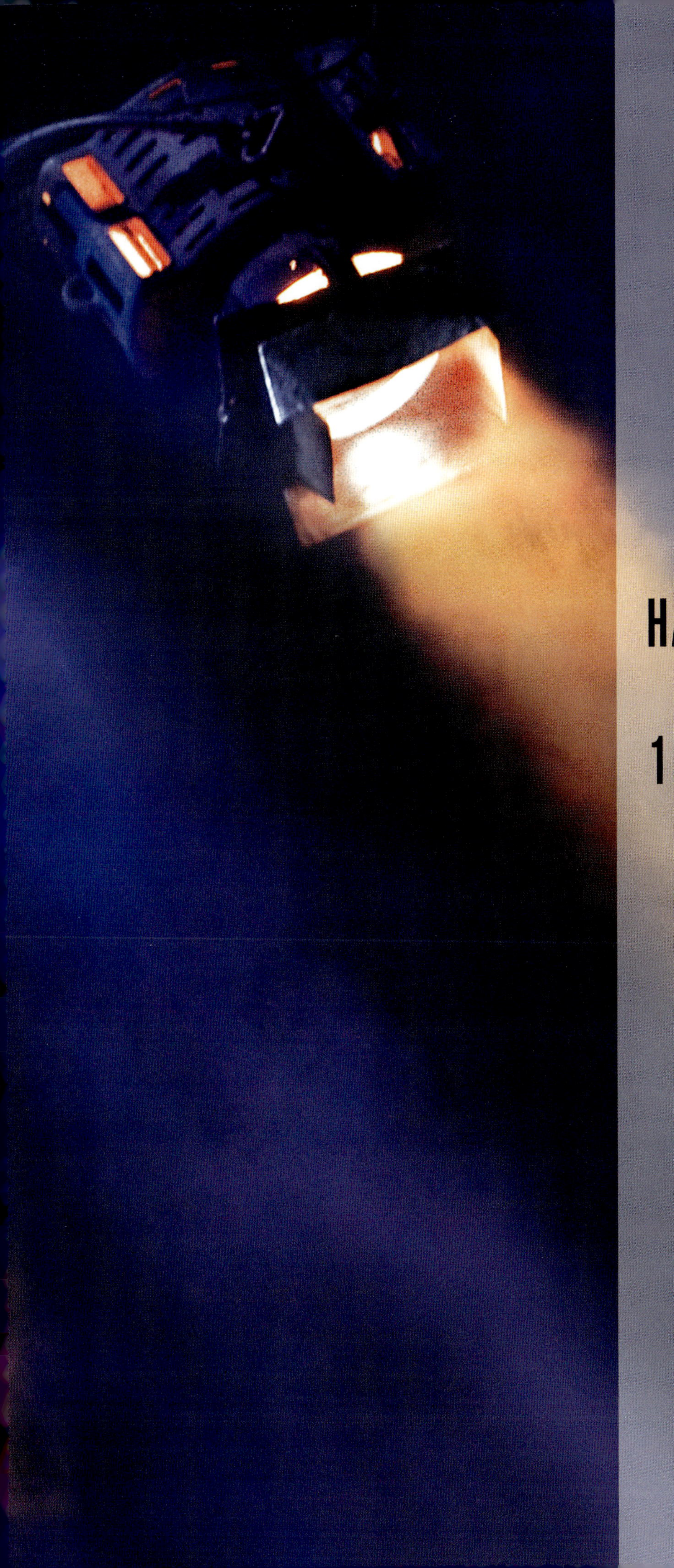

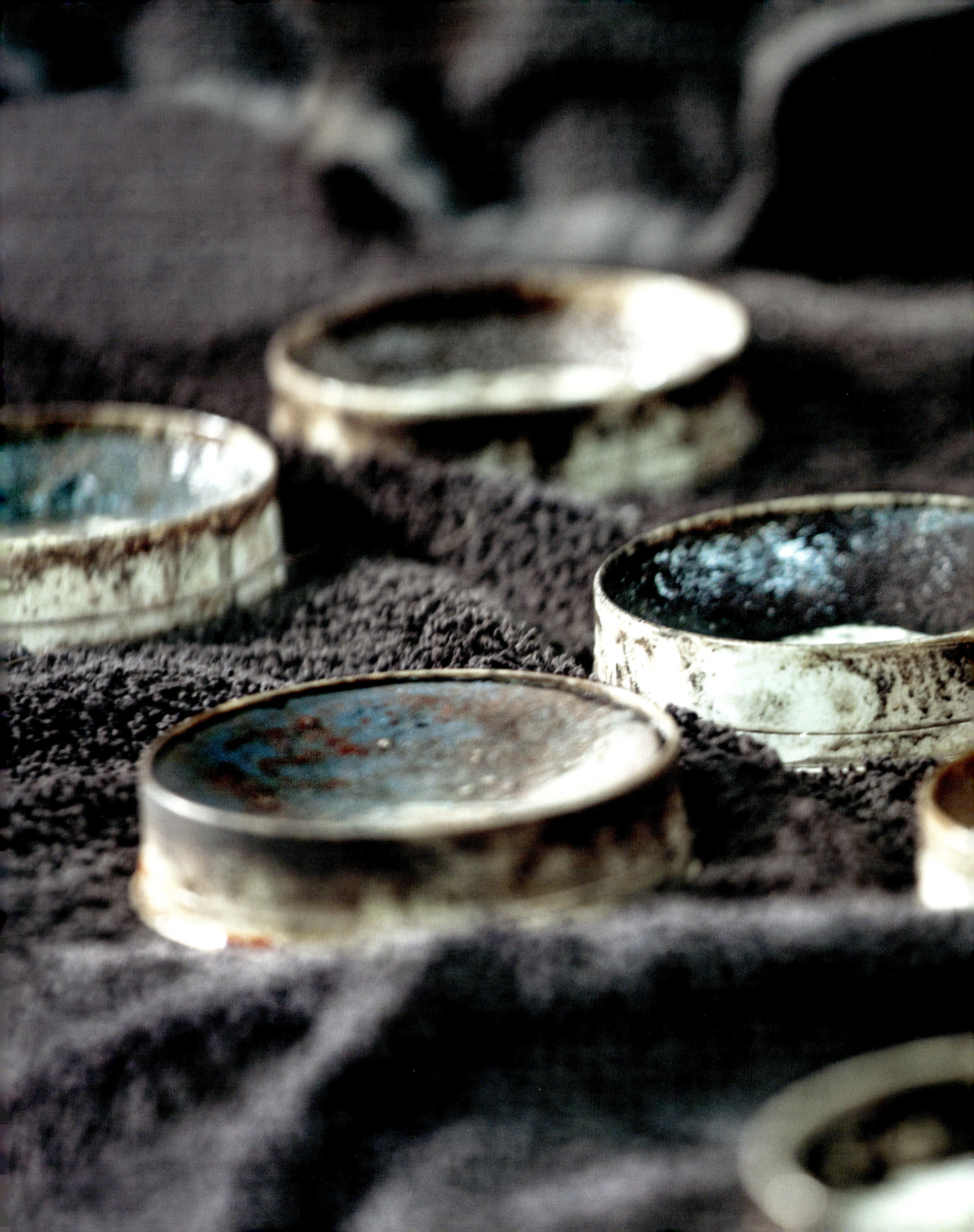

HALF HOUR CALL

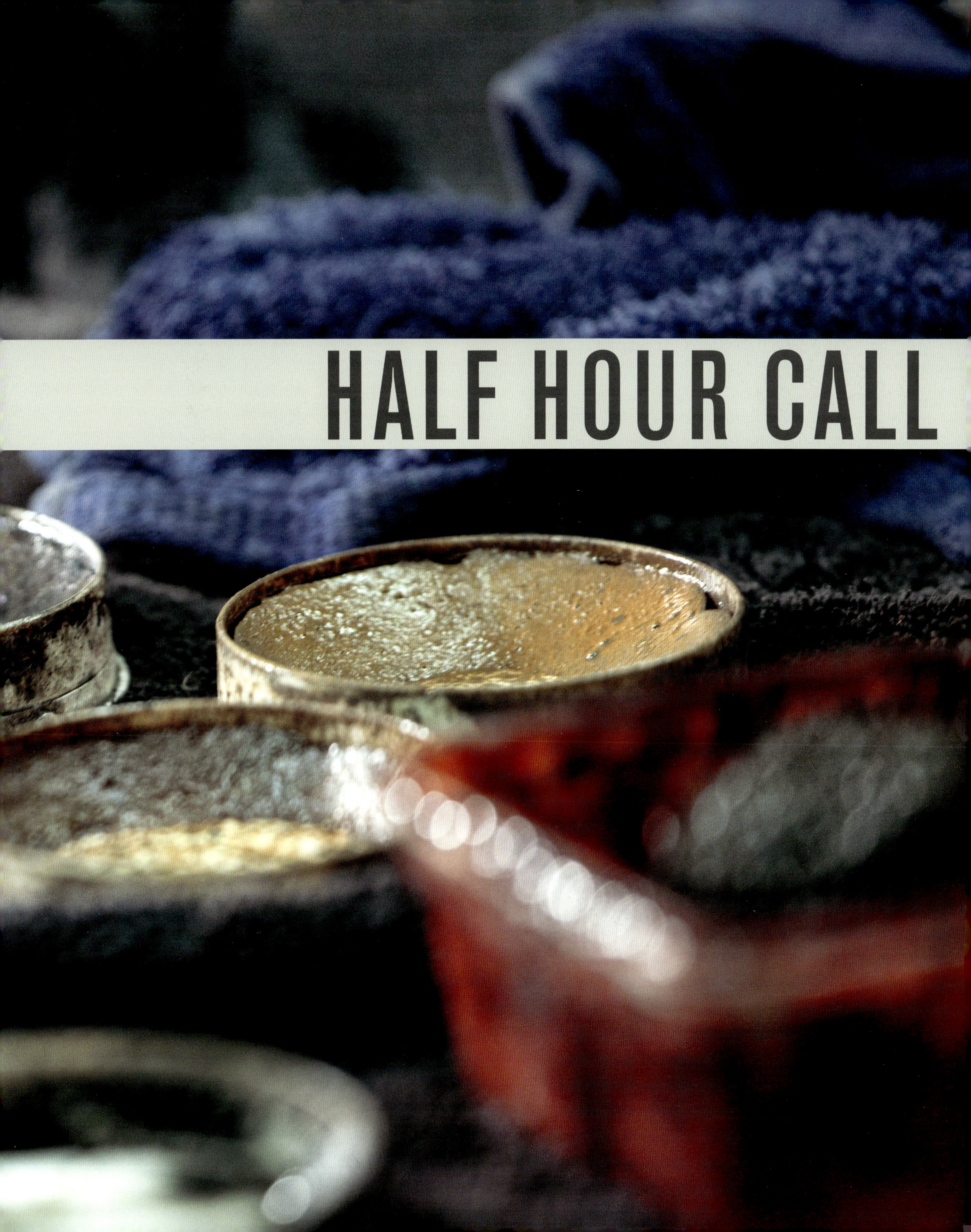

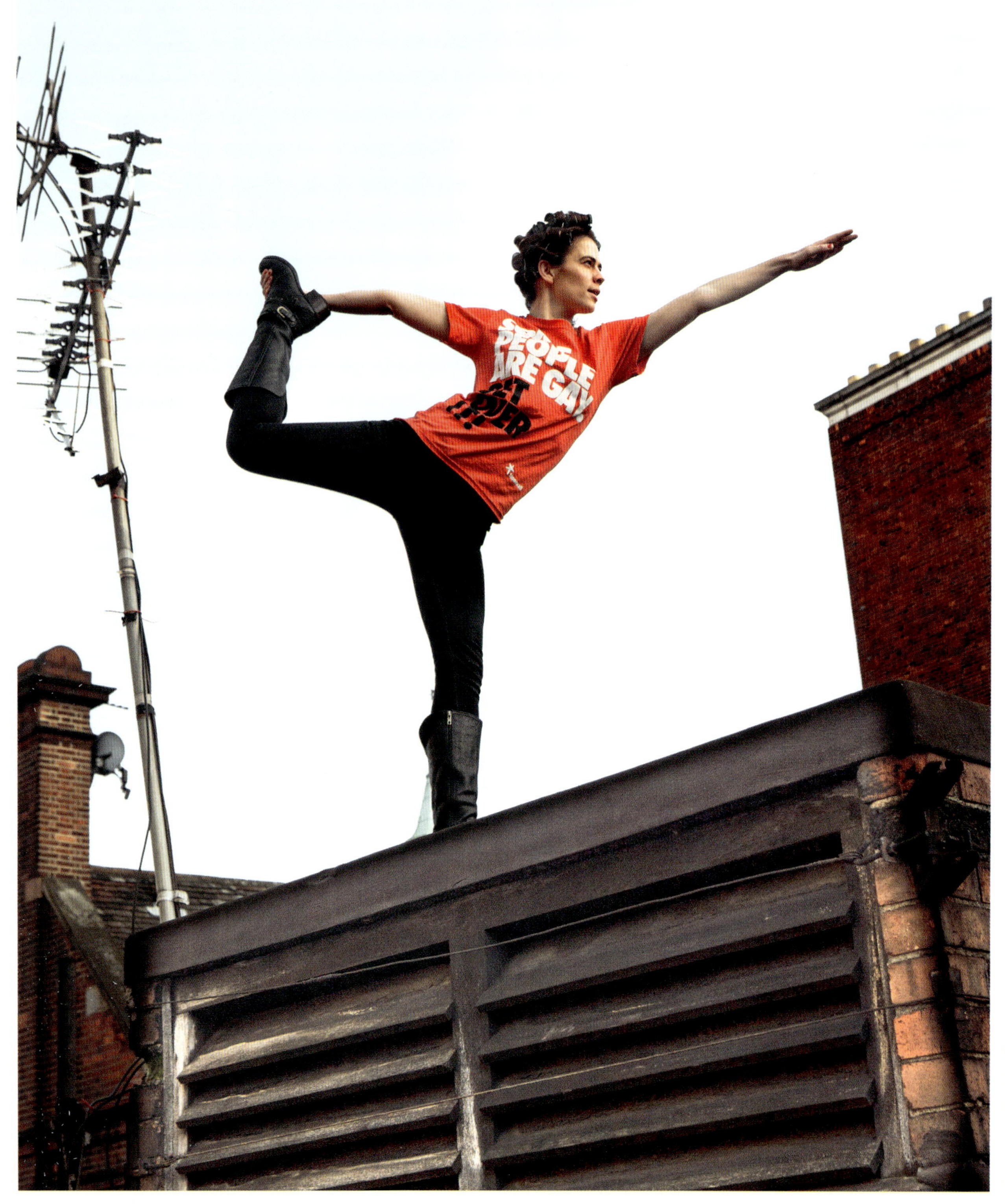

LEFT: HAYLEY ATWELL, *THE PRIDE*, TRAFALGAR STUDIOS, 2013
Hayley likes to have fun. She has lent her immense talent to a variety of projects, including the Captain America films and numerous stage roles. A wonderfully outgoing and inclusive personality, I have never heard a bad word said about her.

OPPOSITE: ANNABEL SCHOLEY, *PASSION PLAY*, DUKE OF YORK'S, 2013
This looks like New York but is actually St Martin's Lane in London.

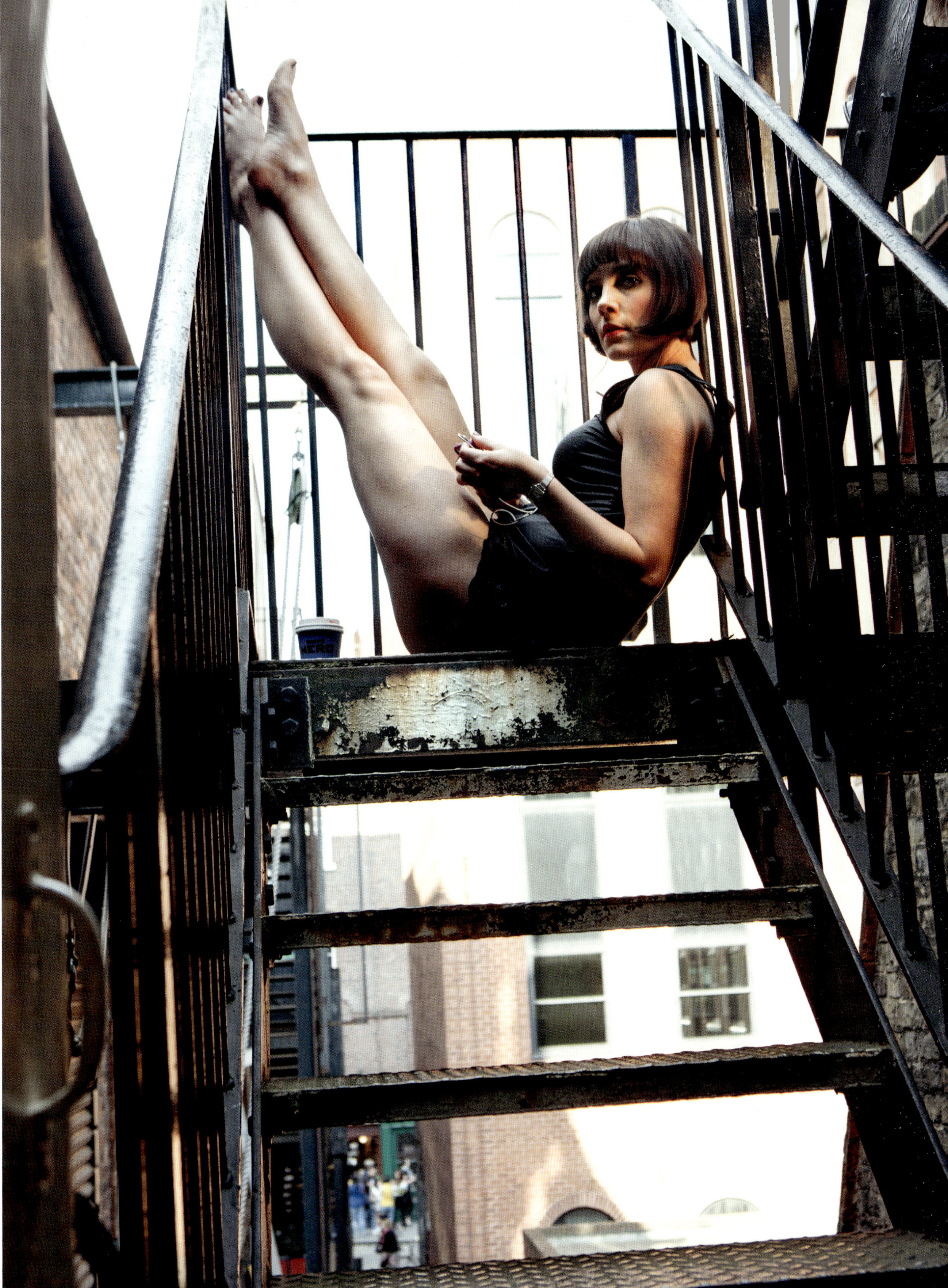

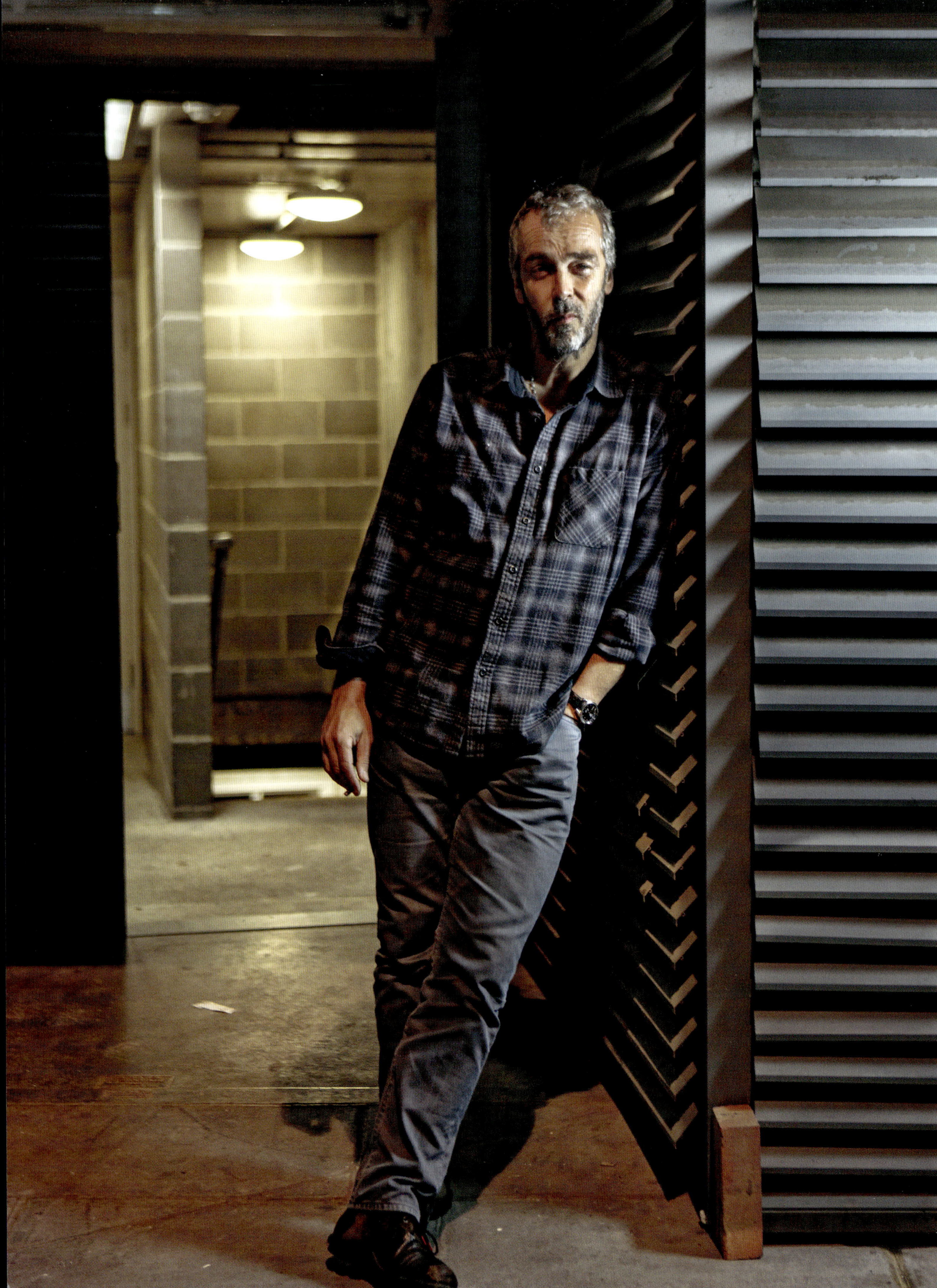

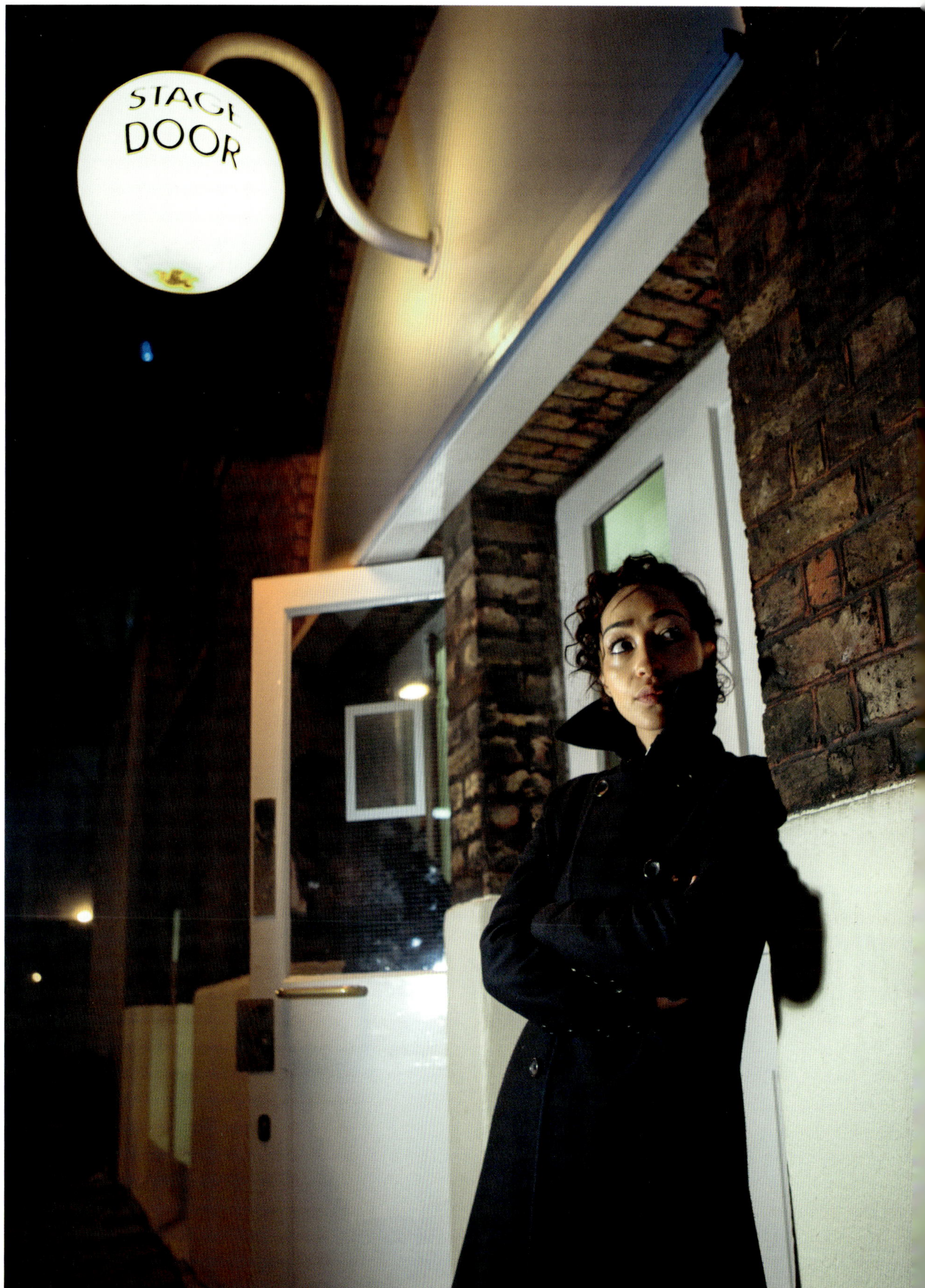

OPPOSITE: **JOHN HANNAH, *UNCLE VANYA*, ST JAMES THEATRE, 2014**
The Scottish actor, whose voice has a distinct timbre all its own, had been asked to play Vanya with a Lincolnshire accent.

RIGHT: **RUTH NEGGA, *PLAYBOY OF THE WESTERN WORLD*, OLD VIC THEATRE, 2011**
In the early days of her career. The physical wall marks the boundary line between the world outside and the world of the play inside.

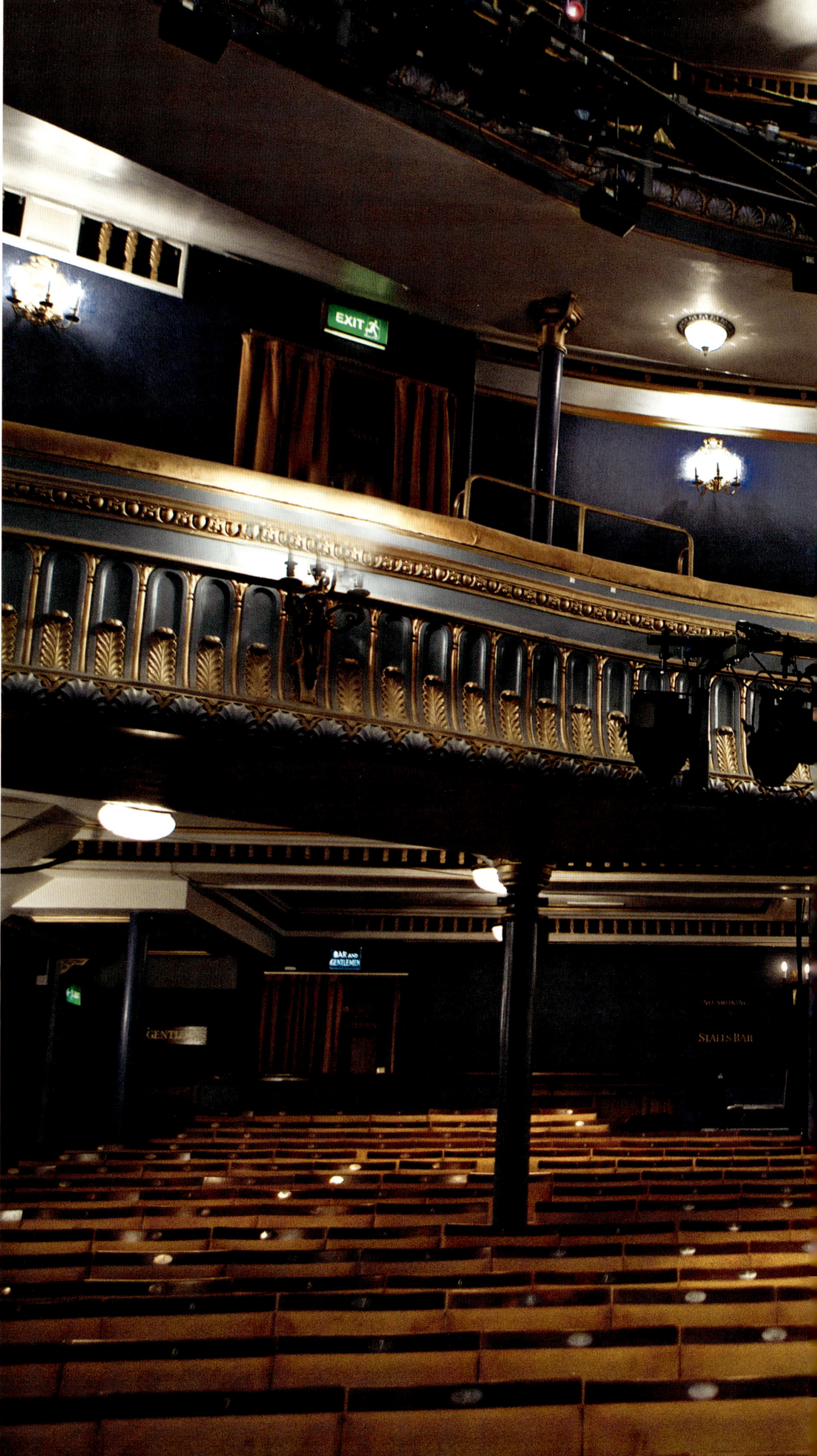

CLAUDIE BLAKLEY, *CHIMERICA*, HAROLD PINTER THEATRE, 2013

The first exercises of the evening and Claudie is getting a sense of the auditorium from her audience's point of view.

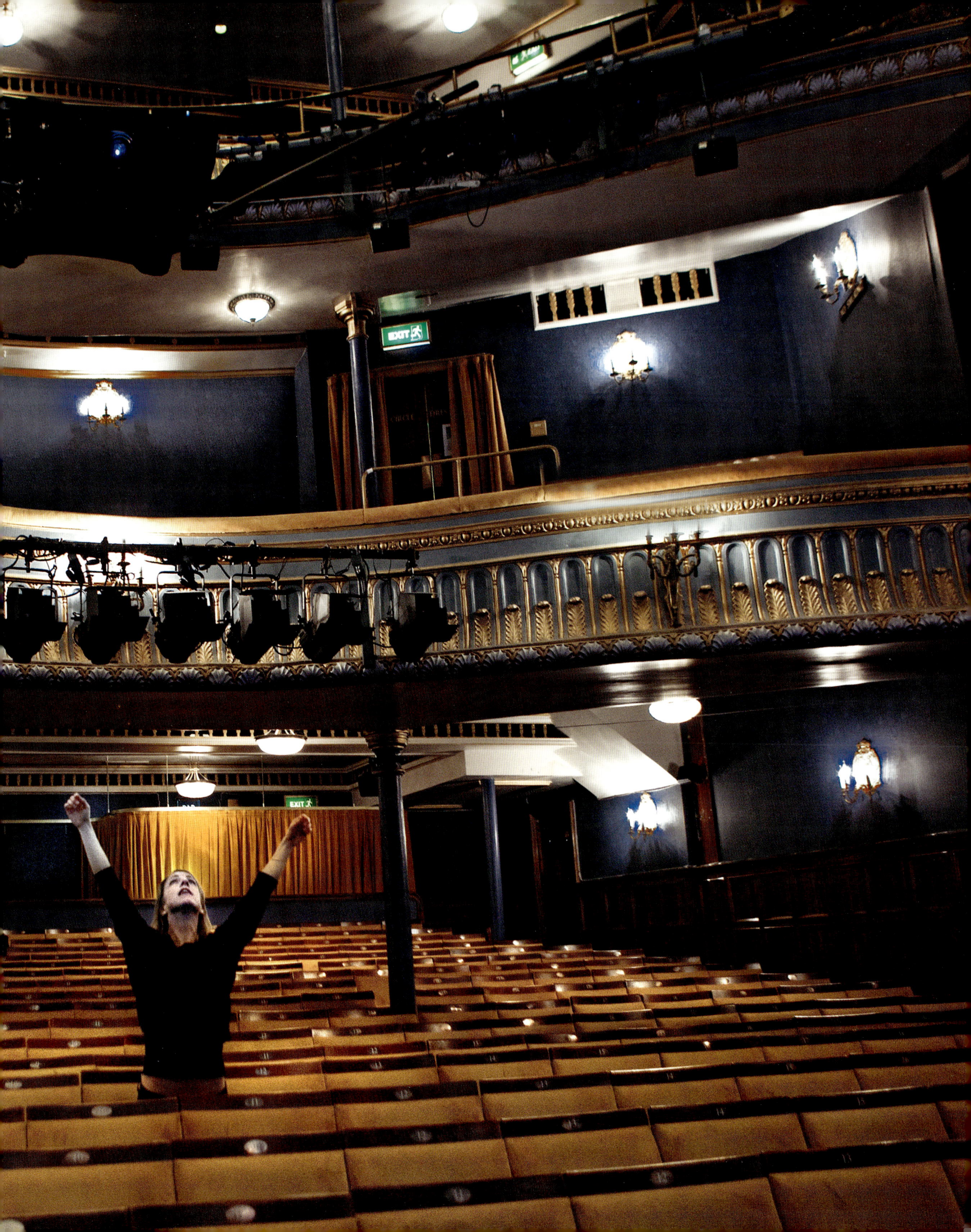
EXIT
EXIT

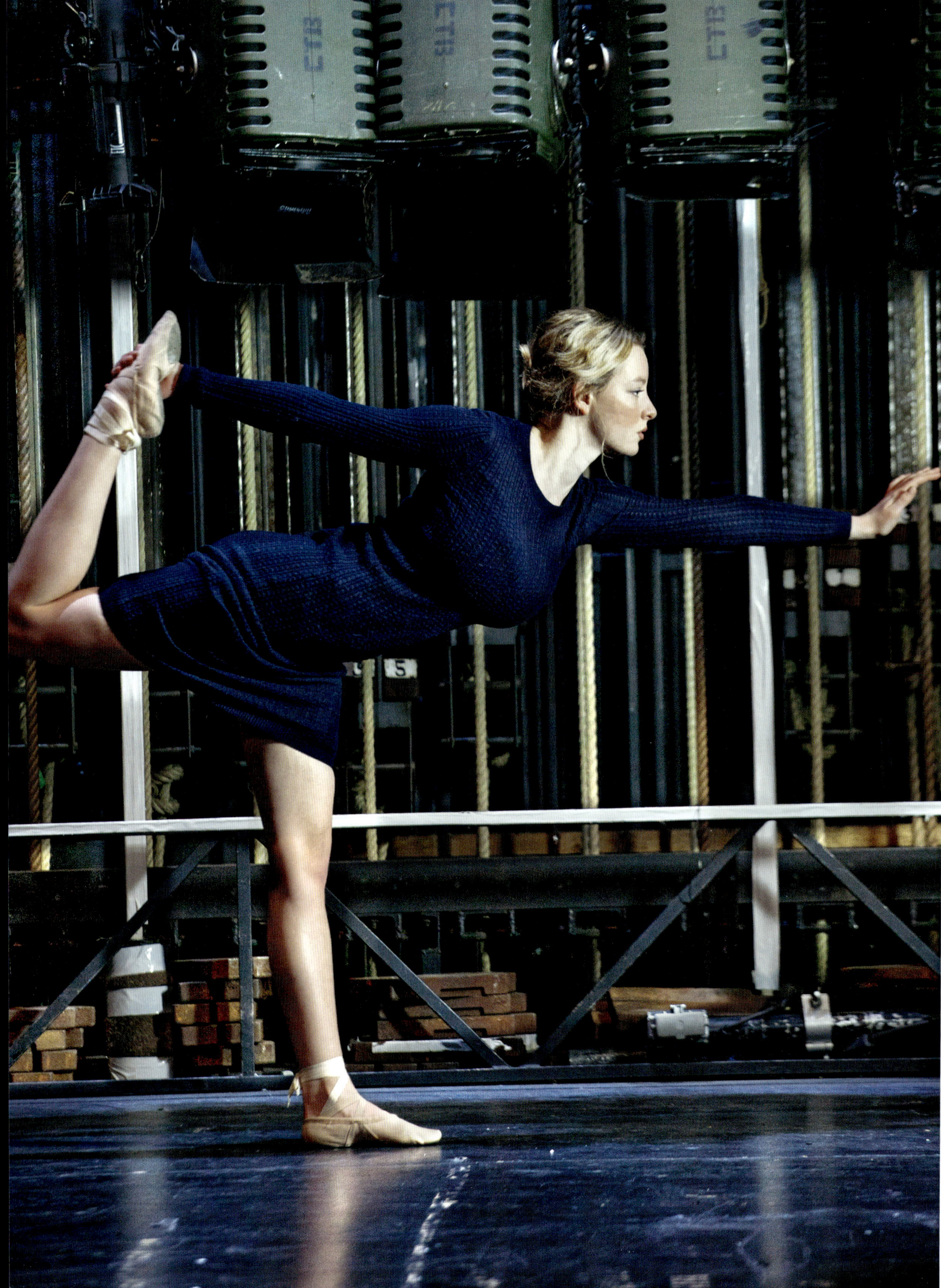
CTB
CTB
CTB
5

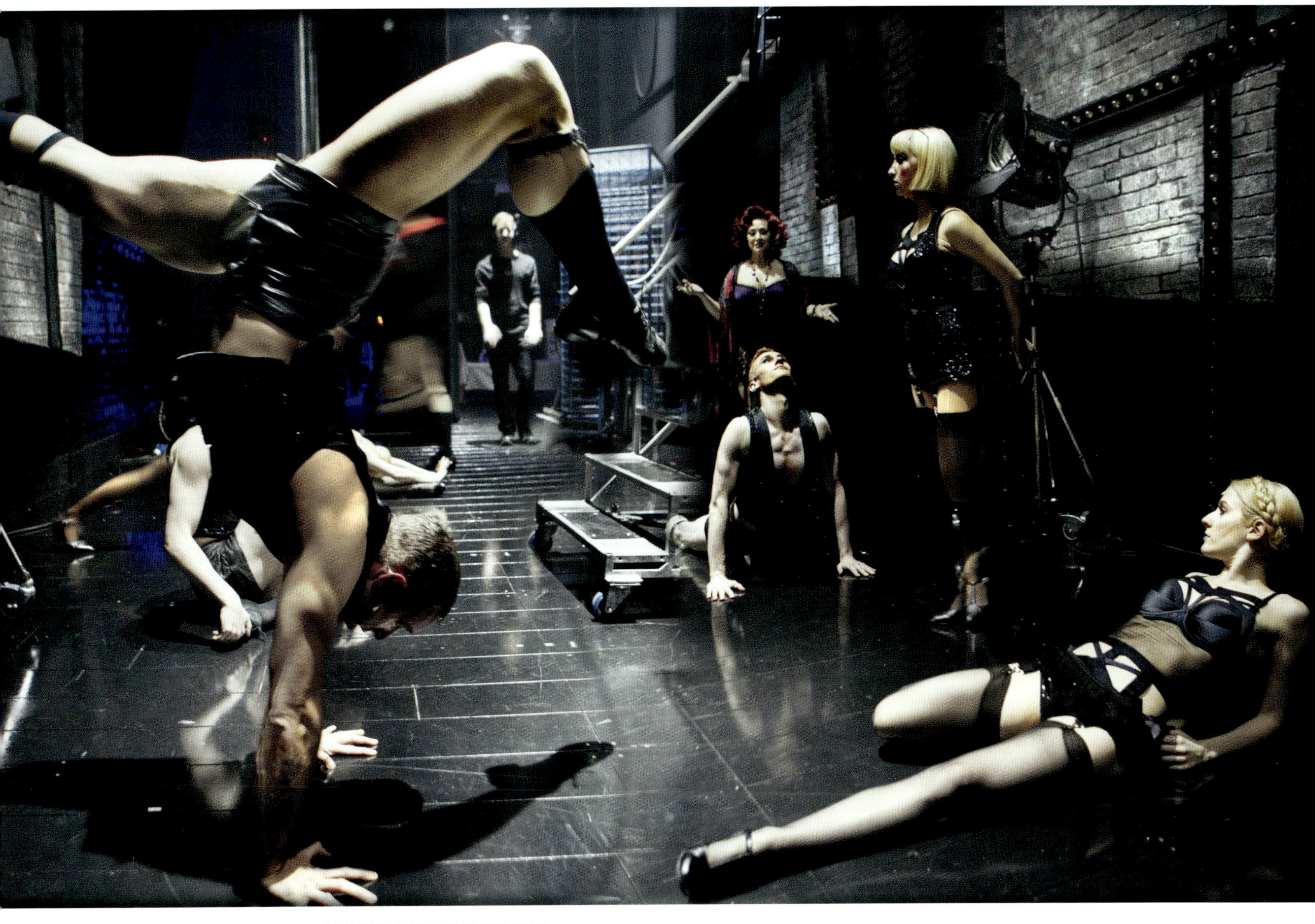

OPPOSITE: **DAKOTA BLUE RICHARDS, *ARCADIA*, CHURCHILL THEATRE BROMLEY, 2015**
Preparation ... making sure her physical muscles are loose and the body is centred.

ABOVE: **NUNO SILVA, CYDNEY UFFINDELL-PHIILLIPS, JESSICA ELLEN, JOHN BRANNOCH, ALLESSIA LUGOBONI, EDD MITTON, LAURA TYRER, *CABARET*, SAVOY THEATRE, 2012**
Warming up.

WARM-UP

Getting the body ready for a performance is vitally important, especially if it is a very physical production. Every actor has their own personal way of warming up.

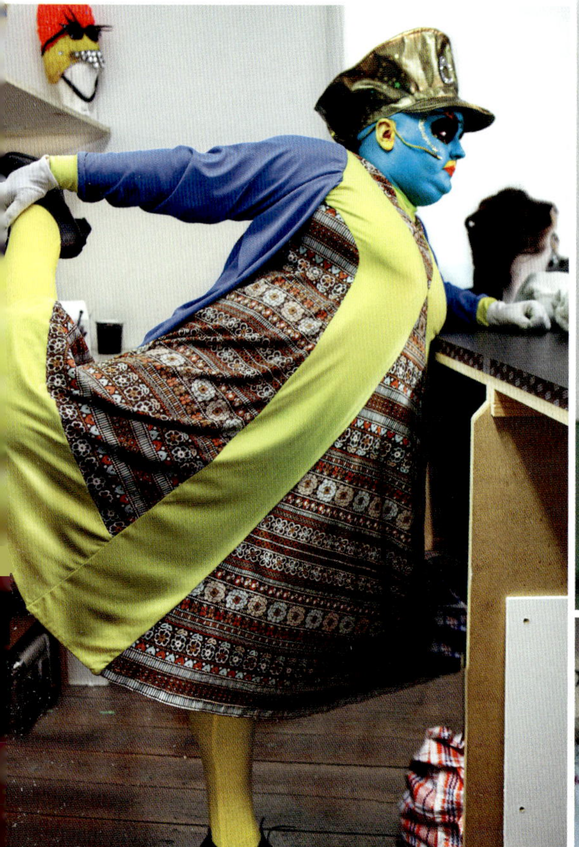

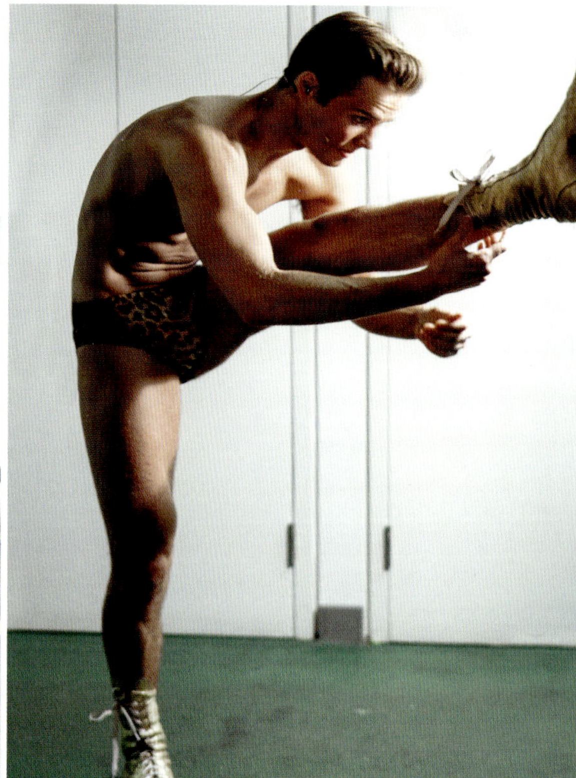

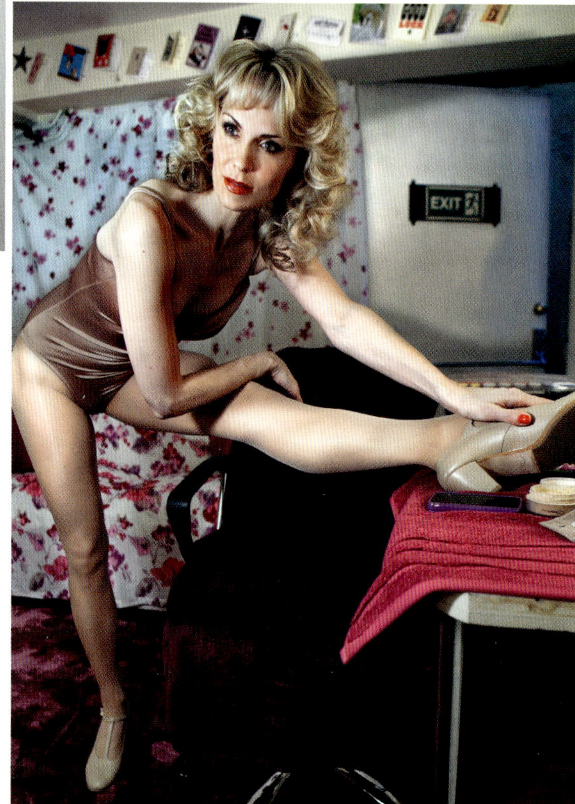

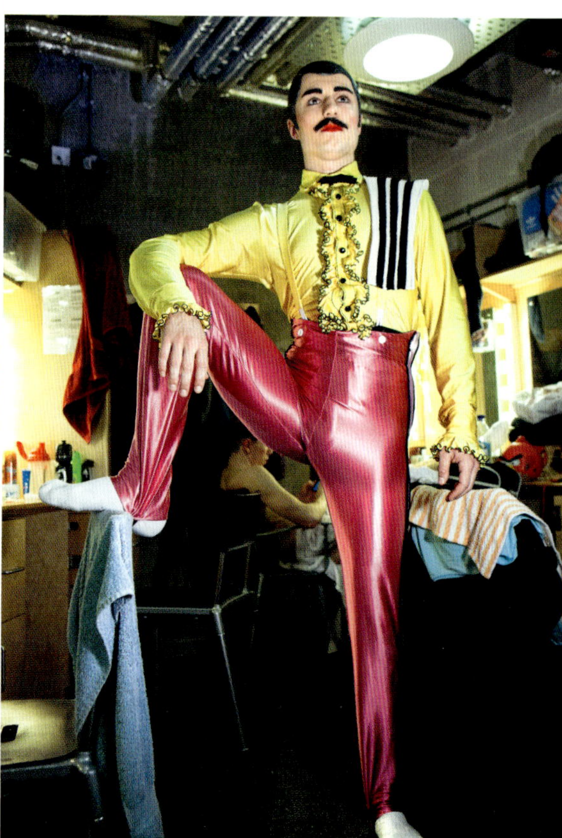

ABOVE: SAM BUTTERY, *TABOO*, BRIXTON CLUB HOUSE, 2012

TOP: CALLUM EVANS, *ROCKY HORROR PICTURE SHOW*, MILTON KEYNES, 2019

RIGHT: LEIGH ZIMMERMAN, *A CHORUS LINE*, PALLADIUM, 2013

FAR RIGHT: LEON MORAN, MATTHEW BOURNE'S *NUTCRACKER!*, SADLER'S WELLS, 2012

OPPOSITE: DAISY LEWIS, *AMAZONIA*, YOUNG VIC, 2008
Daisy has the agility of a circus performer, which she embraces to the full. A larger than life person off stage she reminds me of a character from one of Evelyn Waugh's novels.

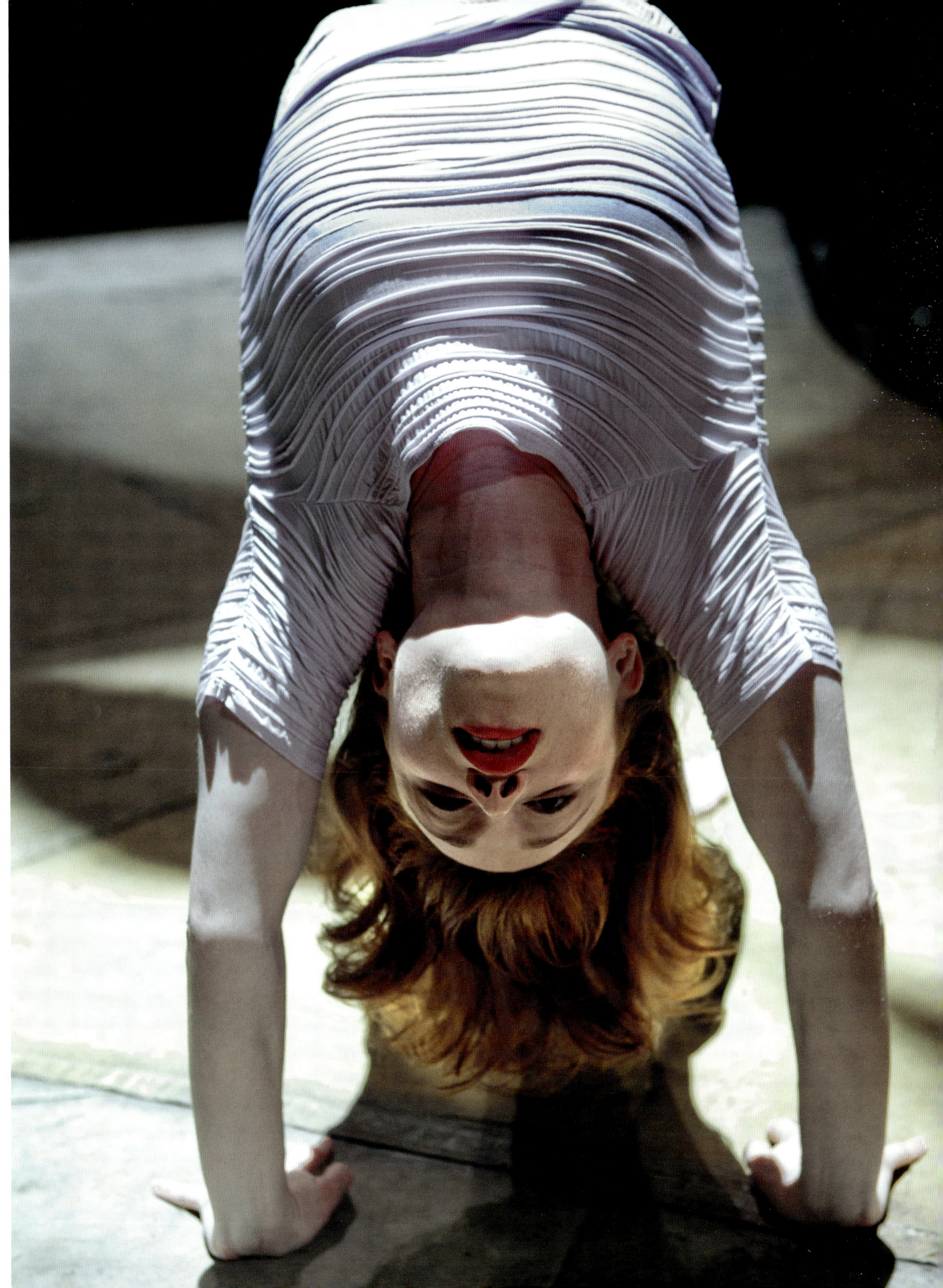

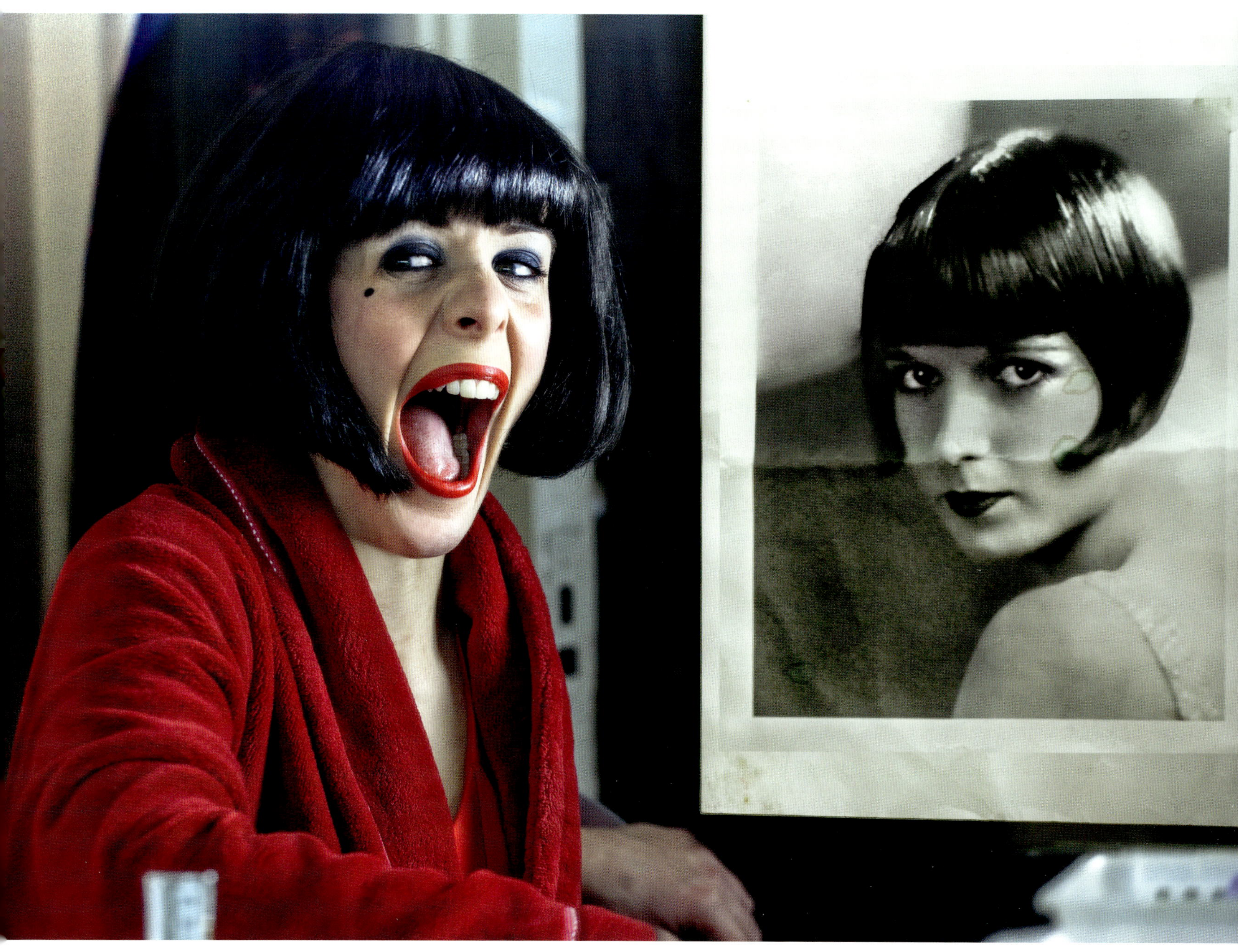

ABOVE: **CHARLIE RUSSELL, *THE PLAY THAT GOES WRONG*, DUCHESS THEATRE, 2014**
Vocal exercises, which are essential to keep the facial muscles as well as the voice in good shape.

OPPOSITE: **JOHN GOODMAN, *AMERICAN BUFFALO*, WYNDHAM'S, 2015**
Everyone said the eminent A-List American star was so polite and professional it might be difficult to take a lively photo. Not so. Wonderful session. Fabulous guy.

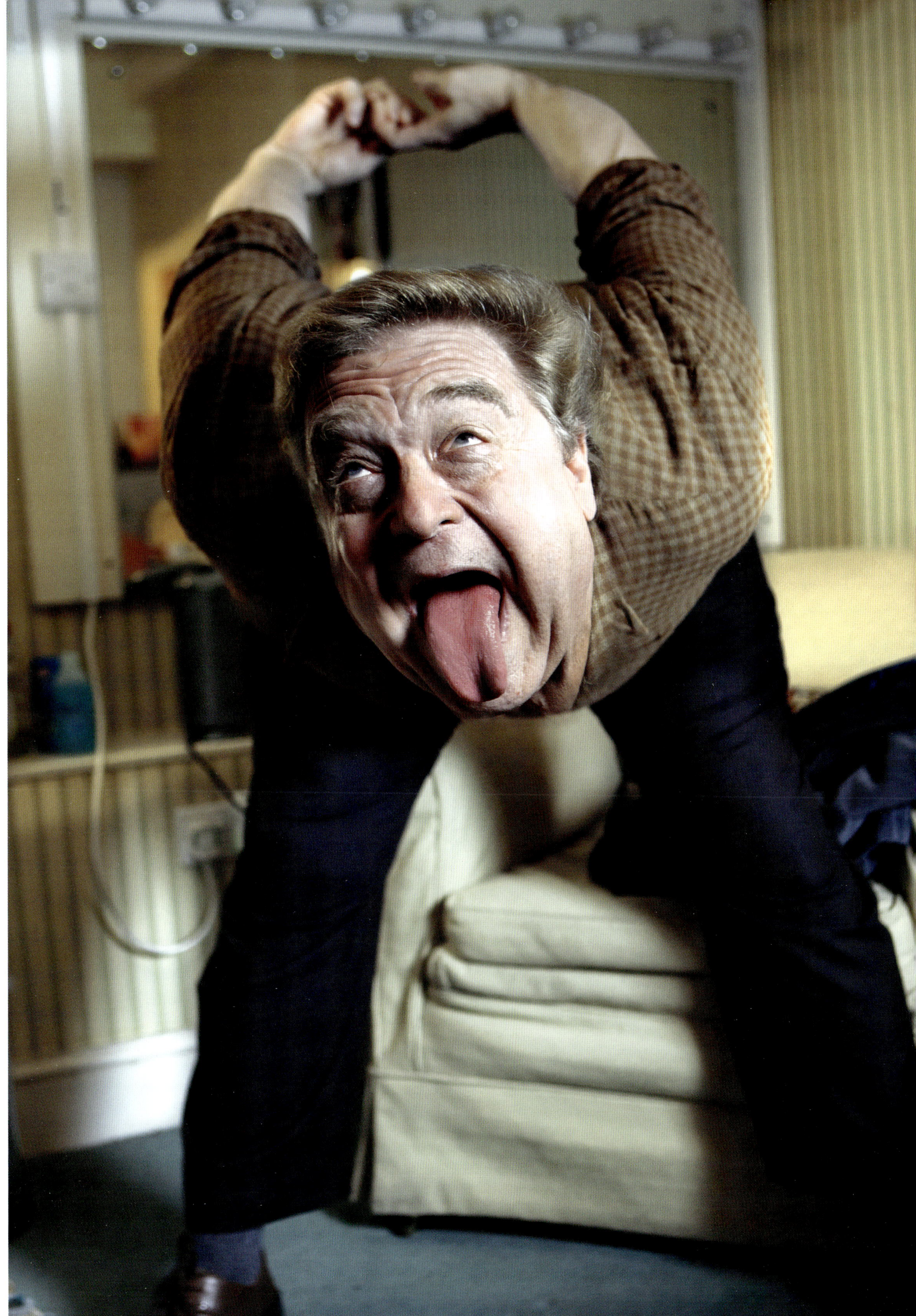

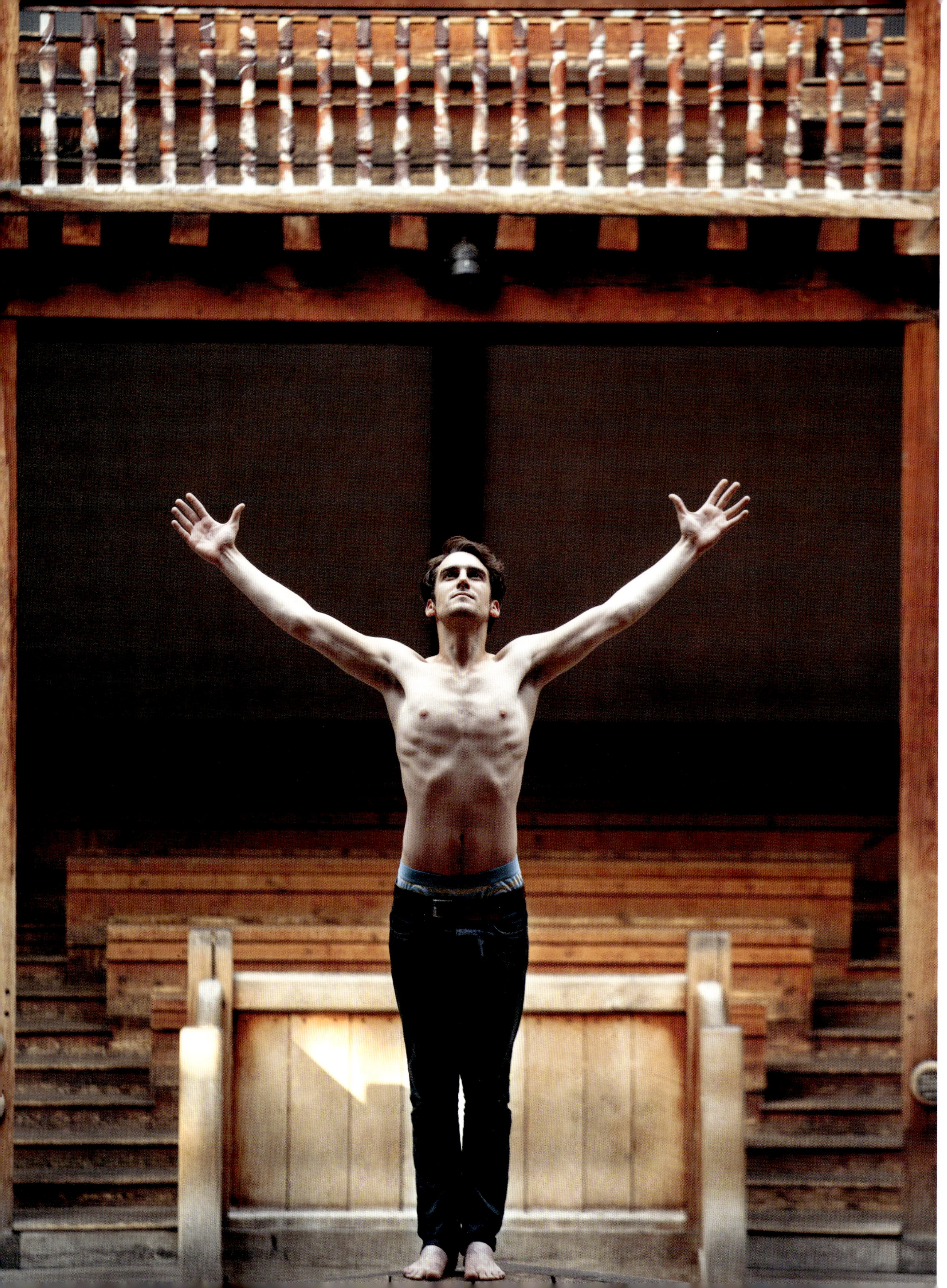

OPPOSITE: JOSHUA SILVER, *A MIDSUMMER NIGHT'S DREAM*, SHAKESPEARE'S GLOBE, 2014
Stretching in the beautiful wooden surroundings of The Globe, which are exposed to the open air.

BELOW: TOM HIDDLESTON, *CORIOLANUS*, DONMAR WAREHOUSE, 2014
Known for *The Avengers, The Night Manager* and *Thor*, Tom is preparing for a role full of physical and mental challenges.

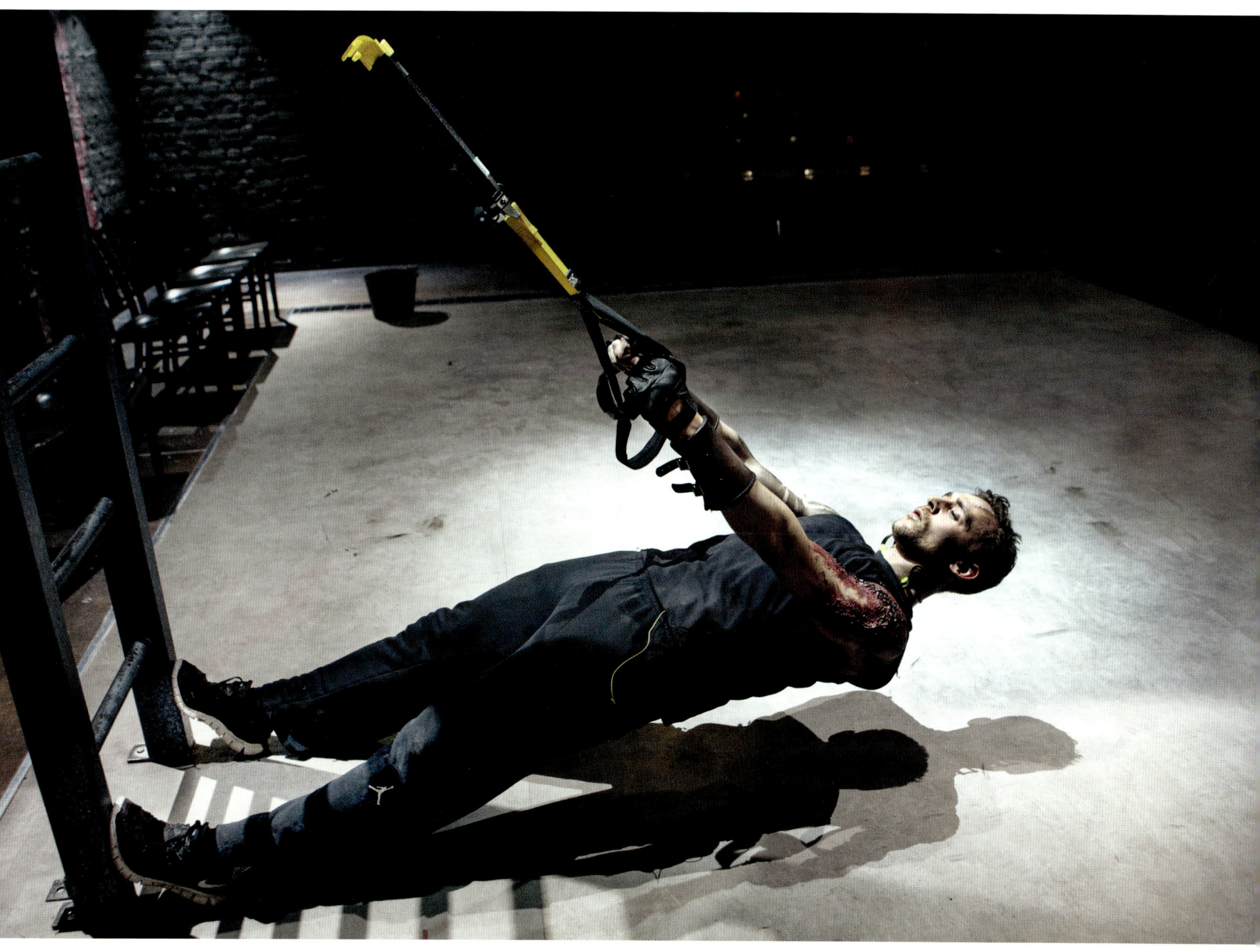

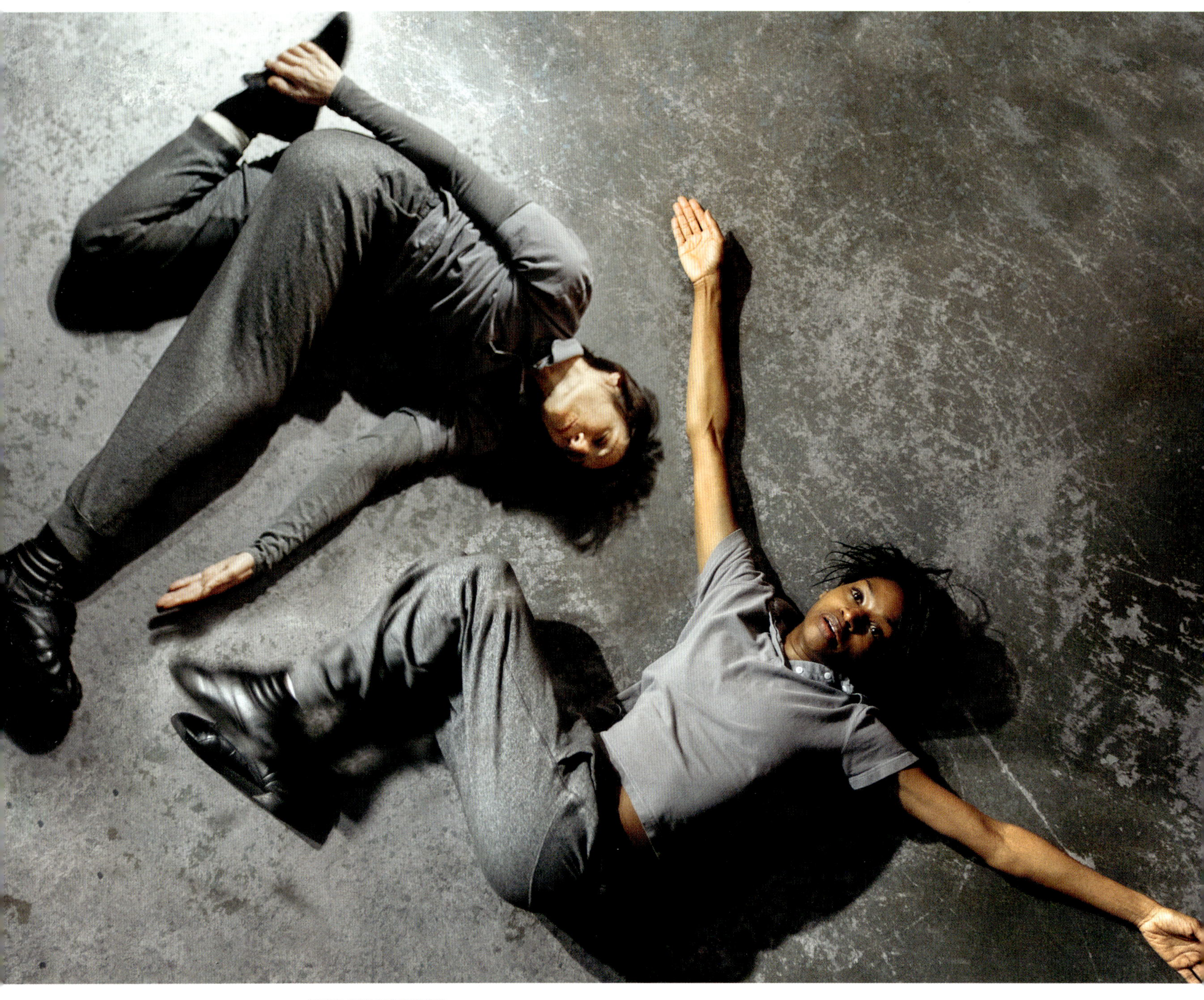

ABOVE: **HARRIET WALTER, JENNY JULES, *JULIUS CAESAR*, DONMAR WAREHOUSE, 2012**
This was an all-female production, with Harriet playing Brutus.

OPPOSITE: **BEN WHISHAW, ANDREW SCOTT, *COCK*, ROYAL COURT, 2009**
Two charismatic stars, early in their successful careers, enjoying an intense discussion during the warm-up.

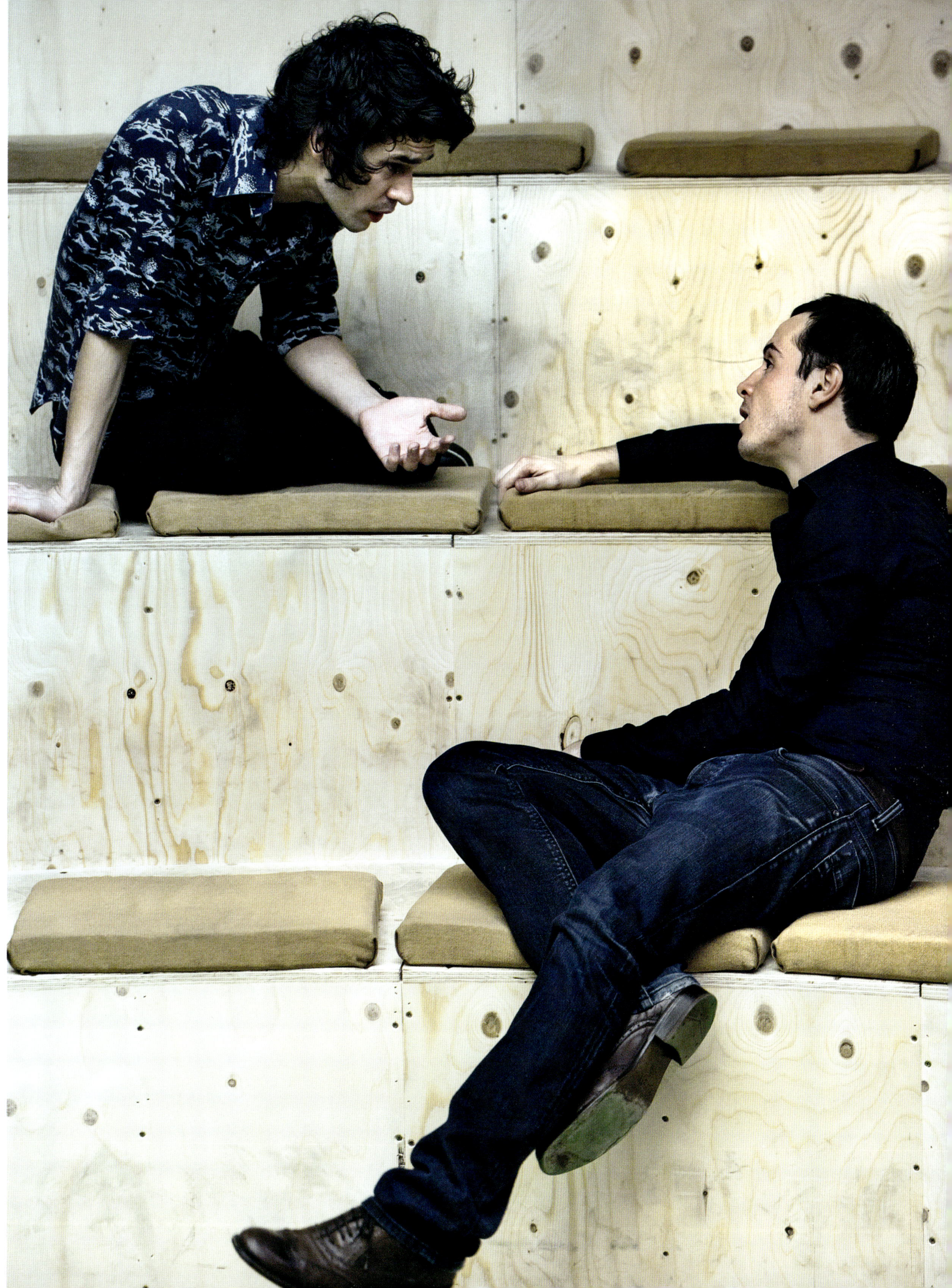

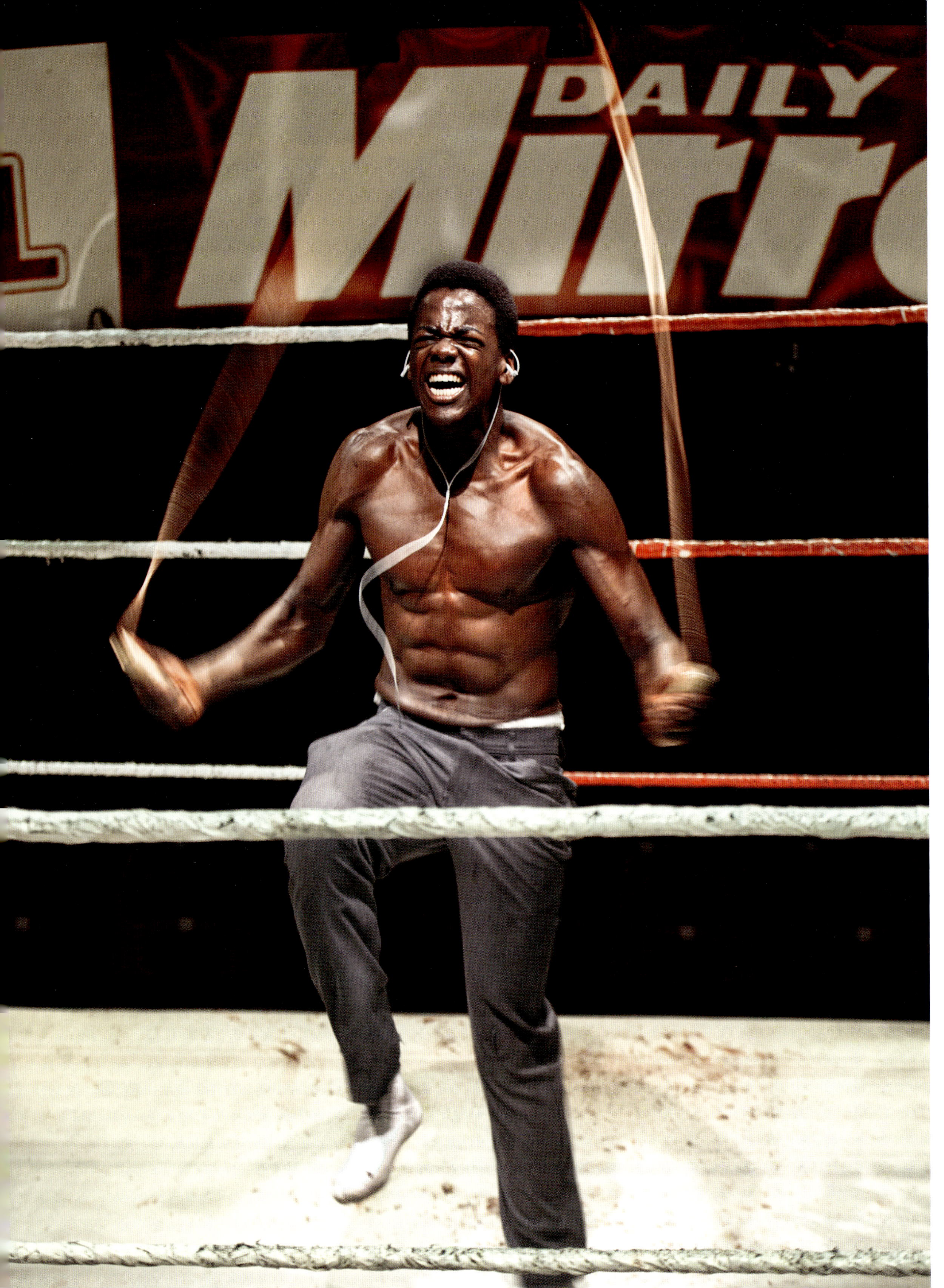
DAILY
Mirr

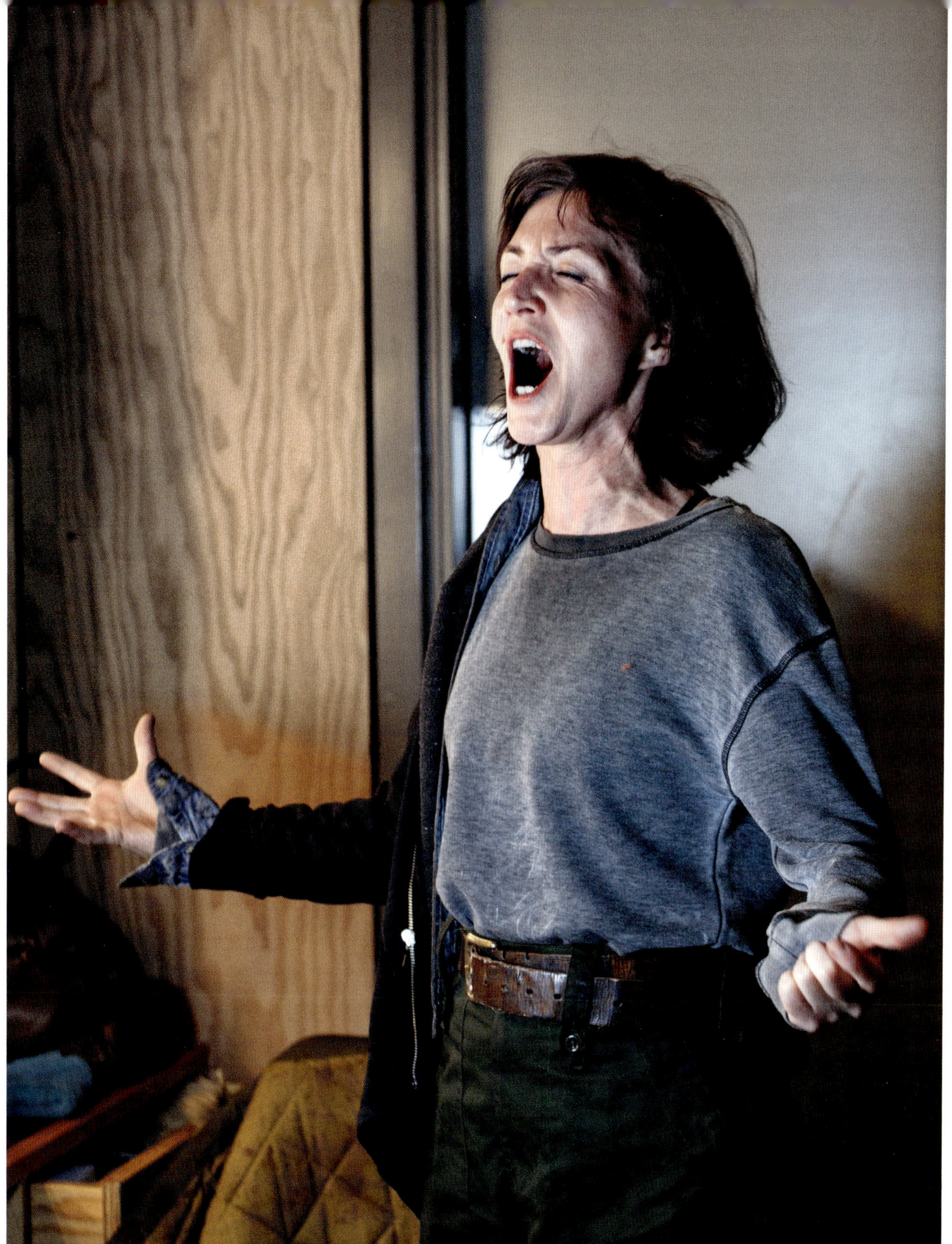

OPPOSITE: **DANIEL KALUUYA, *SUCKER PUNCH*, ROYAL COURT, 2010**
Through intensive training Daniel managed to lose several stone to play the boxer Leroy Davidson in Roy Williams's play.

RIGHT: **MICHELLE FAIRLEY, *JULIUS CAESAR*, BRIDGE THEATRE, 2018**
Michelle has always been highly respected as an actress, and after landing a lead in *Game of Thrones* she now has more casting power. Her sense of satisfaction is palpable.

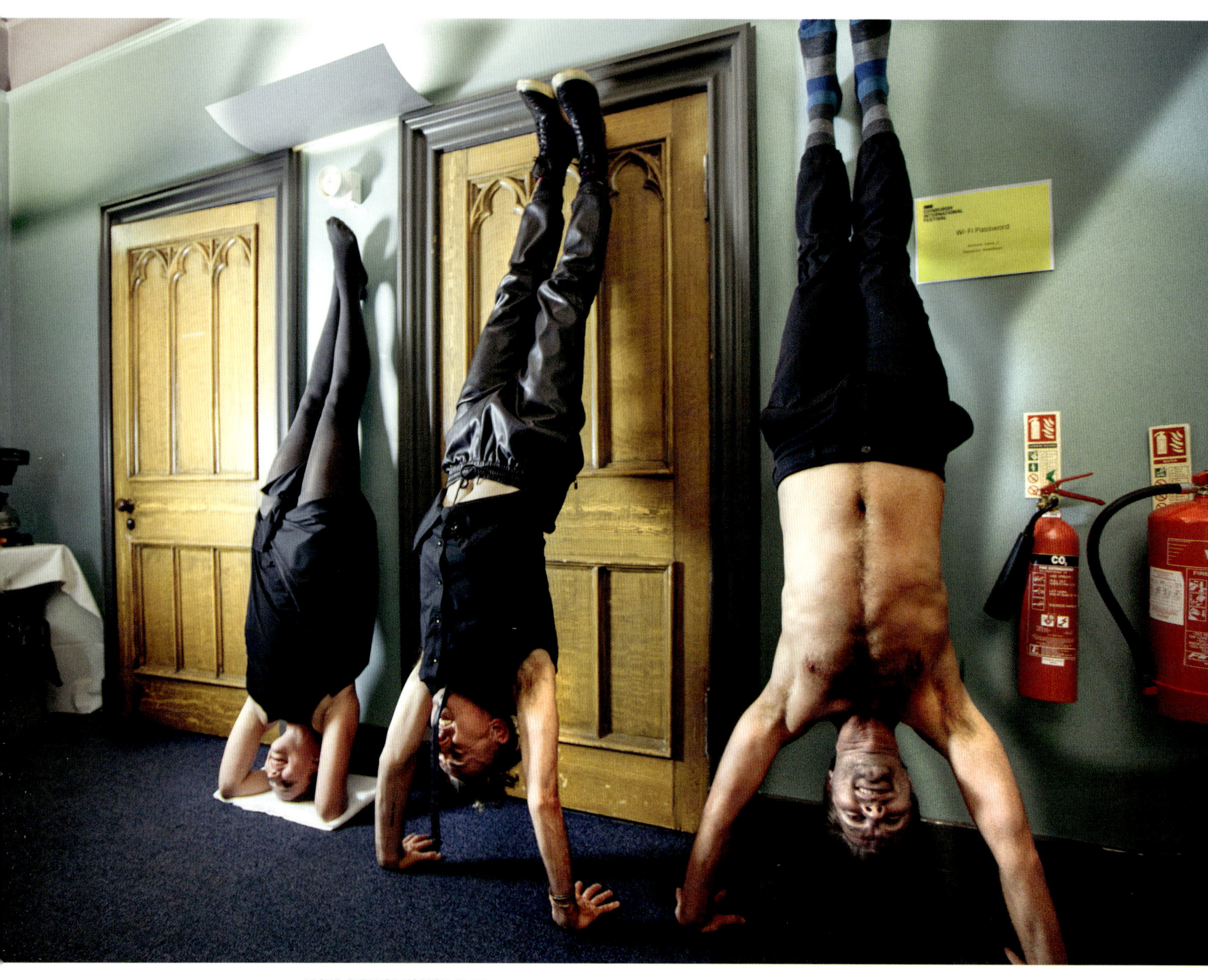

ABOVE: **ELEANOR NORTON, ALAN CUMMING, LANCE HORNE, *ALAN CUMMING SINGS SAPPY SONGS*, THE HUB EDINBURGH, 2016**
The irrepressible Alan is leading a warm-up before an evening of hilarity and music.

OPPOSITE: **SIMON RUSSELL BEALE, *DEATHTRAP*, NOËL COWARD THEATRE, 2010**
It has always been a delight to photograph Simon and witness the unbounded pleasure he takes in playing so many varied roles.

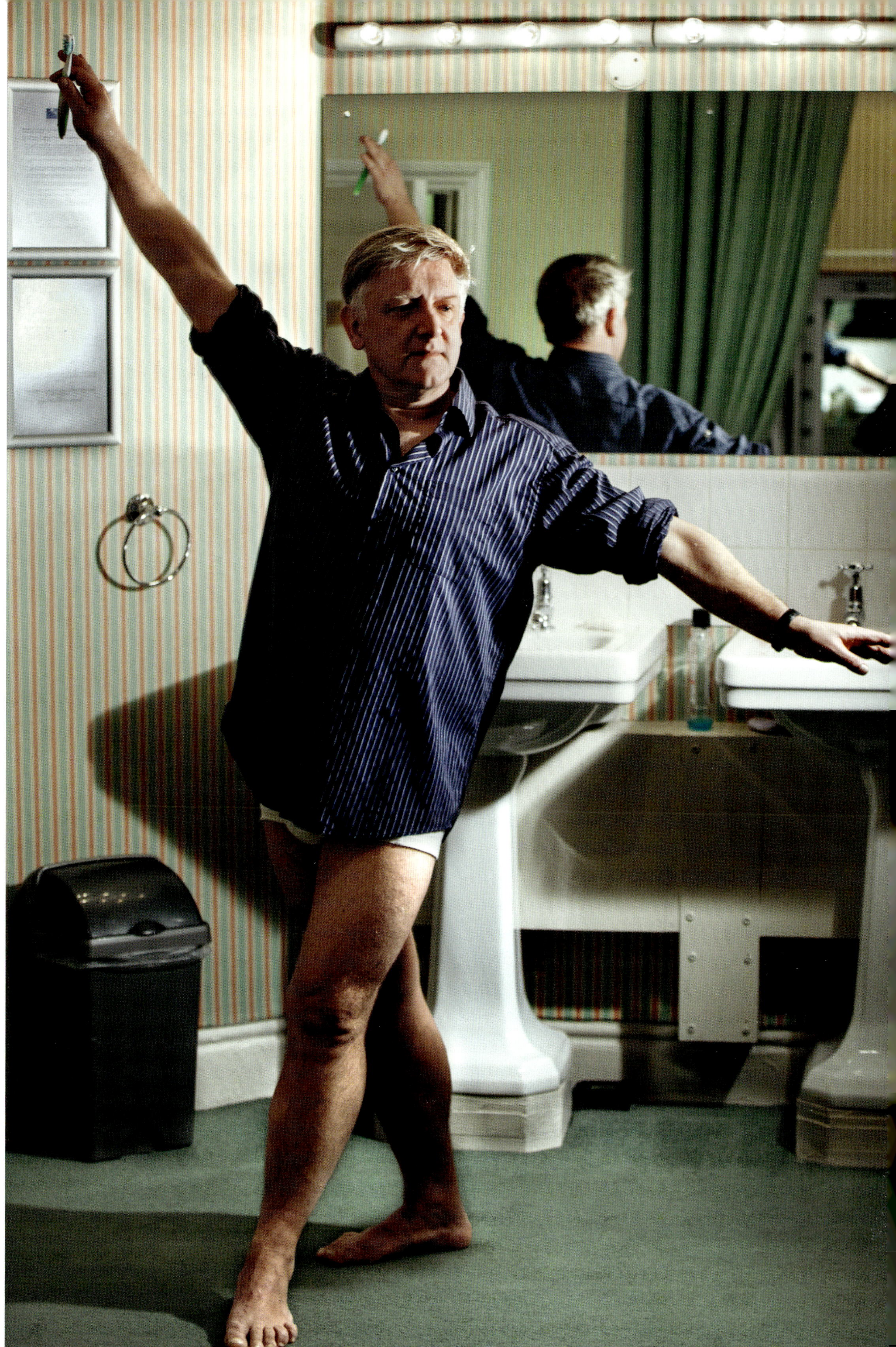

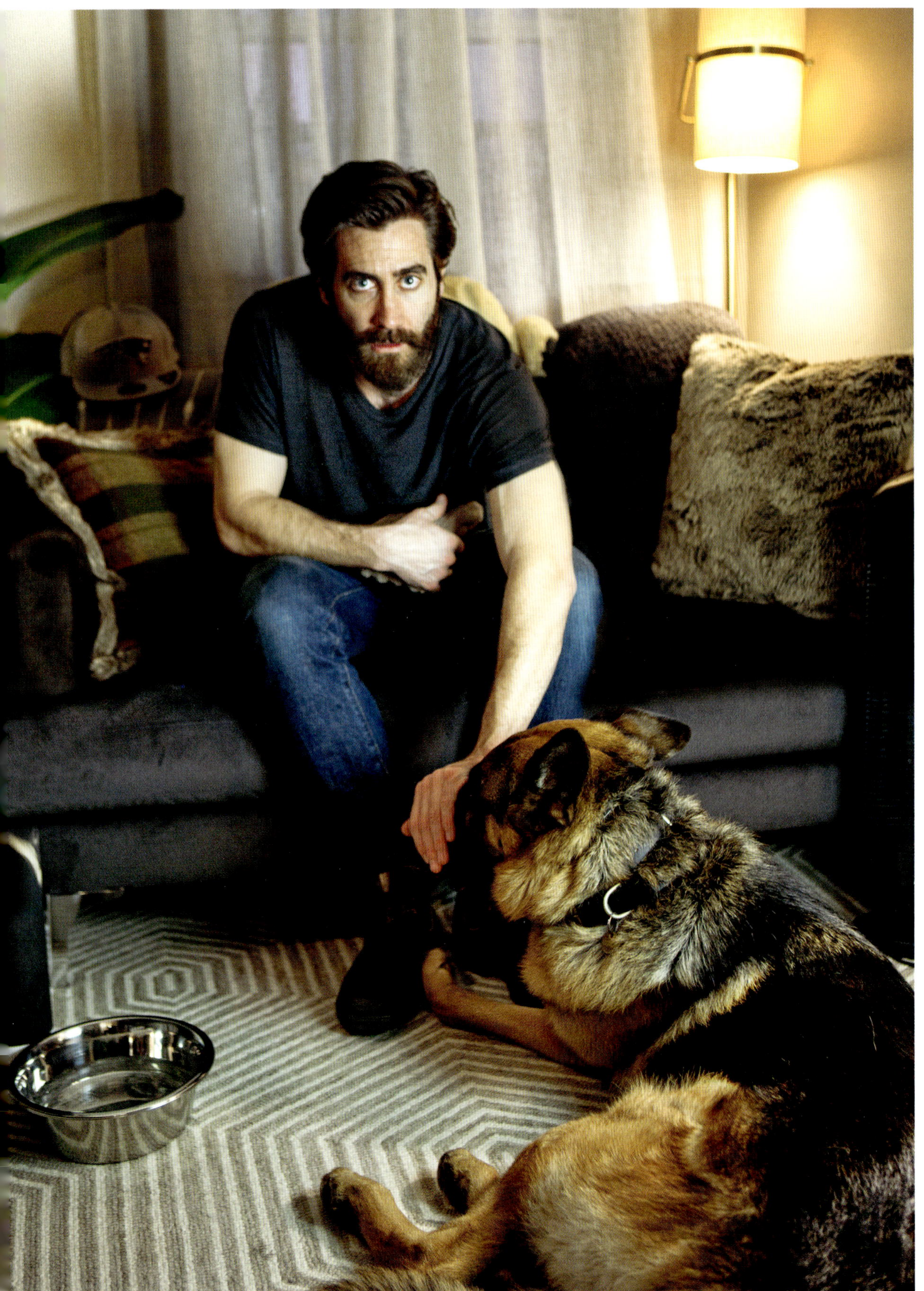

LEFT: **JAKE GYLLENHAAL,**
***SUNDAY IN THE PARK WITH GEORGE*,**
NEW YORK CITY CENTER, 2017
A true gentleman, and his dog seemed to mirror his personality perfectly.

OPPOSITE: **JEREMY IRONS,**
***LONG DAY'S JOURNEY INTO NIGHT*,**
WYNDHAM'S, 2018
One of the few people who makes all heads turn when entering a room. This is the first image of our session. Jeremy is still reminiscing about his day, before preparing for the lengthy role of James Tyrone in Eugene O'Neill's classic.

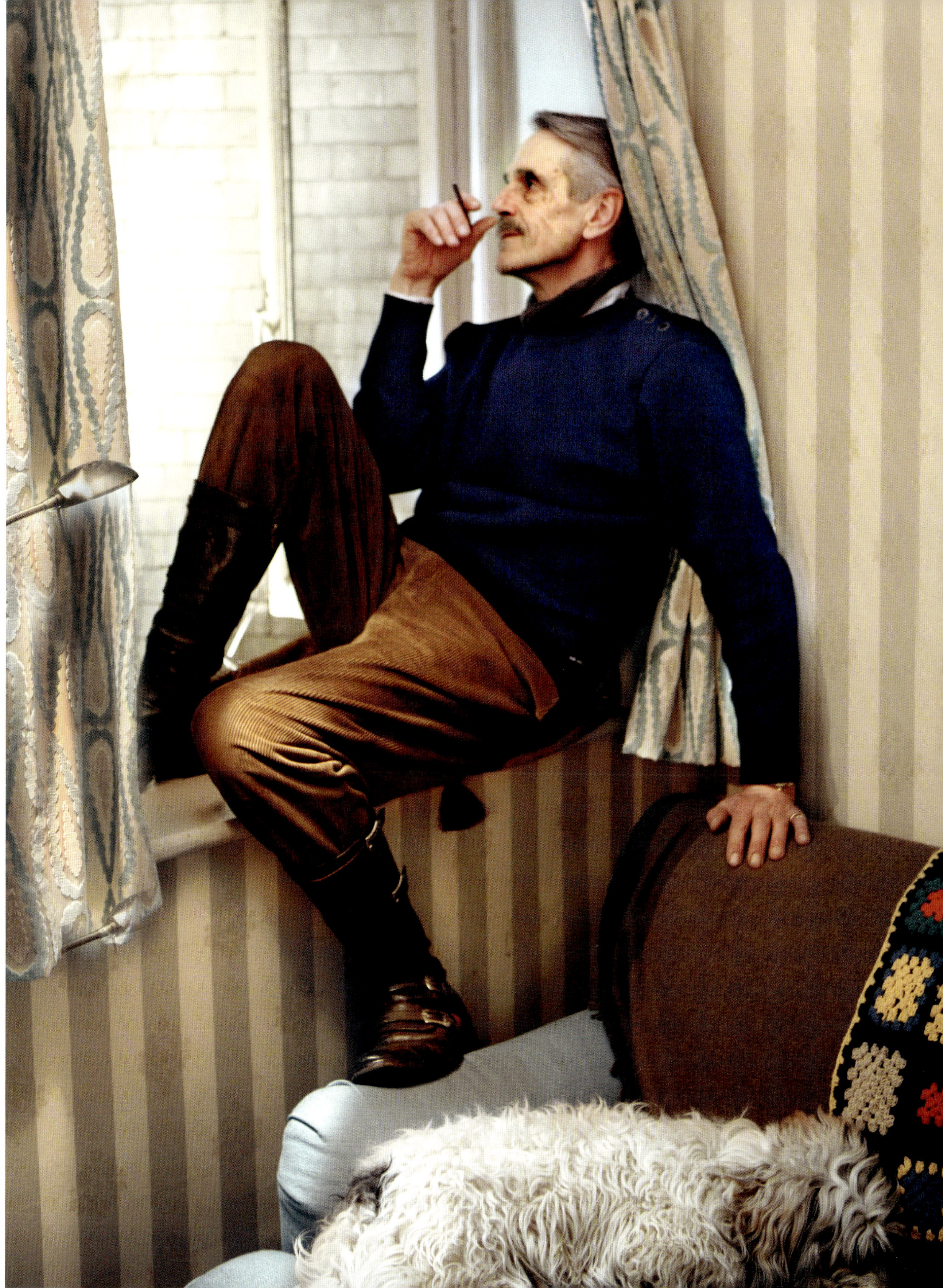

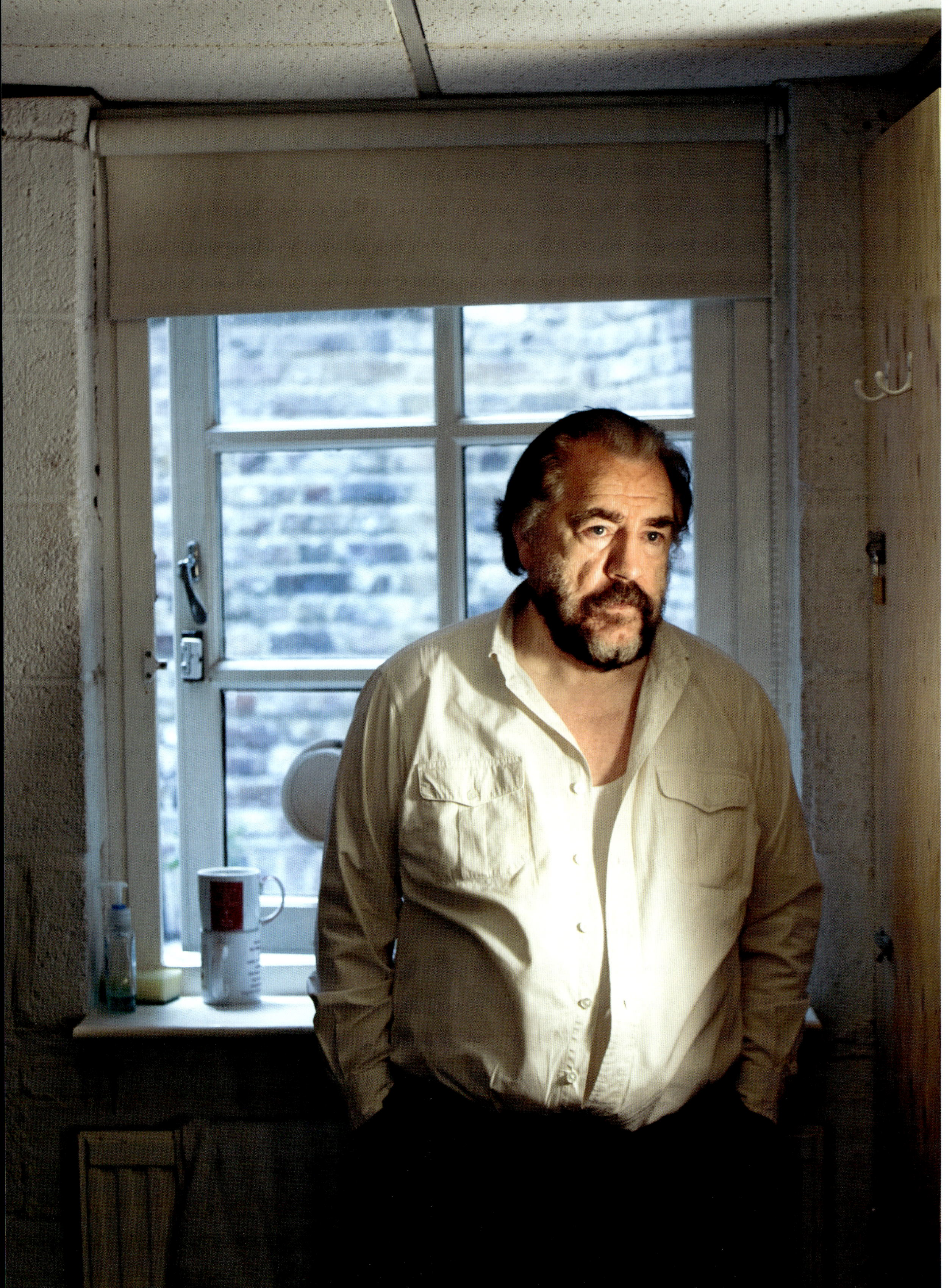

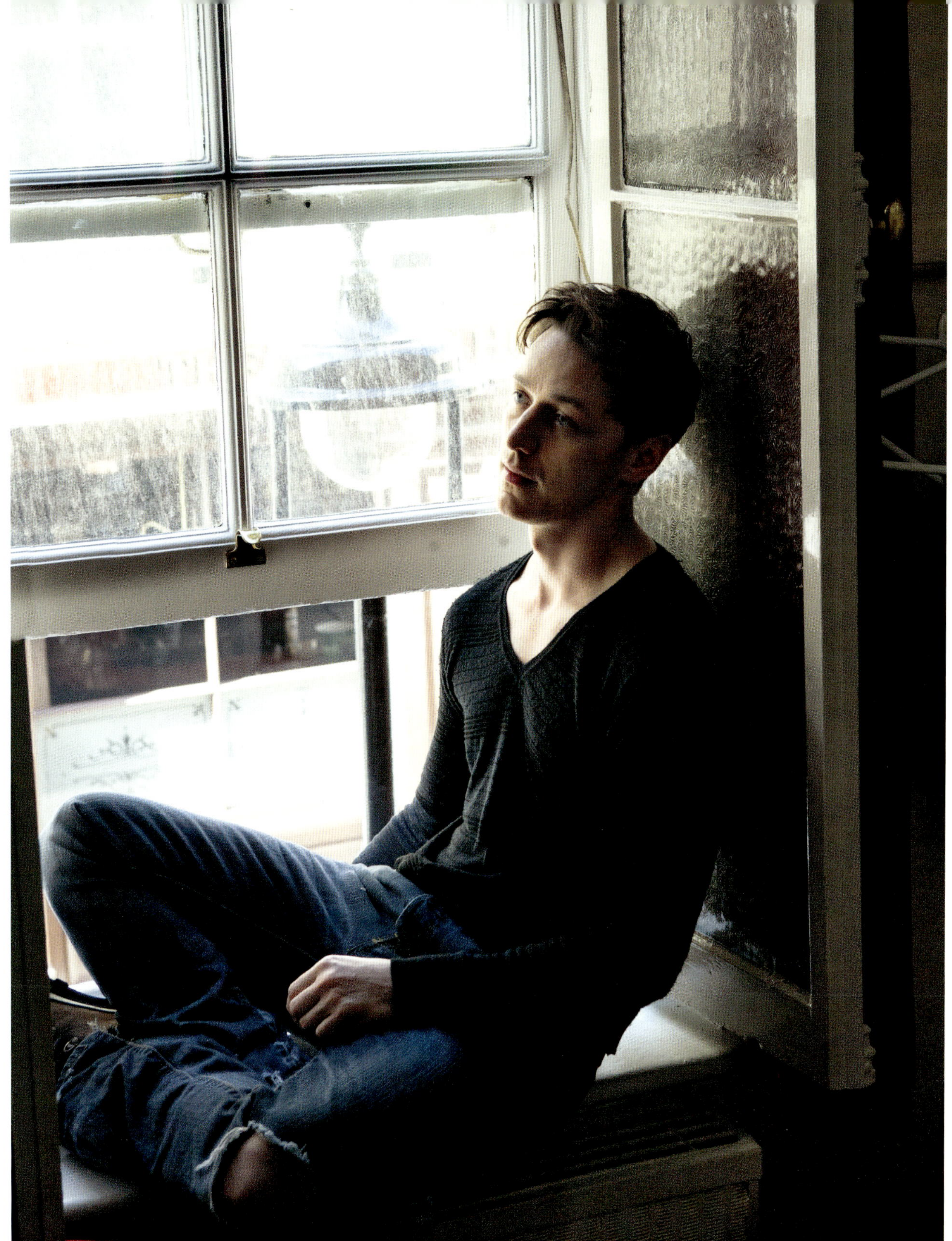

OPPOSITE: **BRIAN COX, *THE WEIR*, DONMAR WAREHOUSE, 2013**
Such a wonderful face, you can see the traces of many fictional characters that have passed through it.

RIGHT: **JAMES McAVOY, *THREE DAYS OF RAIN*, APOLLO THEATRE, 2009**
The often mesmerising and energetic actor is relaxing for a change.

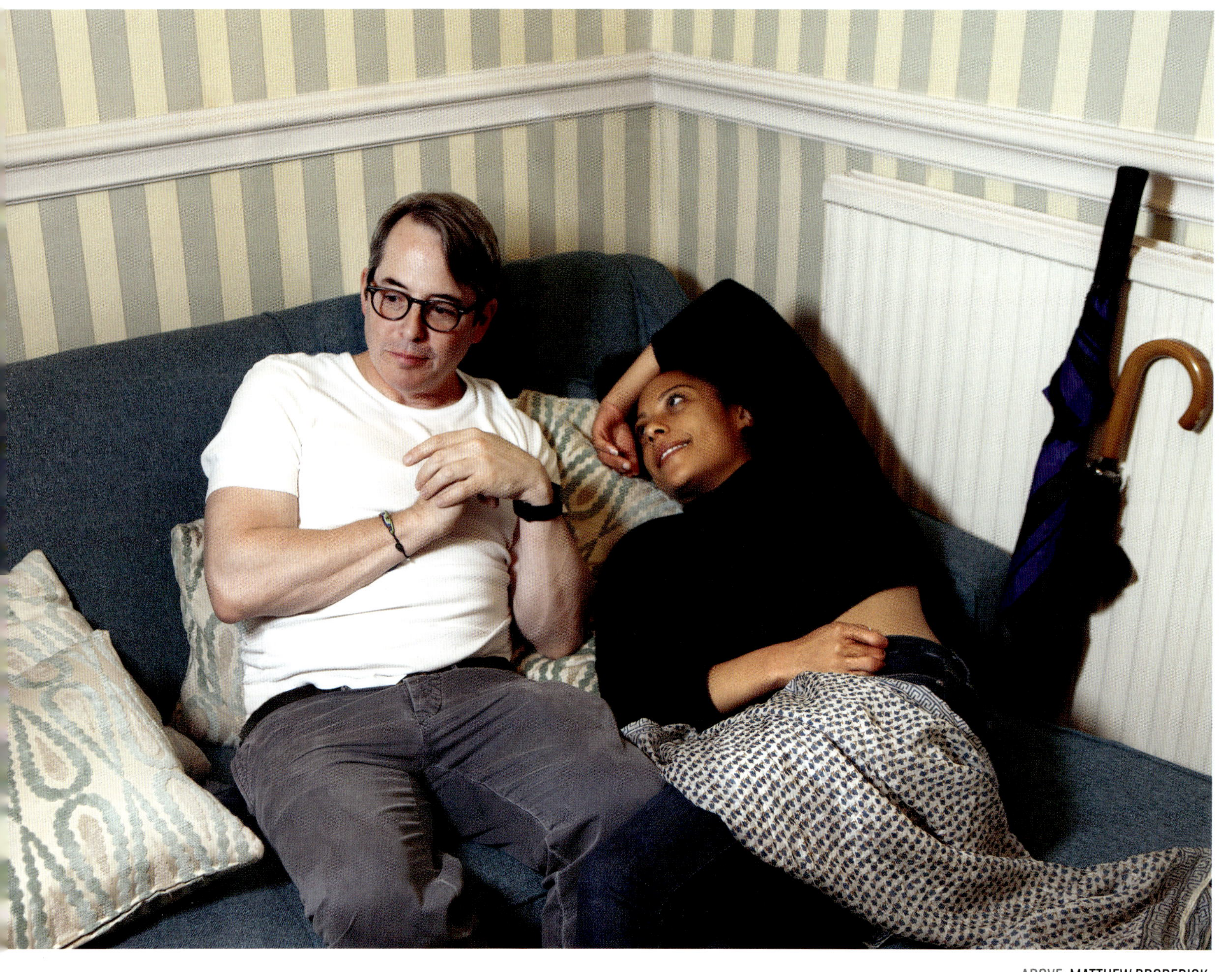

ABOVE: **MATTHEW BRODERICK, ROSALIND ELEAZAR, *THE STARRY MESSENGER*, WYNDHAM'S, 2019**
Matthew's performance was a masterclass in how to make an essentially dull character fascinating to watch. Rosalind's star is rising fast. Taken in the Green Room.

OPPOSITE: **JEFF GOLDBLUM, *THE PRISONER OF SECOND AVENUE*, VAUDEVILLE THEATRE, 2010**
Jeff loves his piano and he played non-stop throughout the twenty-minute session.

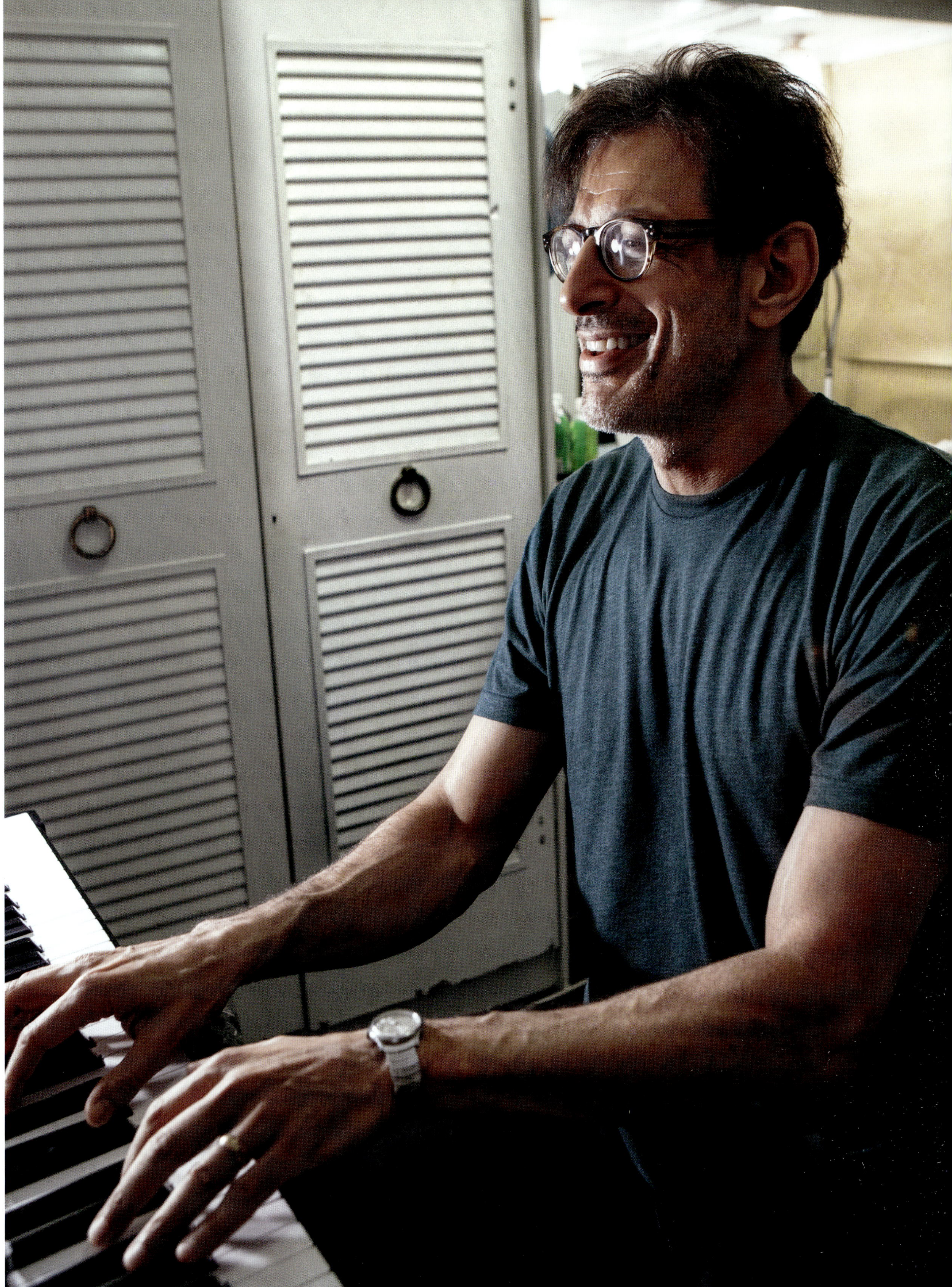

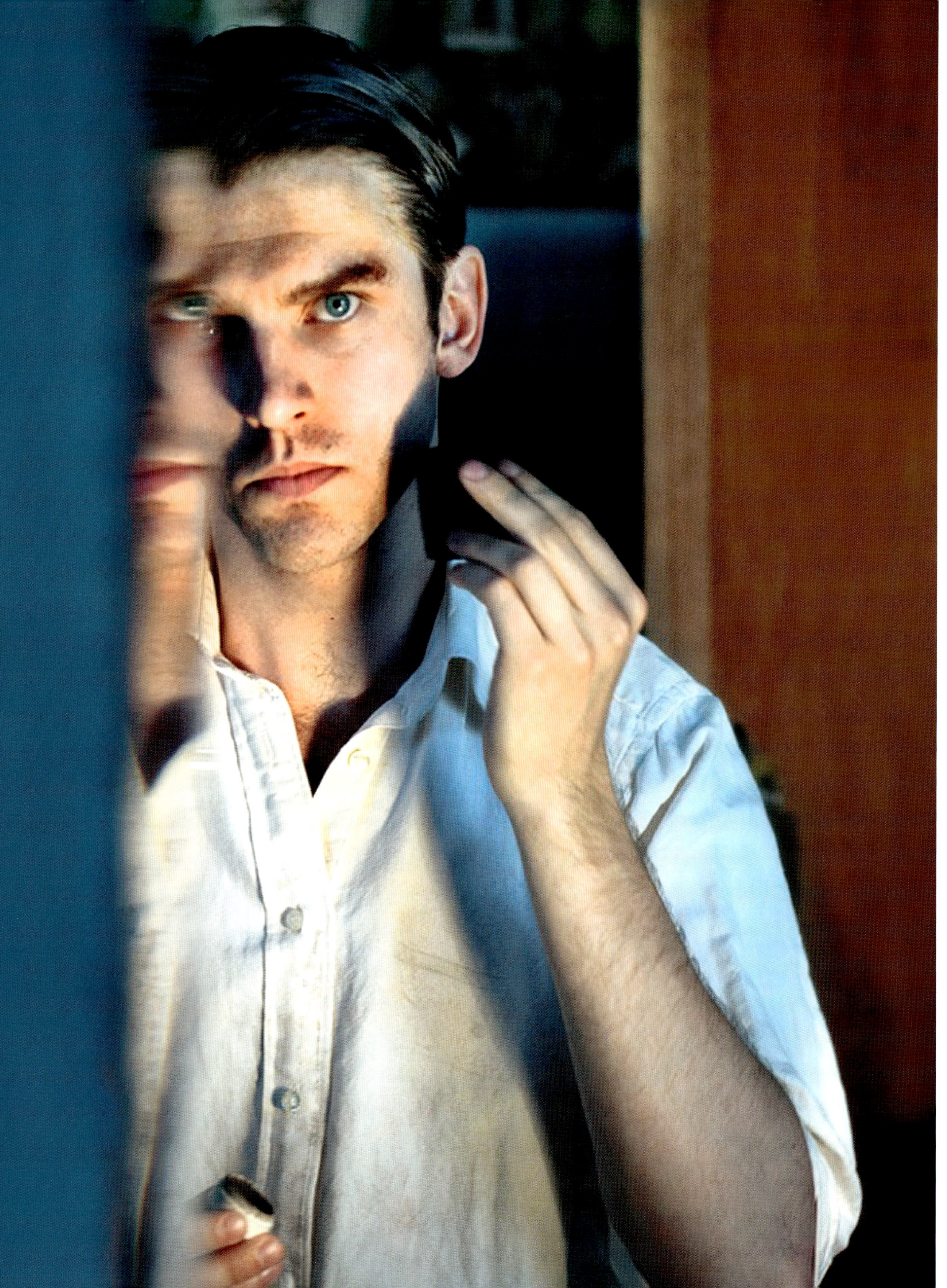

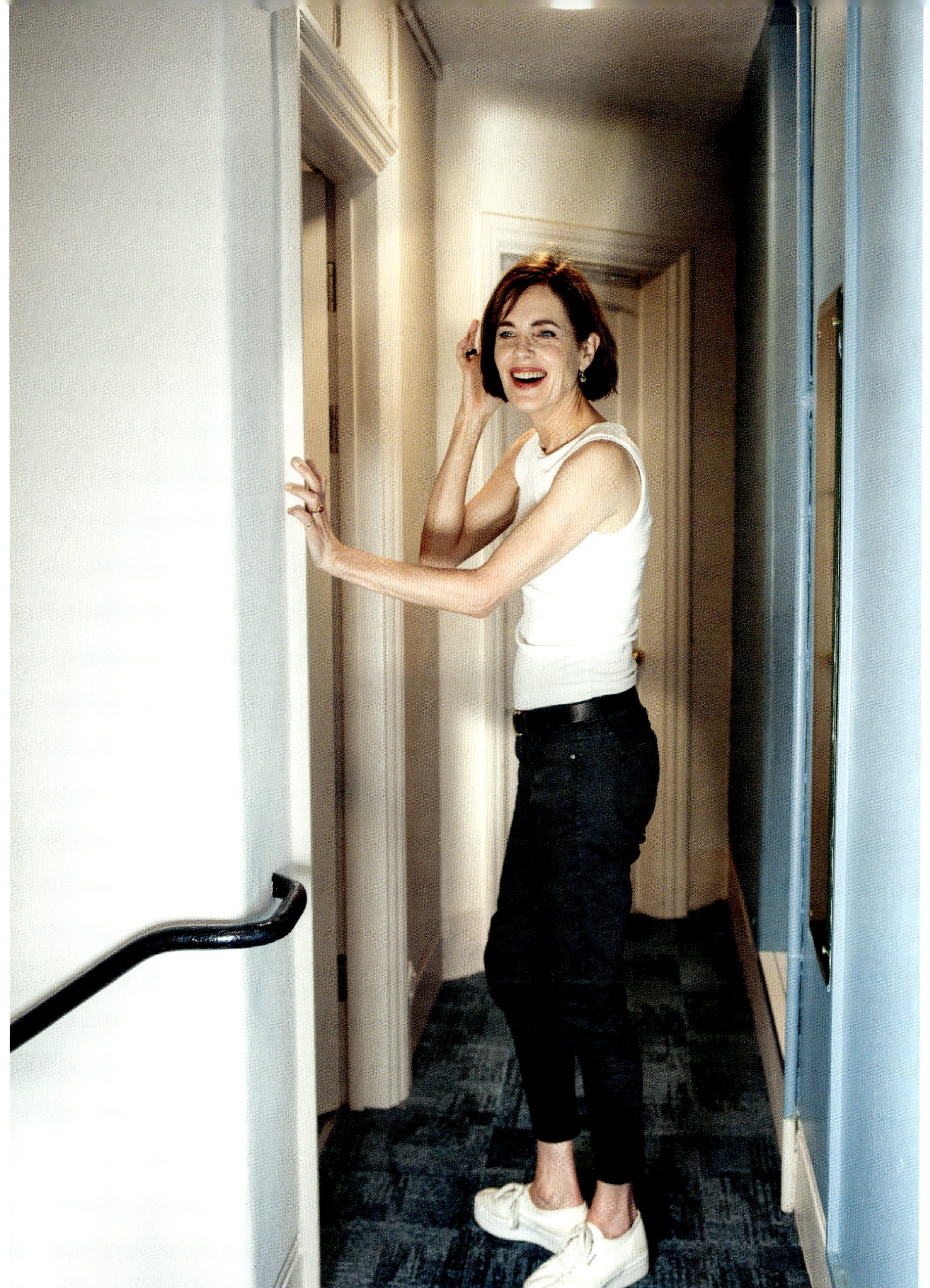

OPPOSITE: **DAN STEVENS, *HAY FEVER*, THEATRE ROYAL HAYMARKET, 2006**
This is the moment where the character begins to take hold.

RIGHT: **ELIZABETH McGOVERN, *THE STARRY MESSENGER*, WYNDHAM'S, 2019**
Elizabeth checking on all her fellow actors to wish them well.

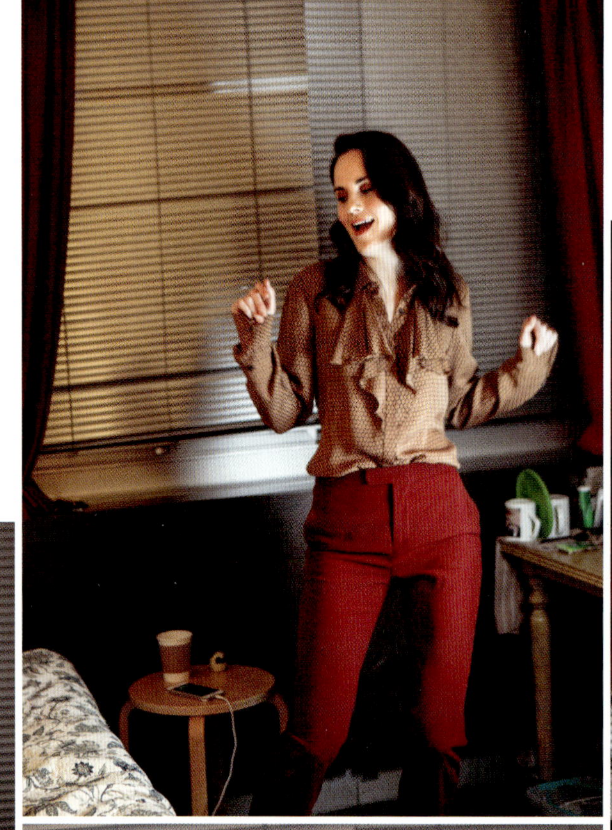

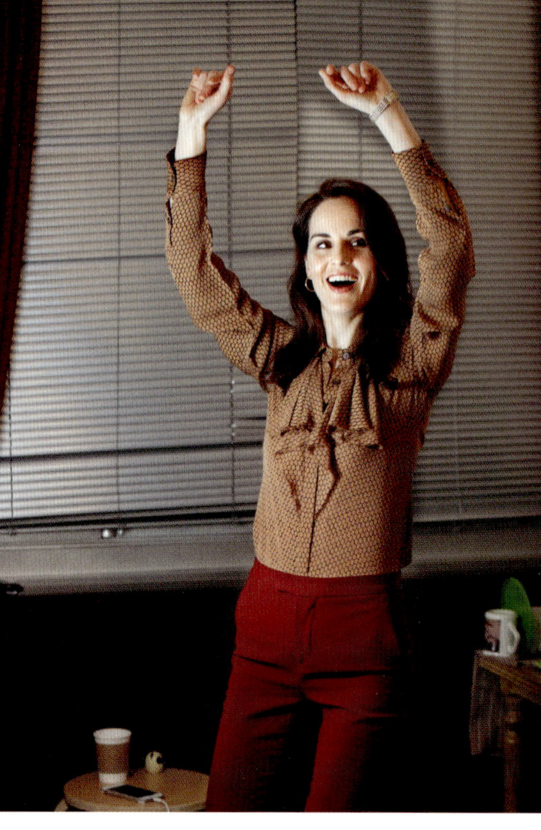

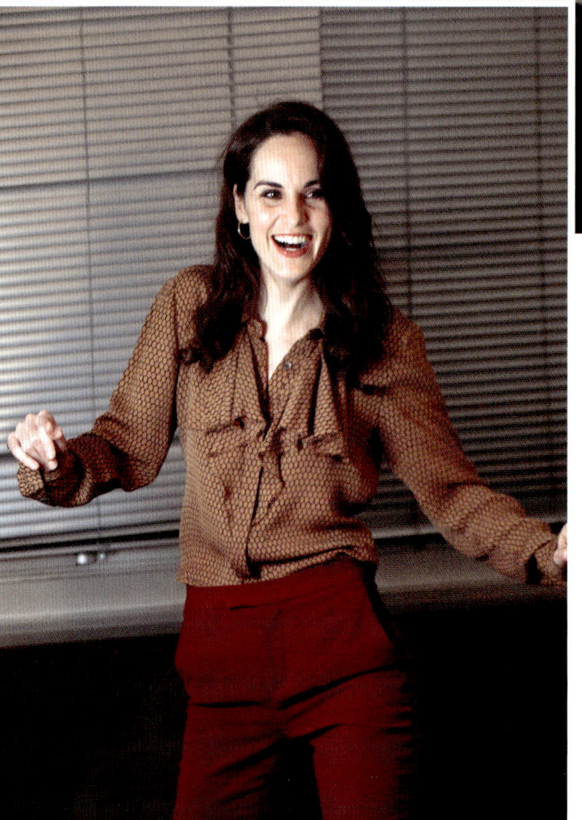

MICHELLE DOCKERY, *NETWORK*, NATIONAL THEATRE, 2017
Michelle loves to dance. Her warm and big-hearted personality is so different from the cold characters she is sometimes asked to play.

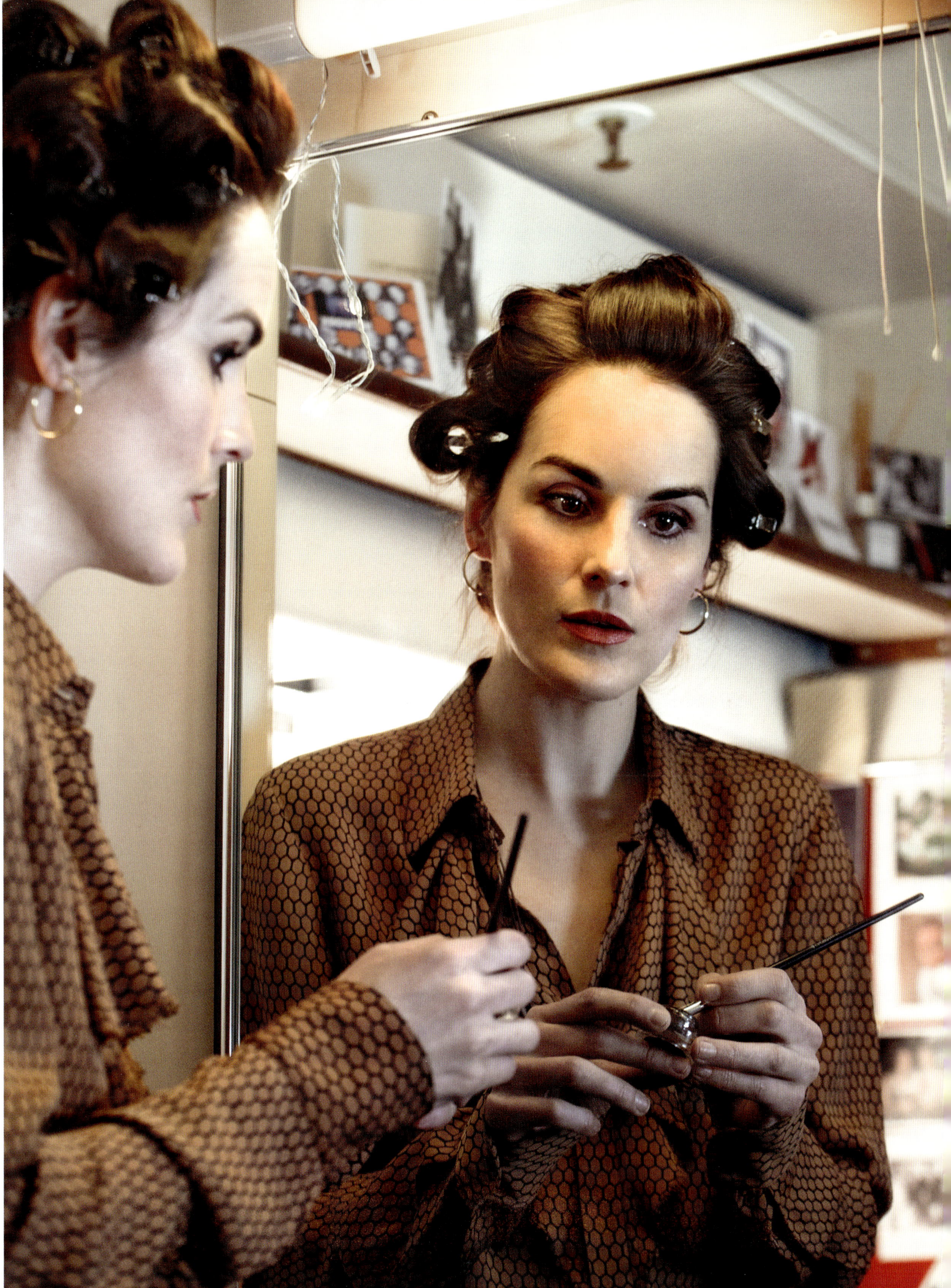

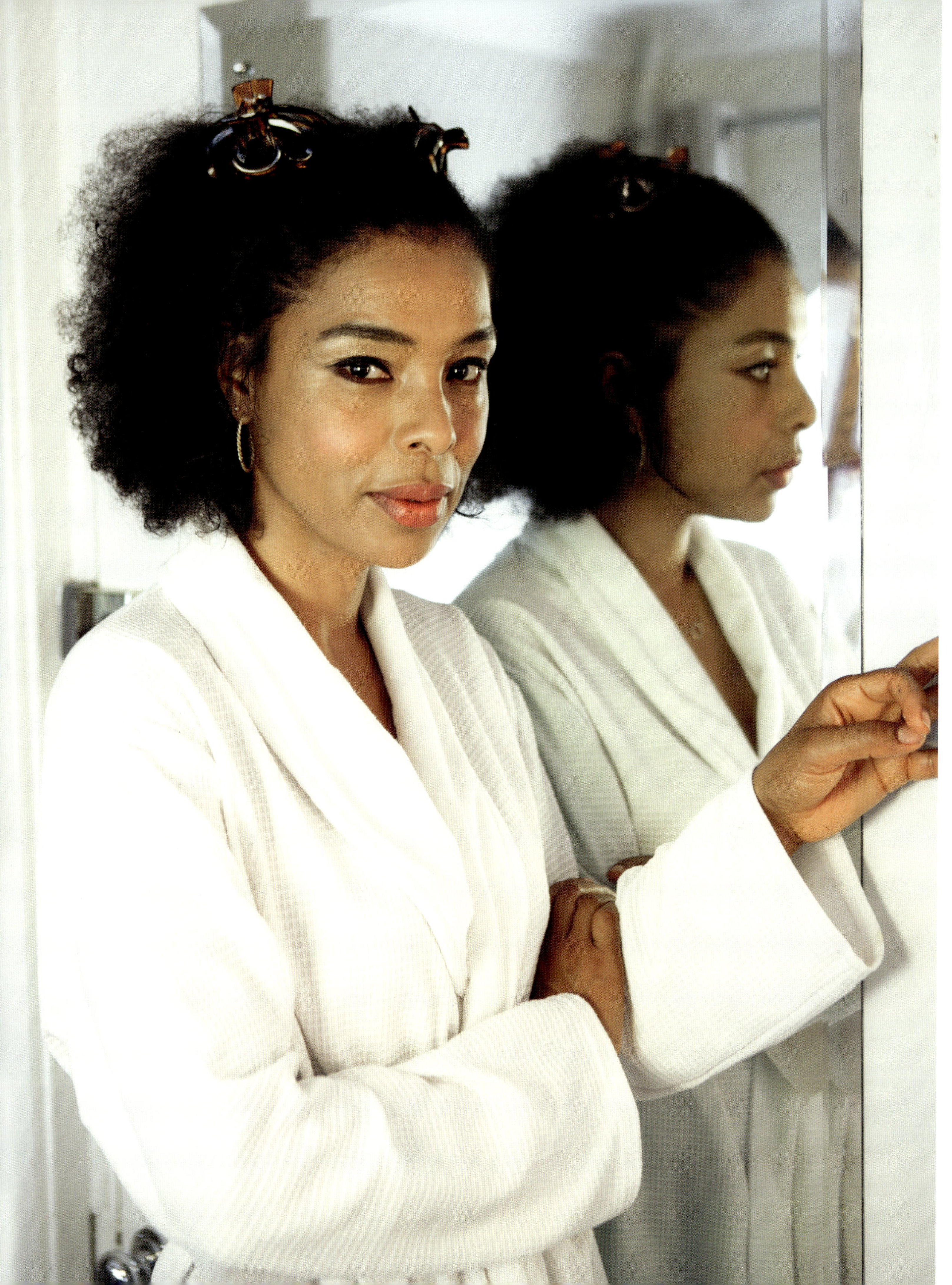

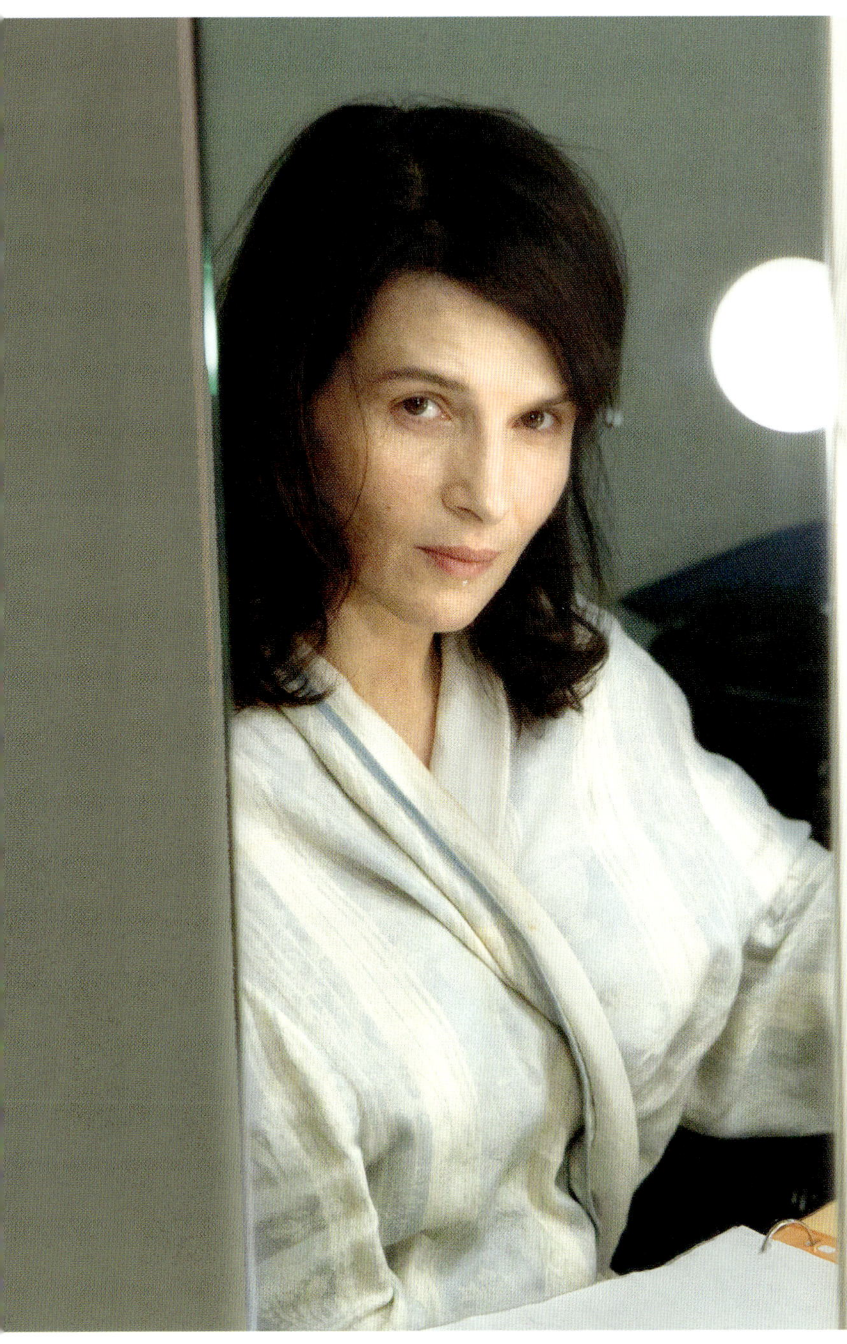
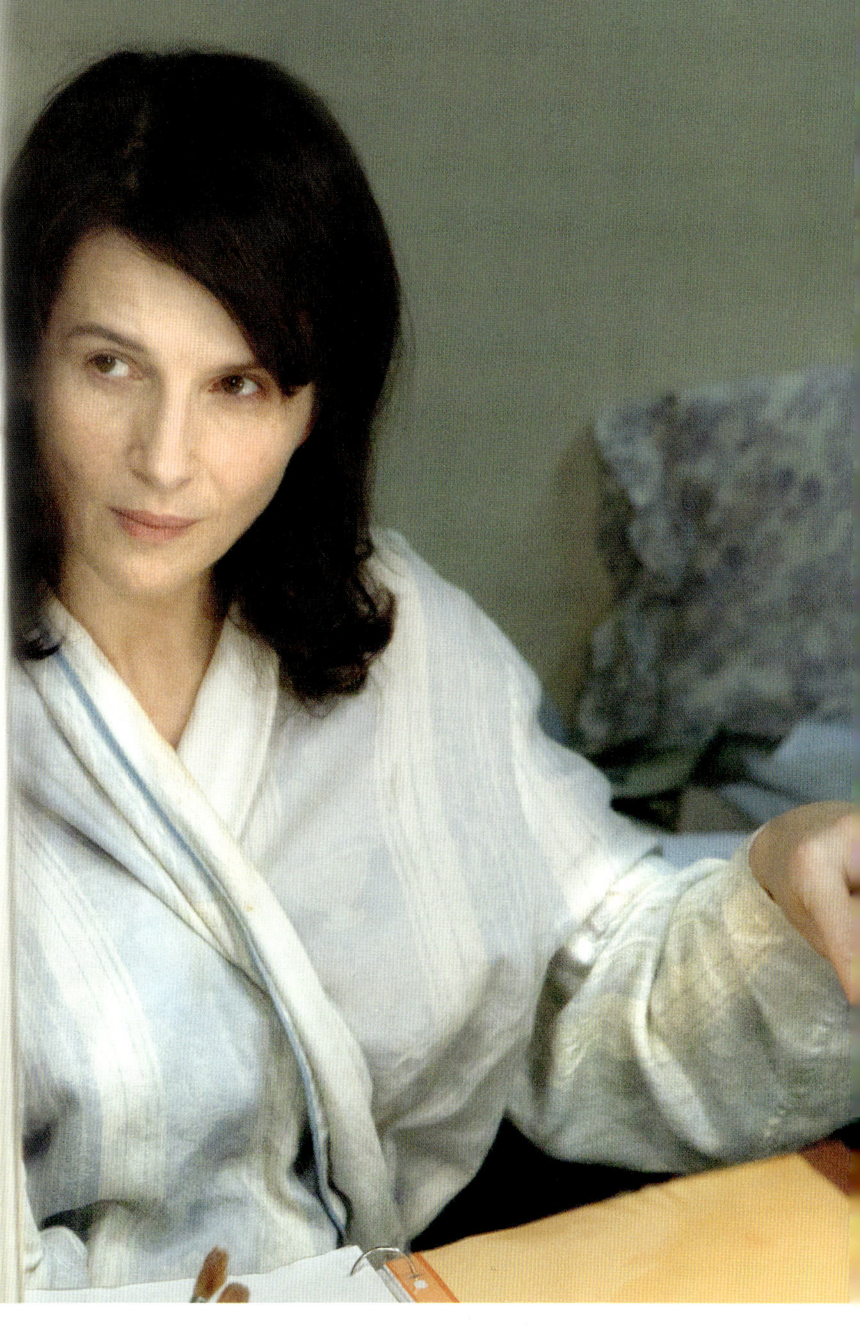

OPPOSITE: **SOPHIE OKONEDO,**
THE GOAT, OR WHO IS SYLVIA?**,**
THEATRE ROYAL HAYMARKET, 2017
For many years casting opportunities for black actors have been unfairly limited. Hopefully this is beginning to change. Sophie's next role was Cleopatra at the National Theatre, which was a triumph.

ABOVE: **JULIETTE BINOCHE, *IN-I*,**
NATIONAL THEATRE, 2010
The great French actress requested a second session. She was keen that her particular process of preparation was recorded, and I was happy to oblige.

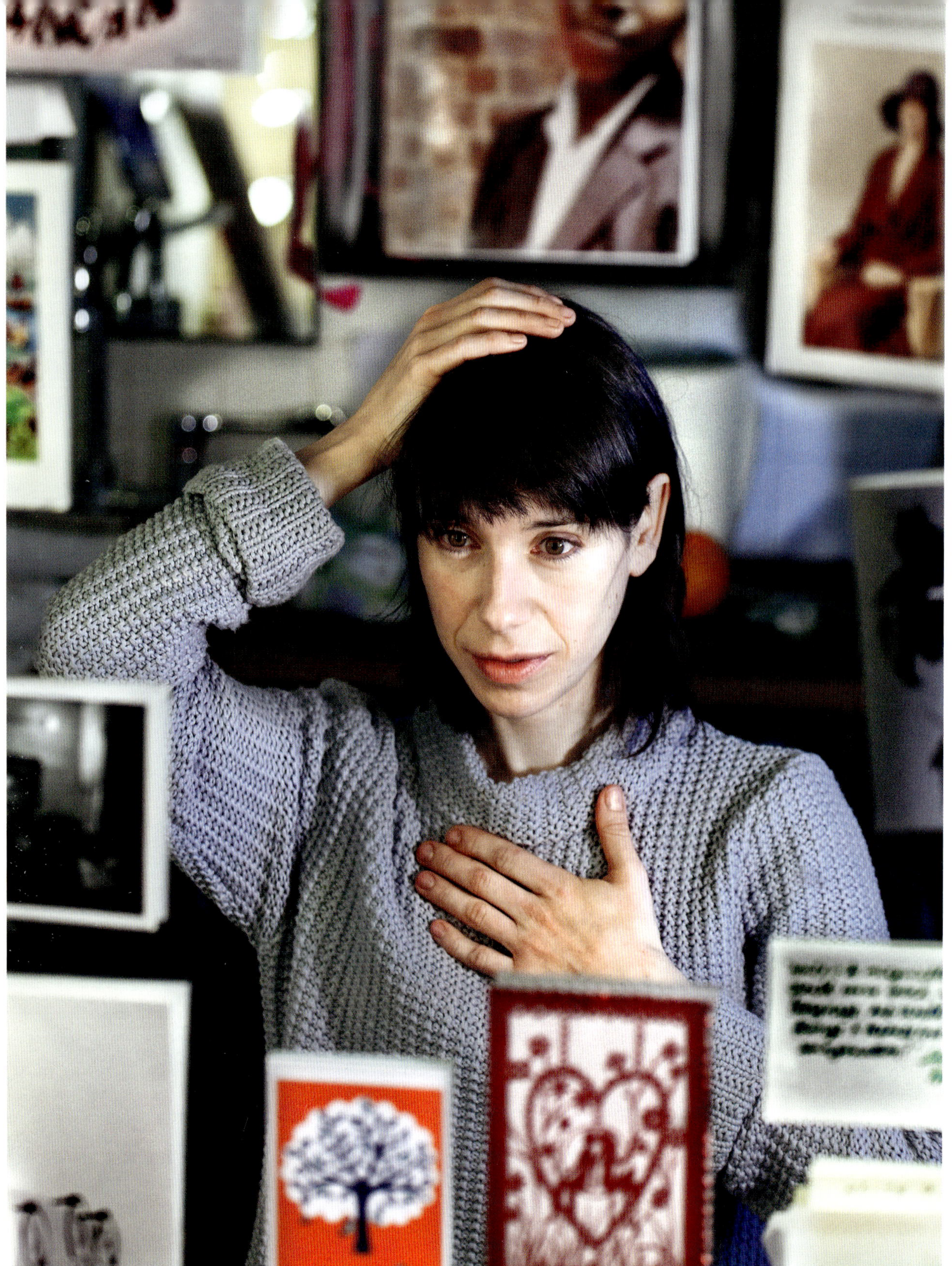

LEFT: **SALLY HAWKINS, *CONSTELLATIONS*, ROYAL COURT, 2012**
Connecting her heart with her mind.

OPPOSITE: **ELISABETH MOSS, *THE CHILDREN'S HOUR*, COMEDY THEATRE, 2011**
The mutual respect between us created much fun during the session and there were many images to choose from. This picture will always remind me how a very talented and focused professional can also let go when trust is there.

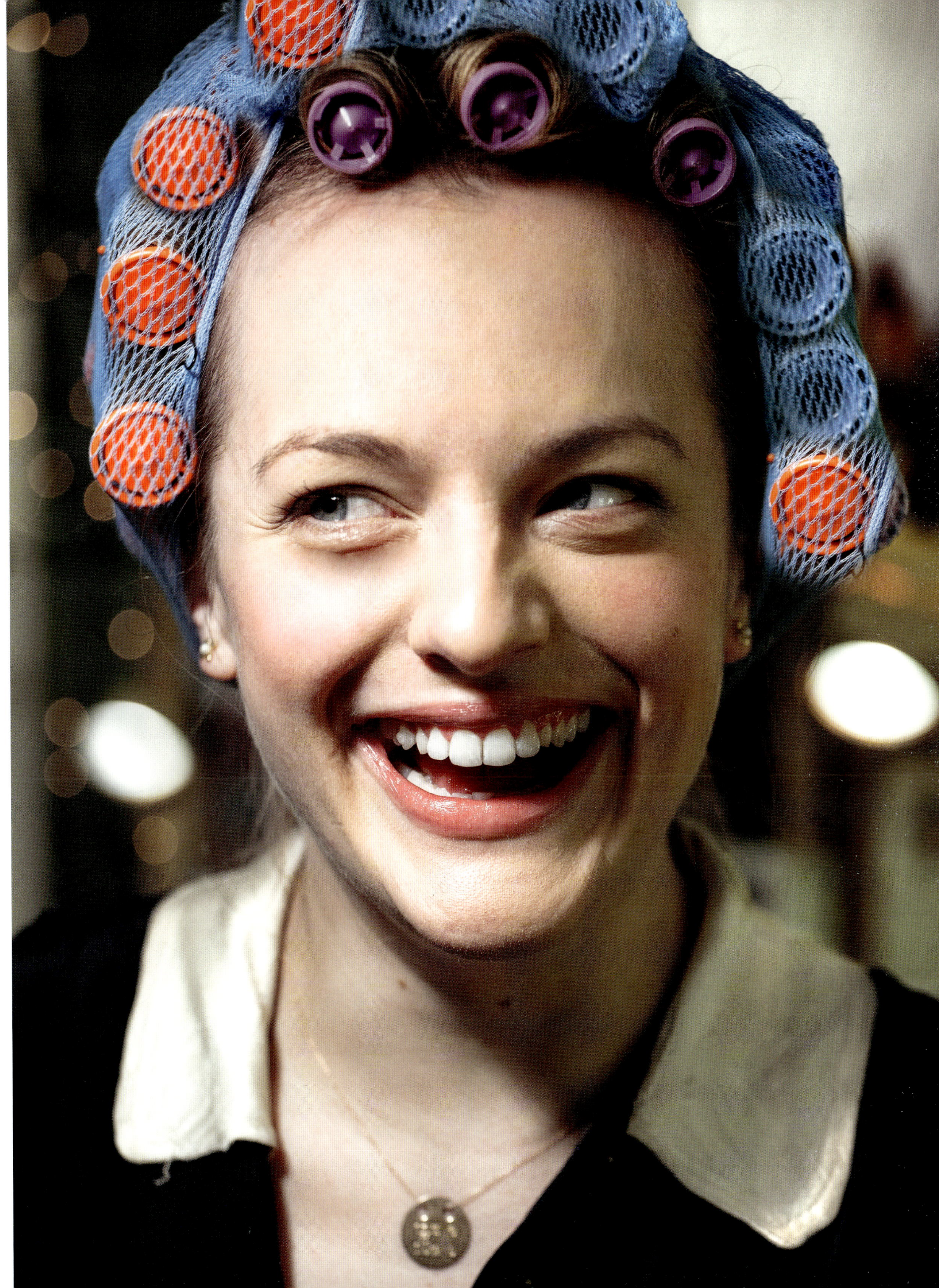

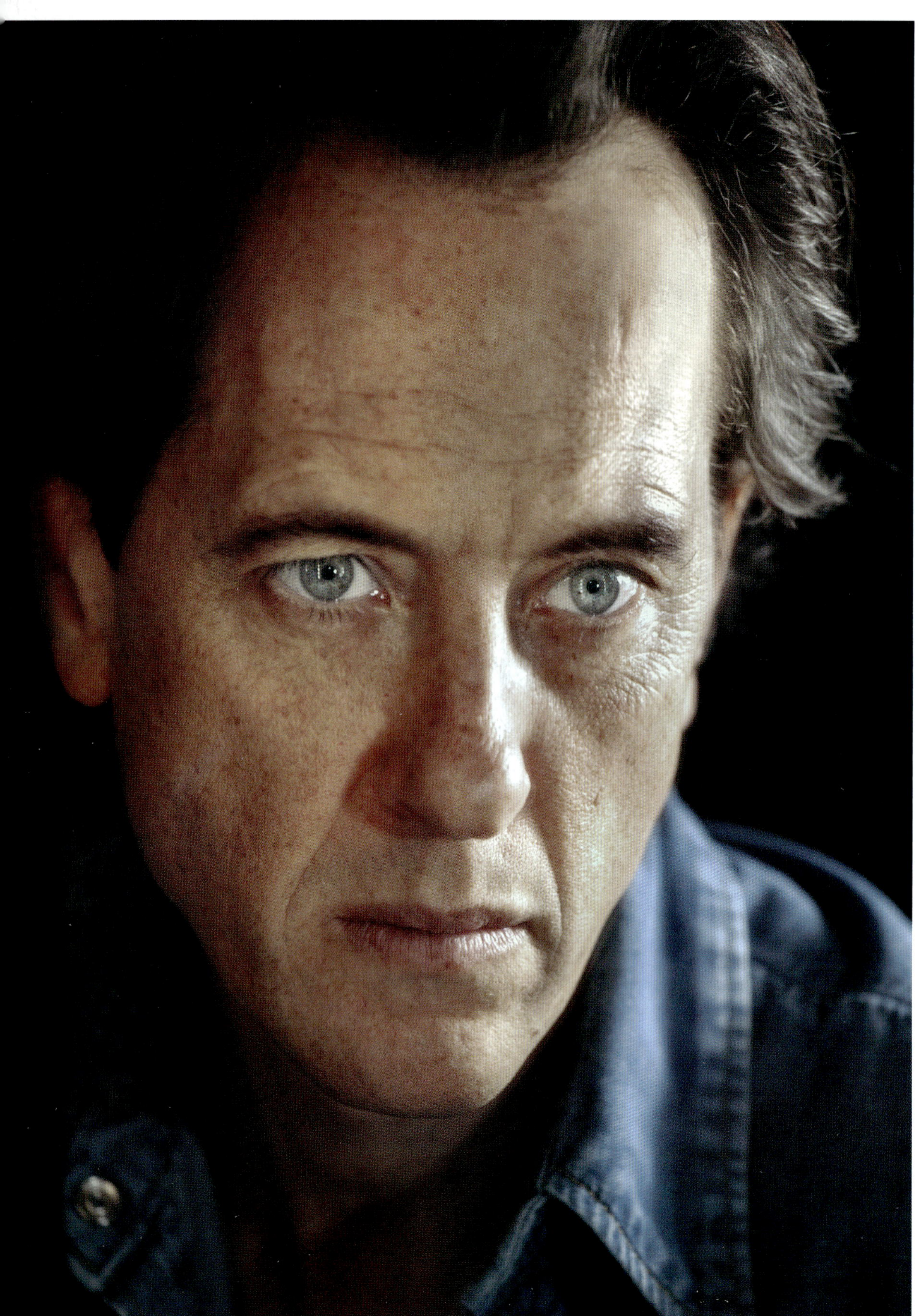

LEFT: **RICHARD E. GRANT, *OTHERWISE ENGAGED*, CRITERION THEATRE, 2005**
Richard personifies an actor who can leave their role behind at the end of the day. My impression is that his personality is not defined by being an actor.

OPPOSITE: **MARK STRONG, *A VIEW FROM THE BRIDGE*, YOUNG VIC, 2015**
Over the years Mark has developed a commanding stage presence, driven by vulnerability, which is an underrated art and much in demand.

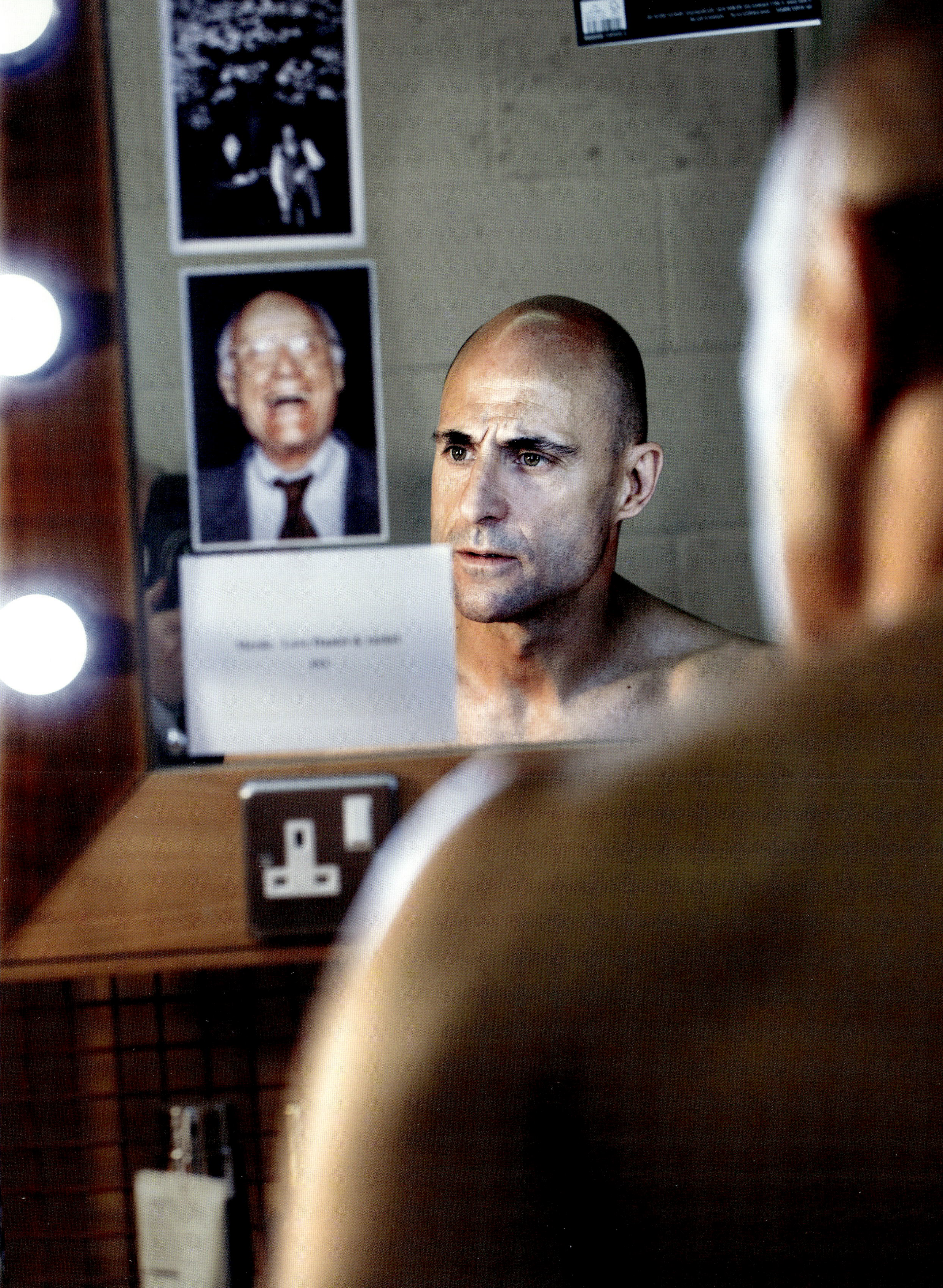

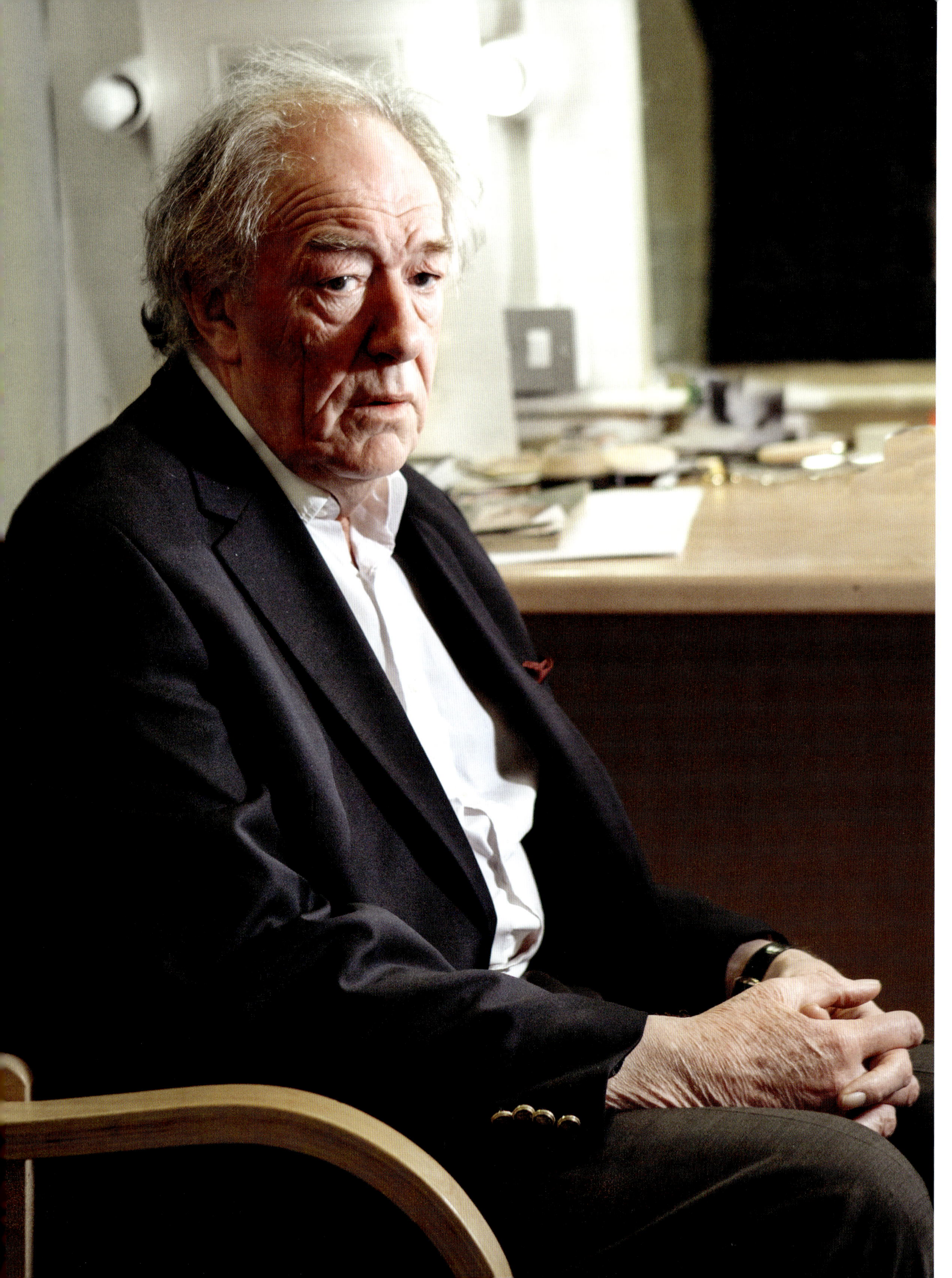

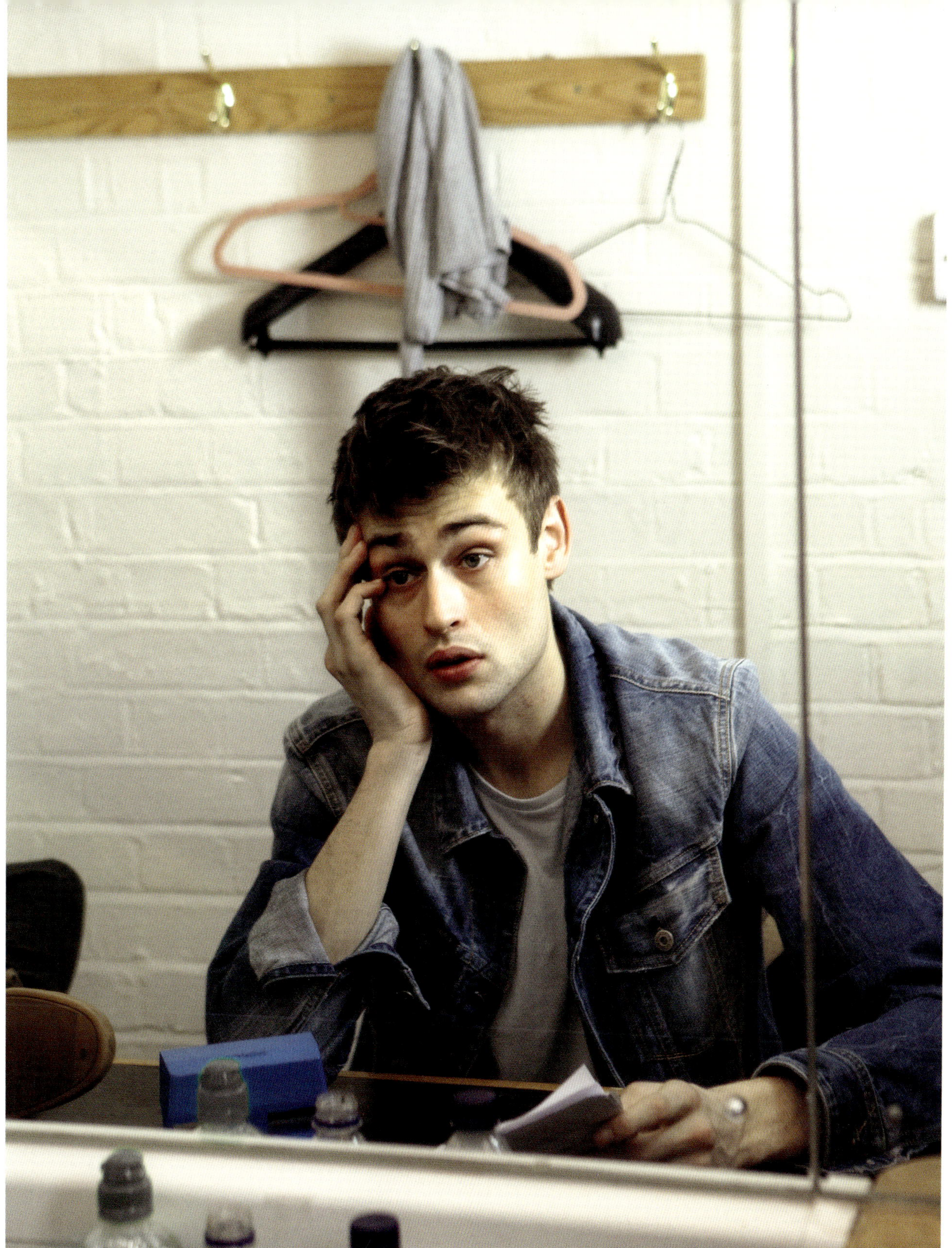

OPPOSITE: MICHAEL GAMBON, *NO MAN'S LAND*, DUKE OF YORK'S, 2008
The Great Gambon, as Ralph Richardson called him, loves theatre history. He is one of the few actors who can show the essence of bullying in Pinter's bleakest plays without a shred of vanity. He fully understands the tough landscape and has no fear of going there.

RIGHT: DOUGLAS BOOTH, *A GUIDE FOR THE HOMESICK*, TRAFALGAR STUDIOS, 2018
Douglas begins his preparation to get in character.

EDWARD FOX, *AN IDEAL HUSBAND*, THEATRE ROYAL BATH, 2018

Close to his eightieth birthday and still touring, Edward loves performing to a live audience. The tradition is very safe in his skilful hands. We had agreed to a session, but it had to be rescheduled to later in the tour. We only had eight minutes in the end, but it was well worth the travel.

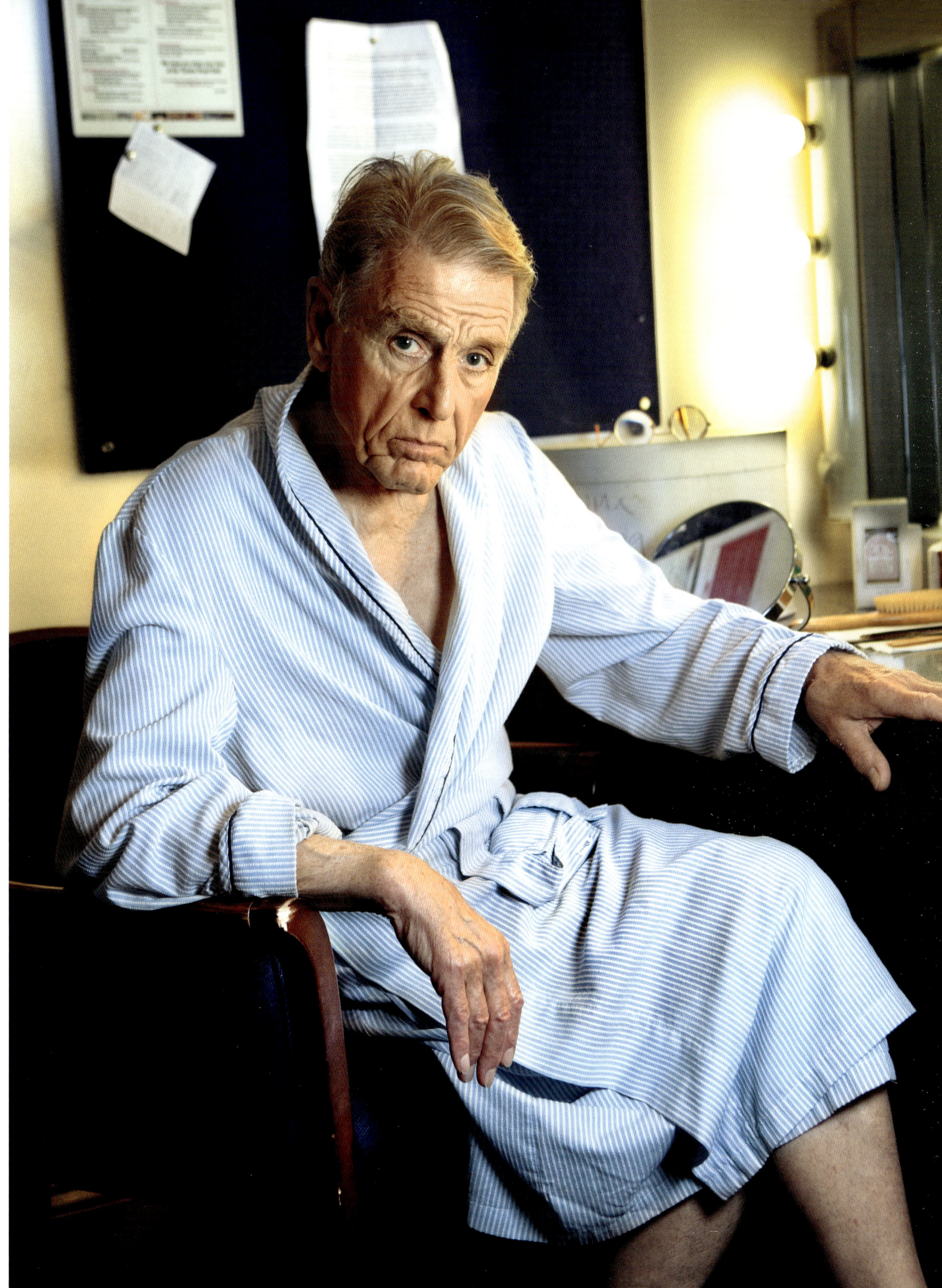

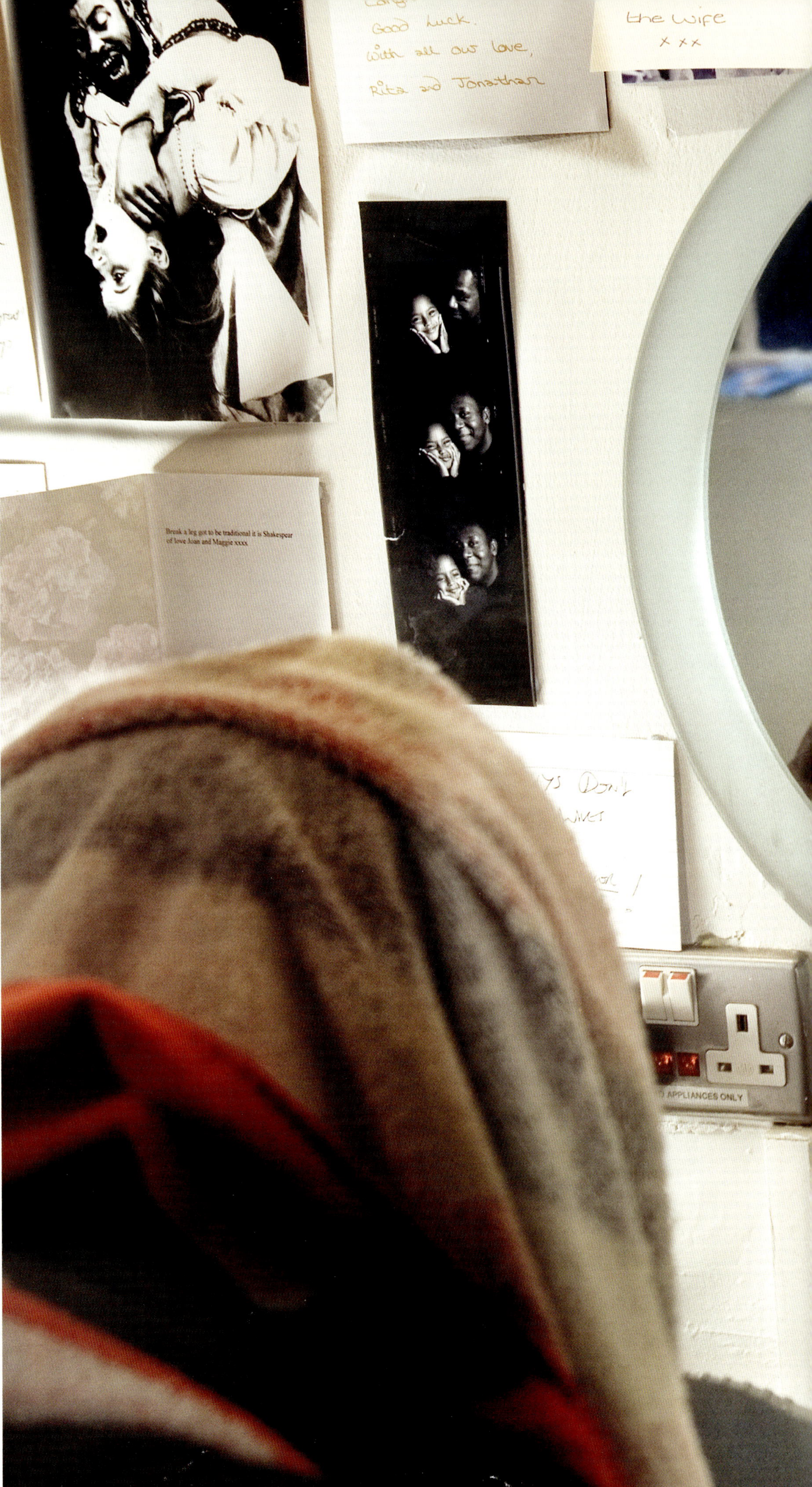

LENNY HENRY, *OTHELLO*, TRAFALGAR STUDIOS, 2009
As Lenny takes on the massive task of playing Othello, he is reminiscent of a boxer before the fight.

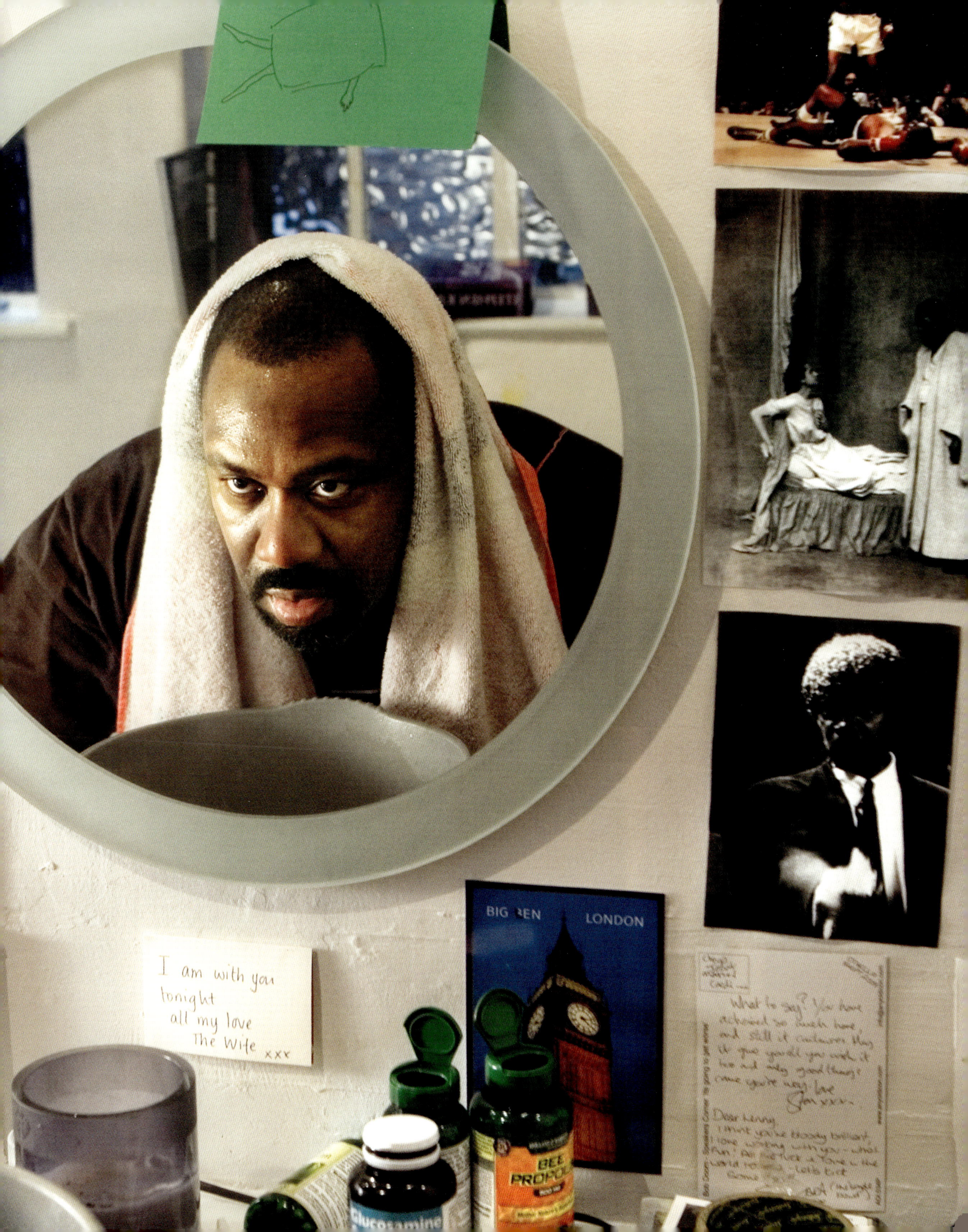
I am with you
tonight
all my love
The Wife xxx
LONDON
BEE
Glucosamine

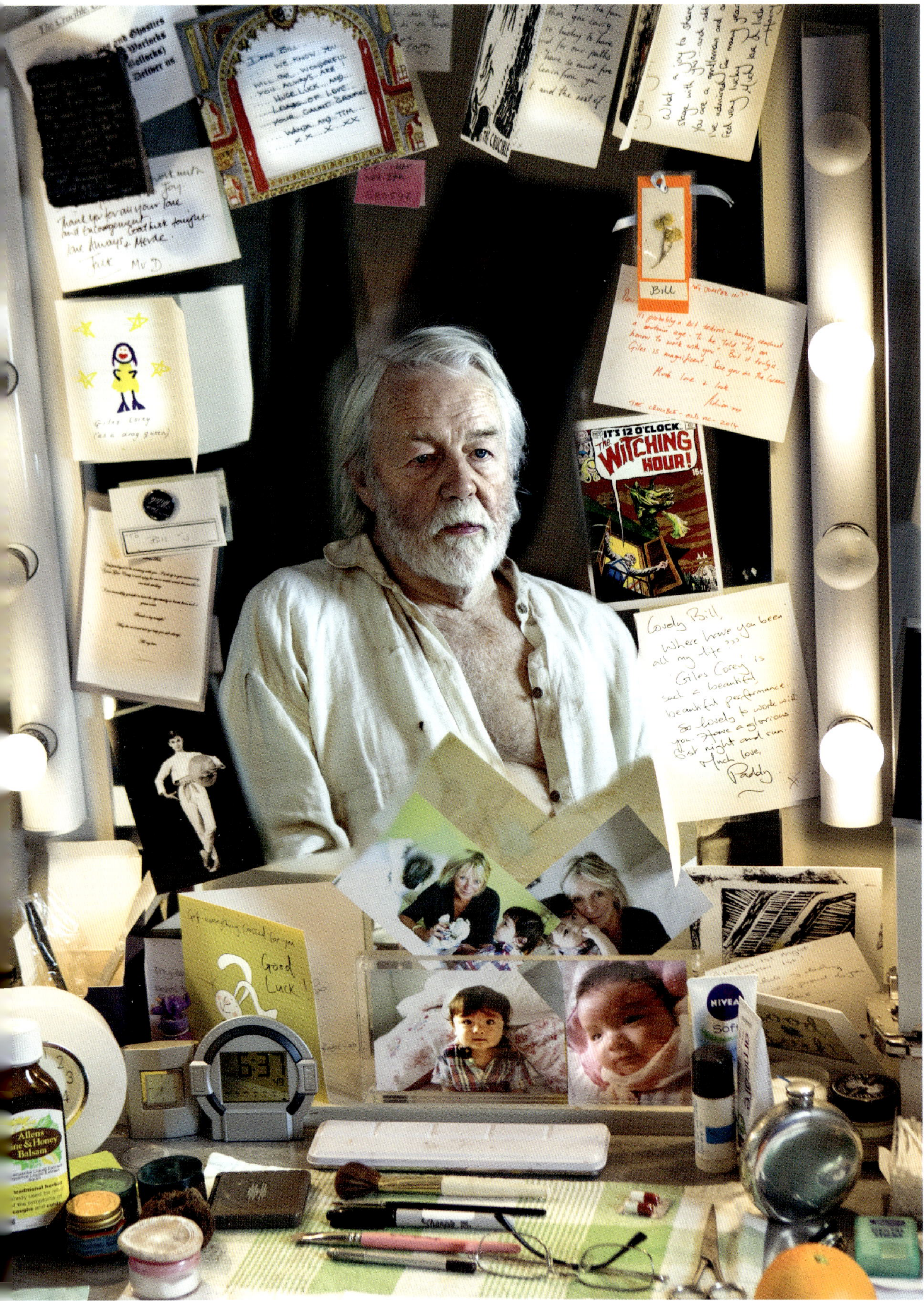

LEFT: WILLIAM GAUNT, *THE CRUCIBLE*, OLD VIC THEATRE, 2014

After a long and distinguished career in TV, William is enjoying a life full of the theatre.

OPPOSITE: ASHLEY JENSEN, *A CHORUS OF DISAPPROVAL*, HAROLD PINTER THEATRE, 2013

Ashley confronts herself and what drew her to play the part.

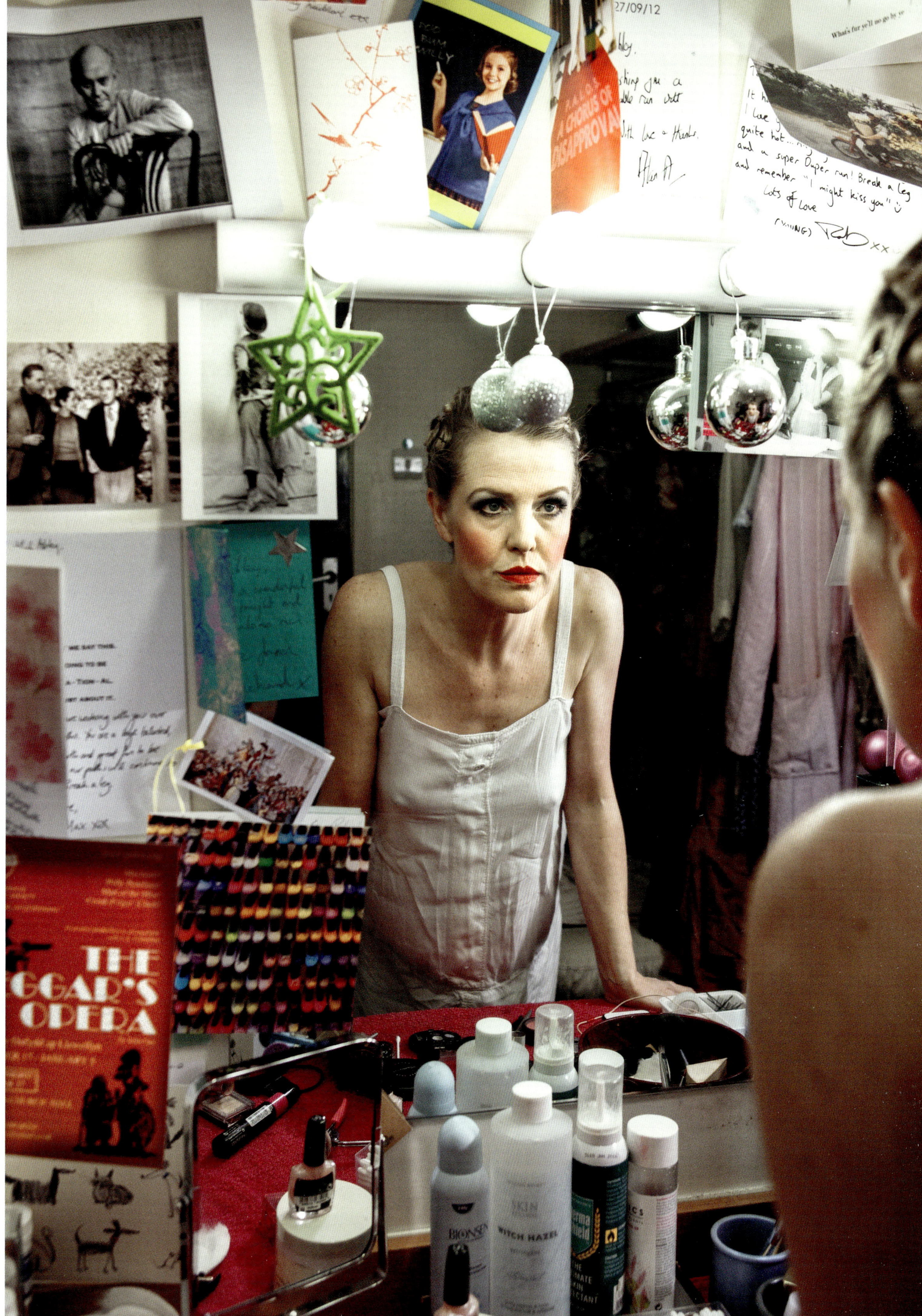

27/09/12
and a super Duper run! Break a leg
and remember "I might kiss you"
Lots of Love
THE
OPERA
WITCH HAZEL

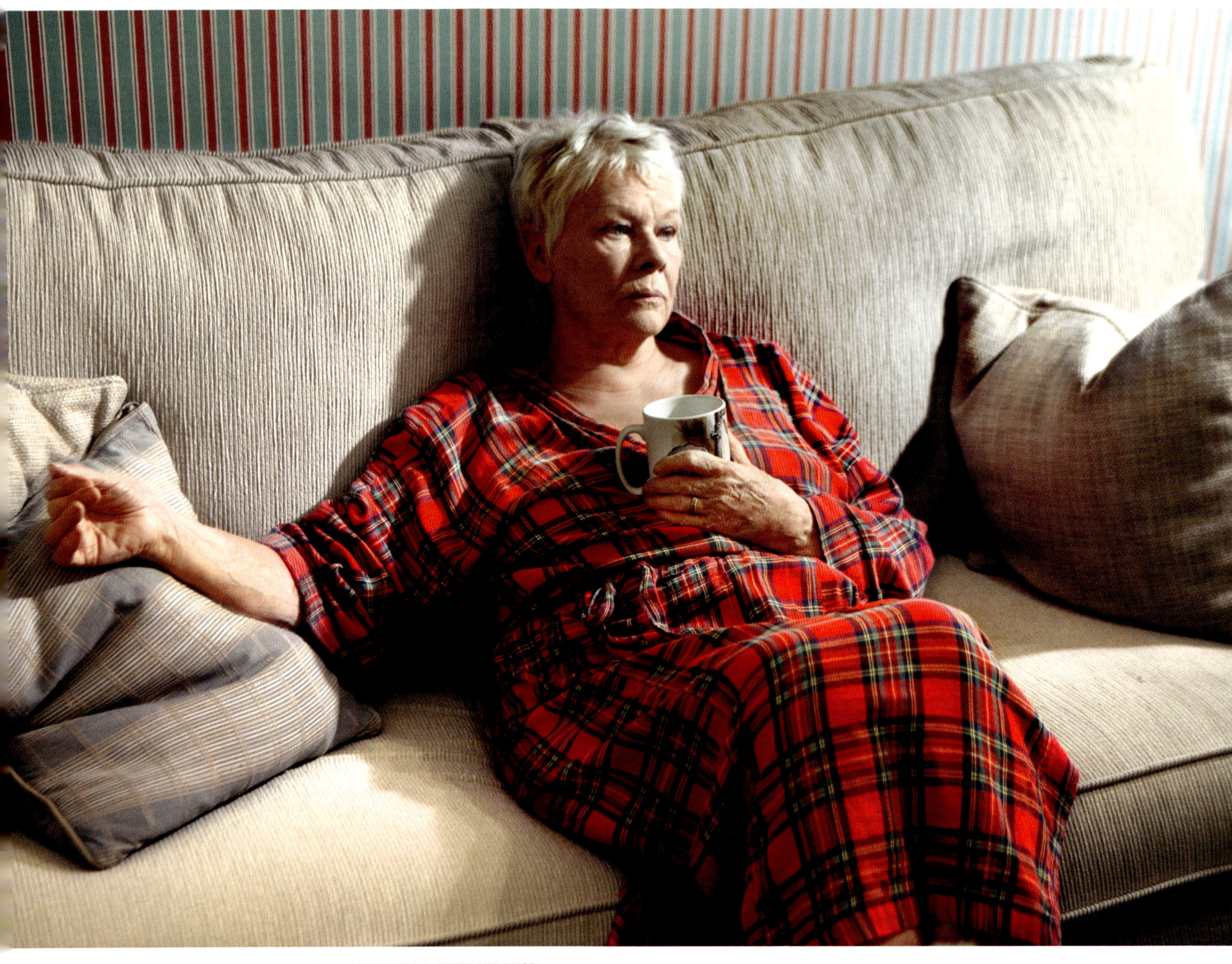

ABOVE: **JUDI DENCH, *PETER AND ALICE*, NOËL COWARD THEATRE, 2013**
Judi in a reflective moment. She is a wonderful host to all the guests who visit her dressing room.

OPPOSITE: **F. MURRAY ABRAHAM, *THE MENTOR*, USTINOV STUDIO, 2017**
A rare sighting of the great actor. The energy he brought to the rehearsal room was ruthless and particular, driven by a wealth of experience.

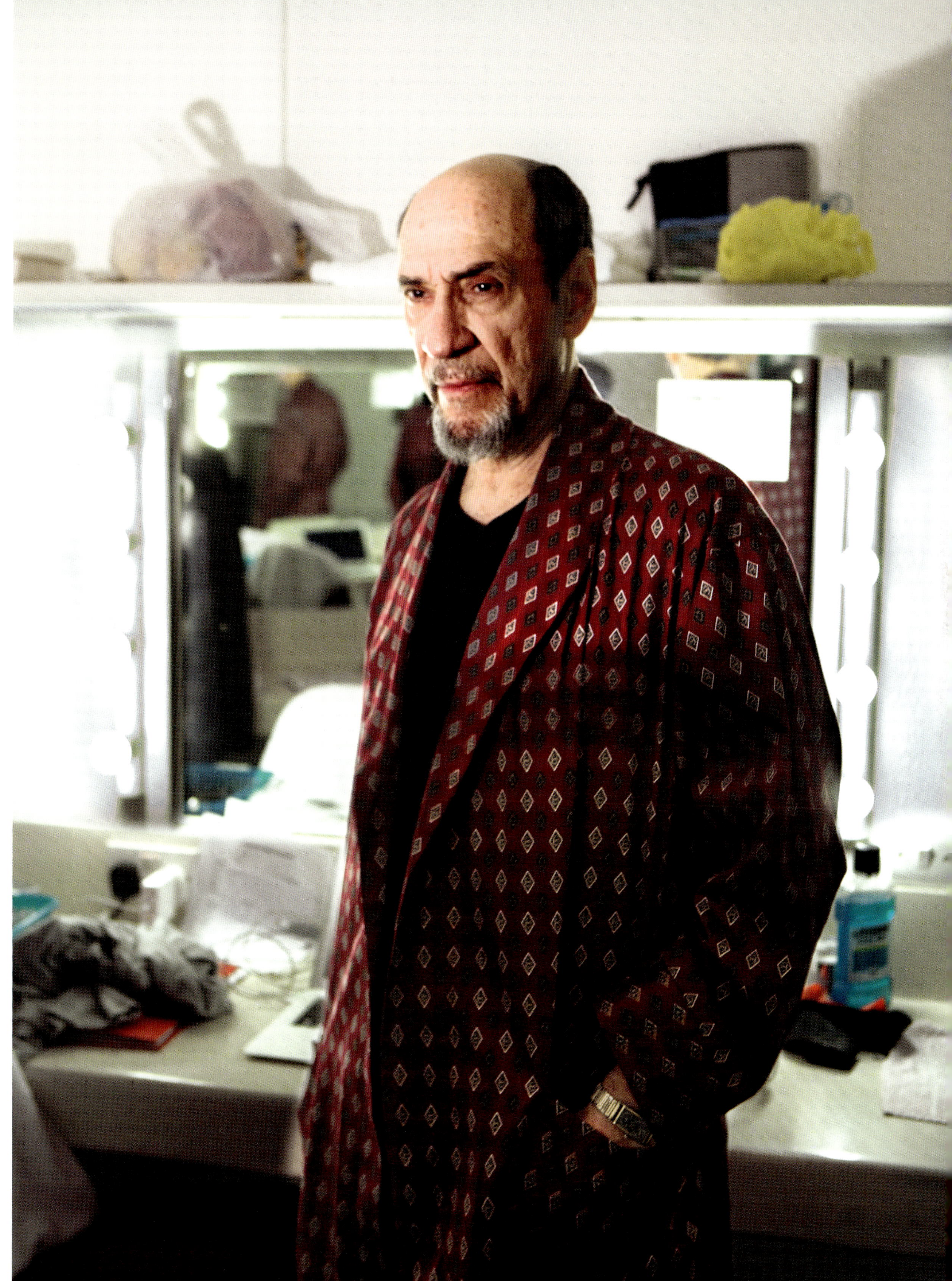

JUDE LAW, *HAMLET*, WYNDHAM'S, 2009
Hamlet is one of the great classical roles, requiring maximum concentration throughout a long play, eight times a week. Jude had a photo of Fred Astaire to lighten the mood of the Prince's melancholia.

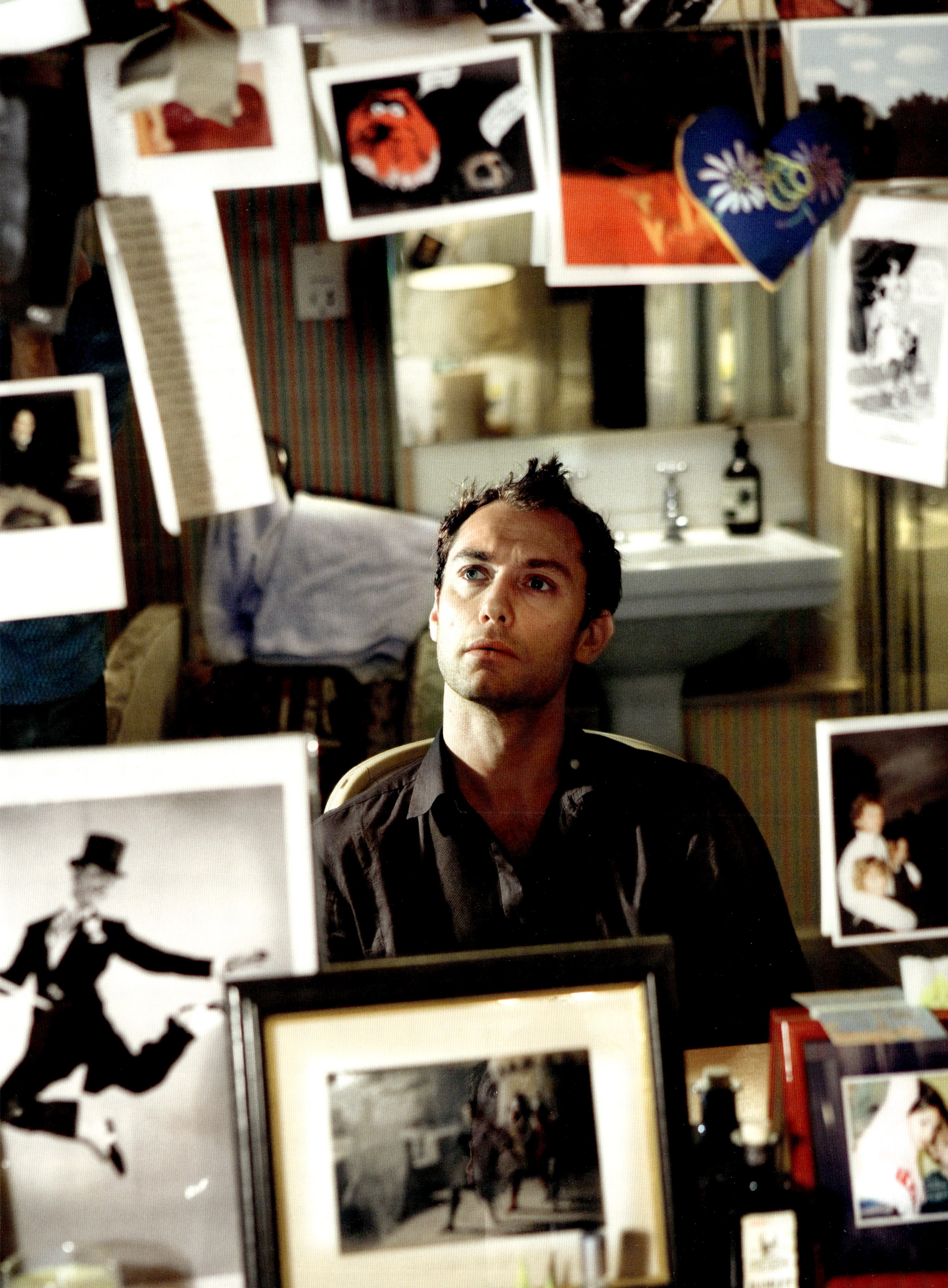

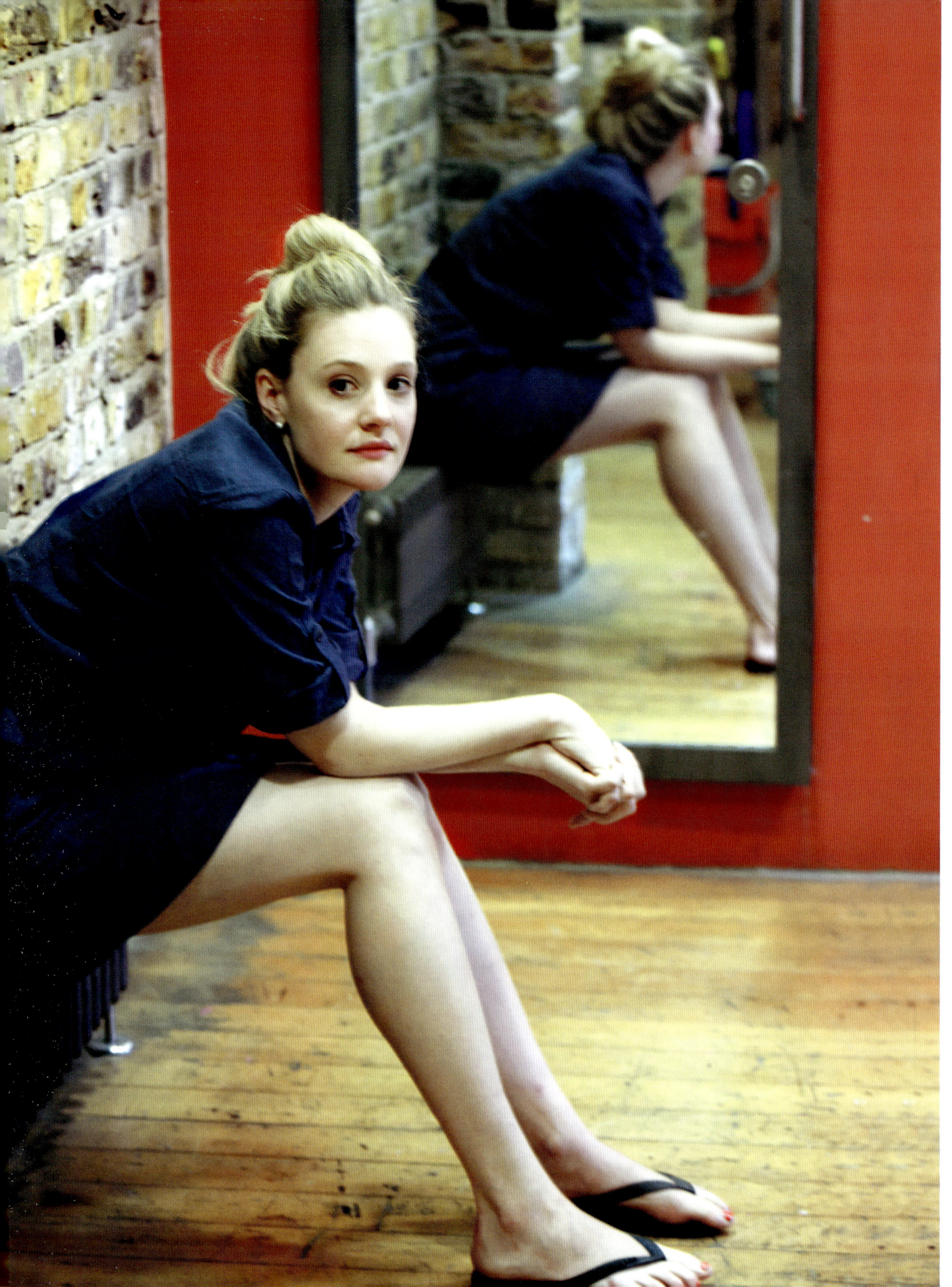

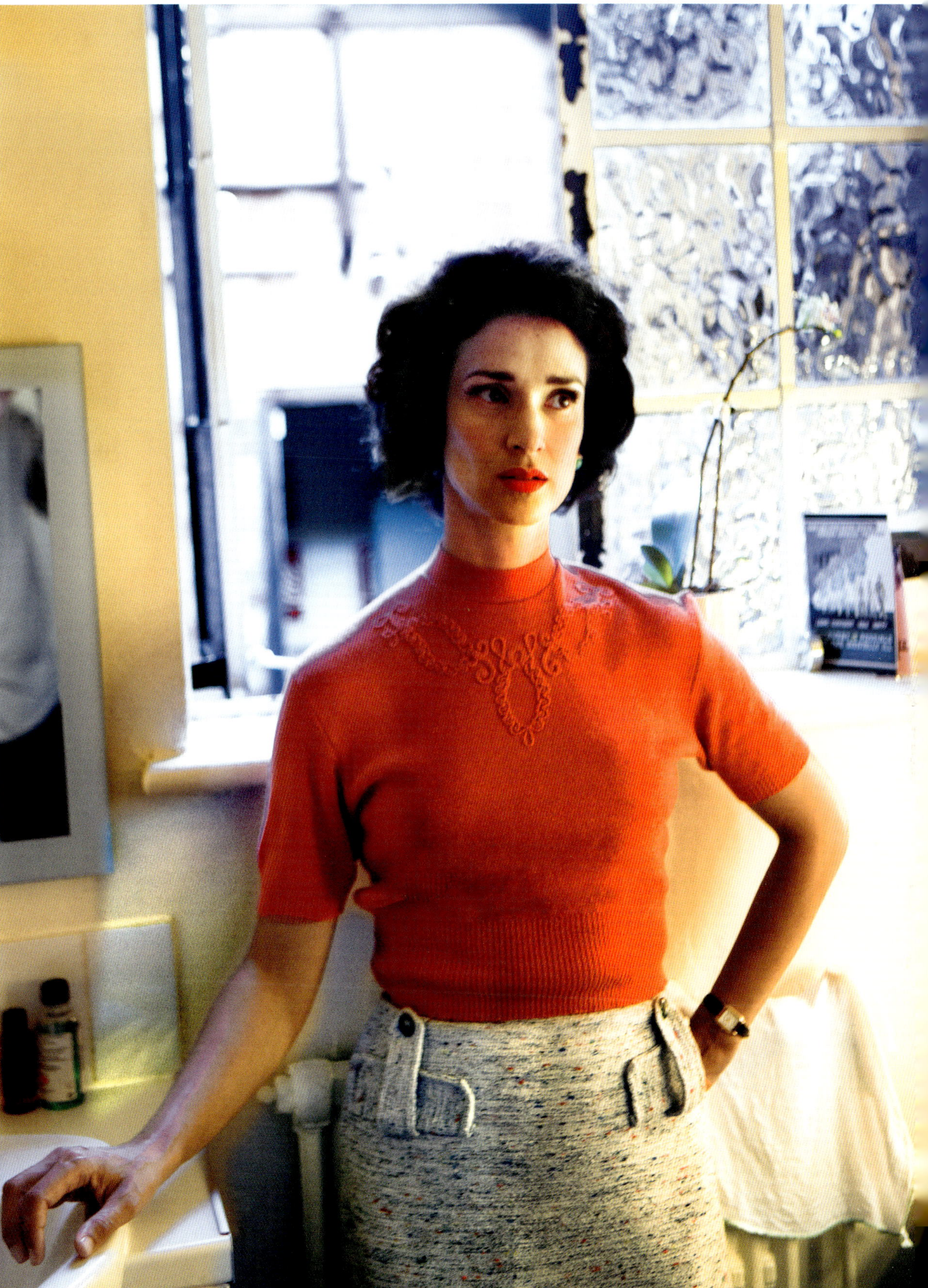

OPPOSITE: **ROMOLA GARAI, *THE VILLAGE BIKE*, ROYAL COURT, 2011**
At the time, Romola was suffering from a few sleepless nights, so the daily performances required her full stamina.

RIGHT: **INDIRA VARMA, *THE HOTHOUSE*, TRAFALGAR STUDIOS, 2013**
A lead in the series *Game of Thrones*, Indira was drawn to Pinter's classic black comedy. The Trafalgar Studios used to be the Whitehall Theatre, on the road that leads to the Houses of Parliament. The original 1930s windowpanes can still be seen.

CLAIRE FOY, *MACBETH*, TRAFALGAR STUDIOS, 2013

Claire has an extraordinary presence in her work. Before the worldwide glamour that came with playing Elizabeth II in *The Crown*, here she is getting down to play Lady M in a relatively small theatre. I shot her first headshot out of drama school.

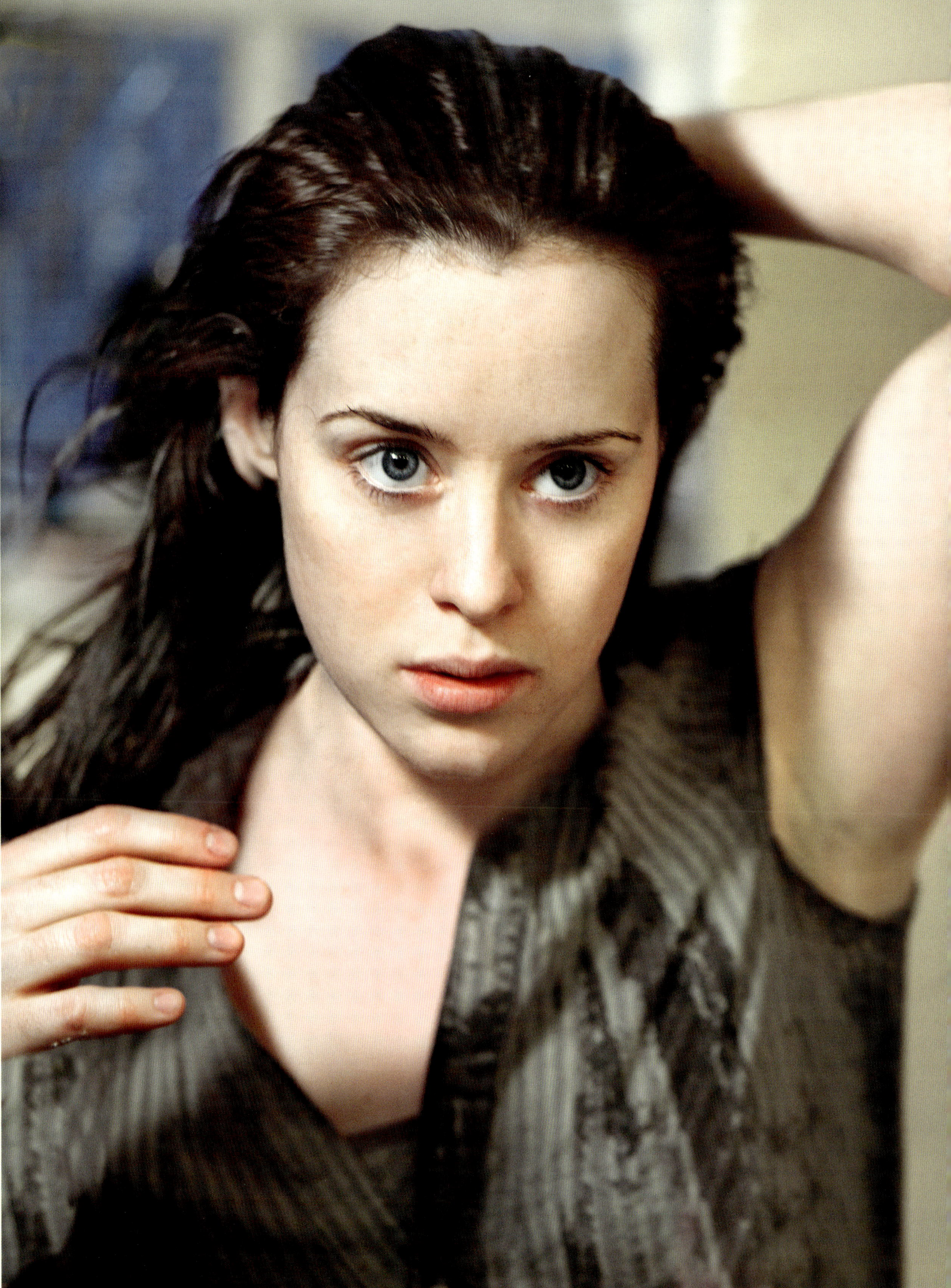

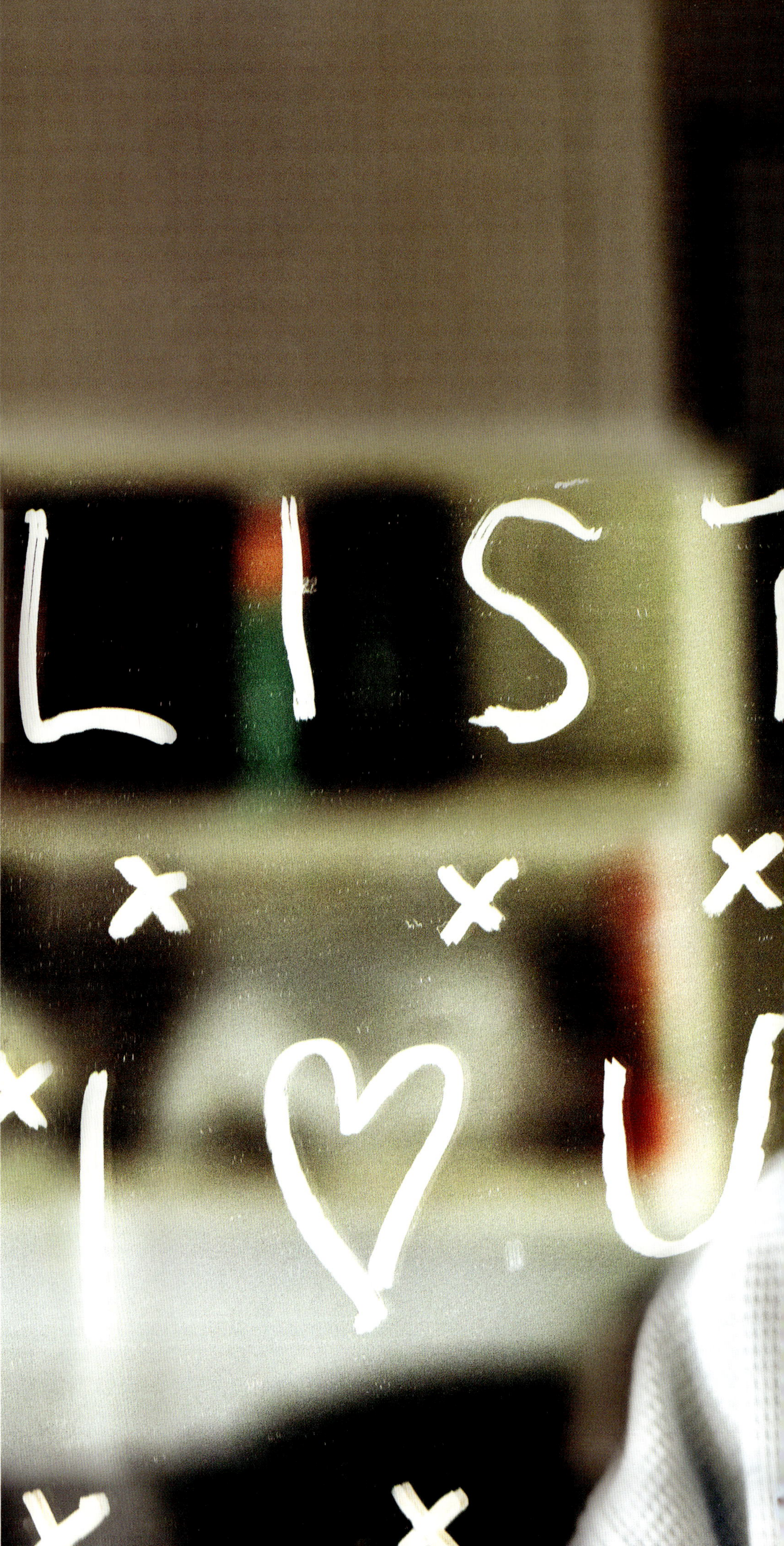

JULIET STEVENSON, *THE HERETIC*, ROYAL COURT, 2011

Juliet wrote 'LISTEN', to remind herself to do so in the performance, and her daughter, visiting that evening, added the rest.

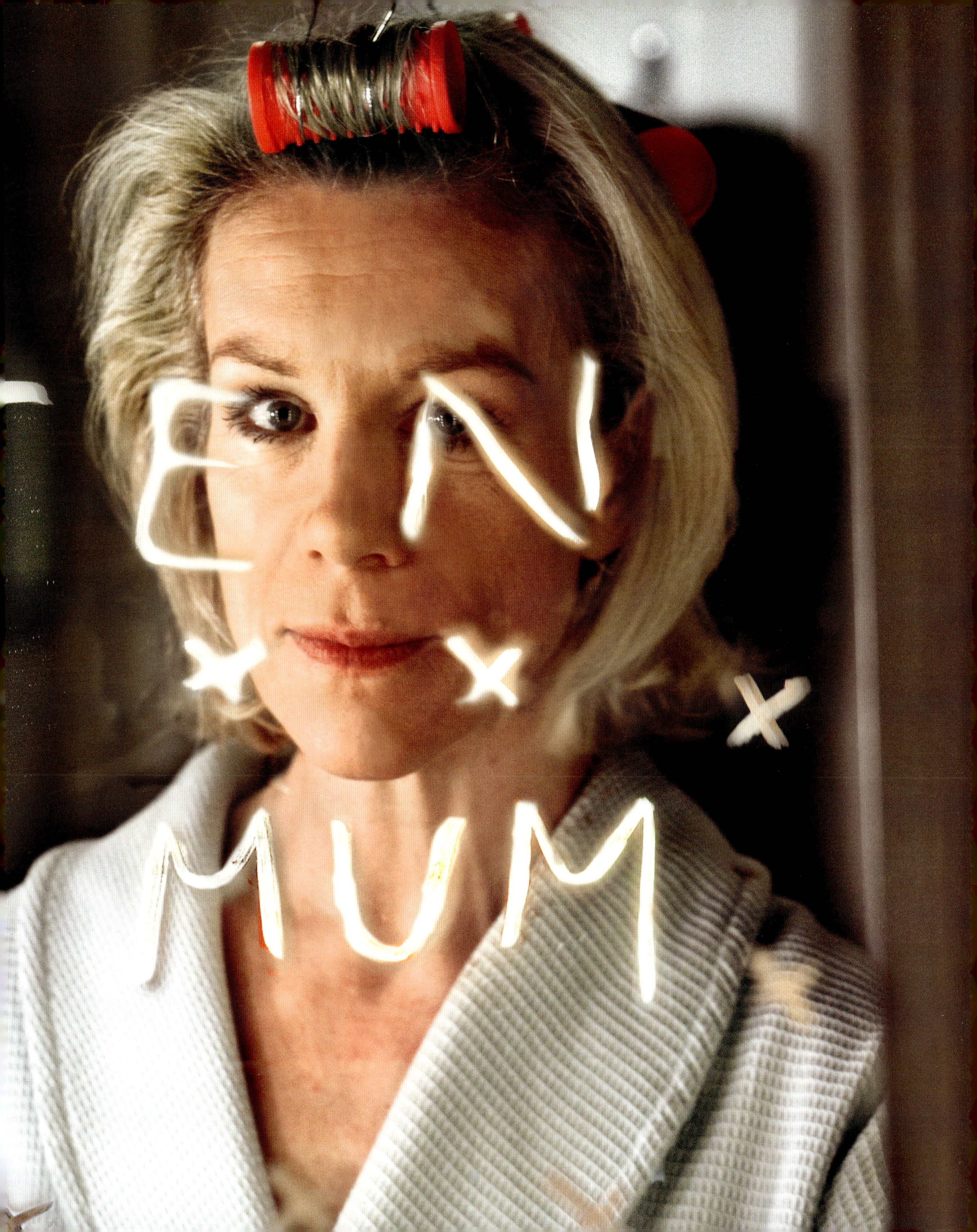
EN
x x x
MUM

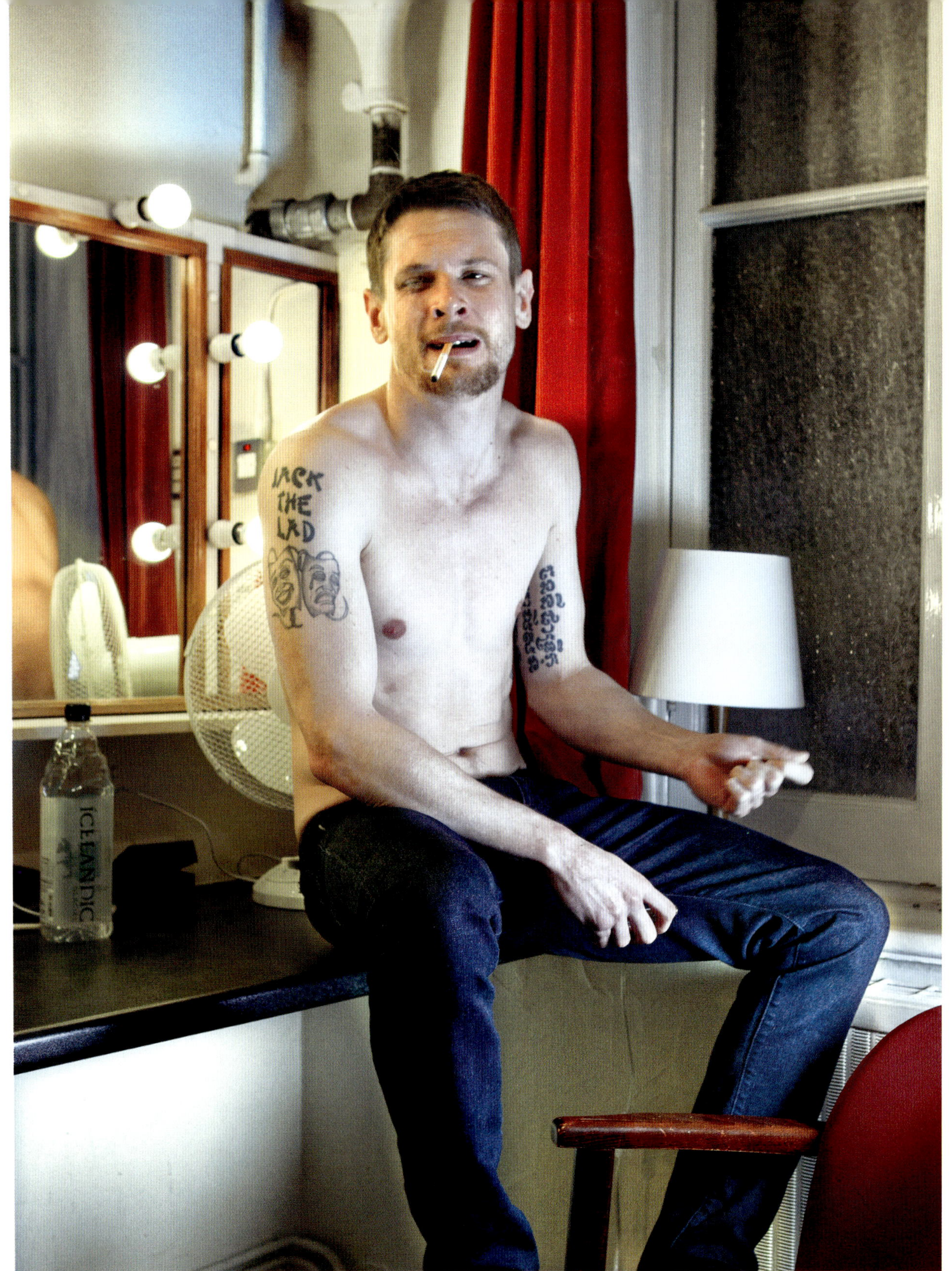

LEFT: **JACK O'CONNELL, *CAT ON A HOT TIN ROOF*, APOLLO THEATRE, 2017**
Jack is edgy, edgy, edgy and entertaining with it. He has a strong following amongst younger actors.

OPPOSITE: **LESLEY MANVILLE, *GHOSTS*, ALMEIDA, 2014**
I have followed Lesley's work for many years and it is a joy to see her landing the top parts. Always patient, kind and generous, she is a delight to photograph.

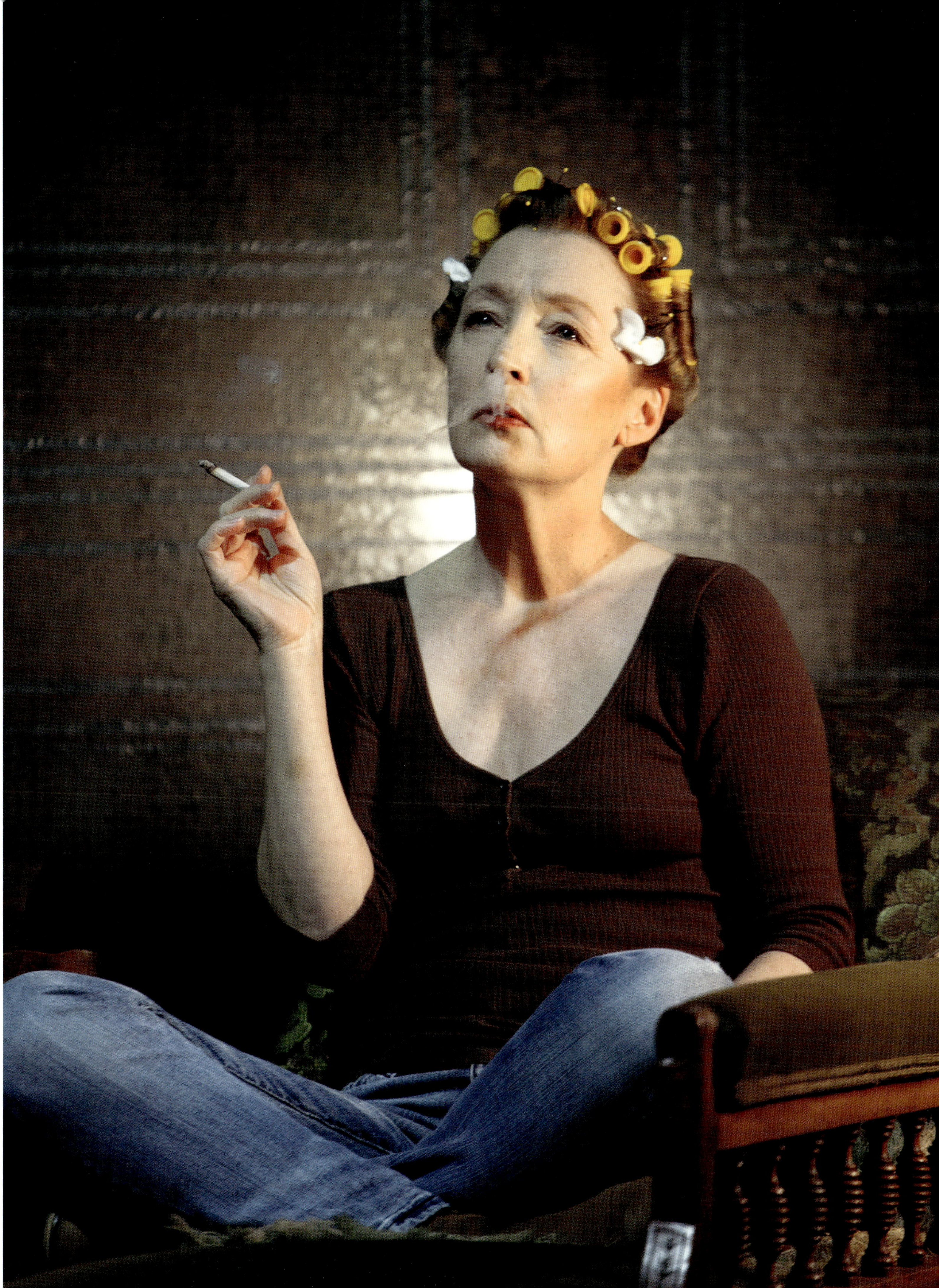

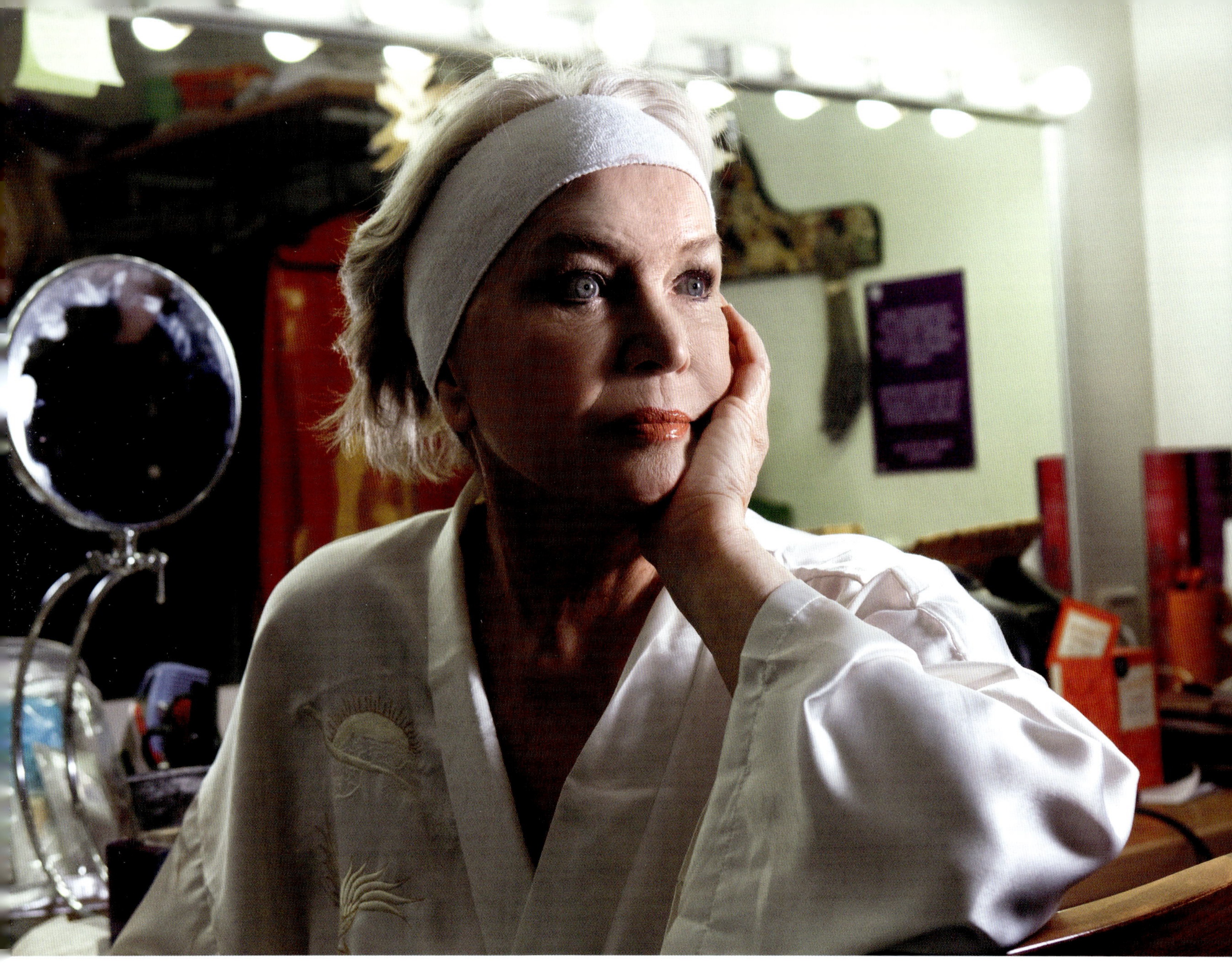

ELLEN BURSTYN, *THE CHILDREN'S HOUR*, COMEDY THEATRE, 2011
Apart from her many achievements in a long and distinguished career, Ellen is Co-President of The Actor's Studio and once campaigned to free the boxer Rubin 'Hurricane', immortalised in Bob Dylan's song 'Hurricane', from jail.

KEIRA KNIGHTLEY, *THE MISANTHROPE*, COMEDY THEATRE, 2009

This was the first time a photographer had been allowed in her dressing room. I had met Keira once before on a photo shoot with her mother, Sharman MacDonald. Sharman was dressed in leather and entangled in a thicket, and Keira aged fourteen, came out into the garden curious to see what was going on.

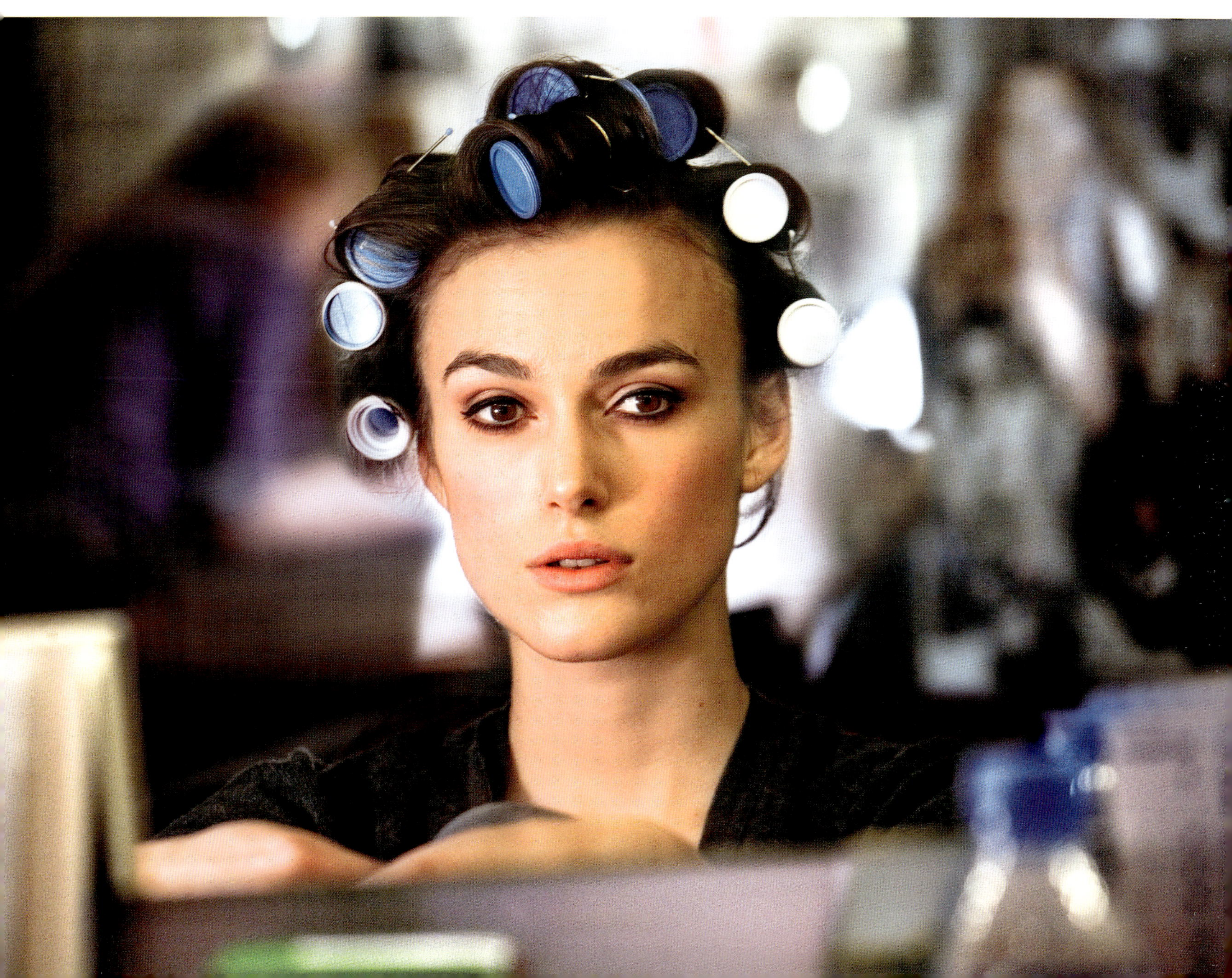

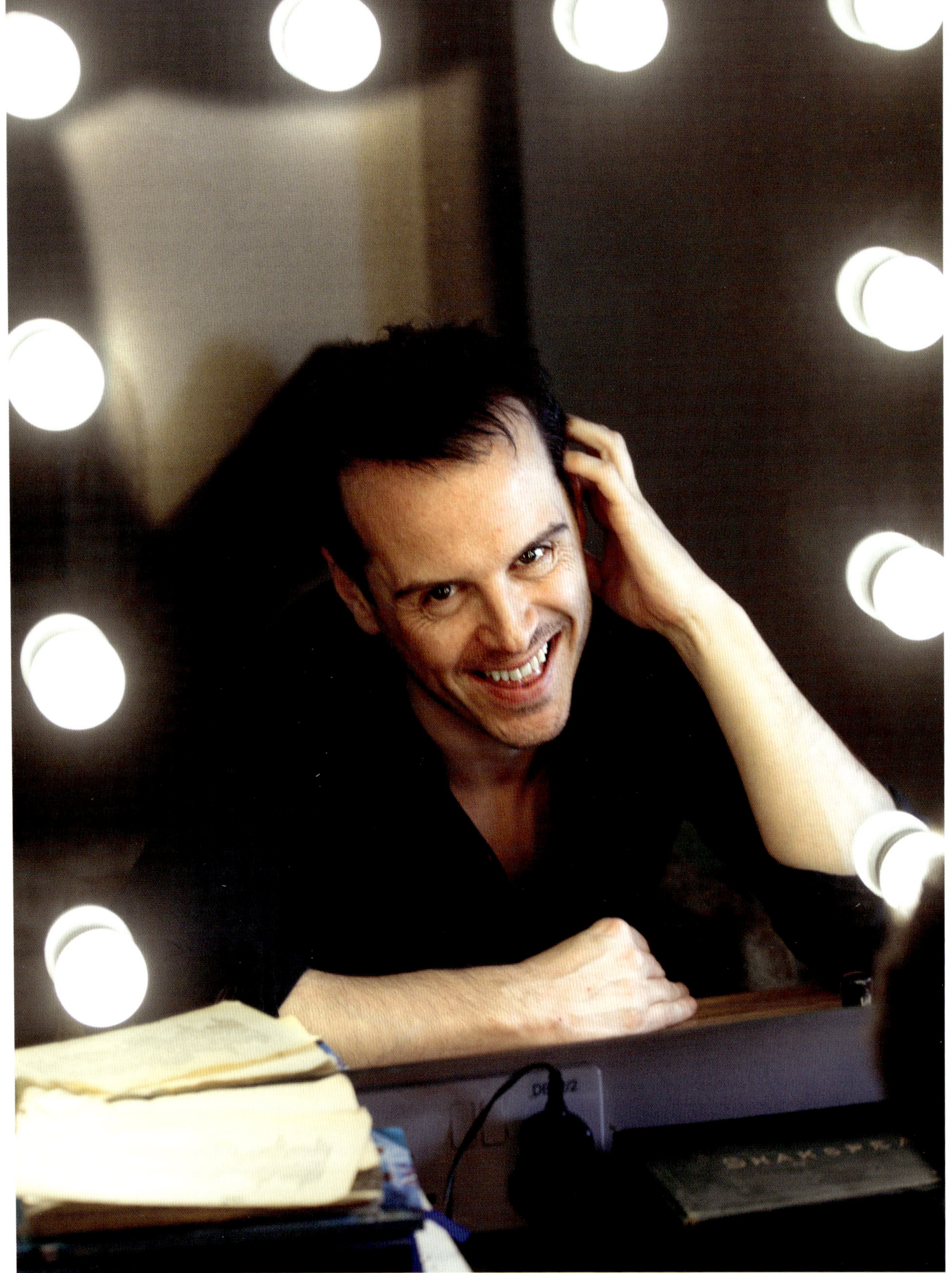

LEFT: **ANDREW SCOTT, *HAMLET*, HAROLD PINTER THEATRE, 2018**
'The Hot Priest' of *Fleabag* doing a very hot Hamlet. Always a pleasure to photograph, Andrew exudes mischief. Deservedly he is a popular member of the acting community, and brilliantly talented.

OPPOSITE: **PHOEBE WALLER-BRIDGE, *ROPE*, ALMEIDA, 2009**
I first shot Phoebe when she was twenty-four and knew then she was too bright to hang around, waiting to be hired. Her writing is an inspiration to a generation of actresses, who now see the possibility of creating work for themselves.

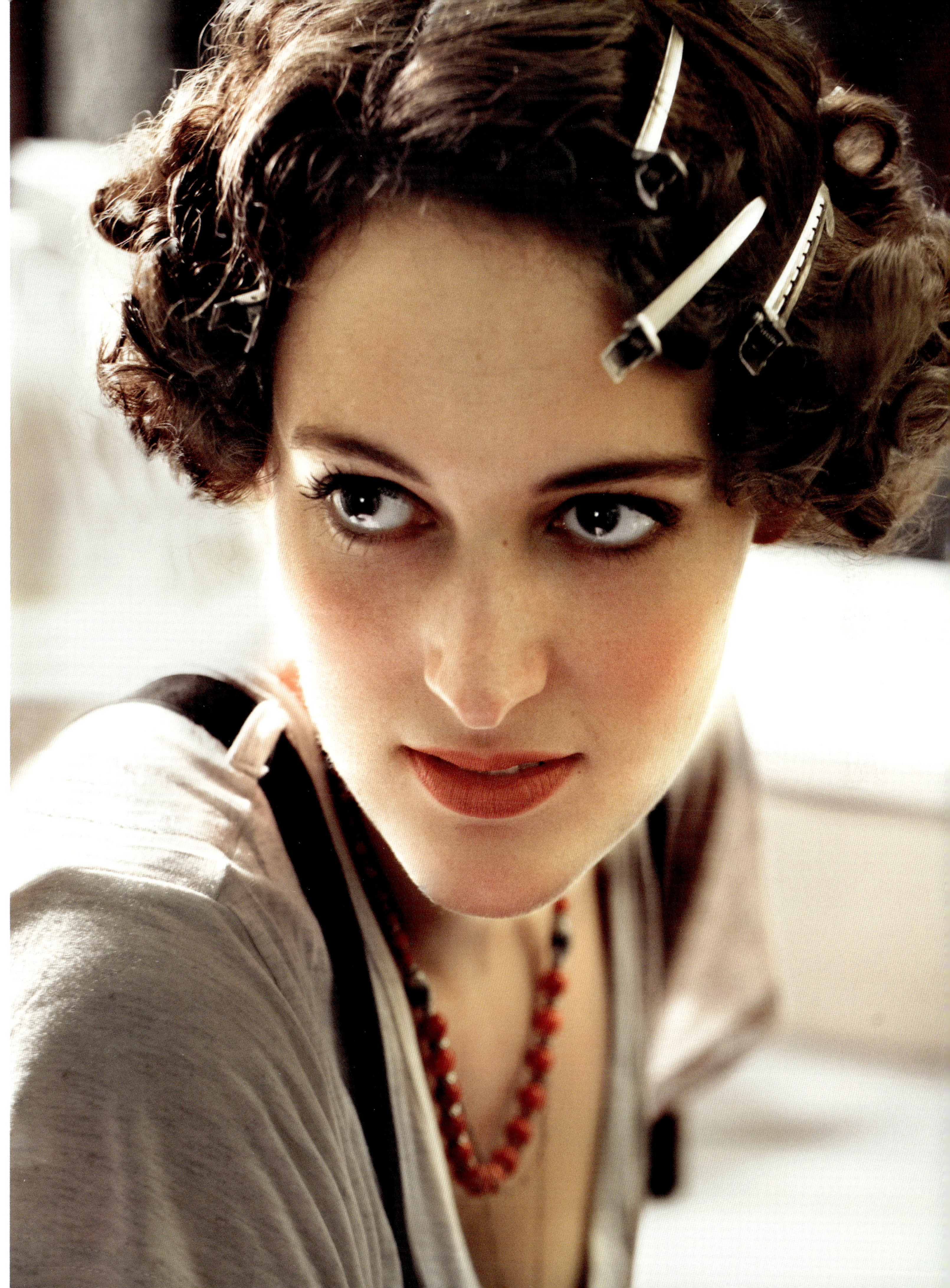

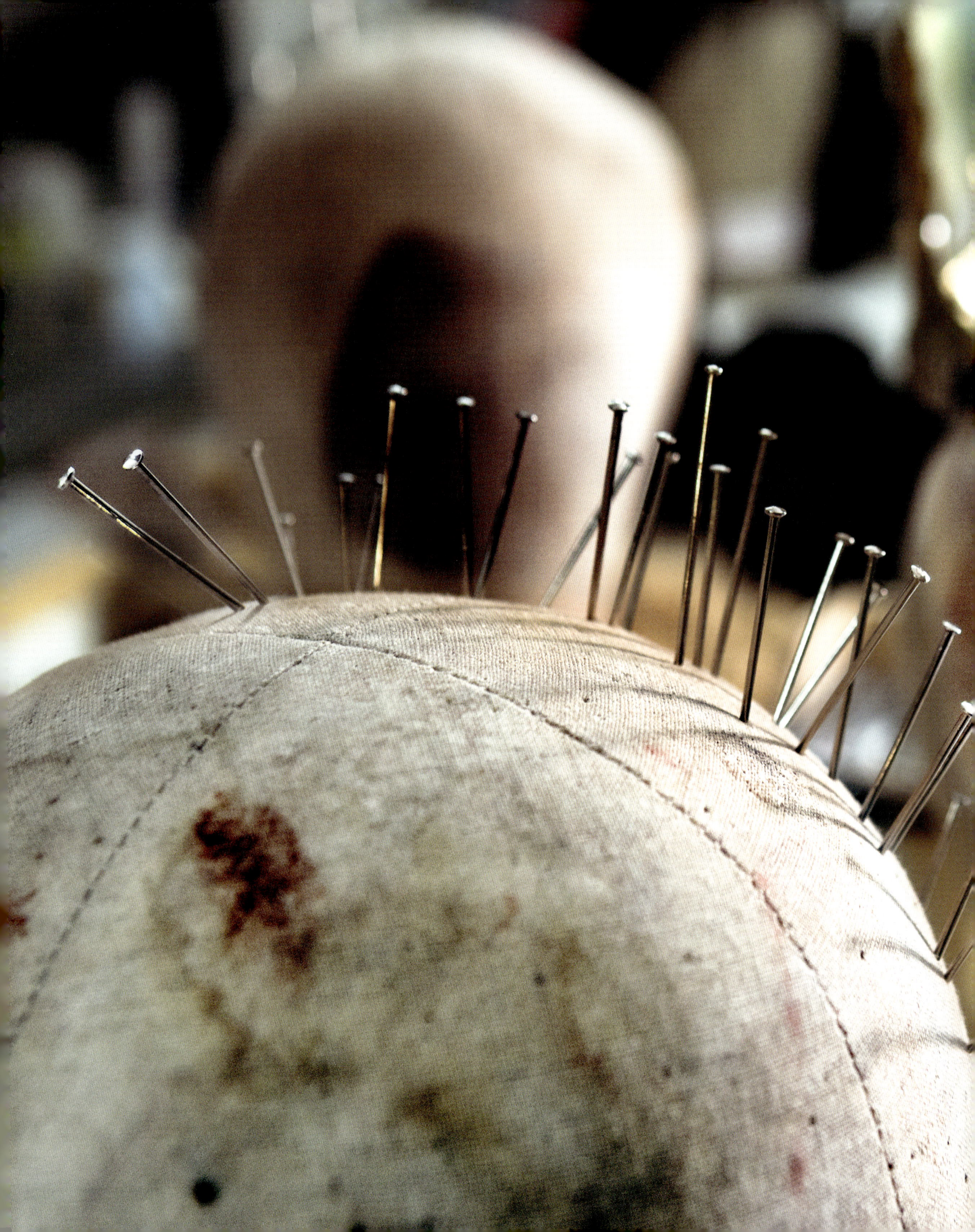

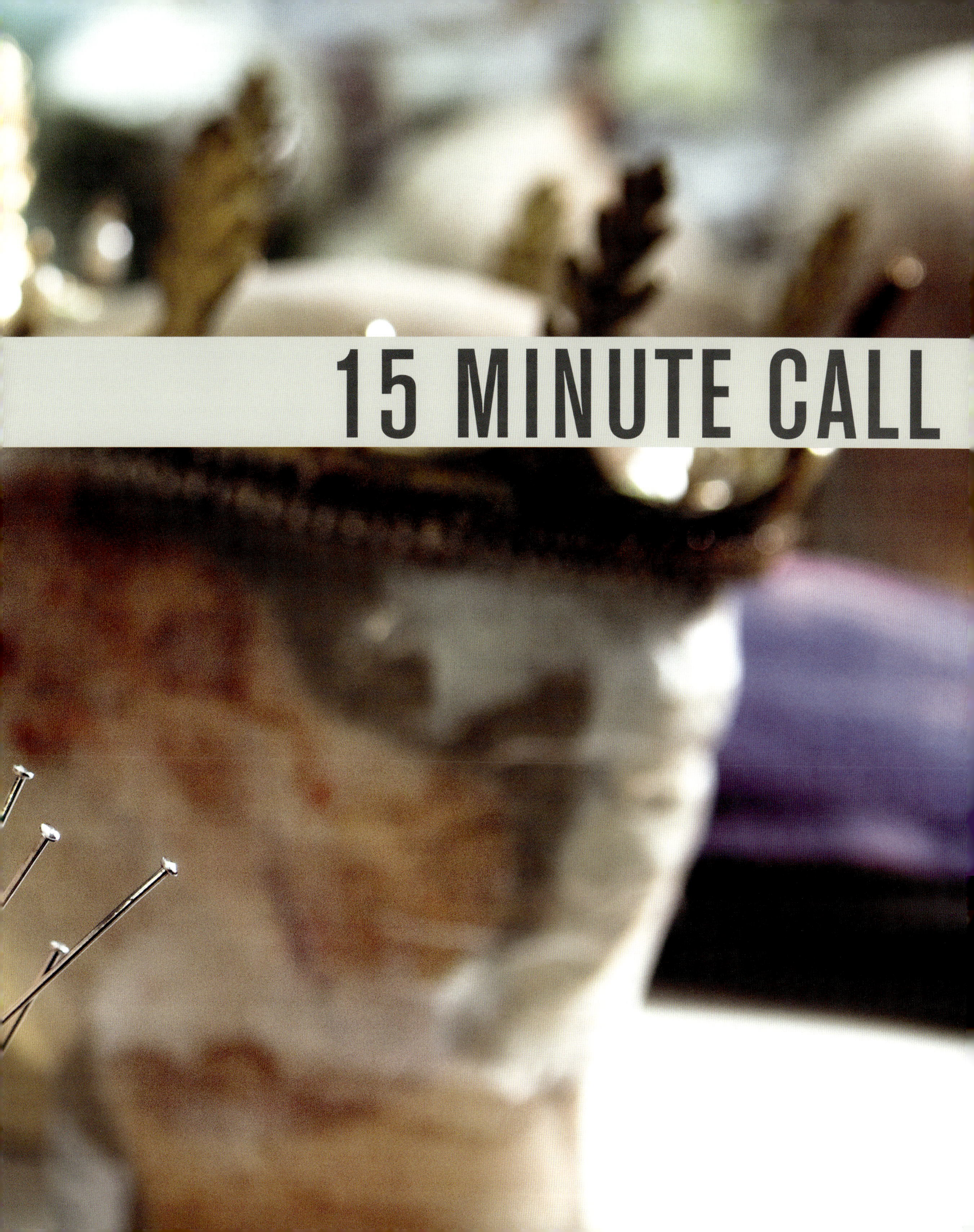

15 MINUTE CALL

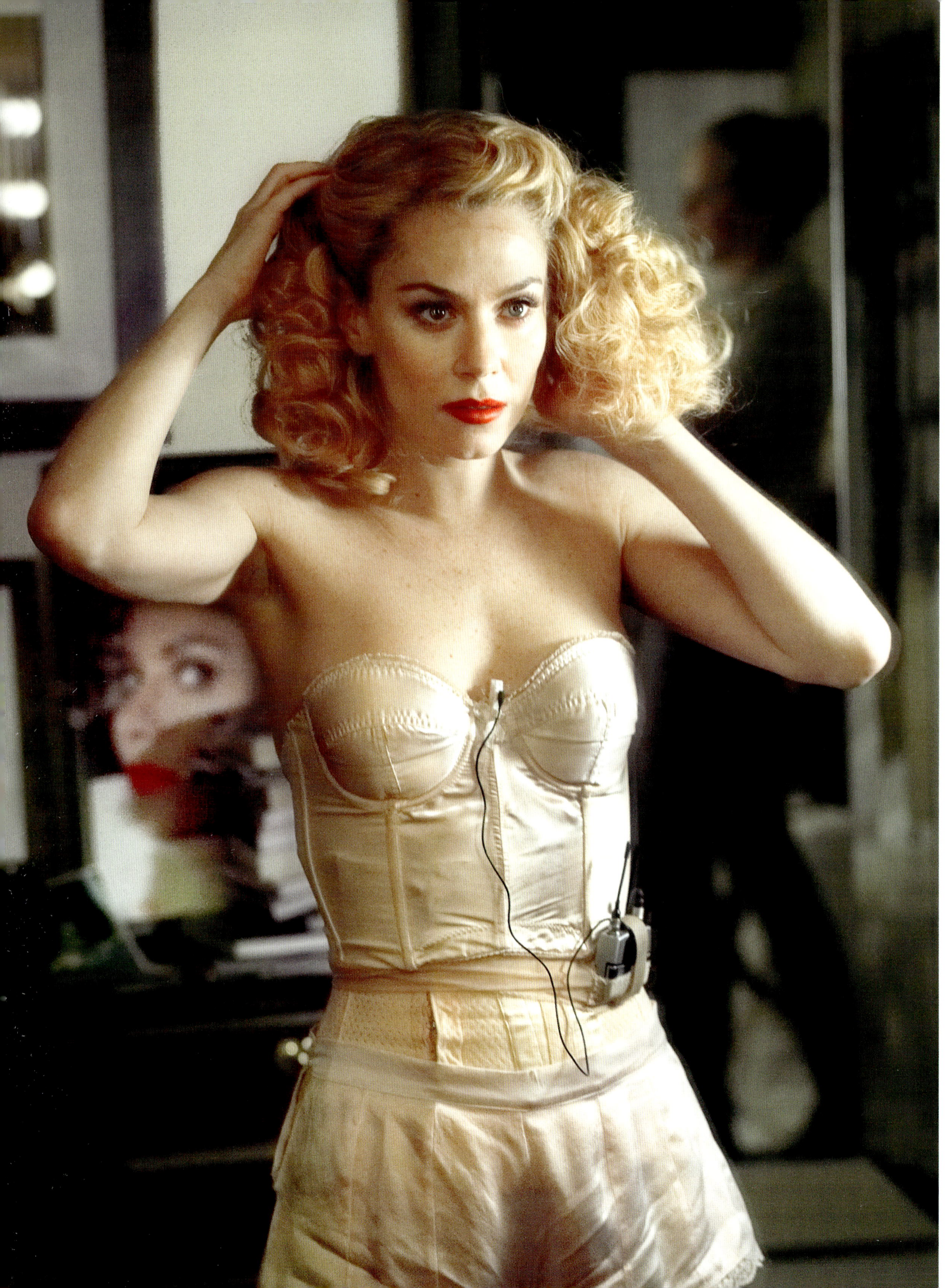

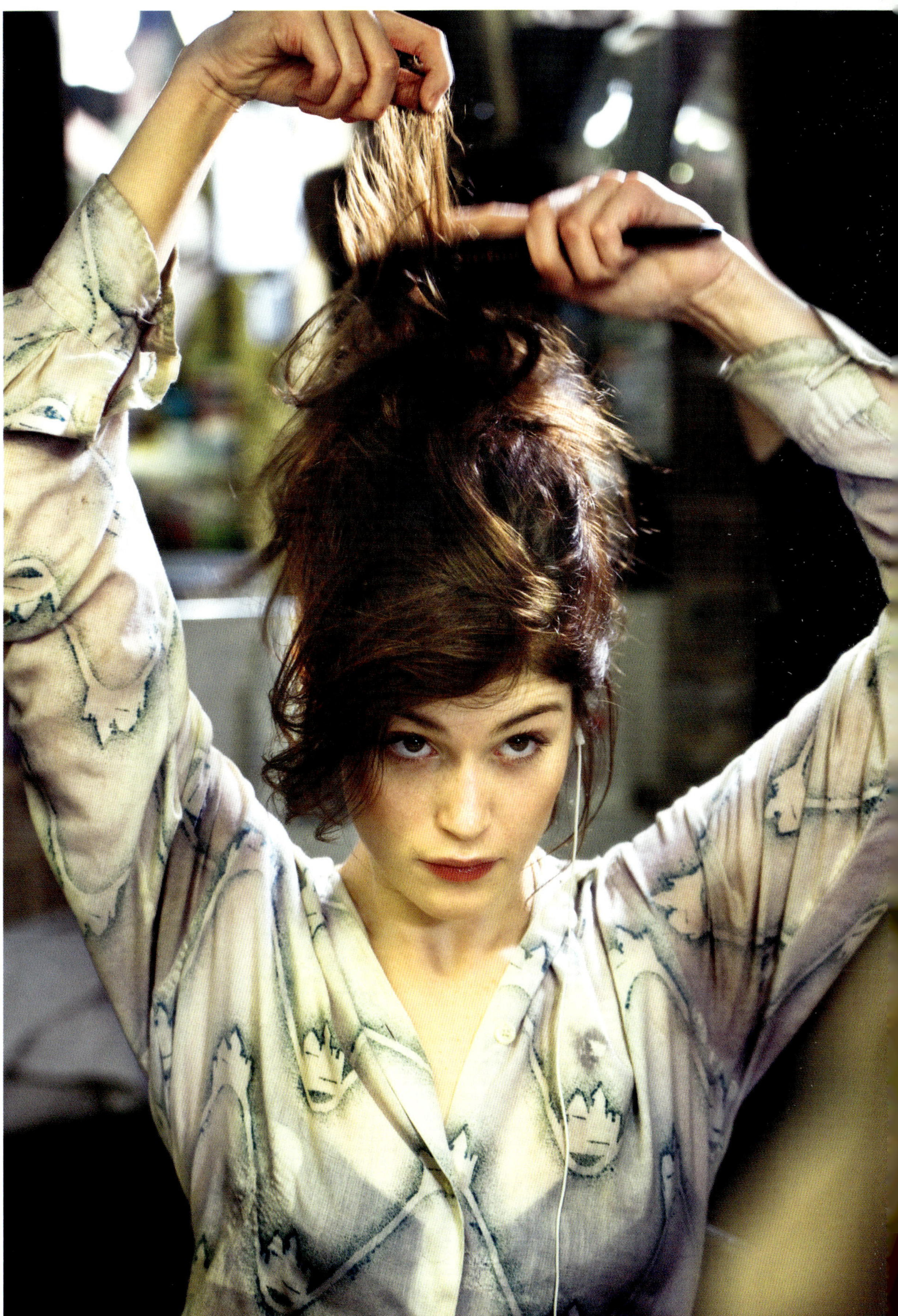

OPPOSITE: **ANNA FRIEL, *BREAKFAST AT TIFFANY'S*, THEATRE ROYAL HAYMARKET, 2009**
Anna in original 1950s lingerie as Holly Golightly. A session with her is an adventure. In the background is Sophie, my assistant at the time.

RIGHT: **GEMMA ARTERTON, *THE MASTER BUILDER*, ALMEIDA, 2010**
Listening to music is a popular way of getting into a role. Gemma's breakthrough role was Bond girl Strawberry Fields in *Quantum of Solace*. Here she is exploring the psychological and social issues raised by Ibsen.

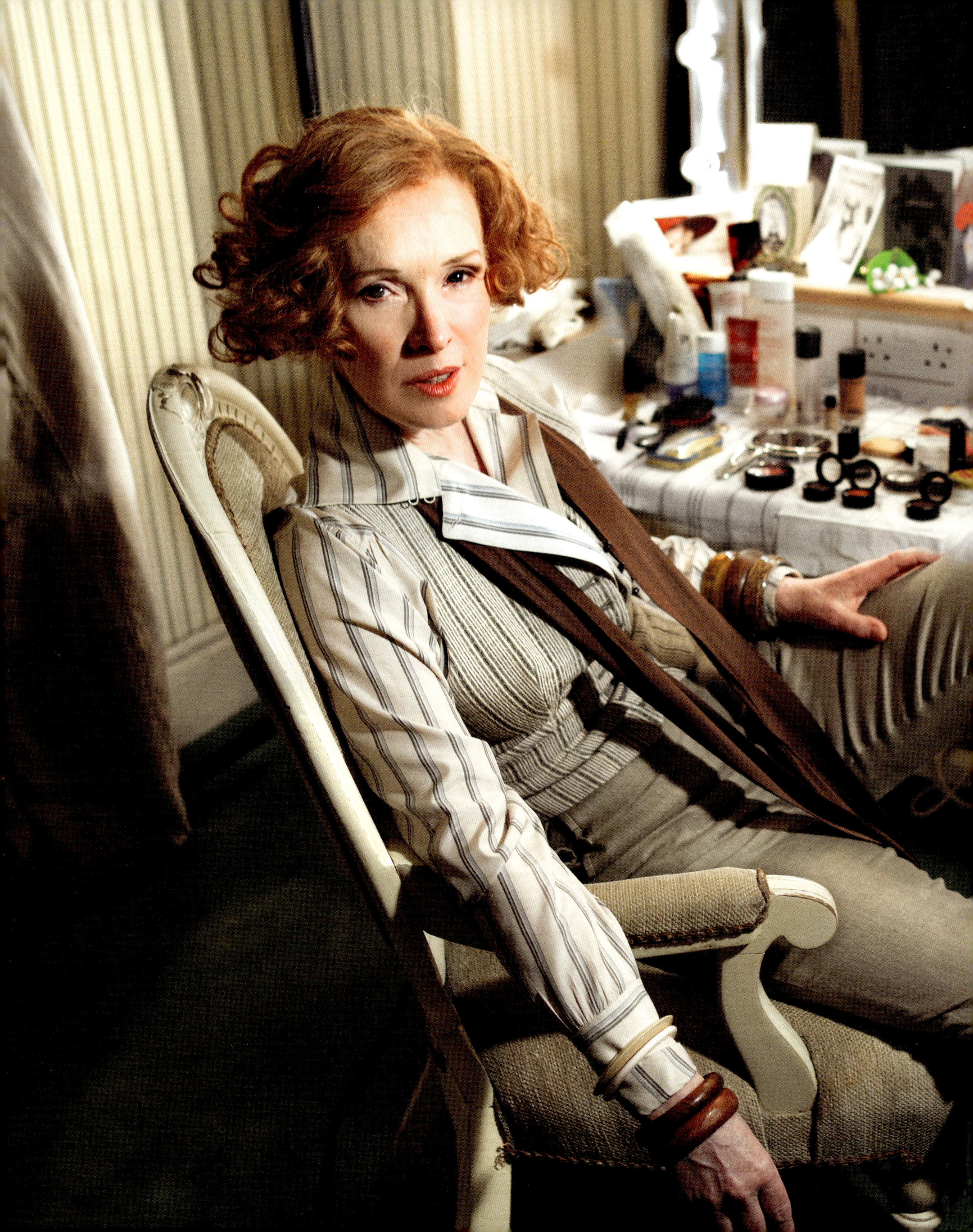

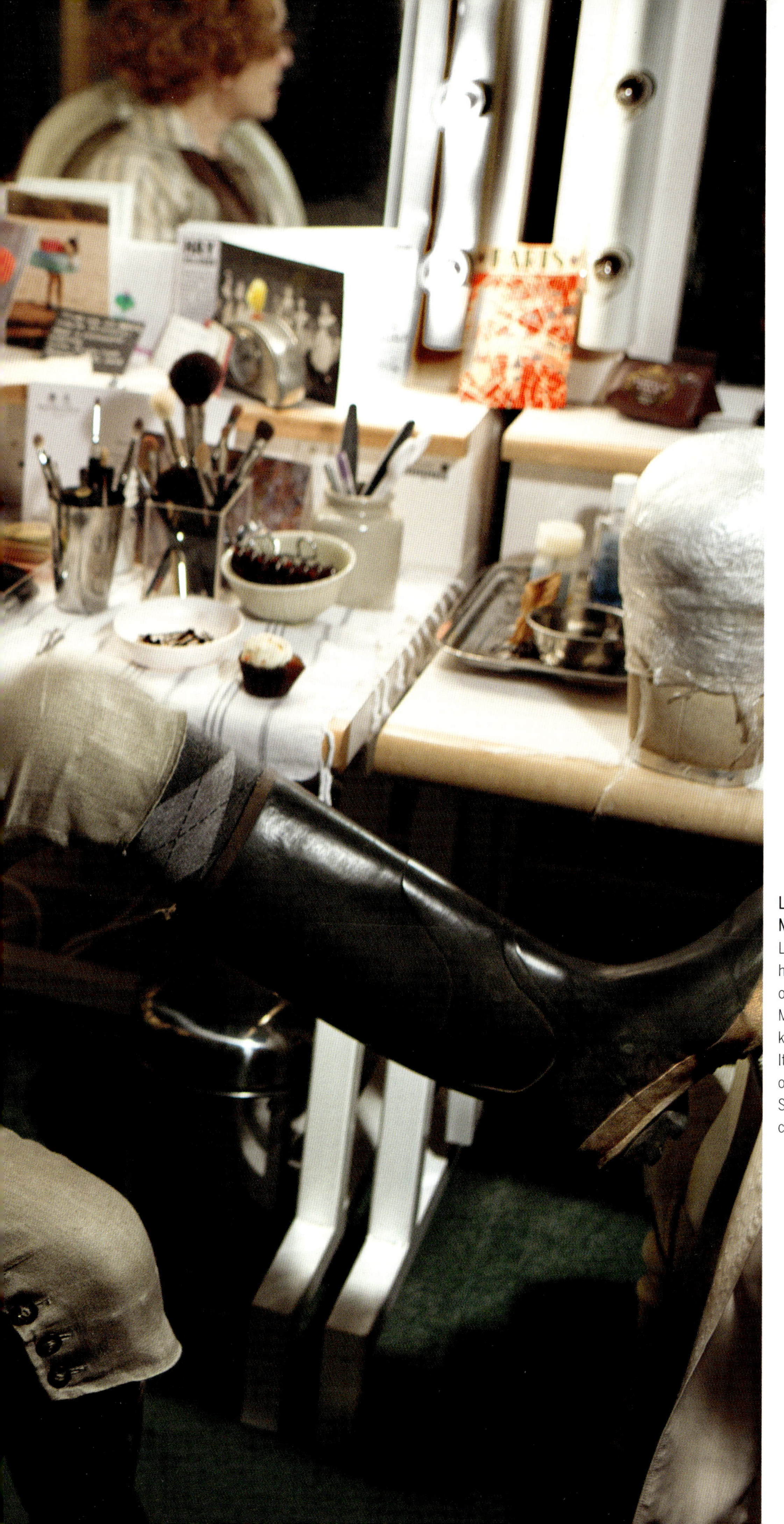

LINDSAY DUNCAN, *HAY FEVER*, NOËL COWARD THEATRE, 2012

Lindsay is an actress of great passion, humour and understanding. In her own words: 'I love a dressing room. Most actors do. We're safe, while knowing it's about to get dangerous. It's a very charged space, an exciting one. It was possible to prepare while Simon was there because his zone of concentration was the same as mine.'

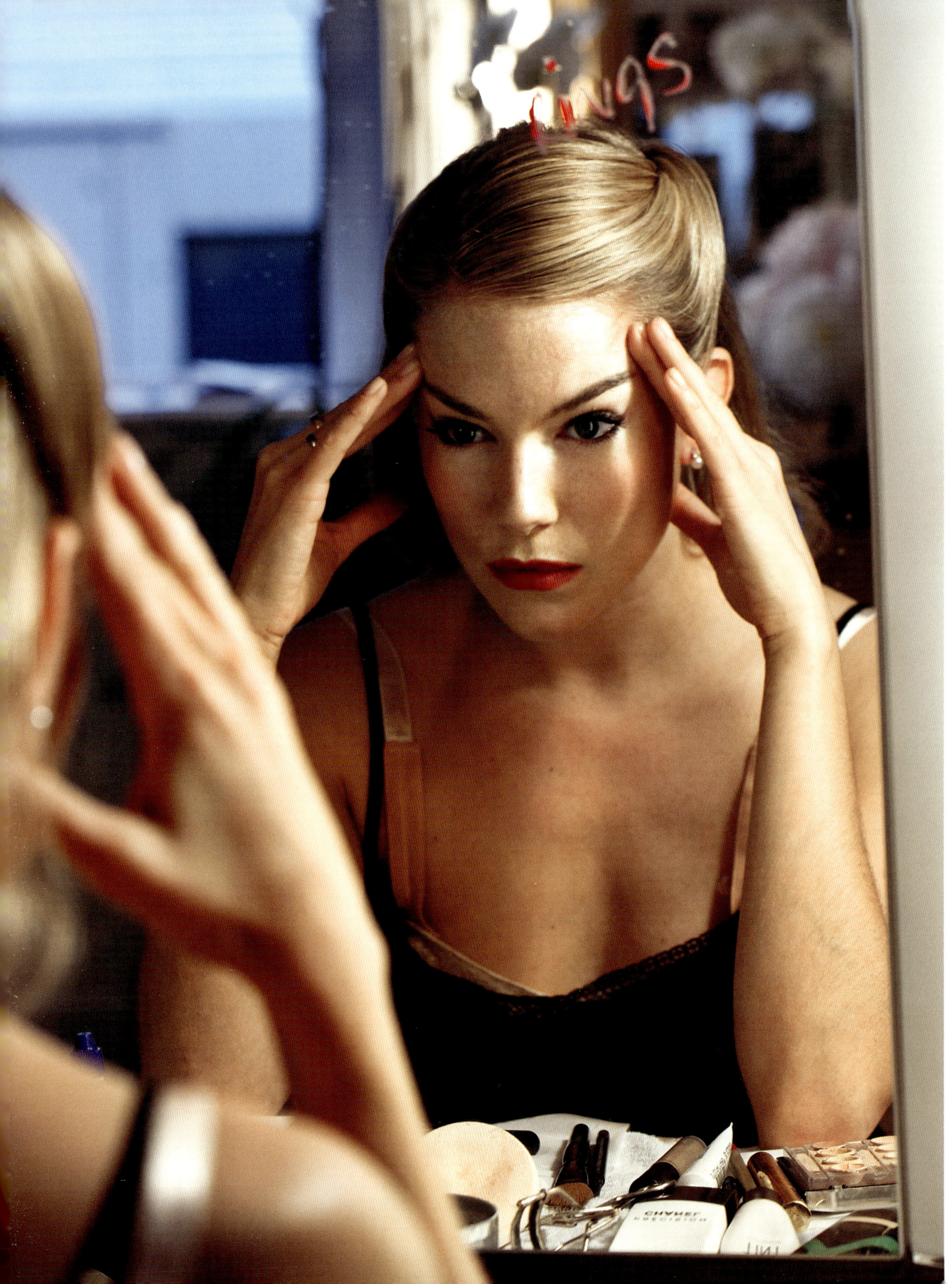

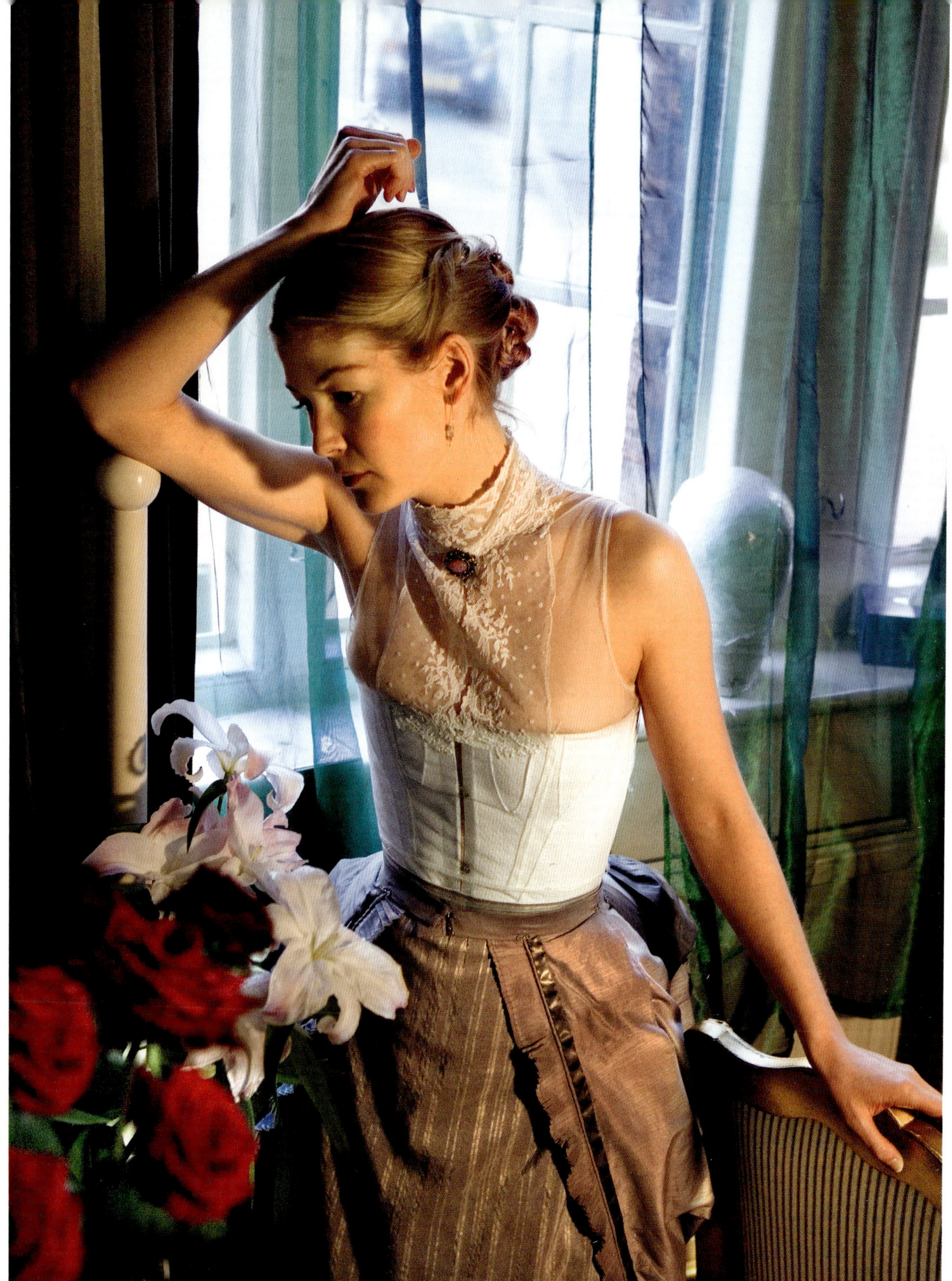

OPPOSITE: **SIENNA MILLER, *FLARE PATH*, THEATRE ROYAL HAYMARKET, 2011**
Zoning into the character for the evening ahead. Sienna's ability to focus is exceptional.

RIGHT: **ROSAMUND PIKE, *GASLIGHT*, OLD VIC THEATRE, 2007**
This was Laurence Olivier's dressing room while he worked at the Old Vic. Rosamund carries the supreme elegance that her name suggests; red roses add to the ambiance.

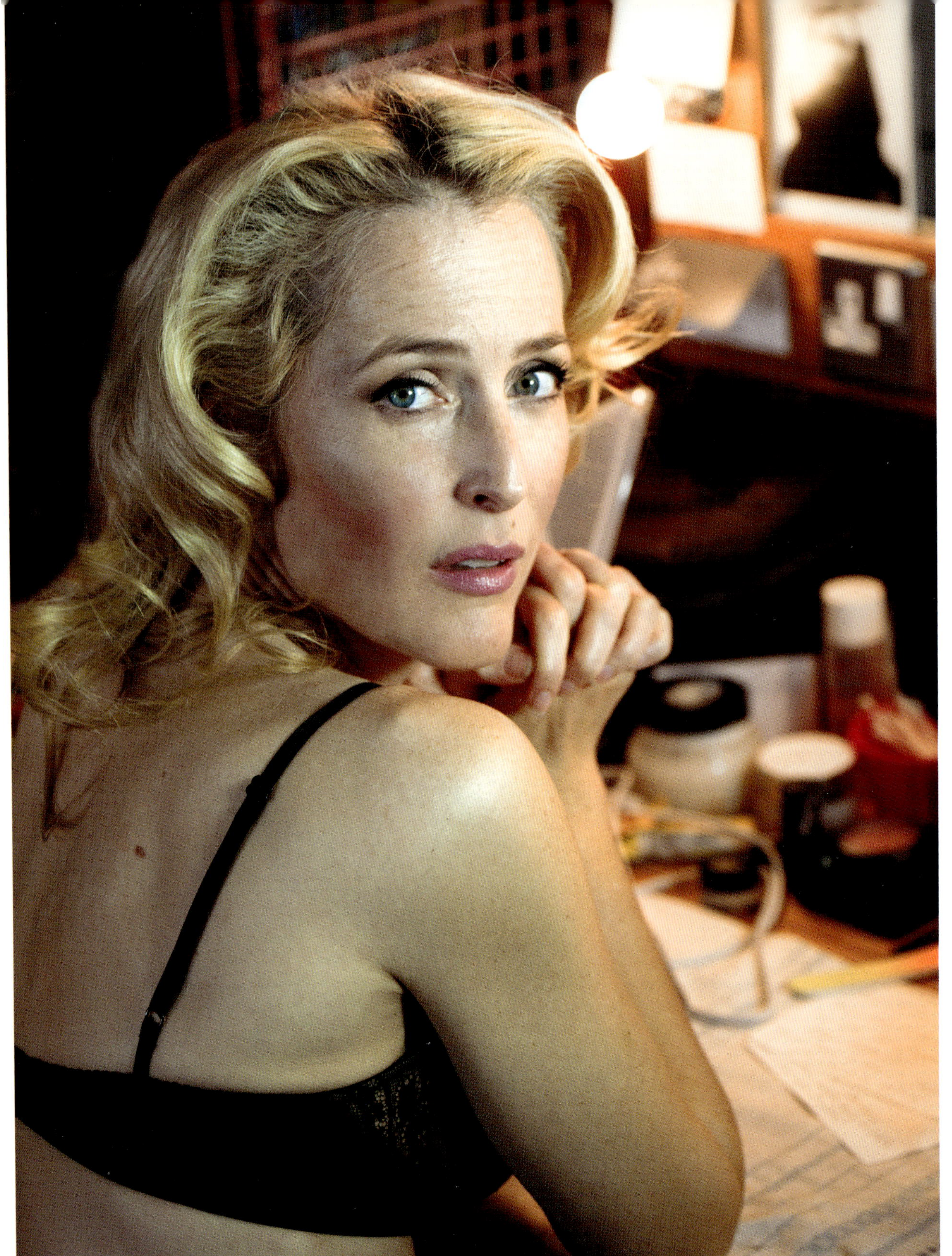

LEFT: **GILLIAN ANDERSON, *A STREETCAR NAMED DESIRE*, YOUNG VIC, 2016**
We knew each other from before, which helped, and this was a brief five-minute session. Her sense of the camera is so finely tuned that the short time available did not prevent an instinctive exchange between us.

OPPOSITE: **KIM CATTRALL, *SWEET BIRD OF YOUTH*, OLD VIC THEATRE, 2013**
The fascinating enigma that is Kim was perfect to play Tennessee Williams. Again in Olivier's old dressing room, this time looking the other way.

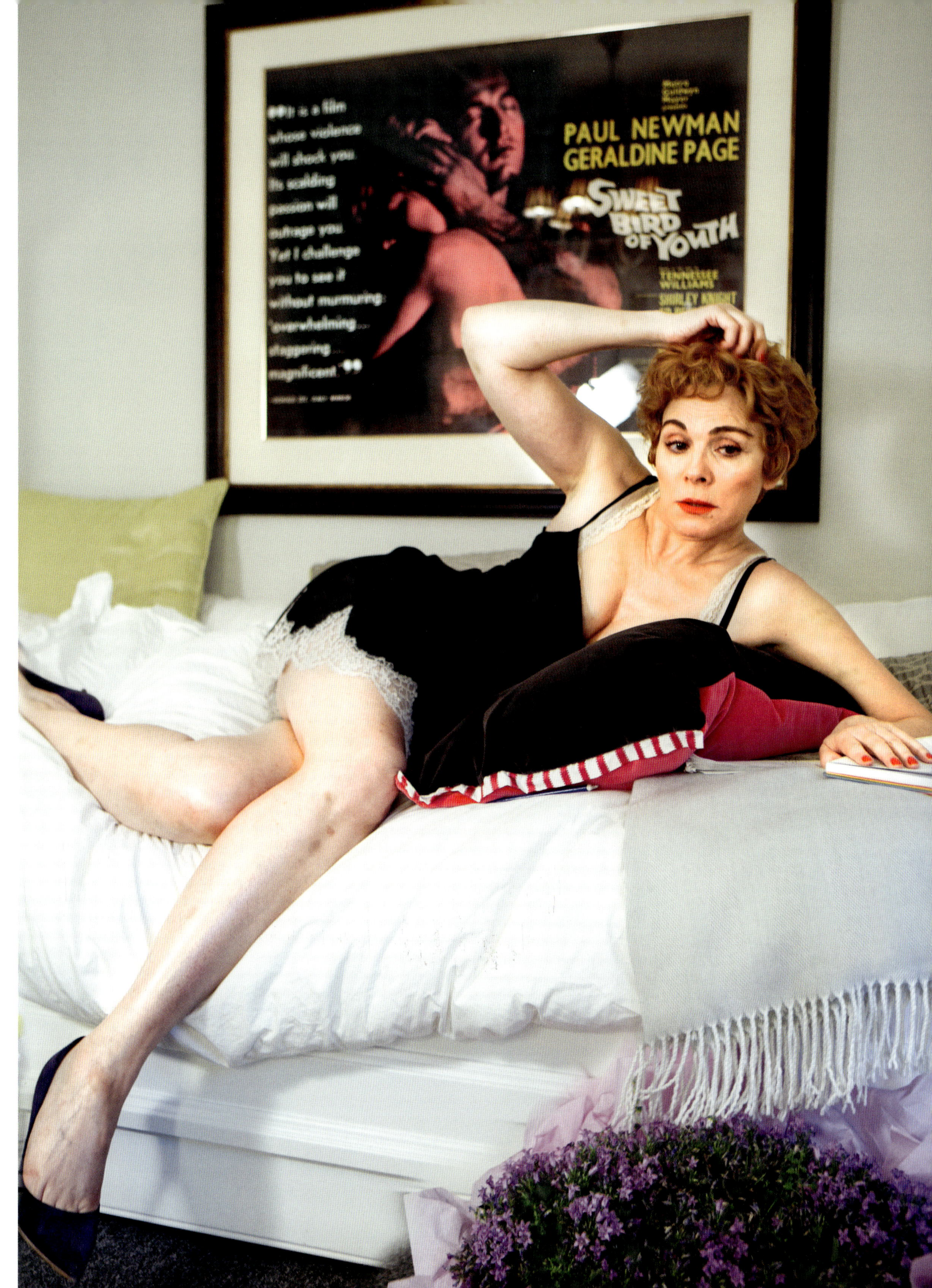
"It is a film
whose violence
will shock you.
Its scalding
passion will
outrage you.
Yet I challenge
you to see it
without murmuring:
'overwhelming...
staggering...
magnificent.'"
PAUL NEWMAN
GERALDINE PAGE
SWEET BIRD OF YOUTH
TENNESSEE
WILLIAMS
SHIRLEY KNIGHT

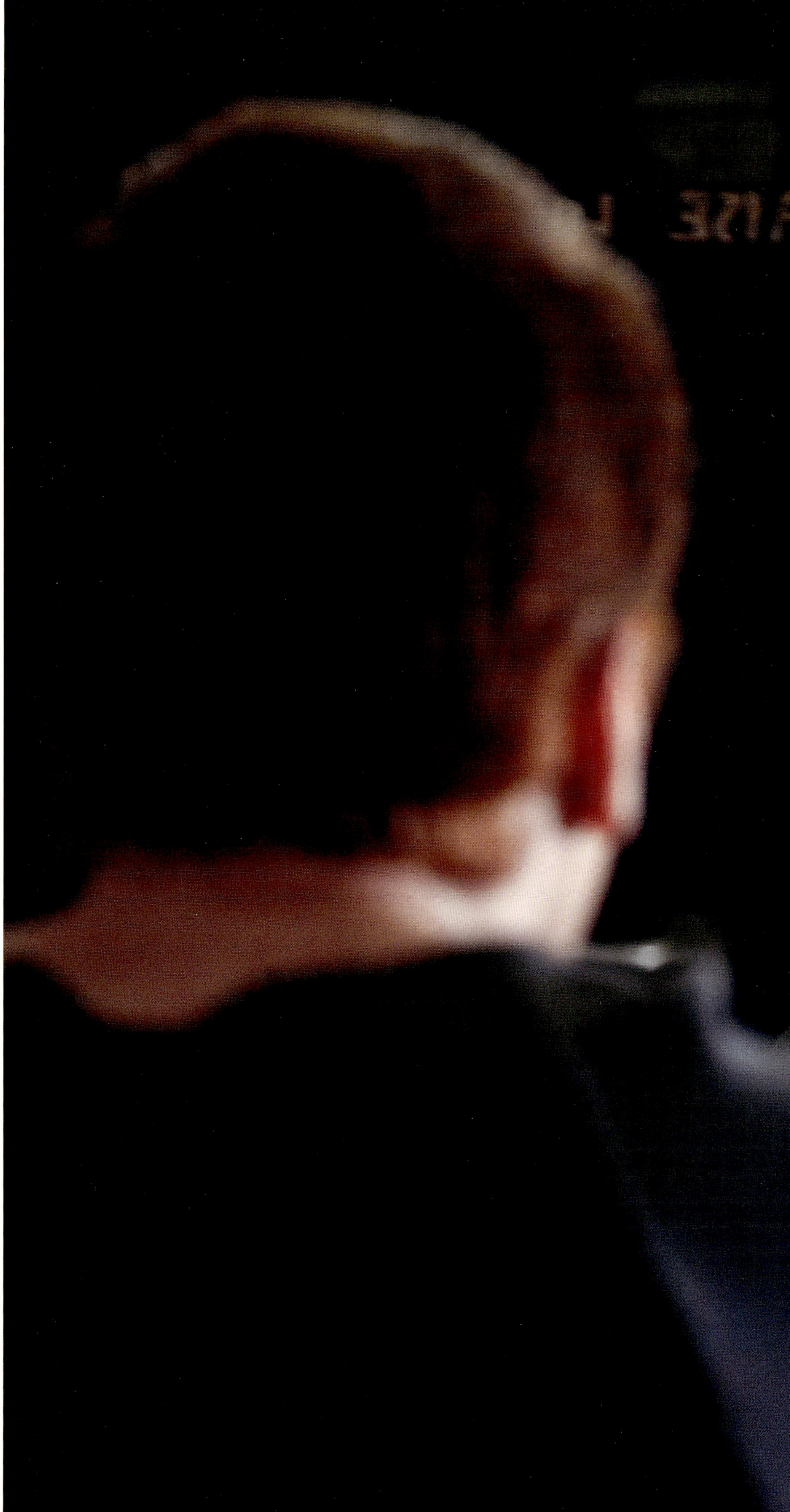

DAMIAN LEWIS, *AMERICAN BUFFALO*, WYNDHAM'S, 2015
Damian has access to a level of truth and honesty which has enabled a long series of brilliant performances in a wide variety of roles.

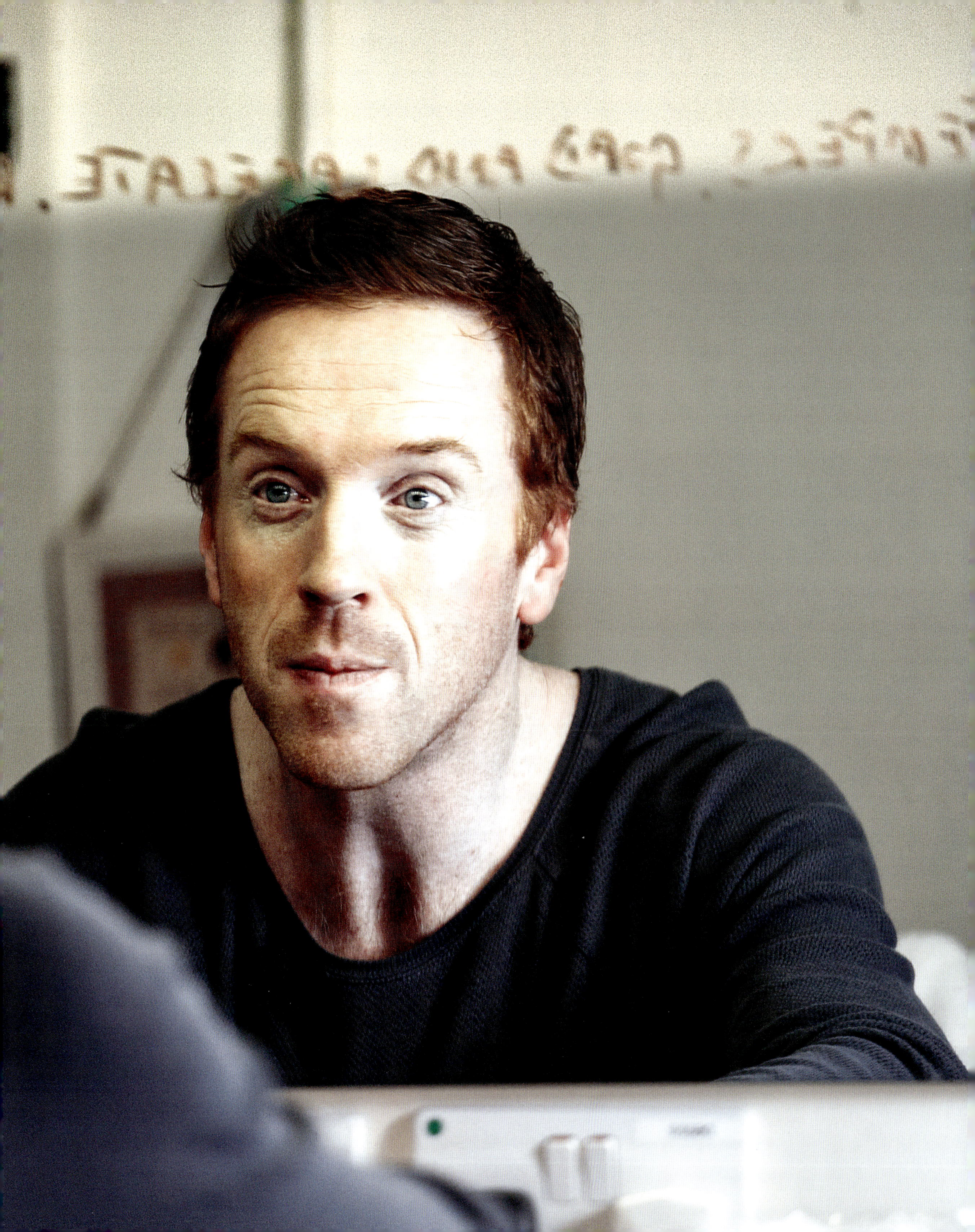

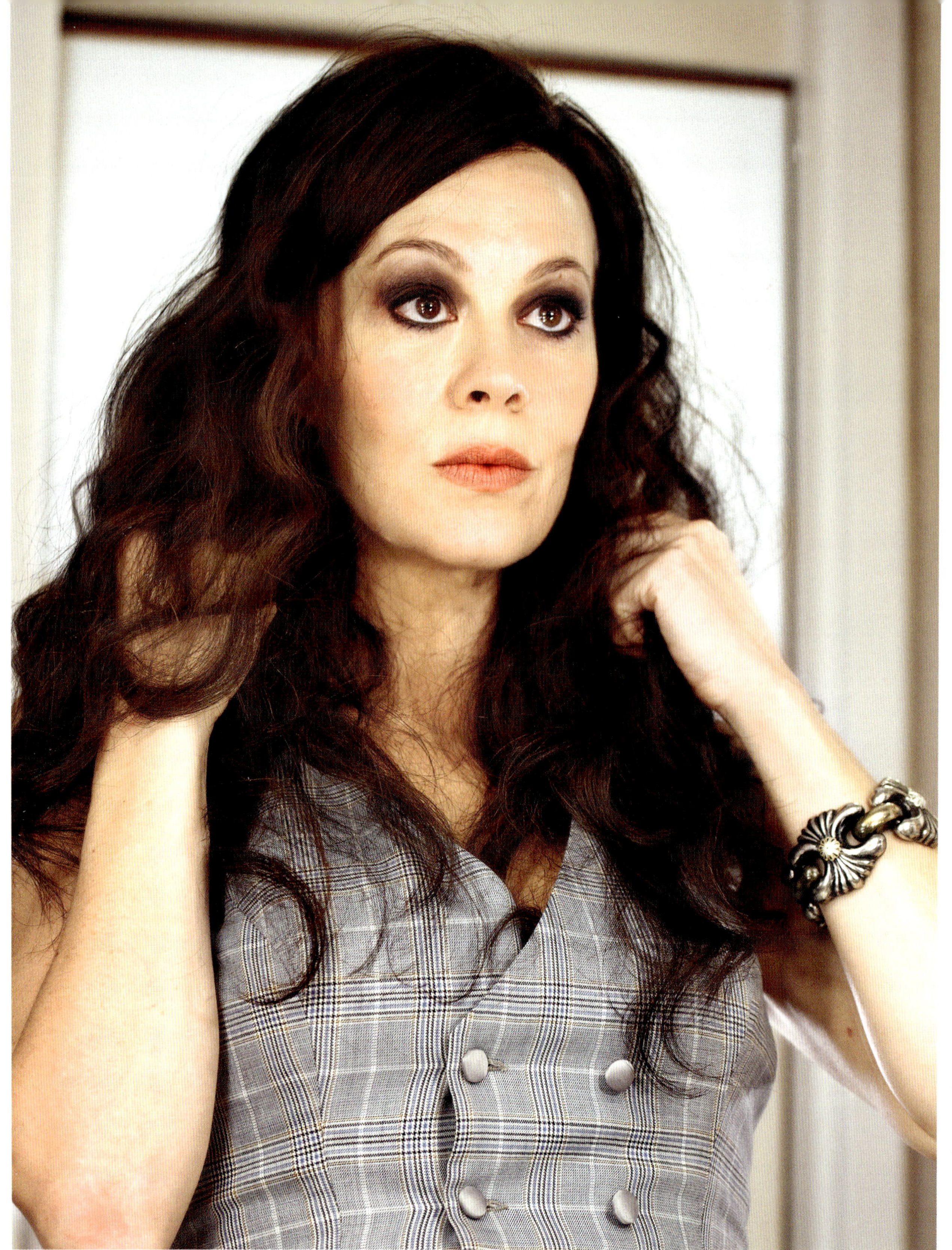

LEFT: **HELEN McCRORY, *THE LAST OF THE HAUSSMANS*, NATIONAL THEATRE, 2012**
Damian jokingly said one day '... you'd better make sure Helen is included'. Interestingly, she has won more awards than him and is firmly placed in the affections of many an adoring fan. Together they are an extraordinary and devoted couple.

OPPOSITE: **KATE FLEETWOOD, *KING LEAR*, NATIONAL THEATRE, 2014**
Putting on her extravagant necklace is a perfect symbol for the ambition of Goneril, Lear's daughter. Using props to get into the role.

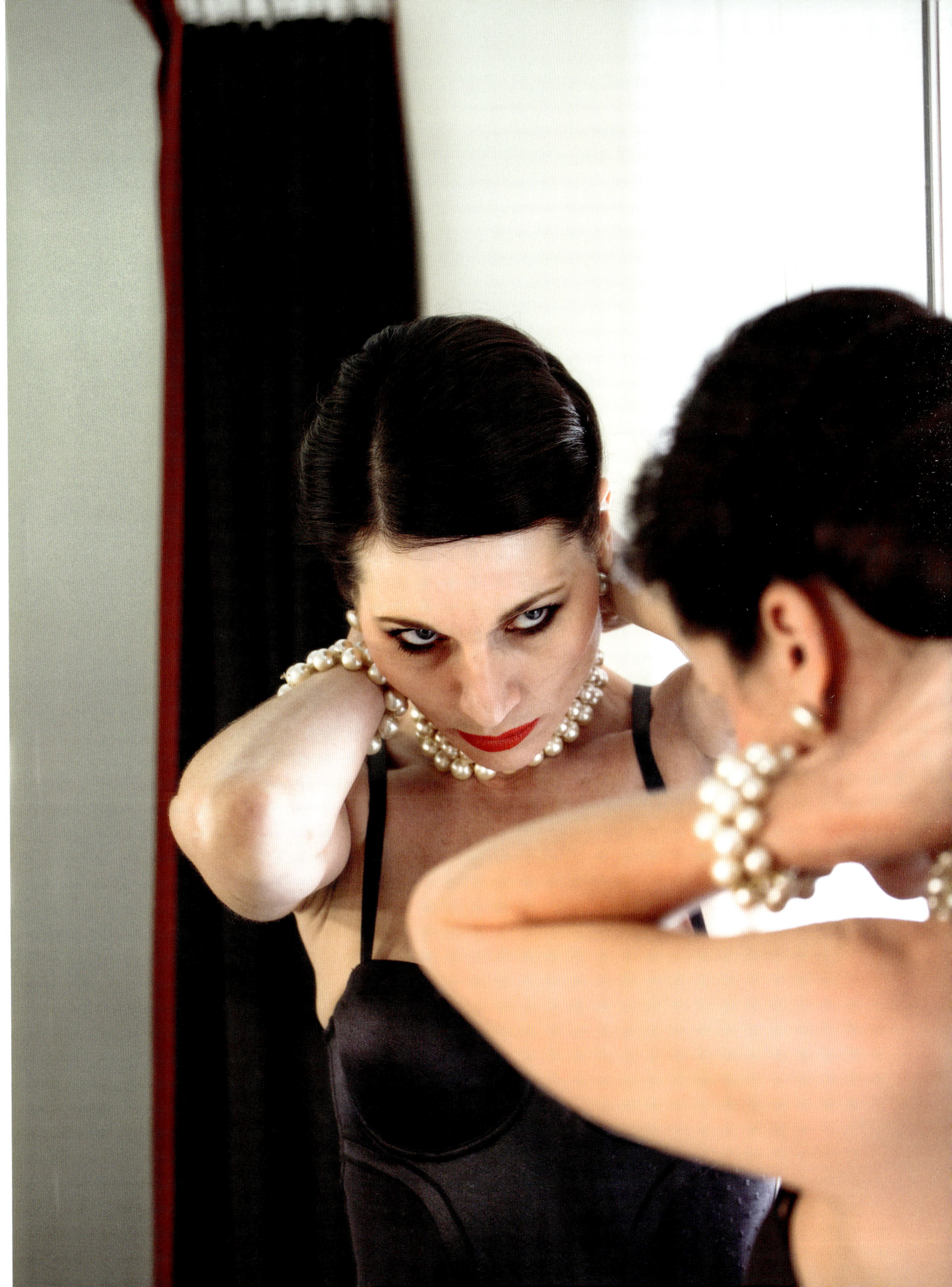

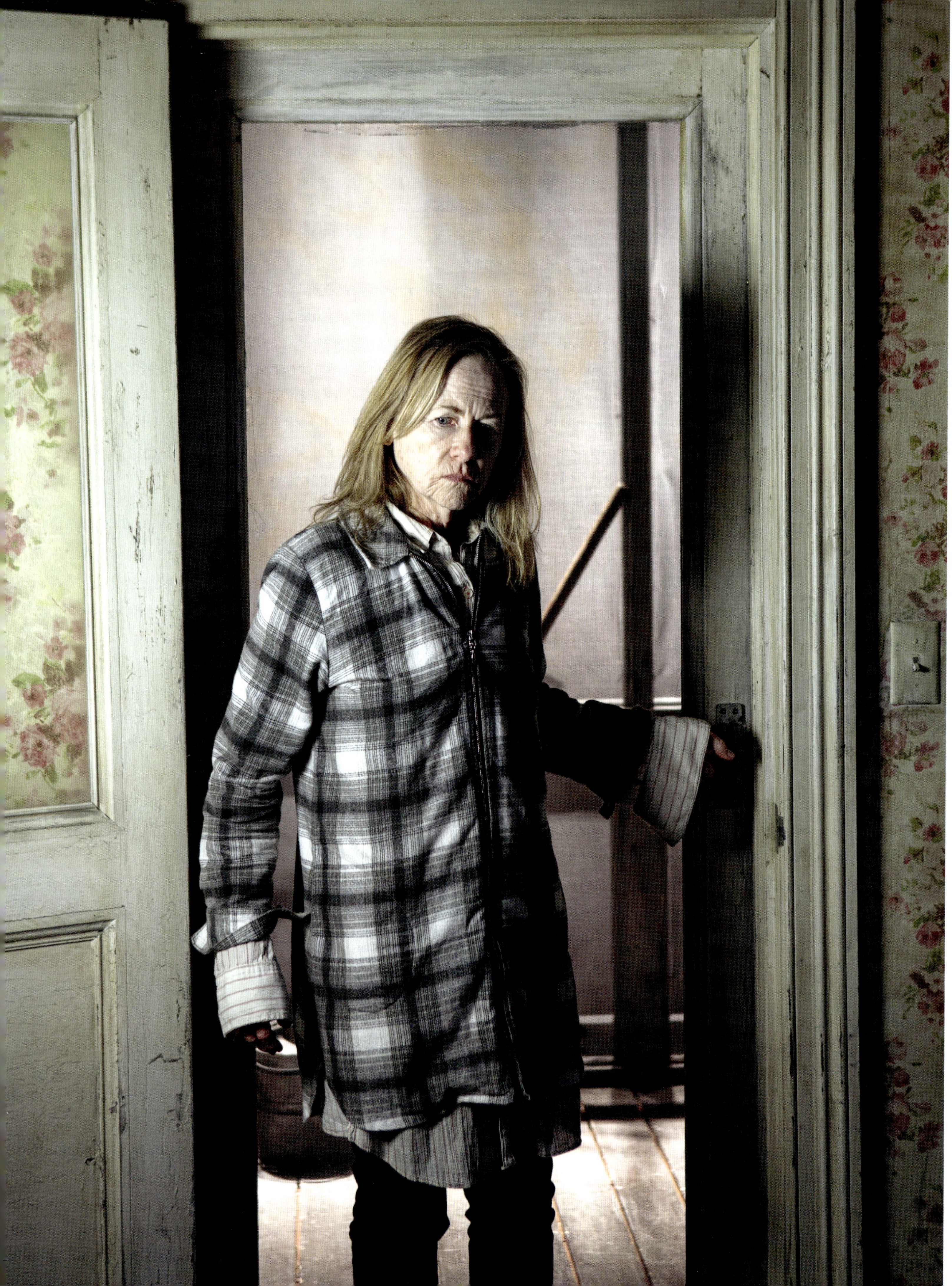

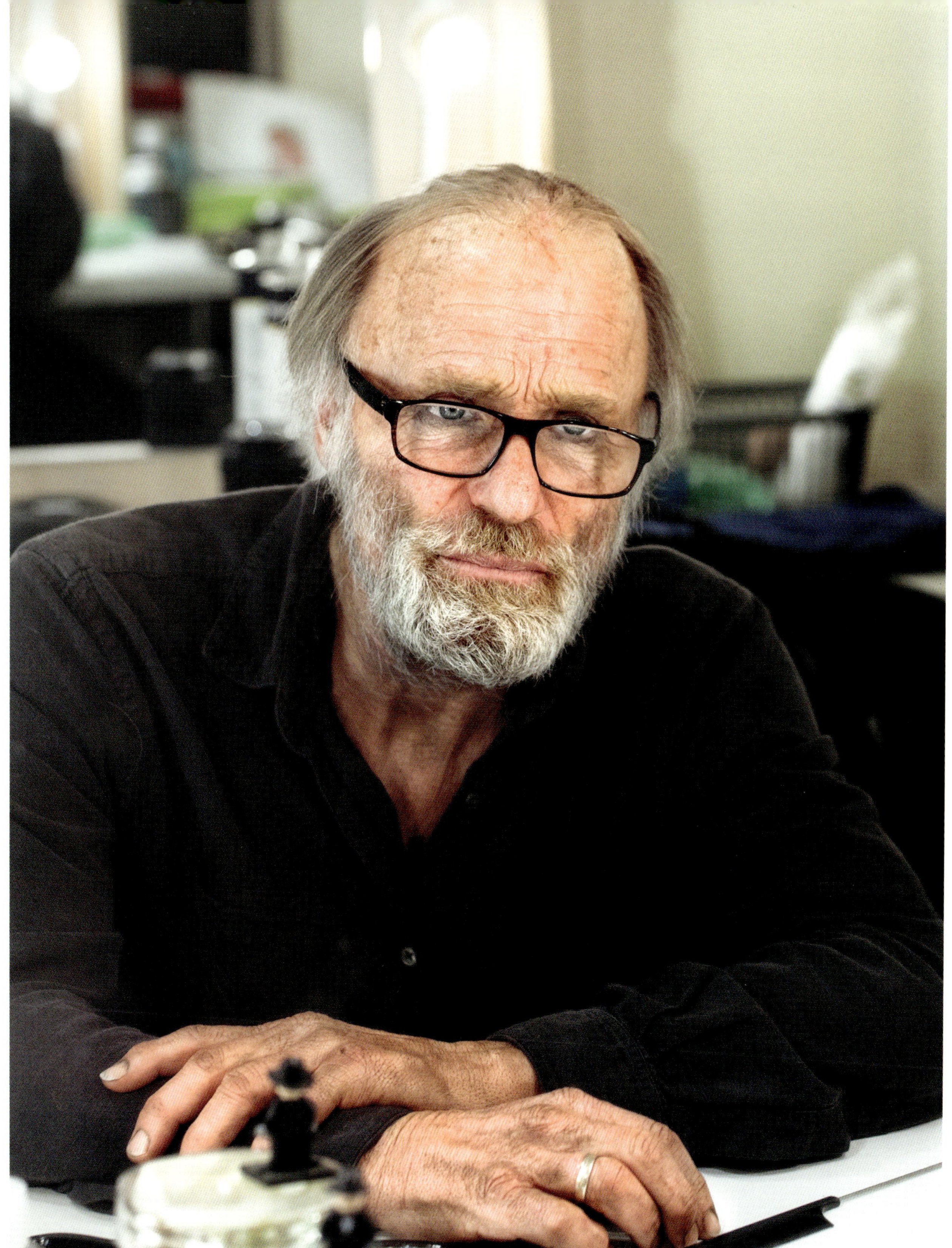

OPPOSITE: **AMY MADIGAN, *BURIED CHILD*, TRAFALGAR STUDIOS, 2016**
For her preparation, Amy went onto the set to physically rehearse the key moments of her character's journey – a comprehensive and Method approach.

RIGHT: **ED HARRIS, *BURIED CHILD*, TRAFALGAR STUDIOS, 2016**
This is a rare image. Not keen on being seen backstage, Ed gave me 90 seconds to take a photo. So as not to disturb his rhythm, I made sure it was completed in 85.

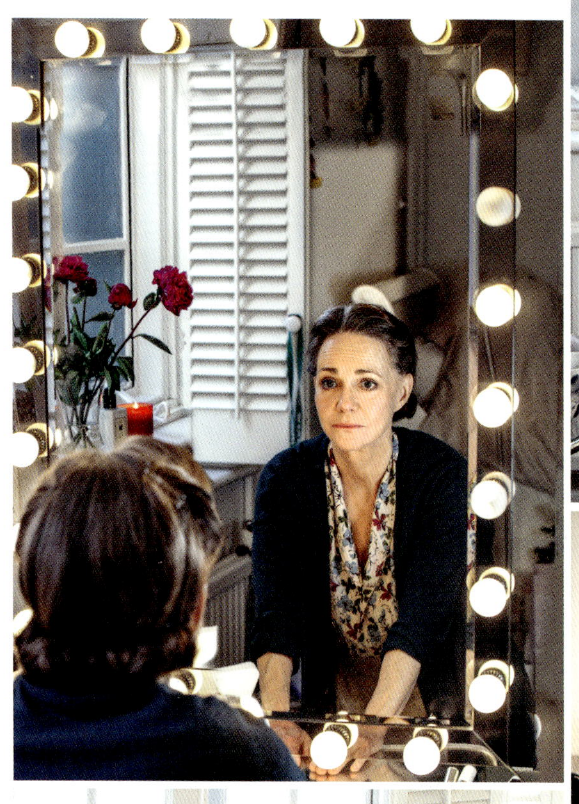

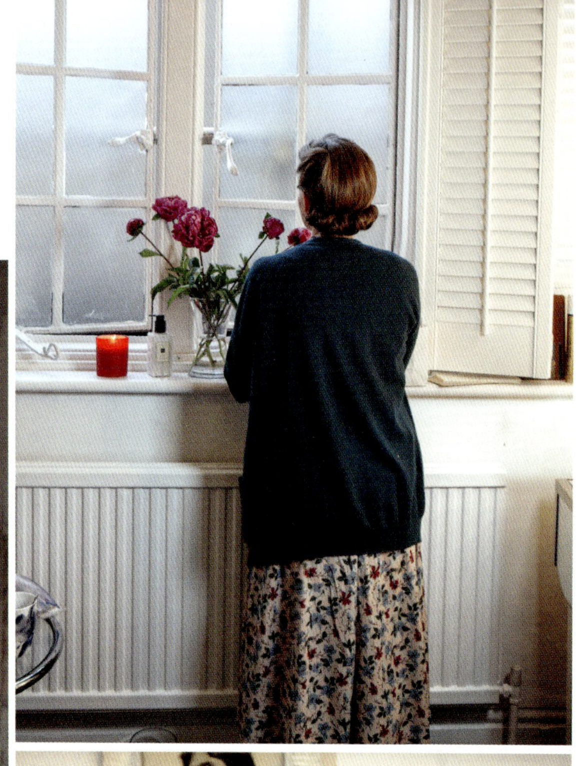

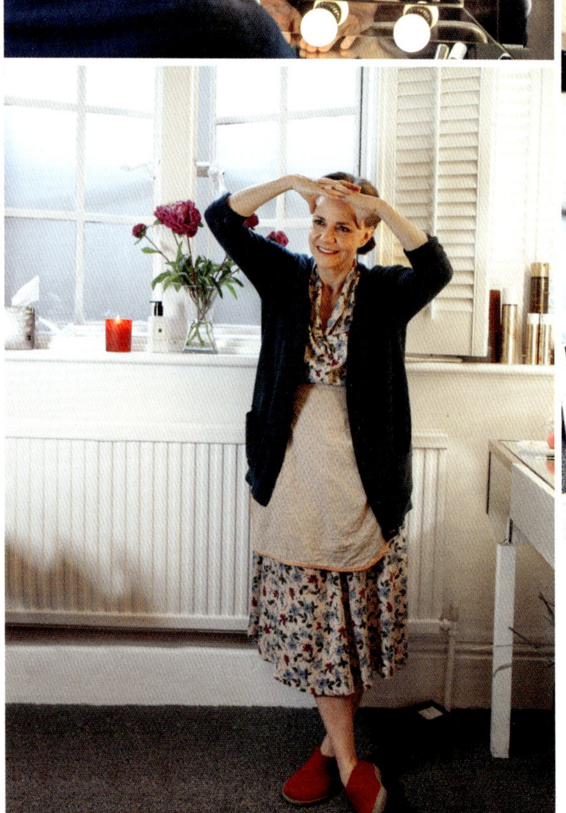

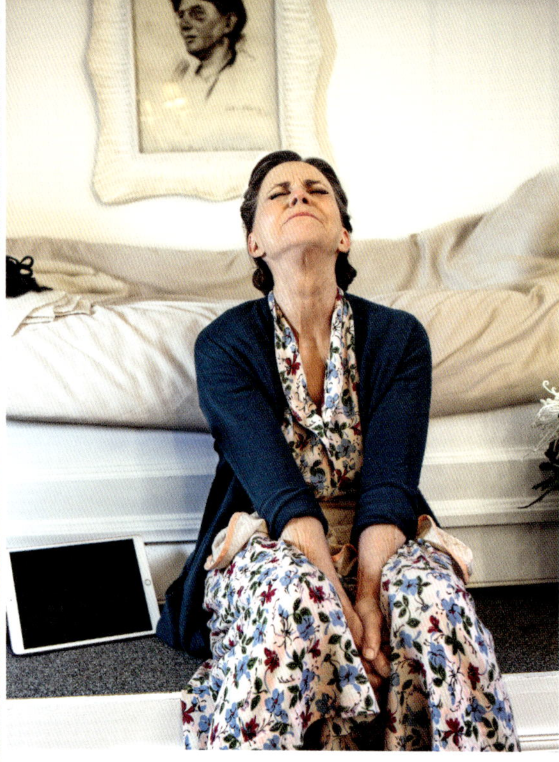

SALLY FIELD, *ALL MY SONS*, OLD VIC THEATRE, 2019

Sally uses the room, again Olivier's, to inhabit the character long before reaching the stage. A portrait of Lillian Bayliss, the proprietor of the Old Vic in the 1930s and who made it successful as a theatre, is above the bed.

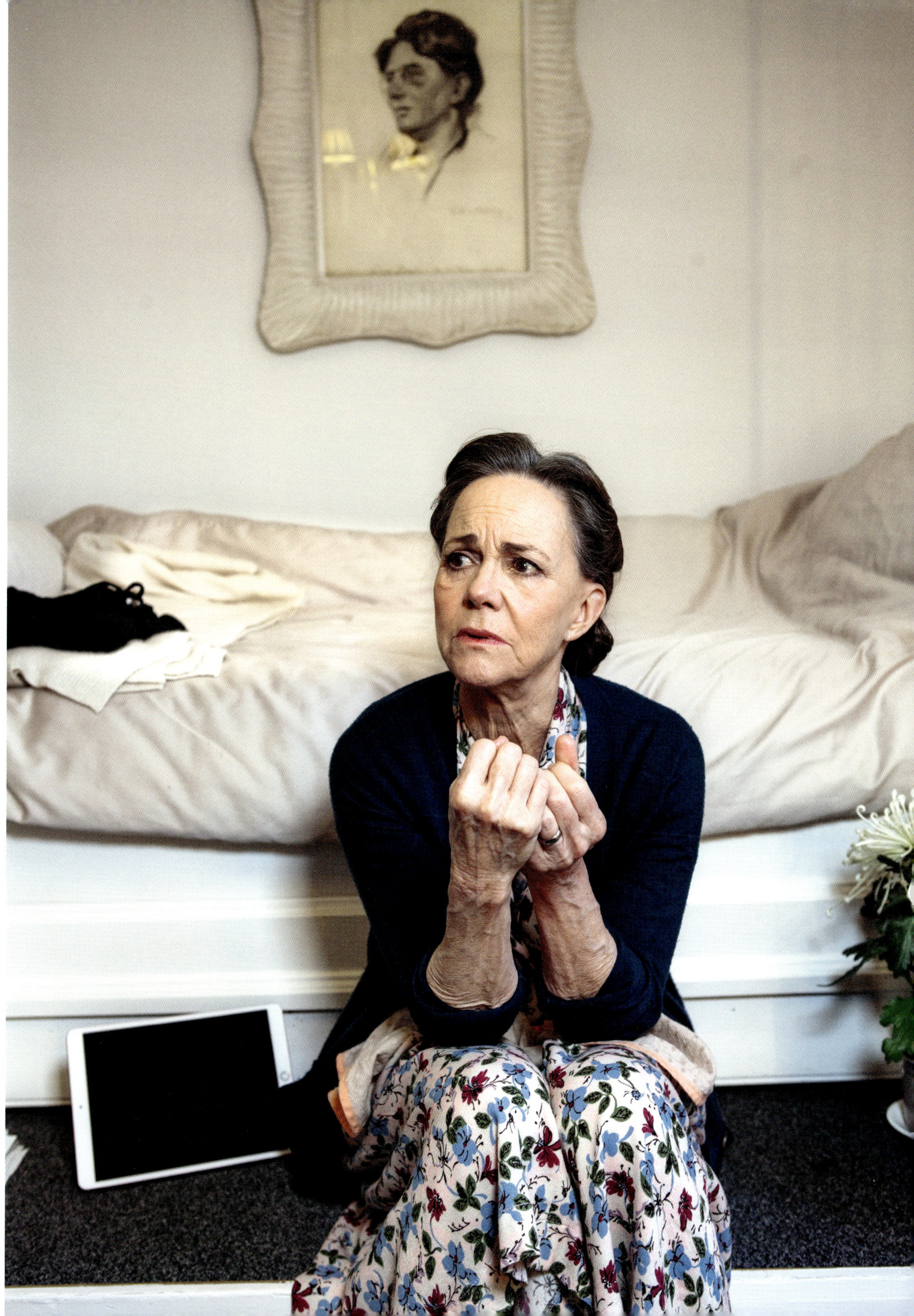

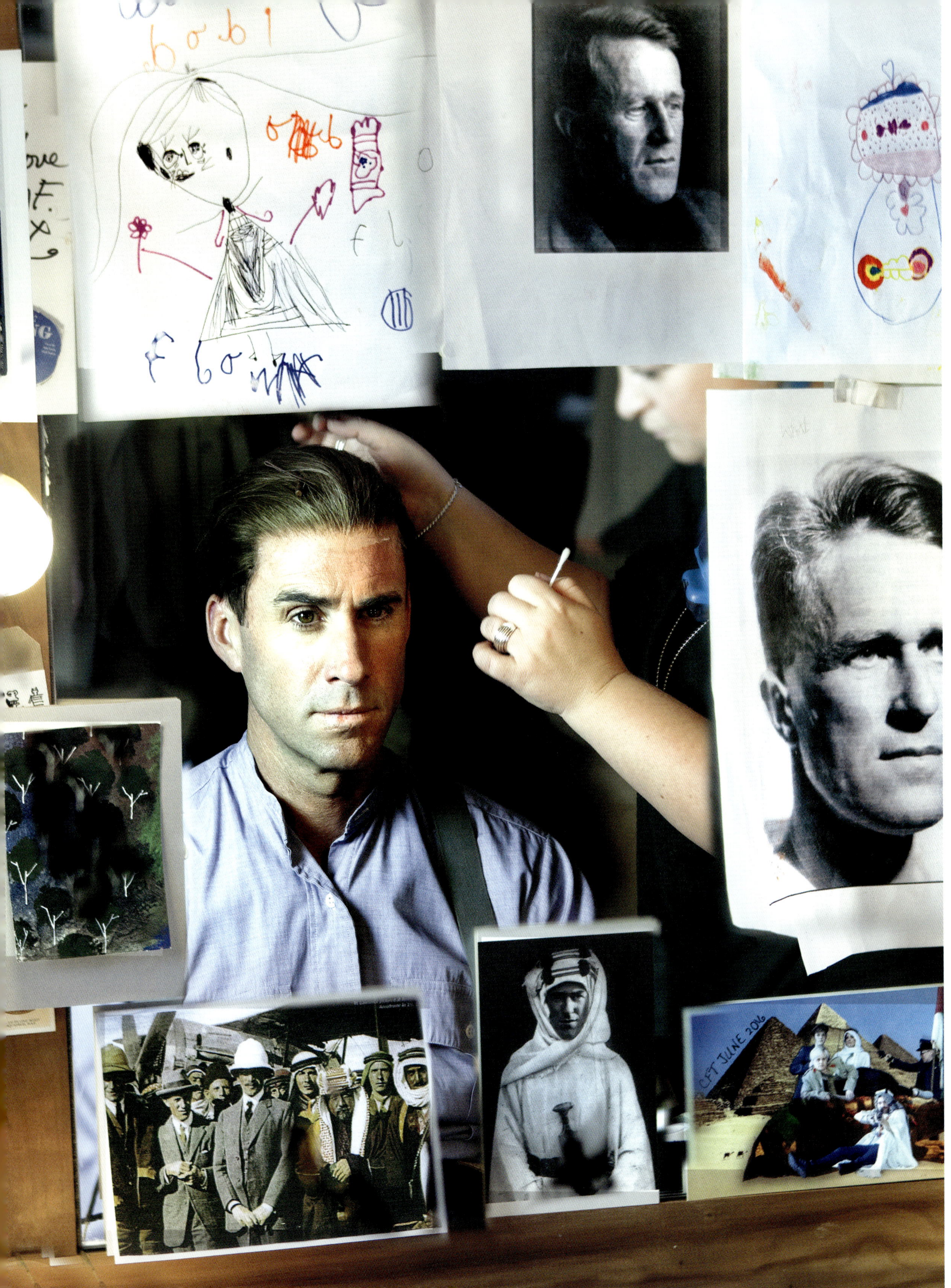
bobi
CFT JUNE 2016

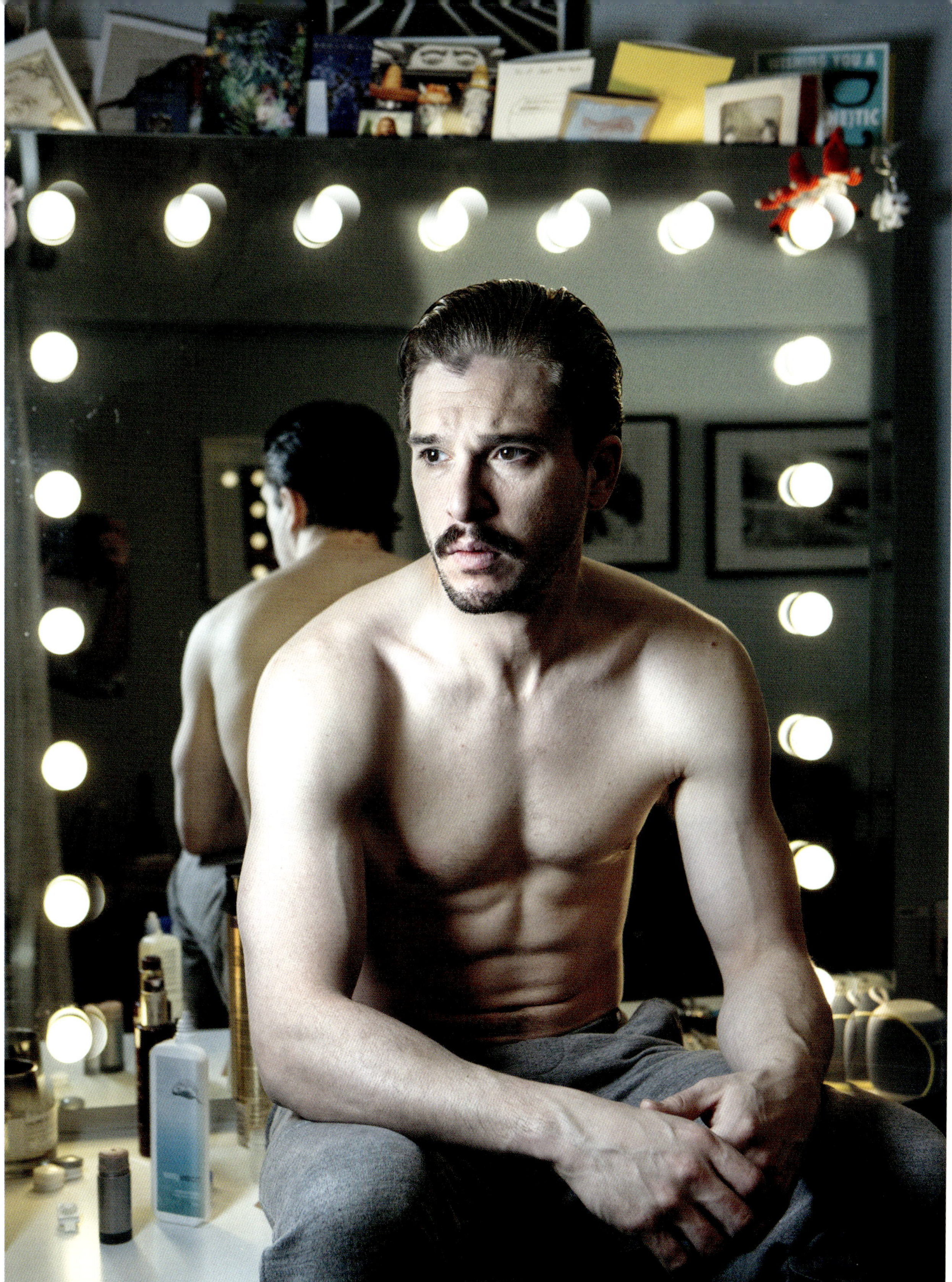

OPPOSITE: **JOSEPH FIENNES, *ROSS*, CHICHESTER FESTIVAL THEATRE, 2016**
Playing the historical character Laurence of Arabia. The choice for an actor to make, is how much to impersonate him, or not.

RIGHT: **KIT HARINGTON, *TRUE WEST*, VAUDEVILLE THEATRE, 2018**
After his monumental success in *Game of Thrones*, Kit returns to the theatre.

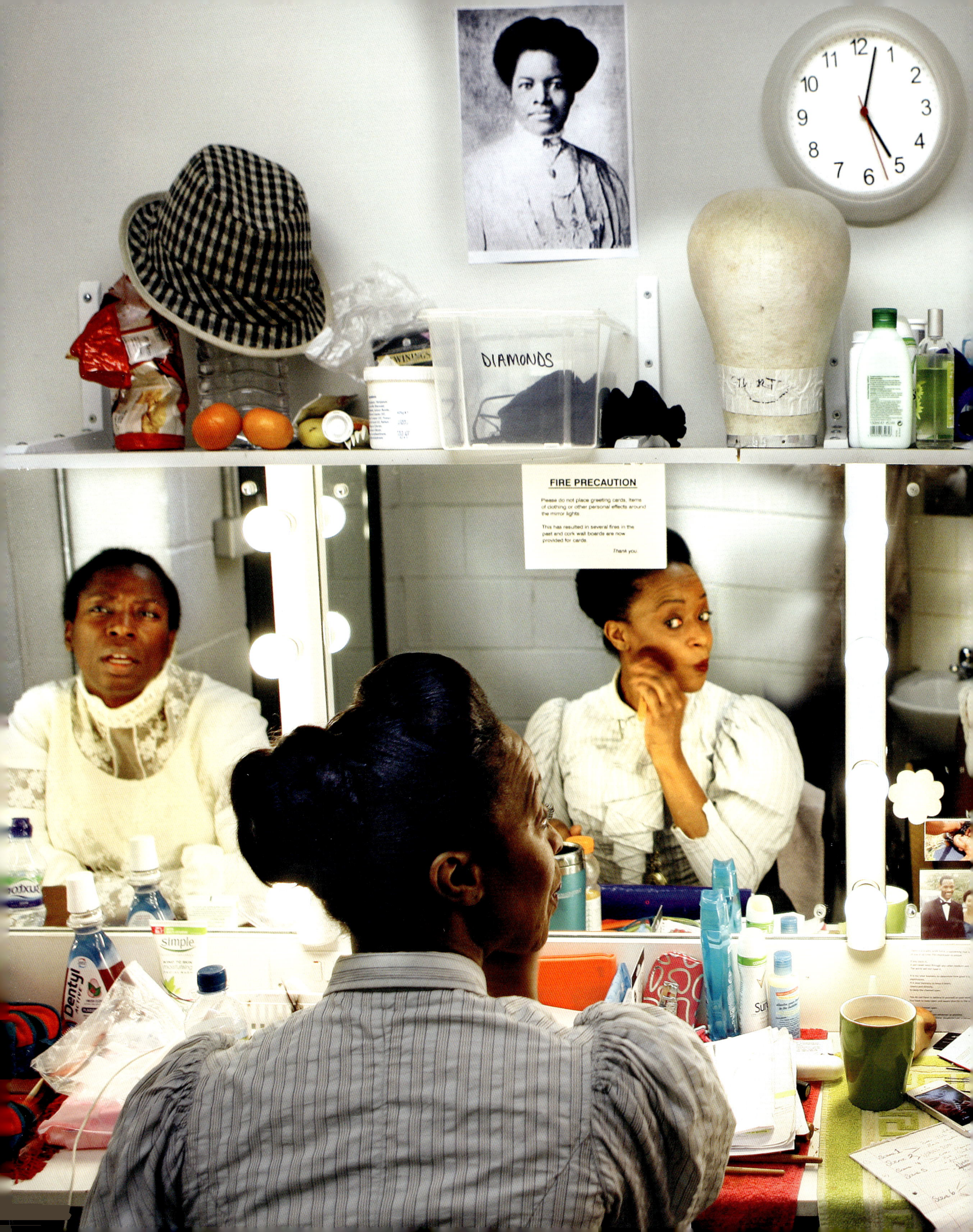
DIAMONDS
FIRE PRECAUTION
Please do not place greeting cards, items of clothing or other personal effects around the mirror lights.
This has resulted in several fires in the past and cork wall boards are now provided for cards.
Thank you.
TWININGS
Dentyl
simple

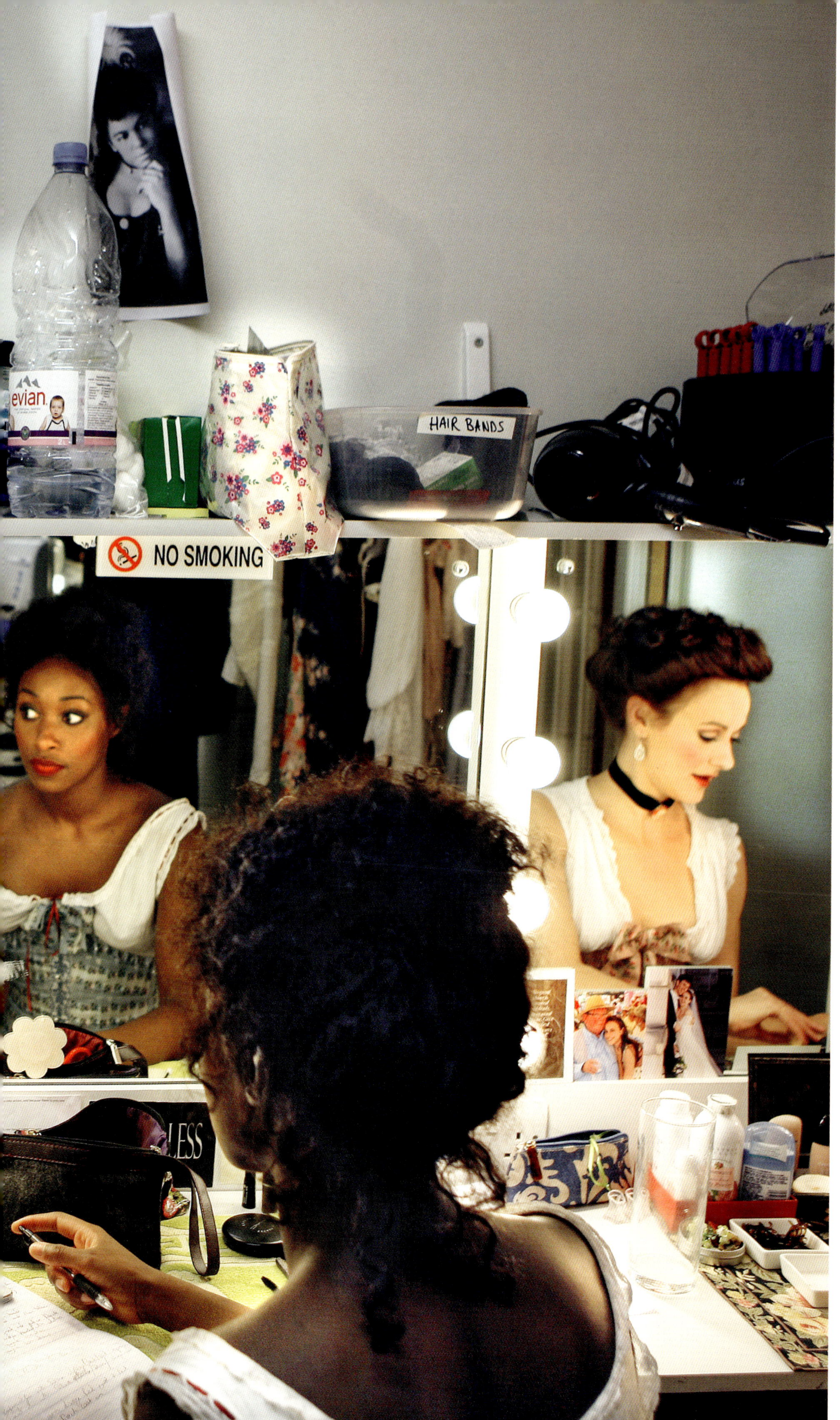

TANYE MOODIE, DAWN HOPE, ROCHELLE NEIL, SARA TOPHAM, *INTIMATE APPAREL*, USTINOV THEATRE, 2014

Sharing a dressing room is a skill in itself.

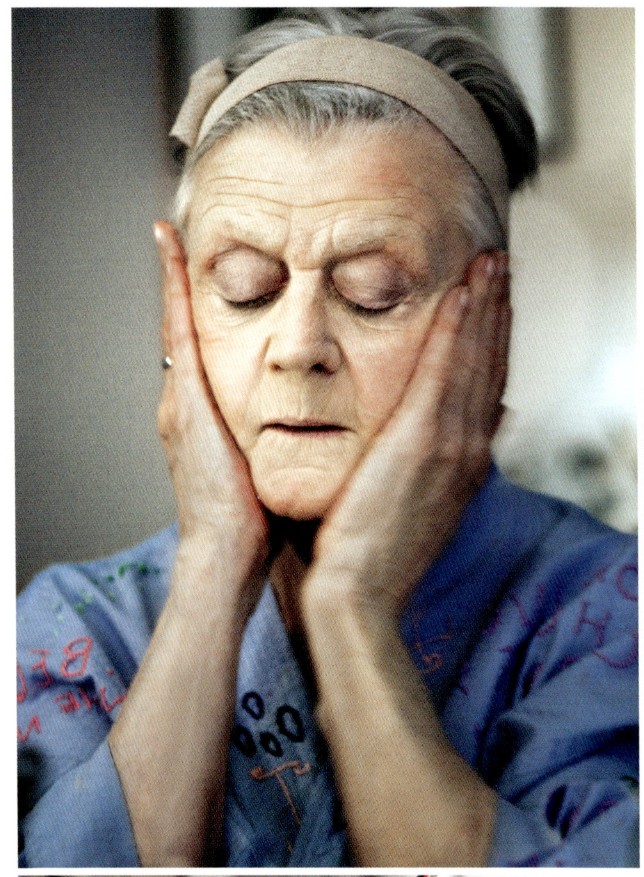

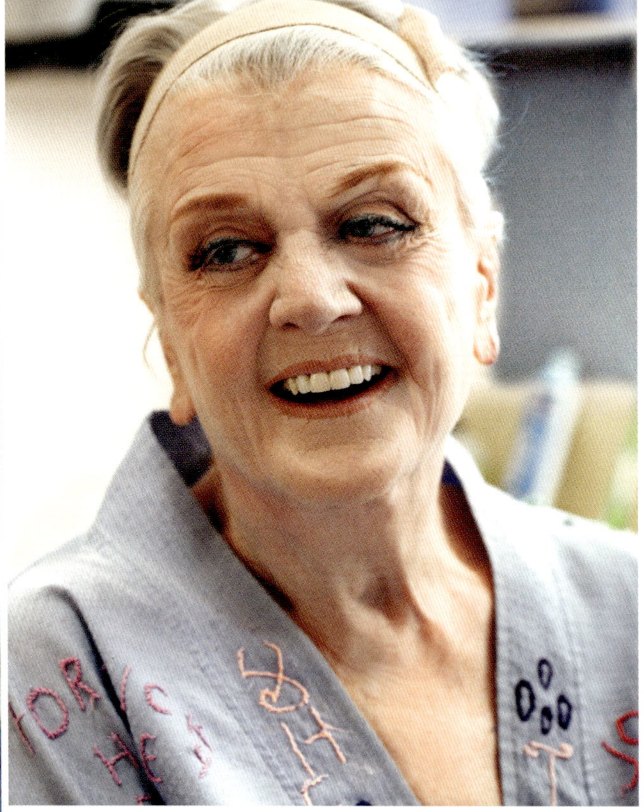

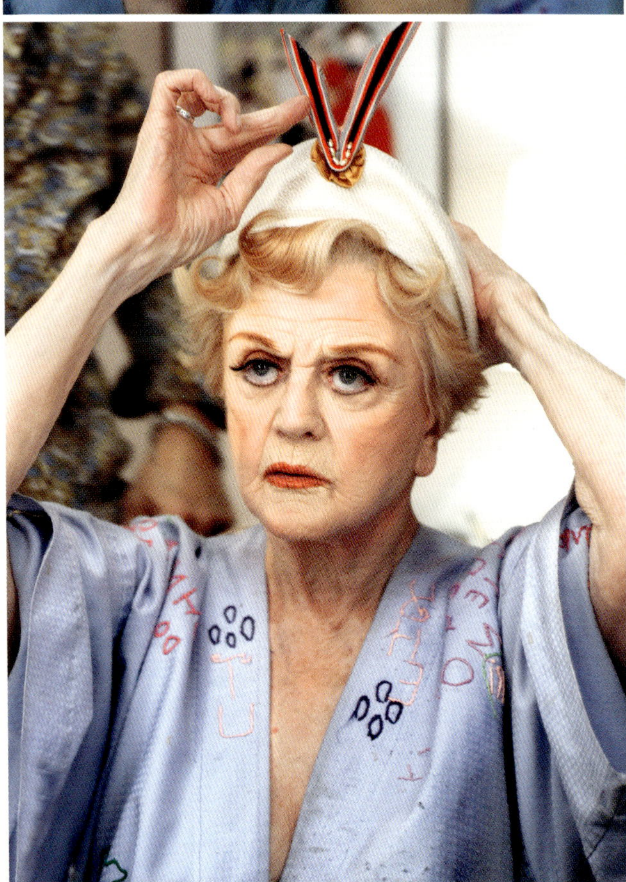

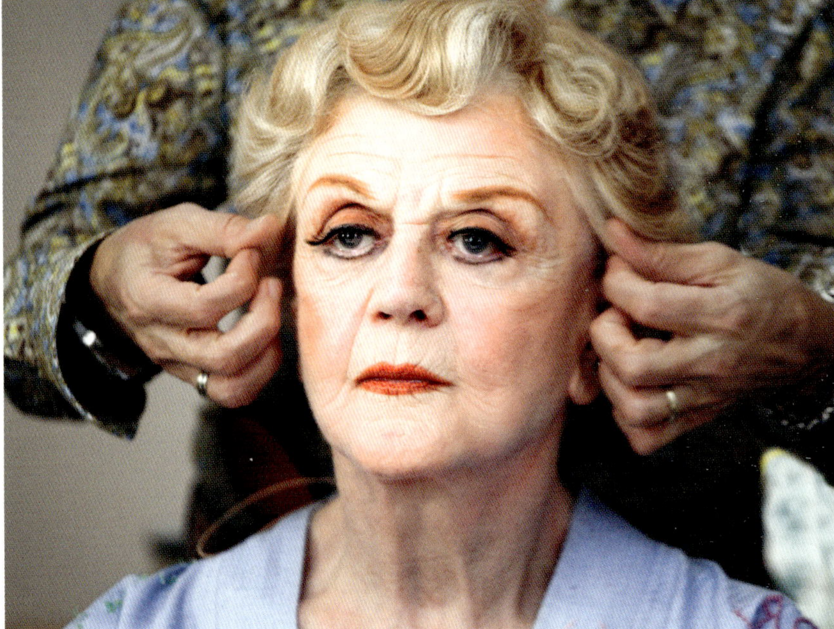

ANGELA LANSBURY, *BLITHE SPIRIT*, GIELGUD THEATRE, 2014

Angela's spirit and generosity astounded me. A magnificent trouper, an extraordinary talent, grace and humour all rolled into one.

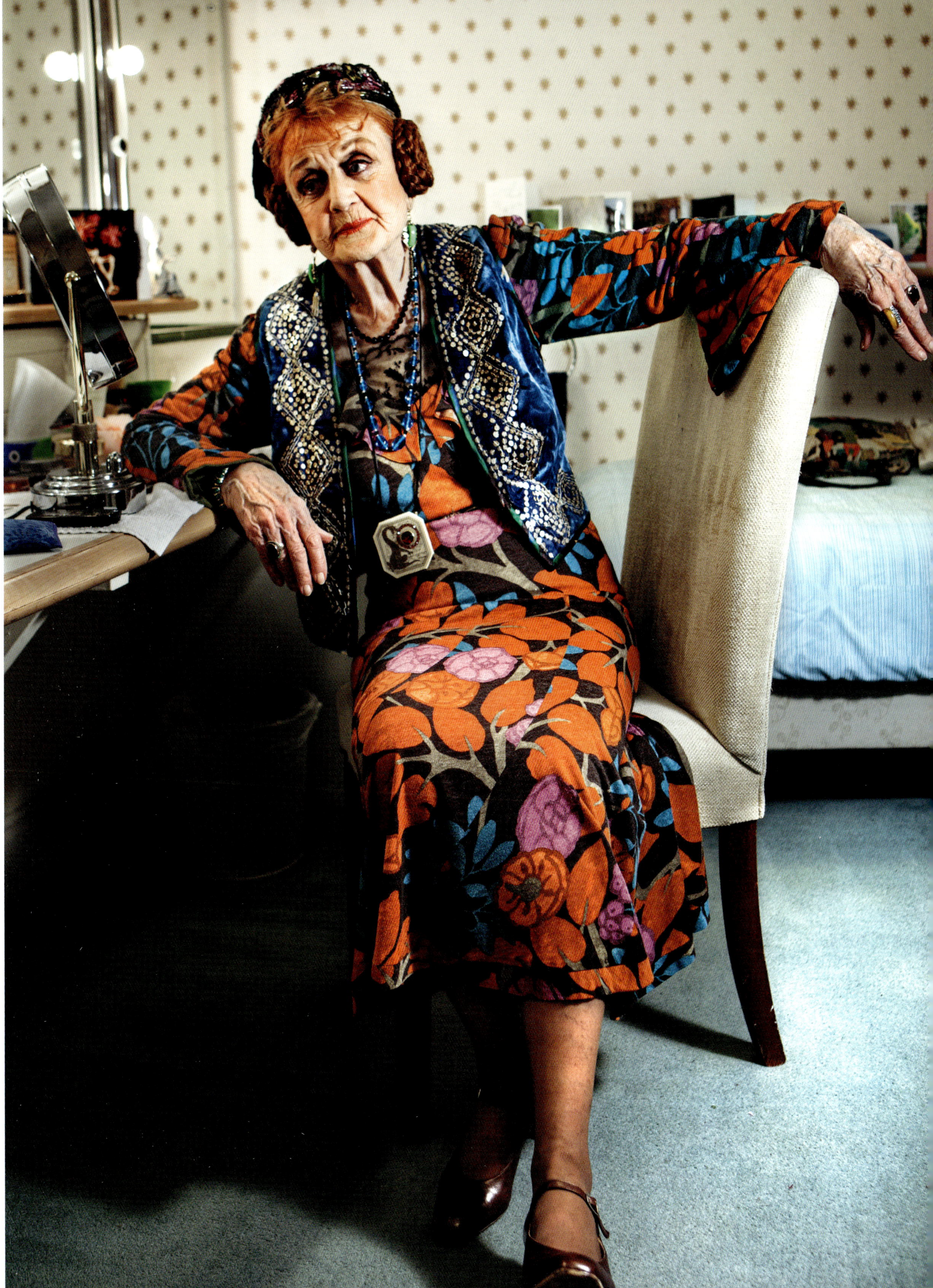

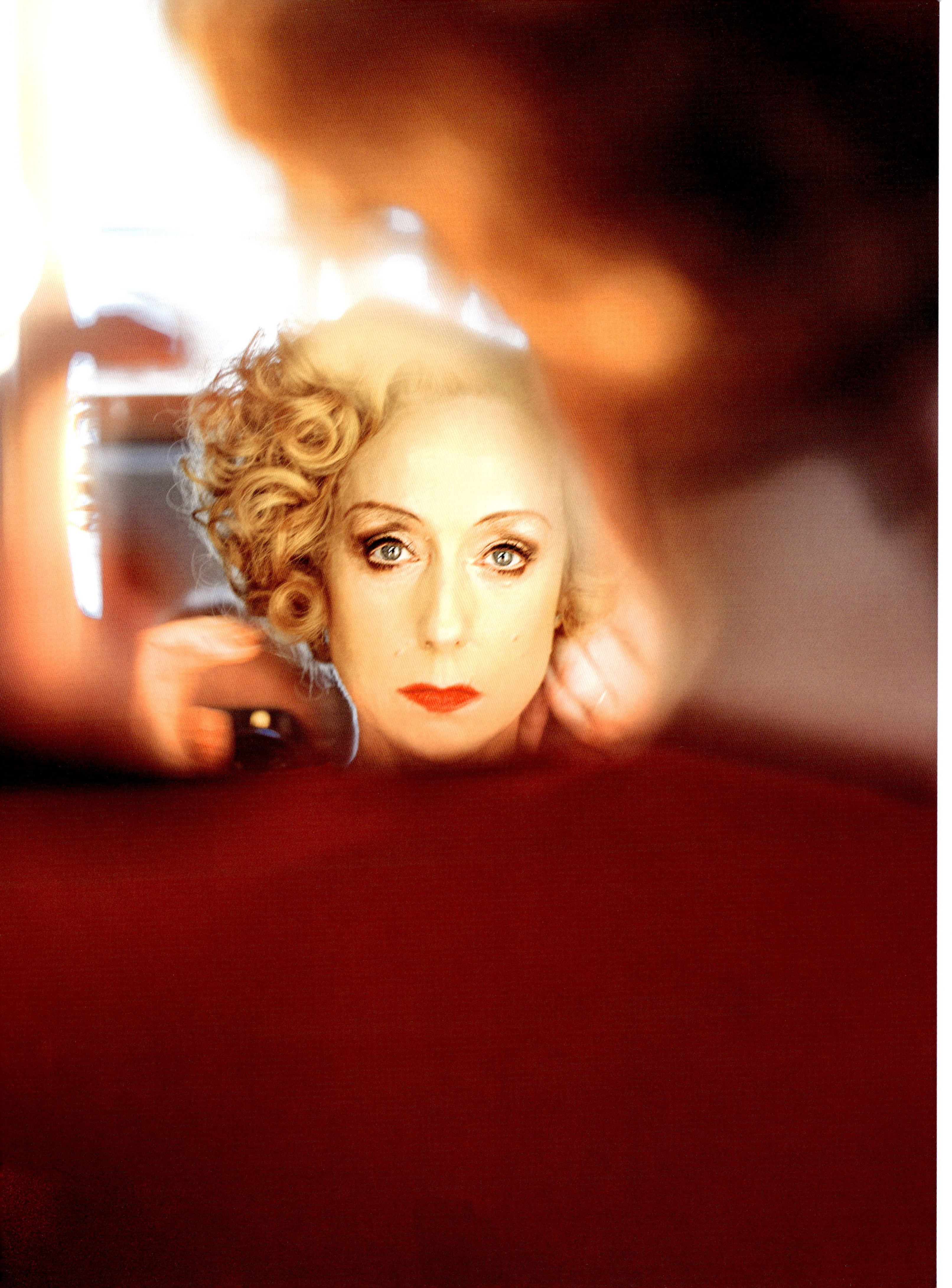

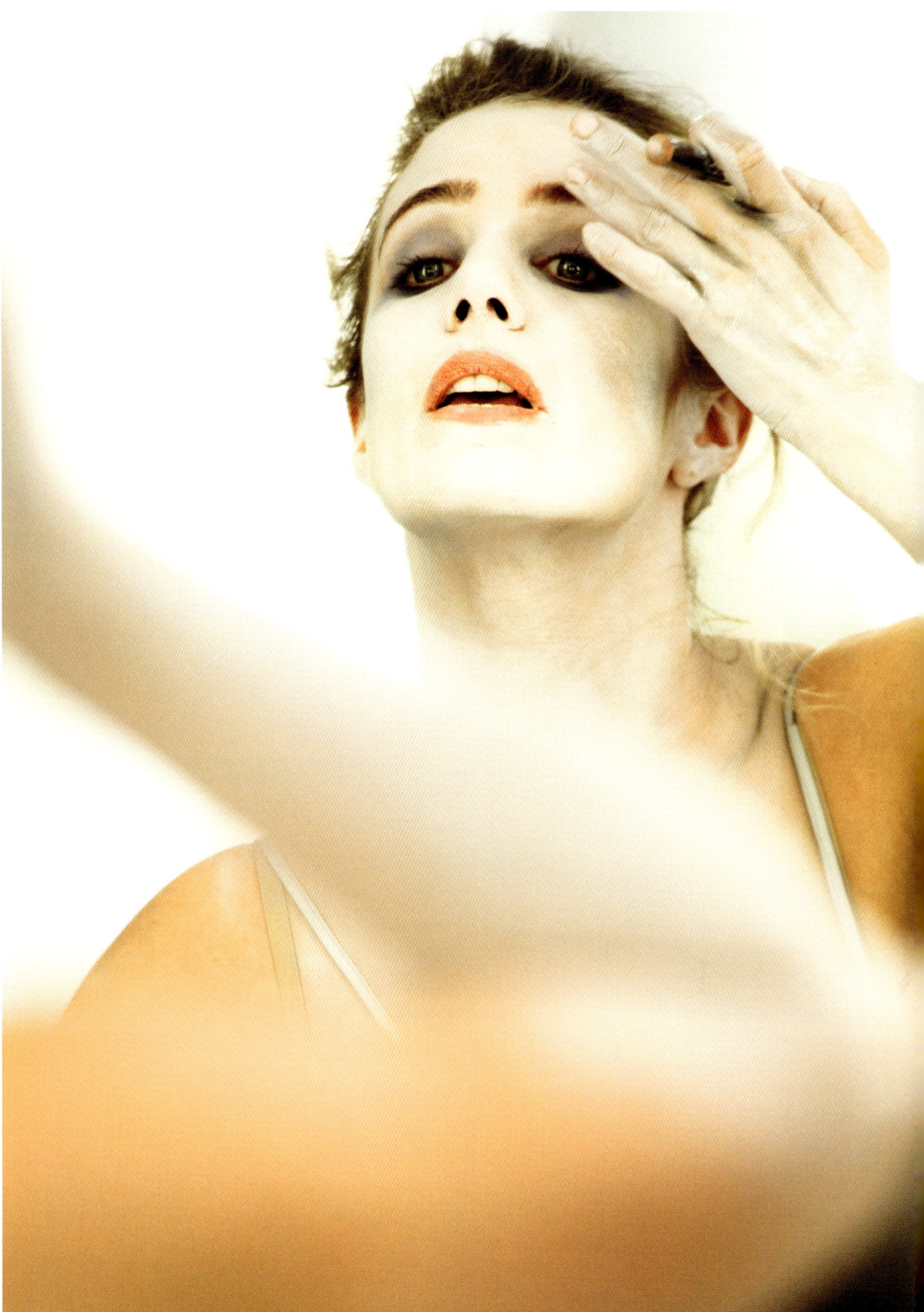

OPPOSITE: **LIA WILLIAMS, *THE PRIME OF MISS JEAN BRODIE*, DONMAR WAREHOUSE, 2018**

Lia is one of the most underrated actresses of her generation. Once the muse of Pinter and totally without vanity, she tells the story as it is. Here she takes on the Scottish school mistress, originally made famous by Maggie Smith.

RIGHT: **LISA DWAN, *ROCKABY*, ROYAL COURT, 2014**

Lisa has taken over the mantle from Billie Whitelaw as the foremost interpreter of Samuel Beckett's work.

HAIR

Wigs help an actor to interpret a character. Mark Gatiss, co-writer of *Sherlock* and *Dr Who*, is also a distinguished comic and dramatic actor who often builds his performance when deciding the hairstyle of a character.

OPPOSITE PAGE TOP, FROM LEFT TO RIGHT: DAVID THRELFALL, *DON QUIXOTE*, GARRICK THEATRE, 2018; SIMON CALLOW, *WAITING FOR GODOT*, THEATRE ROYAL HAYMARKET, 2009; ROGER LLOYD PACK, *TWELFTH NIGHT*, GLOBE THEATRE, 2013

OPPOSITE PAGE BOTTOM: STEFFAN RHODRI, *A MAD WORLD MY MASTERS*, RSC, 2013

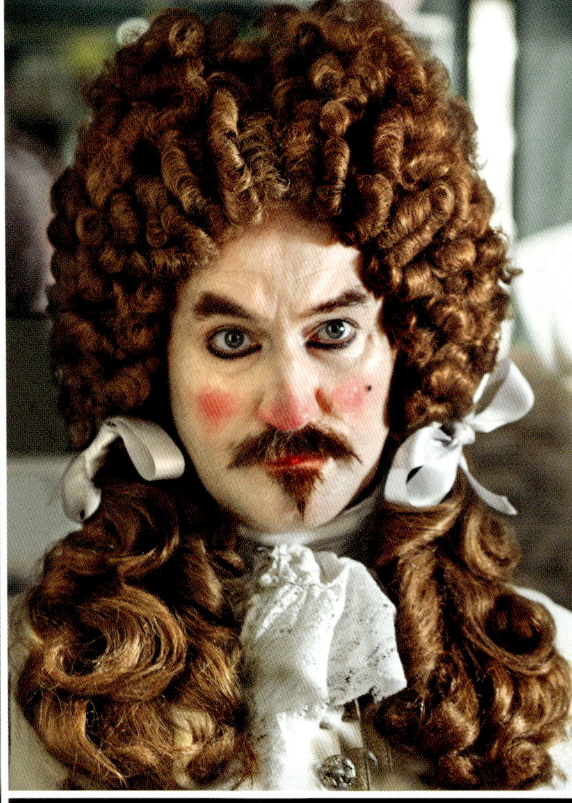

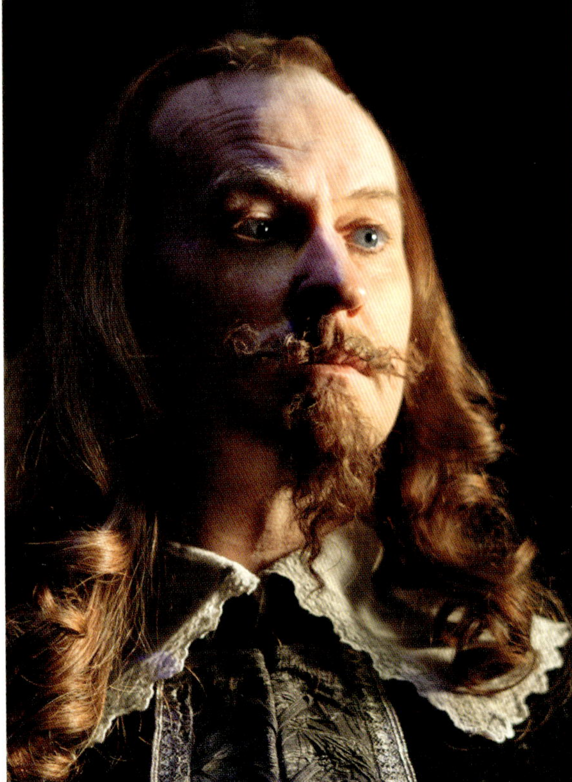

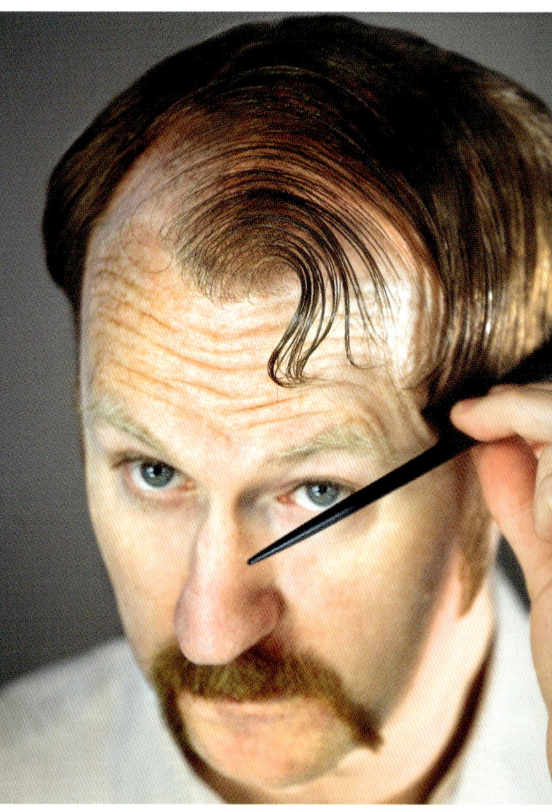

THIS PAGE: MARK GATISS,
ABOVE: *THE BOYS IN THE BAND*, VAUDEVILLE THEATRE, 2017
TOP: *THE RECRUITING OFFICER*, DONMAR WAREHOUSE, 2012
RIGHT: *55 DAYS*, HAMPSTEAD THEATRE, 2012
FAR RIGHT: *SEASON'S GREETINGS*, NATIONAL THEATRE, 2010

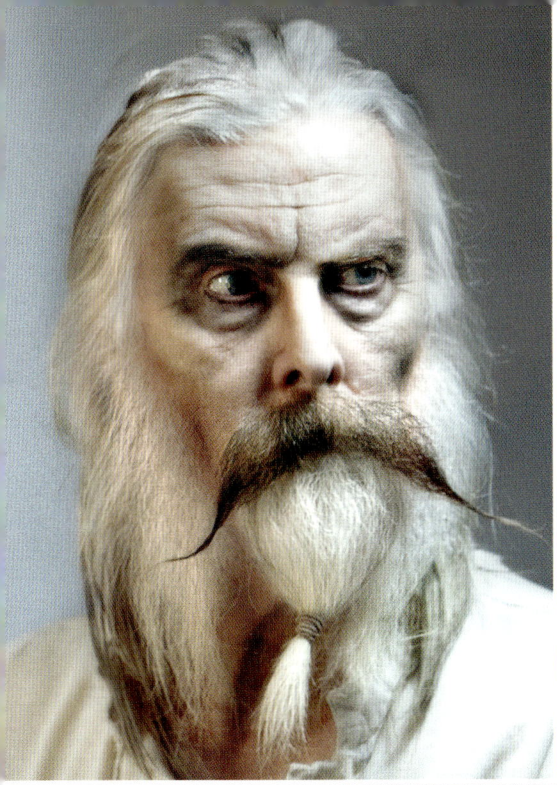

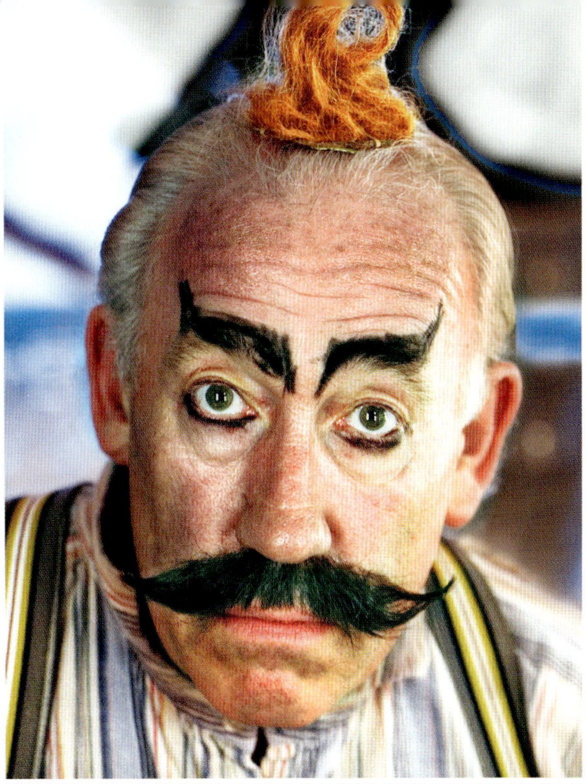

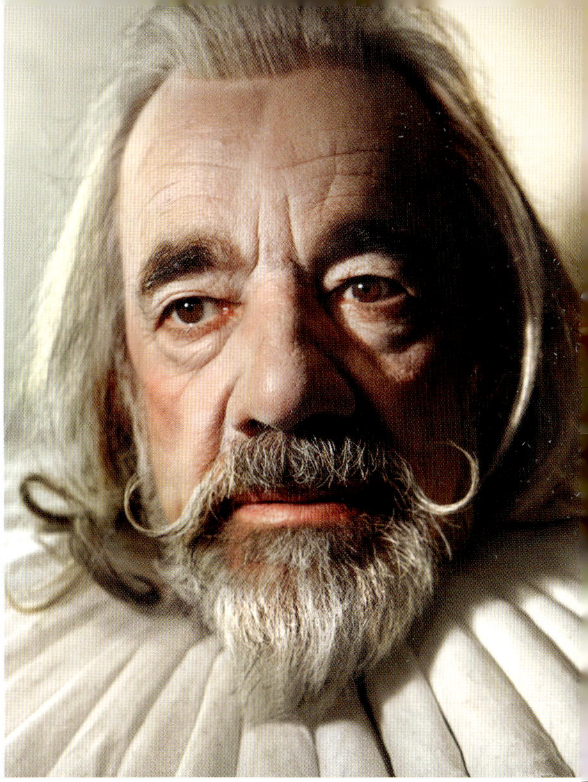

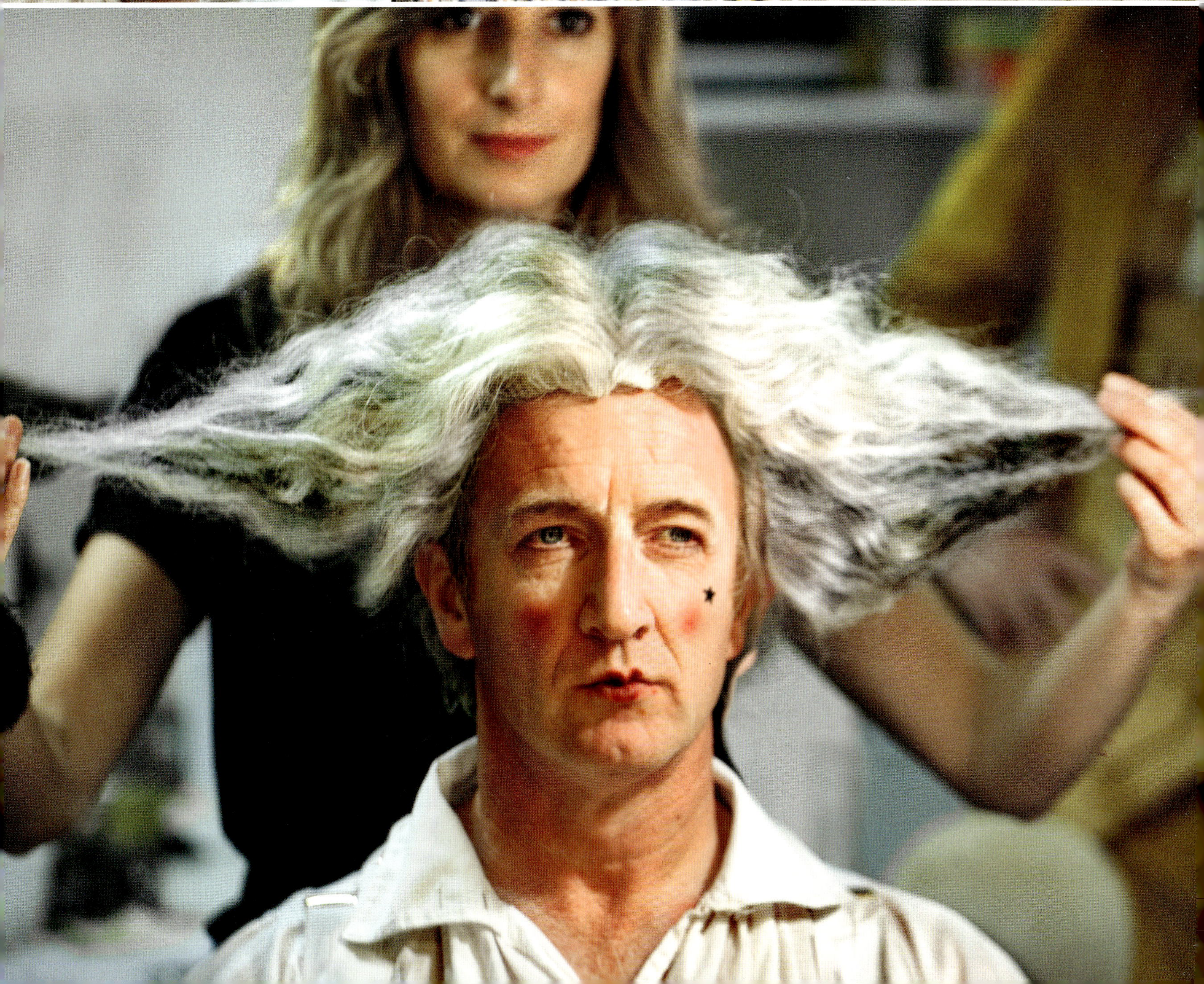

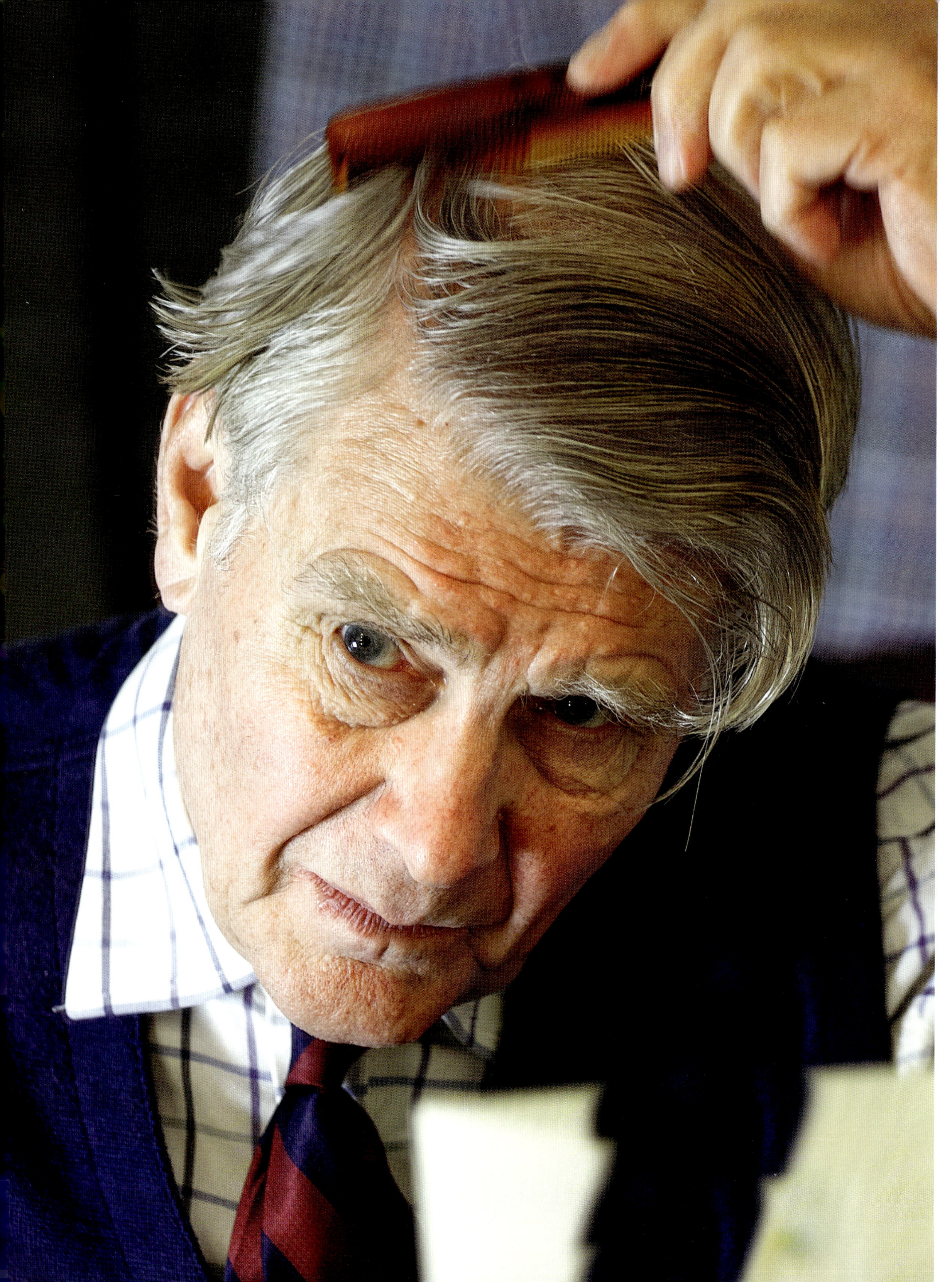

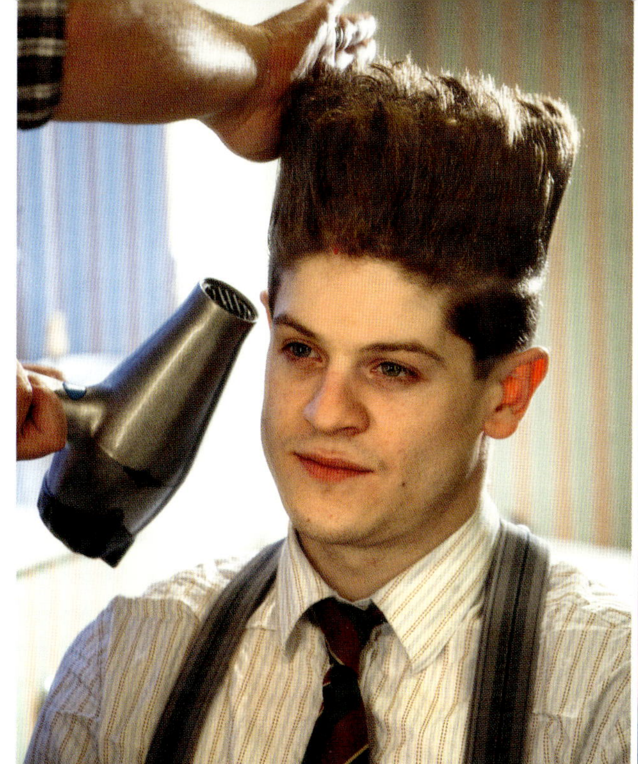

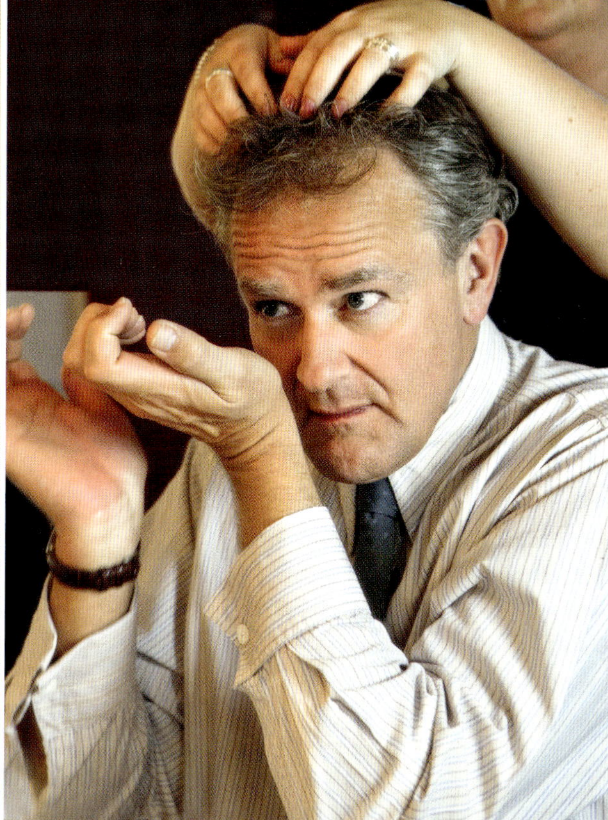

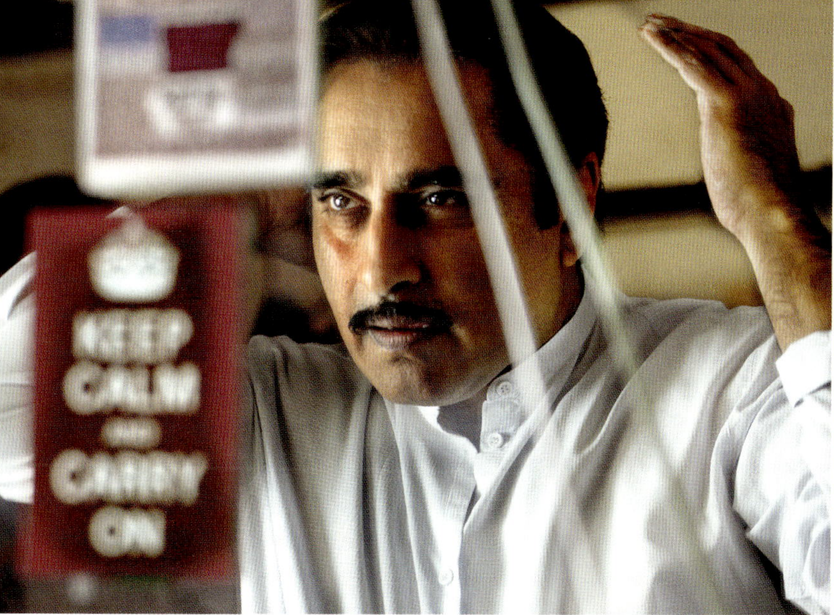

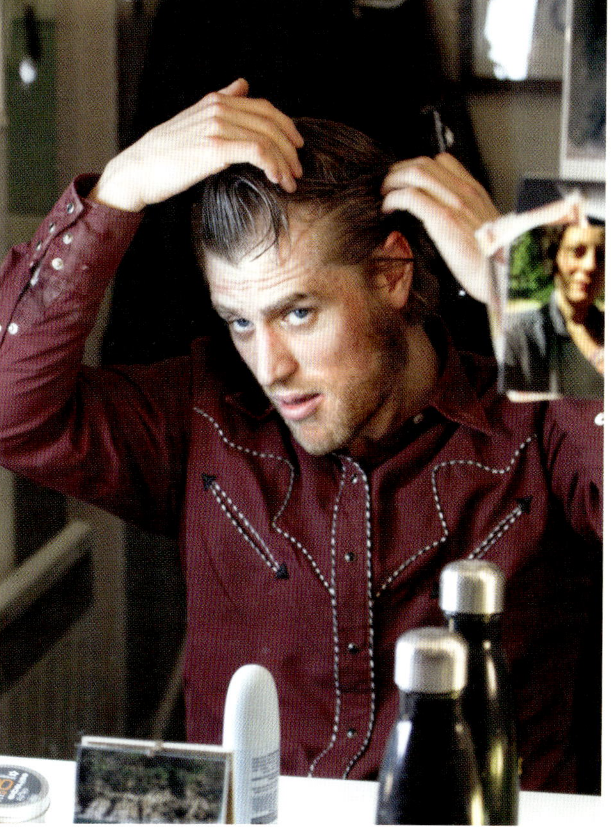

OPPOSITE: JAMES FOX, *DEAR LUPIN*, APOLLO THEATRE, 2015
The way James brushes his hair reminds me of my father. In the mirror, a man trying to make sense of what sometimes seems untameable.

ABOVE: SANJEEV BHASKAR, *DINNER WITH SADDAM*, MENIER CHOCOLATE FACTORY, 2015

TOP LEFT: IWAN RHEON, *SPRING AWAKENING*, NOVELLO THEATRE, 2009

TOP RIGHT: HUGH BONNEVILLE, *AN ENEMY OF THE PEOPLE*, CHICHESTER FESTIVAL THEATRE, 2016

RIGHT: JOHNNY FLYNN, *TRUE WEST*, VAUDEVILLE THEATRE, 2018

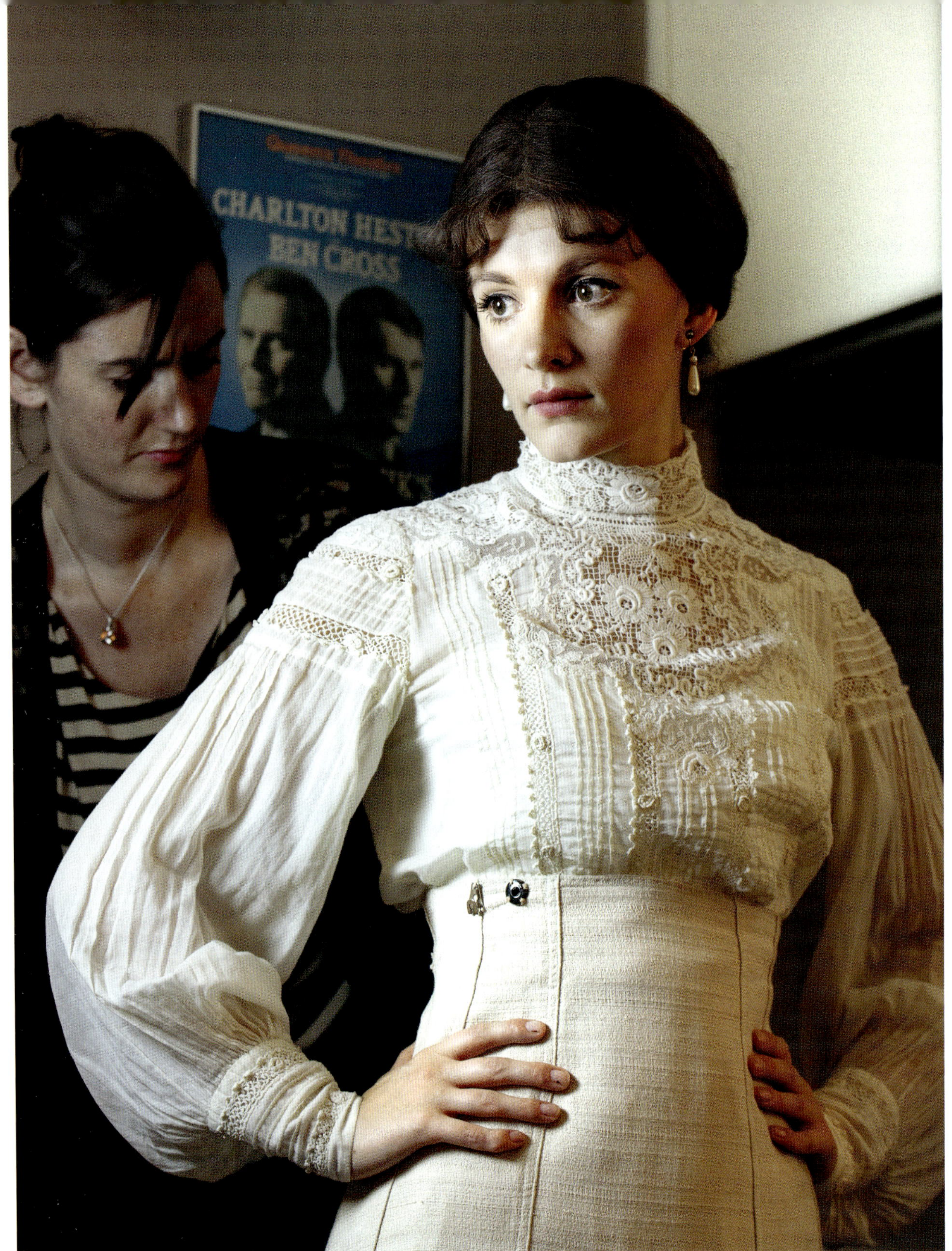

LEFT: **EMILY BARBER, *THE IMPORTANCE OF BEING EARNEST*, VAUDEVILLE THEATRE, 2015**
Emily is a fast-rising young actress, with an unmistakable star quality.

OPPOSITE: **OLIVIA COLMAN, *HAY FEVER*, NOËL COWARD THEATRE, 2012**
When choosing the photos, I wanted to show another side of Olivia Colman, but her consistent and cheerful disposition is hard to resist.

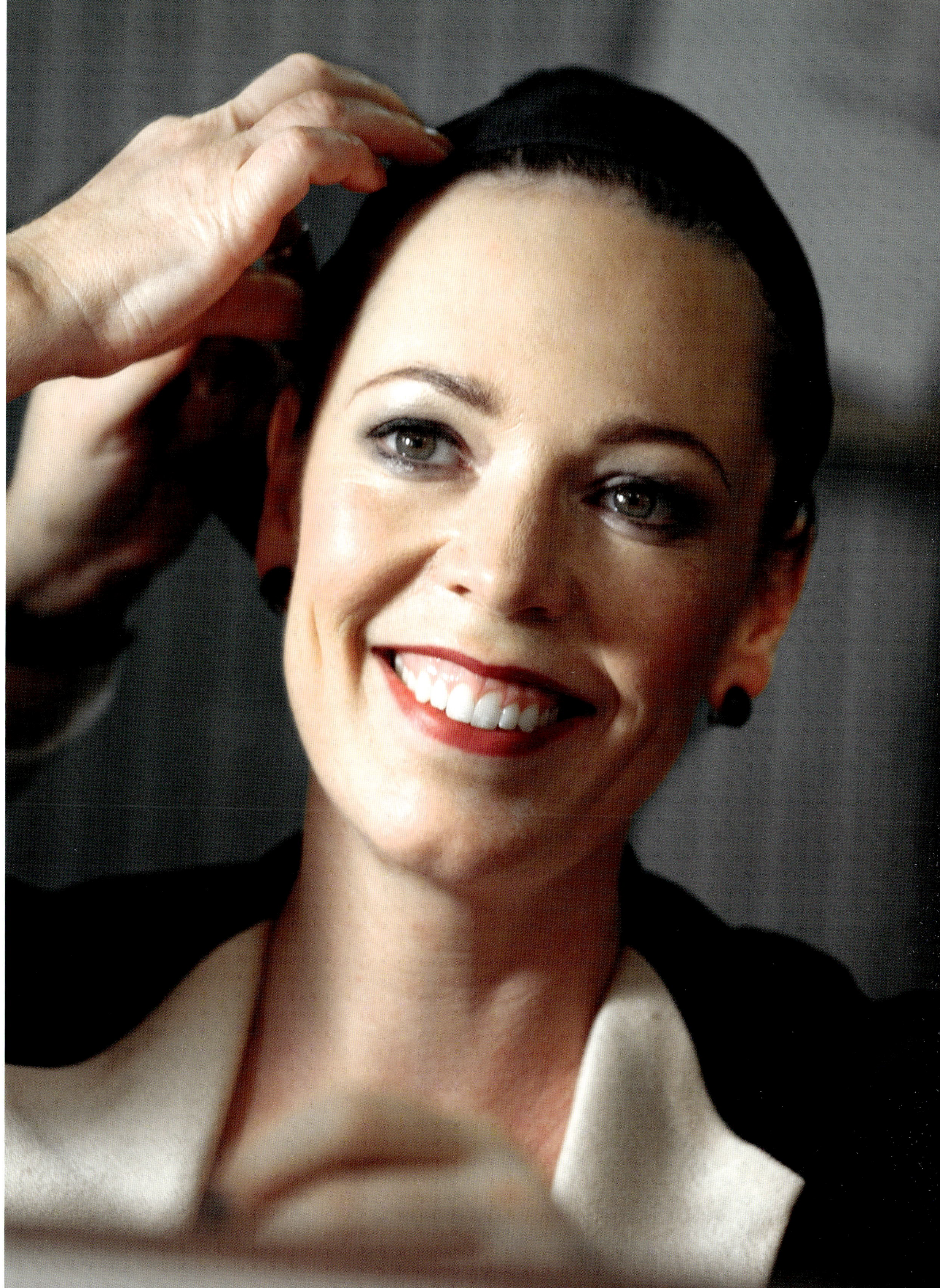

BENJAMIN ASKEW, DOMINIC TIGHE, MATHEW HORNE, STEVEN PACEY, NORMAN PACE, CHARLES KAY, *CHARLEY'S AUNT*, MENIER CHOCOLATE FACTORY, 2012

Some theatres have space for only one male and one female dressing room. The joys of sharing a room.

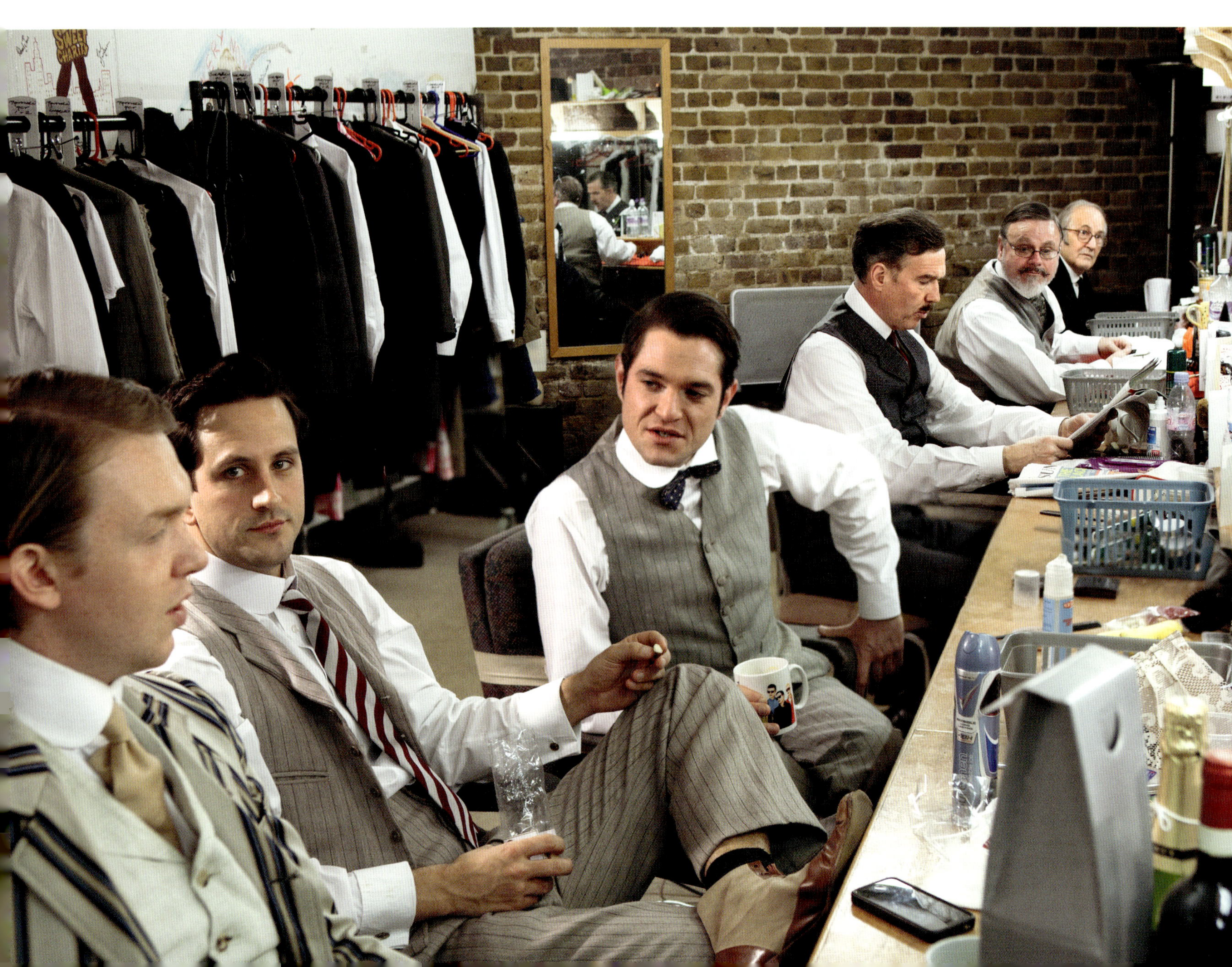

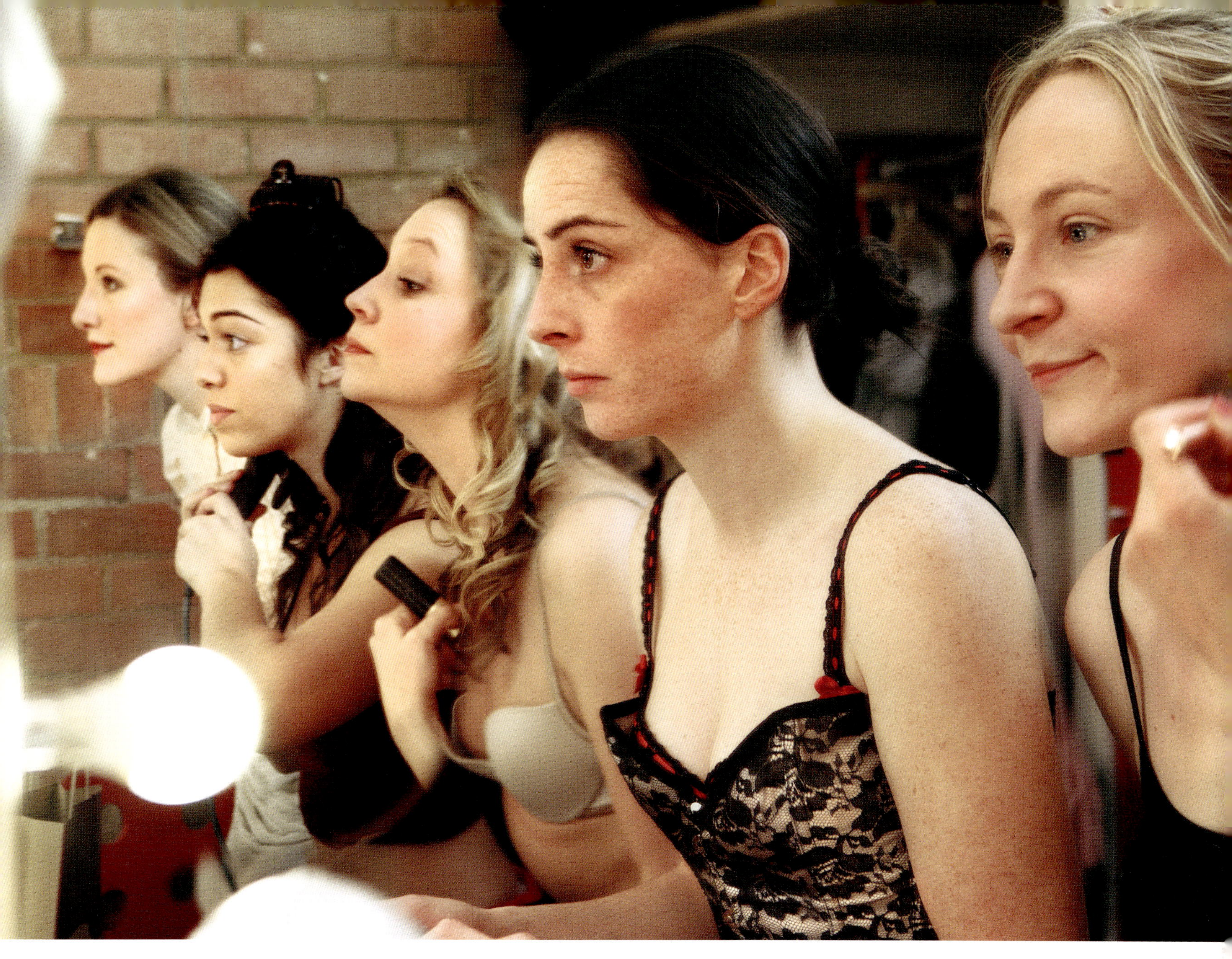

MARIE FORTUNE, CHLOE WIGMORE, SCARLETT CLIFFORD, KATY DAGHORN, AMY CHRISTIE, *HAMLET*, PARK THEATRE, 2014
A shared dressing room for actresses in a fringe theatre. There is little space and often the actors work for minimal wages, but the passion to perform is strong.

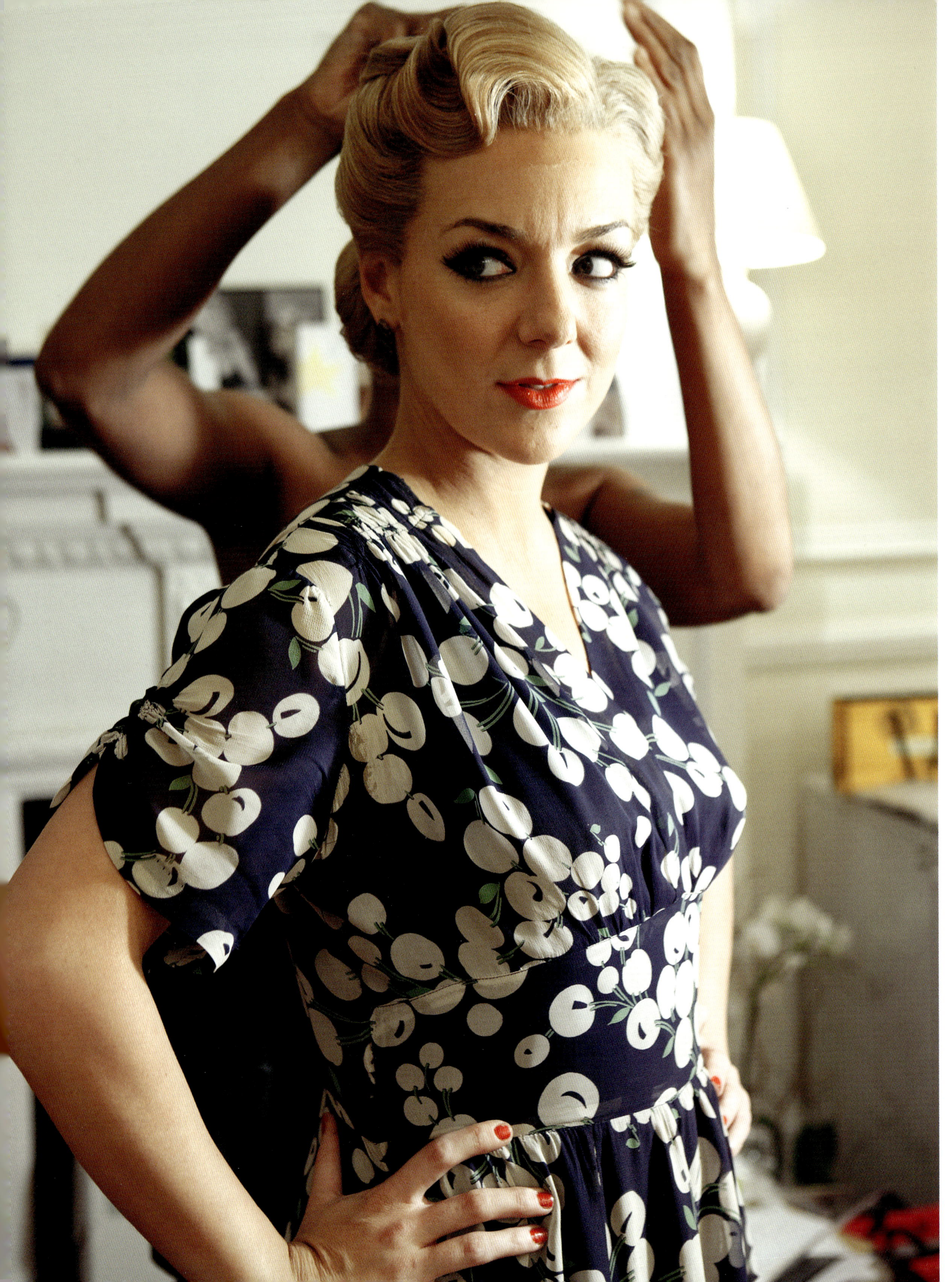

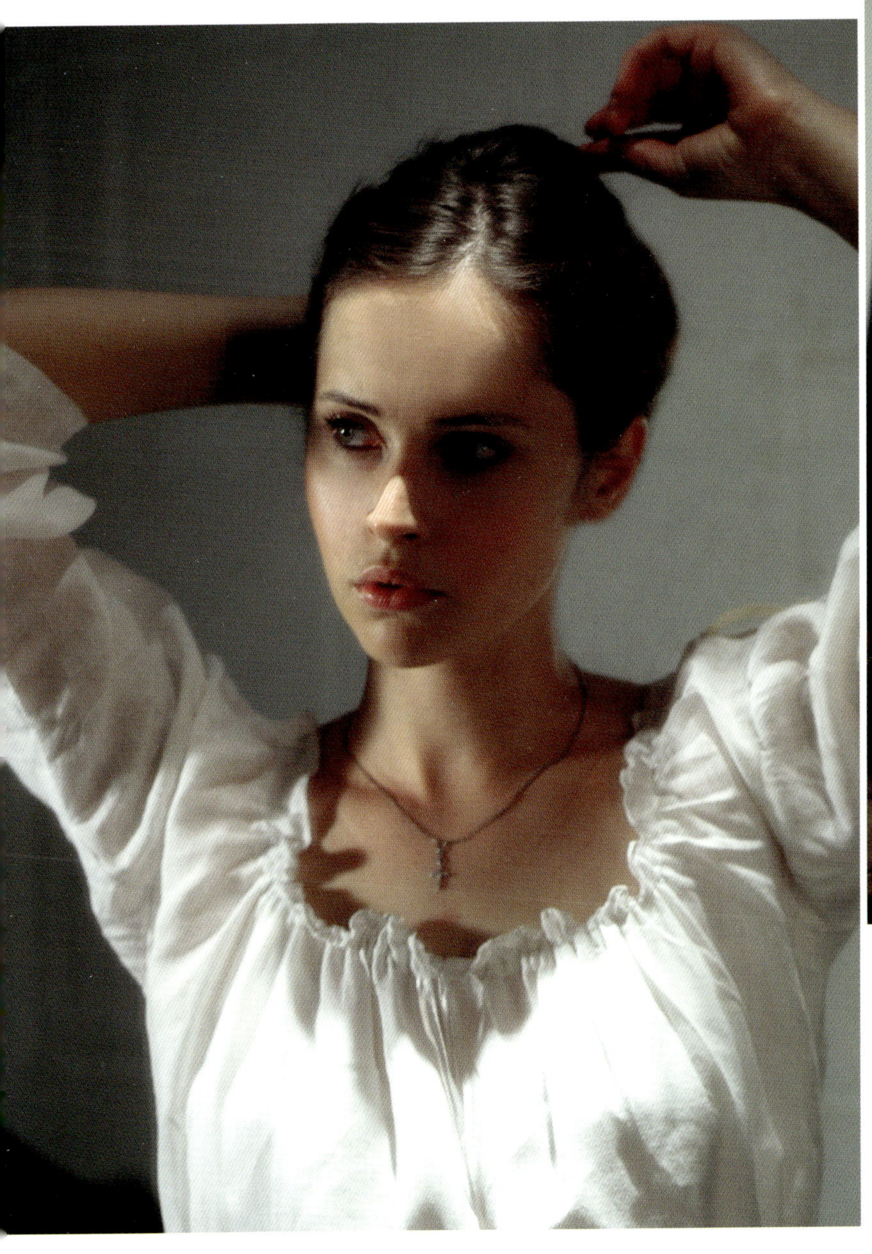

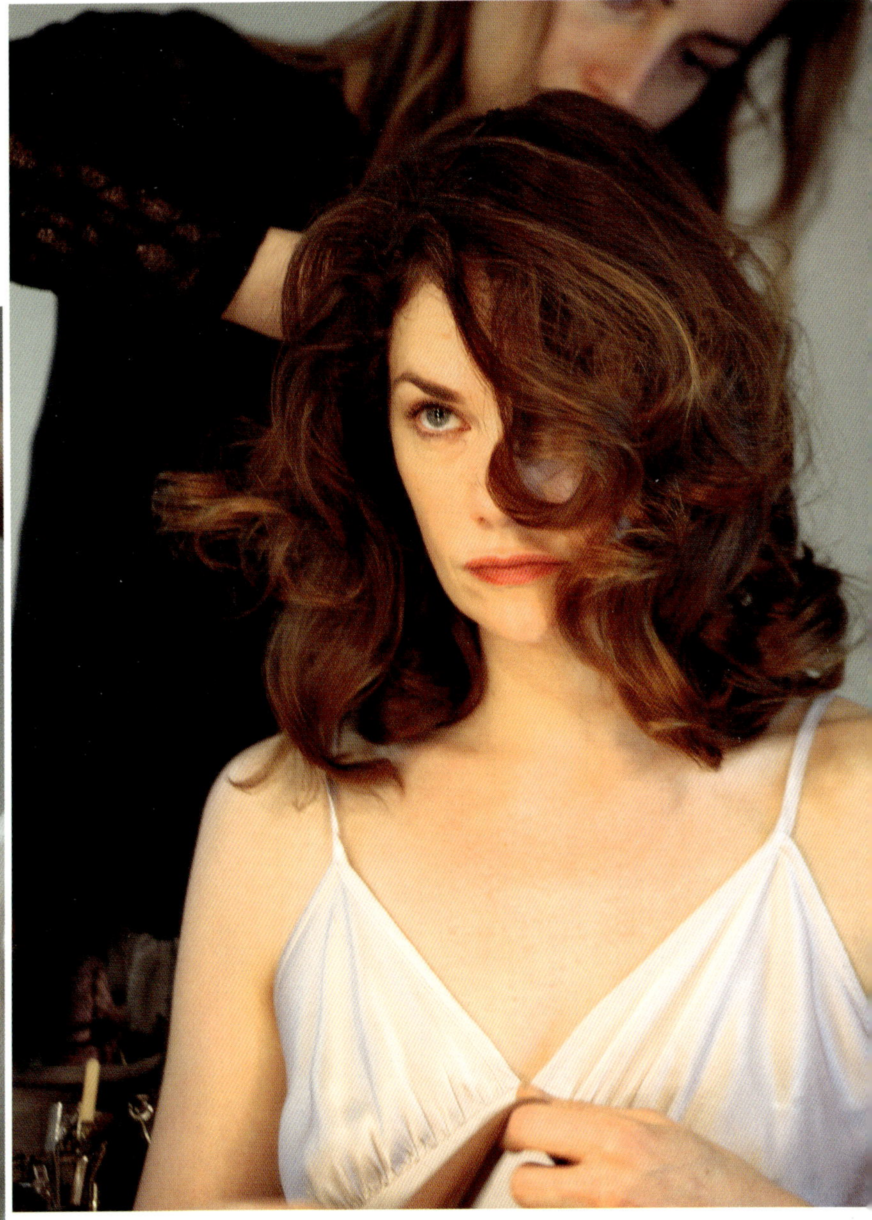

OPPOSITE: **SHERIDAN SMITH, *FLARE PATH*, THEATRE ROYAL HAYMARKET, 2011**
The star of TV comedy and drama won an Olivier Award for this performance at the Theatre Royal Haymarket.

LEFT: **FELICITY JONES, *LUISE MILLER*, DONMAR WAREHOUSE, 2011**
She was just about to burst through as a film star. We all knew somehow, and a team was forming around her. Here she is working on her last theatre show for a while…

ABOVE: **RUTH WILSON, *HEDDA GABLER*, NATIONAL THEATRE, 2017**
It might seem odd to choose an image where half of Ruth's very expressive face is hidden, but somehow it adds to the mystery of this very intriguing actress.

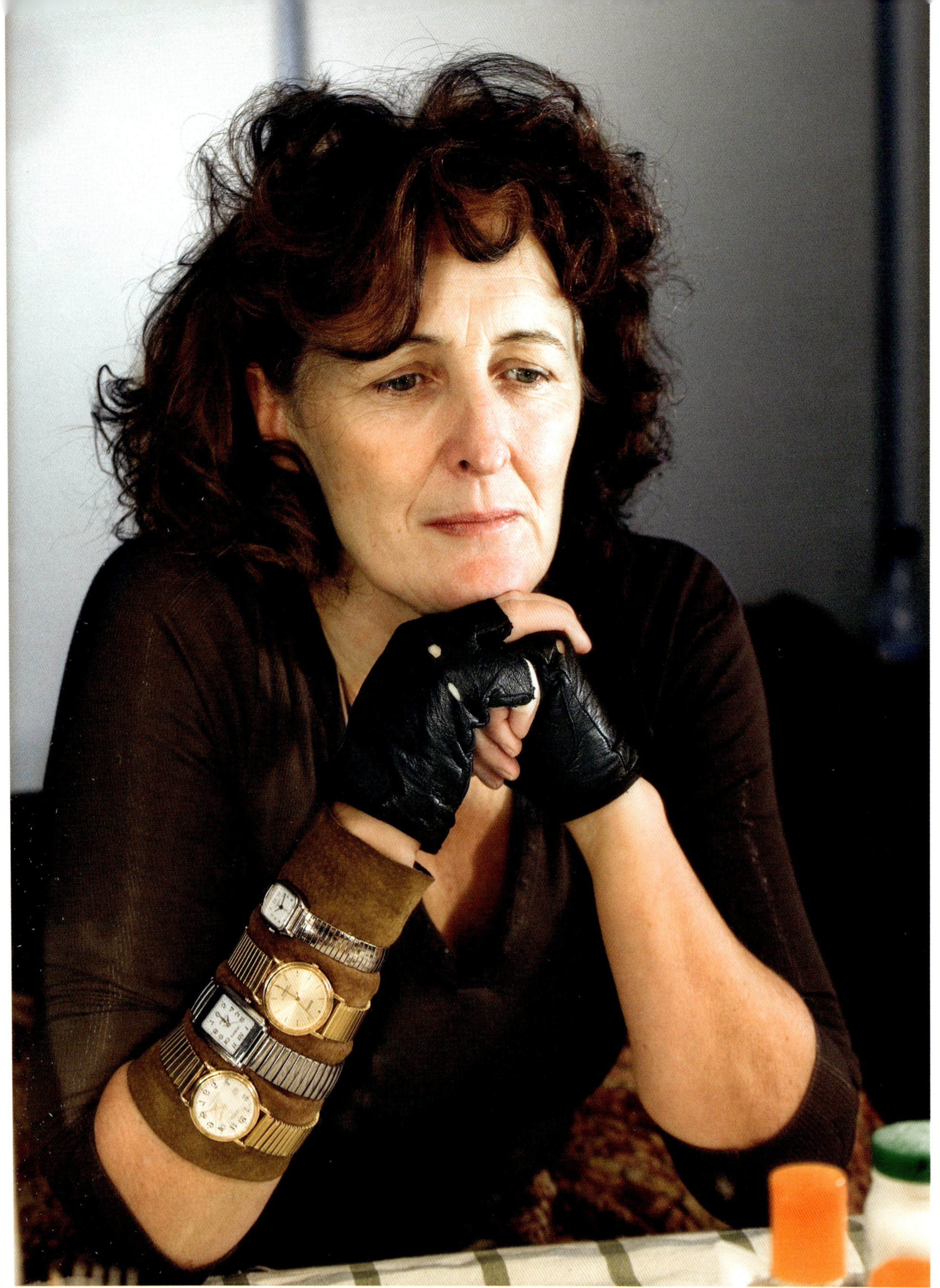

LEFT: **FIONA SHAW, *MOTHER COURAGE AND HER CHILDREN*, NATIONAL THEATRE, 2009**
The great classical actress taking on the Brechtian role of Mother Courage, directed by her long-time friend Deborah Warner.

OPPOSITE: **JENNIFER EHLE, *OSLO*, VIVIAN BEAUMONT THEATER, 2017**
It is often thought that starting a family will inhibit a successful career. Jennifer is the perfect example of how to combine the two.

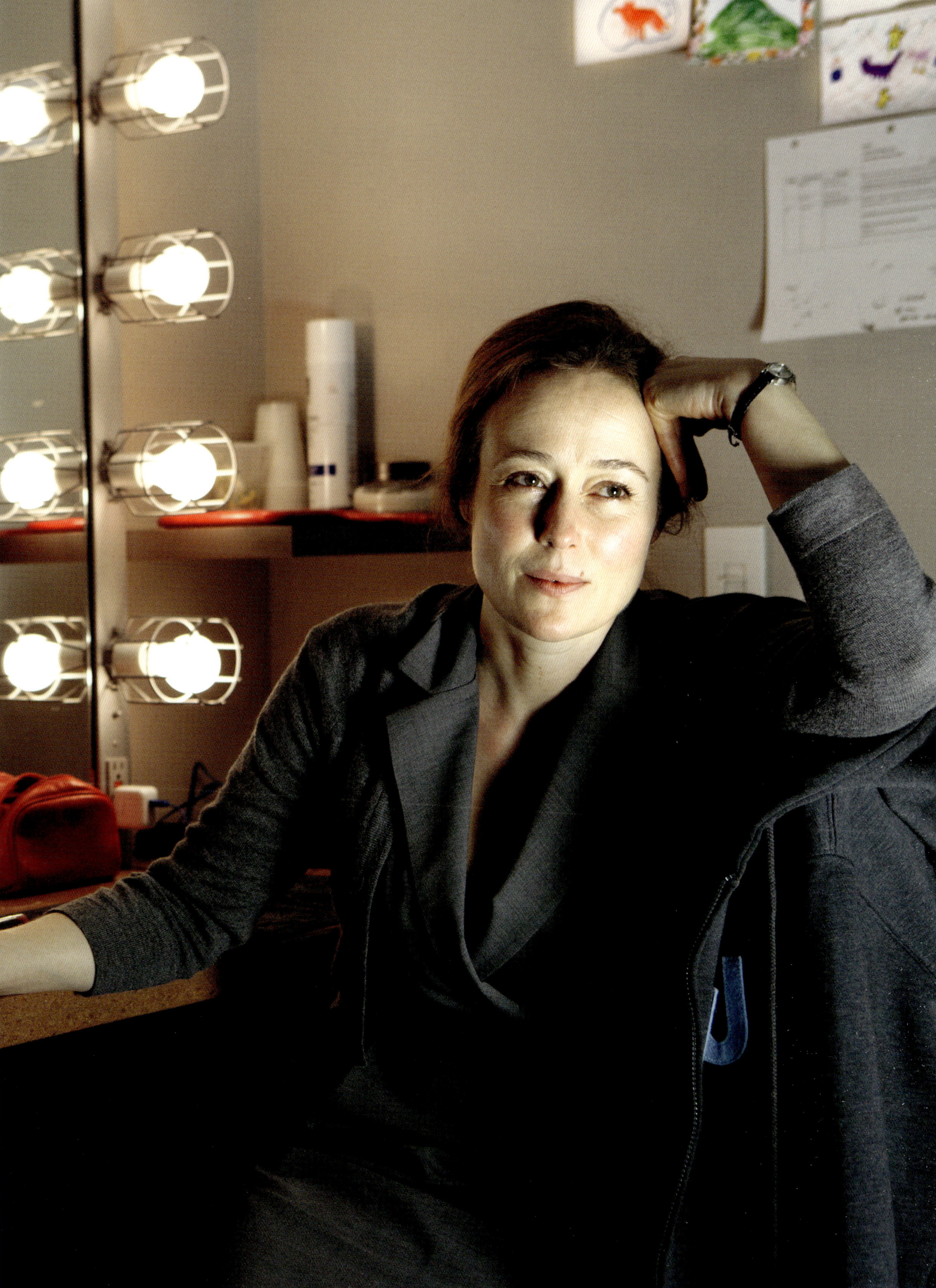

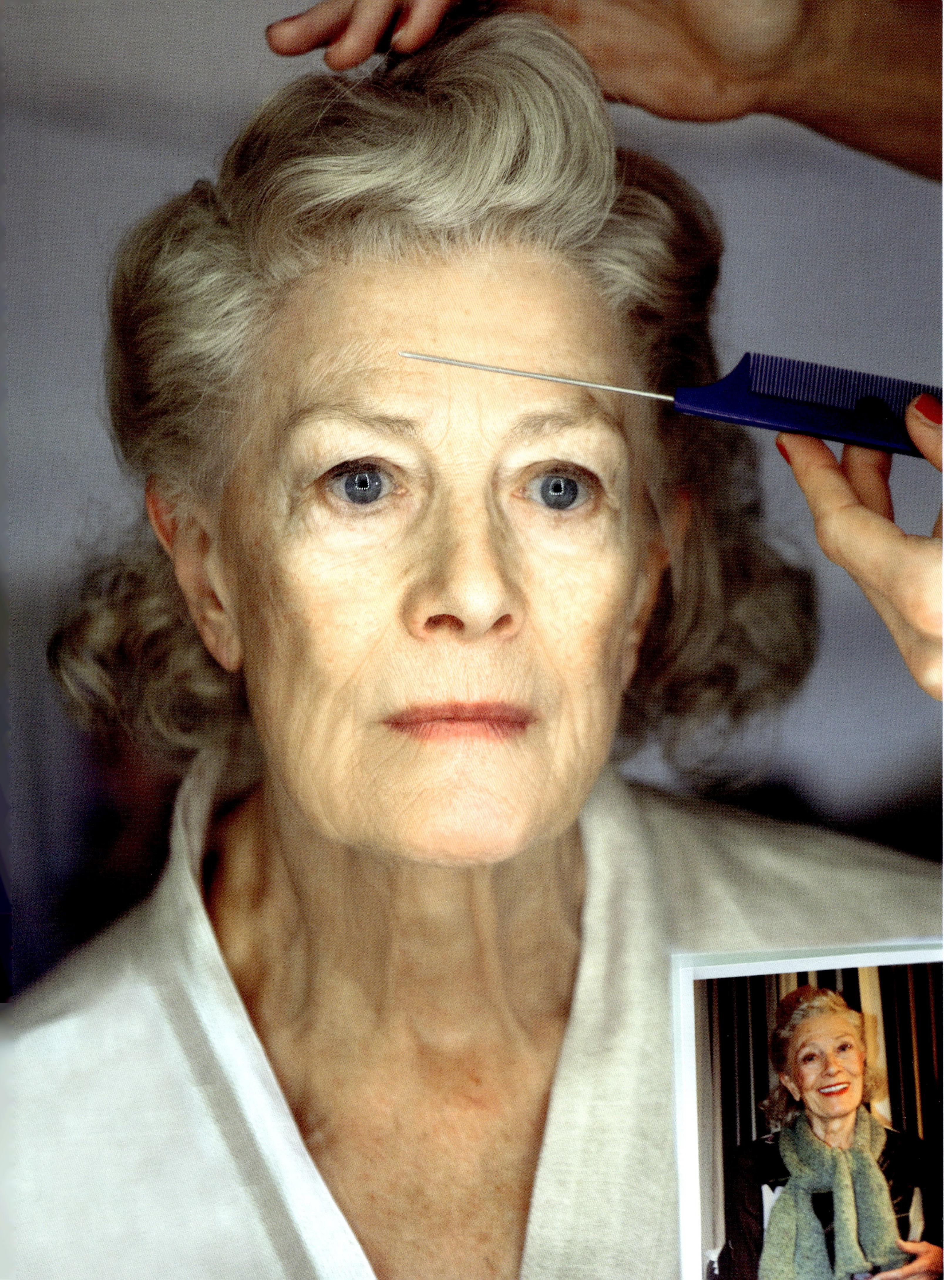

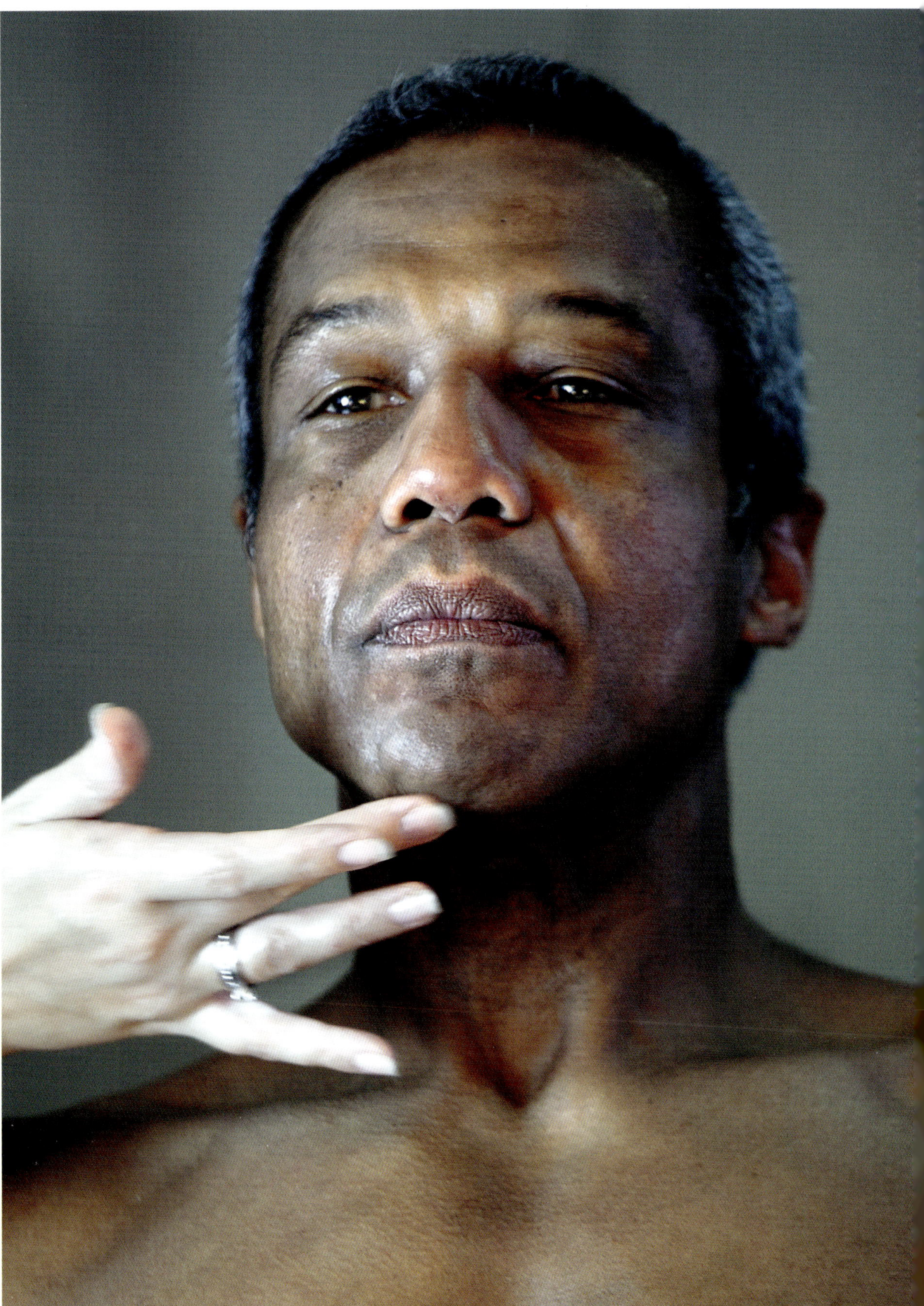

OPPOSITE: **VANESSA REDGRAVE, *MUCH ADO ABOUT NOTHING*, OLD VIC THEATRE, 2013**

Given her extraordinary life and career, it is perhaps surprising that this was her first appearance at the Old Vic in a Shakespeare play. Vanessa had been a life-long smoker and she decided to stop only ten days before this photo was taken.

RIGHT: **HUGH QUARSHIE, *OTHELLO*, RSC, 2015**

If the current shift towards non-racial casting had been in place thirty years ago, Hugh would be more recognised than he already is and acknowledged as one of the great actors of his generation.

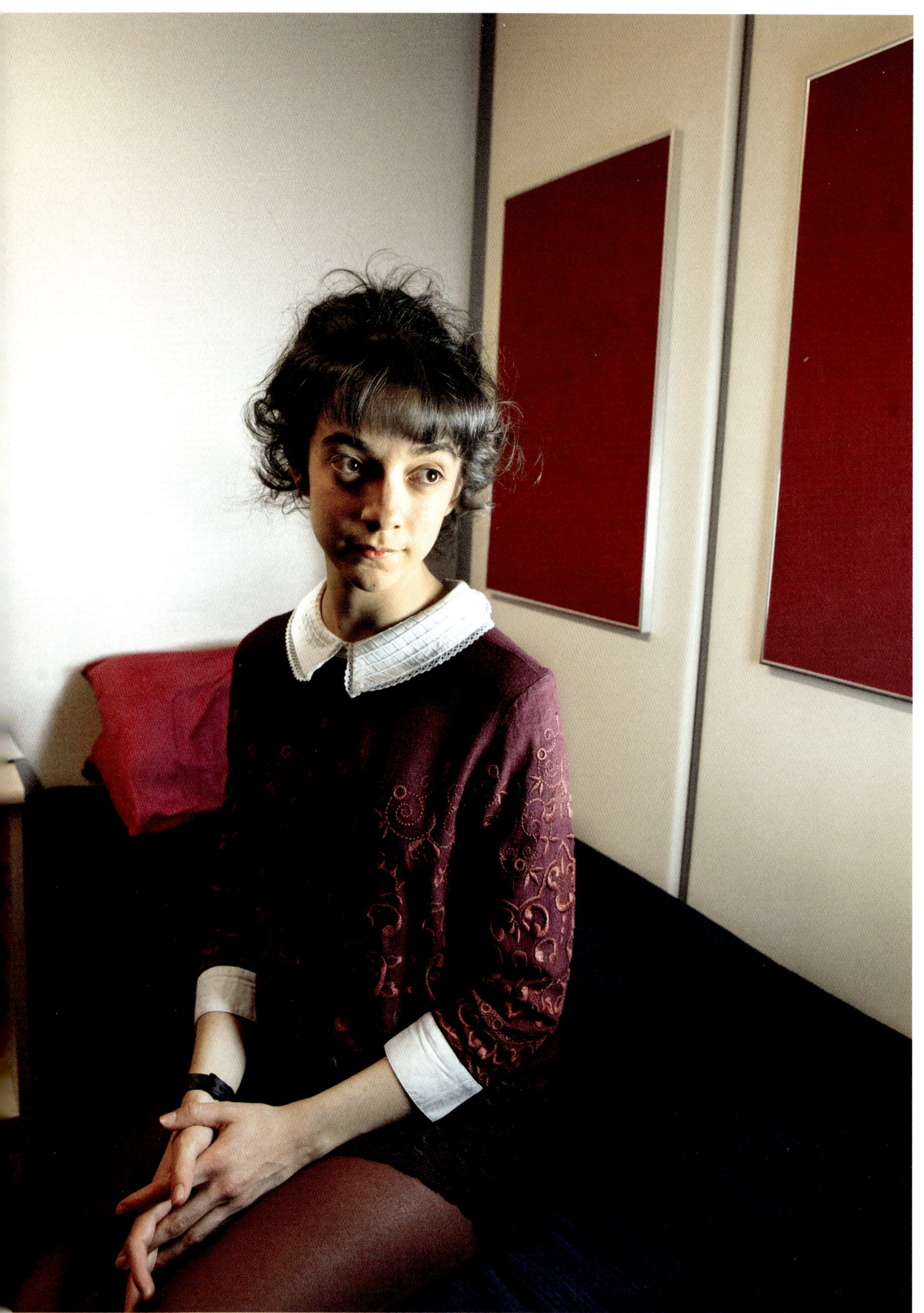

LEFT: **PATSY FERRAN, *AS YOU LIKE IT*, NATIONAL THEATRE, 2016**
It is always a pleasure to photograph a young actor who clearly has a bright and productive future. The talent seems so natural and abundant.

OPPOSITE: **OLIVIA WILLIAMS, *MOSQUITOES*, NATIONAL THEATRE, 2017**
The point during 'the half' where aspects of a fictional character start to take over. The dressing room is a physical place, which allows this psychological crossover to happen in a private environment.

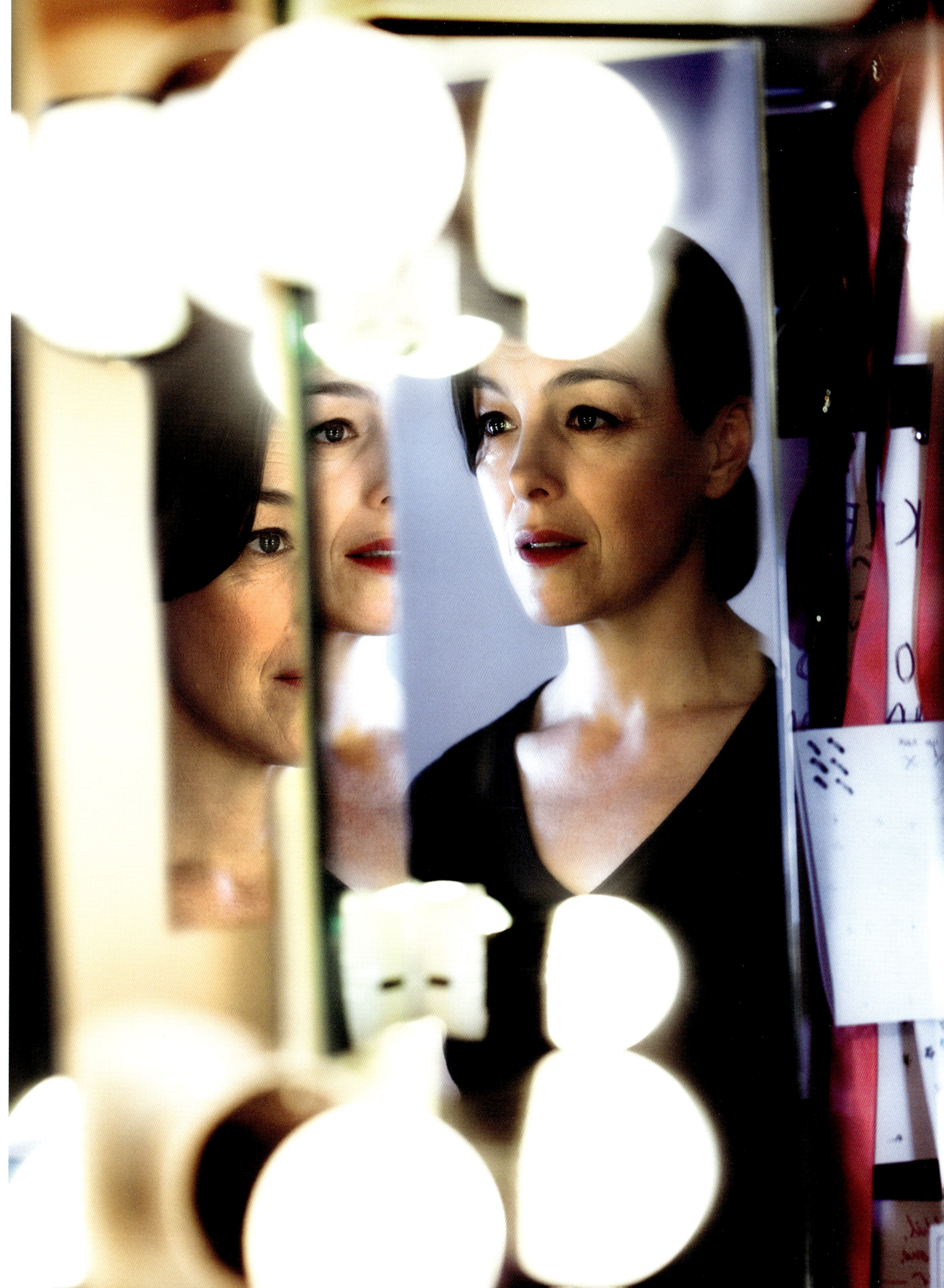

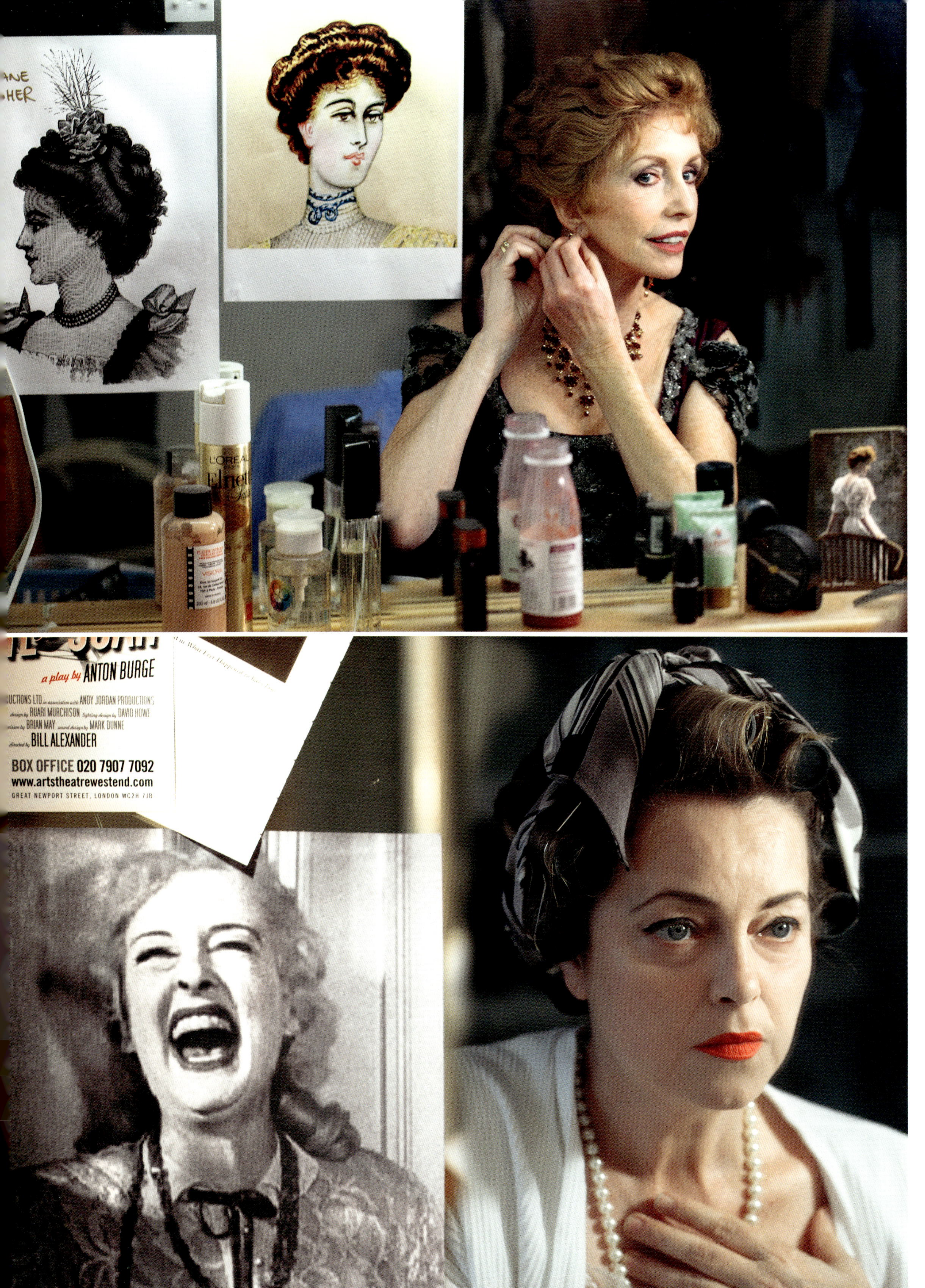
a play by ANTON BURGE
directed by BILL ALEXANDER
BOX OFFICE 020 7907 7092
www.artstheatrewestend.com
GREAT NEWPORT STREET, LONDON WC2H 7JB

MIRRORS

The mirror is the focal point of every dressing room. Actors use it not only to scrutinise themselves, but to display good-luck cards and inspirational photos. These are some of my favourite actresses.

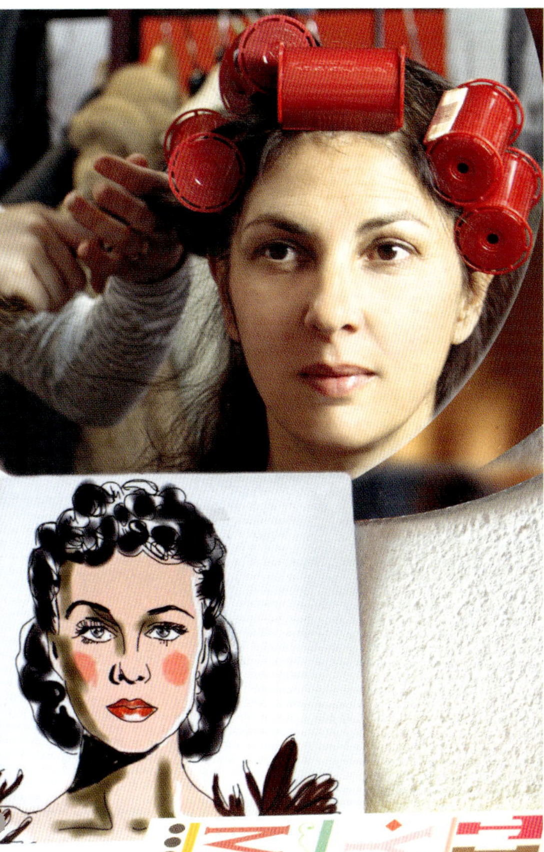

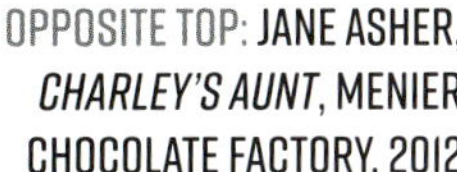

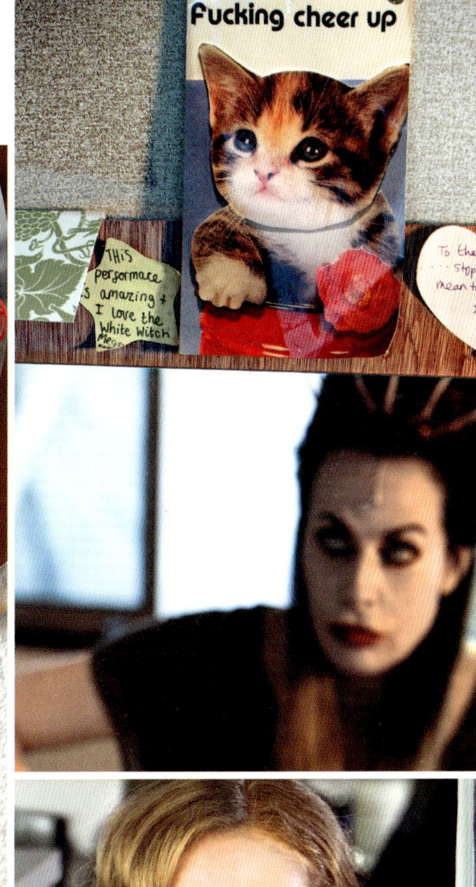

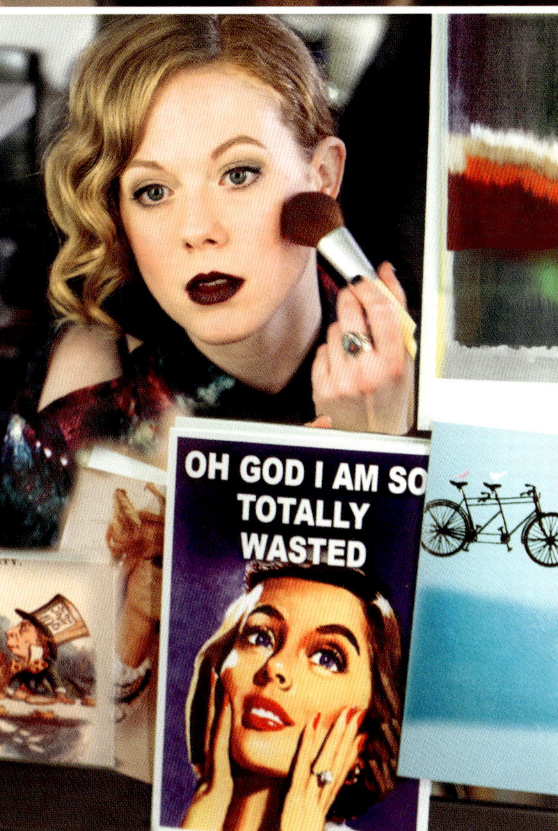

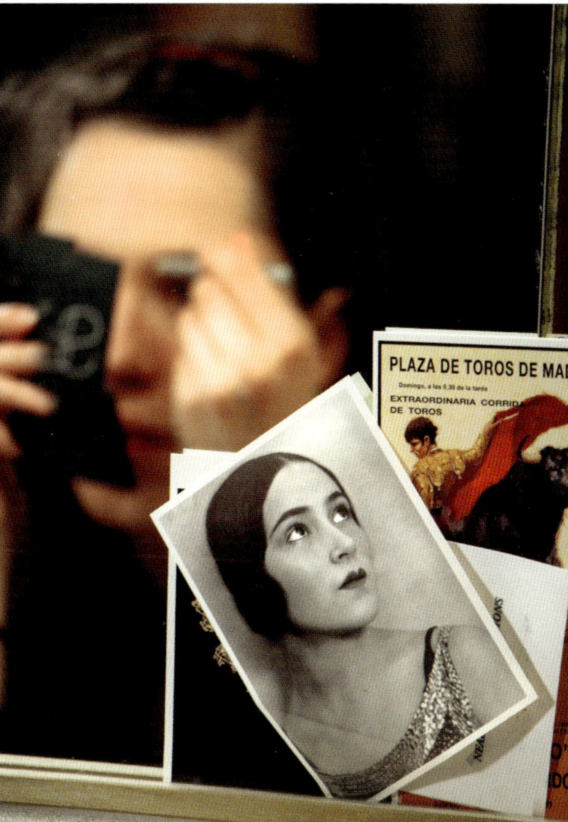

OPPOSITE TOP: JANE ASHER, *CHARLEY'S AUNT*, MENIER CHOCOLATE FACTORY, 2012

OPPOSITE BOTTOM: GRETA SCACCHI, *BETTE & JOAN*, ARTS THEATRE, 2011

ABOVE: GINA BELLMAN, *ORSON'S SHADOW*, SOUTHWARK PLAYHOUSE, 2015

TOP: SALLY DEXTER, *THE LION, THE WITCH AND THE WARDROBE*, KENSINGTON GARDENS, 2012

RIGHT: ZOE BOYLE, *NO QUARTER*, ROYAL COURT, 2013

FAR RIGHT: REBECCA HALL, *THE WINTER'S TALE*, OLD VIC THEATRE, 2009

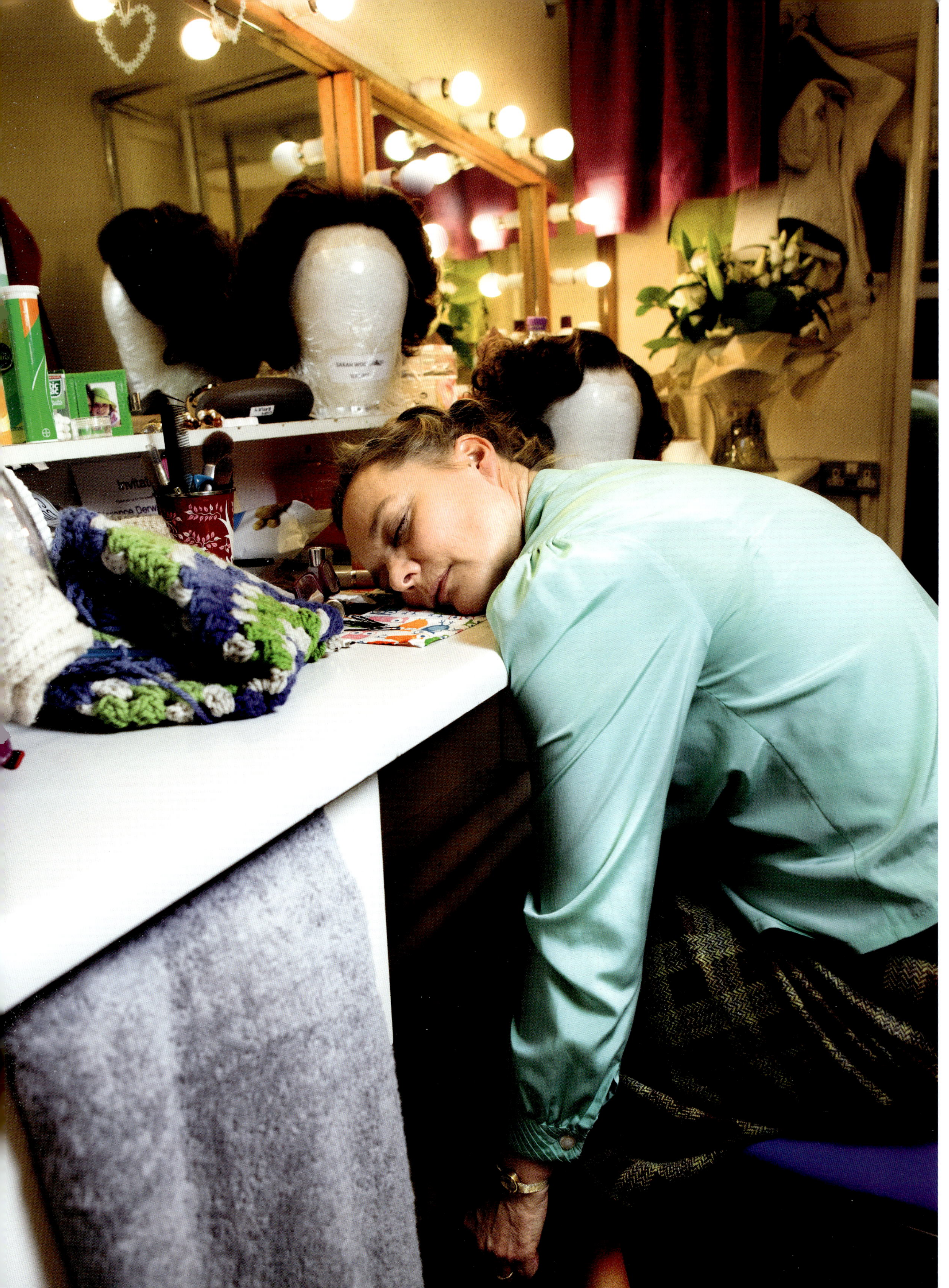

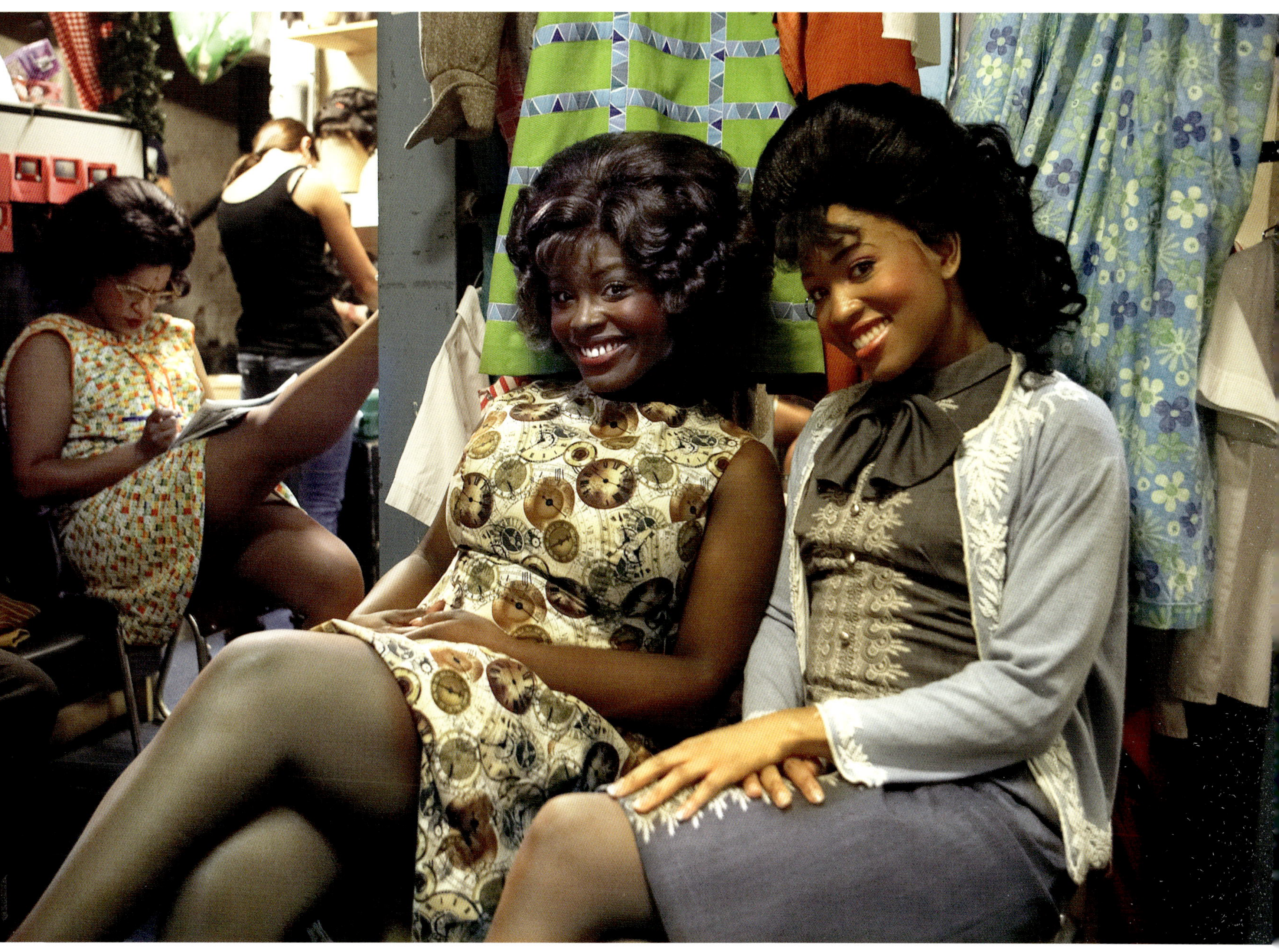

OPPOSITE: **SARAH WOODWARD, *THIS HOUSE*, GARRICK THEATRE, 2017**
This is genuine fatigue. On entering the room I found Sarah in this position and asked her to retain it for a photograph.

ABOVE: **NADINE HIGGIN, KEISHA ATWELL, *HAIRSPRAY*, SHAFTESBURY THEATRE, 2010**
Down in the basement of the theatre, in the boiler room, with wigs on, it is difficult to stay this cheerful.

PAAPA ESSIEDU, *HAMLET*, RSC, 2016
Paapa's account of Hamlet was a revelation to many, and his complete focus is evident in this image.

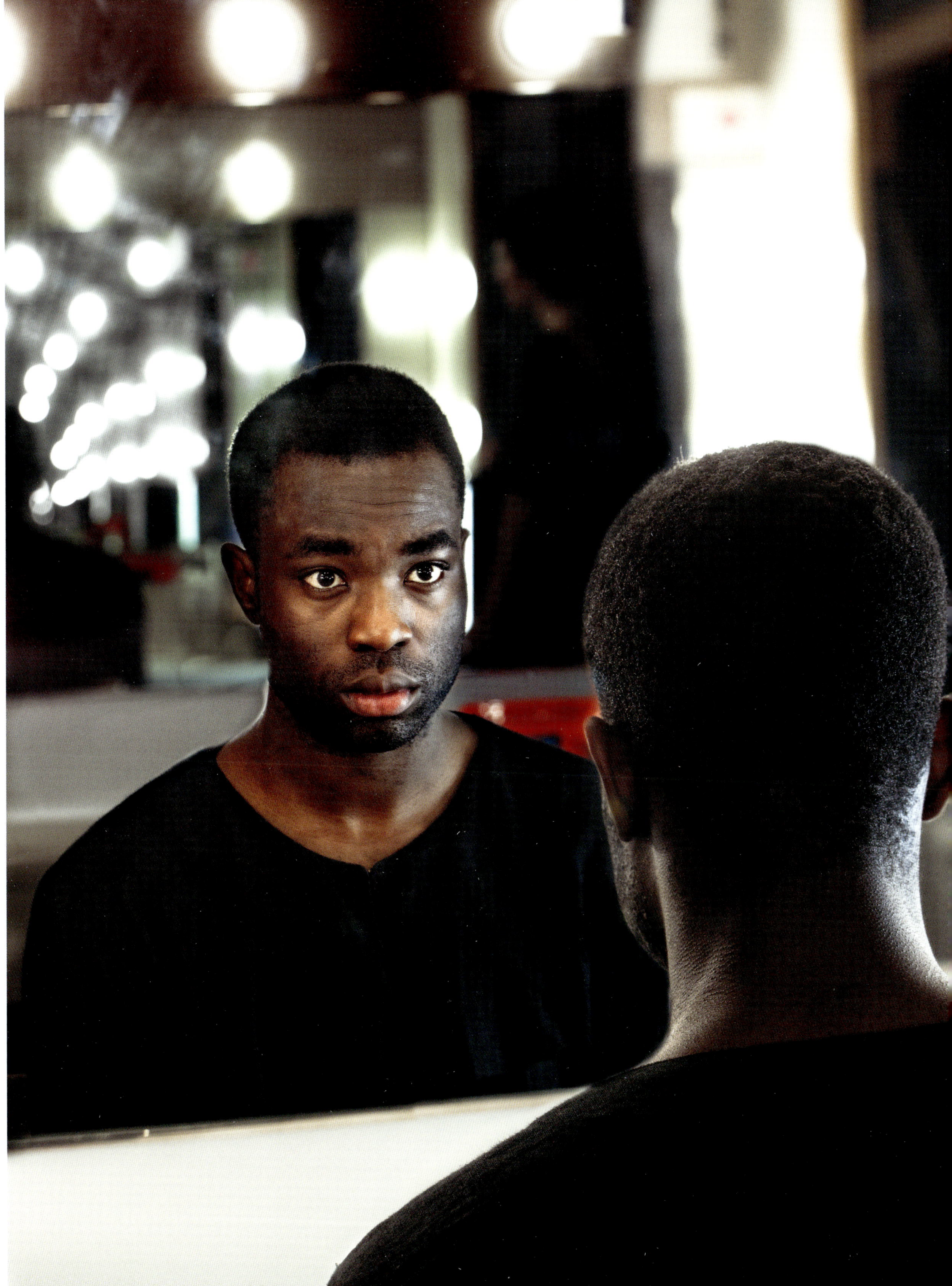

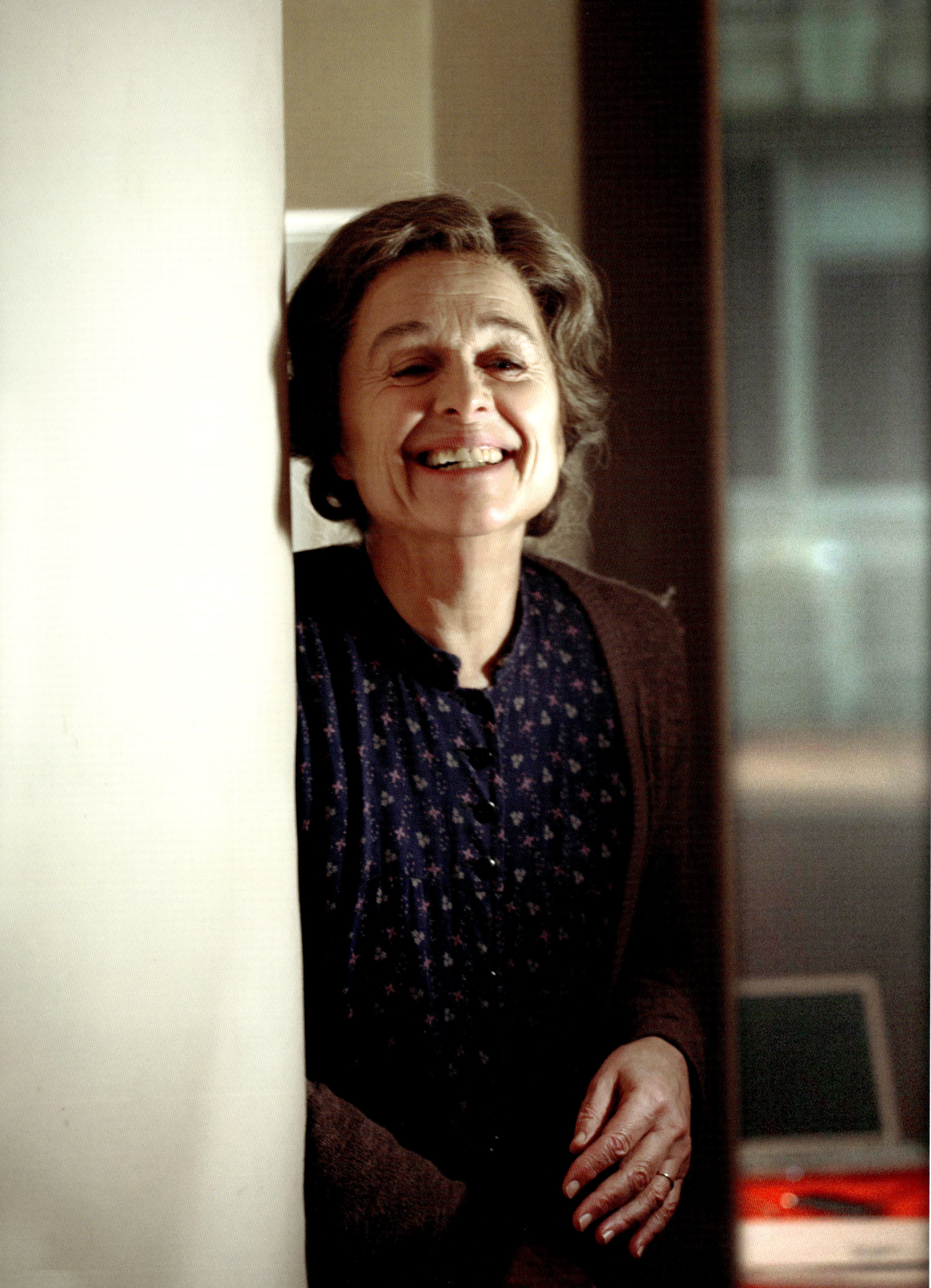

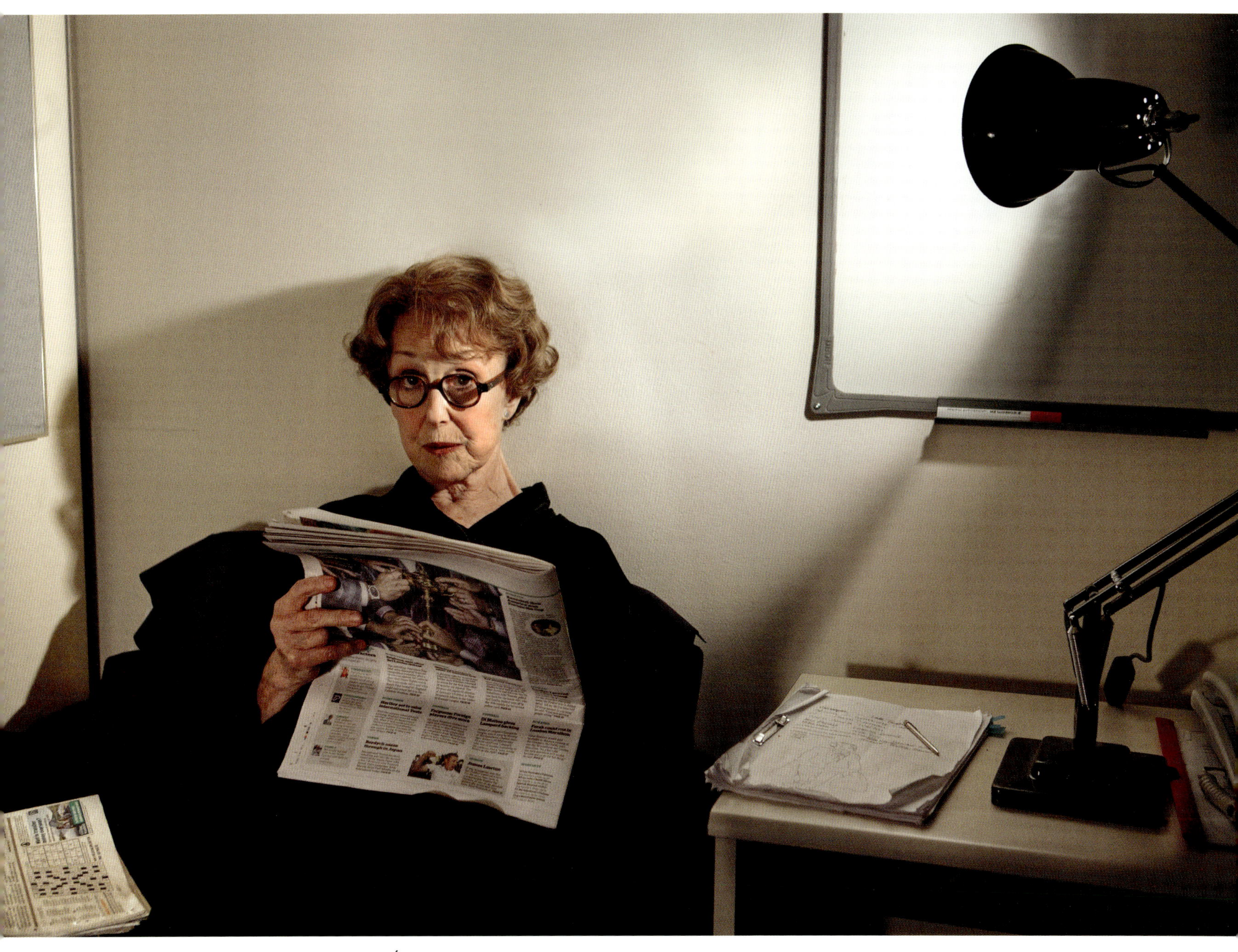

OPPOSITE: SINÉAD CUSACK, *JUNO AND THE PAYCOCK*, NATIONAL THEATRE, 2012
It was a privilege to see Sinéad performing in an Irish classic. My house in Chiswick in the 1980s was round the corner from where her father, Cyril Cusack, lived and I was fortunate to be friends with this special family.

ABOVE: UNA STUBBS, *THE CURIOUS INCIDENT OF THE DOG IN THE NIGHT-TIME*, NATIONAL THEATRE, 2012
Reading is a favourite activity for many actors. Una is a treasured member of any company lucky enough to have her.

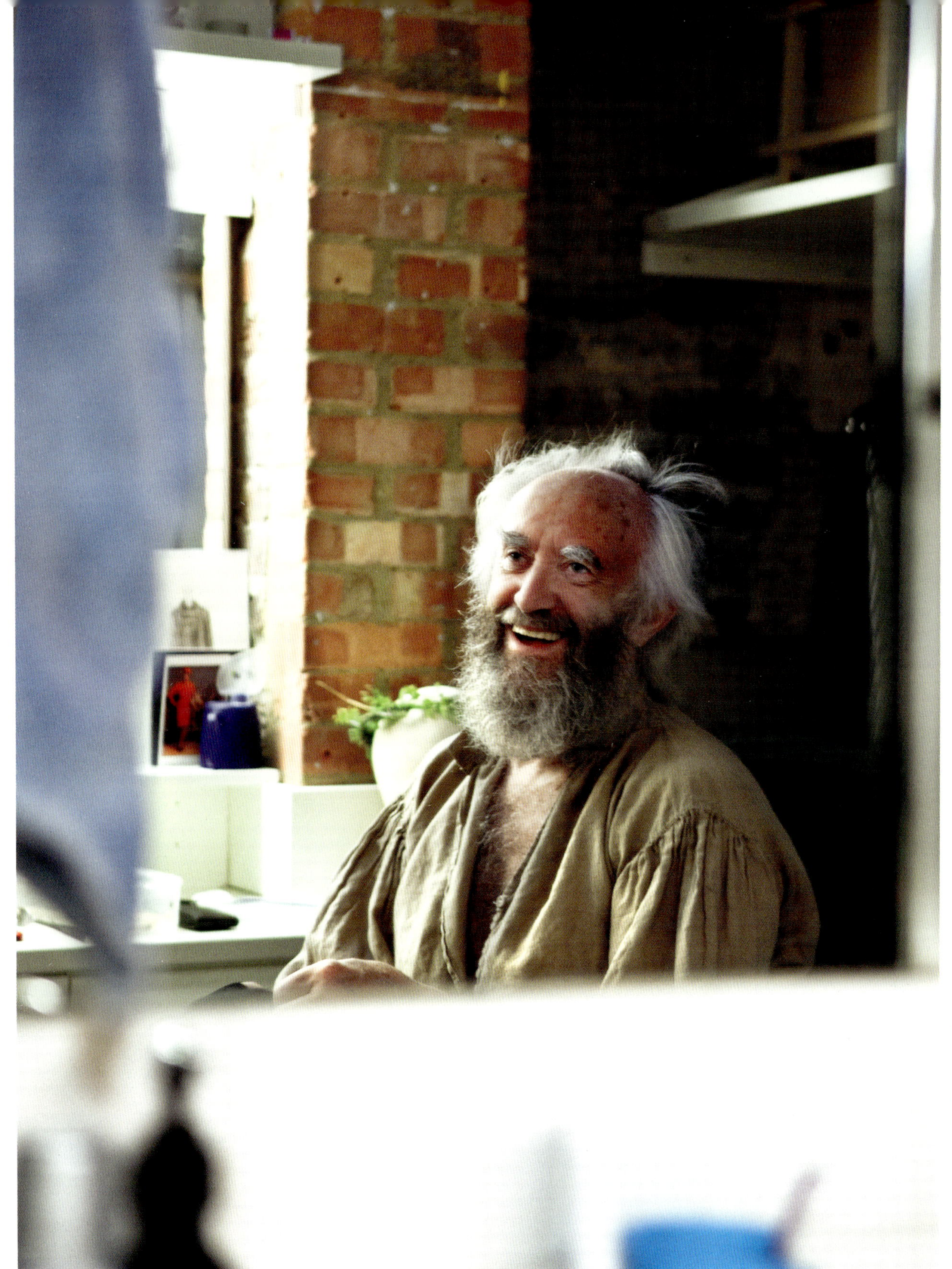

LEFT: **JONATHAN PRYCE, *KING LEAR*, ALMEIDA, 2012**
When I asked Jonathan if it was true that *Lear* was the 'Everest' for actors, he laughed it off and said 'Definitely not. It's the badly written plays which are difficult to play.'

OPPOSITE: **DAVID OYELOWO, DANIEL CRAIG, *OTHELLO*, NEW YORK THEATRE WORKSHOP, 2016**
The two of them had committed to playing Othello at the tiny New York venue with a capacity of 198. The production was a triumph and proof that the theatre has its own particular challenges and satisfactions.

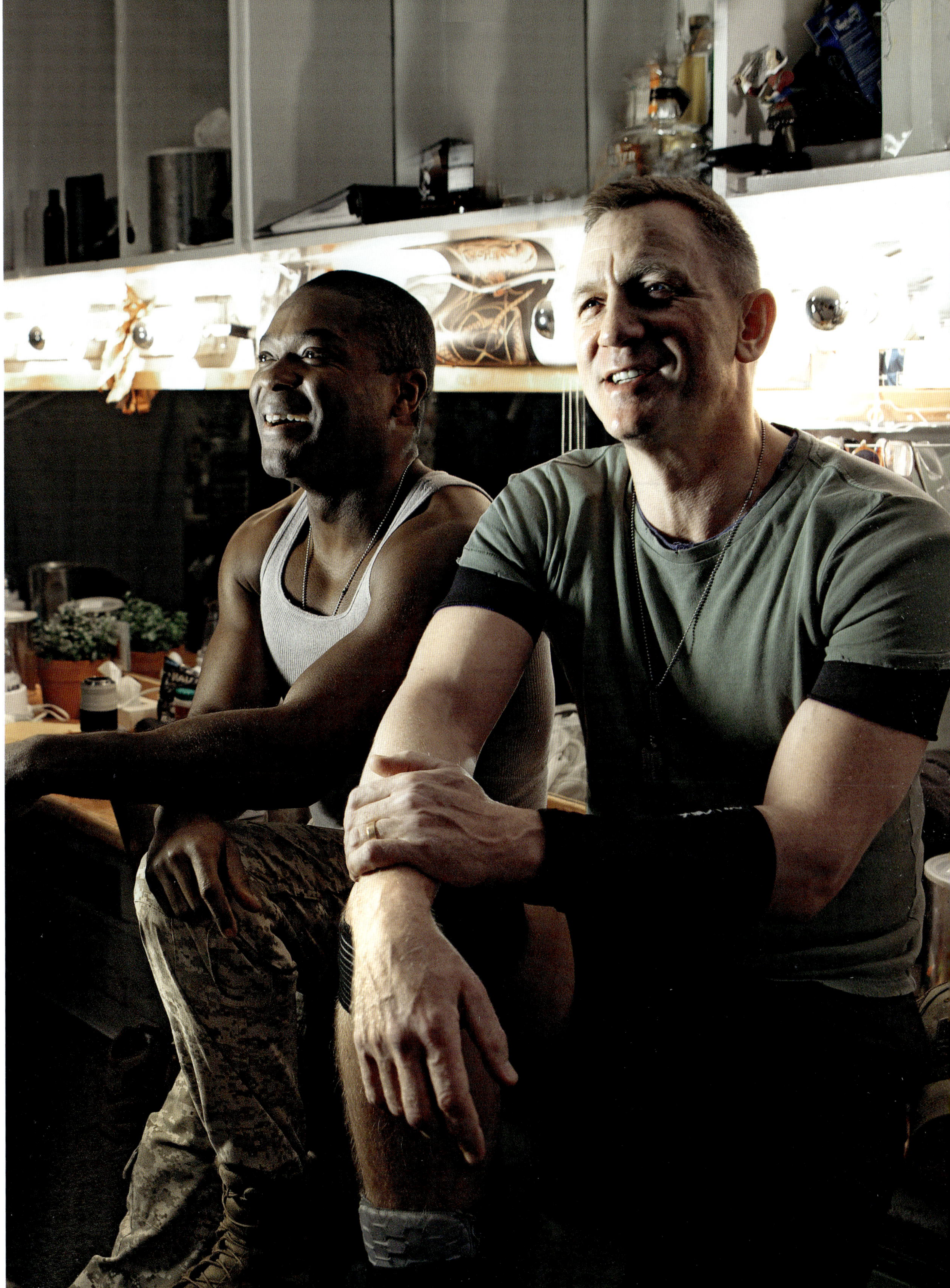

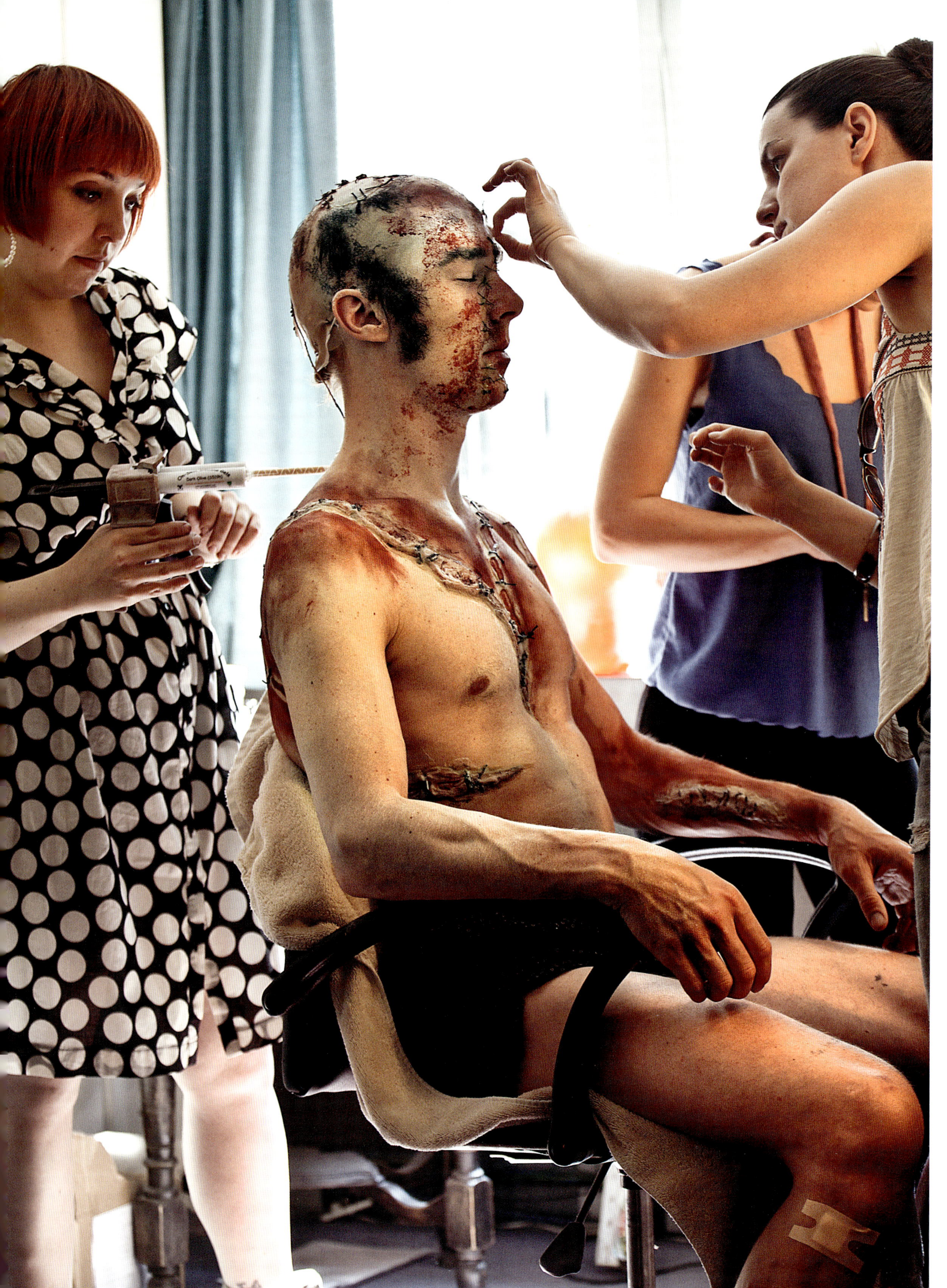

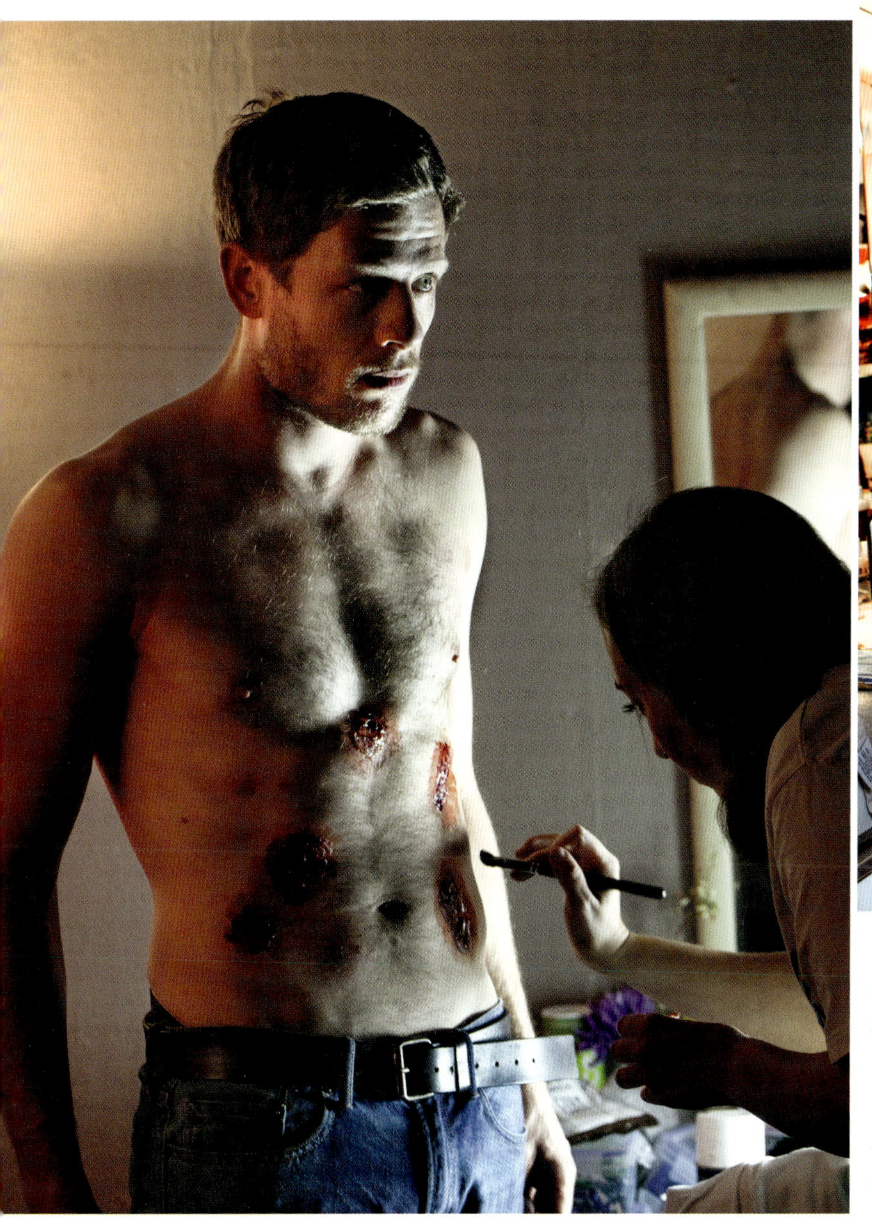

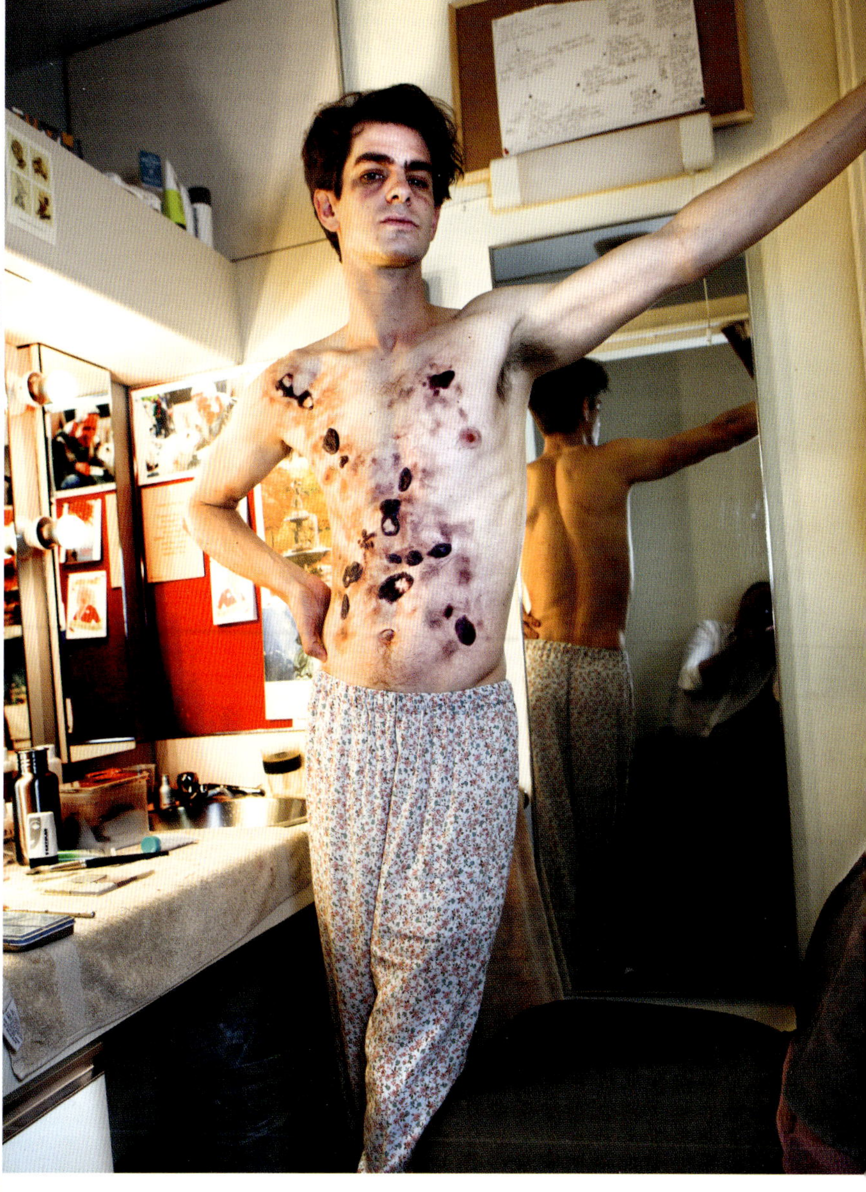

OPPOSITE: **BENEDICT CUMBERBATCH, *FRANKENSTEIN*, NATIONAL THEATRE, 2011**
He had just returned from the US, had a cold, was jetlagged, and had to learn how to ride a horse in two days' time for the filming of *War Horse*. And then he had to endure hours in make-up.

LEFT: **JAMES NORTON, *BUG*, FOUND III, 2016**
Performed in an old office block converted into a tiny theatre, the character James played was being eaten by bugs.

ABOVE: **ANDREW GARFIELD, *ANGELS IN AMERICA*, NATIONAL THEATRE, 2017**
Andrew's extraordinary and heroic performance of a man conflicted by AIDS. The make-up was underneath his shirt and revealed later in the story.

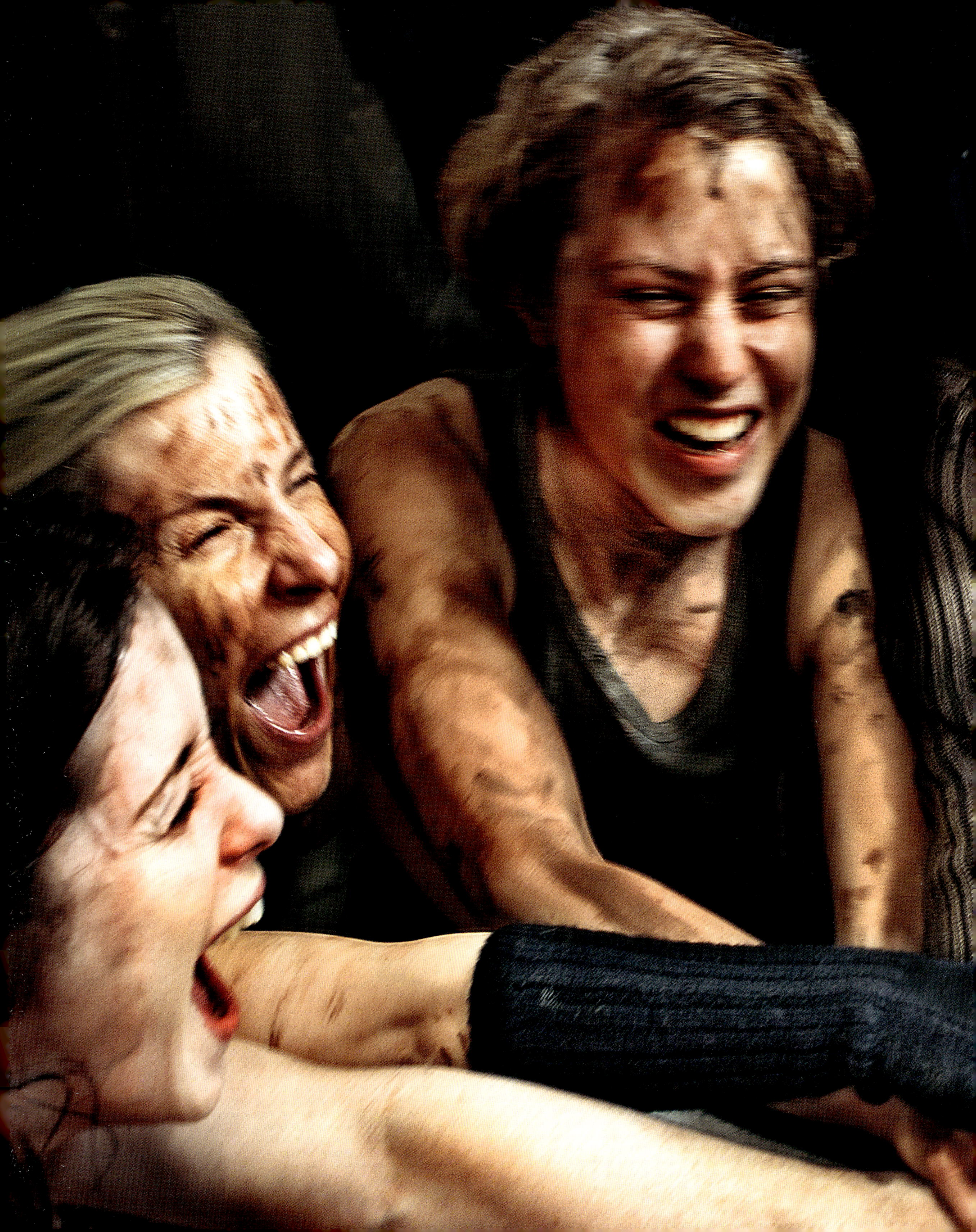

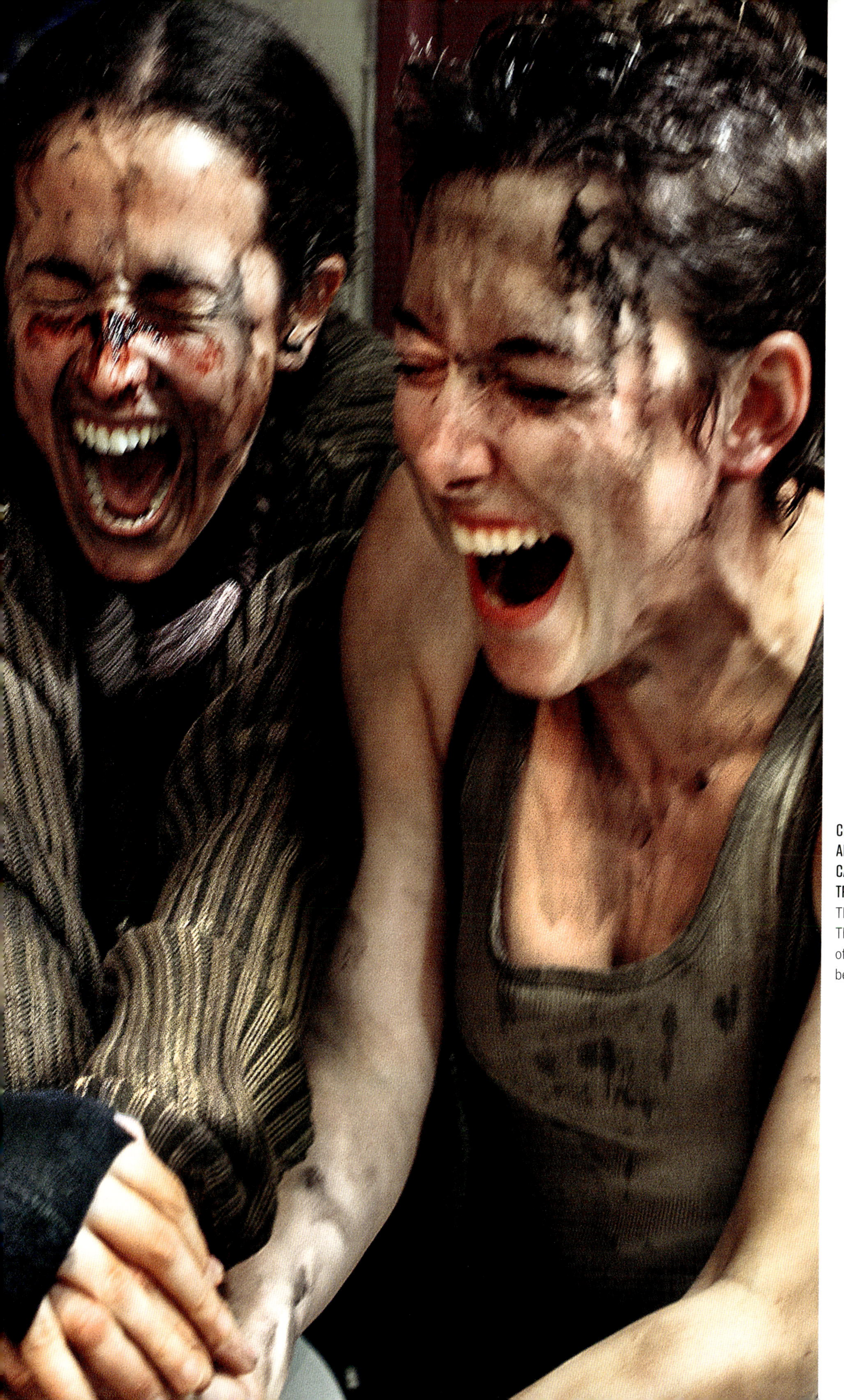

CLAIRE FOY, LISA GARDINER, ALLISON McKENZIE, OLIVIA MORGAN, CATHERINE MURRAY, *MACBETH*, TRAFALGAR STUDIOS, 2013
They shared a dressing room. This is the final group affirmation of the witches, Caithness and Lady M before they go on stage.

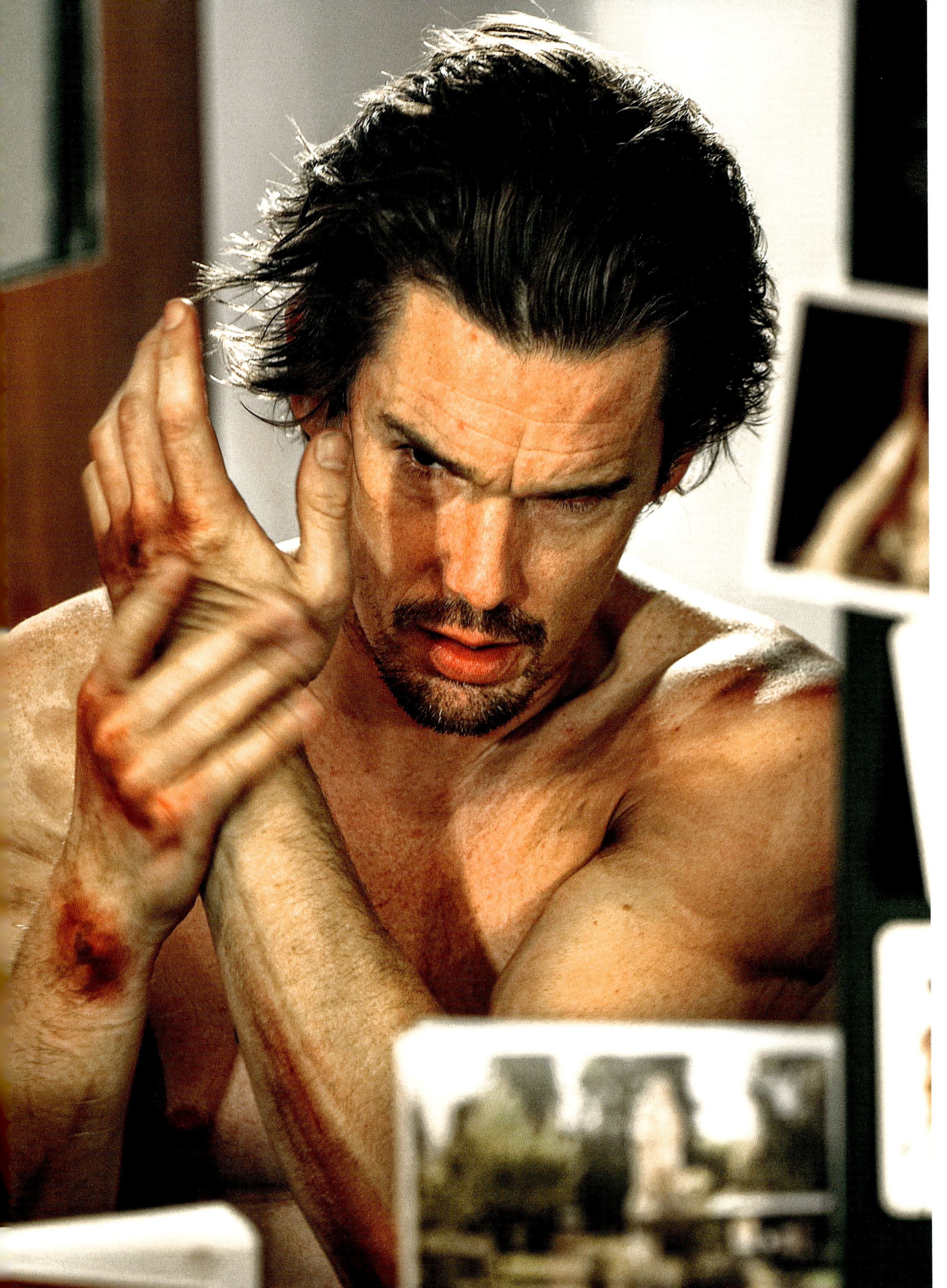

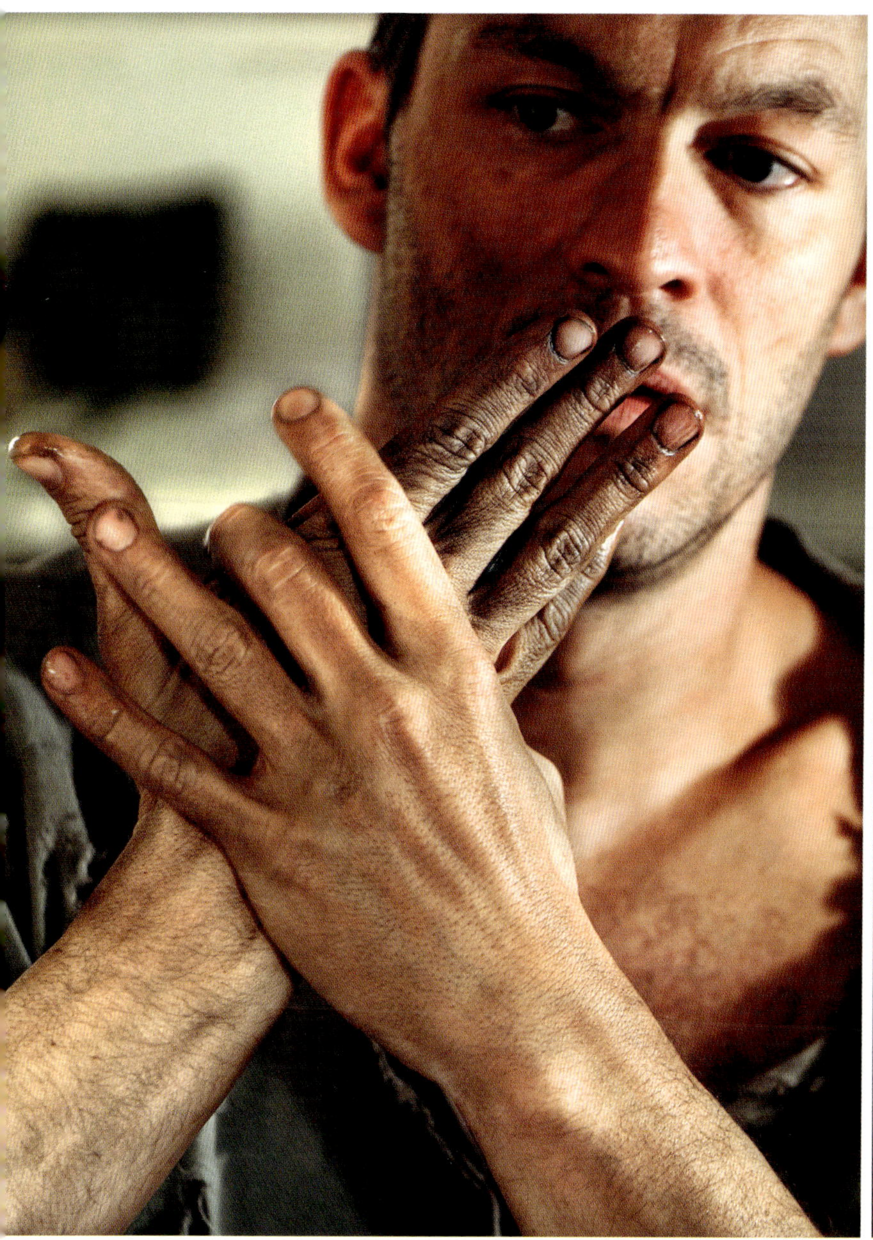

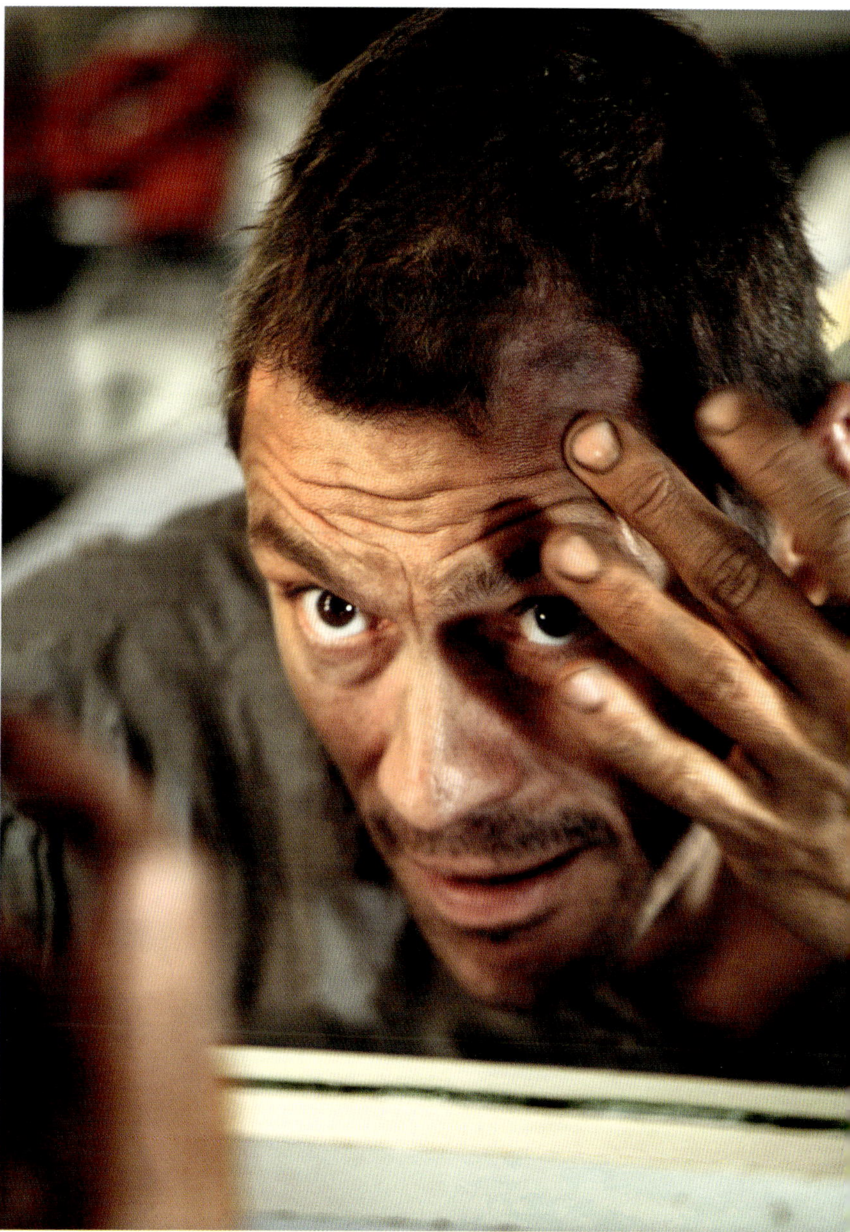

OPPOSITE: **ETHAN HAWKE, *THE WINTER'S TALE*, OLD VIC THEATRE, 2009**
American actors, performing on the London stage, bring a different dynamic to the party. The audience will feel it immediately.

ABOVE: **DOMINIC WEST, *LIFE IS A DREAM*, DONMAR WAREHOUSE, 2009**
Hands are always interesting to photograph and the interest is doubled when an actor applies make-up to portray the hands of somebody else.

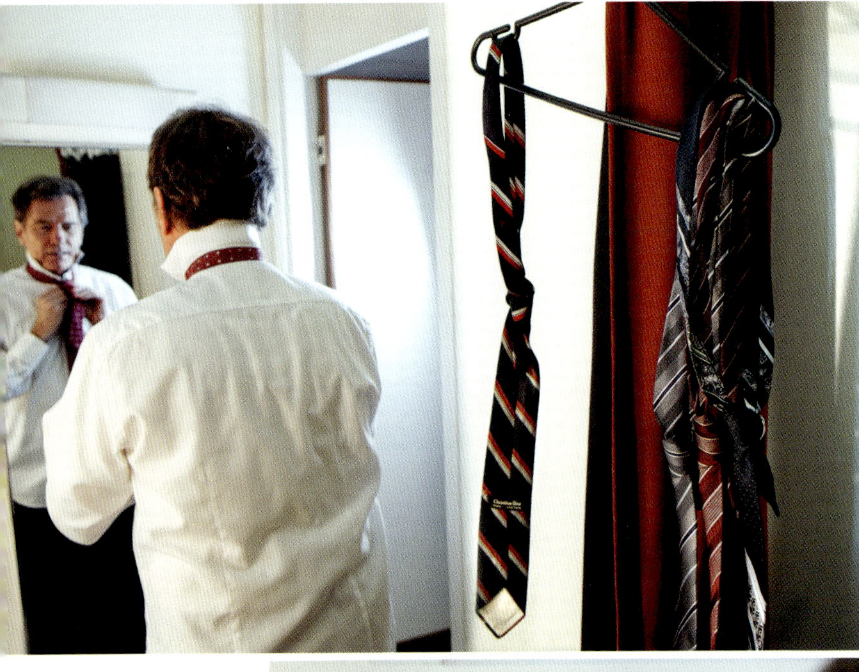
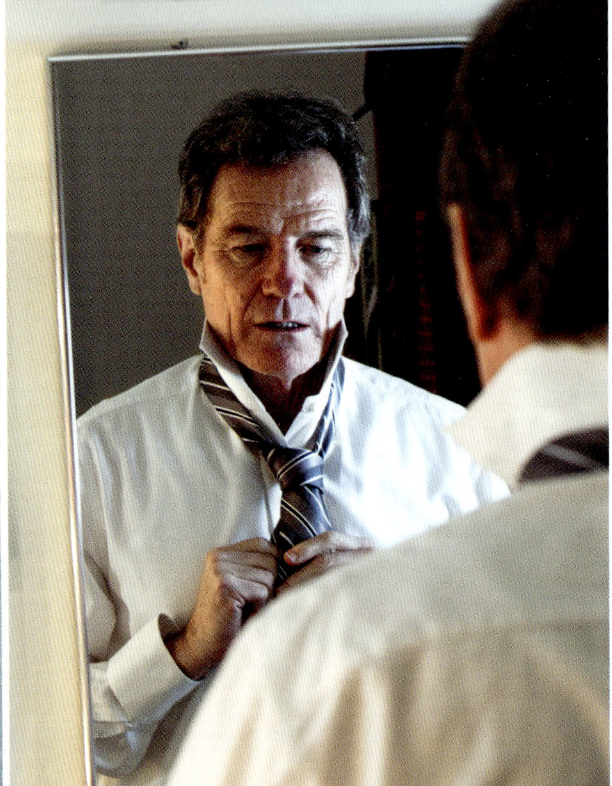
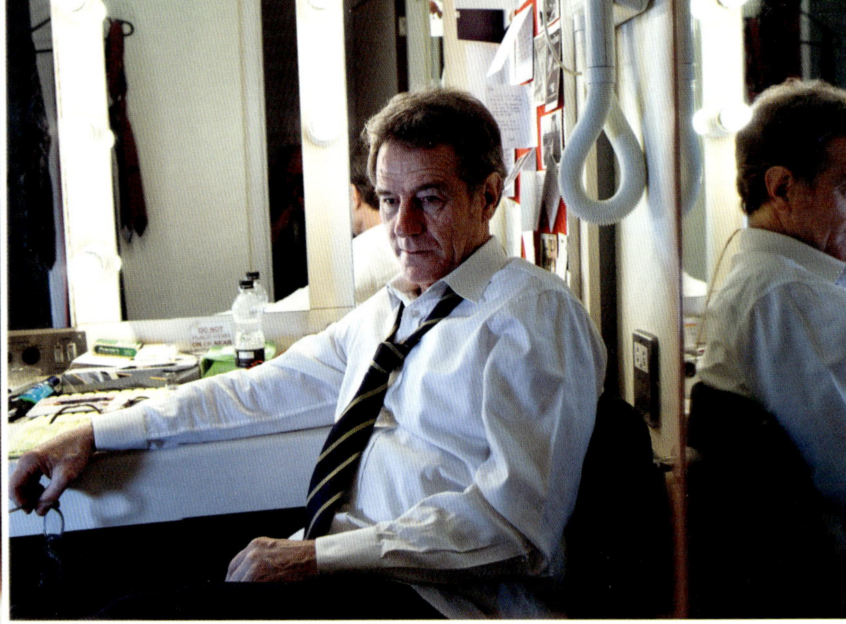
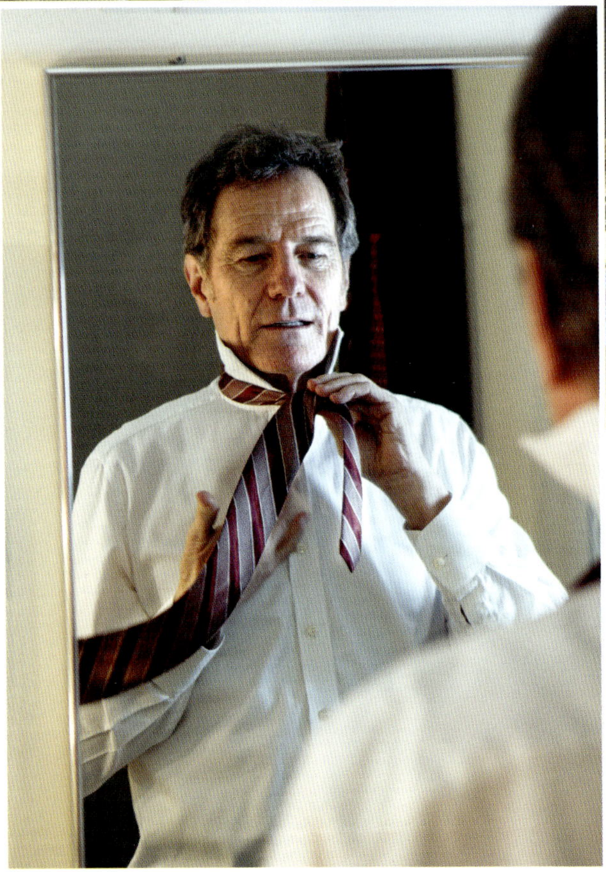

BRYAN CRANSTON, *NETWORK*, NATIONAL THEATRE, 2018
Bryan is the star of the legendary *Breaking Bad*. There are many different ways to find the character through props. For some it is a wig, a pair of shoes, a hat, a waistcoat, maybe some cufflinks. For Bryan, in this show, it was a tie, his character being a TV anchor. He tried on a number of different ones to get the right feel.

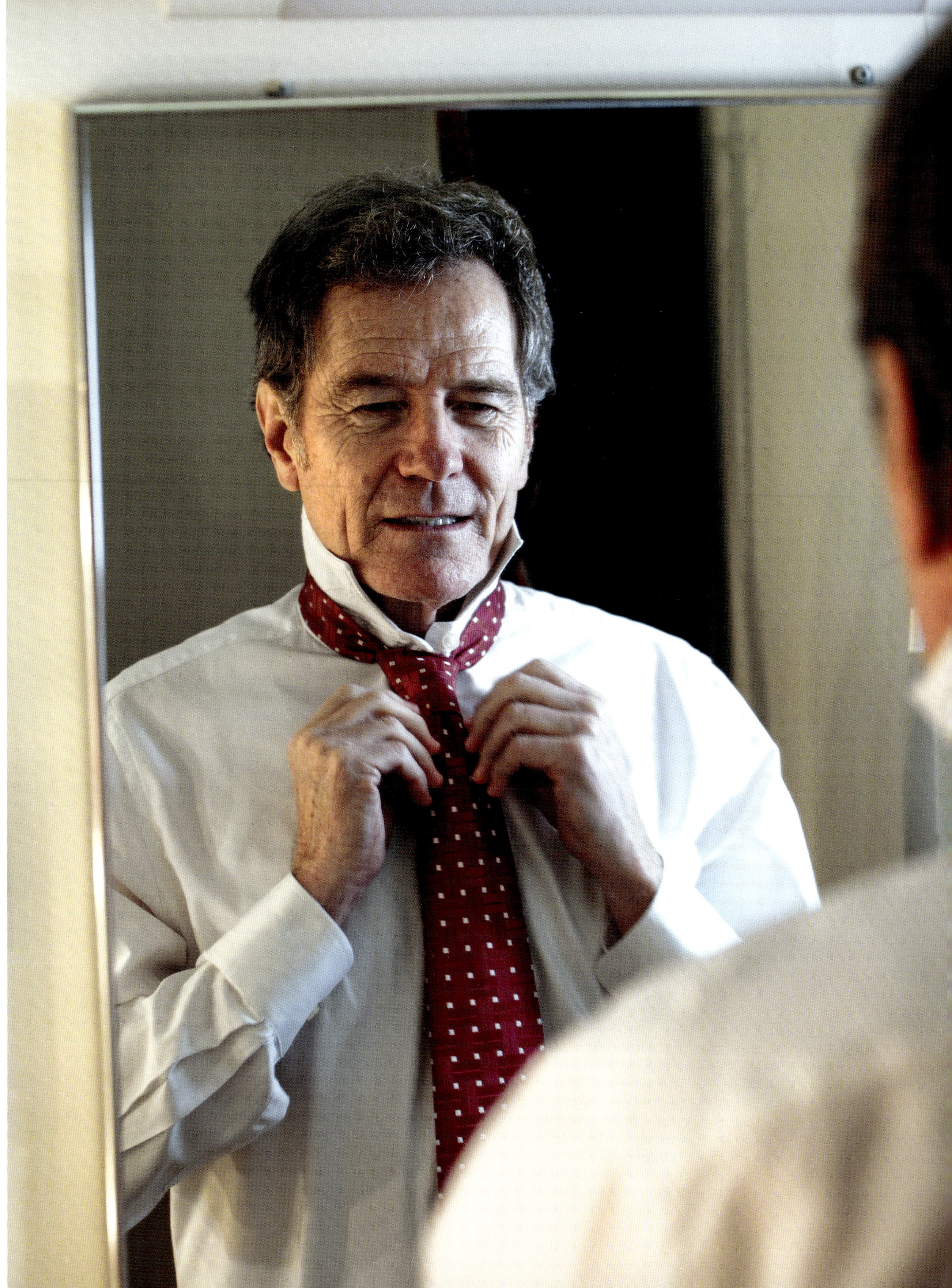

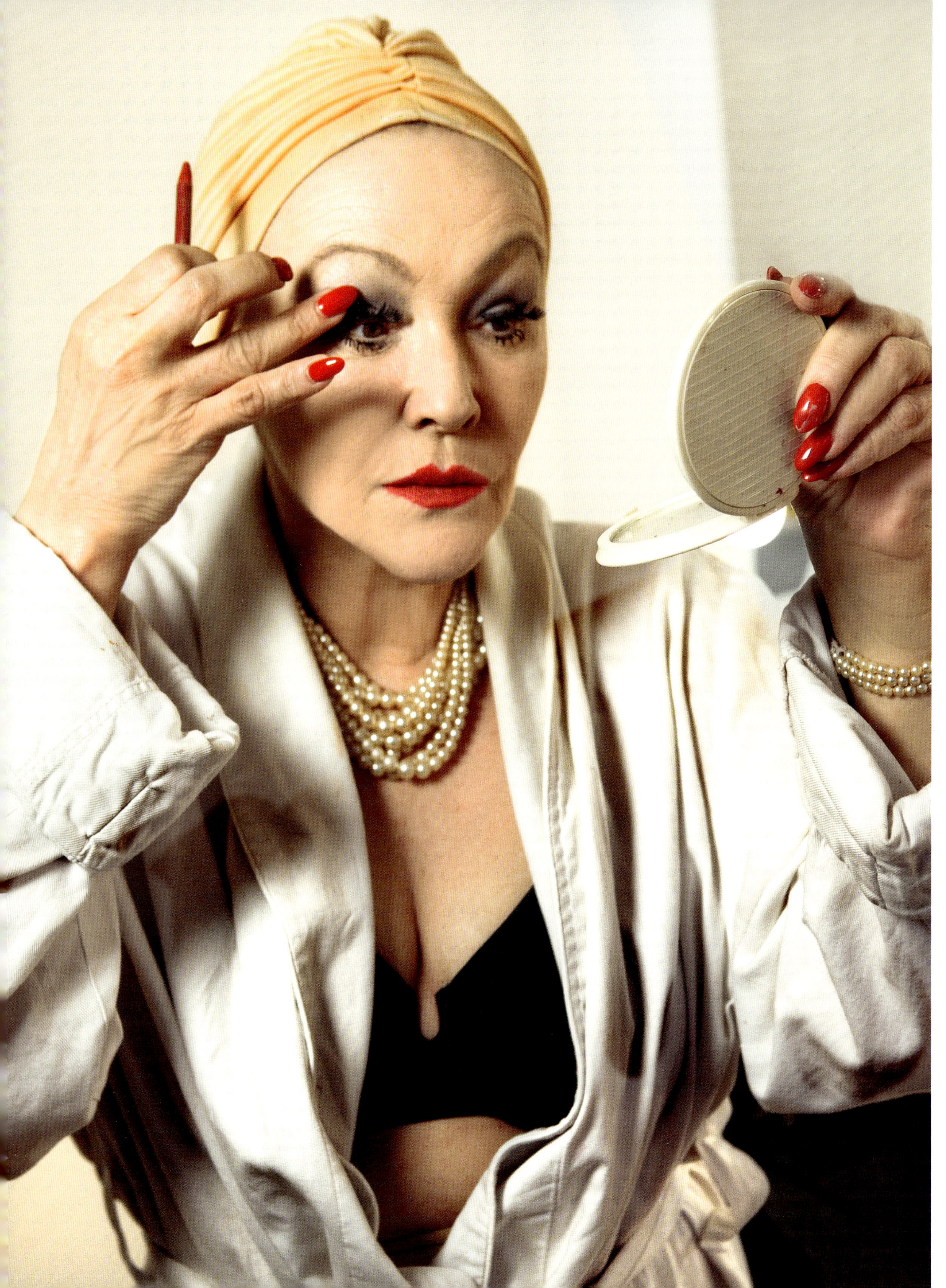

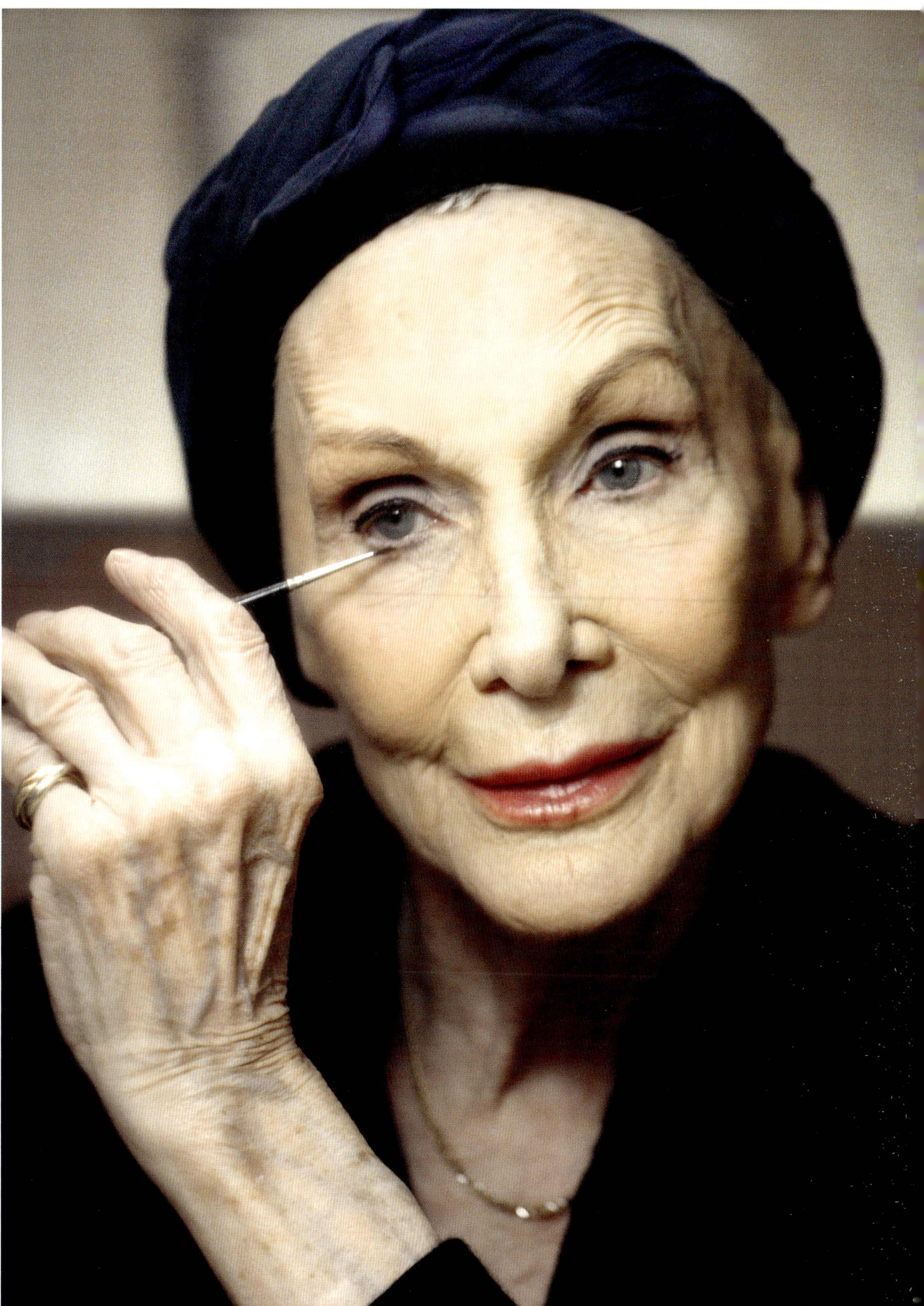

OPPOSITE: **FRANCES BARBER, *MADAME RUBINSTEIN*, PARK THEATRE, 2017**
Frances was playing the cosmetic guru Elizabeth Arden, opposite Miriam Margolyes as Helena Rubinstein. They were famously fierce competitors.

RIGHT: **SIÂN PHILLIPS, *LES BLANCS*, NATIONAL THEATRE, 2016**
Siân has such clarity, combined with her enigma. Bilingual, she dreams in Welsh.

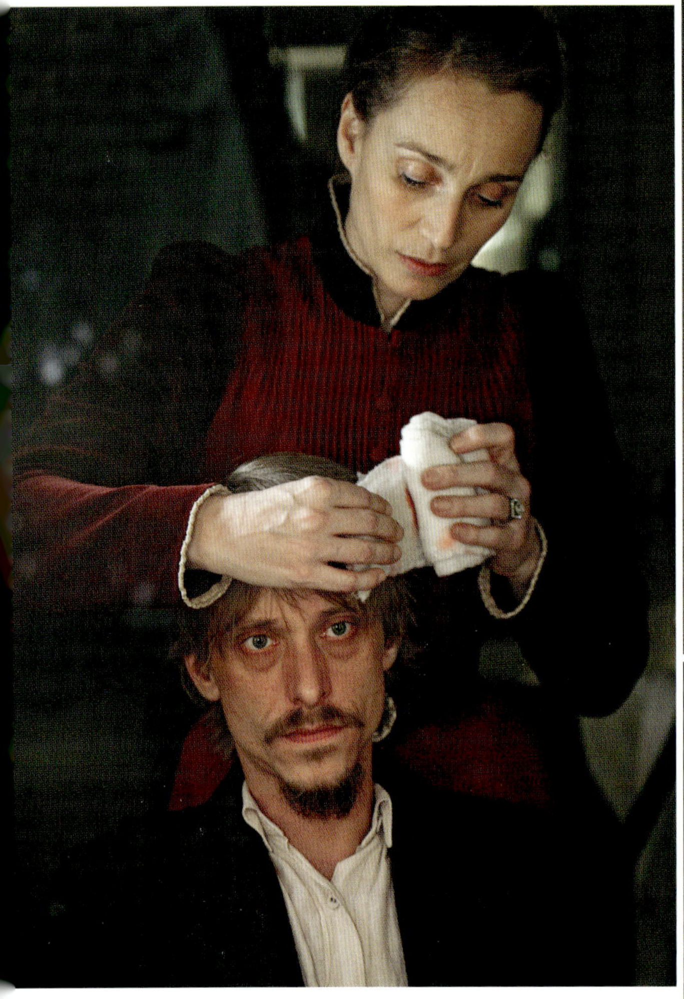

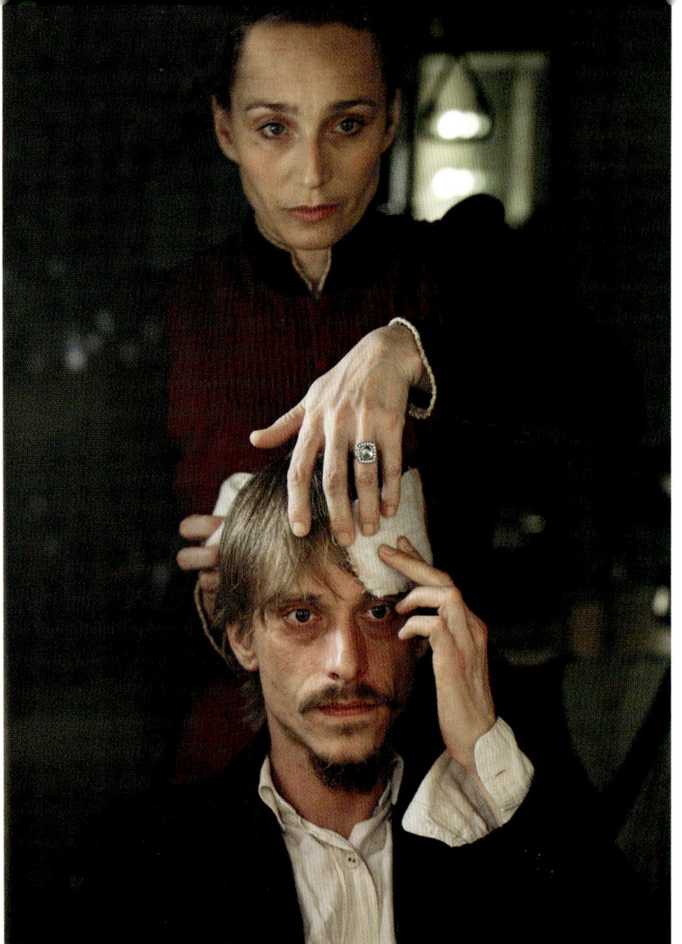

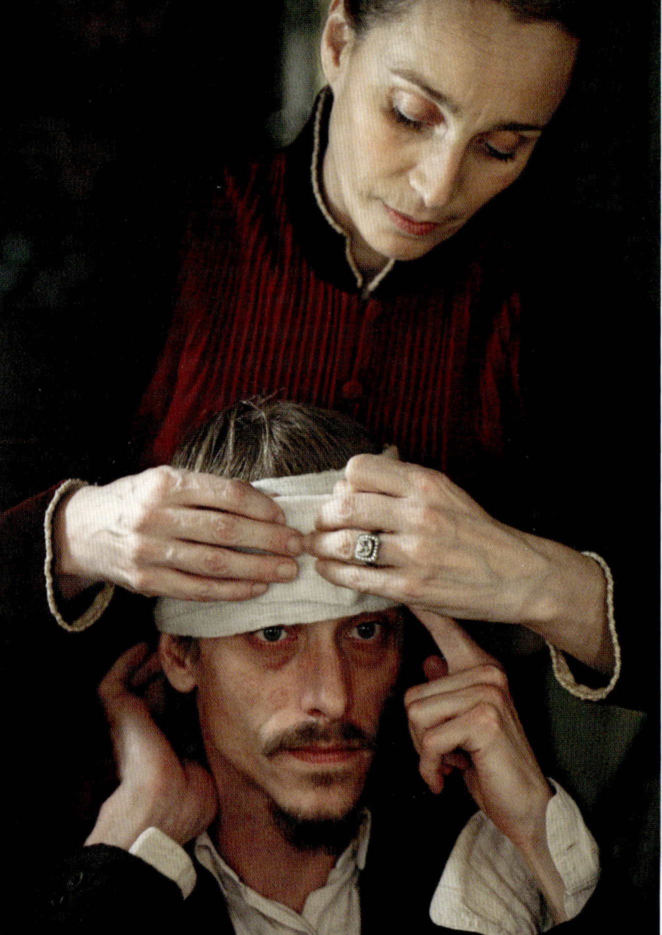

KRISTIN SCOTT THOMAS, MACKENZIE CROOK, *THE SEAGULL*, ROYAL COURT, 2007

The application of a bandage was a ritual they had before going on as Arkadina and Treplyov. This was the last performance of their run, which added an extra level of poignancy to the daily familiarity.

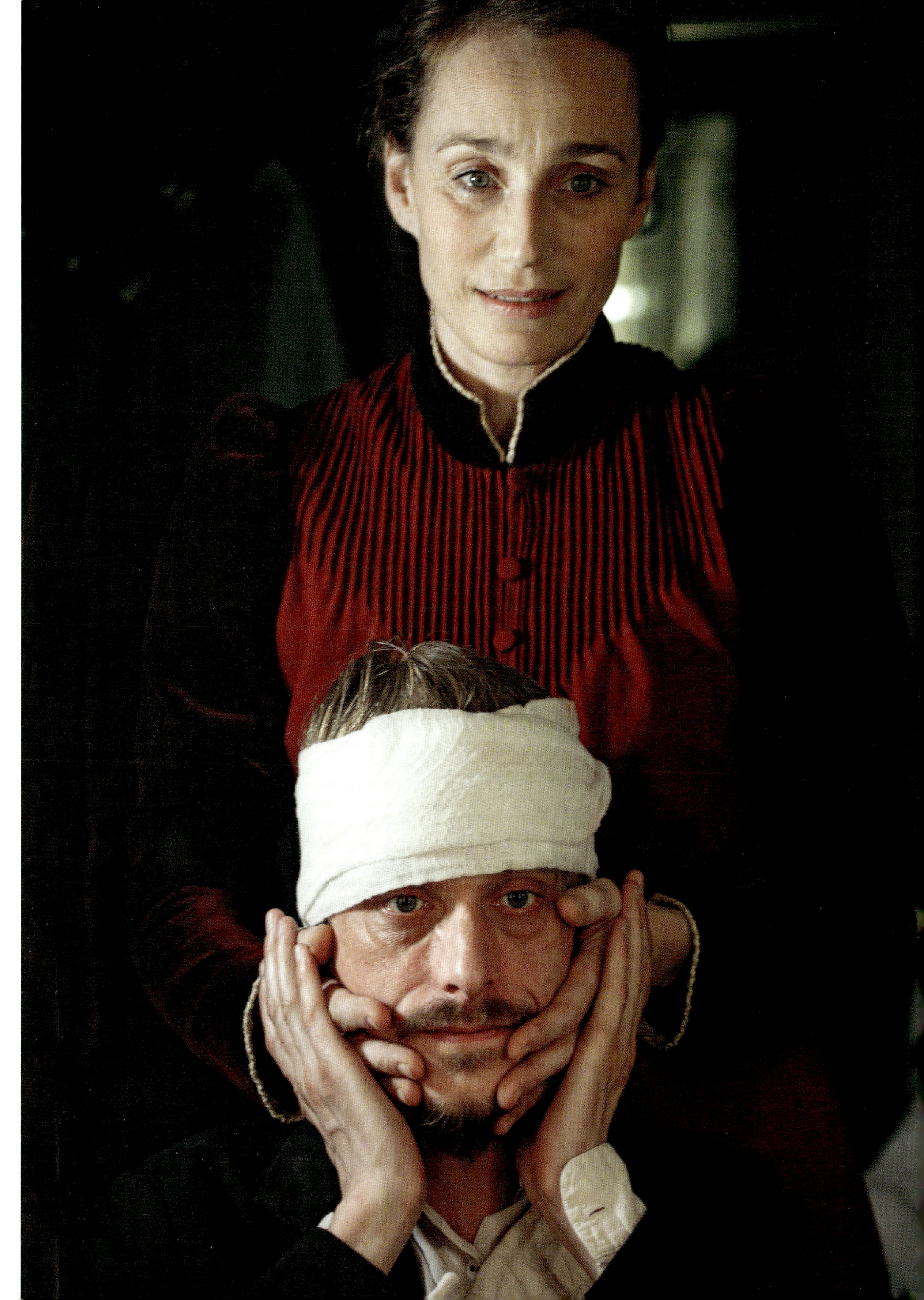

PETER BOWLES, *THE RIVALS*, THEATRE ROYAL HAYMARKET, 2011

Peter has played many characters from the Restoration canon, always injecting a high degree of mischief and pleasure into the proceedings.

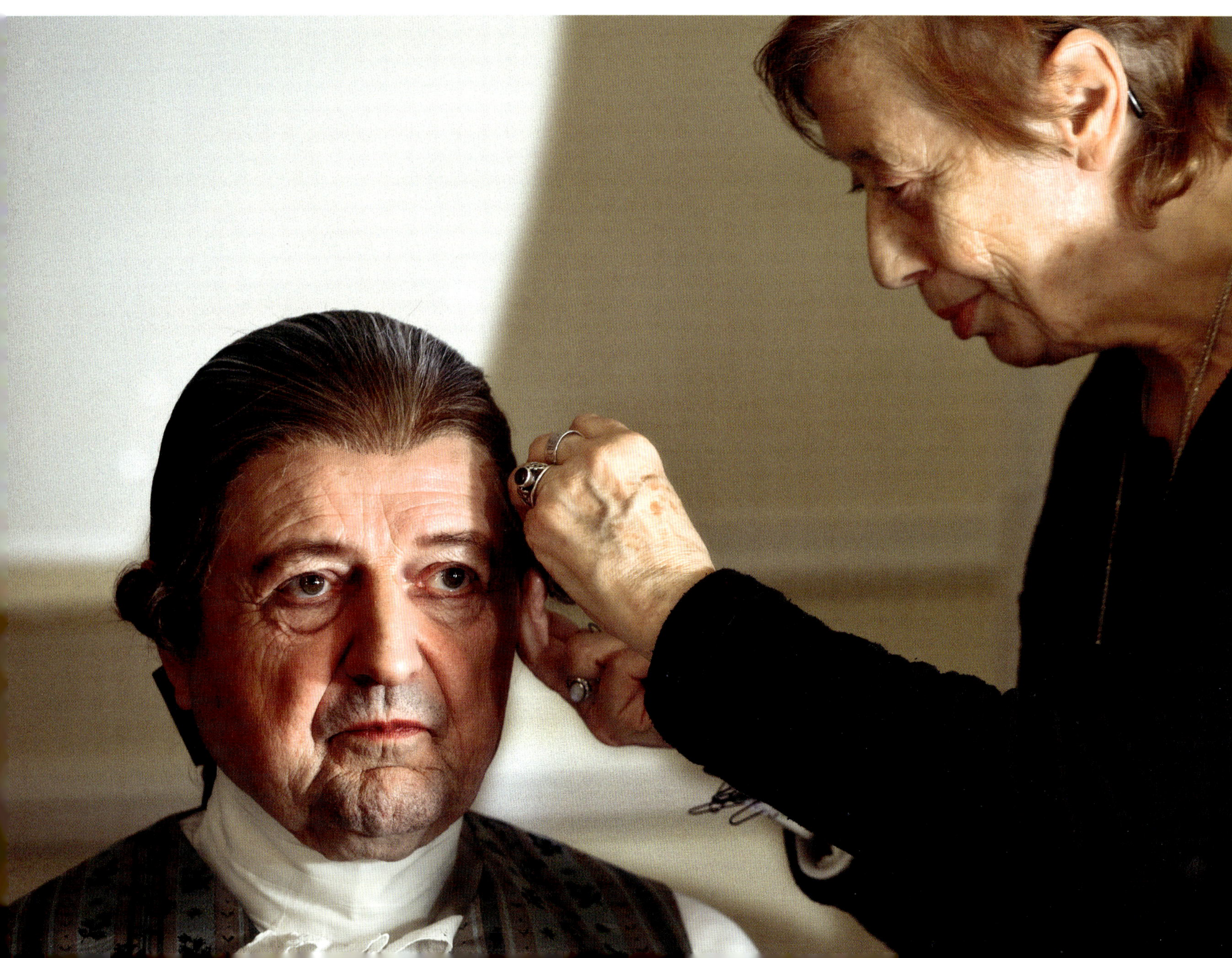

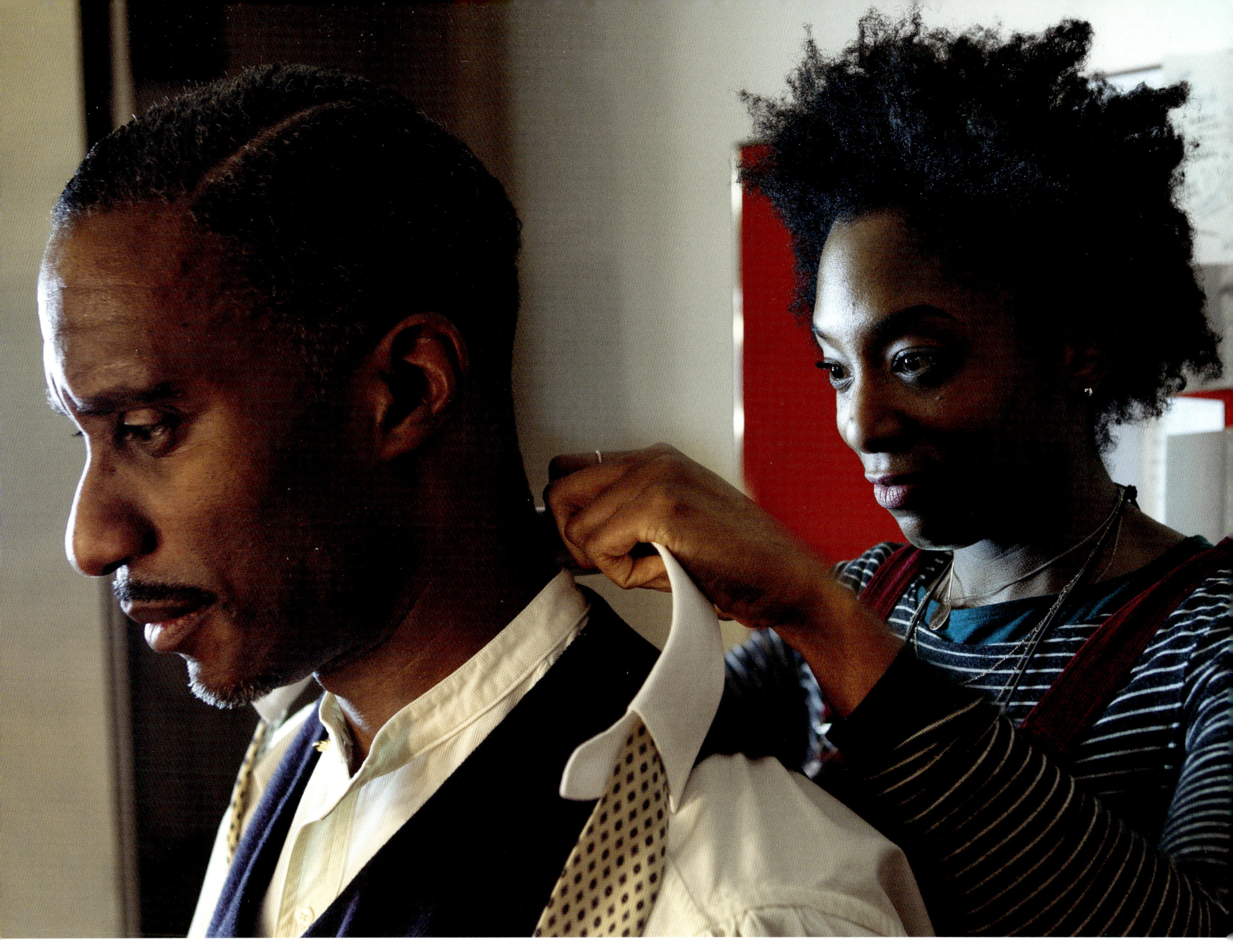

CLINT DYER, *MA RAINEY'S BLACK BOTTOM*, NATIONAL THEATRE, 2016
Final adjustments to a costume are all-important, especially the view from behind, which is hard for an actor to see. Turning one's back to the audience can be as powerful as facing front.

ORLANDO BLOOM, *IN CELEBRATION*, DUKE OF YORK'S, 2007

A moment of calm. Having had the lead in a number of highly popular film franchises, Orlando definitely lent some star power to this revival. There were camera flashes and shrieks on his entrance, and apparently his picture was pinned to the wall of many an admirer.

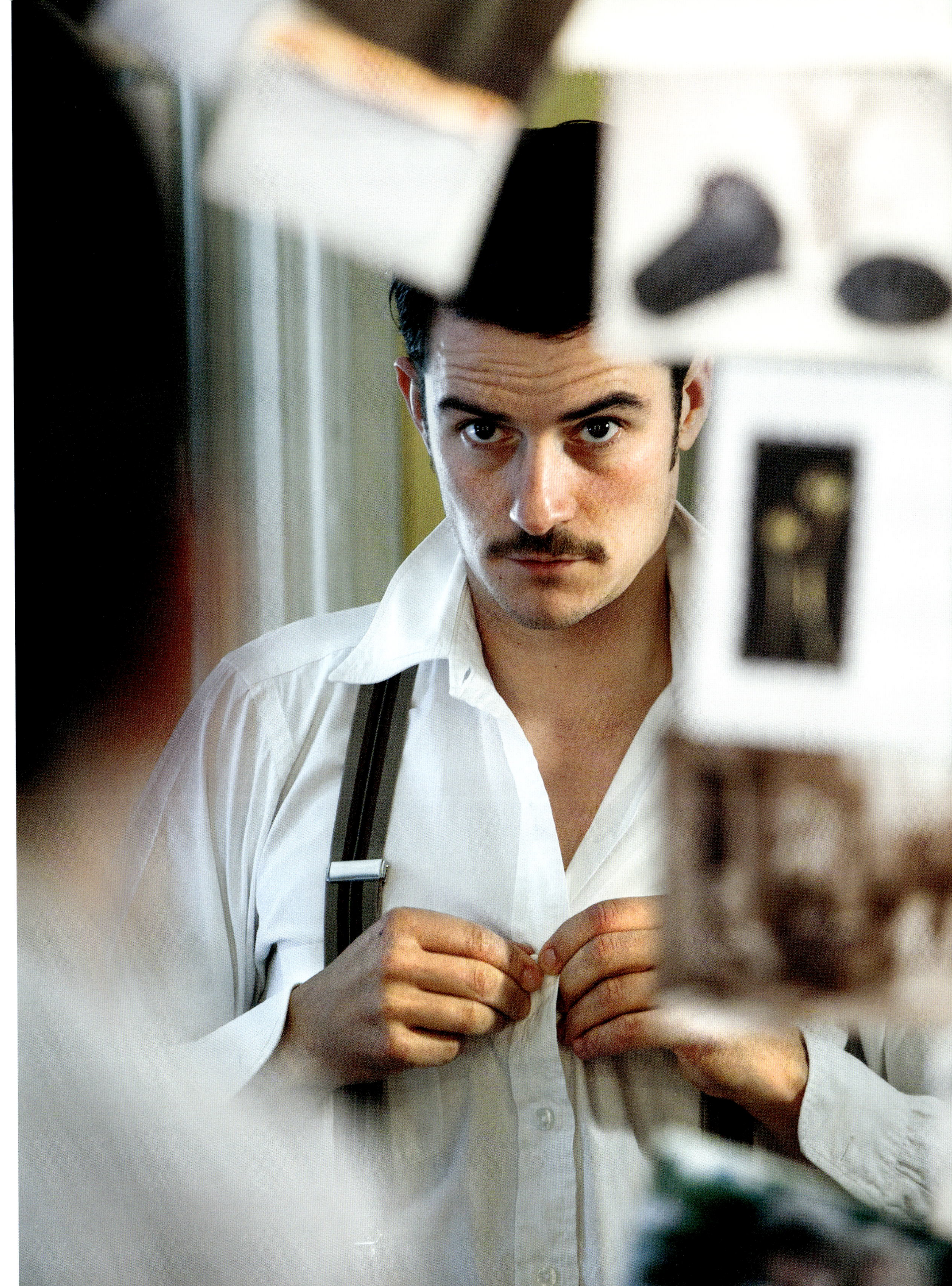

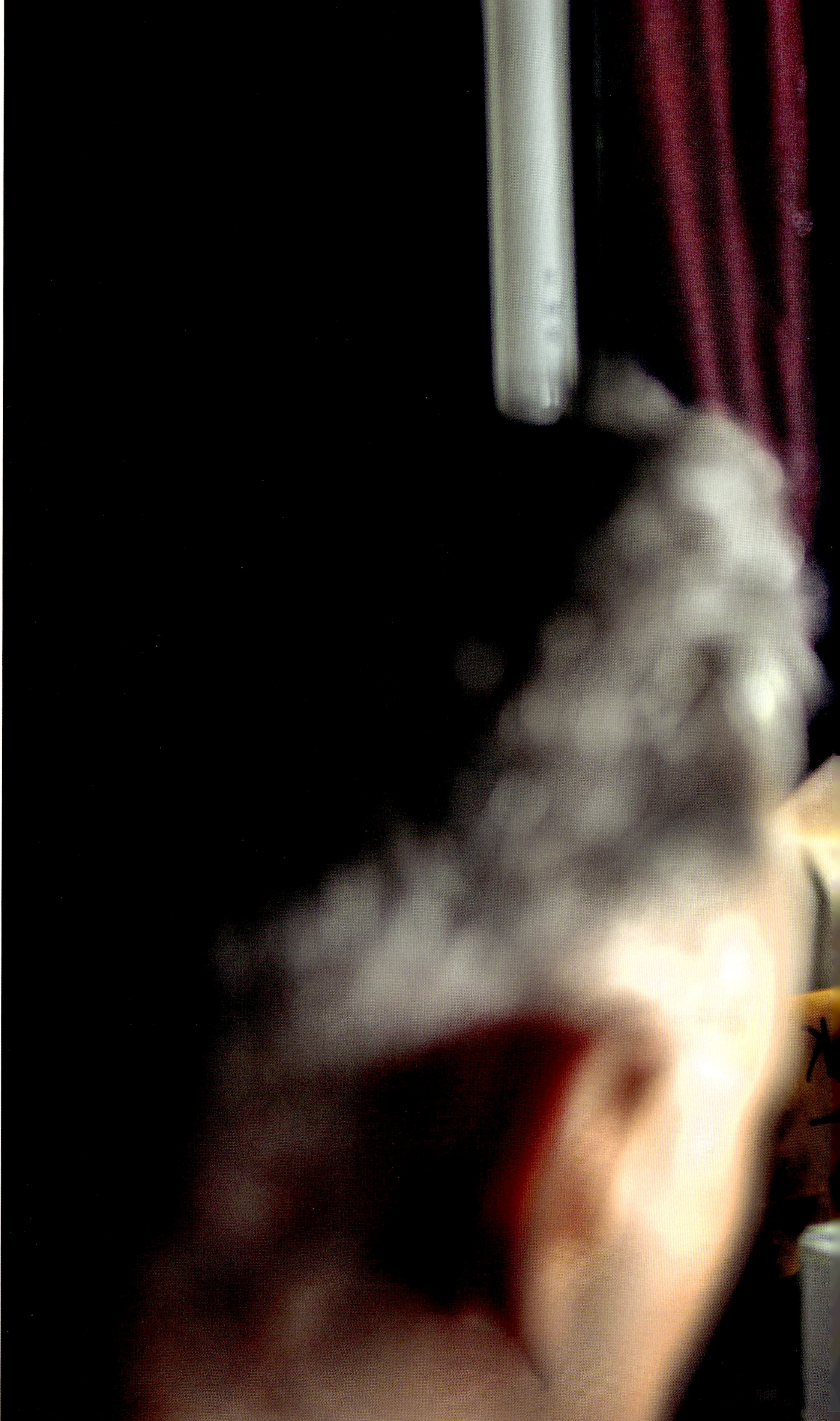

ALAN CUMMING, *ALAN CUMMING SINGS SAPPY SONGS*, THE HUB EDINBURGH, 2016

I hadn't seen Alan since 1992. When the Edinburgh Festival booked him, I drove up there from London for a twenty-minute session in the back room, and then watched the performance.

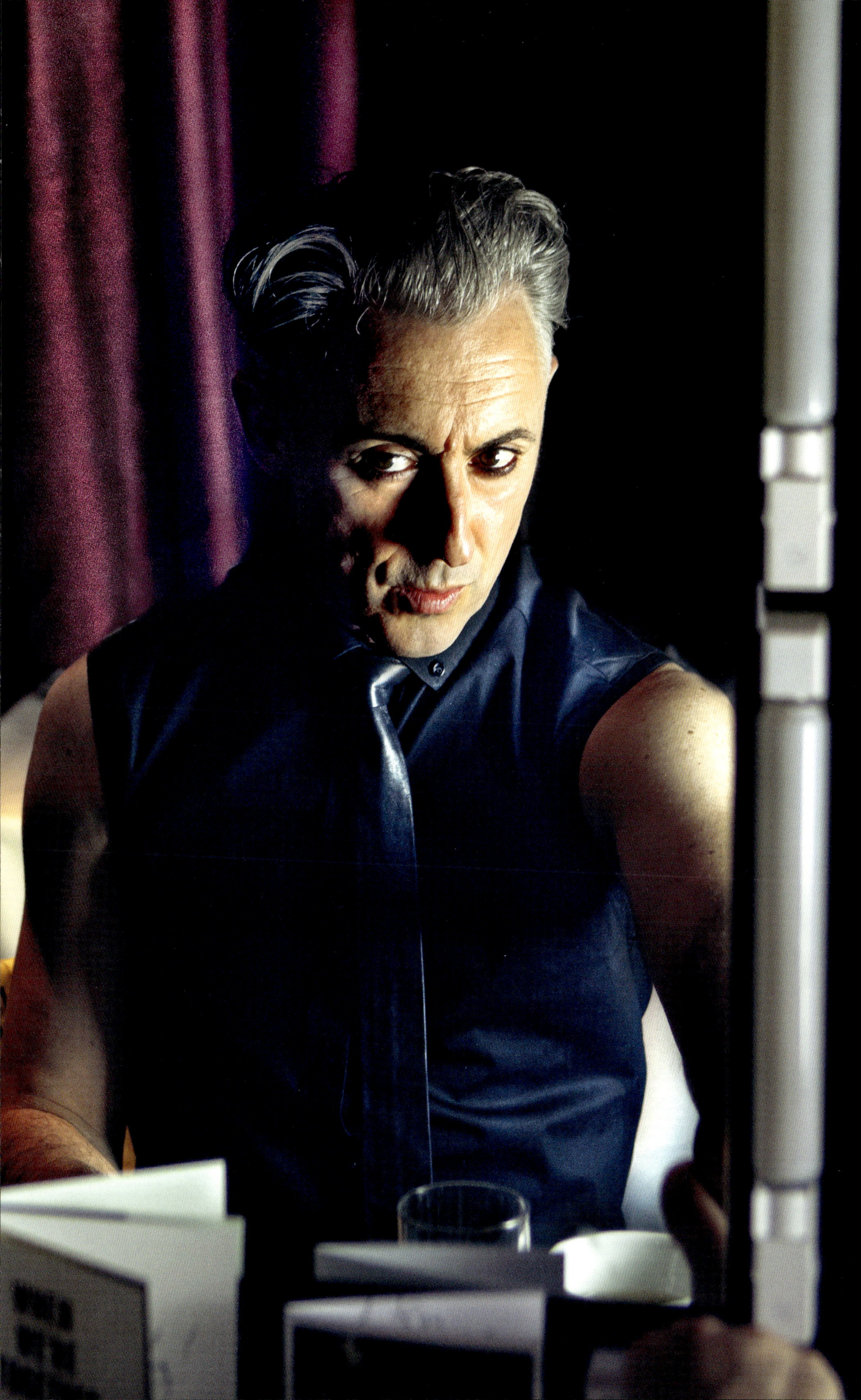

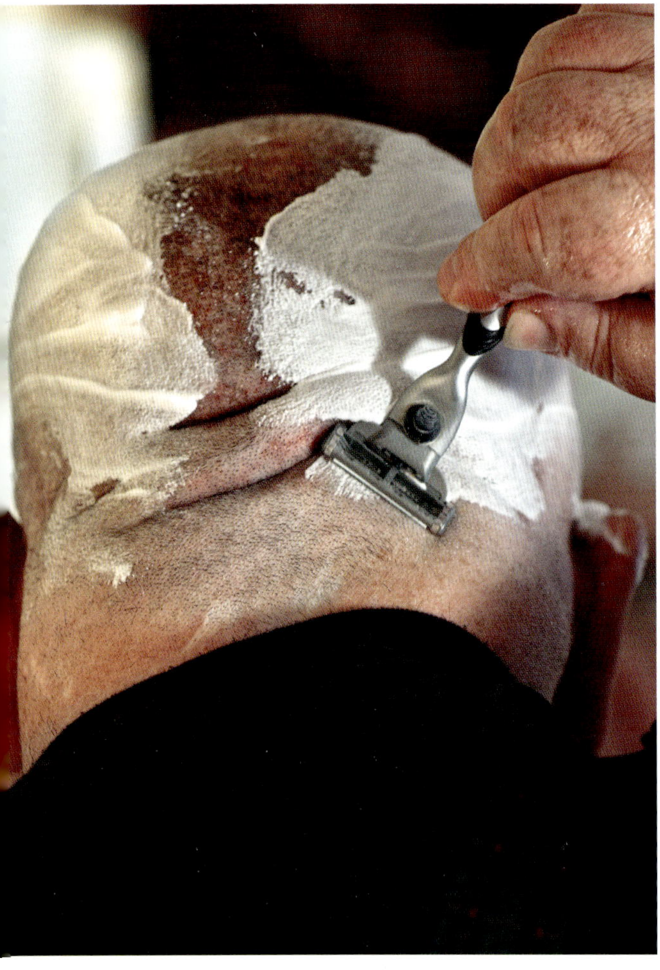

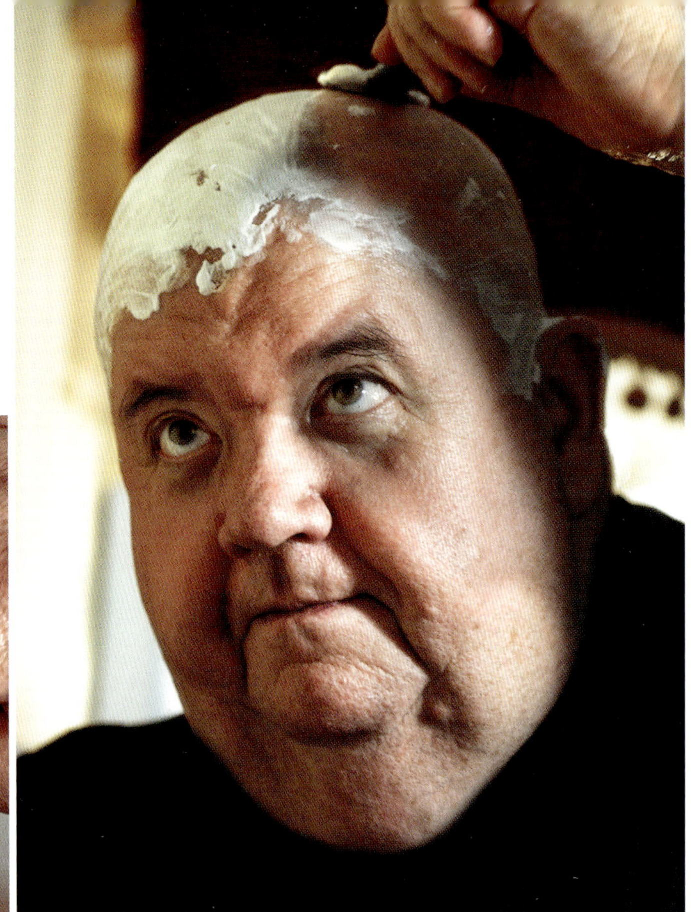

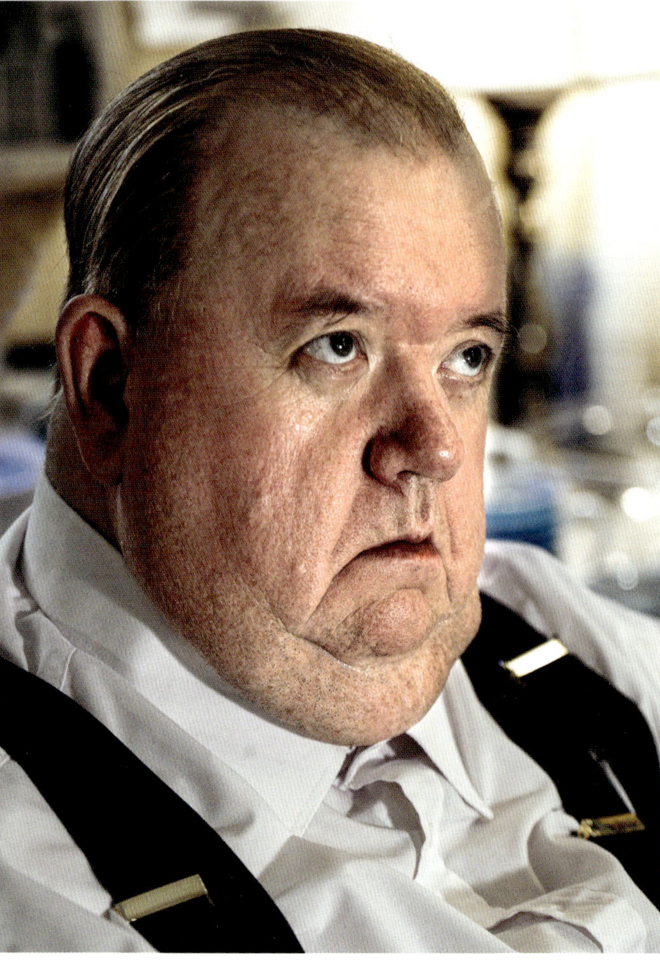

IAN McNEICE, *THE KING'S SPEECH*, WYNDHAM'S, 2012

The difficulty of playing such a well-known historical figure is immense. The actor has to make their performance real without it being a cliché. Ian had to create the portrayal in only a few scenes, which takes consummate skill.

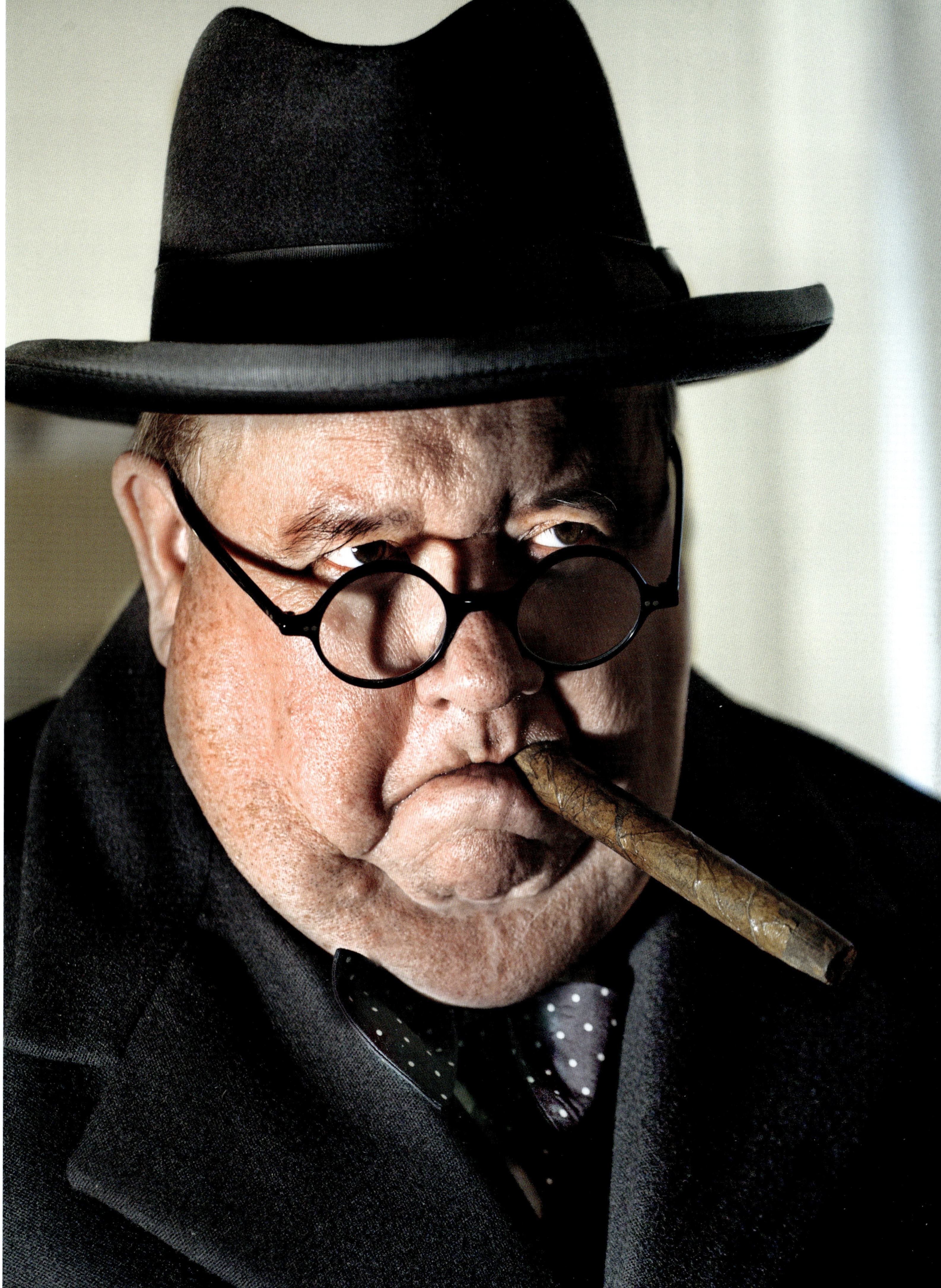

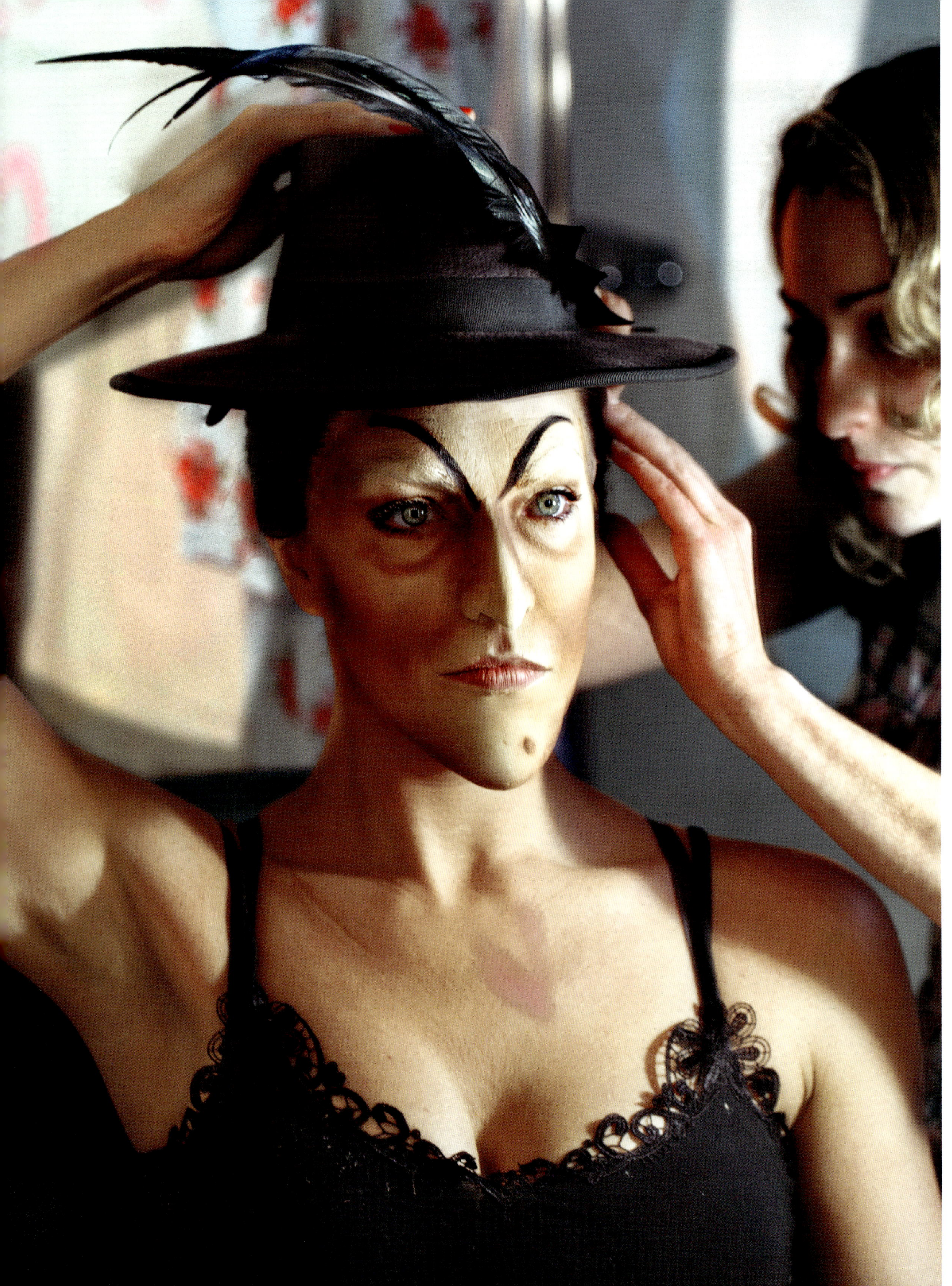

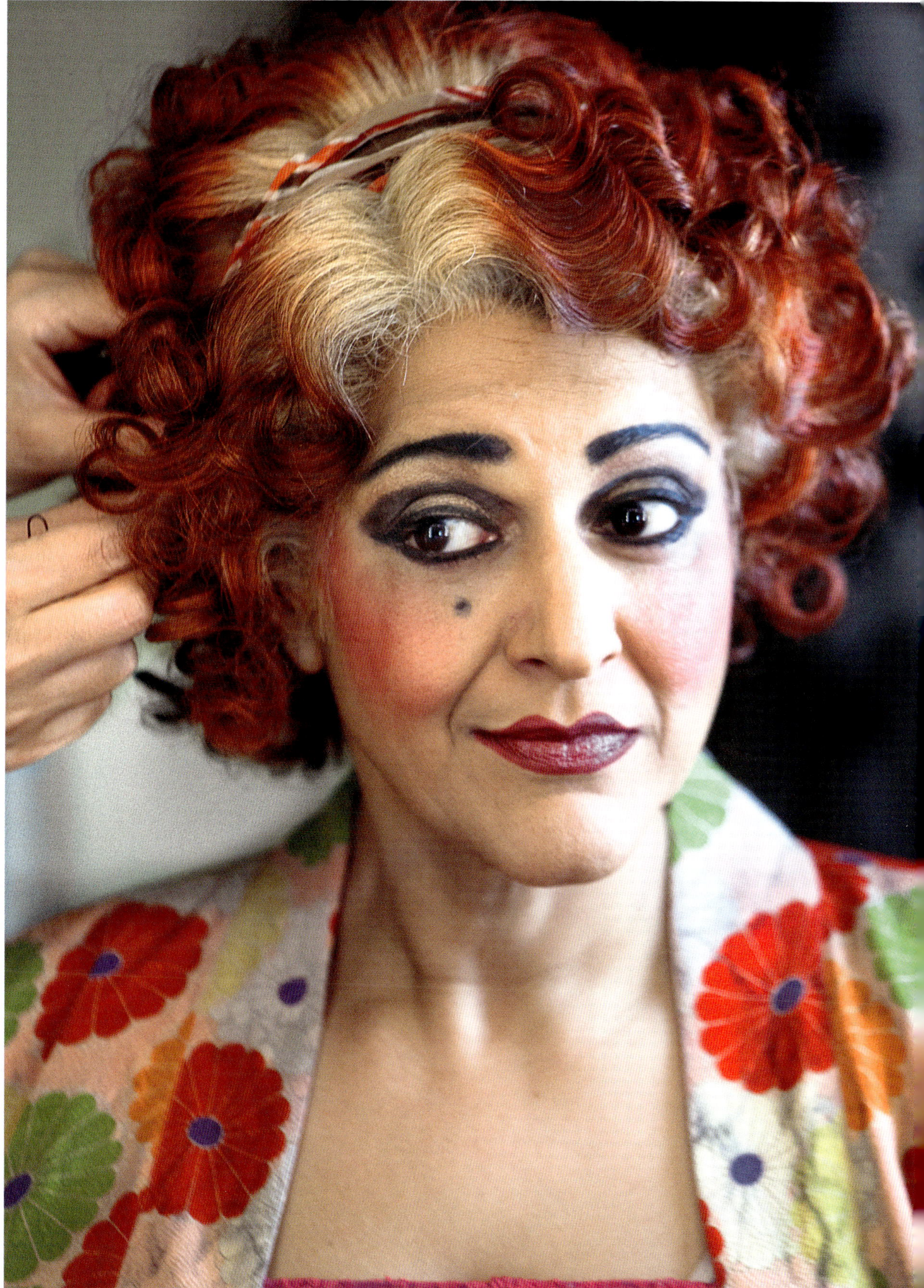

OPPOSITE: **HANNAH WADDINGHAM, *THE WIZARD OF OZ*, PALLADIUM, 2011**
To play the dark side of a character, Hannah is prepared to trash her own beauty. She does it without a shred of vanity. The more the audience love to hate her, the better her performance.

RIGHT: **MEERA SYAL, *ANNIE*, PICCADILLY THEATRE, 2018**
Meera chose very particular make-up to play the cruel and slovenly drunkard Miss Hannigan, who runs the orphanage where Annie is taken.

BELOW: **MARK RYLANCE, *TWELFTH NIGHT*, APOLLO THEATRE, 2012**
Meticulous with his make-up for Olivia for this all-male Original Practices production.

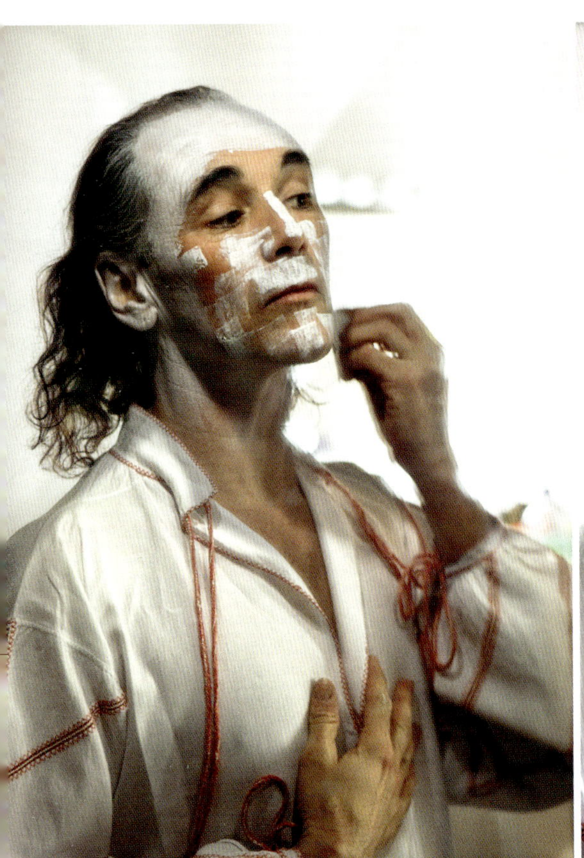

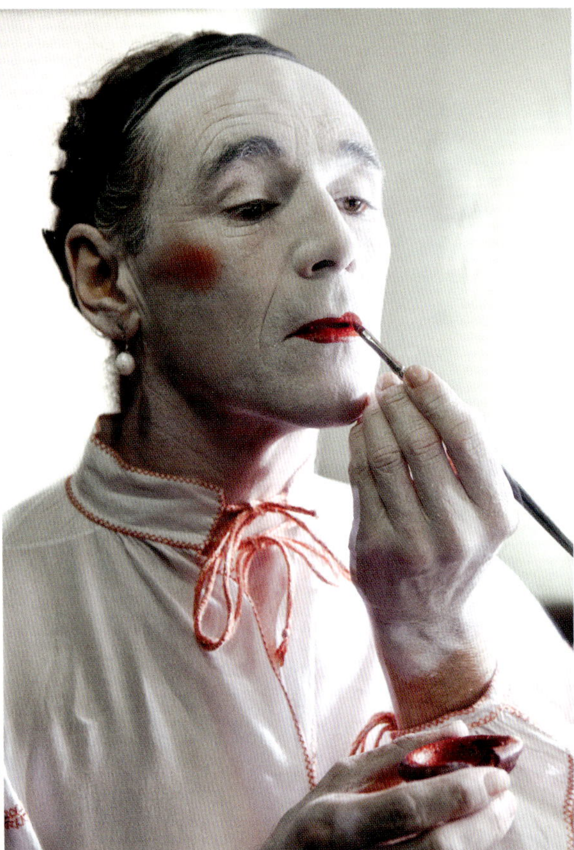

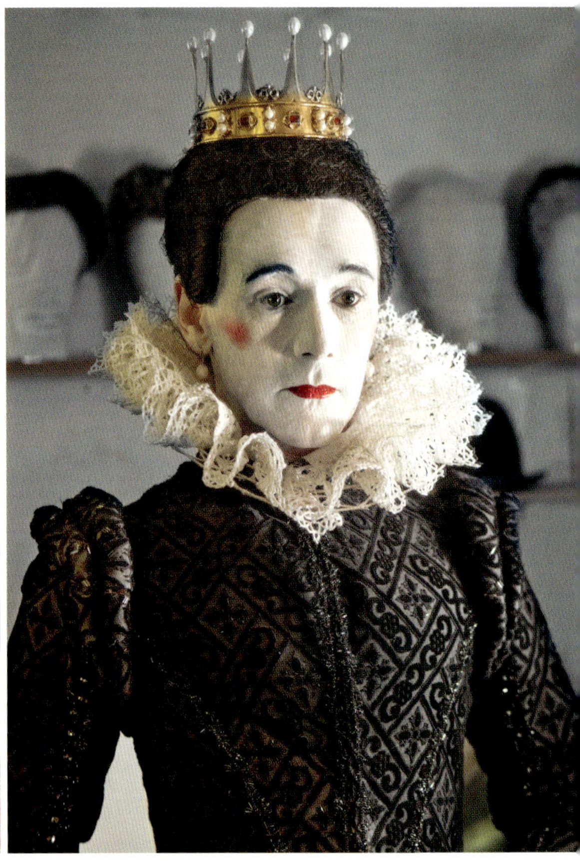

OPPOSITE: **MARK RYLANCE, *JERUSALEM*, APOLLO THEATRE, 2010**
These are two of Mark's finest roles. They are in complete contrast, both legendary. In *Jerusalem* he shared a room with Mackenzie Crook who drew the roosters on the wall, which alluded to his character's name, Rooster Byron.

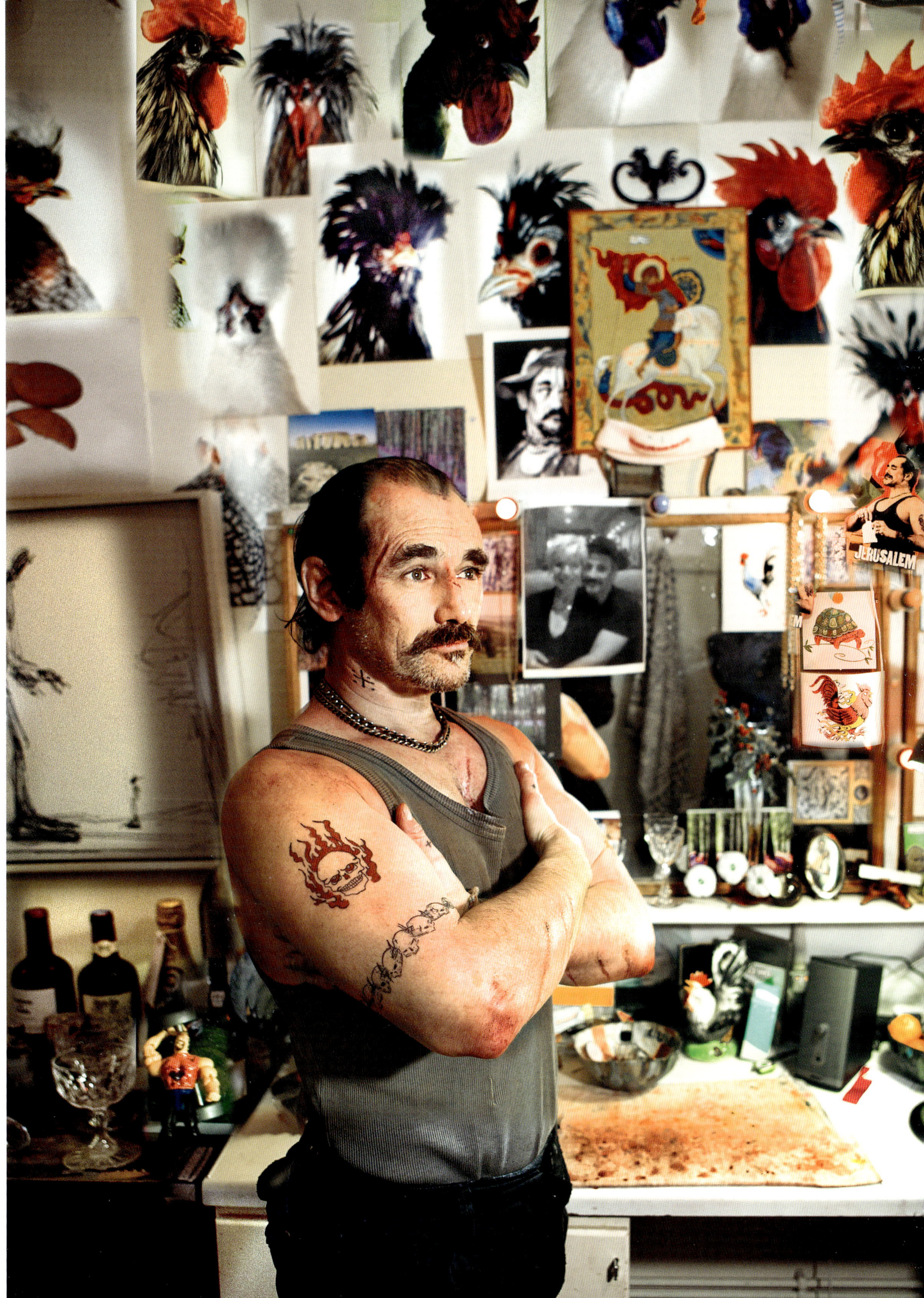
JERUSALEM

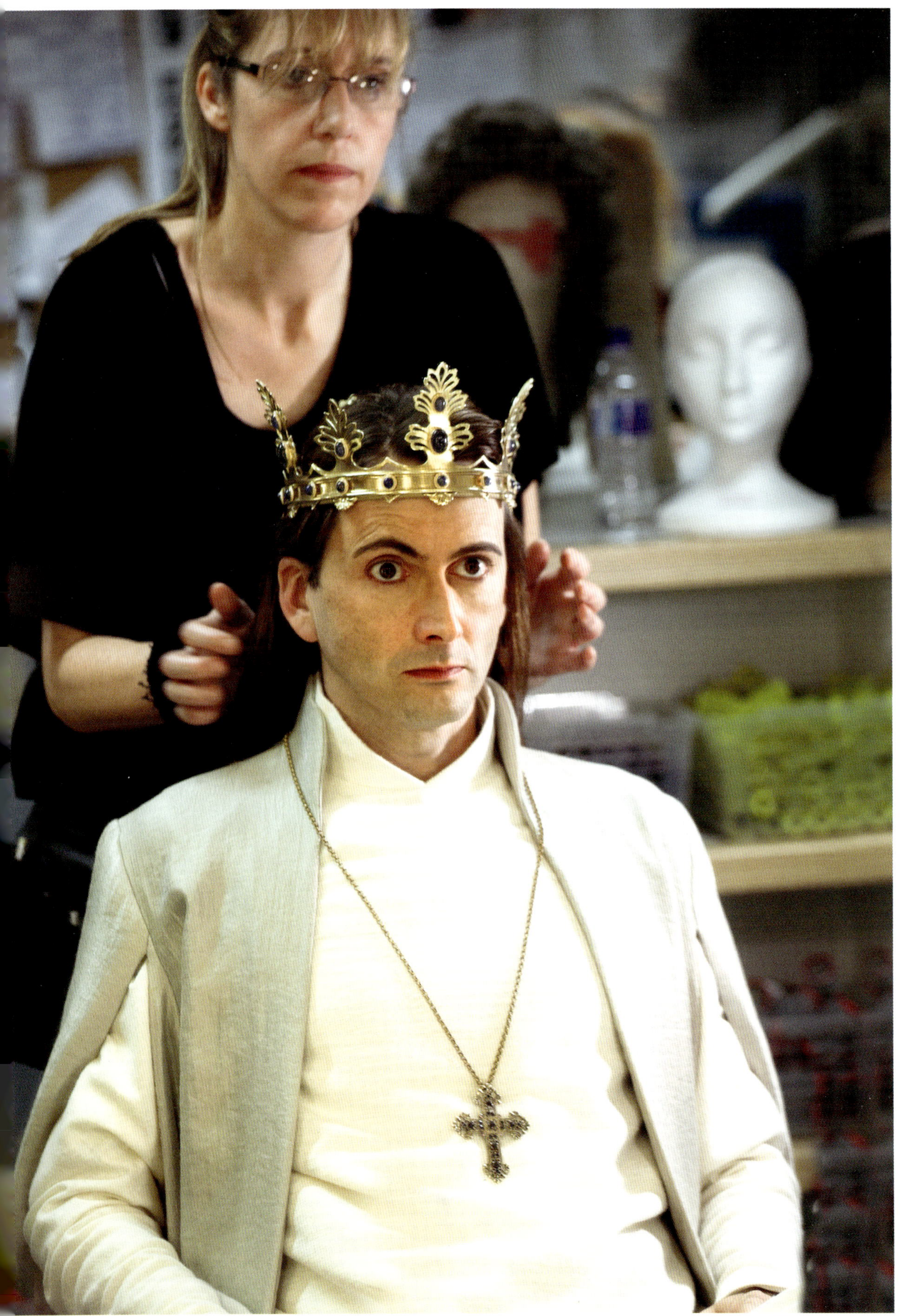

LEFT: **DAVID TENNANT, *RICHARD II*, RSC, 2013**
David has charisma to burn. Luckily it is coupled with a genuine sense of spreading well-being amongst all the company he works with. Here, in the wig chair, is a quiet opportunity to gather his thoughts.

OPPOSITE: **EDDIE REDMAYNE, *RICHARD II*, DONMAR WAREHOUSE, 2012**
By this time Eddie was a certified film star. The Donmar has two main dressing rooms – male and female – so it's all in together. Eddie had no difficulty adjusting to a shared room and neither did the others.

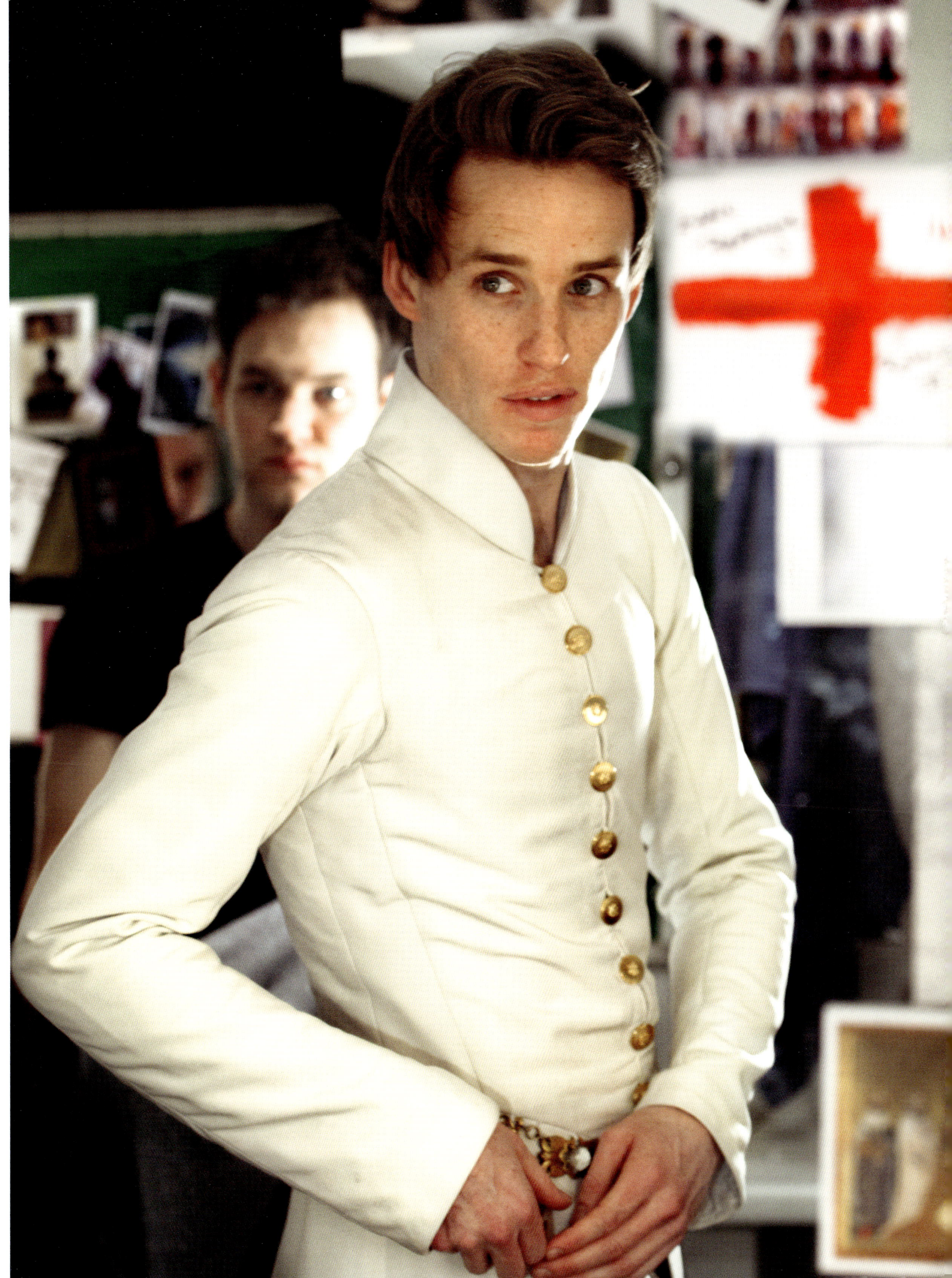

CATE BLANCHETT, *THE PRESENT*, ETHEL BARRYMORE THEATER, 2017

Cate has been an ally since we first met in 1999. When asked in interviews the dreaded question, 'Who is your favourite actor to photograph?', invariably I will say Cate. Her capacity for vulnerability in front of a camera is truly extraordinary.

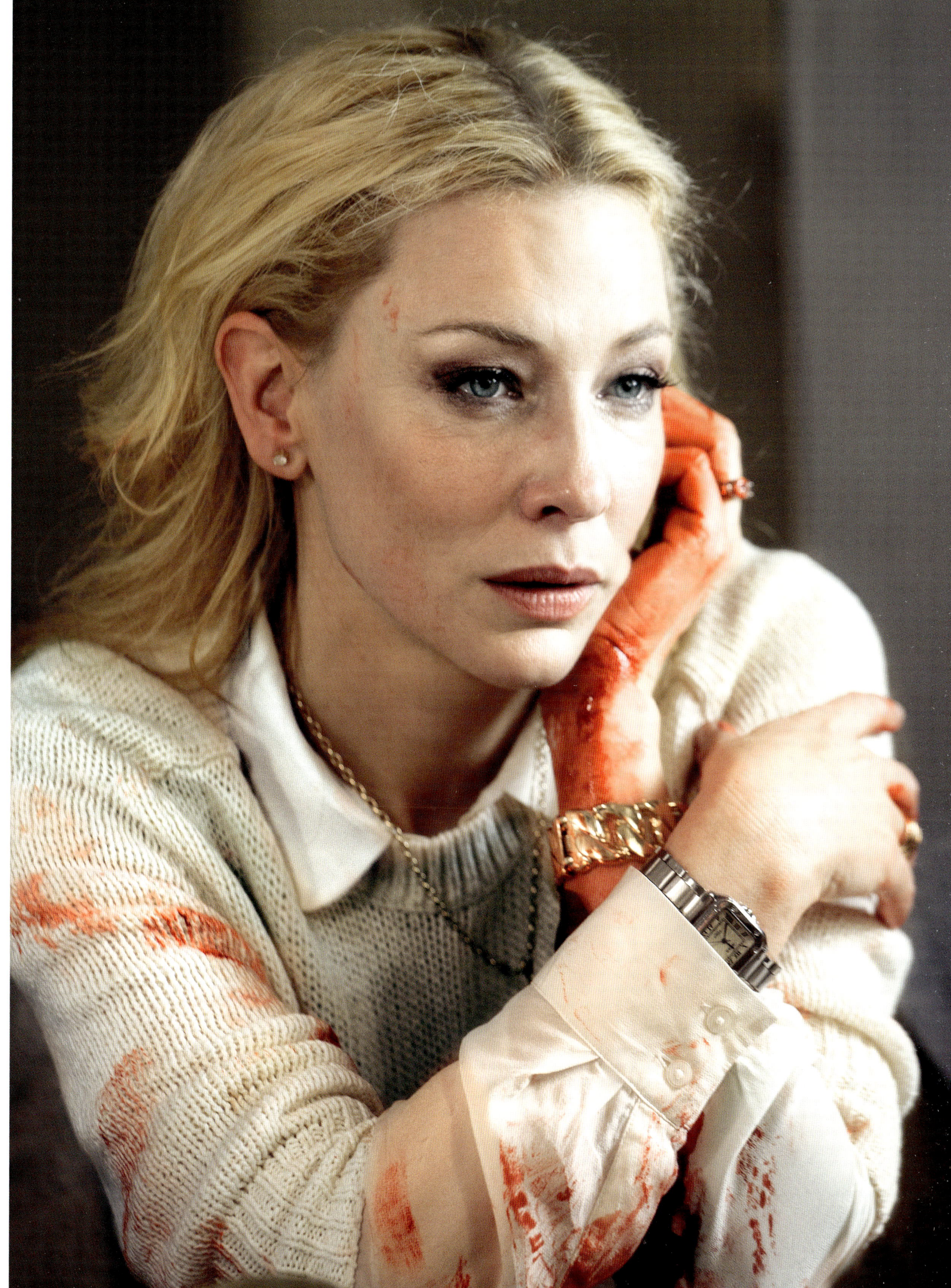

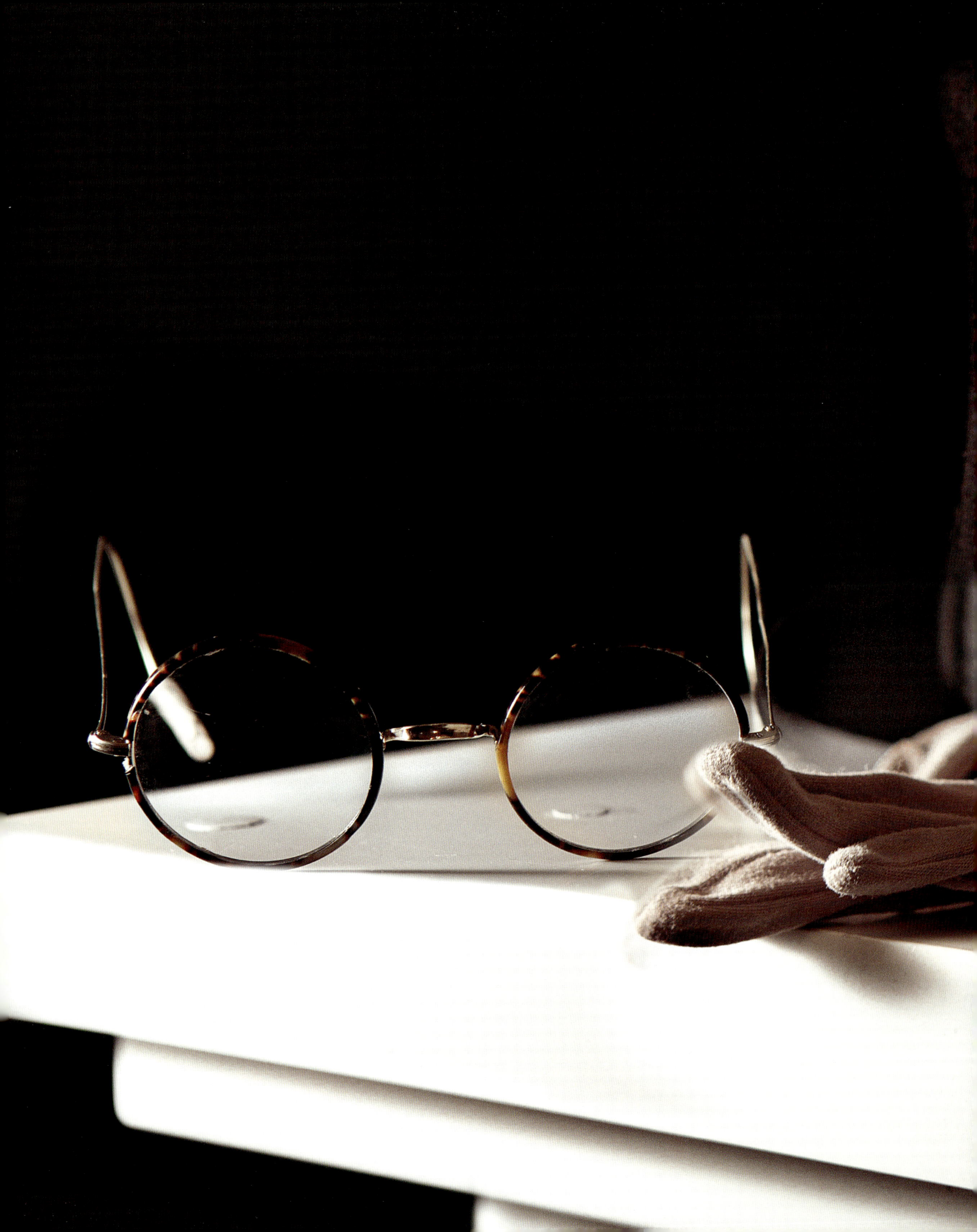

5 MINUTE CALL

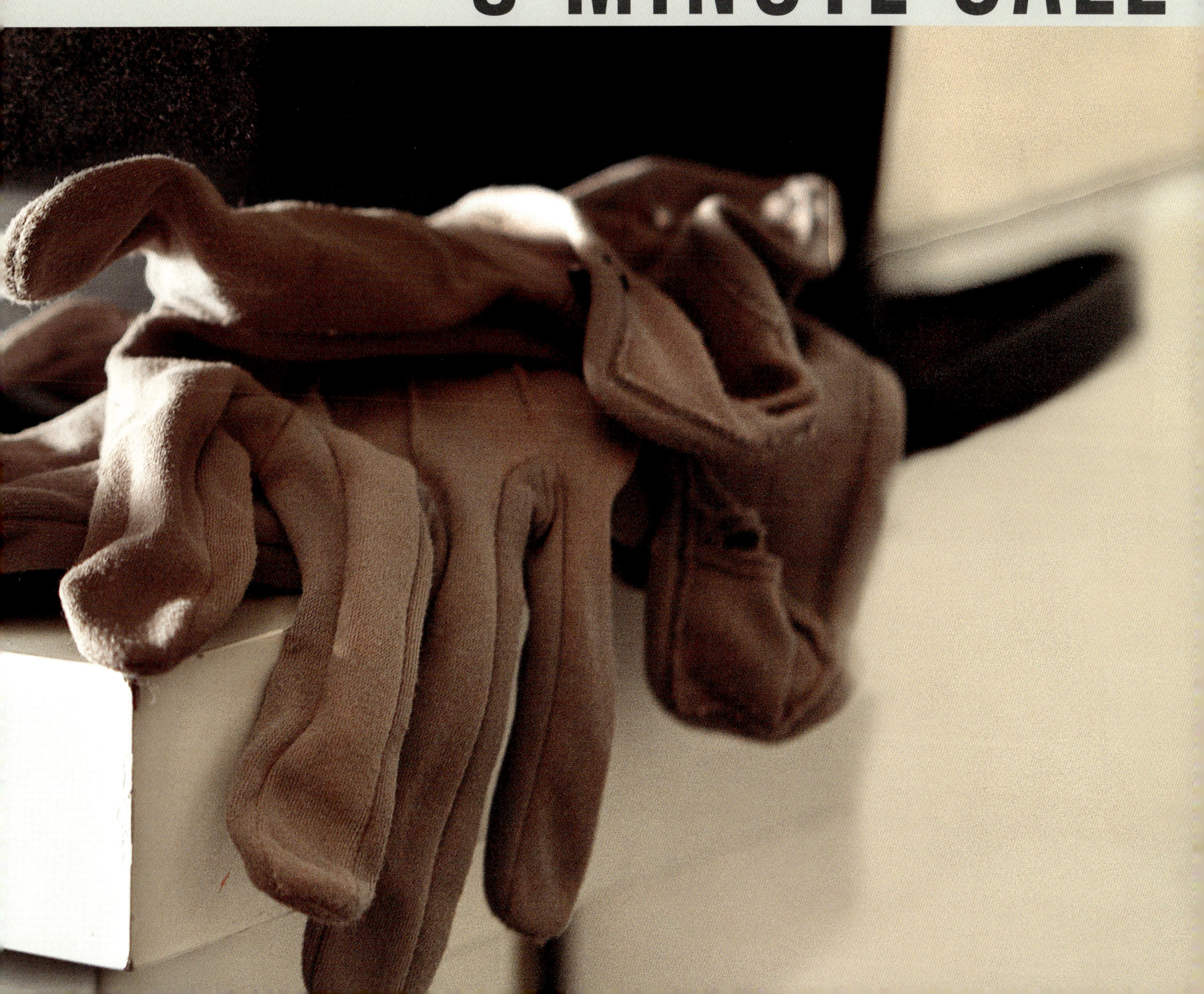

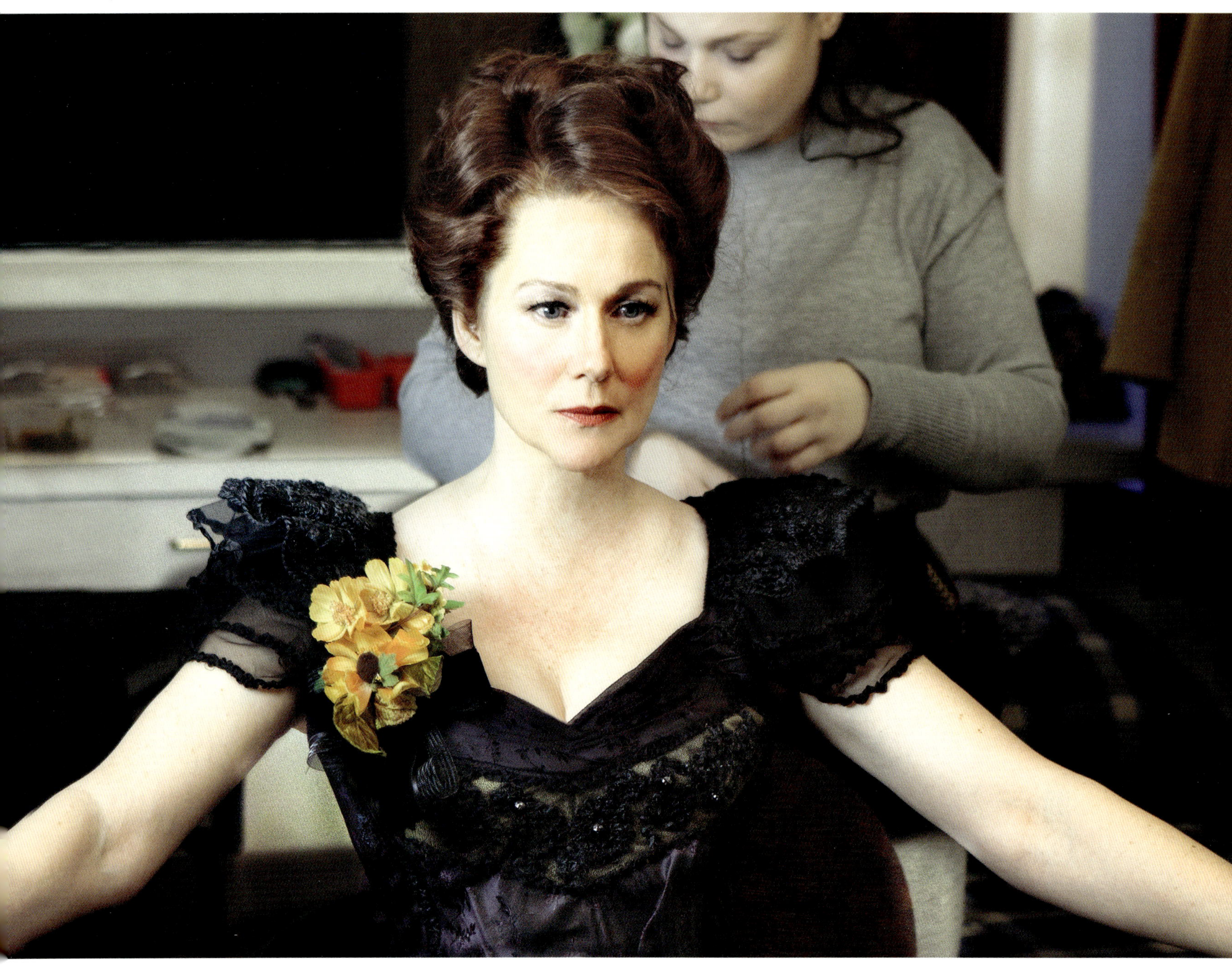

ABOVE: **LAURA LINNEY, *THE LITTLE FOXES*, MANHATTAN THEATRE CLUB, 2017**
Laura alternated the lead role with Cynthia Nixon every other night. That evening it was her turn. It is interesting how a perfect black dress can set the mood for its wearer.

OPPOSITE: **ZOË WANAMAKER, *THE CHERRY ORCHARD*, NATIONAL THEATRE, 2011**
Earlier in the session, Zoë had been playing an amusing game with her dresser. At this point, five minutes before leaving the room, the character of Ranyevskaya is taking hold.

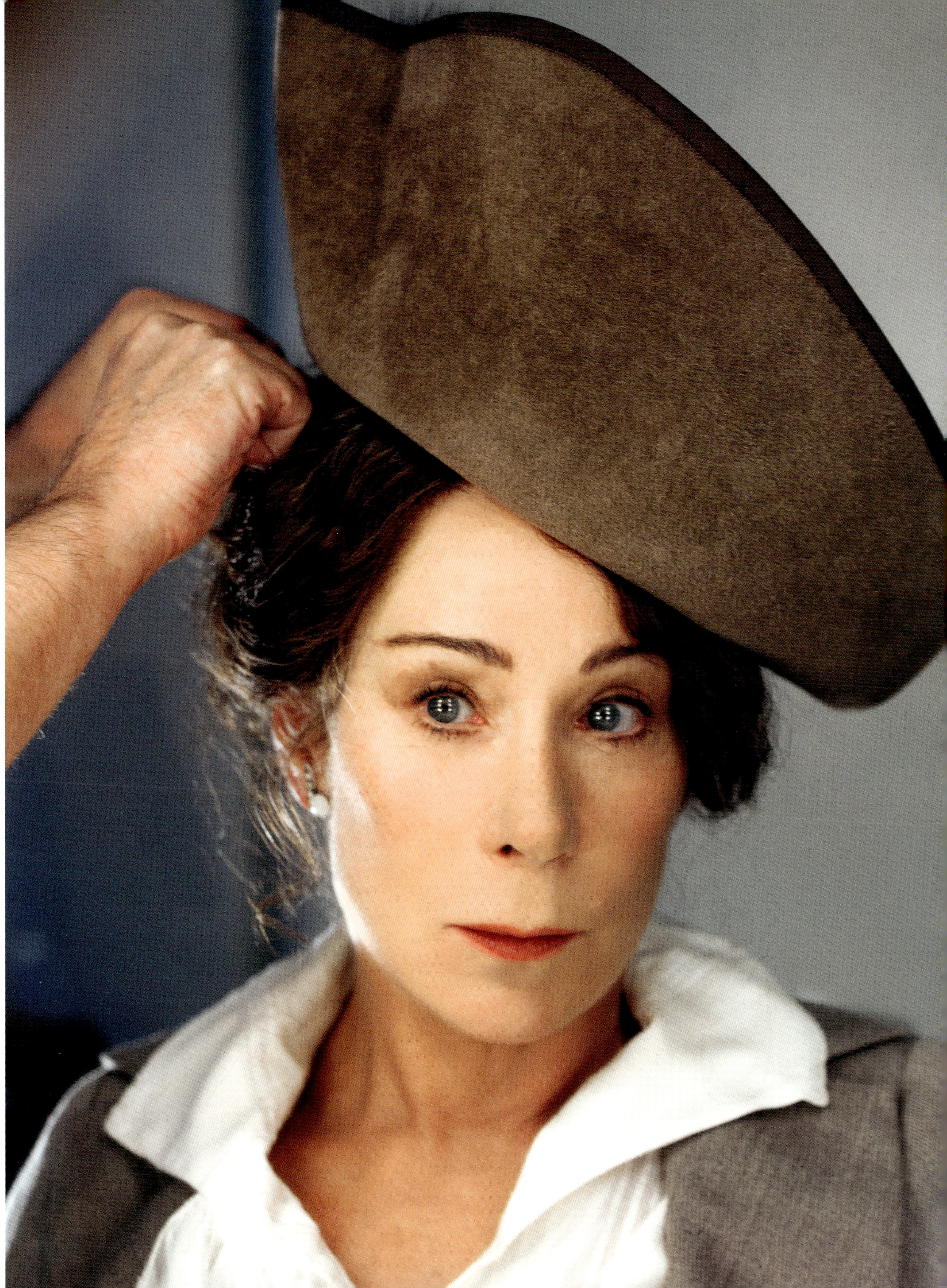

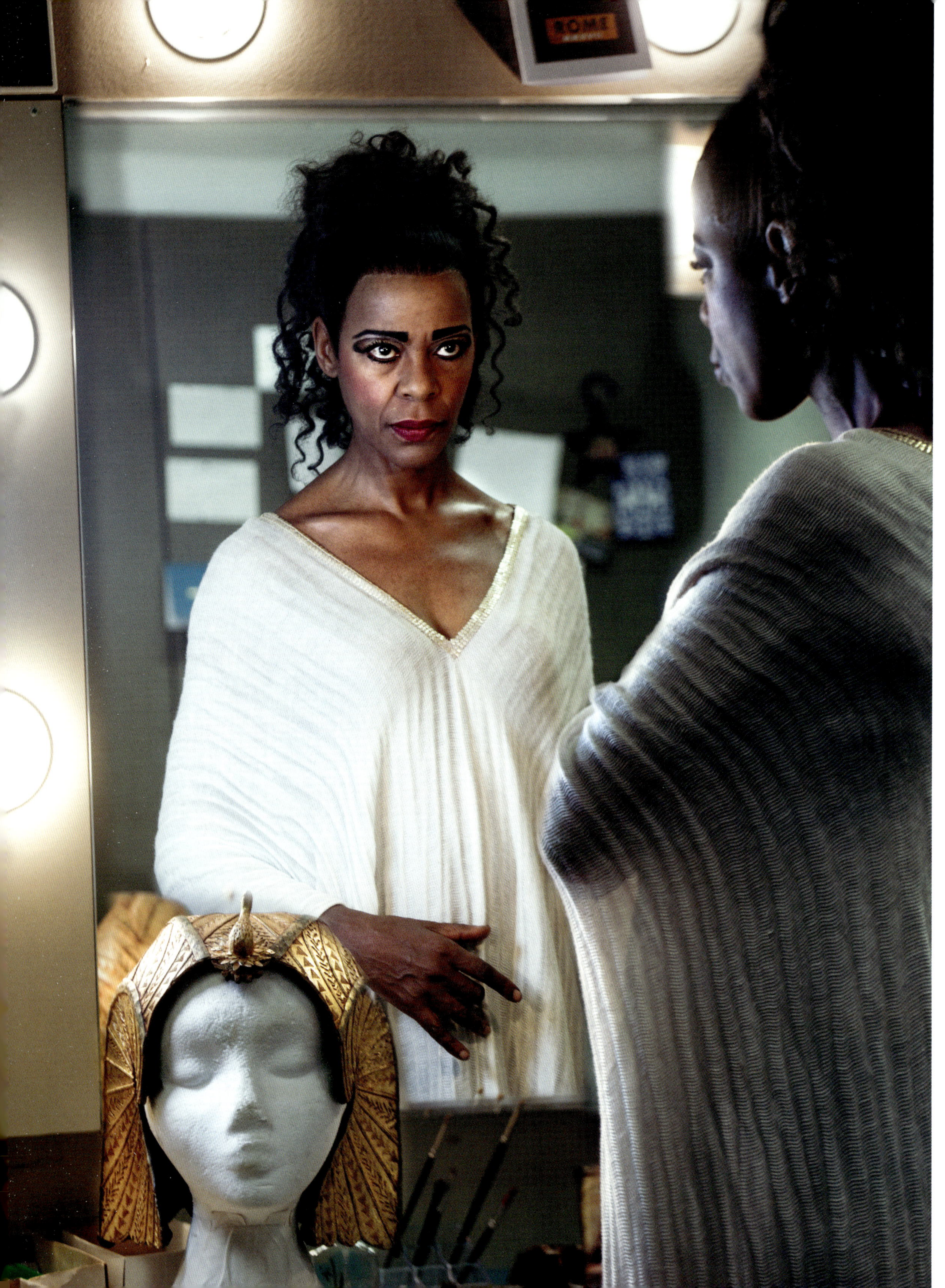
ROME

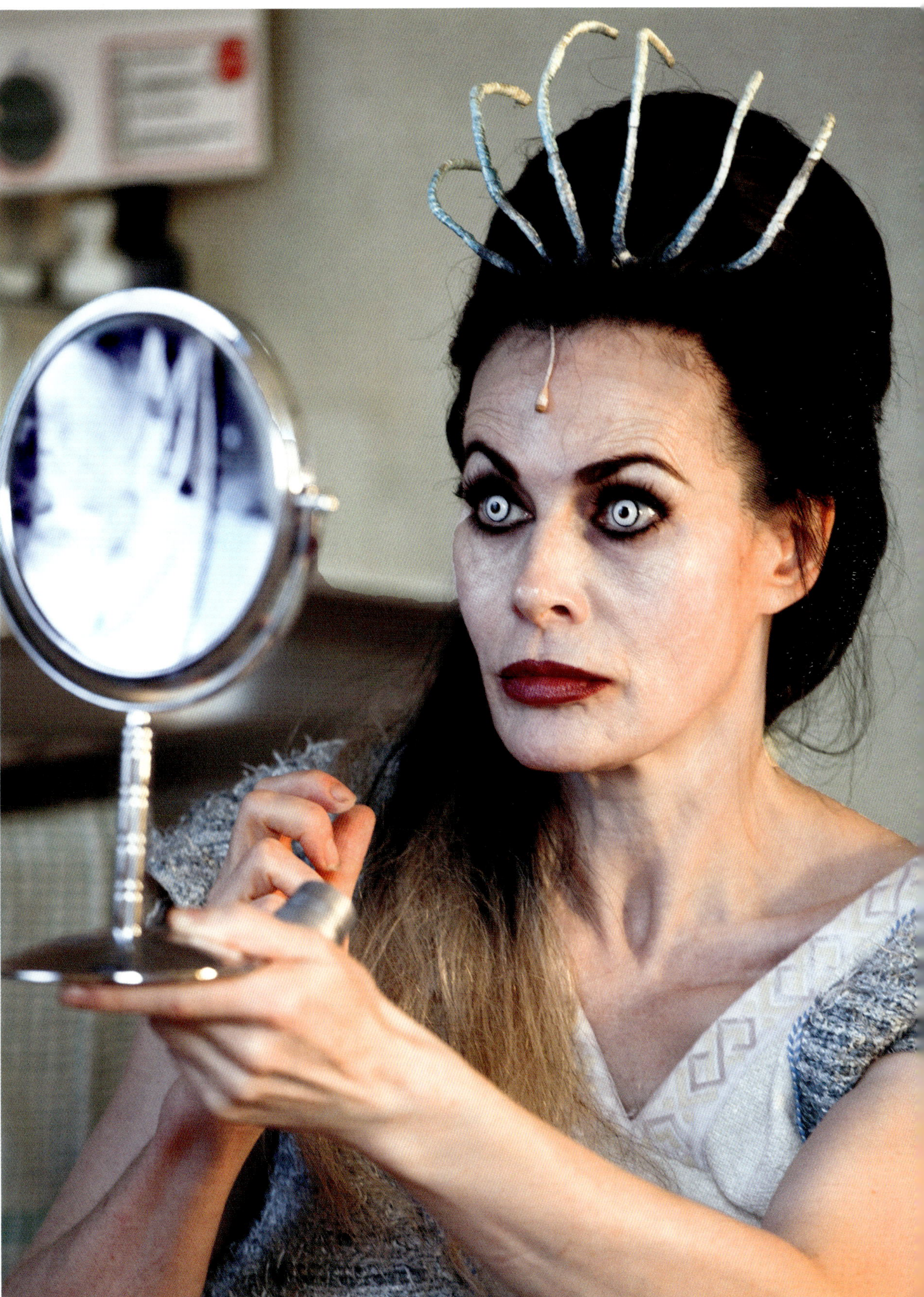

OPPOSITE: **JOSETTE SIMON, *ANTONY AND CLEOPATRA*, RSC, 2017**
It appears as if the fictional character, Cleopatra, is goading the actress into her part.

RIGHT: **SALLY DEXTER, *THE LION THE WITCH AND THE WARDROBE*, KENSINGTON GARDENS, 2012**
Over the years Sally has been a delightful and generous woman to spend time with. I always think of her laughing, but here she is drawn to playing a witch.

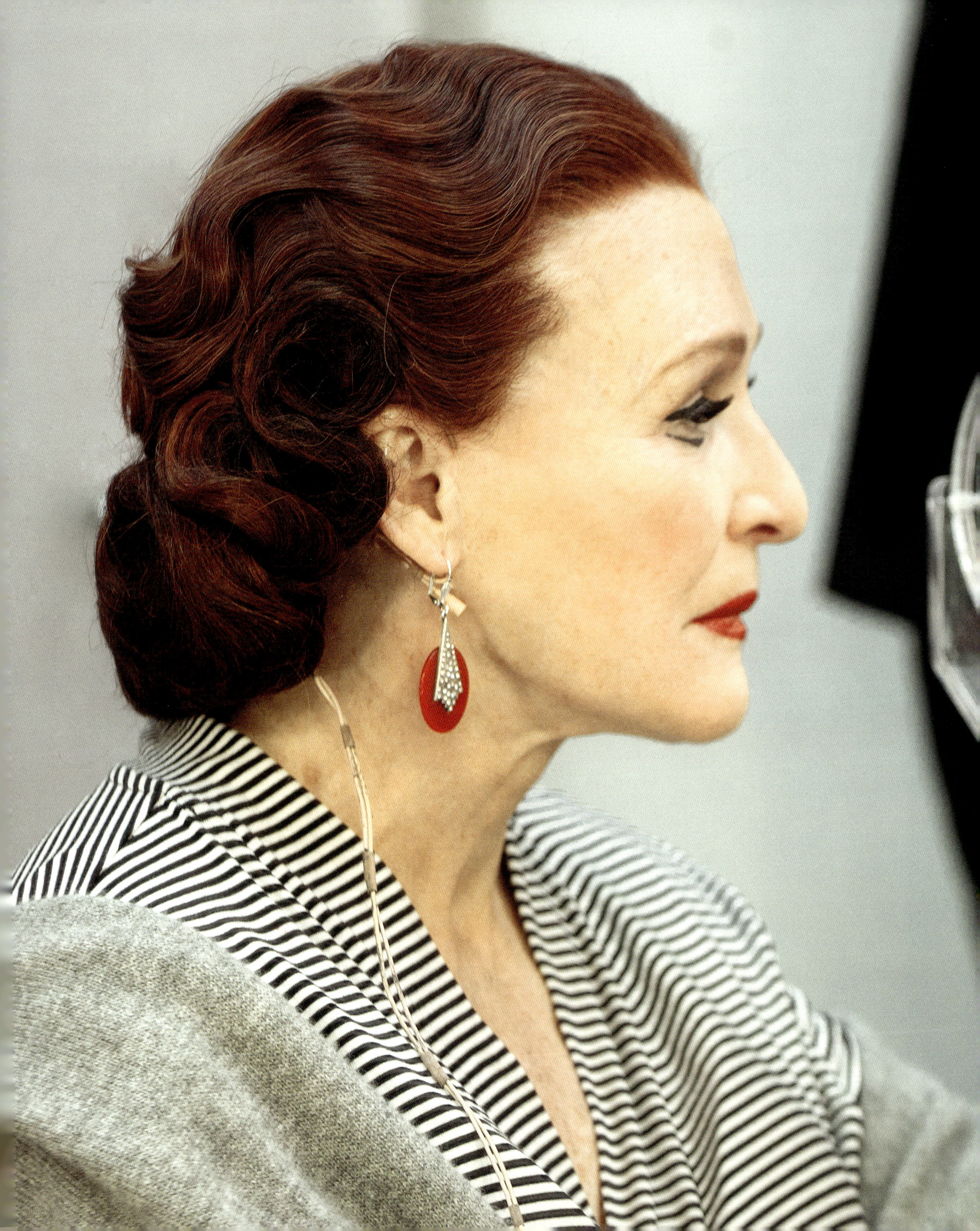

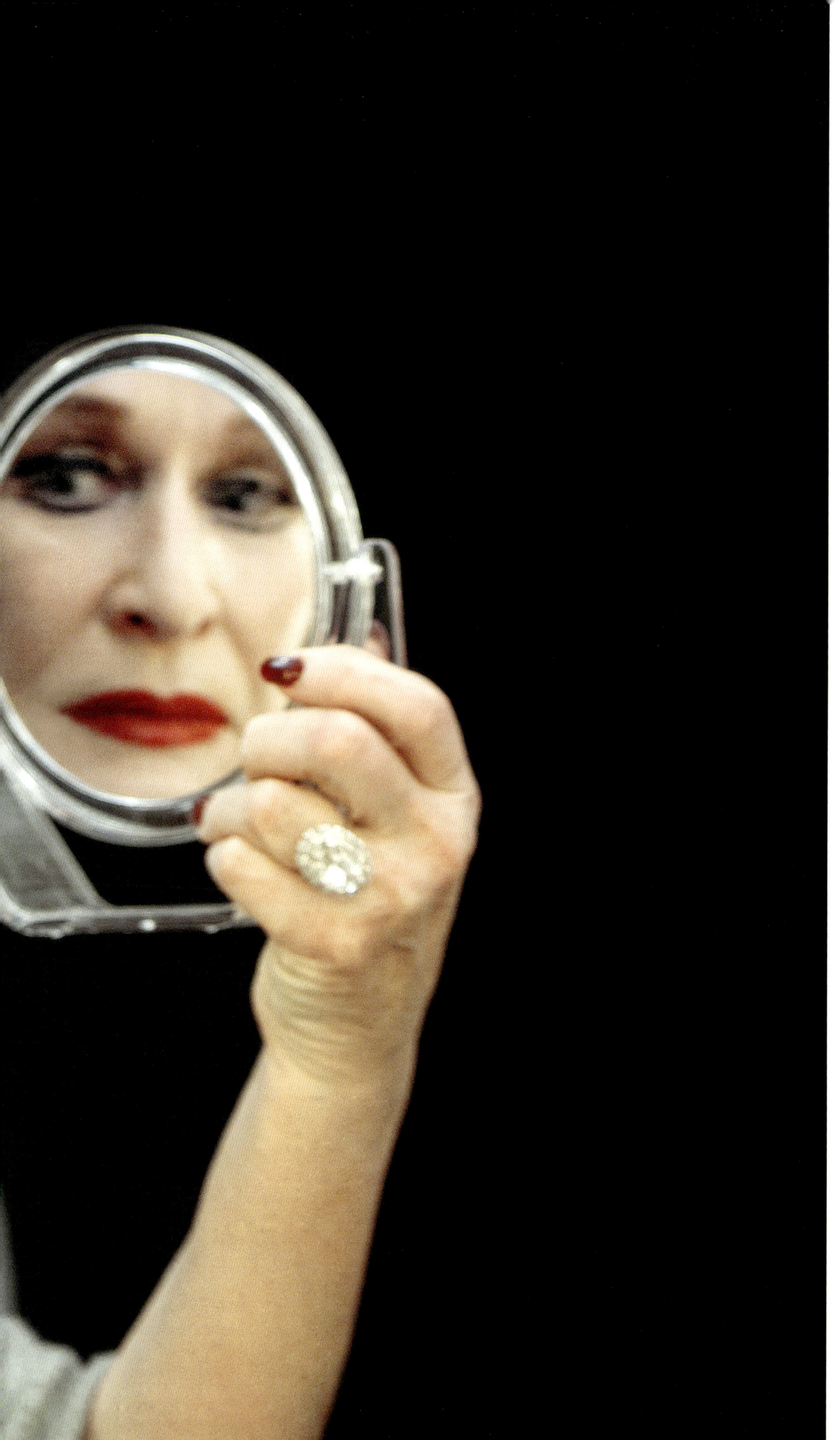

GLENN CLOSE, *SUNSET BOULEVARD*, ENO, LONDON COLISEUM, 2015
Glenn is charming, empathetic and warm-hearted. At the same time, she is a master at playing hard, ambitious characters. The contrasted background draws attention to this paradox. Looking through the lens at Glenn Close feels like a direct line back to Hollywood stars of the past such as Joan Crawford. Intense discipline and focus to succeed.

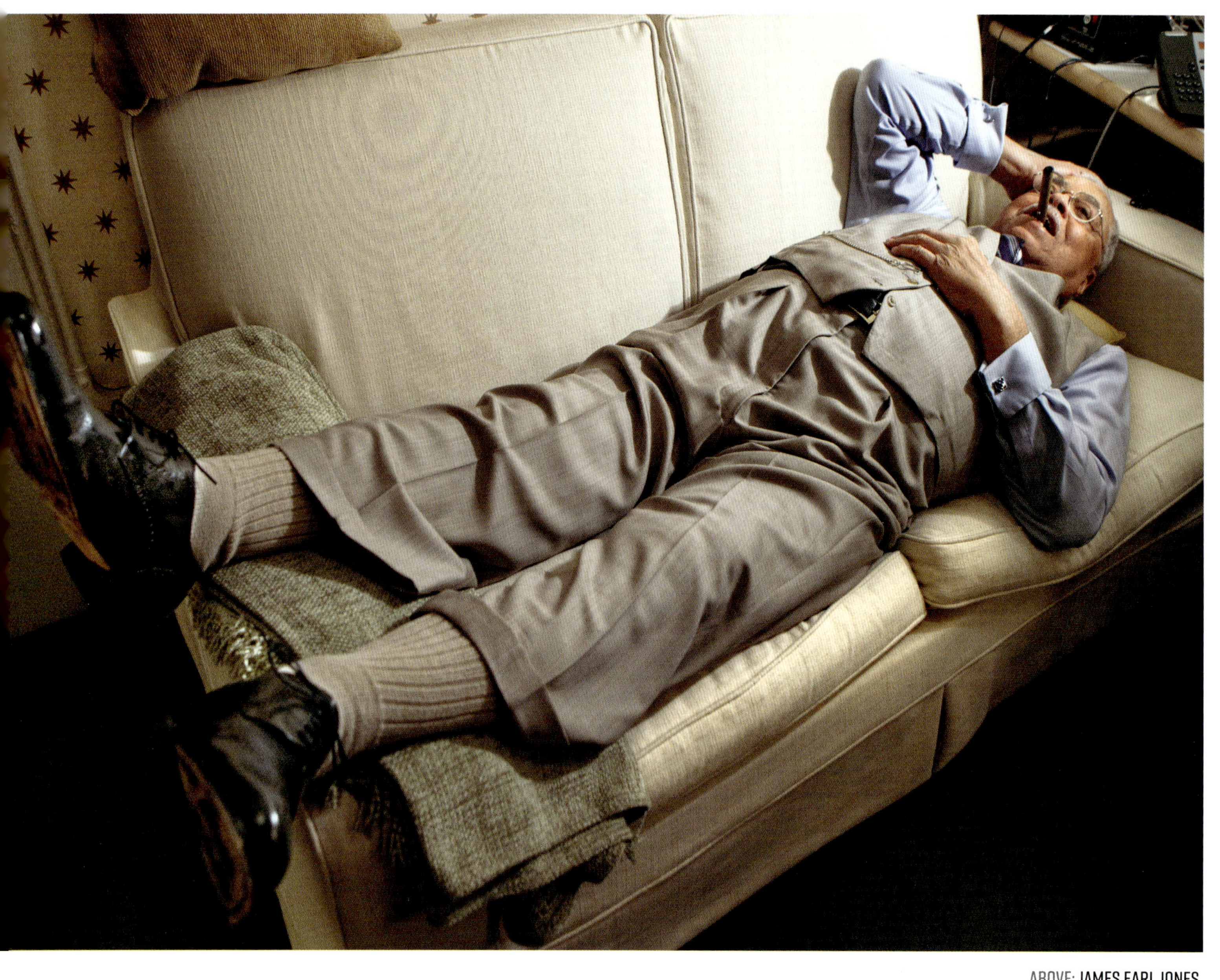

ABOVE: **JAMES EARL JONES, *CAT ON A HOT TIN ROOF*, NOVELLO THEATRE, 2010**
He said to me, 'Whatever you do, don't tell my doctor I'm smoking.' One of the titan actors and I'd love to see him playing King Lear.

OPPOSITE: **JIM BROADBENT, *A CHRISTMAS CAROL*, NOËL COWARD THEATRE, 2016**
Jim is the most charming, gentle man, with a riotous tongue when he feels like it. Here he is quietly contemplating the part of Scrooge, the miser.

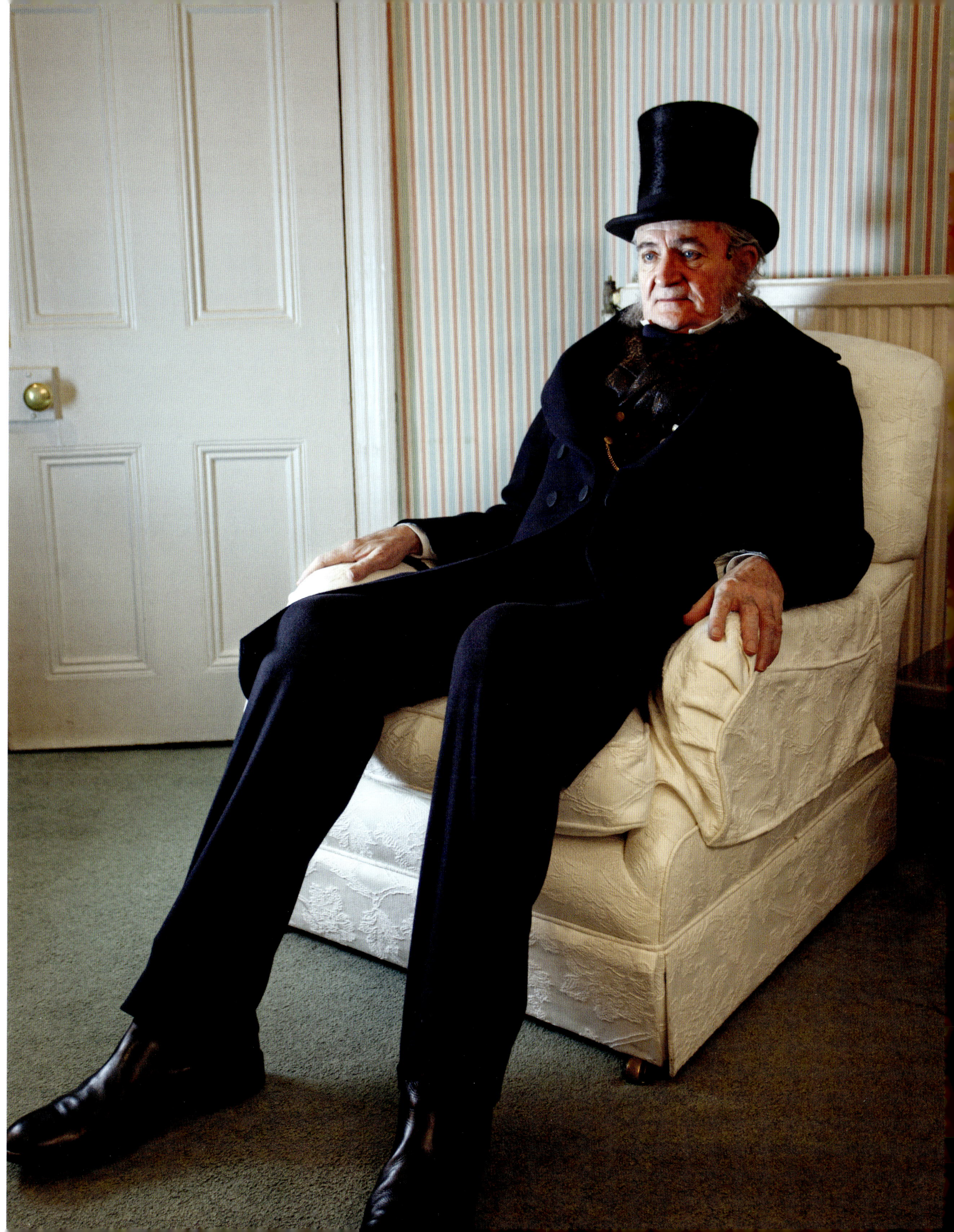

MEMBERS OF THE CAST, *ALICE'S ADVENTURES UNDERGROUND*, VAULT FESTIVAL, 2015
Waiting to be called can be an art in itself.

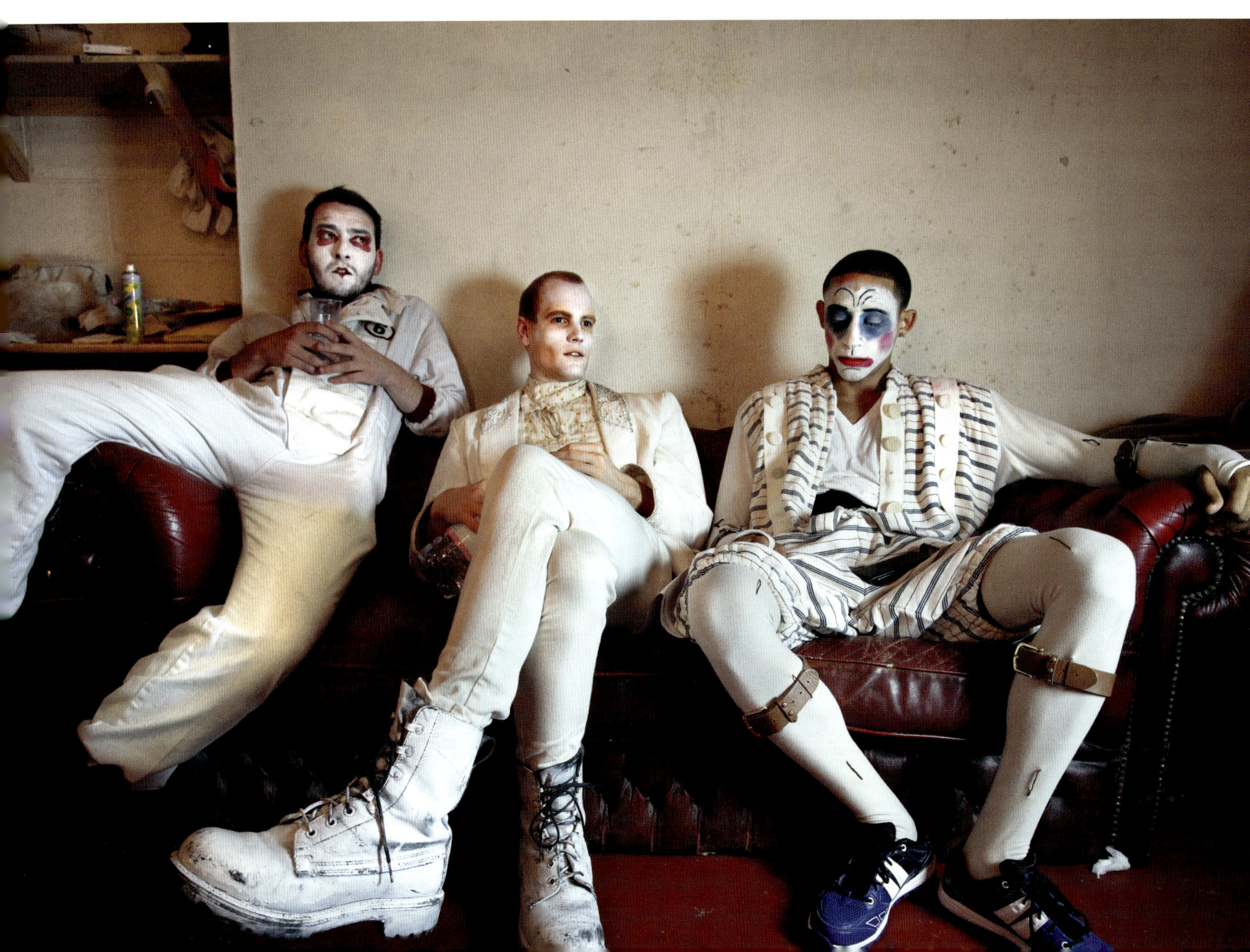

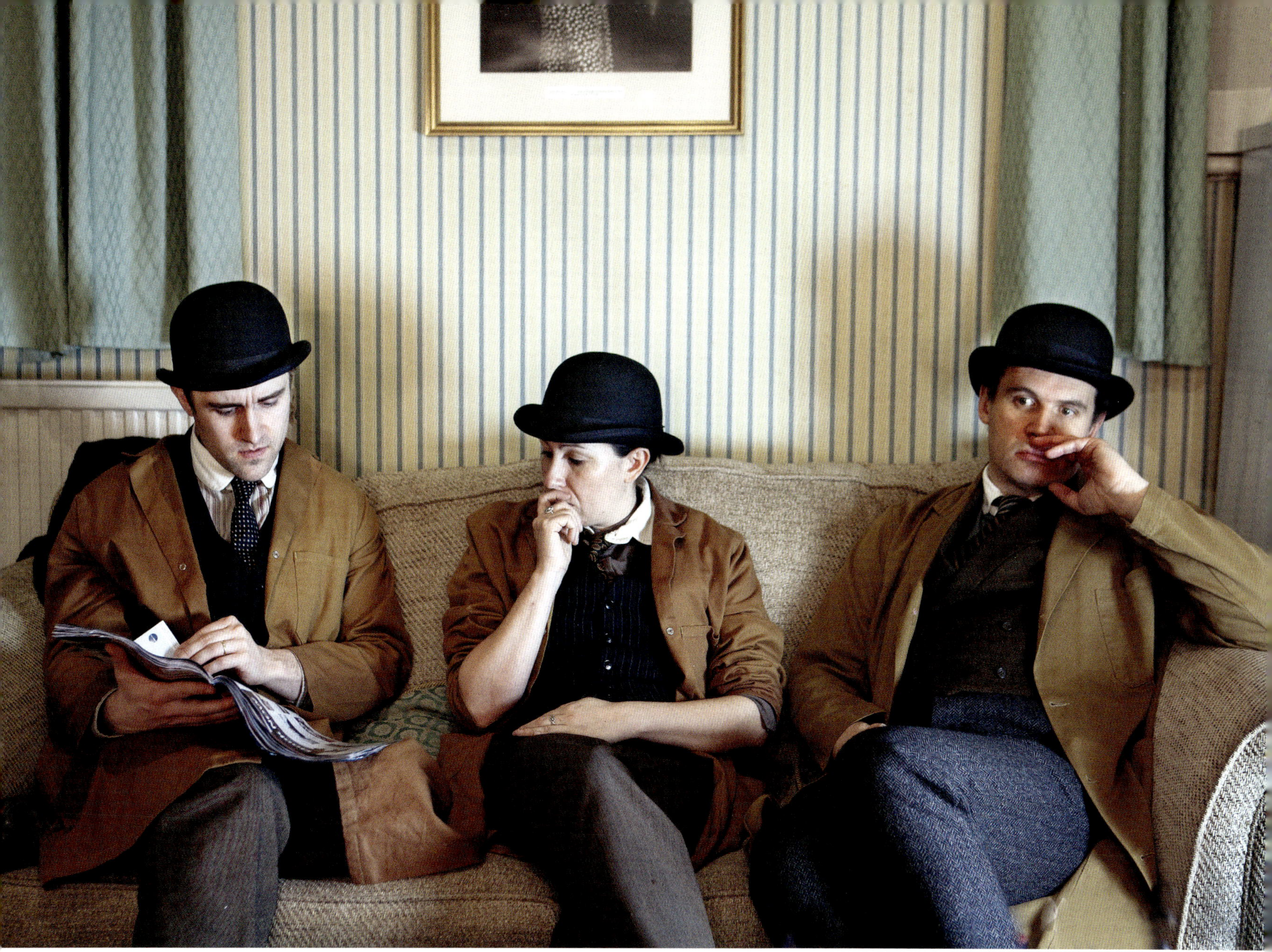

MEMBERS OF THE CAST, *A CHRISTMAS CAROL*, NOËL COWARD THEATRE, 2016
Sitting on a sofa in the room which Gertrude Lawrence made her own in the 1930s and looking relaxed, but always alert for their cue.

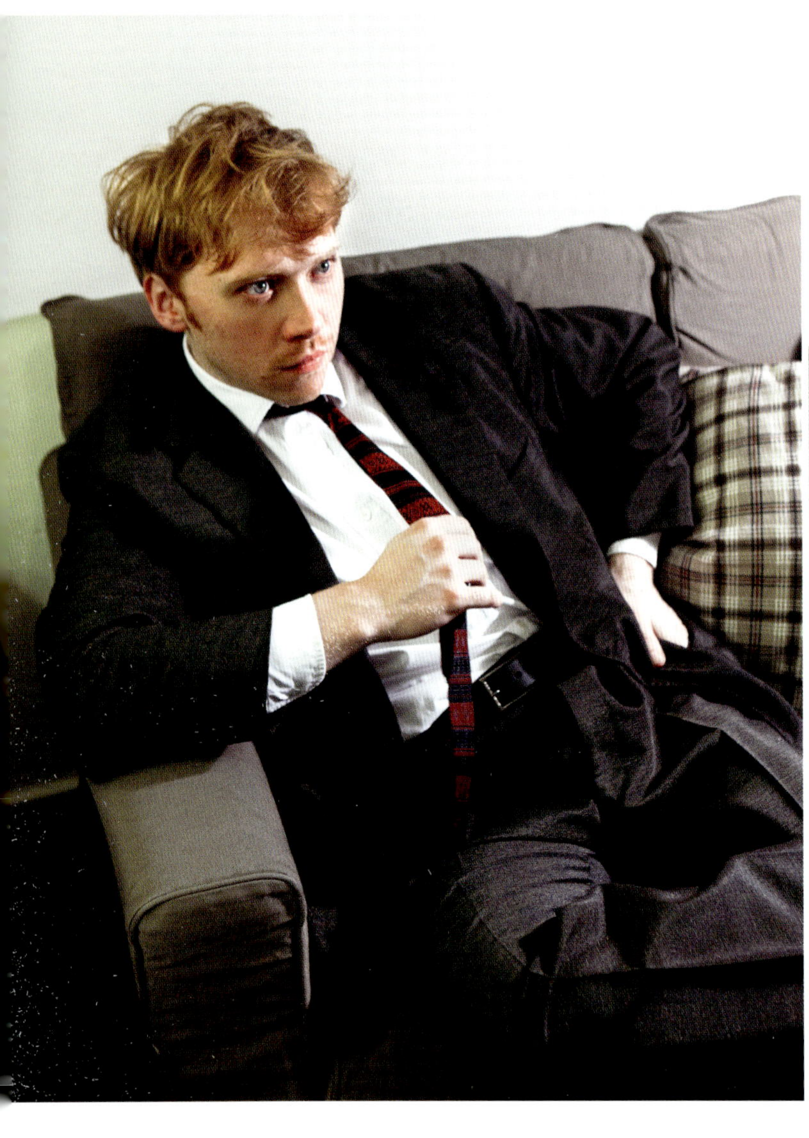

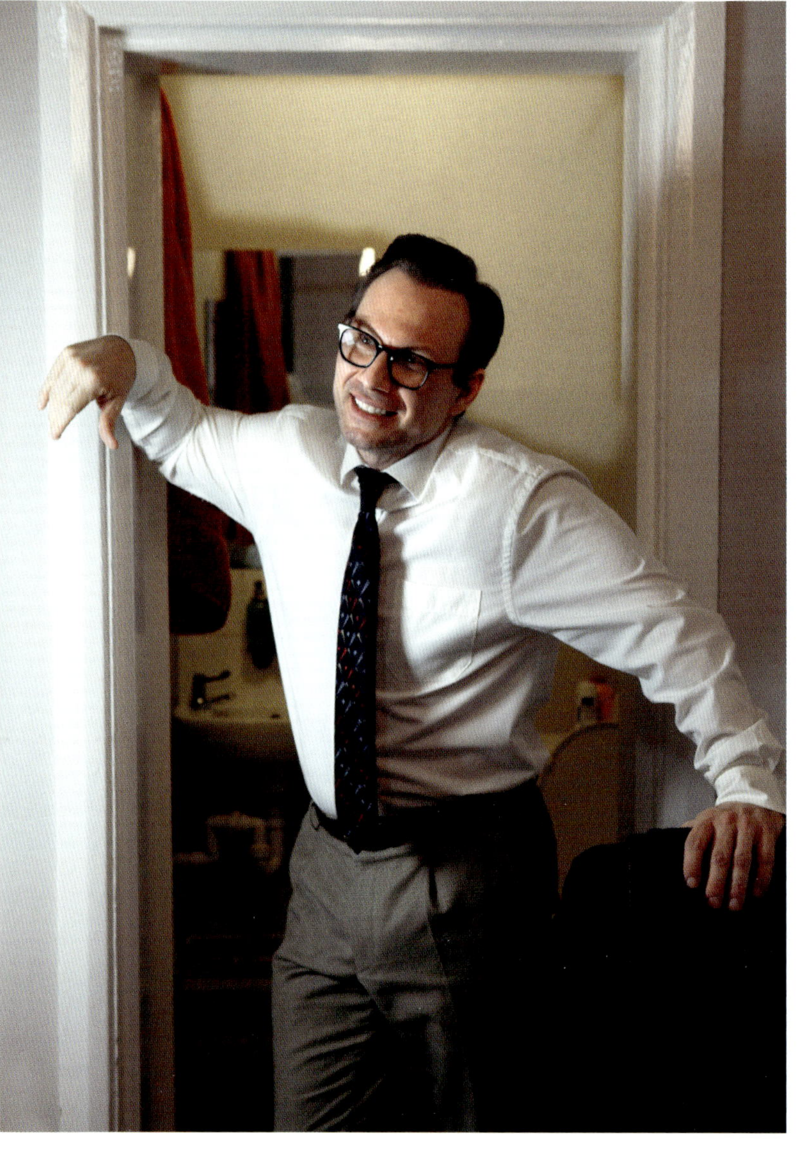

ABOVE: **RUPERT GRINT, *MOJO*, HAROLD PINTER THEATRE, 2014**
Rupert, incredibly famous thanks to Harry Potter, was on less familiar ground in the theatre. By the end of the run his performance prompted other actors in the company to say he was the best player.

RIGHT: **CHRISTIAN SLATER, *GLENGARRY GLEN ROSS*, PLAYHOUSE THEATRE, 2018**
I hope that more top American film actors are asked to play in London. They love it. And the public loves them.

OPPOSITE: **ROBERT VAUGHN, *TWELVE ANGRY MEN*, GARRICK THEATRE, 2013**
It is my hunch that Robert knew he had a serious illness and gave himself a present to perform on the stage in London. He was a perfect American gentleman. Thank you, Robert.

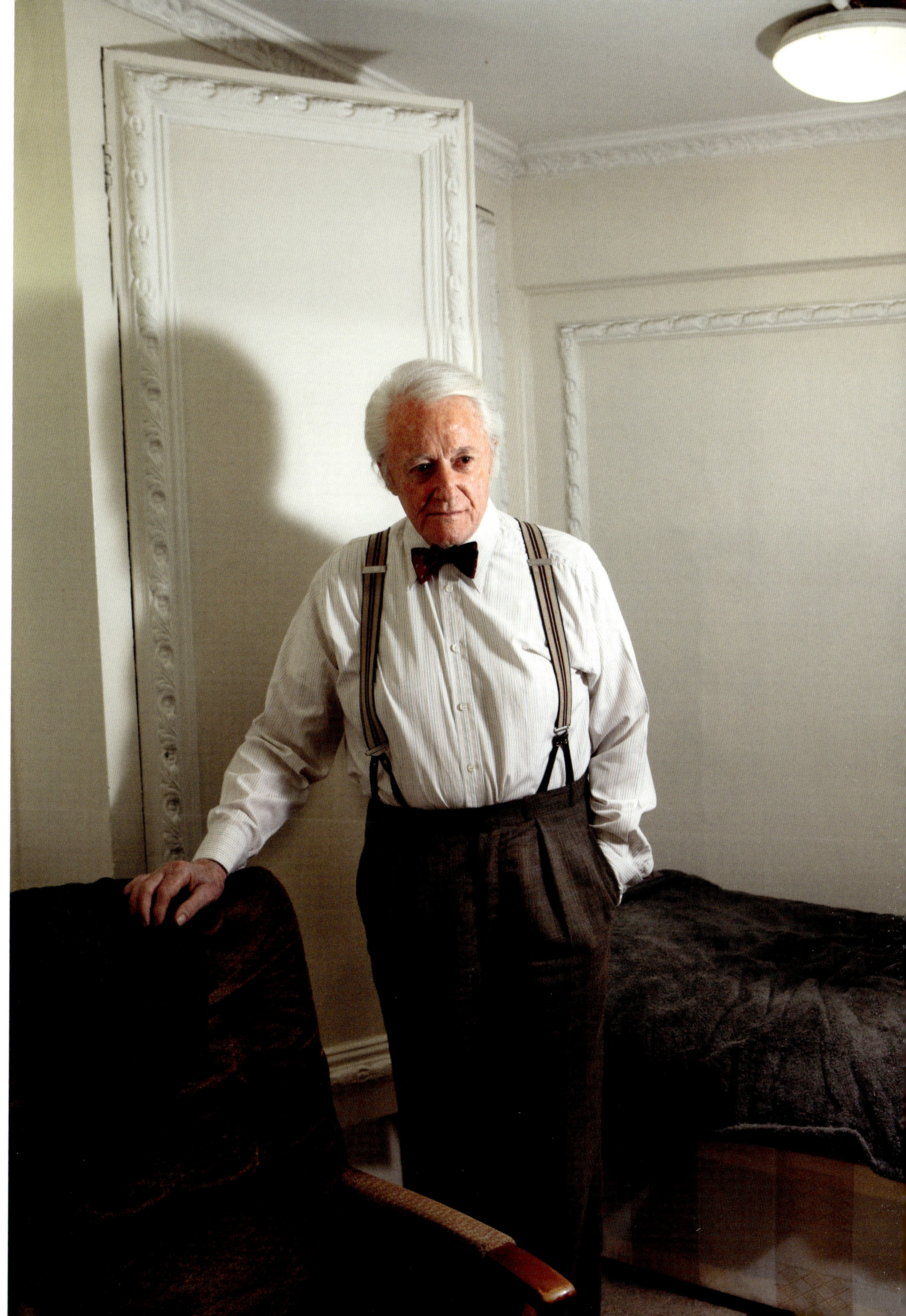

JANET SUZMAN, *ROSE*,
HOME, MANCHESTER, 2017

The tour de force that is Janet Suzman, performing a one-woman show about the Holocaust, aged 79. Whenever I shoot Janet, I am reminded of my very first encounter with her. My life as a photographer was just beginning and Jonathan Miller gave me my first paid job, shooting *Andromache* at the Old Vic. Janet played the lead. Buckets of enthusiasm on my part was not yet tempered by experience and during a rehearsal I took one too many shots, in an attempt to capture a powerful scene. I was politely asked to leave.

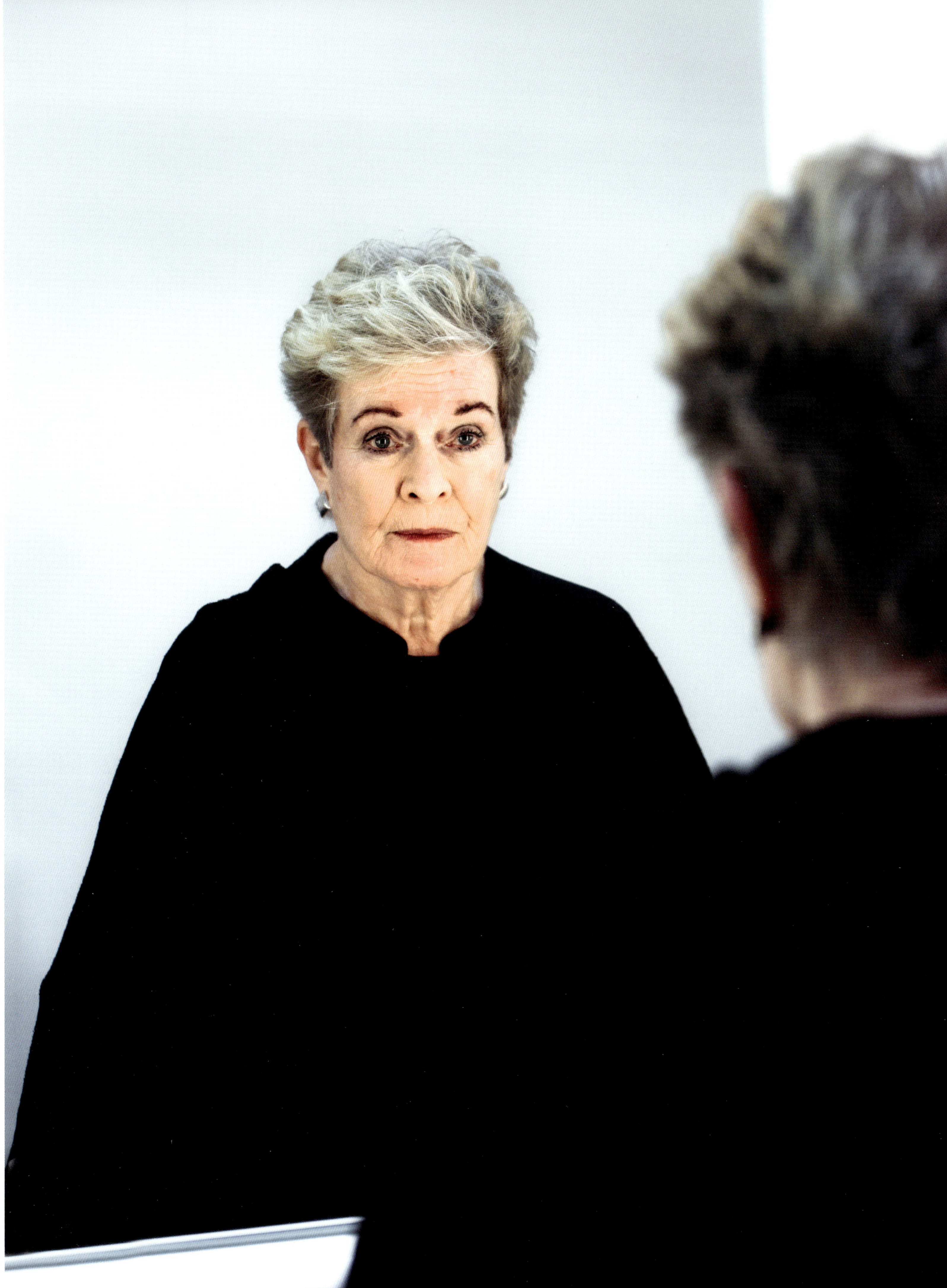

ANTONY SHER, *HENRY IV PART ONE*, RSC, 2016
Antony's astounding versatility here extends to the tragi-comic Falstaff. He is a virtuoso of make-up and physical performance.

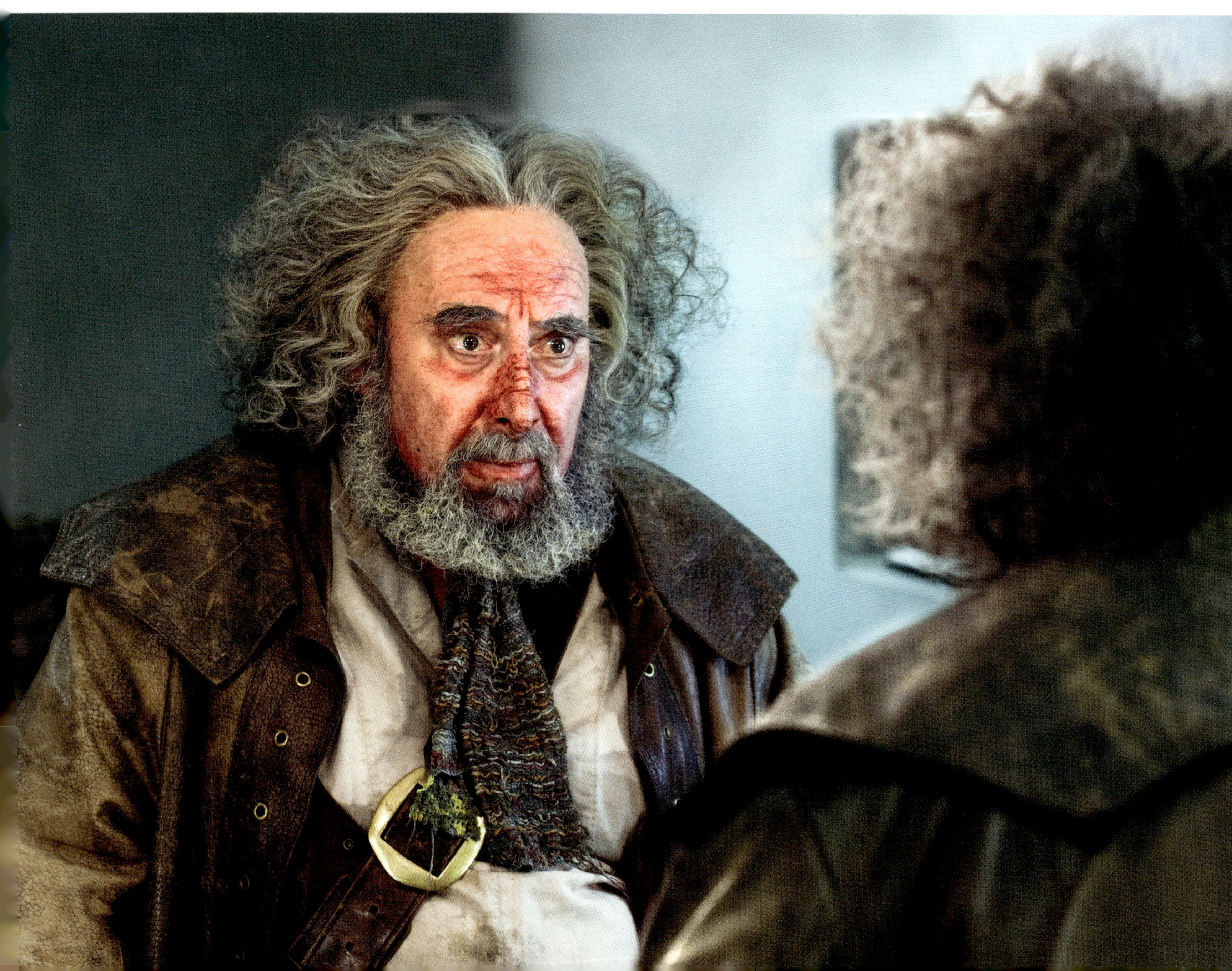

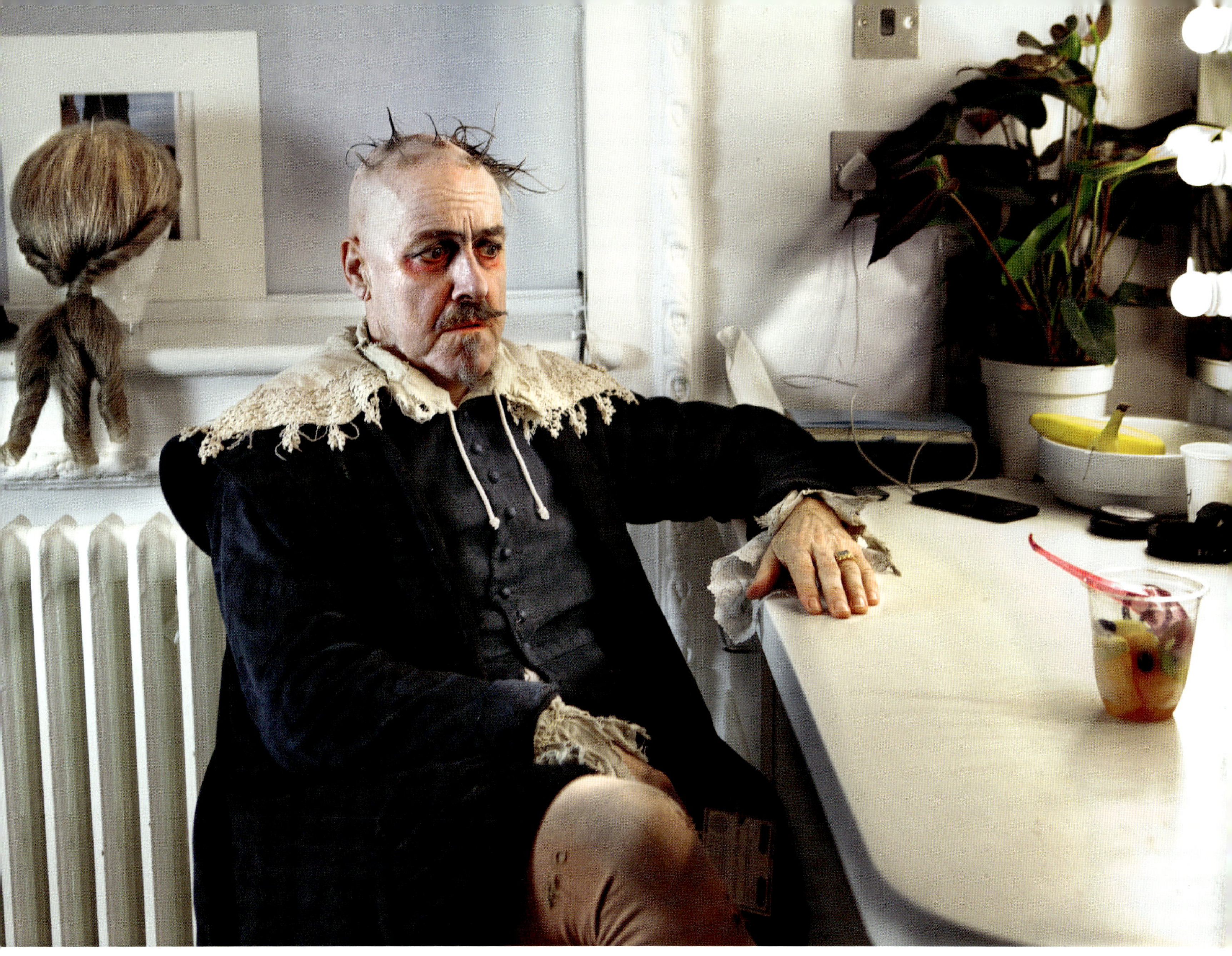

GRIFF RHYS JONES, *THE MISER*, GARRICK THEATRE, 2017

By the time I saw Griff again, thirty-four years later, (see p.17), the bottle of red wine had turned into a fruit salad. Griff is a master of playing farce.

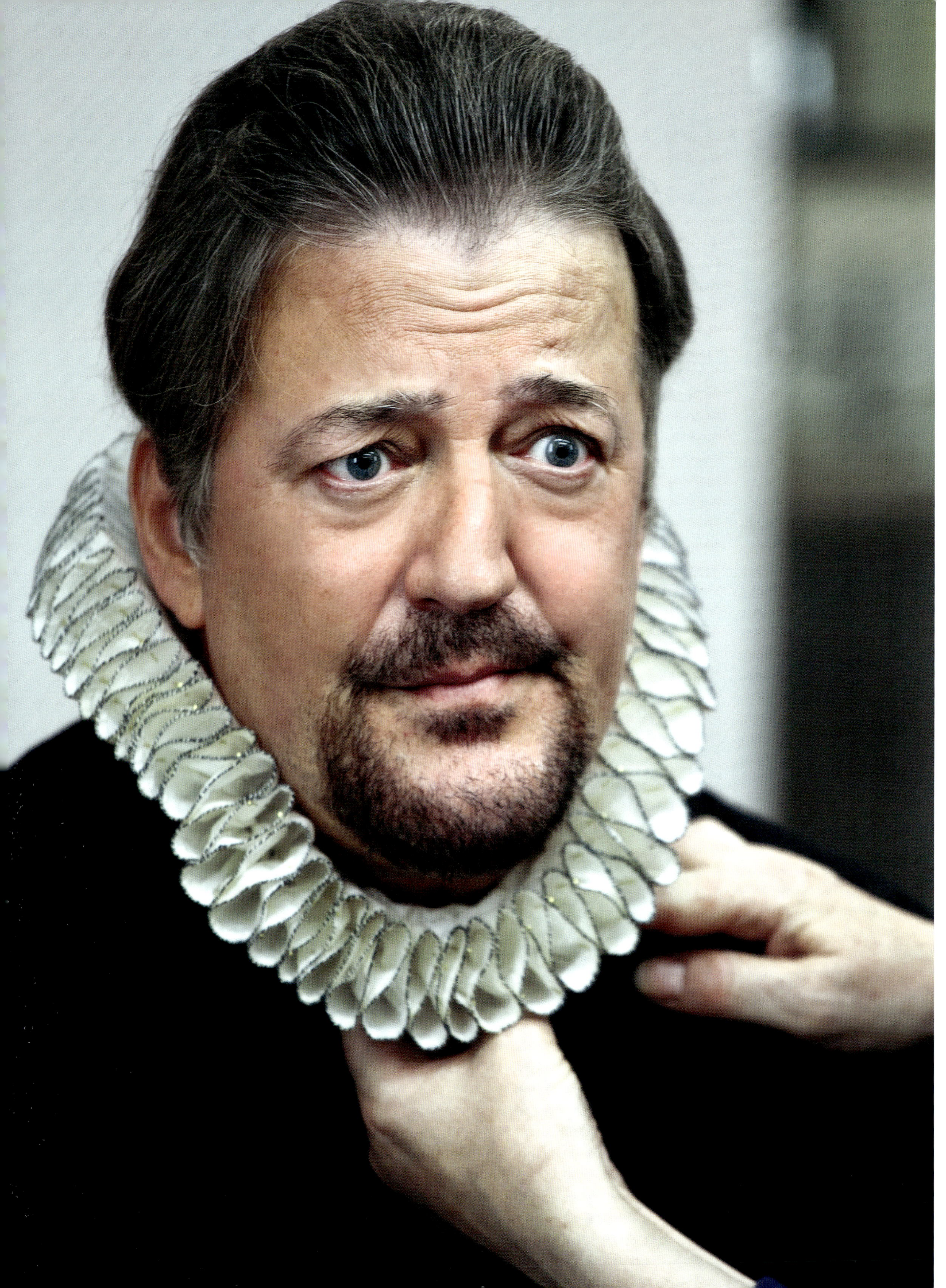

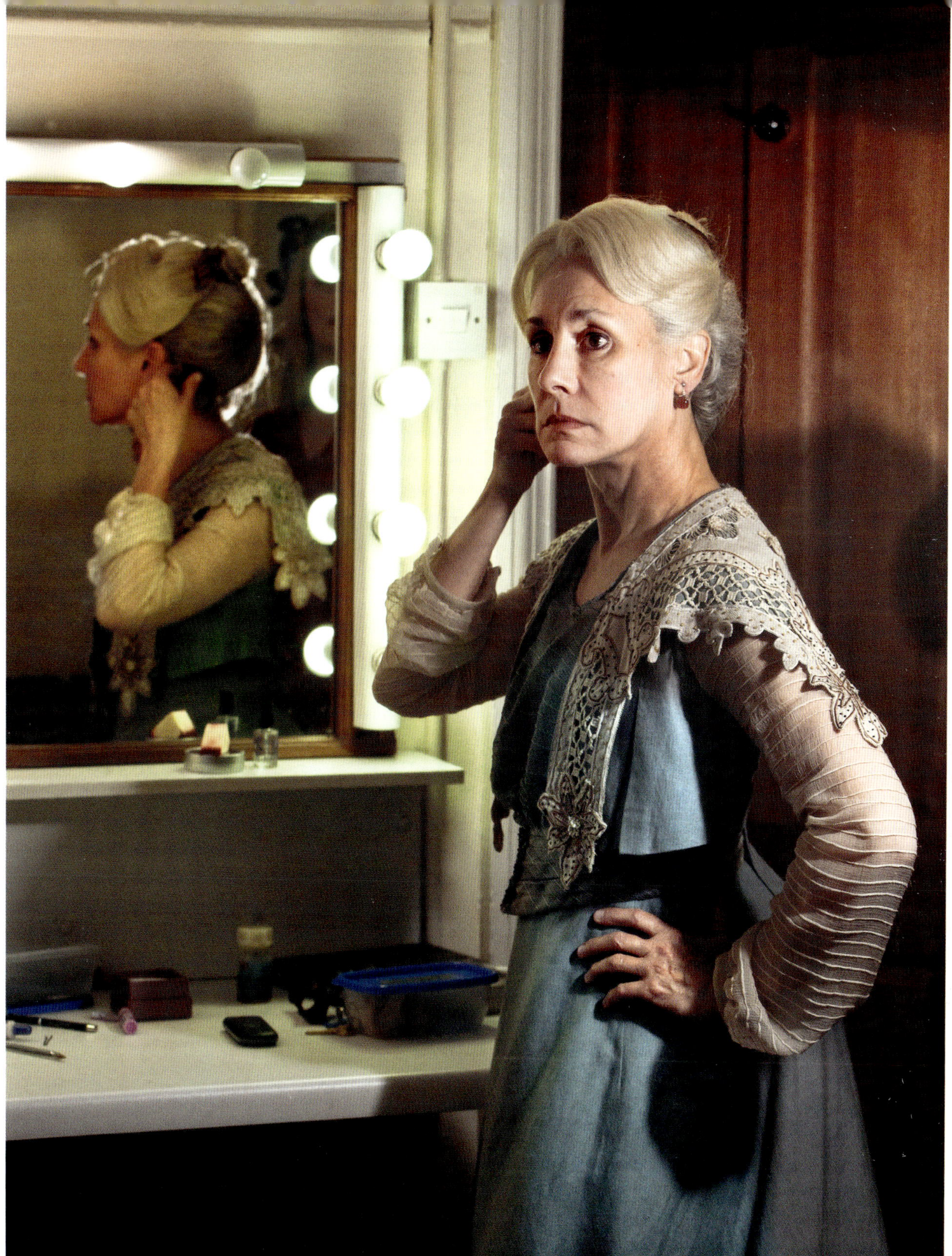

OPPOSITE: **STEPHEN FRY, *TWELFTH NIGHT*, APOLLO THEATRE, 2012**
This was the first time Stephen had played in the theatre since a case of stage fright seventeen years before. To perform the melancholic Malvolio was an incredibly bold choice to make for his return.

RIGHT: **LAURIE METCALF, *LONG DAY'S JOURNEY INTO NIGHT*, APOLLO THEATRE, 2012**
Laurie had a prosthetic hand, made to simulate the arthritic hands of her character Mary Tyrone. I can't remember whether she strapped it on before, or after, playing cards almost every night with her fellow actor Kyle Stoller.

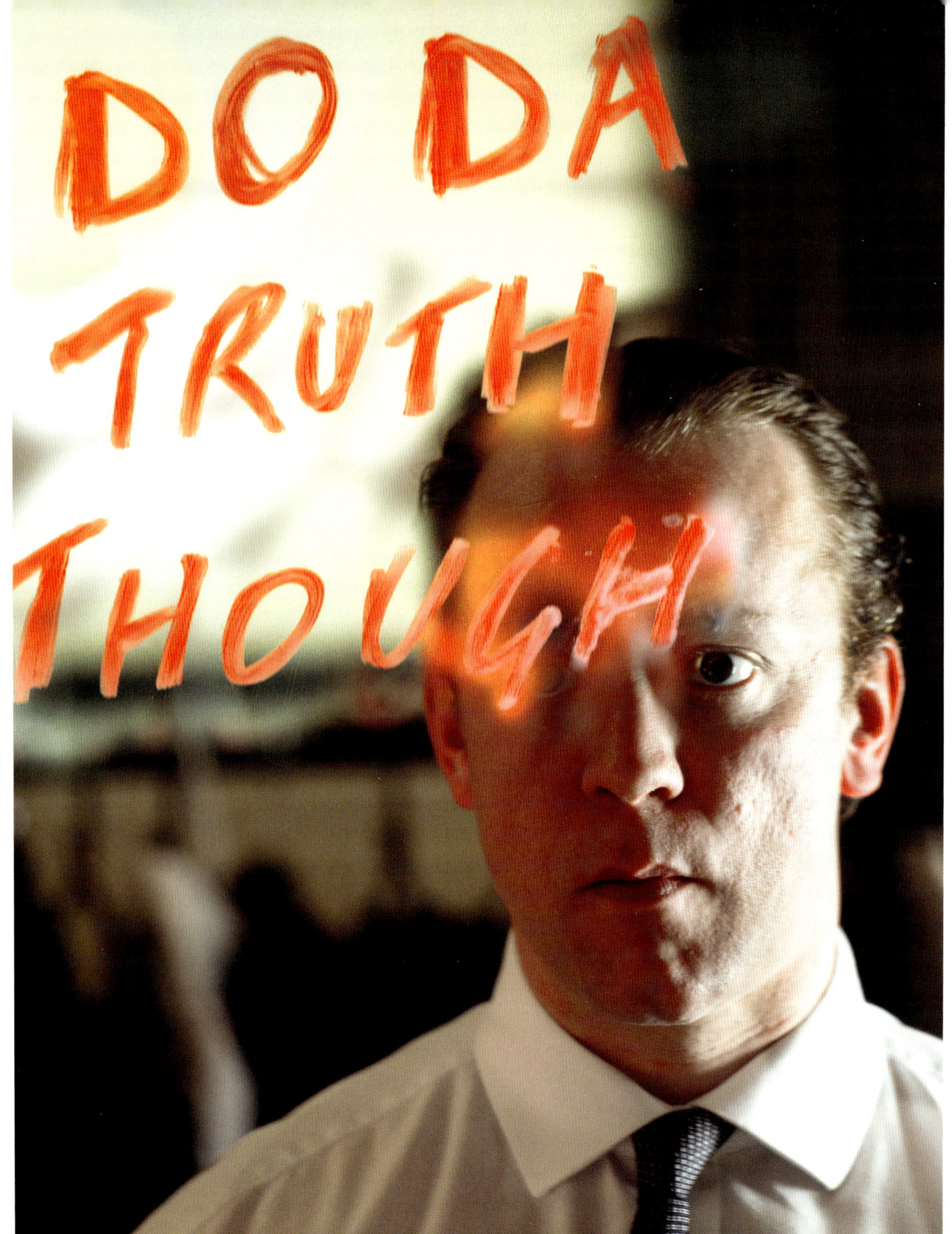

LEFT: SAM TROUGHTON, *BULL*, YOUNG VIC, 2015
'Truth' is a vital concept of acting. Although the truth is often relative, and not ultimate, there's no way a great performance can be fake.

OPPOSITE: SOPHIE THOMPSON, *SHE STOOPS TO CONQUER*, NATIONAL THEATRE, 2012
Due to a willingness to be physical in her performances, Sophie, an Olivier Award winner, is also a specialist at wearing extra padding for tumbles and falls, necessary for many farce and Restoration comedies.

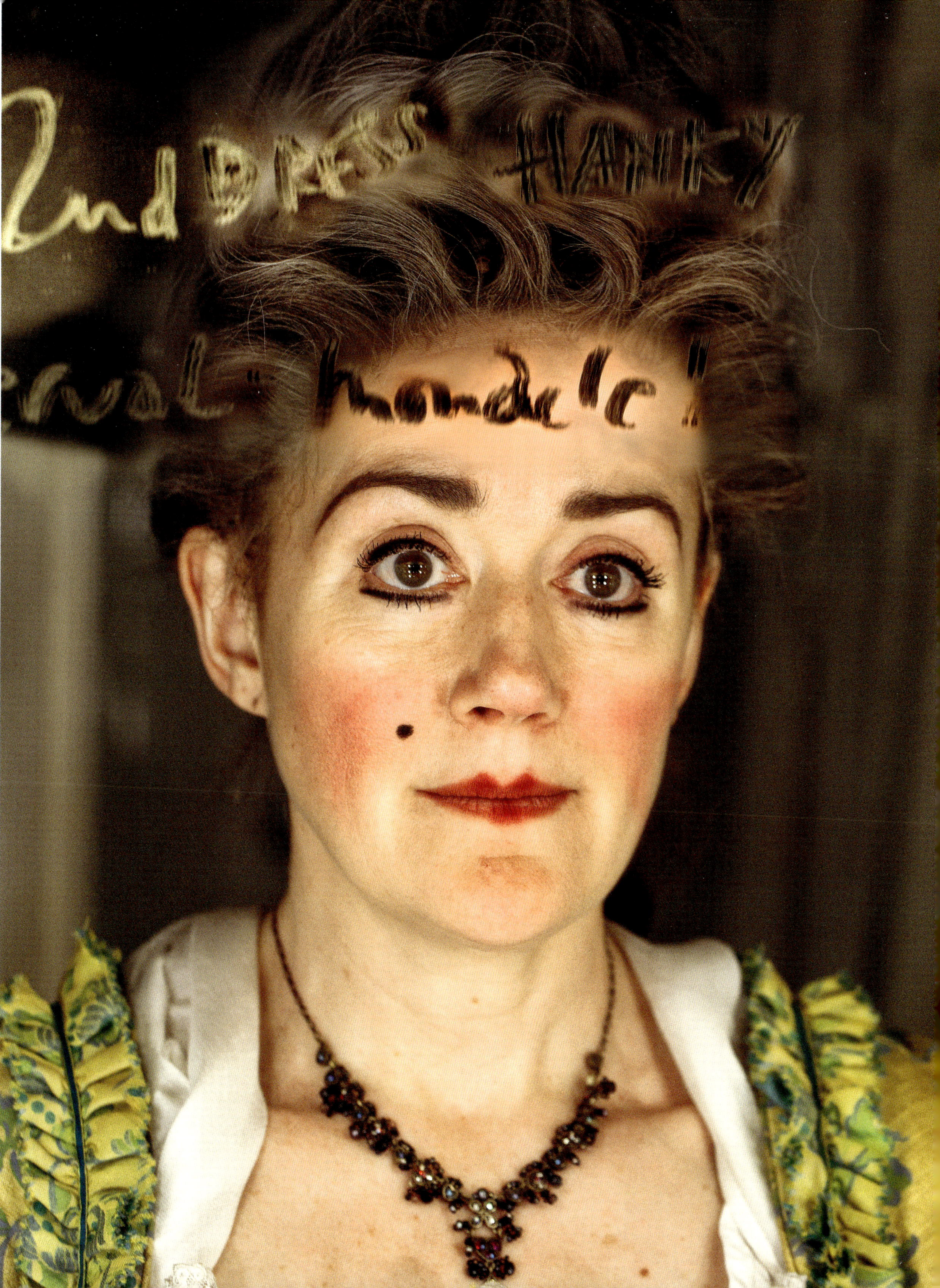
2nd DRESS HANKY

TIM PIGOTT-SMITH, *KING CHARLES III*, WYNDHAM'S, 2015

A truly versatile actor, Tim was the most popular of actors in whatever context he worked. His premature death in 2017 was a shock to all who knew him and the many fans he had around the world.

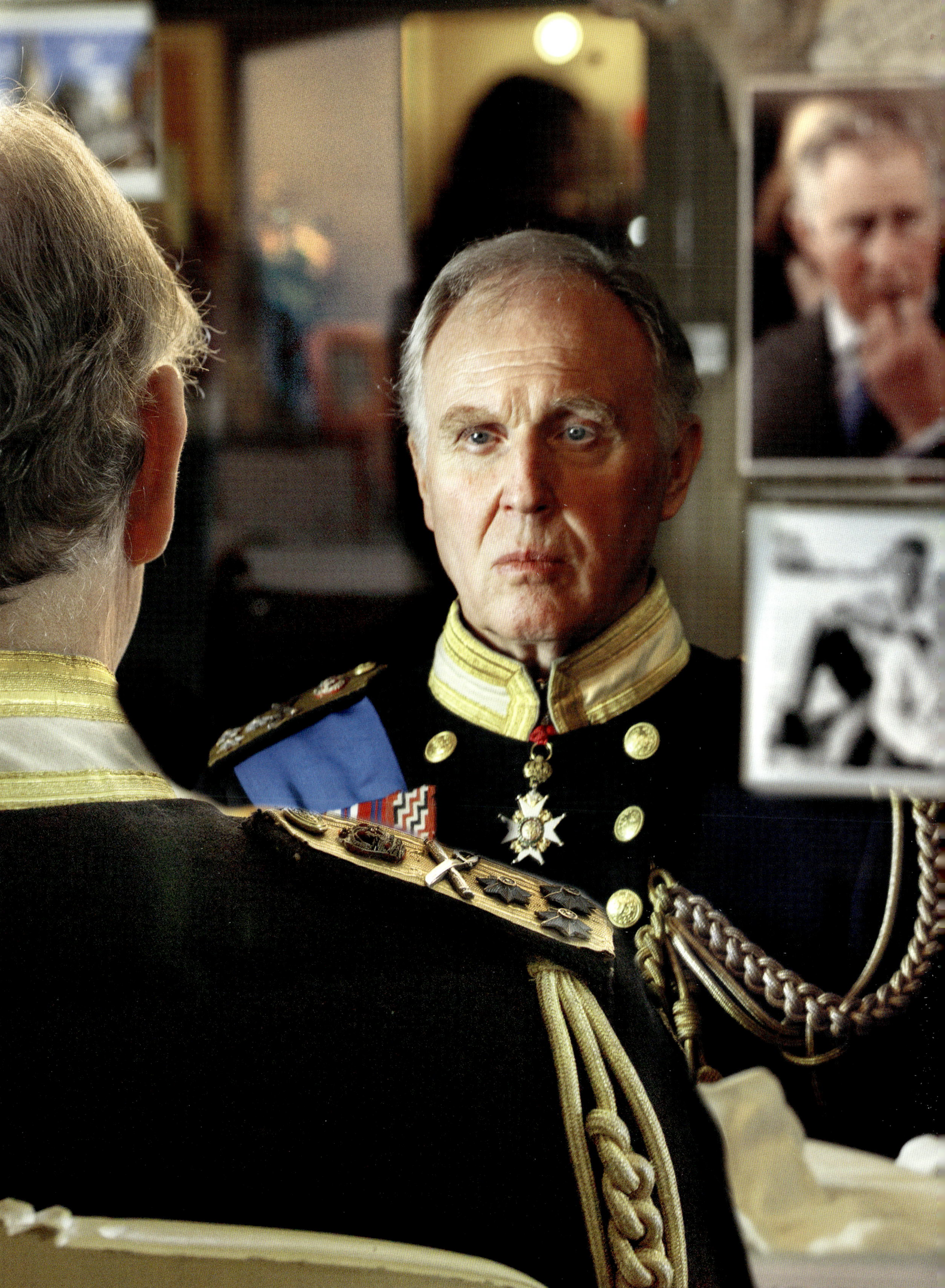

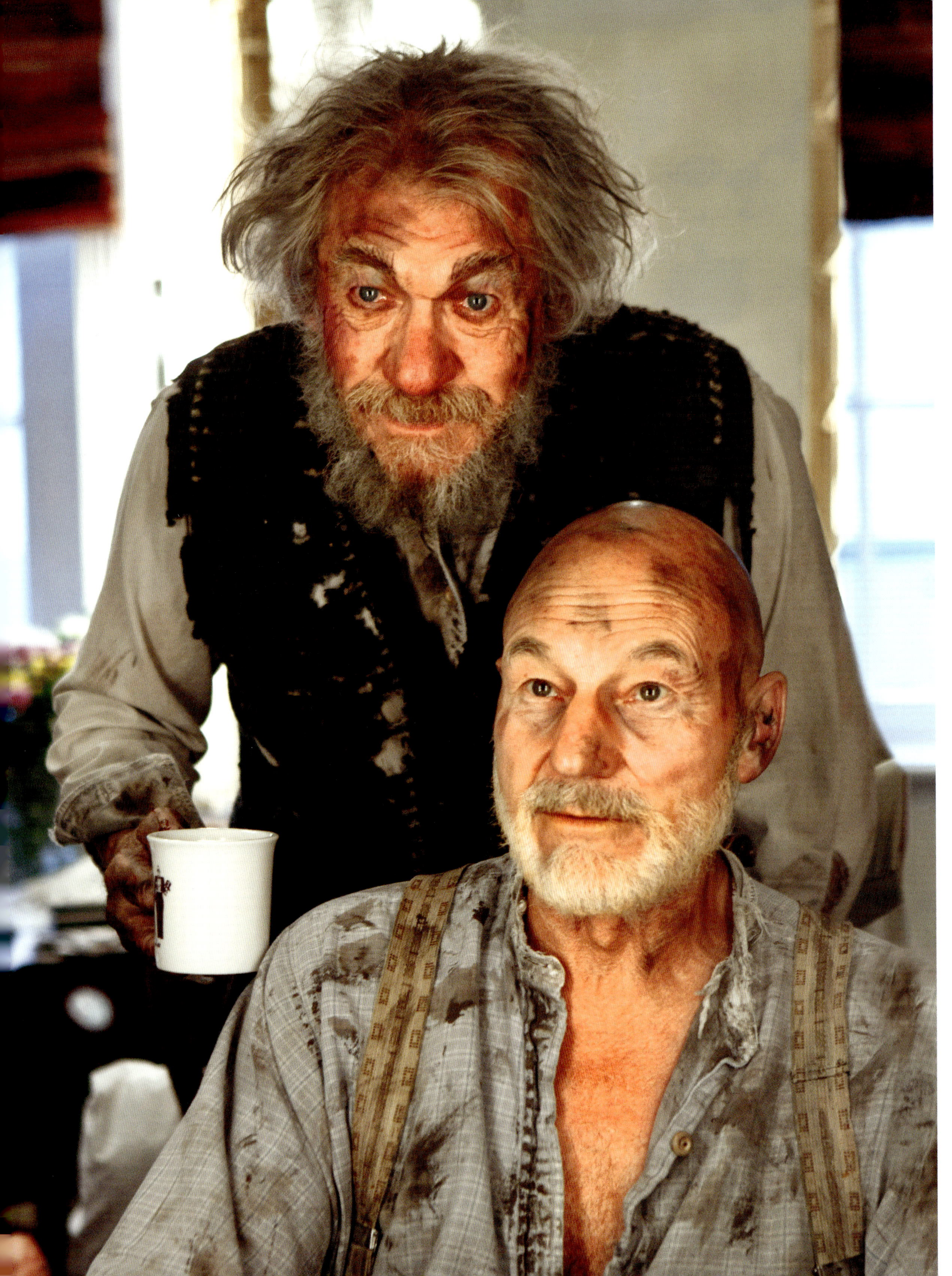

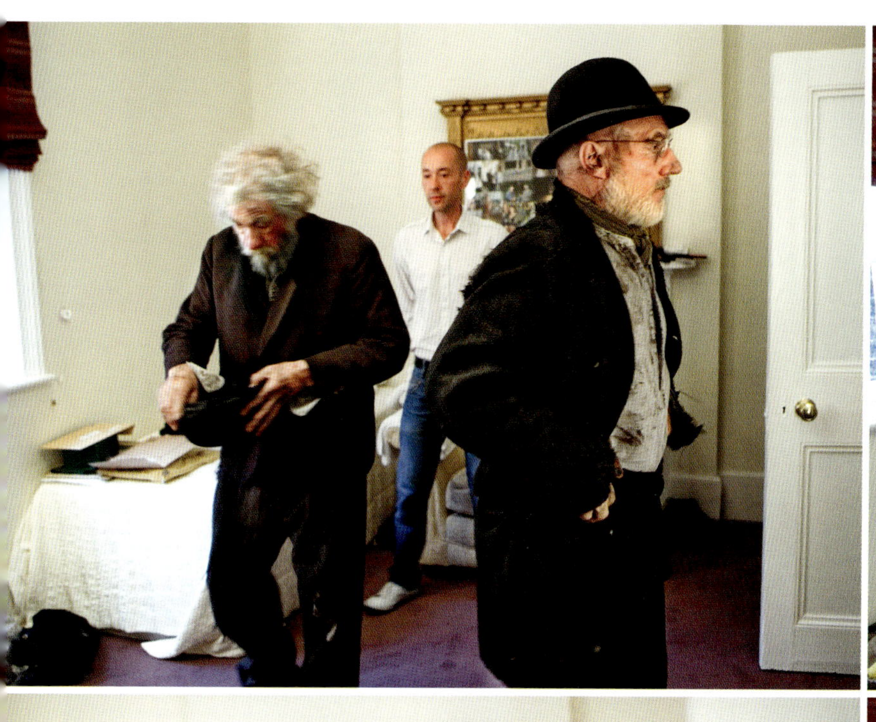
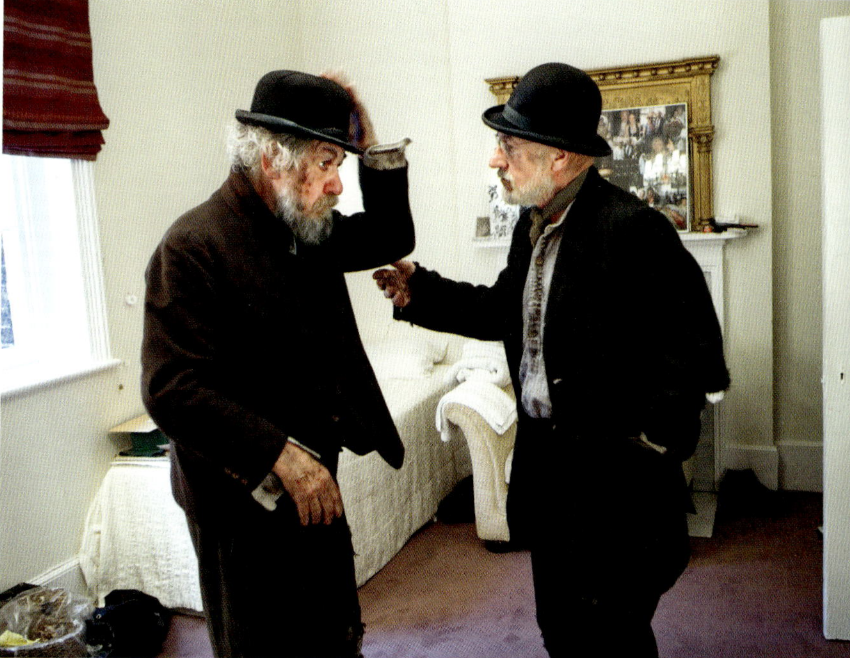
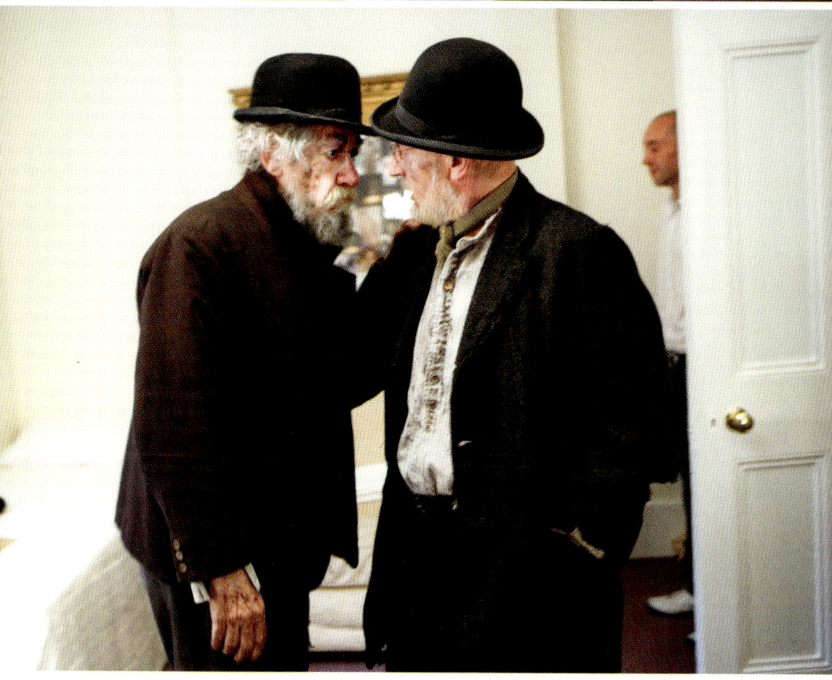
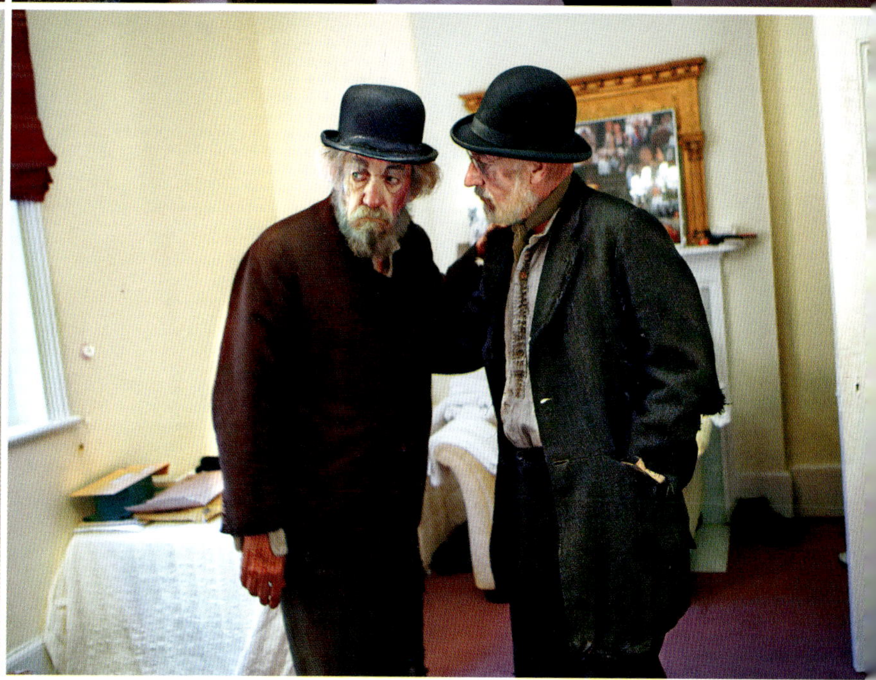

IAN McKELLEN, PATRICK STEWART, *WAITING FOR GODOT*, THEATRE ROYAL HAYMARKET, 2009

This is the well-known No. 10 dressing room used by John Gielgud as a flat during the London Blitz. Ian and Patrick shared the room. The world knows these two men as huge movie stars, but their natural habitat is the theatre. The joy they share in performing live is palpable.

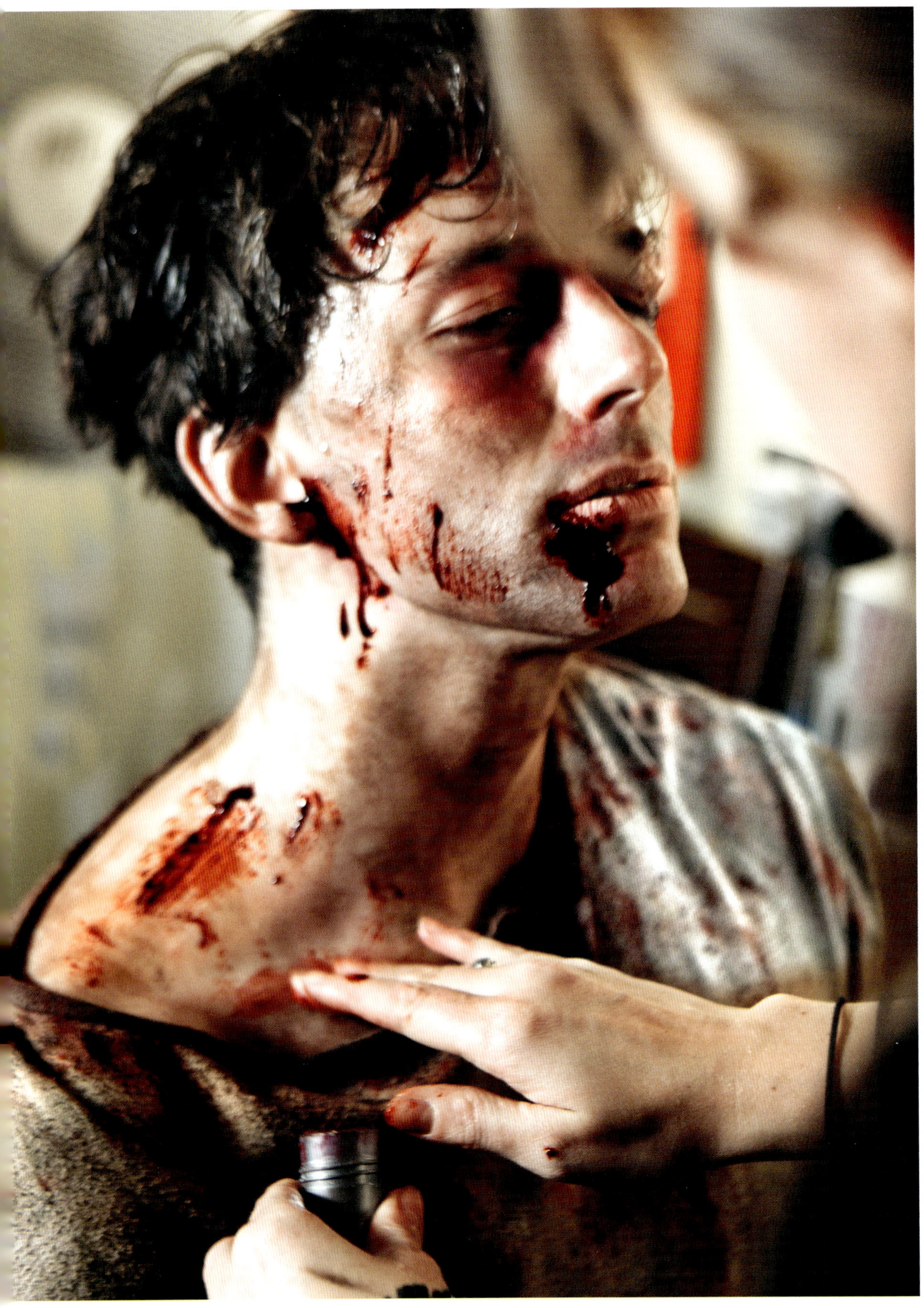

LEFT: SAM MARKS, *RICHARD II*, RSC, 2013
The application of blood has to be convincing. It requires stillness on the part of the actor, which can be difficult if you are in the middle of a scene and about to be murdered.

OPPOSITE: STEPHEN BOXER, *TITUS ANDRONICUS*, RSC, 2013
Using blood as a prop, vital for the tale of Titus Andronicus. Stephen is well known for being fully committed to all his roles.

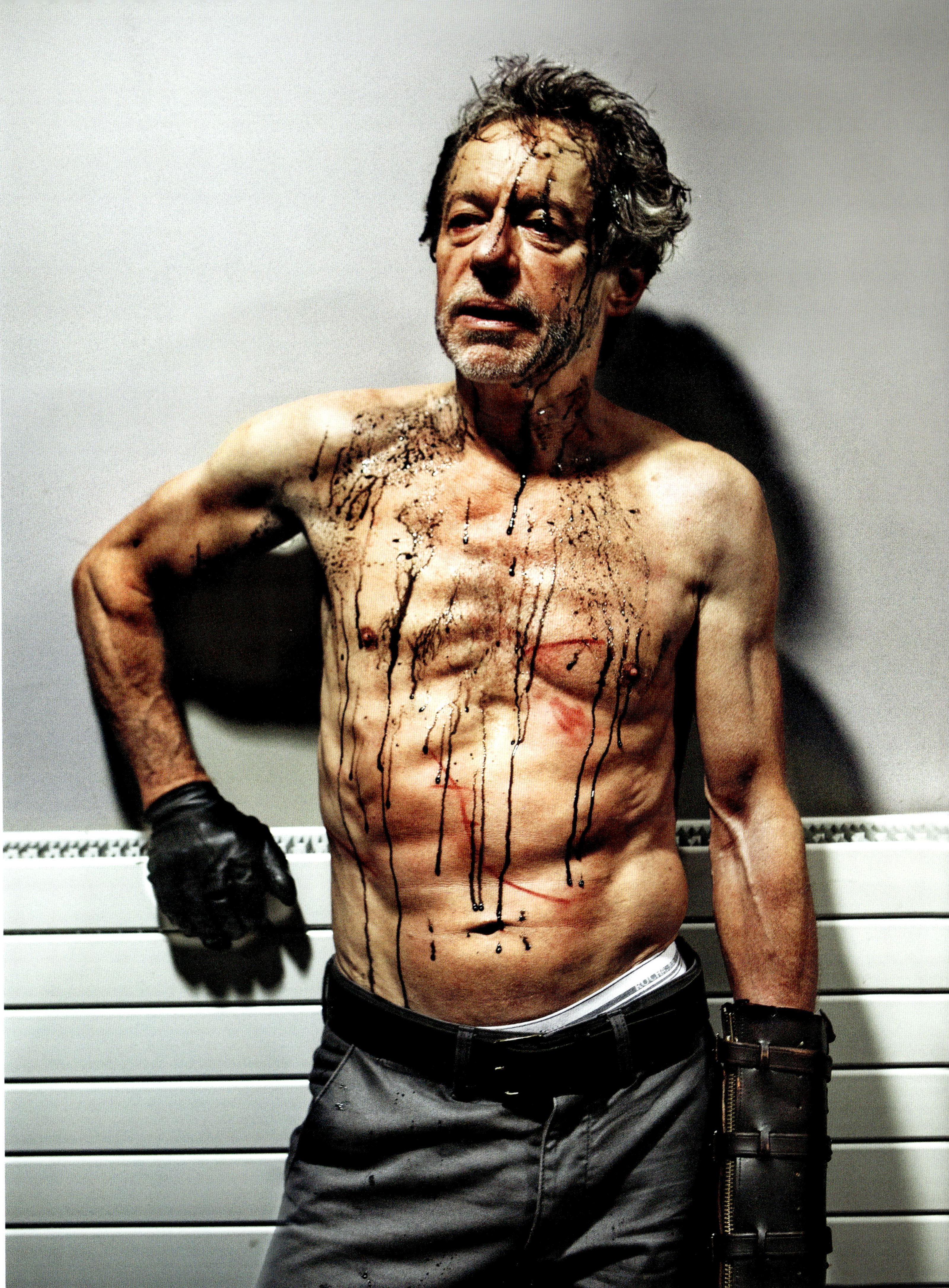

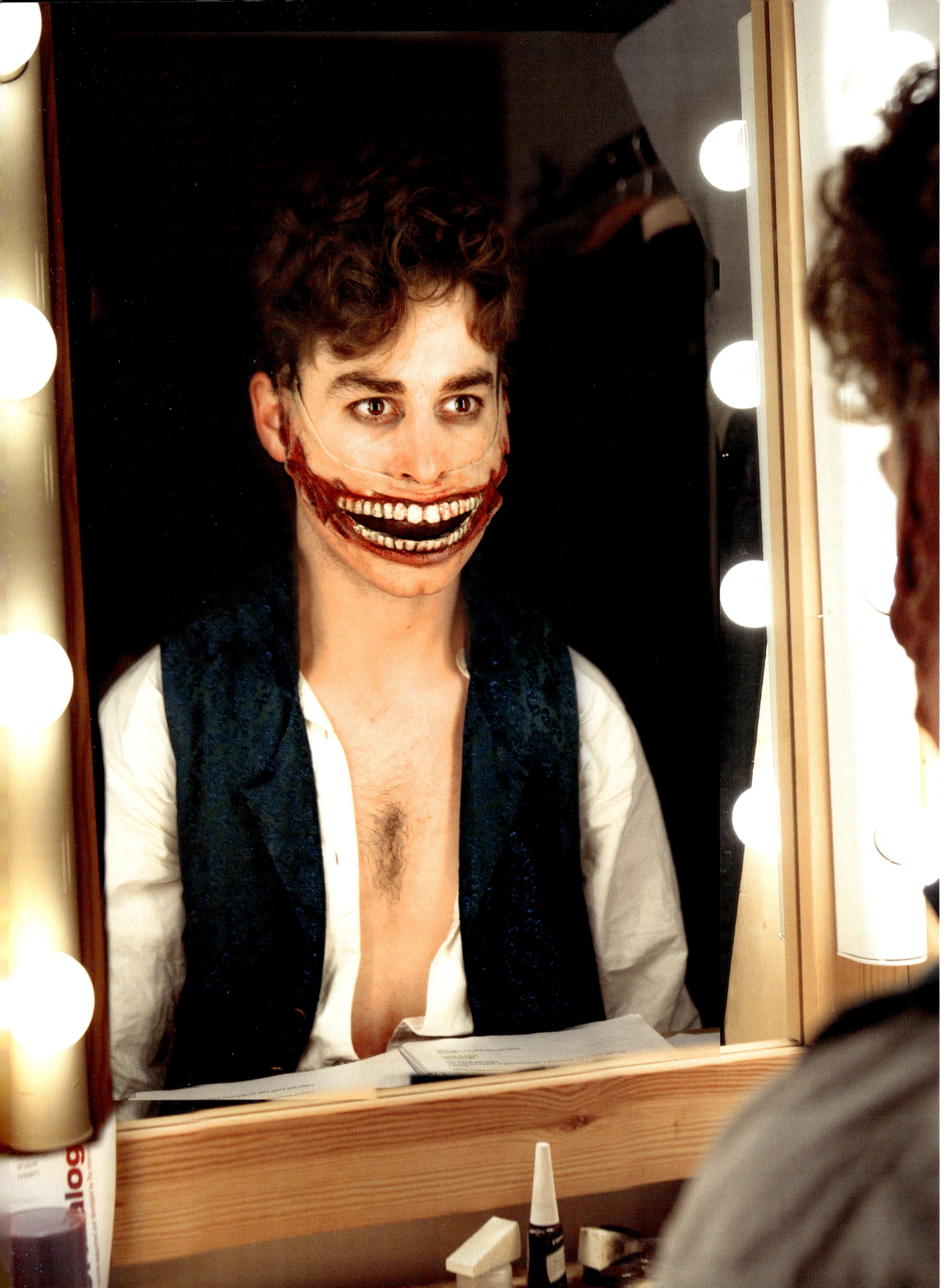

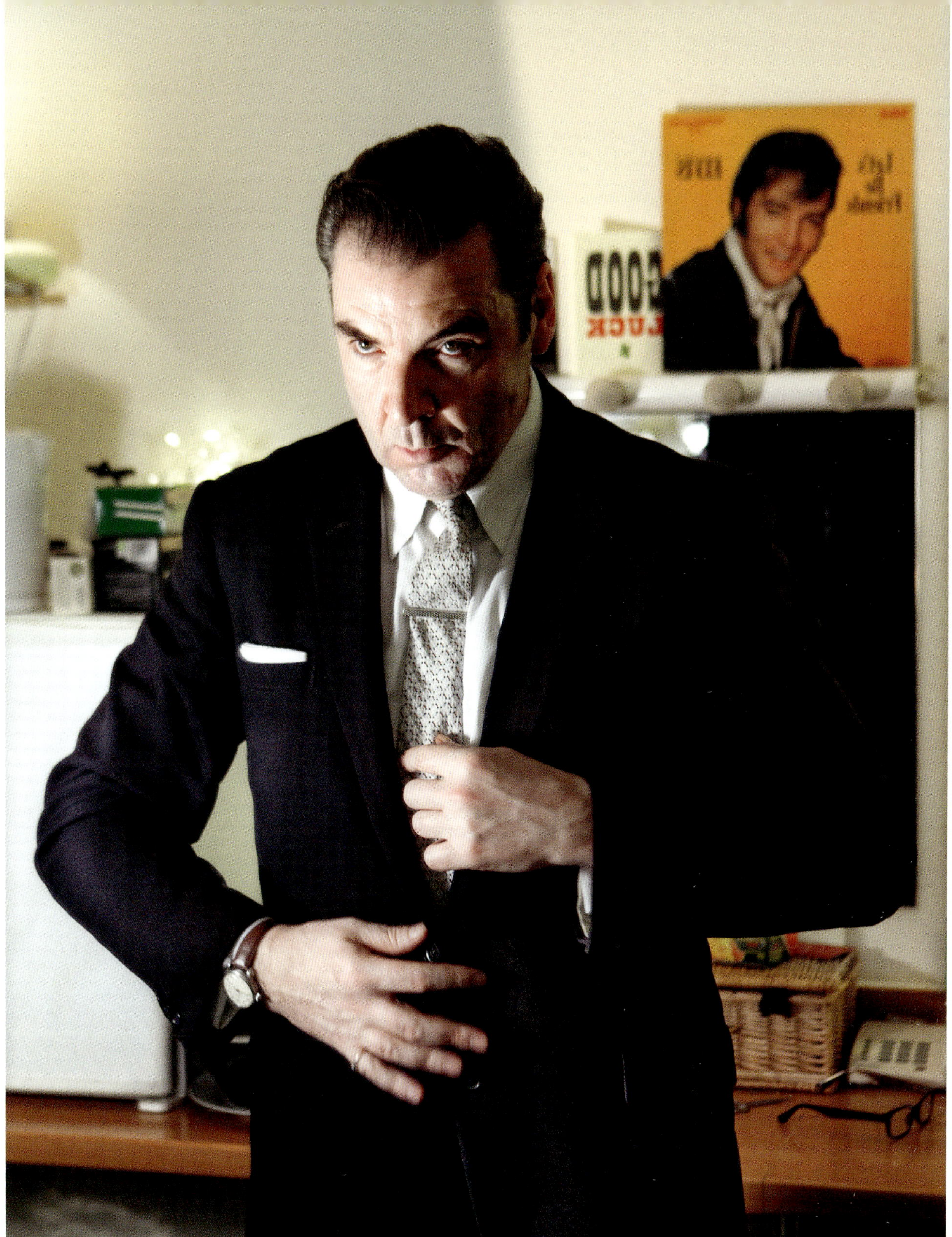

OPPOSITE: **LOUIS MASKELL, *THE GRINNING MAN*, BRISTOL OLD VIC, 2016**
This image sums up the thrill, but also the terror, of going out there to perform live eight times a week.

RIGHT: **BRENDAN COYLE, *MOJO*, HAROLD PINTER THEATRE, 2014**
A man who likes his privacy, I was fortunate that Brendan gave me a rare session. As Mr Bates he was a central character in the long-running *Downton Abbey*. He also won an Olivier Award for his wonderful performance in Conor McPherson's *The Weir*.

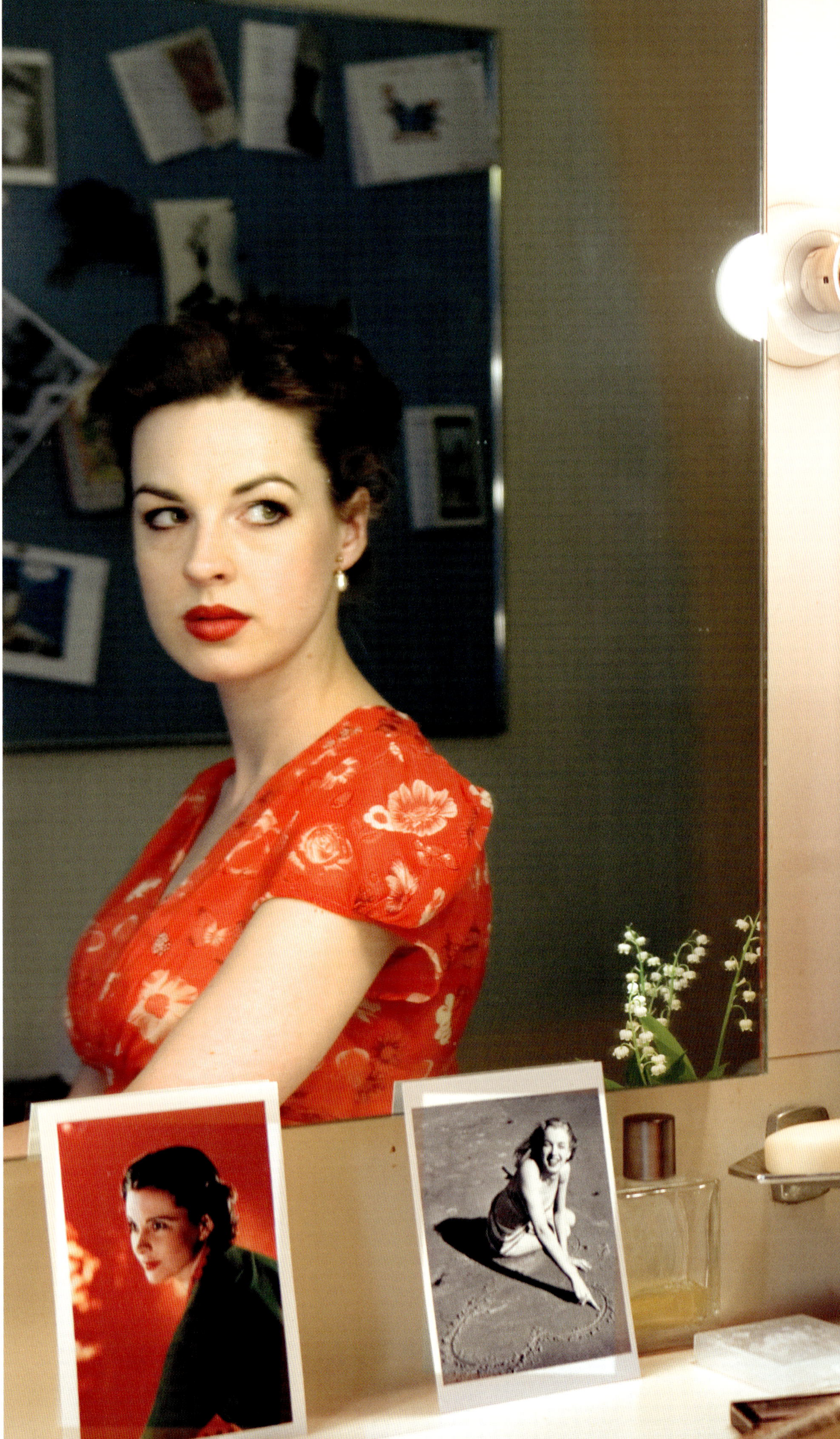

JESSICA RAINE, *ROCKET TO THE MOON*, NATIONAL THEATRE, 2011

One of Jessica's many talents is to hold back her power and energy before it boils over. There are few people who can wear red lipstick better than her.

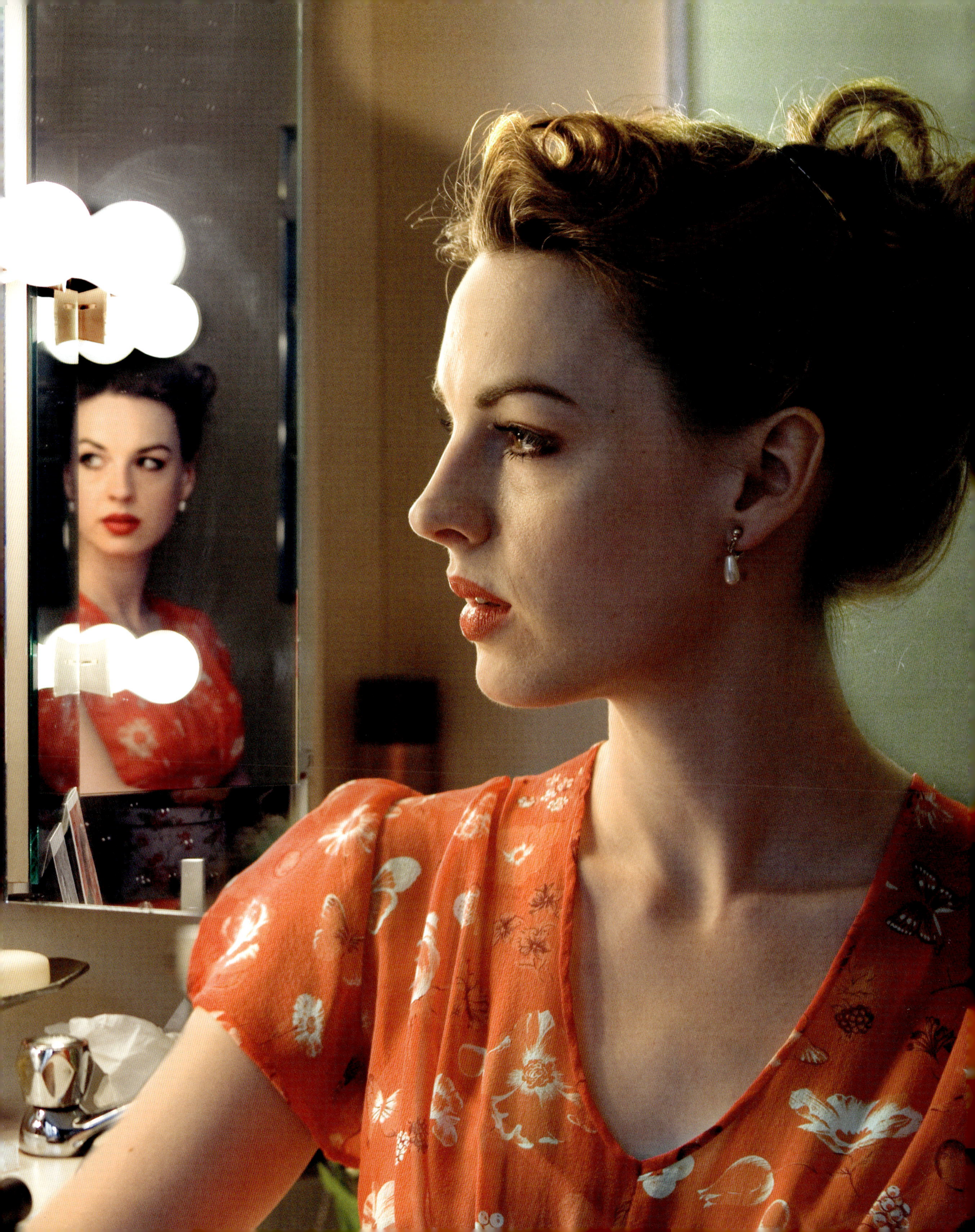

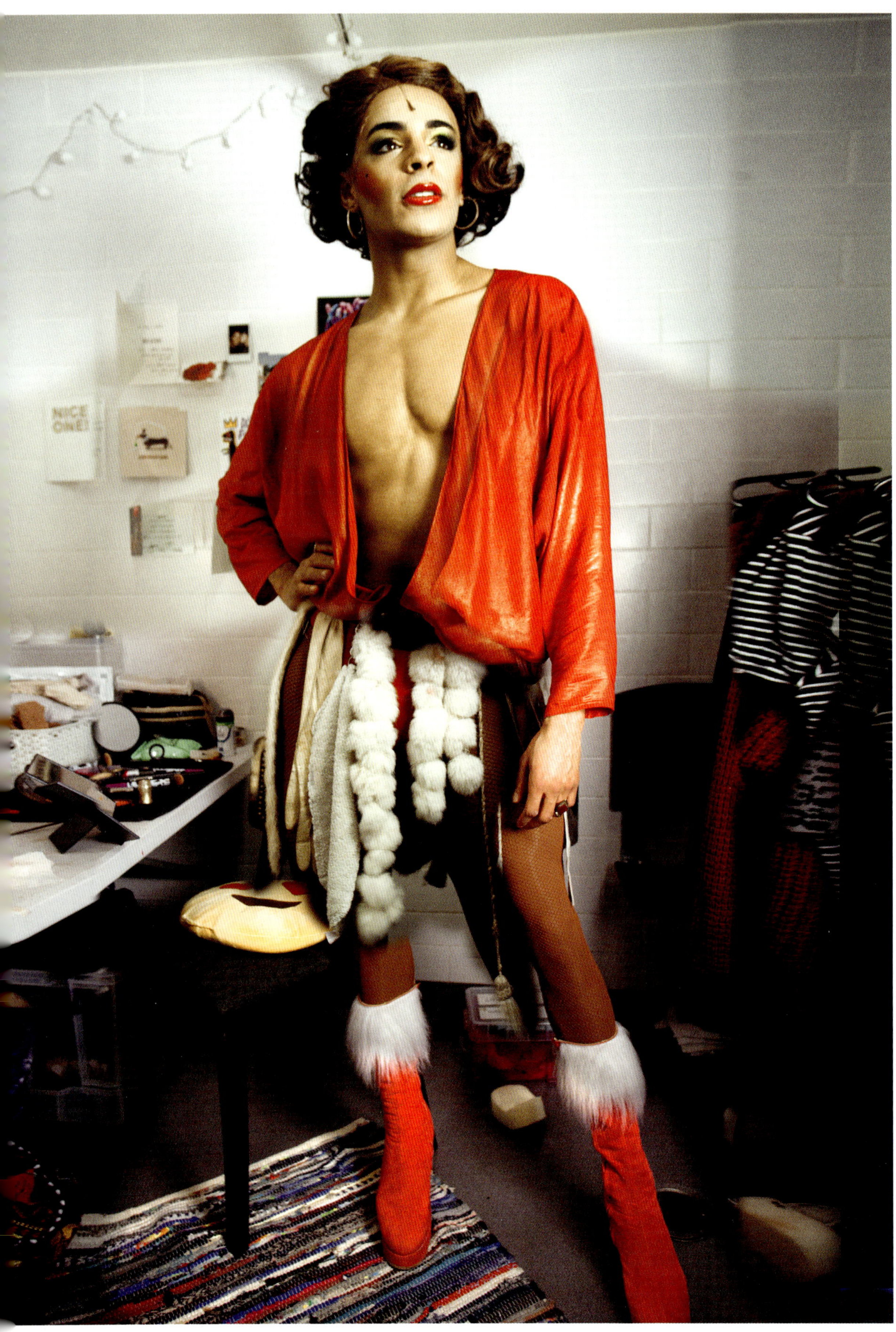

LEFT: **LAYTON WILLIAMS, *RENT*, ST JAMES THEATRE, 2017**
His dressing room was a converted toilet. Layton shared the tiny space with another actor, but still managed to create this elaborate look every evening.

OPPOSITE: **SIMON CALLOW, *PETER PAN*, RICHMOND THEATRE, 2009**
Simon has tremendous vigour as a performer. Playing over the Christmas period demands a punishing schedule. With the hot and heavy costumes, the cramped space and a demanding audience, he was relieved to complete the run. This is five minutes before the last matinee, on a Sunday.

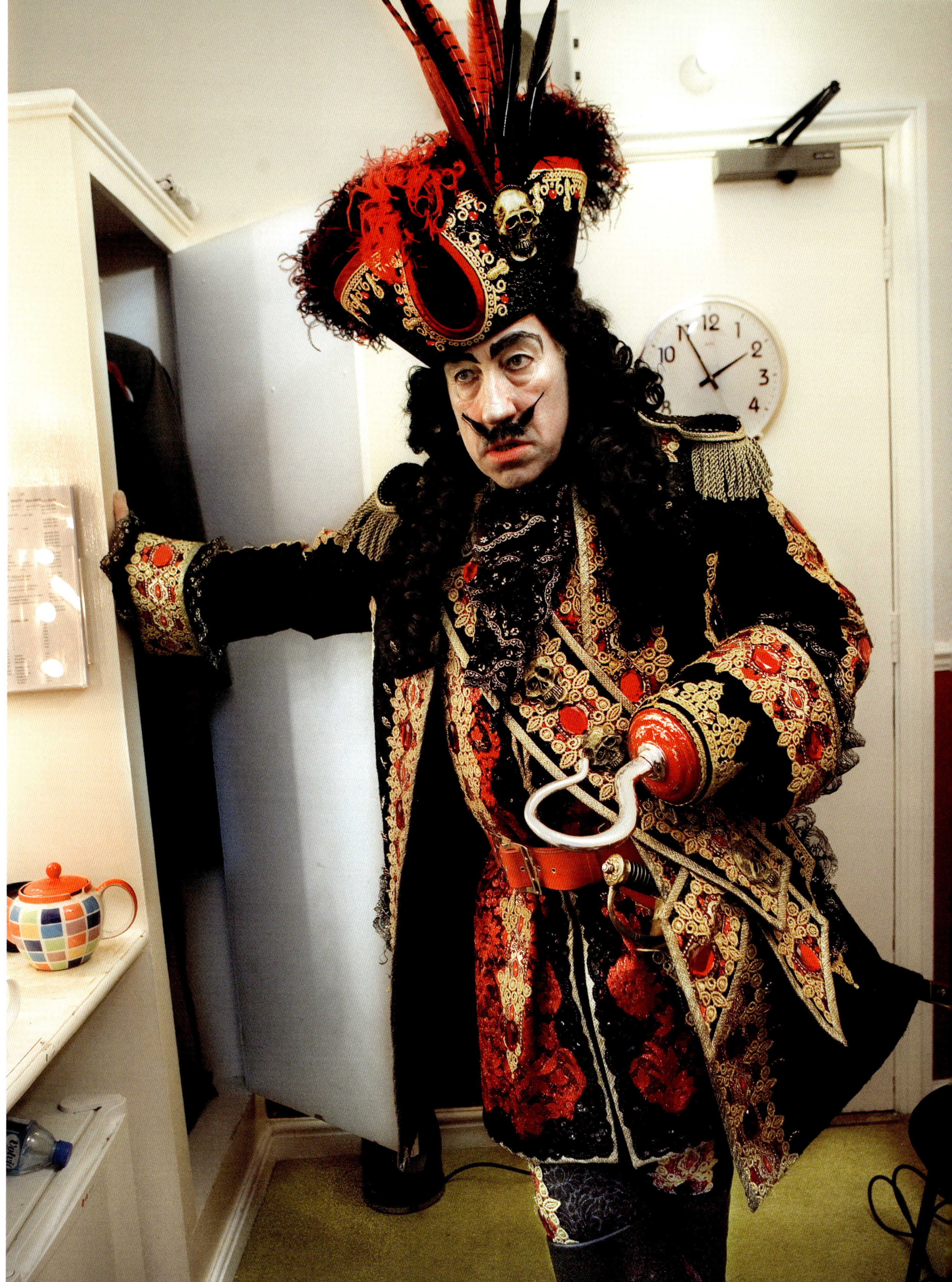

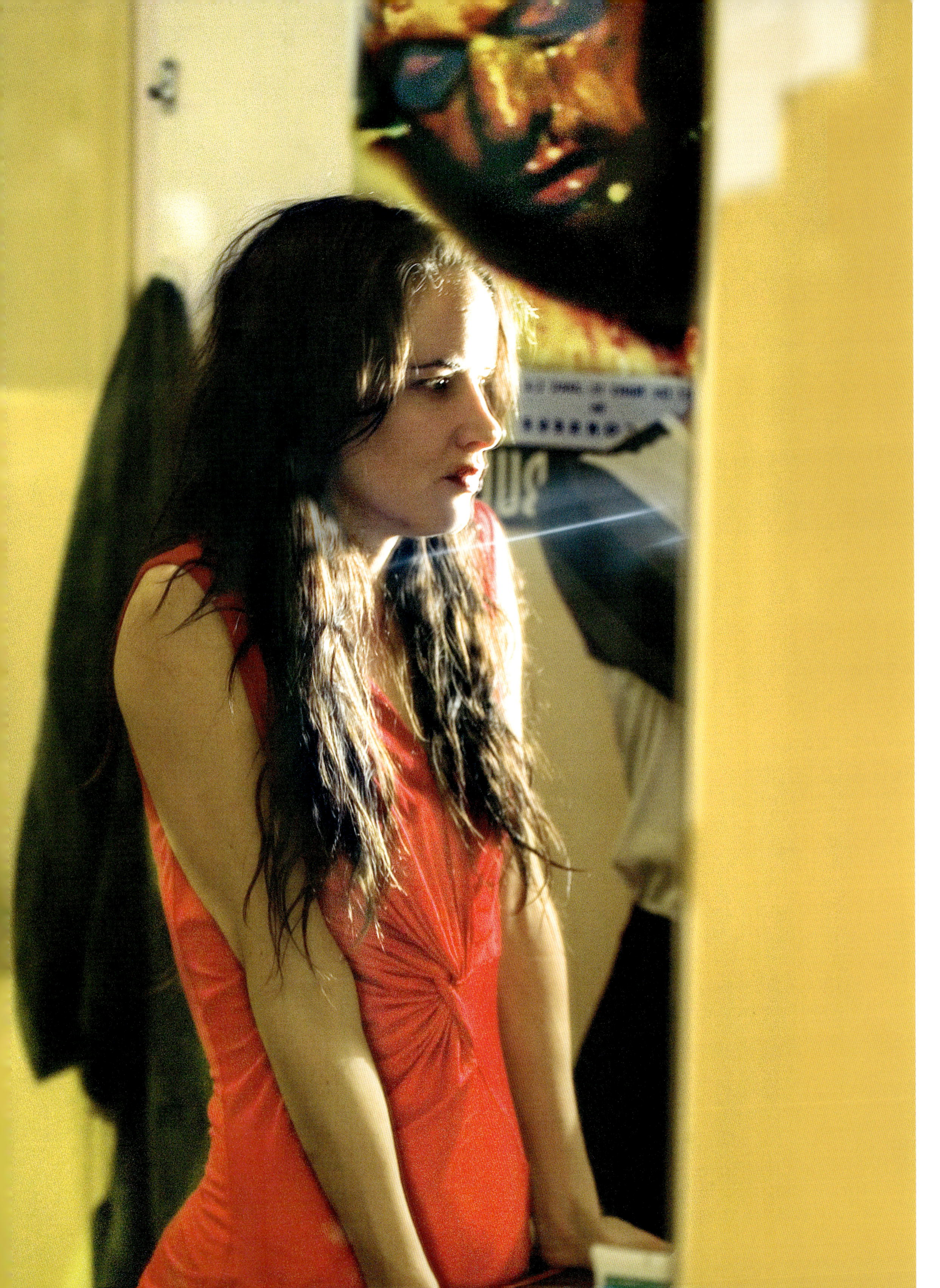

OPPOSITE: **JULIETTE LEWIS, *FOOL FOR LOVE*, APOLLO THEATRE, 2006**
Brave and committed, Juliette still found the time to be seen before her last performance of the run, on a Saturday. The following Monday she started a world tour as a singer with her band. She is the best kind of American spirit.

BELOW: **KELLY BROOK, *CALENDAR GIRLS*, NOËL COWARD THEATRE, 2009**
In terms of knowing about what works in front of a camera, Kelly is one of the brightest people I have photographed. She lay down for perhaps a minute. The photographer has to be quick.

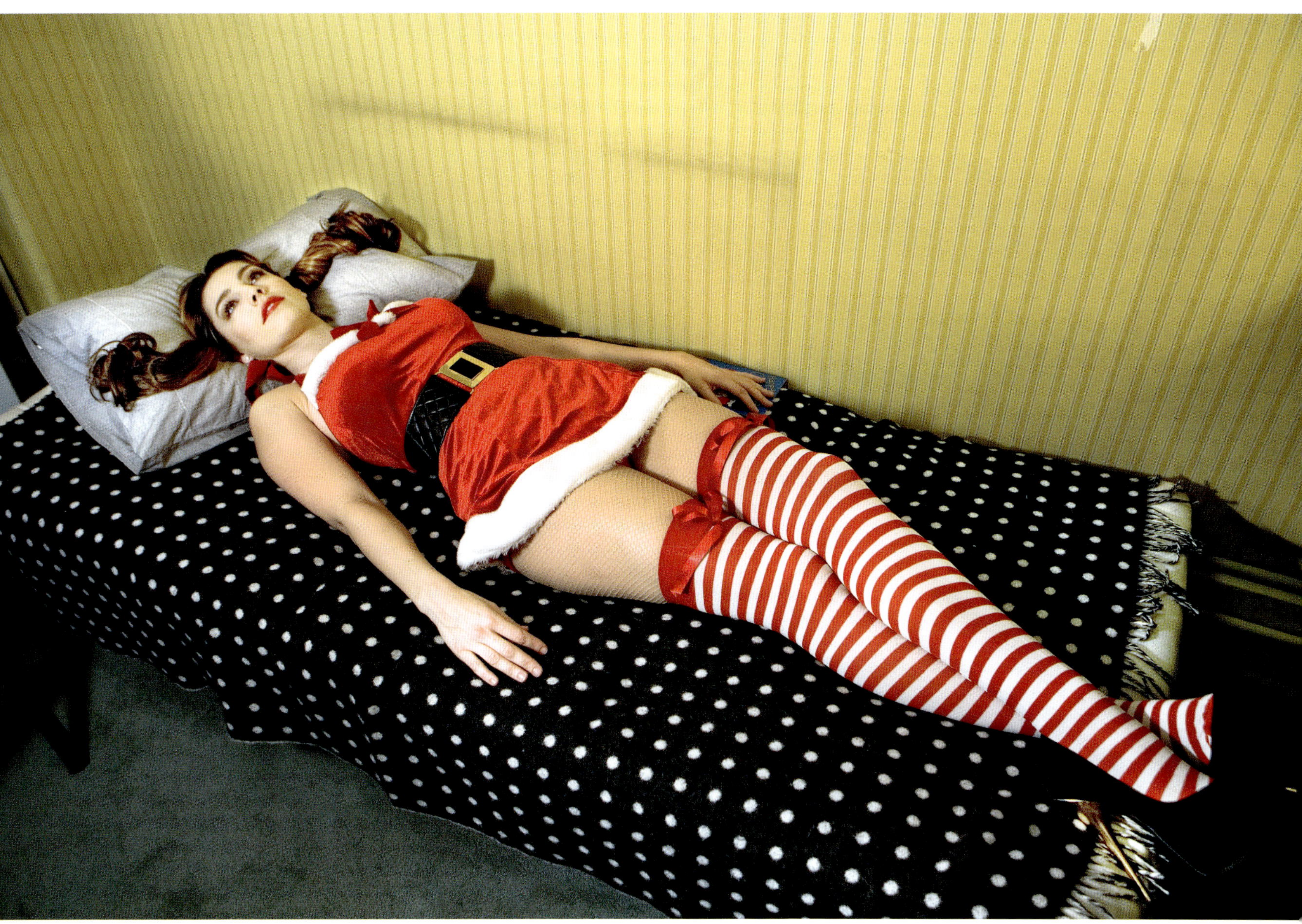

RACHEL WEISZ, *A STREETCAR NAMED DESIRE*, DONMAR WAREHOUSE, 2009

Rachel is making the final adjustments to her costume before leaving the room. Totally focused and zoned in to play Blanche, she won the Best Actress Award that year.

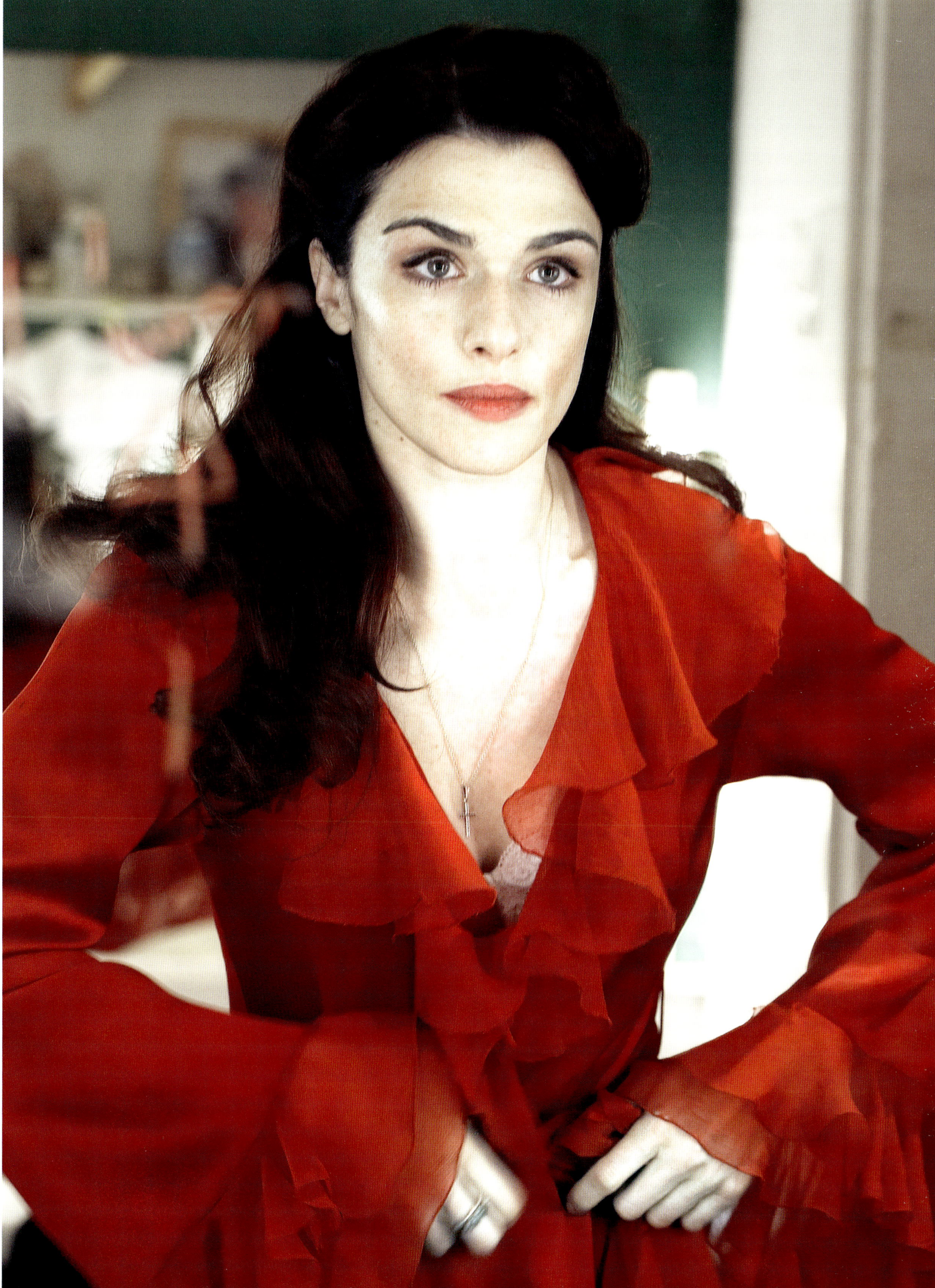

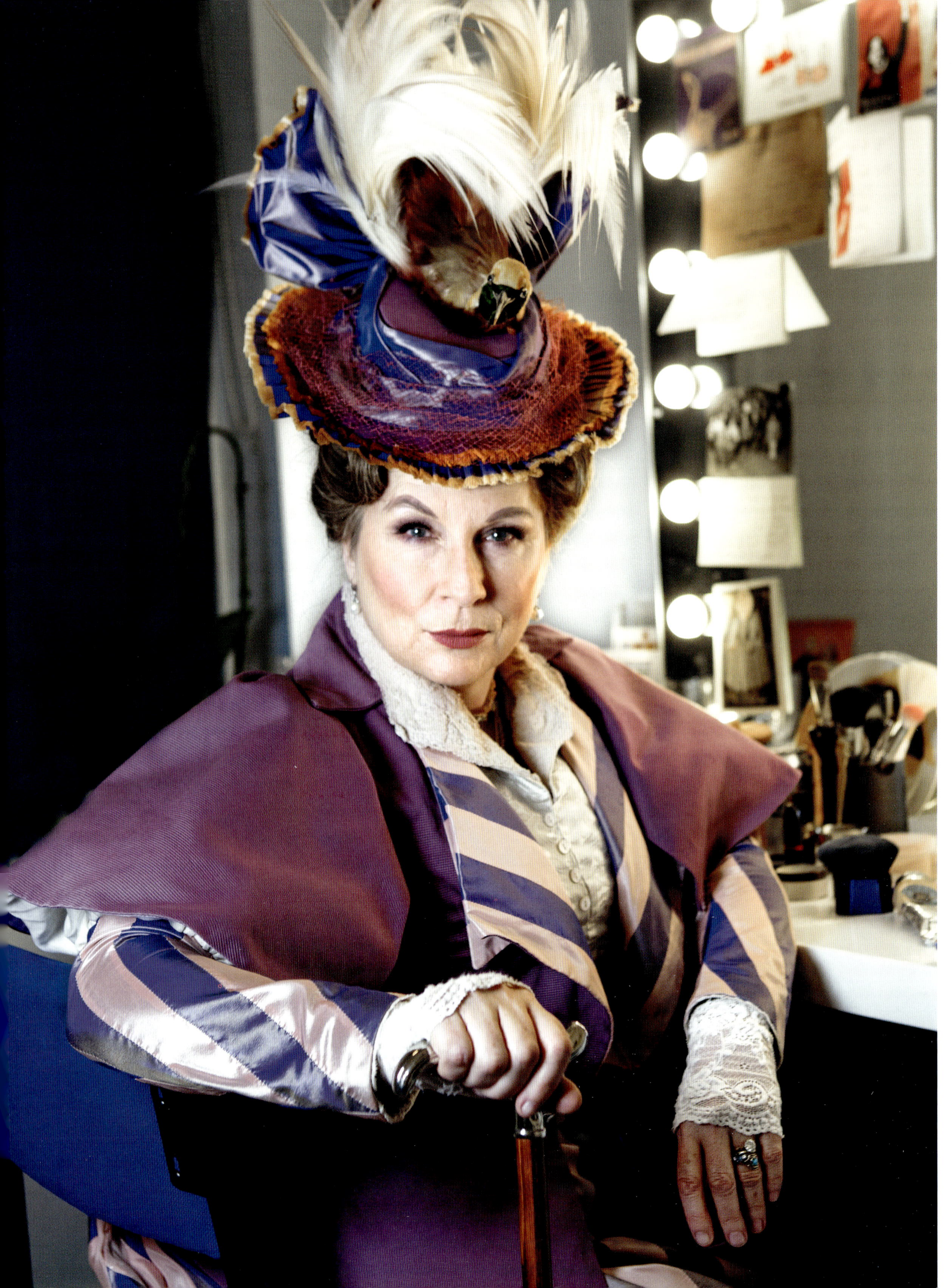

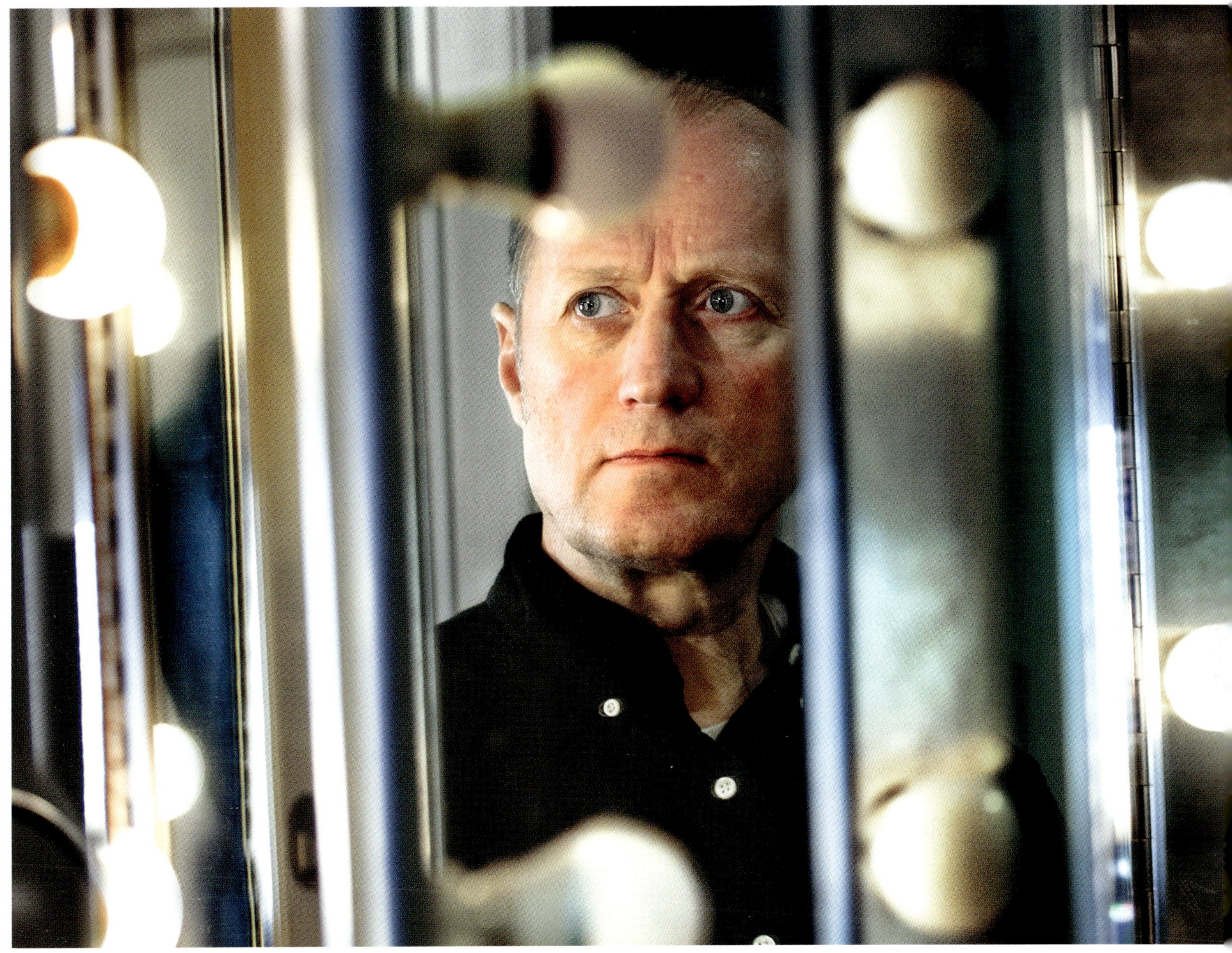

OPPOSITE: **JENNIFER SAUNDERS,**
***LADY WINDERMERE'S FAN*,**
VAUDEVILLE THEATRE, 2018
There is something irresistible about the irreverent mischief of Jennifer in tandem with the wit of Oscar Wilde.

ABOVE: **ADRIAN EDMONDSON,**
***BITS OF ME ARE FALLING APART*,**
SOHO THEATRE, 2016
The husband and wife phenomenon that are Jennifer and Ade. Both members of TV Comedy Royalty, they have undertaken the rigours of daily live performance on stage, in scripts that are not their own.

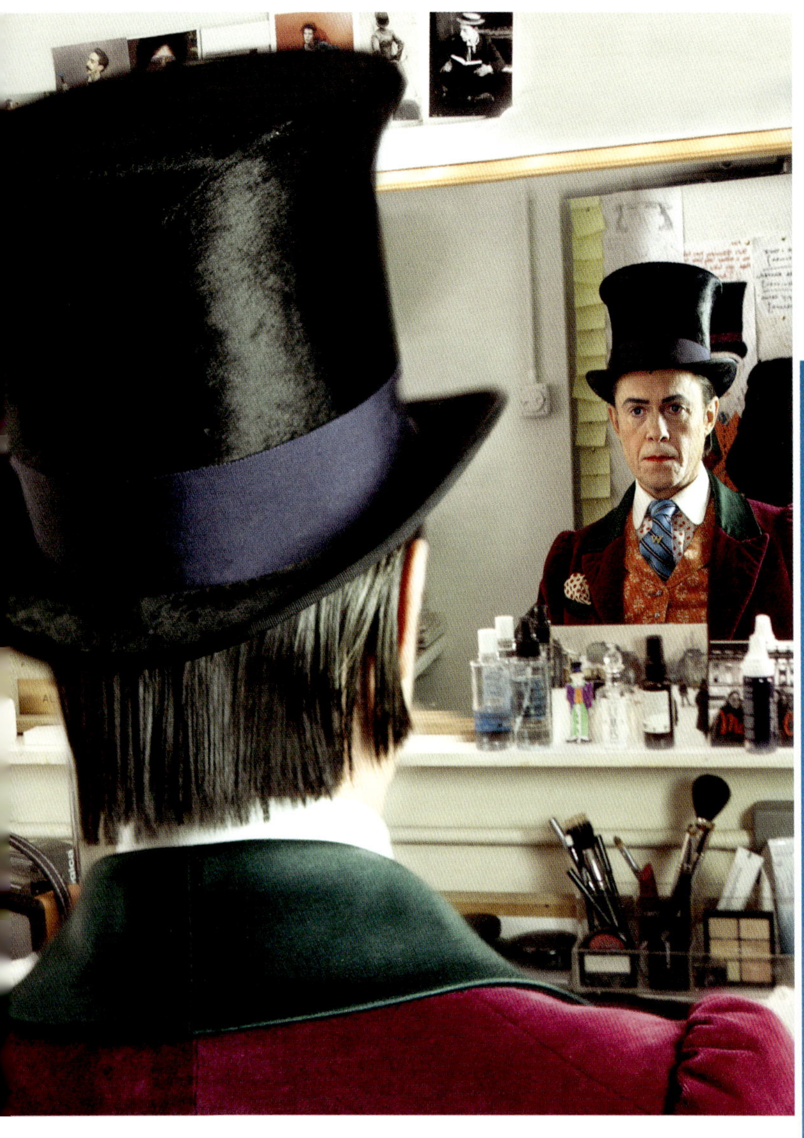

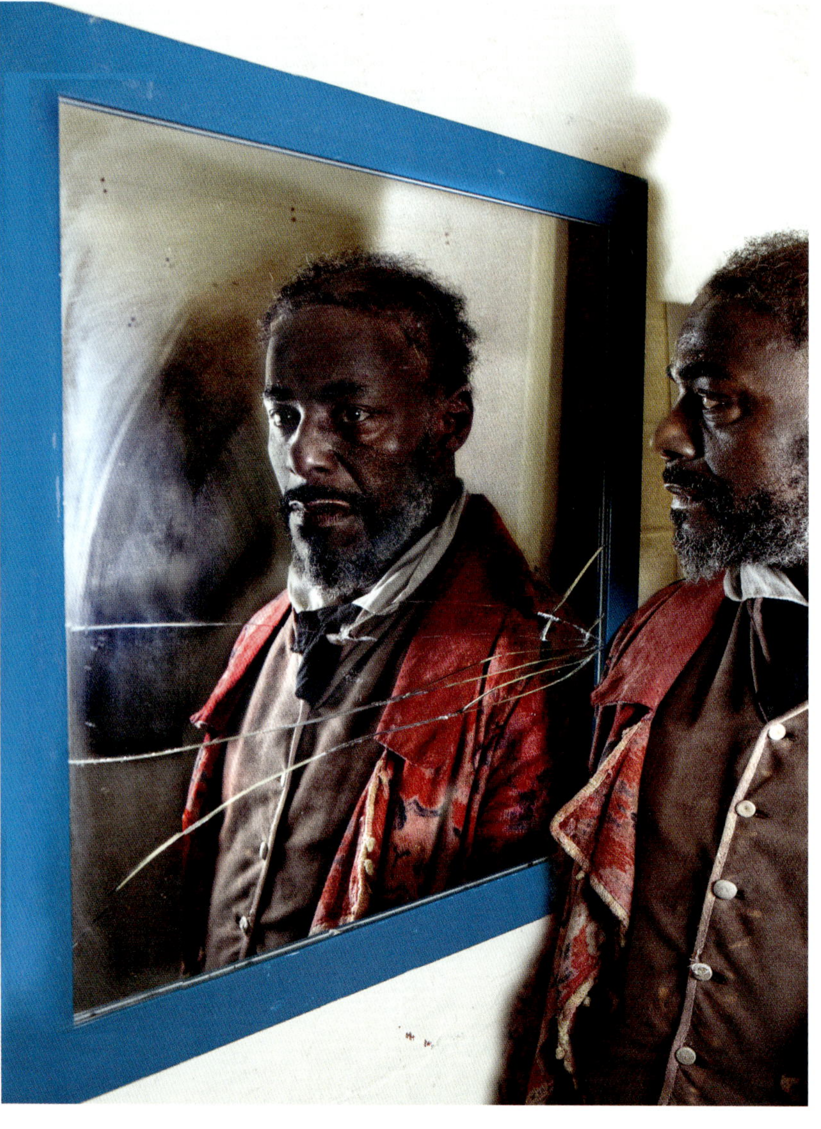

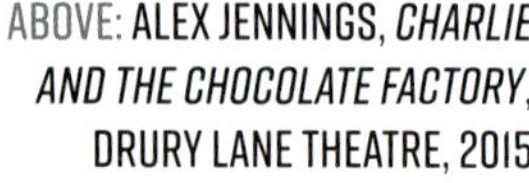

ABOVE: **ALEX JENNINGS, *CHARLIE AND THE CHOCOLATE FACTORY*, DRURY LANE THEATRE, 2015**
I first shot Alex in his breakthrough part as the lead in *Too Clever by Half* in 1988. Since then his voice, a glorious instrument, has weaved its magic in many different genres. Here he gives his Wonka.

RIGHT: **PATERSON JOSEPH, *A CHRISTMAS CAROL*, OLD VIC THEATRE, 2019**
Paterson's Scrooge was a very different version to the one played by Jim Broadbent (see p. 175). Both won critical acclaim.

OPPOSITE: **WENDELL PIERCE, *DEATH OF A SALESMAN*, PICCADILLY THEATRE, 2019**
This was before the last Saturday matinee. Although exhausted by flu, he was determined to make the last performances of the run. During the session I didn't say a word.

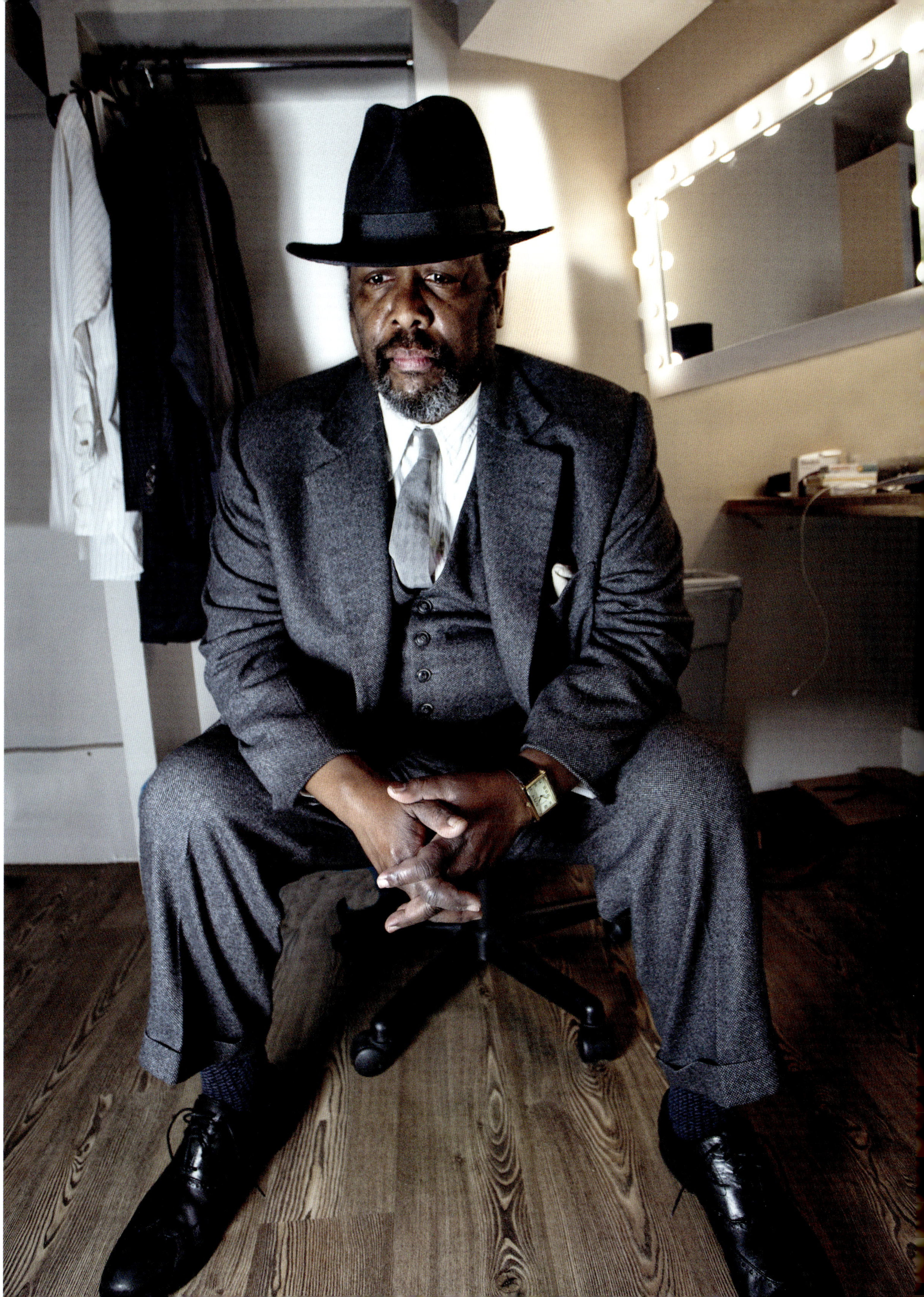

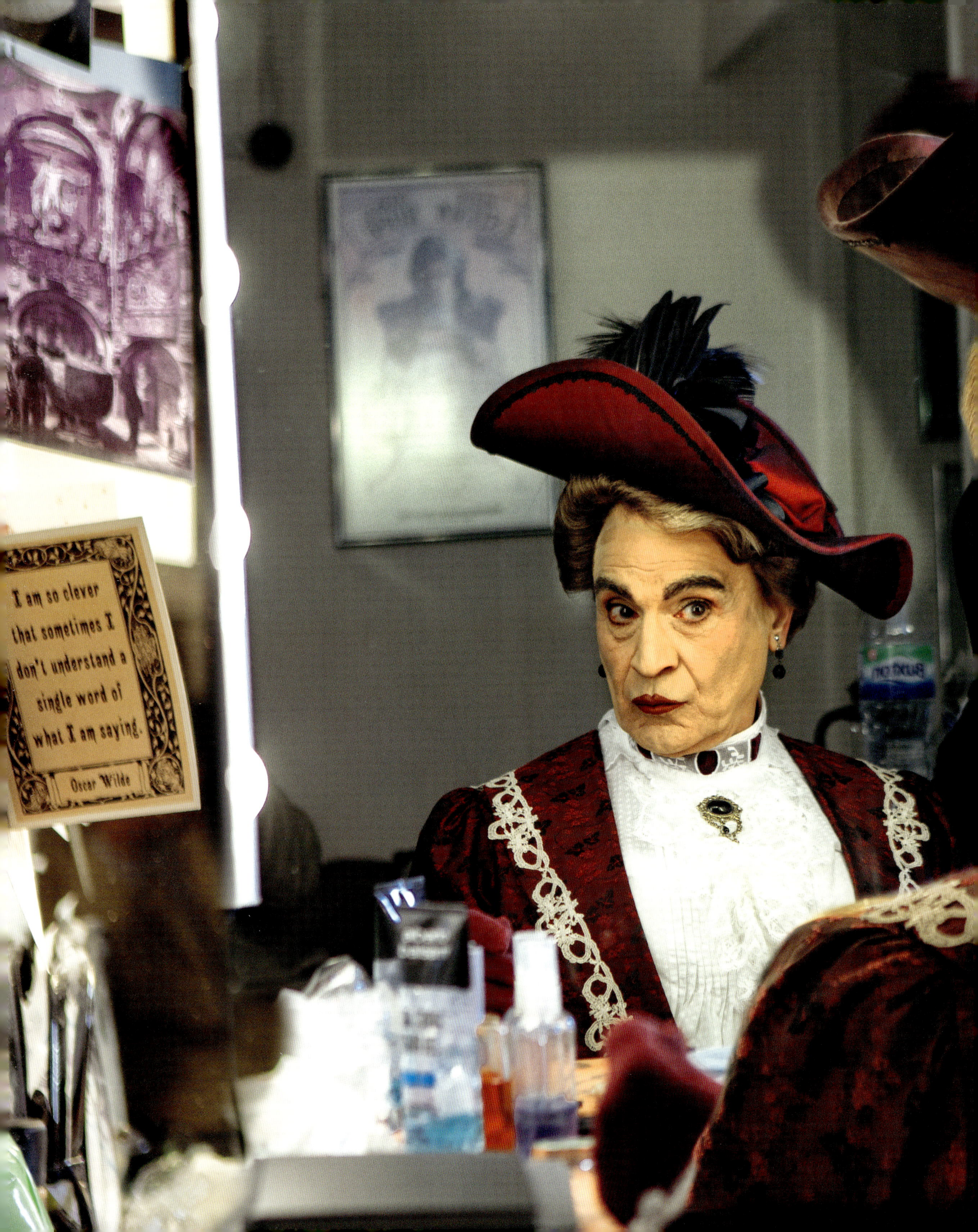
I am so clever
that sometimes I
don't understand a
single word of
what I am saying.
Oscar Wilde

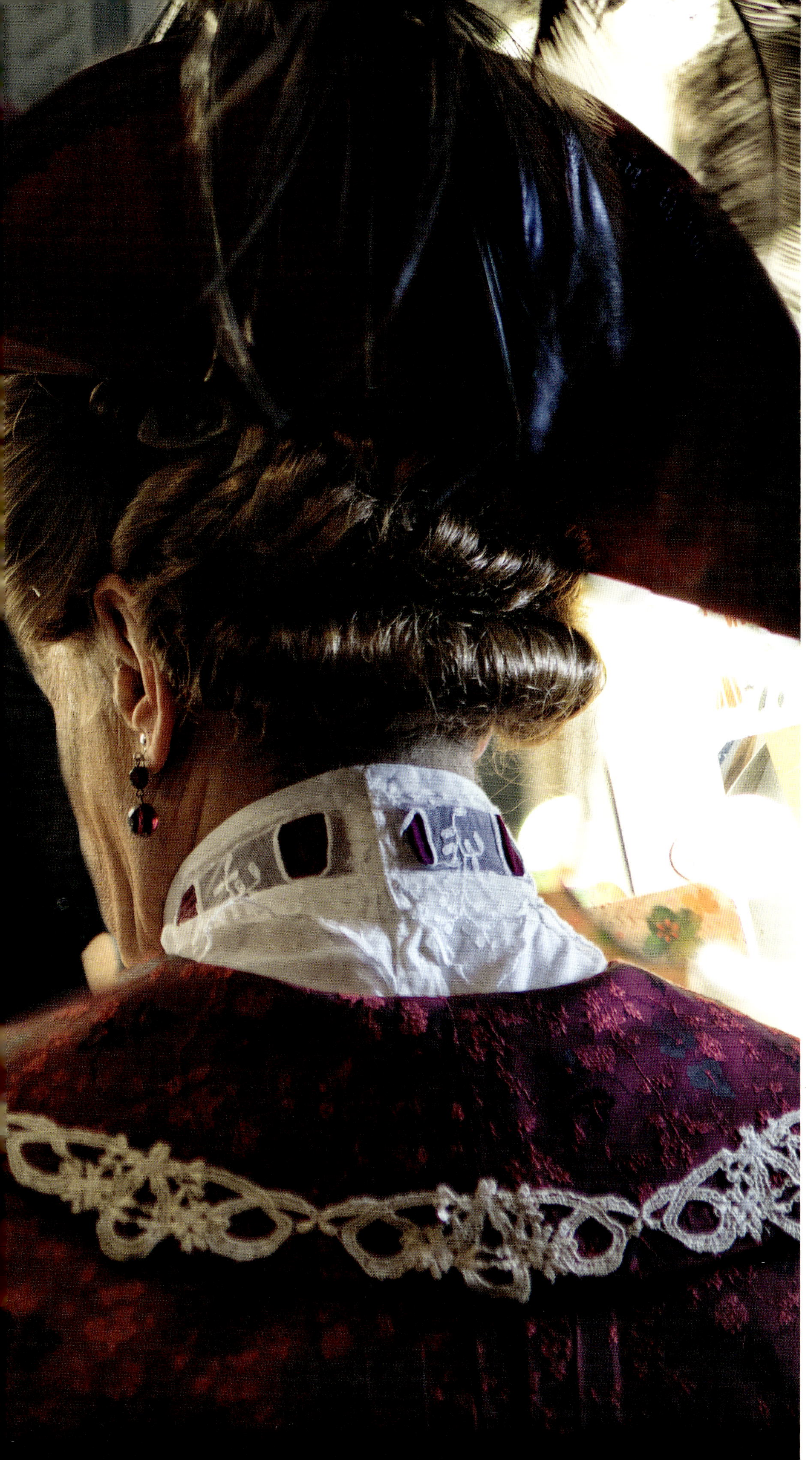

DAVID SUCHET, *THE IMPORTANCE OF BEING EARNEST*, VAUDEVILLE THEATRE, 2015

David checking in the mirror that his version of the legendary Lady Bracknell is ready for action. It was a brave choice for him to take on, after many successes as Hercule Poirot. The transformation into a woman was meticulously detailed.

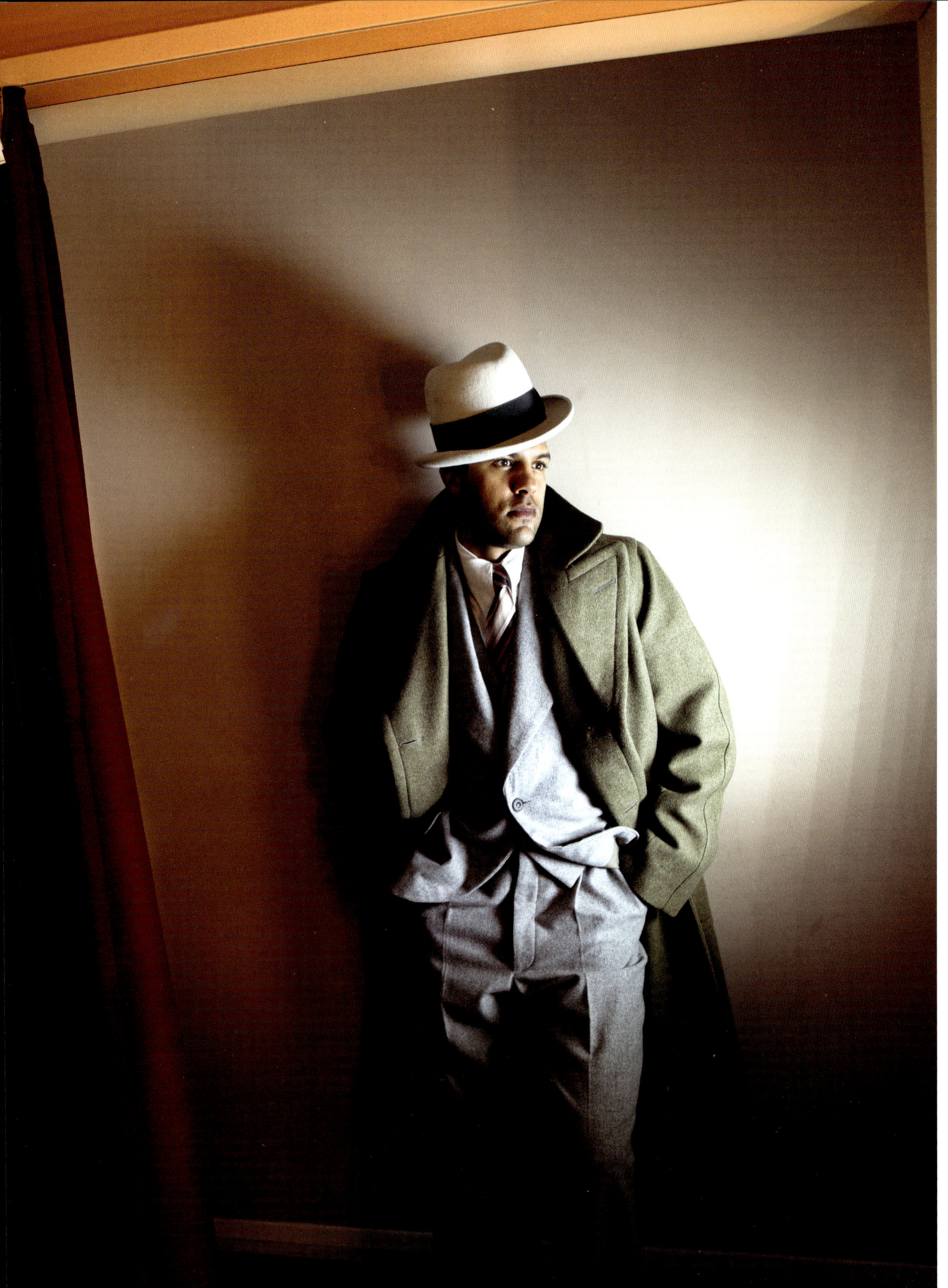

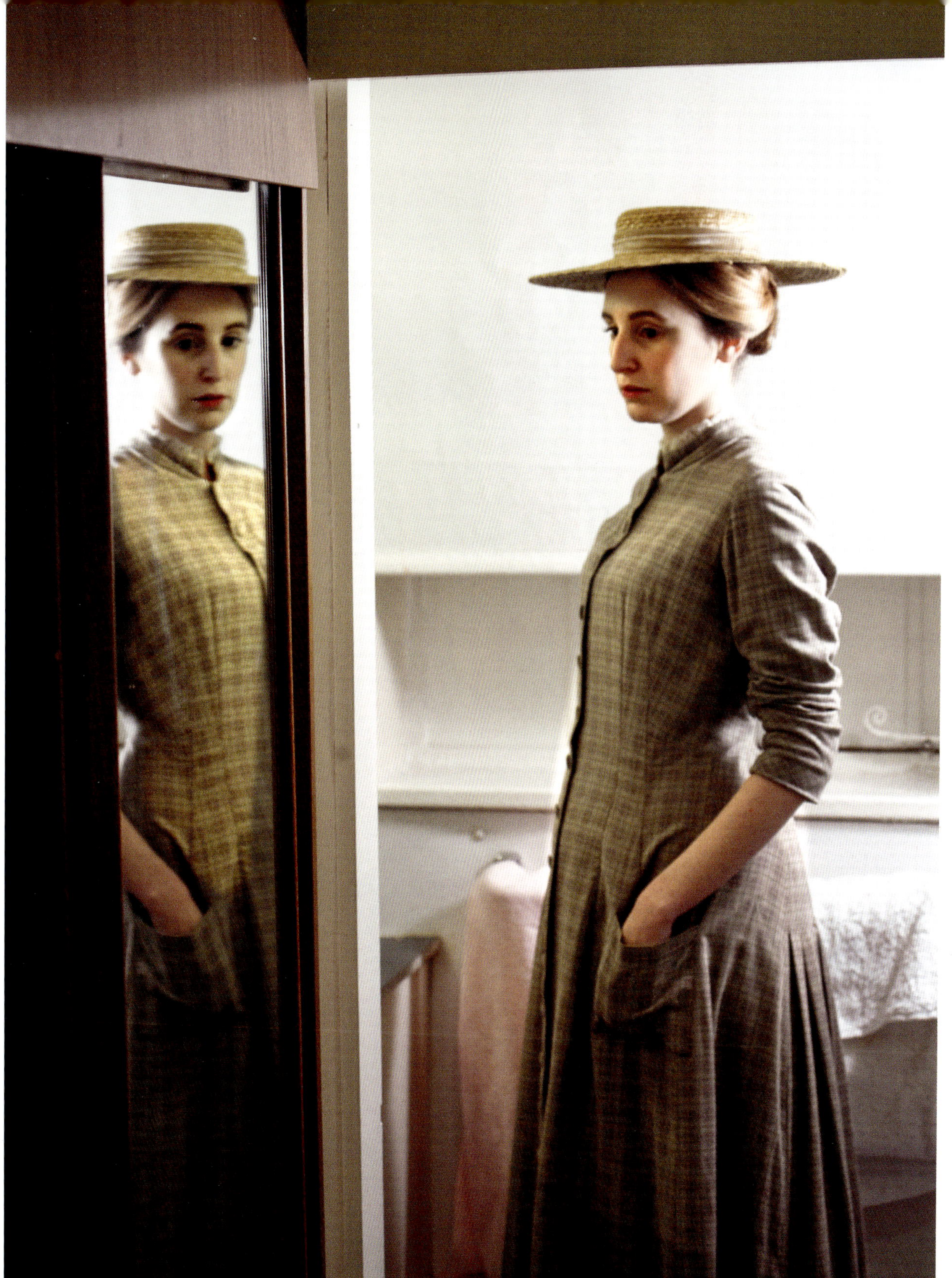

OPPOSITE: **O-T FAGBENLE, *MA RAINEY'S BLACK BOTTOM*, NATIONAL THEATRE, 2016**
Before leaving his room for the stage, he pauses for some cool.

RIGHT: **LAURA CARMICHAEL, *UNCLE VANYA*, VAUDEVILLE THEATRE, 2012**
Here Laura, a star from *Downton Abbey*, is immersed in taking on the character of Sonya, one of the great unsung leads in the canon. The costume is a subtle palette, perhaps suggesting an interior world.

HELEN MIRREN, *PHÈDRE*, NATIONAL THEATRE, 2009

It's rare for Helen to be photographed backstage so I am grateful that five minutes could be found. When I arrived at her dressing room she knew what the photo could be: an image of 'Phèdre' walking down to the stage (in bare feet). She would start walking down the corridor and when passing the open door of her dressing room, on the left, the photo would be taken as the light caught her. She started walking and passed the door before I was ready, and then kept on walking. A photo was taken, just in time, before she continued down to the stage. The flex of a light can be seen on the frame of the door.

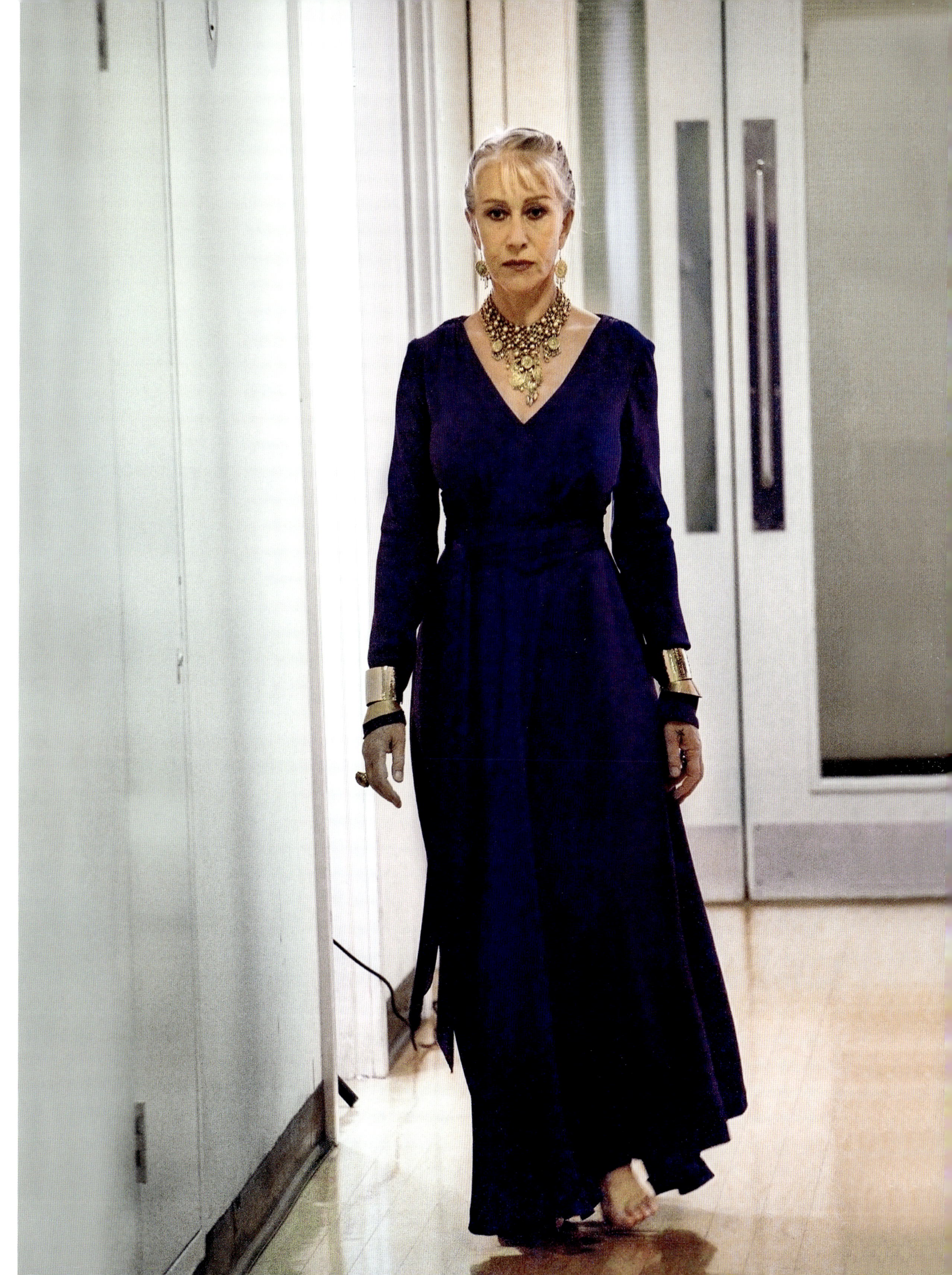

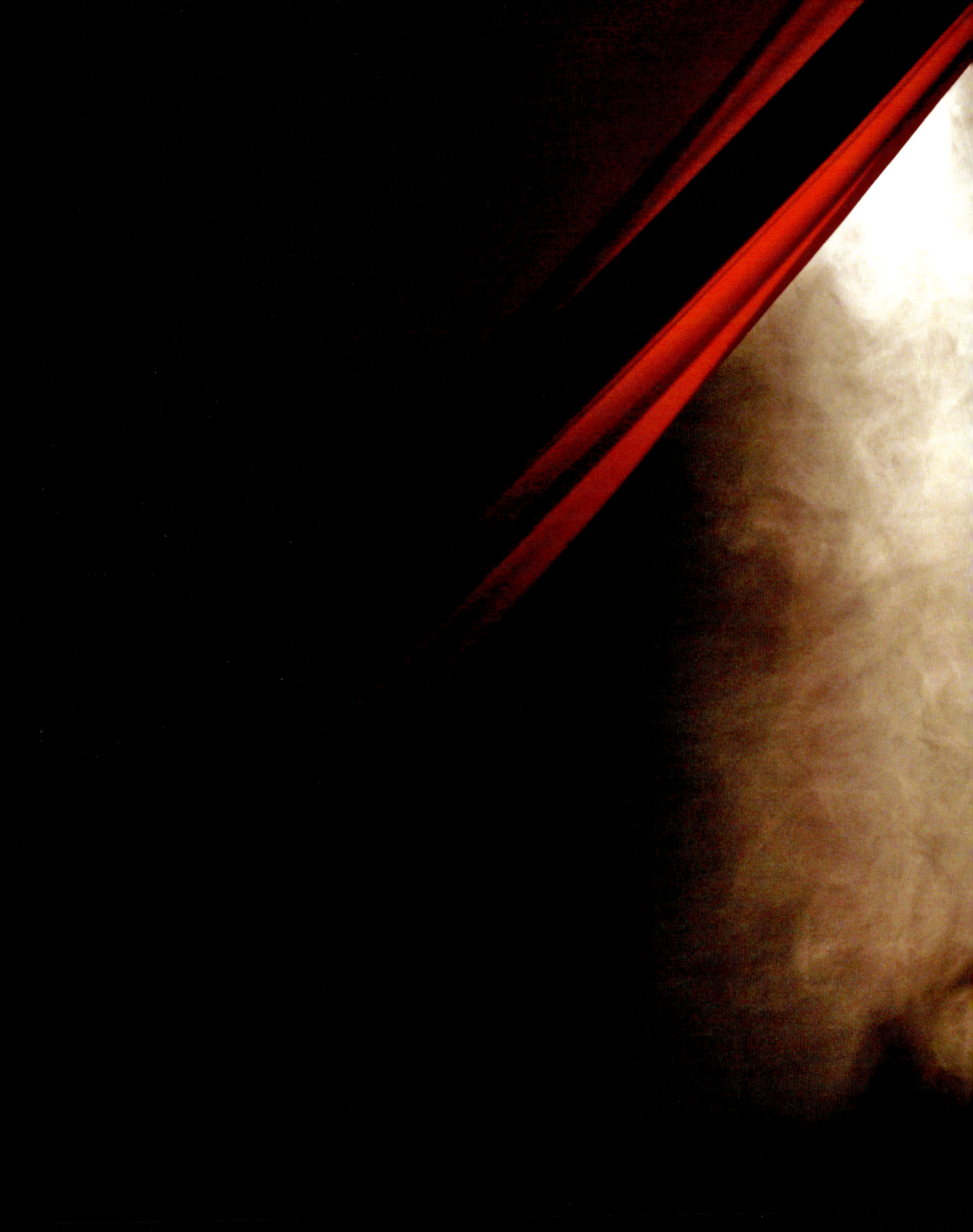

CURTAIN UP

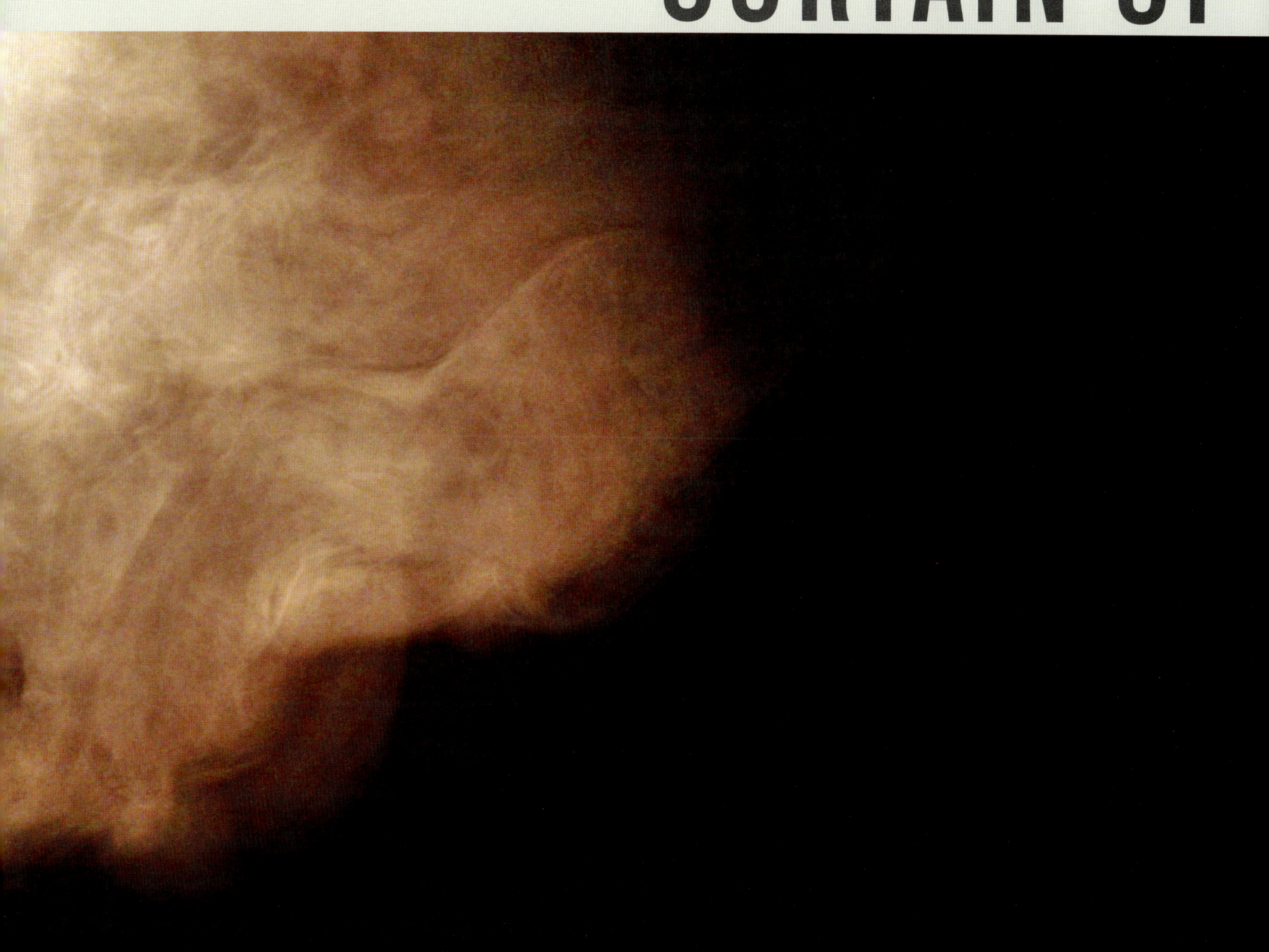

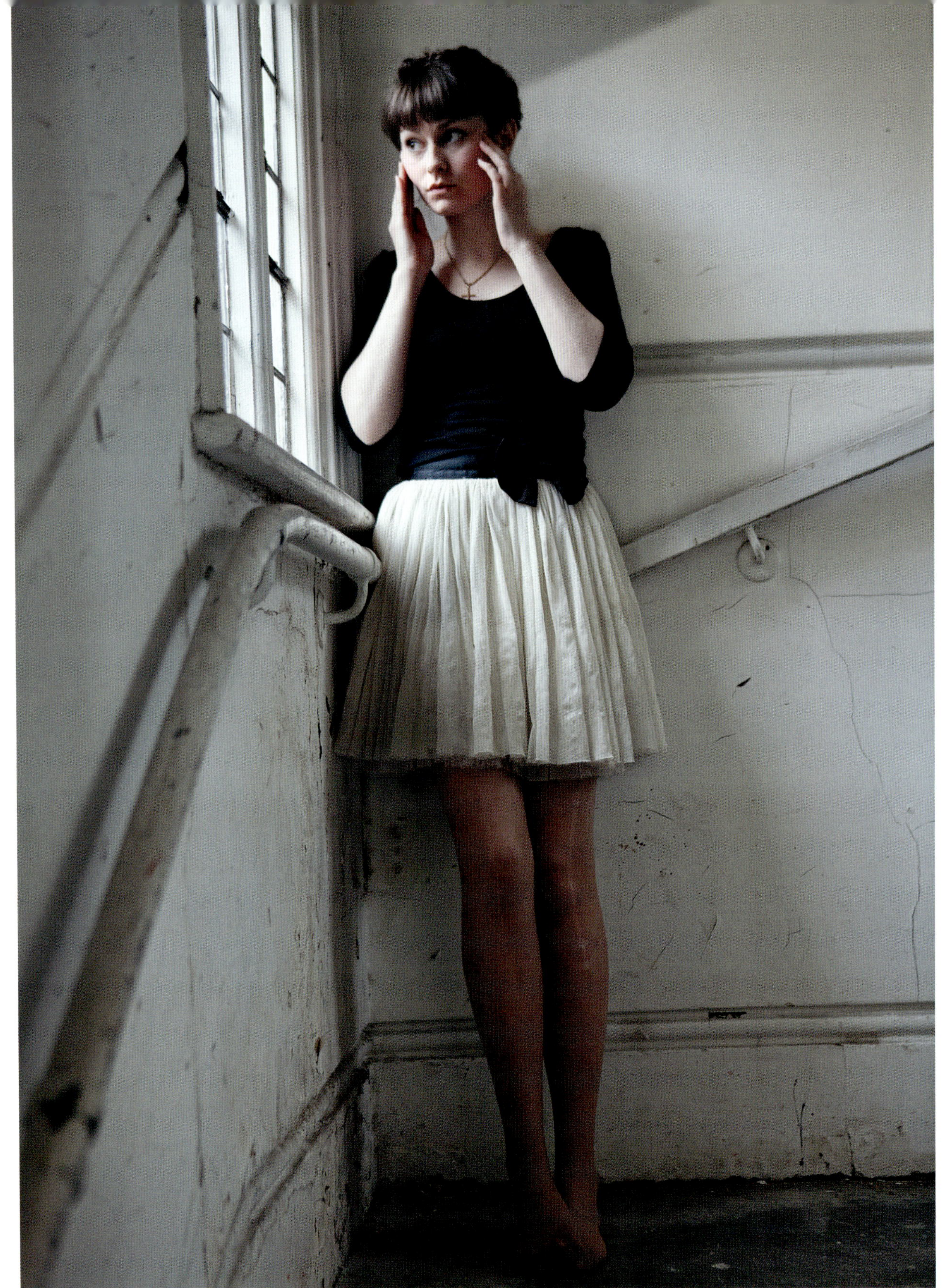

LEFT: **VICTORIA EMSLIE, *NORTHANGER ABBEY*, UPSTAIRS AT THE GATEHOUSE, 2011**
Going down the stairs, towards the stage there is often a window, reminding the actor of the world outside. A rising star, Victoria also has a Masters in Arabic and French.

OPPOSITE: **TOBY JONES, *THE PAINTER*, ARCOLA THEATRE, 2011**
Toby had recently returned from high-profile film jobs in Hollywood. He agreed to play the part of JMW Turner at the wonderful Arcola theatre. The building was originally a paint factory from which Turner and Constable collected their materials.

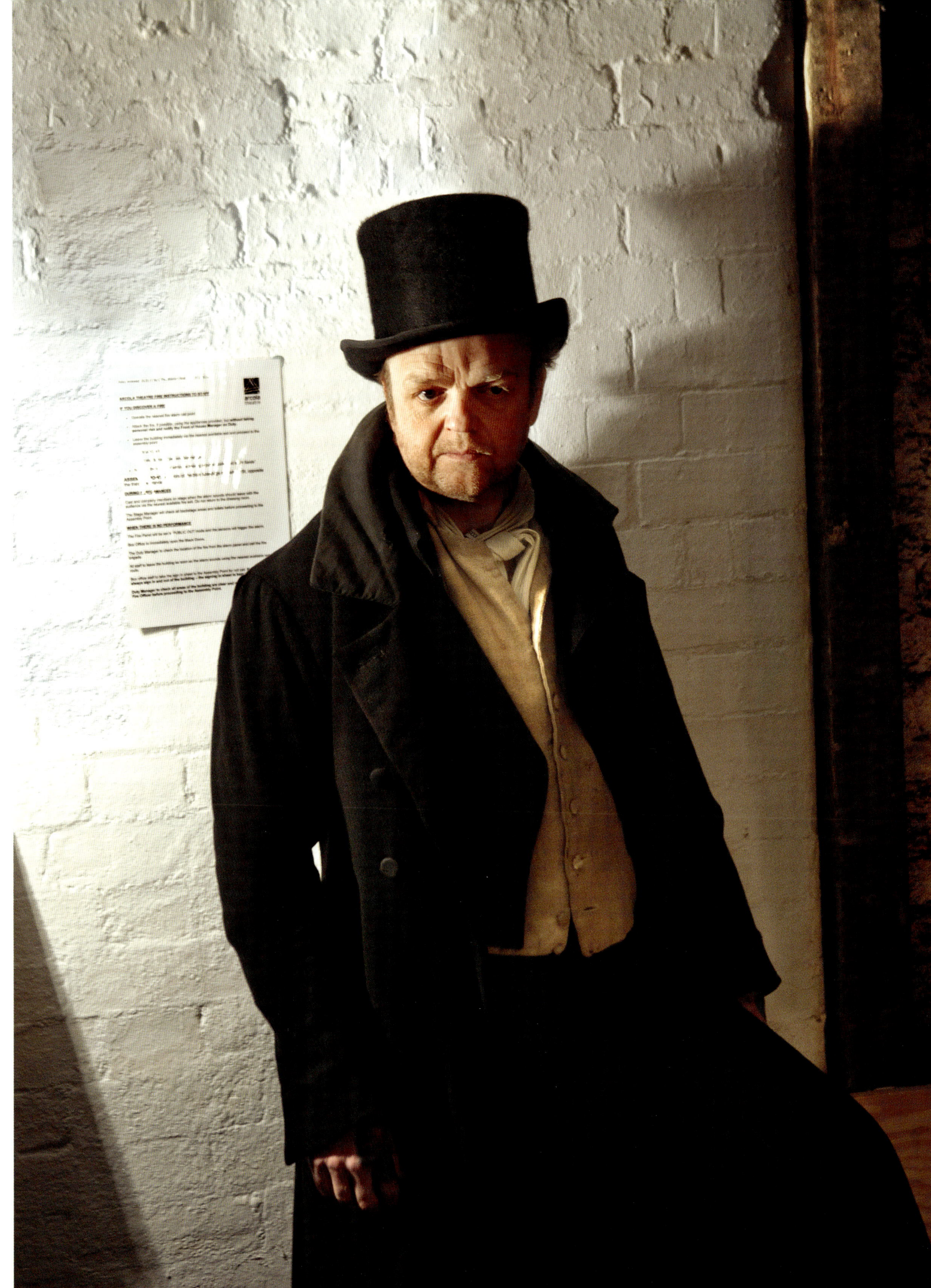

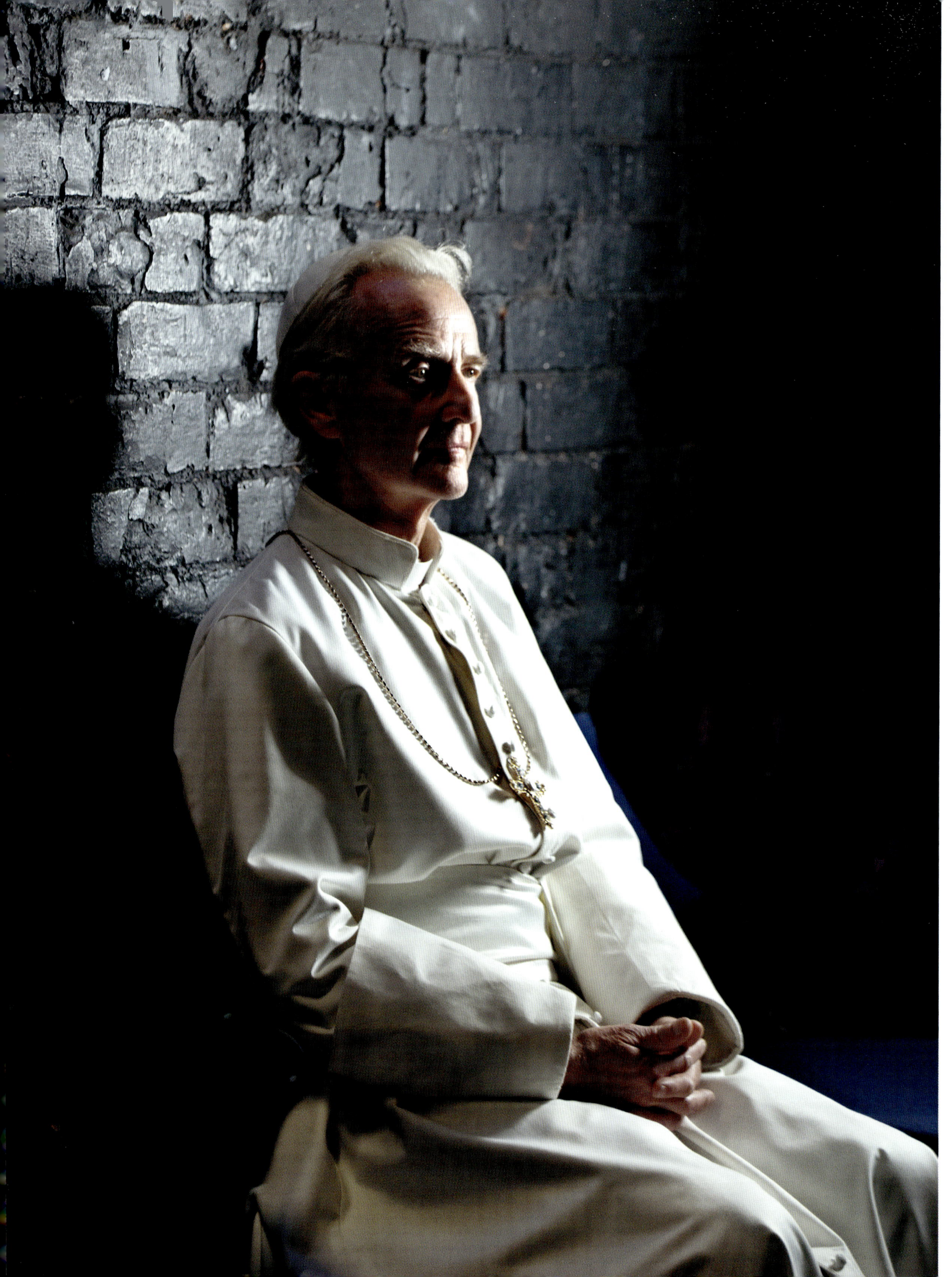

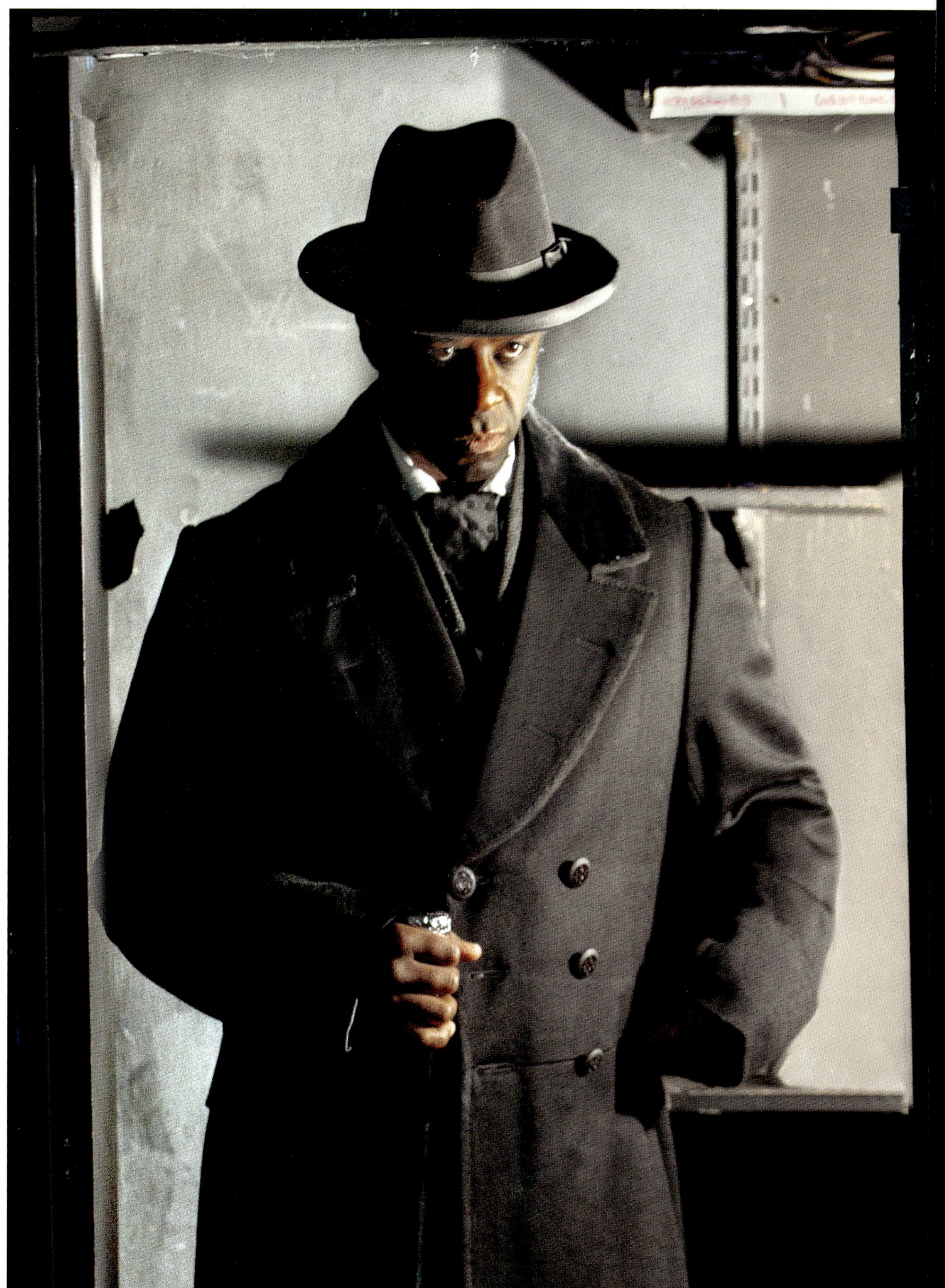

OPPOSITE: **ANTON LESSER, *THE POPE*, ROYAL & DERNGATE, NORTHAMPTON, 2019**
This is a rare sighting of the great actor after ten years' absence from the stage. I drove up to Northampton for the fifteen-minute session before the performance. Anton's presence, his stillness, was beyond compare.

RIGHT: **ADRIAN LESTER, *RED VELVET*, TRICYCLE THEATRE, 2014**
Adrian had created his own personal make-up to suit the look he wanted. Intense concentration as he makes his entrance.

CAREY MULLIGAN, *THE SEAGULL*, ROYAL COURT, 2007

Perfectly cast as Nina, Carey is here on the brink of a bright career in film and TV. She also maintains a deep interest in philanthropy.

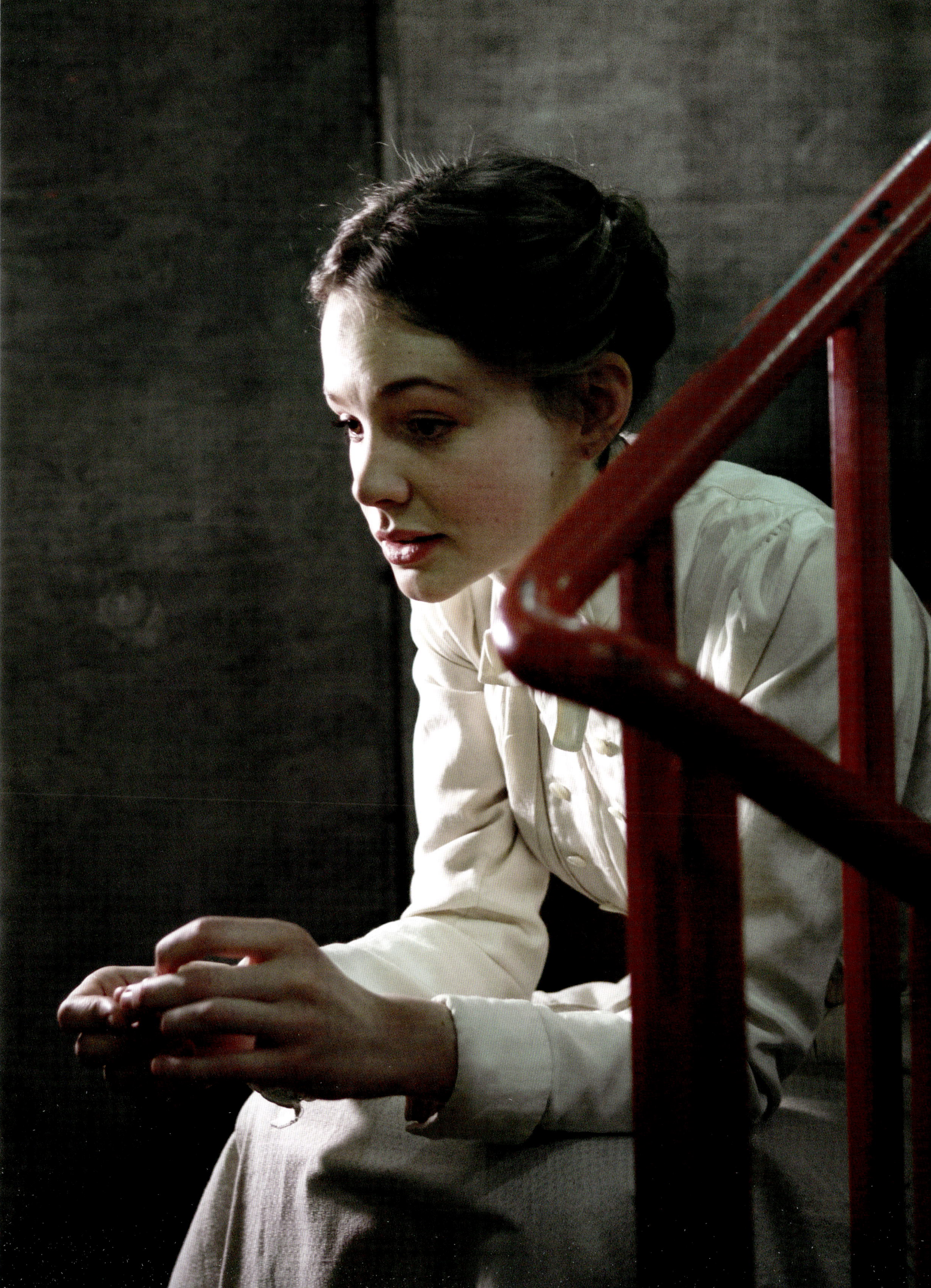

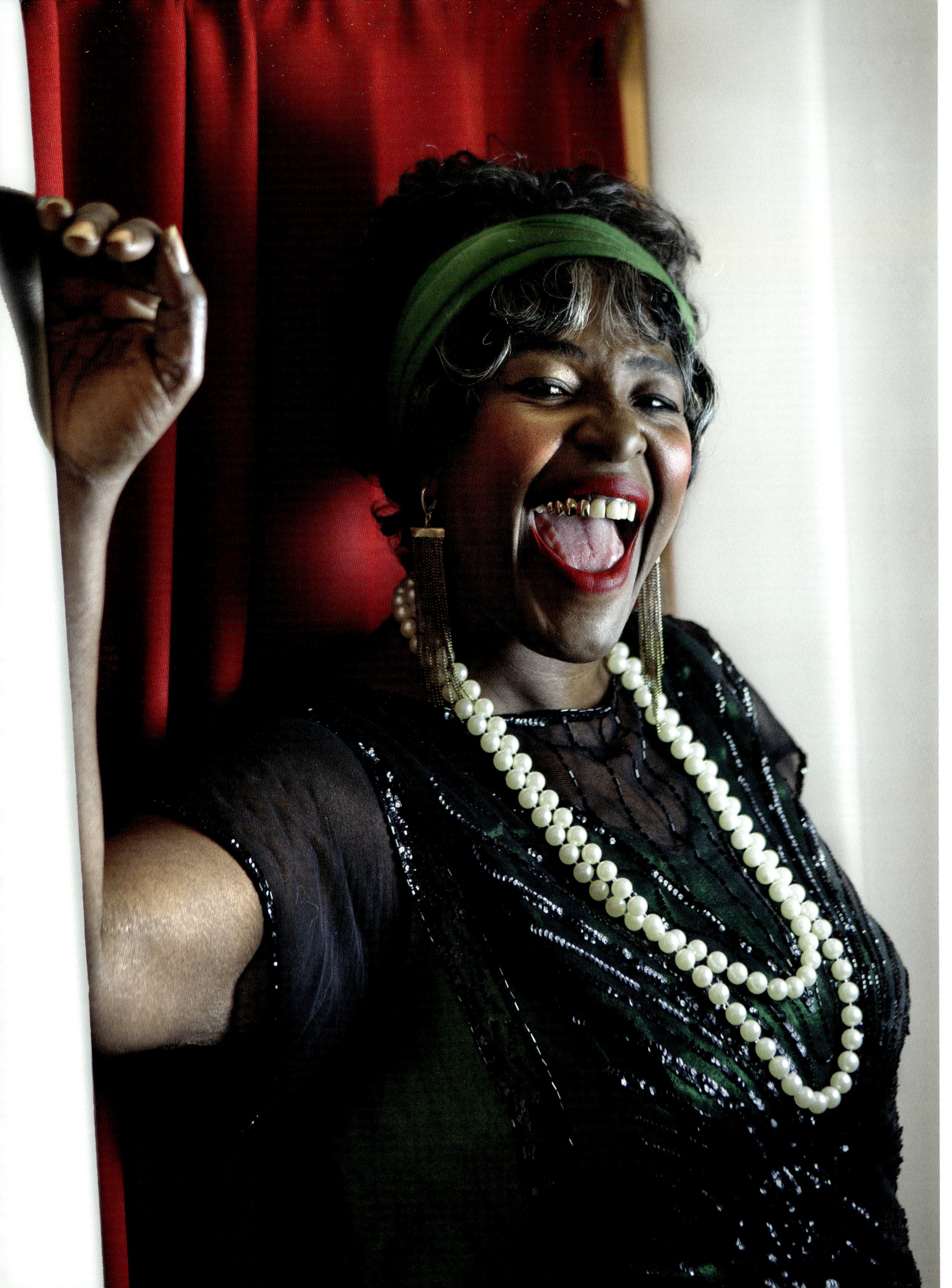

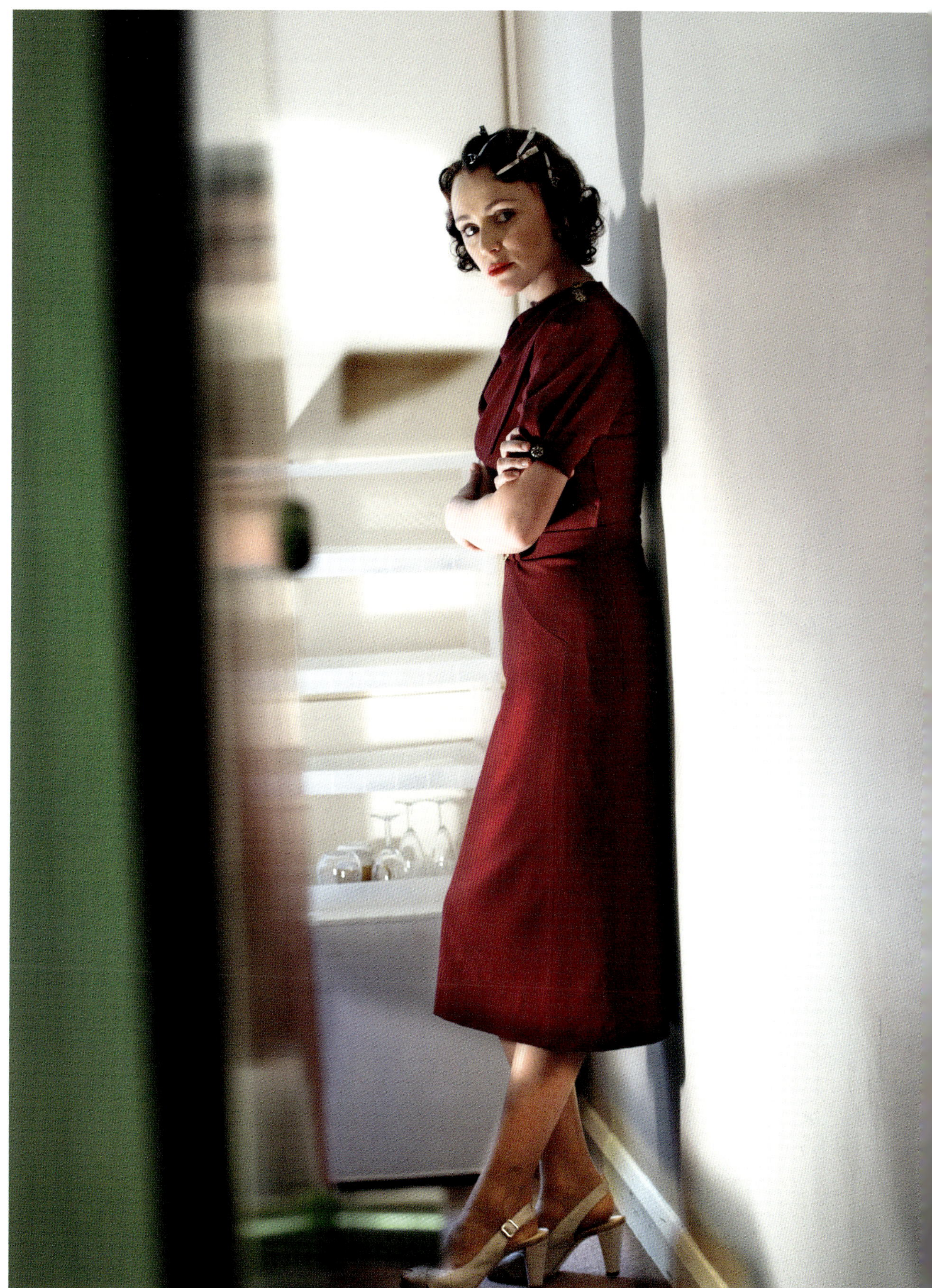

OPPOSITE: **SHARON D. CLARKE, *MA RAINEY'S BLACK BOTTOM*, NATIONAL THEATRE, 2016**
The extraordinarily talented Sharon is now being given the work she richly deserves.

RIGHT: **KEELEY HAWES, *ROCKET TO THE MOON*, NATIONAL THEATRE, 2011**
Keeley's endless versatility in many different genres has been remarkable to see over the last twenty years.

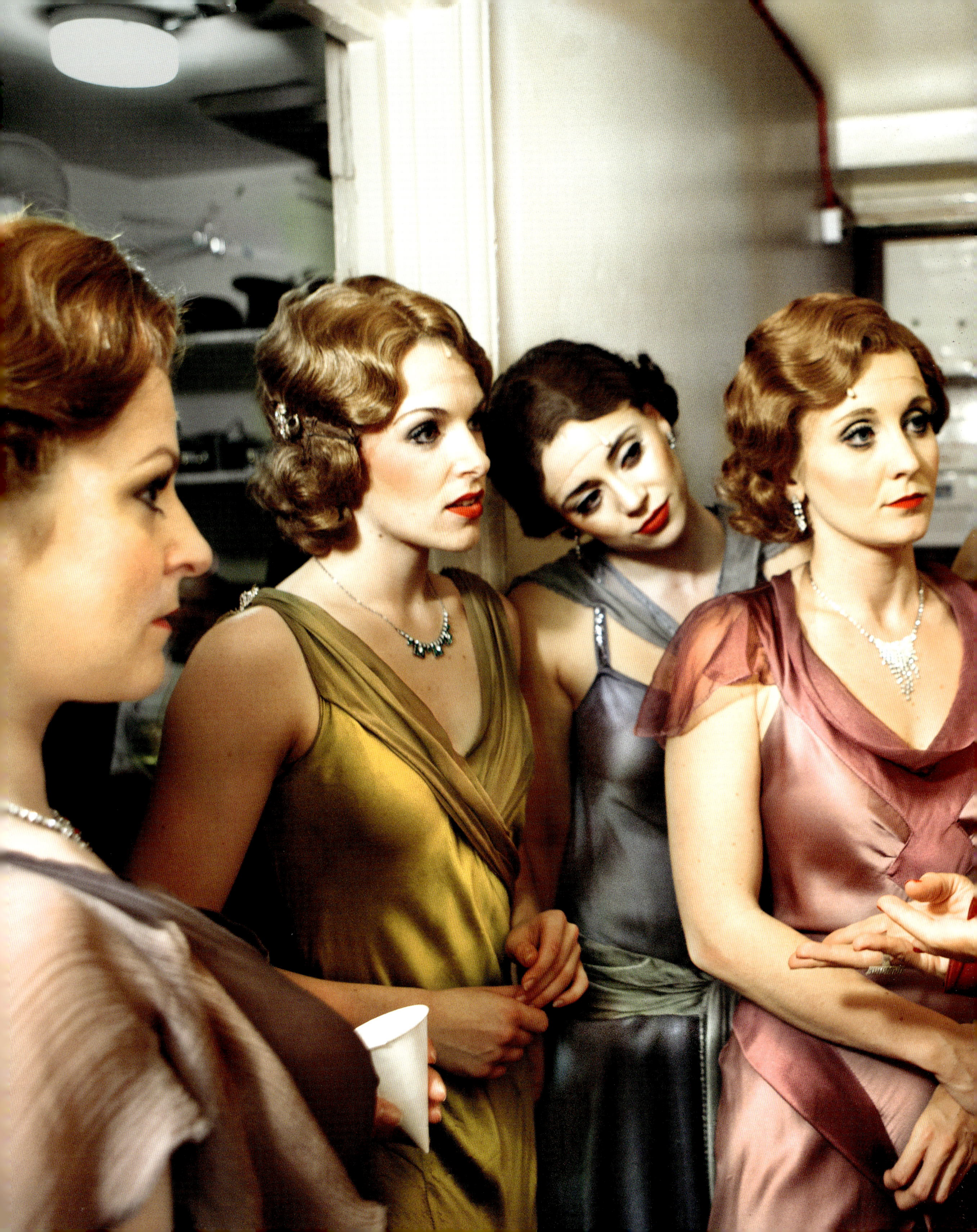

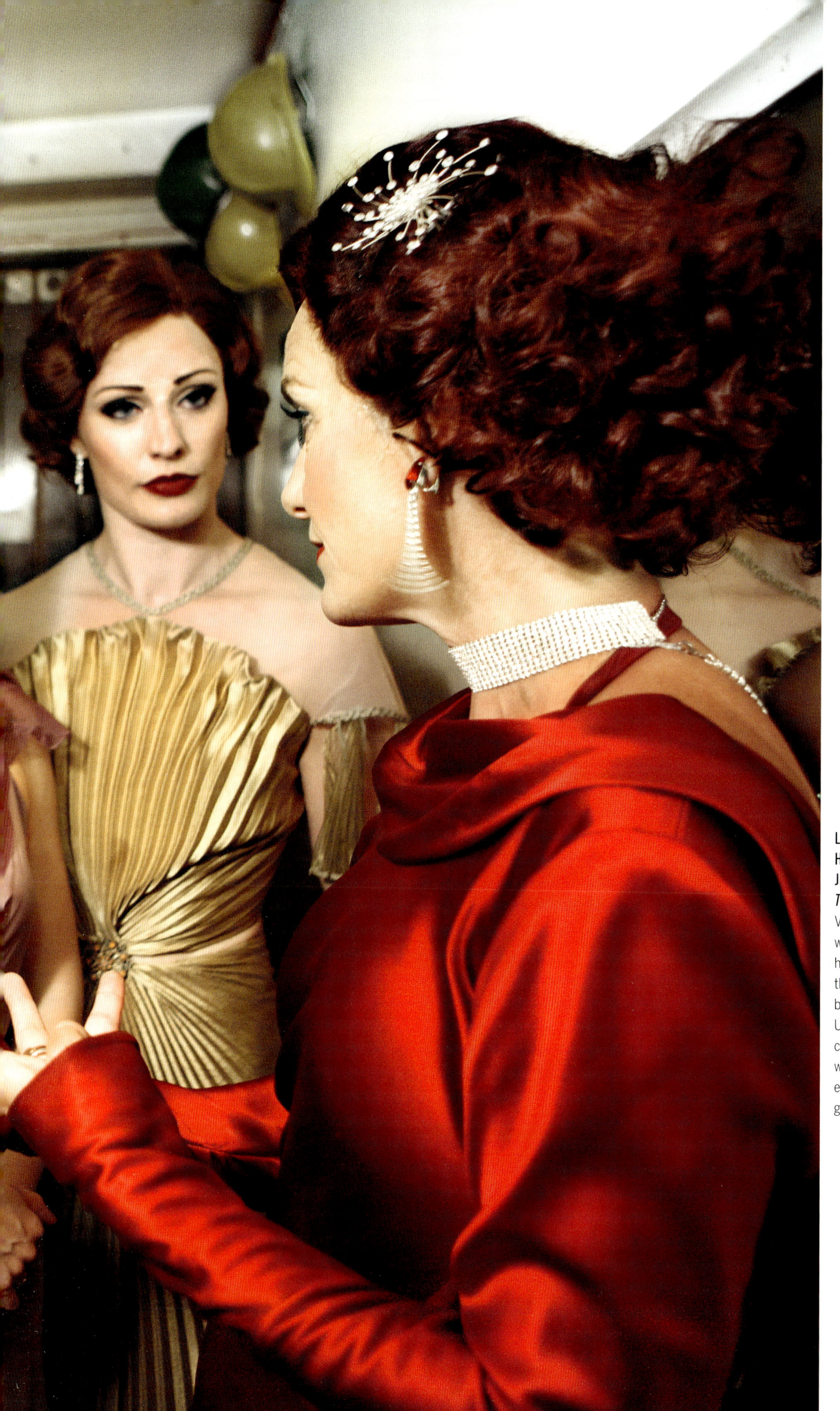

LAUREN APPLEBY, HOLLY ROSTRON, HANNAH CAUCHI, CHARLOTTE GALE, JENNY LEGG, VIVIEN PARRY, *TOP HAT*, ALDWYCH THEATRE, 2012

Vivien told me: 'I have no idea what we were talking about. It was the happiest job. I had just got married, the Olympics came to London, I'd been at the 100-metre final watching Usain Bolt win gold. We had a book club, a politics and info corner. Each week we'd meet and discuss current events. It seems like a beautiful, golden time, a long time ago.'

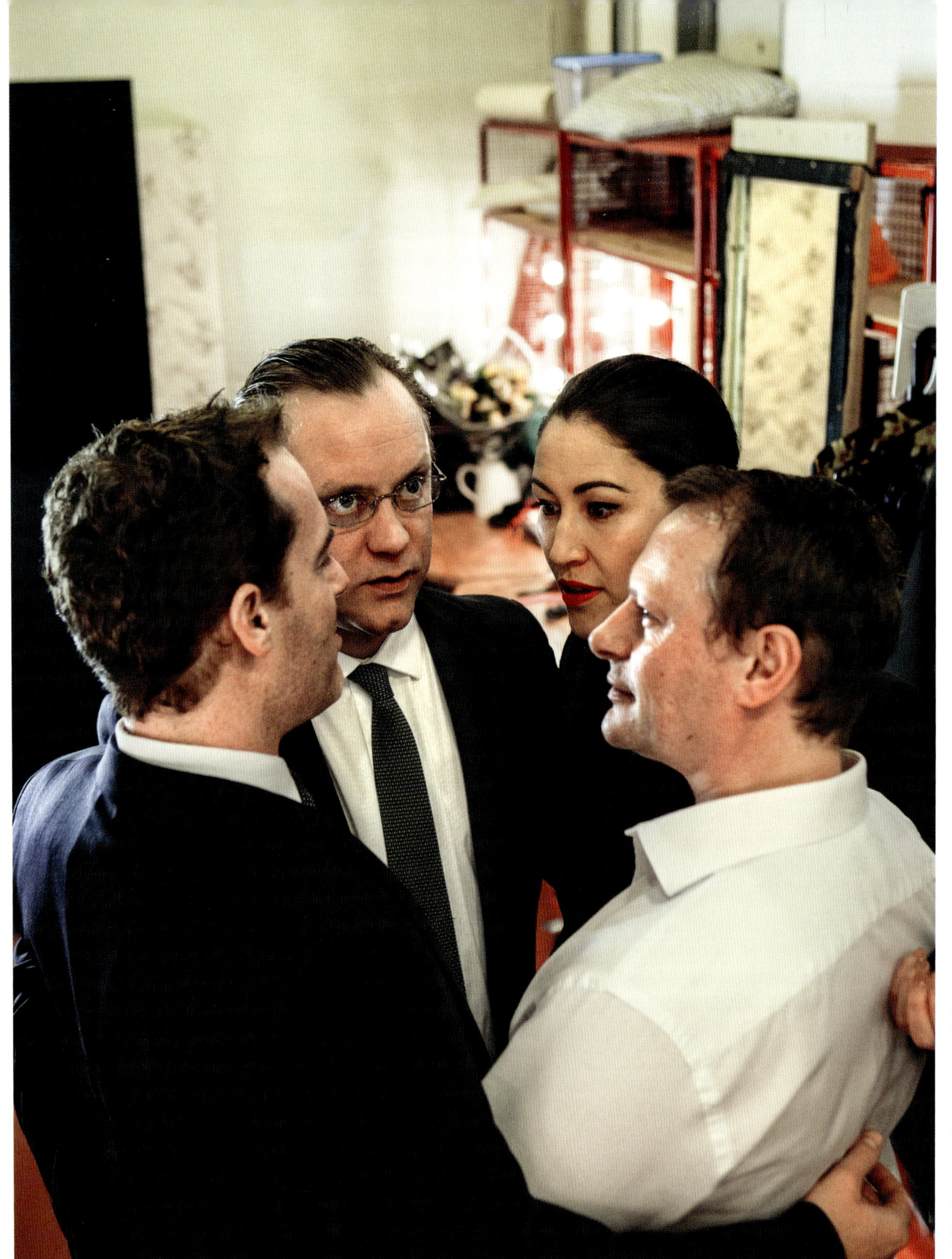

LEFT: **ADAM JAMES, SAM TROUGHTON, ELEANOR MATSUURA, NEIL STUKE, *BULL*, YOUNG VIC, 2015**
The quartet hugs just before they leave the room to play a tight and brilliantly written play by Mike Bartlett, directed by his wife Clare Lizzimore. They also shared the dressing room.

OPPOSITE: **ANNA GUNN, *THE NIGHT OF THE IGUANA*, NOËL COWARD THEATRE, 2019**
Anna is waiting for her moment to enter the stage. A star of the legendary *Breaking Bad* TV series, this was a rare appearance on the London stage.

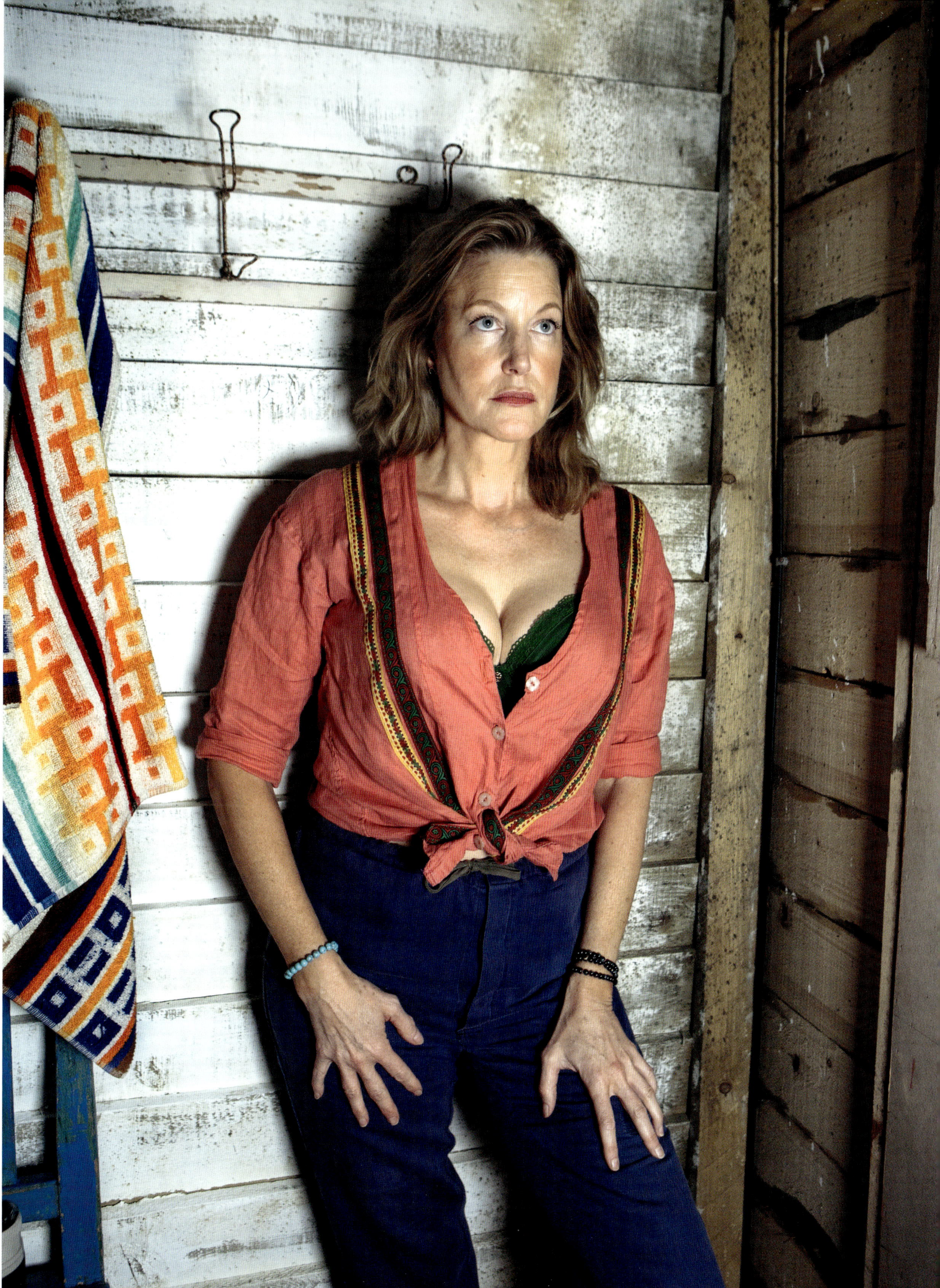

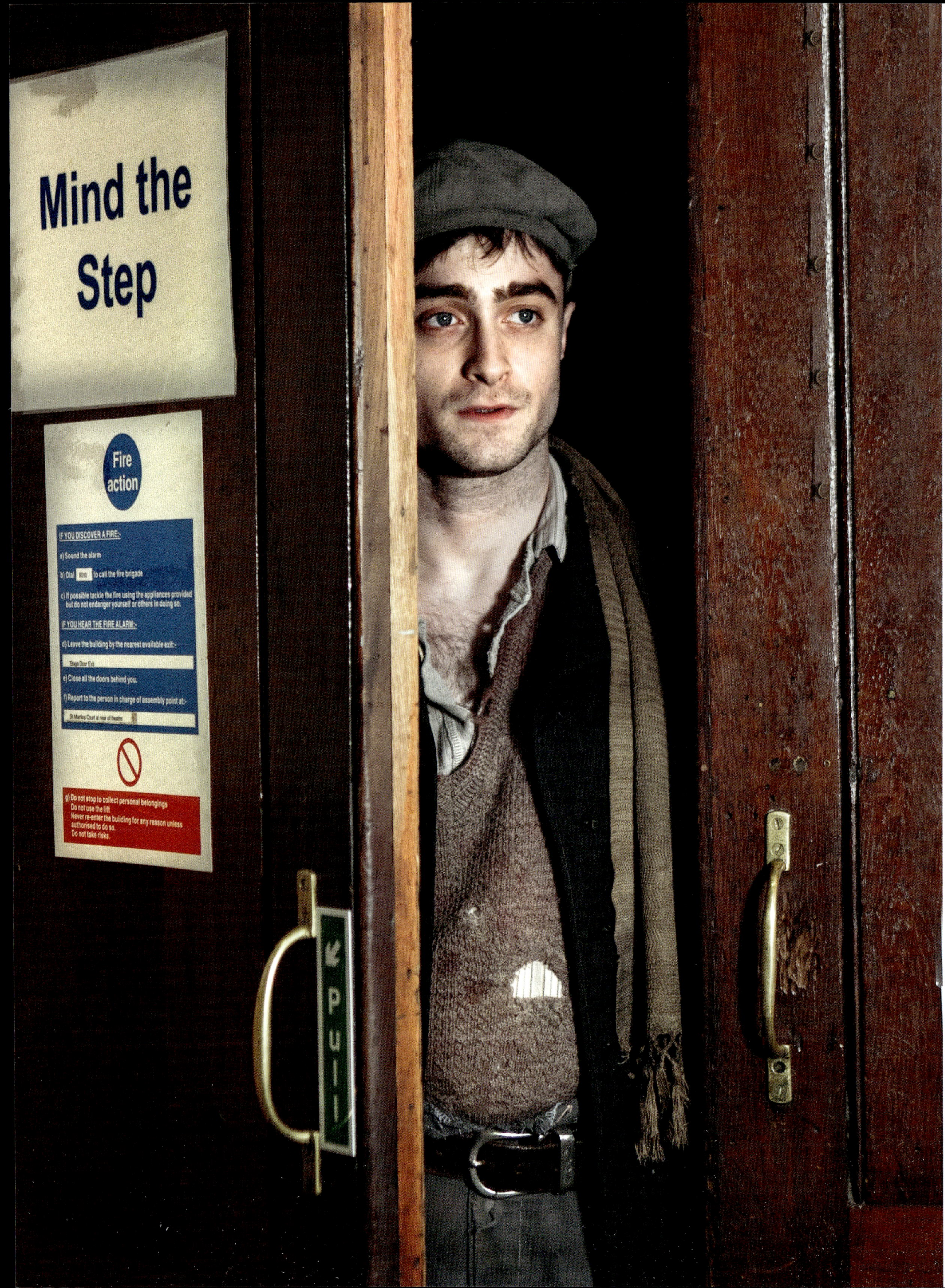

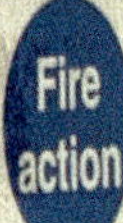
Mind the Step
Fire action
IF YOU DISCOVER A FIRE:-
a) Sound the alarm
b) Dial to call the fire brigade
c) If possible tackle the fire using the appliances provided but do not endanger yourself or others in doing so.
IF YOU HEAR THE FIRE ALARM:-
d) Leave the building by the nearest available exit:-
Stage Door Exit
e) Close all the doors behind you.
f) Report to the person in charge of assembly point at:-

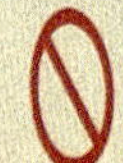
g) Do not stop to collect personal belongings
Do not use the lift
Never re-enter the building for any reason unless authorised to do so.
Do not take risks.
Pull

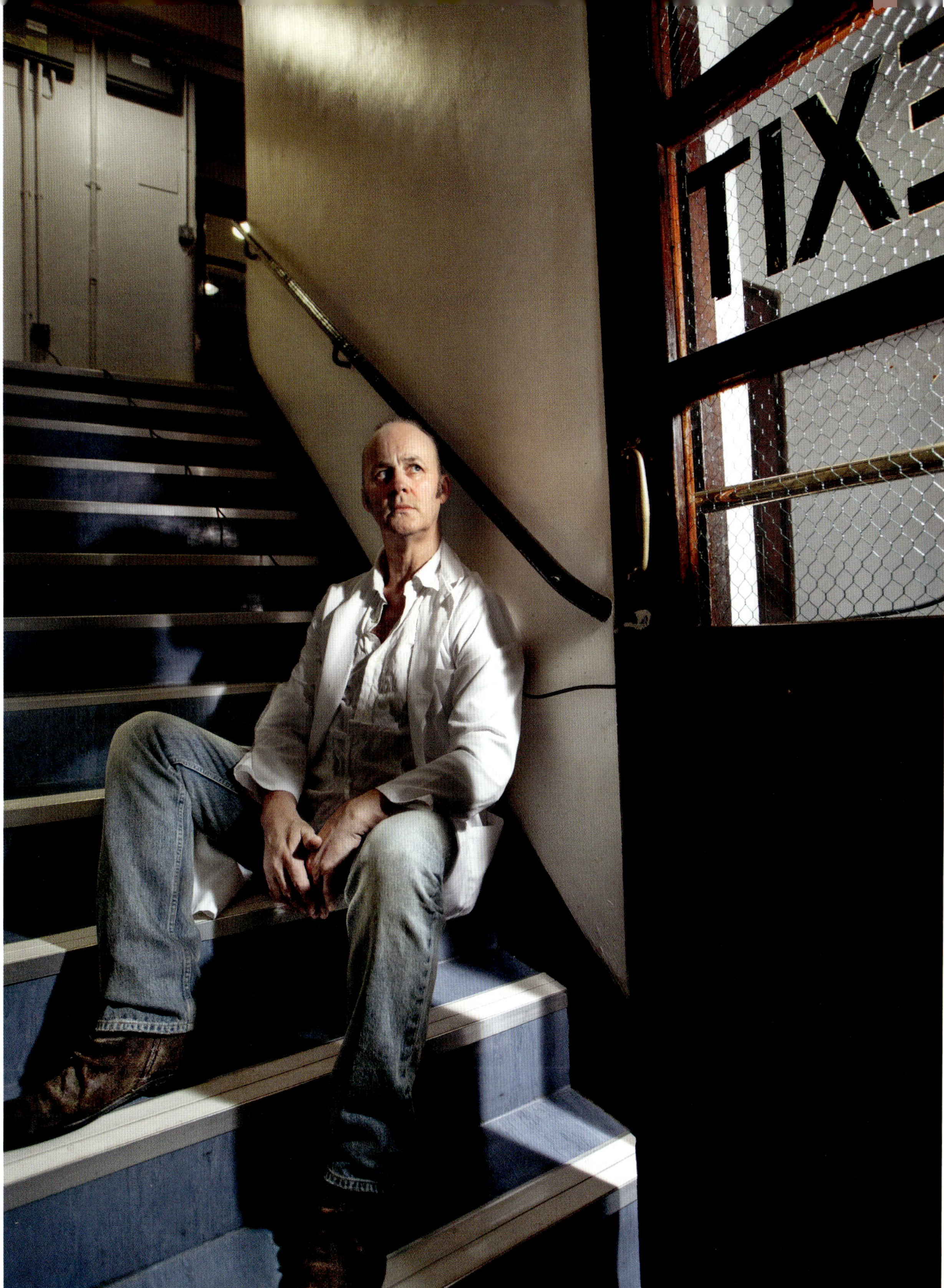

OPPOSITE: **DANIEL RADCLIFFE, *THE CRIPPLE OF INISHMAAN*, NOËL COWARD THEATRE, 2013**
Daniel is coming offstage, through the famous doors that Olivier, Gielgud and Richardson passed through in the legendary seasons of 1947, which gave sustenance to Londoners after the Blitz.

RIGHT: **TIM McINNERNY, *WHAT THE BUTLER SAW*, VAUDEVILLE THEATRE, 2012**
In the theatre, when the call is announced for the play to begin, there is no escape. Tim has journeyed from masterful comic performances with Rowan Atkinson to many dramatic roles on TV and film. This range is an uncommon and difficult feat to achieve.

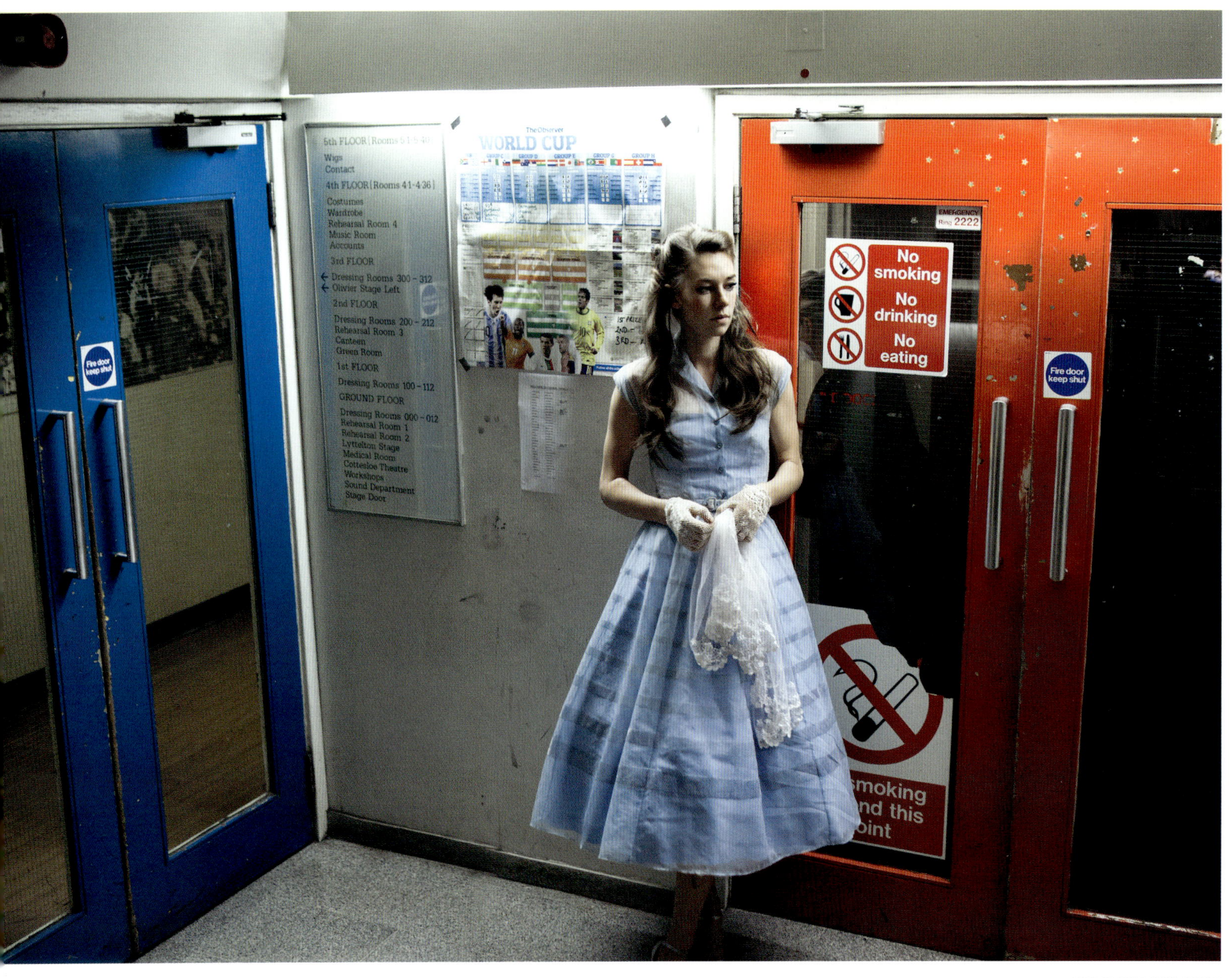

ABOVE: **VANESSA KIRBY, *WOMEN BEWARE WOMEN*, NATIONAL THEATRE, 2010**
The young actress before her TV breakthrough in *The Crown* as Princess Margaret; she is waiting to enter onto the National Theatre stage.

OPPOSITE: **PETER CAPALDI, *THE LADYKILLERS*, GIELGUD THEATRE, 2011**
Just before he took on the role of *Dr Who*, gathering himself prior to his entrance. A warm, kind and generous man, he is a master at portraying some of the vicious, unkinder tendencies in human nature.

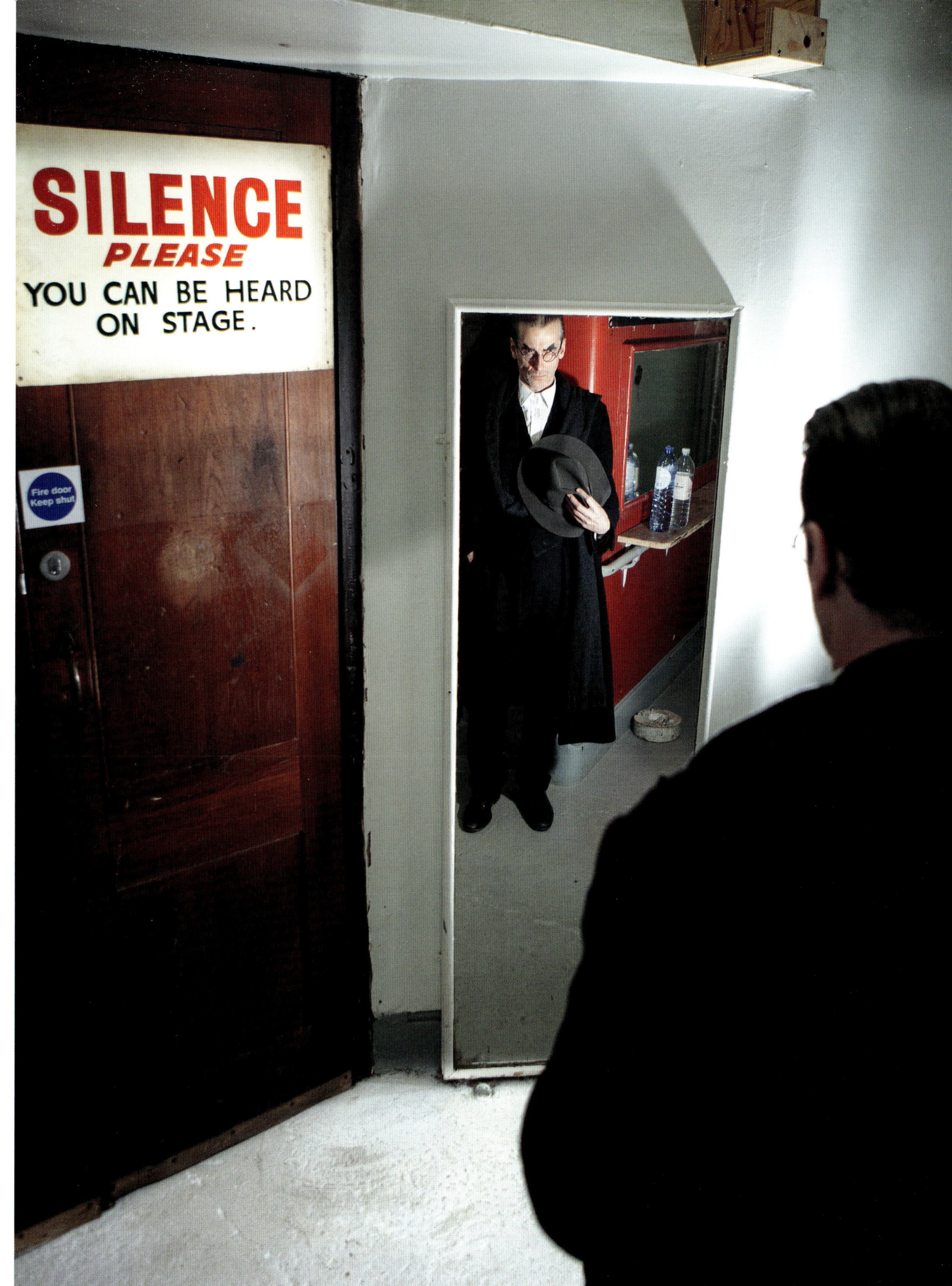
SILENCE
PLEASE
YOU CAN BE HEARD
ON STAGE.
Fire door
Keep shut

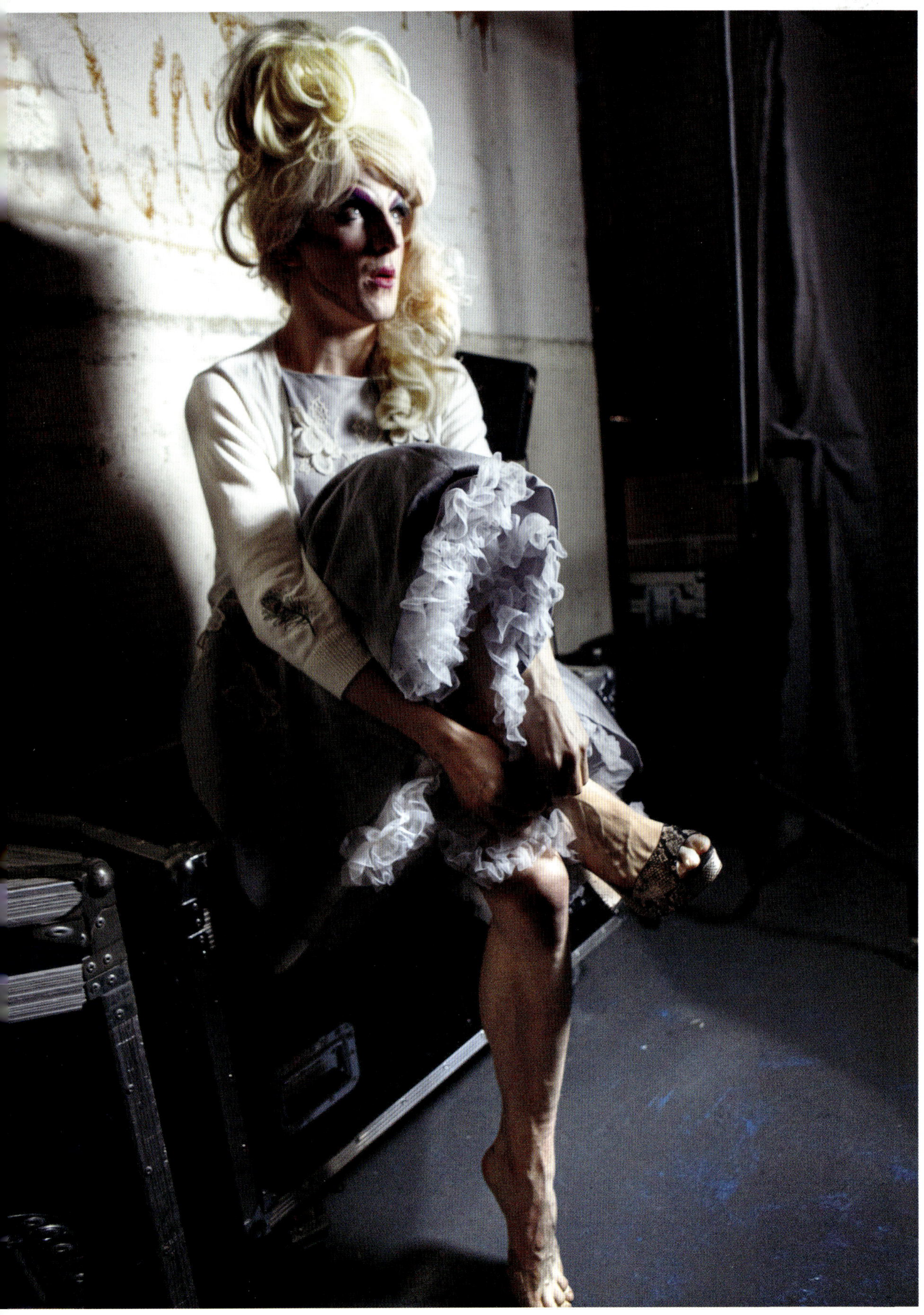

LEFT: **SHIRLEY DU NAUGHTY, *DENIM*, VAULT FESTIVAL, 2016**
Making sure the shoes are ready before going on.

OPPOSITE: **THE CHORUS, *VIVID*, FRIEDRICHSTADT-PALAST, 2018**
Backstage in Berlin. The adult sensibility of fetish treated with ease by the inheritors of a particular tradition in that city.

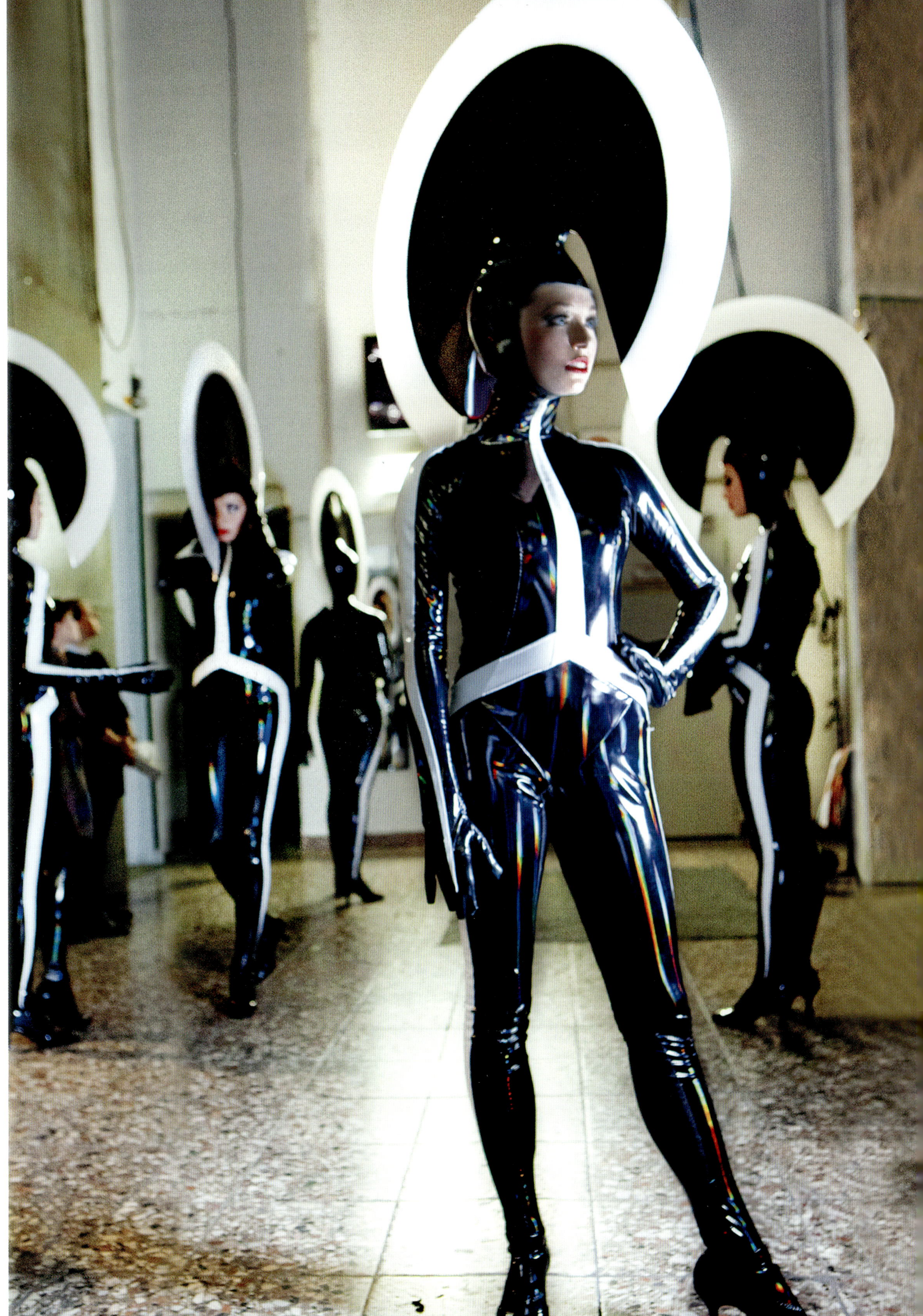

KATY STEPHENS, *TITUS ANDRONICUS*,
RSC, 2013

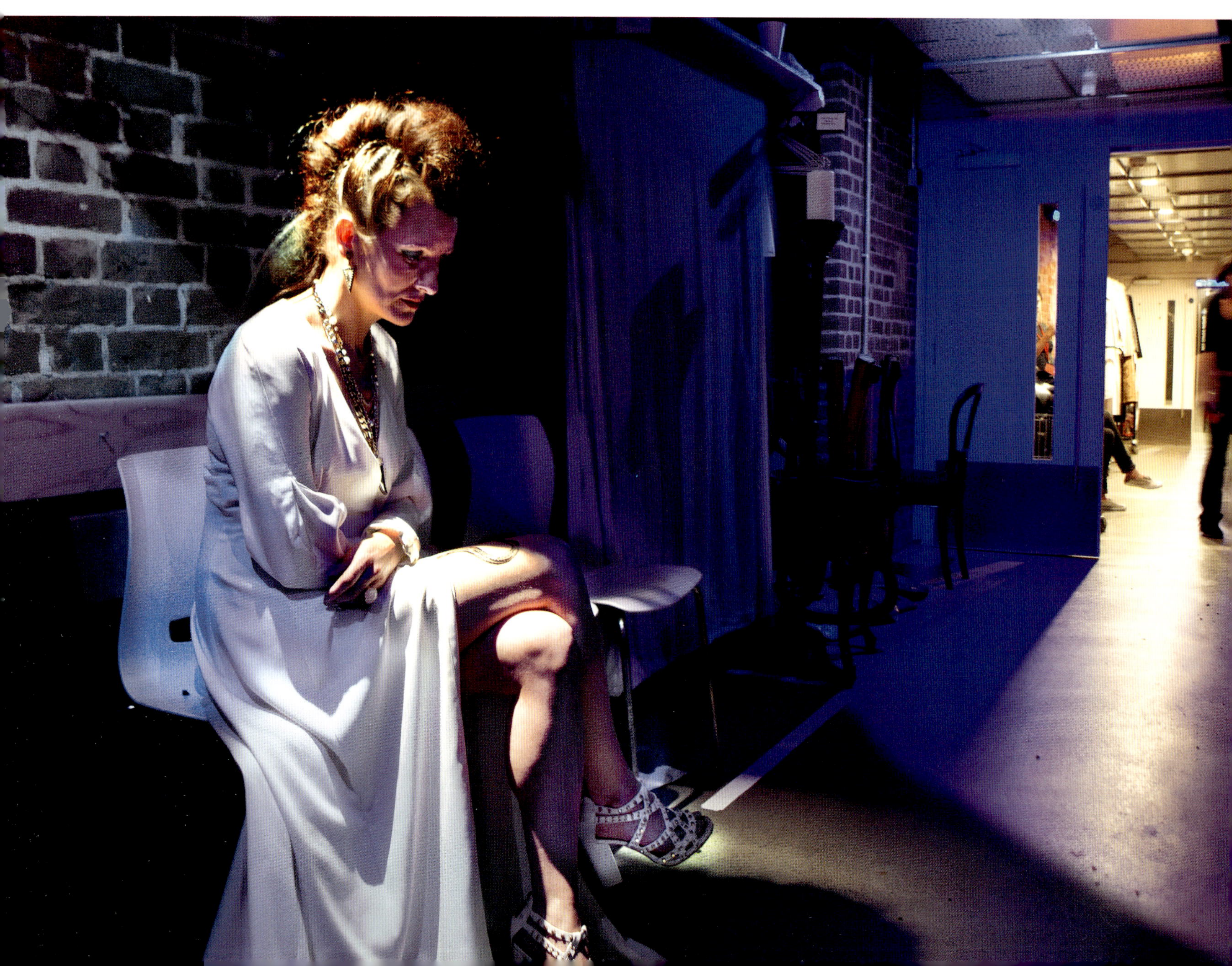

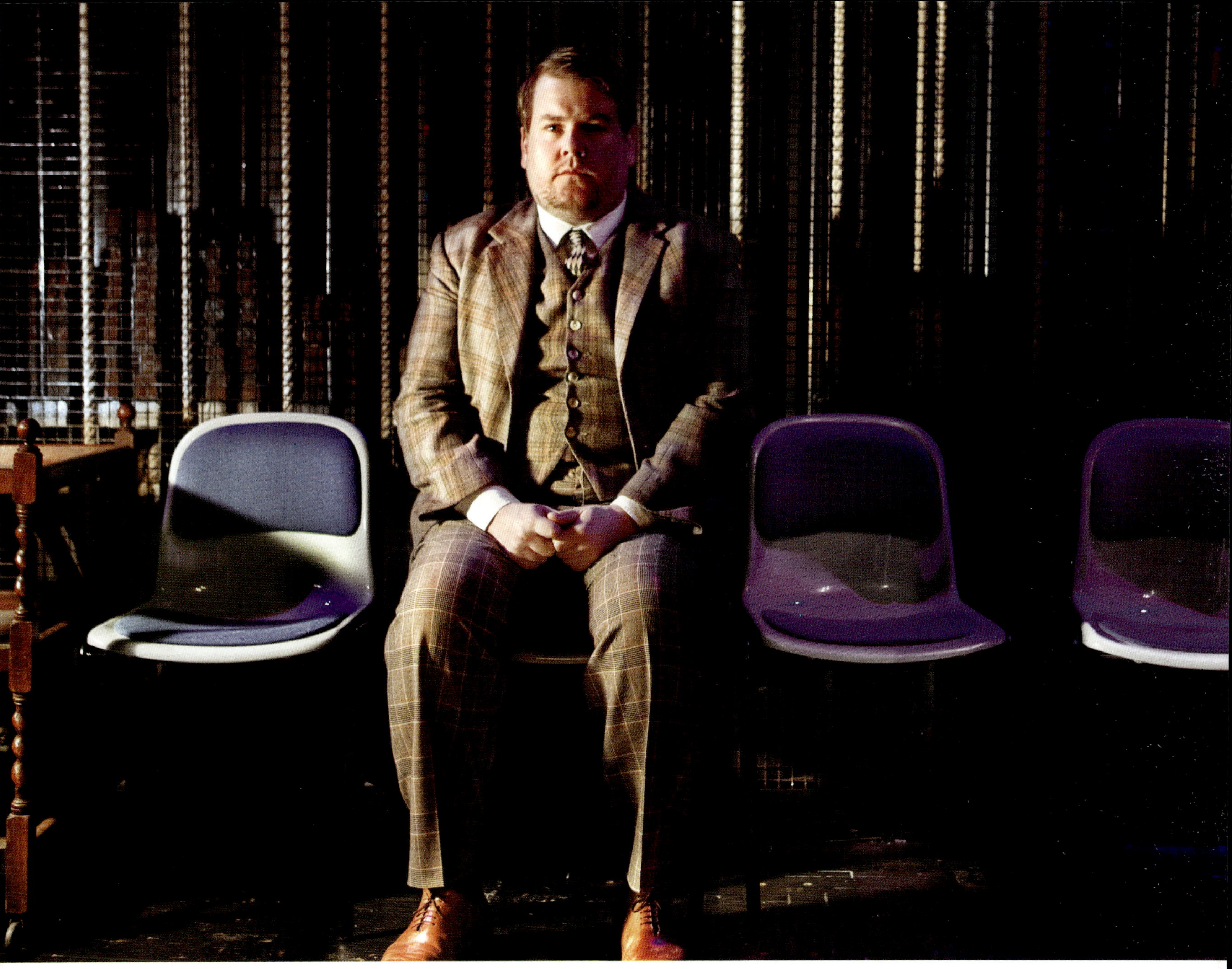

JAMES CORDEN, *ONE MAN, TWO GUVNORS*, NATIONAL THEATRE, 2012
James and Katy are focusing before shows that required an enormous amount of physical and mental energy to perform. One a Shakespearean tragedy, the other a rollicking farce by Richard Bean. Both were a critical success and highly popular.

LILY JAMES, *THE SEAGULL*, SOUTHWARK PLAYHOUSE, 2012

Just before she broke through as a film star, this is Lily playing in Chekhov at a fringe venue. She is blessed with an irrepressible energy that can be fine-tuned into a moment of great subtlety with the click of a finger. There was never any doubt she would make it.

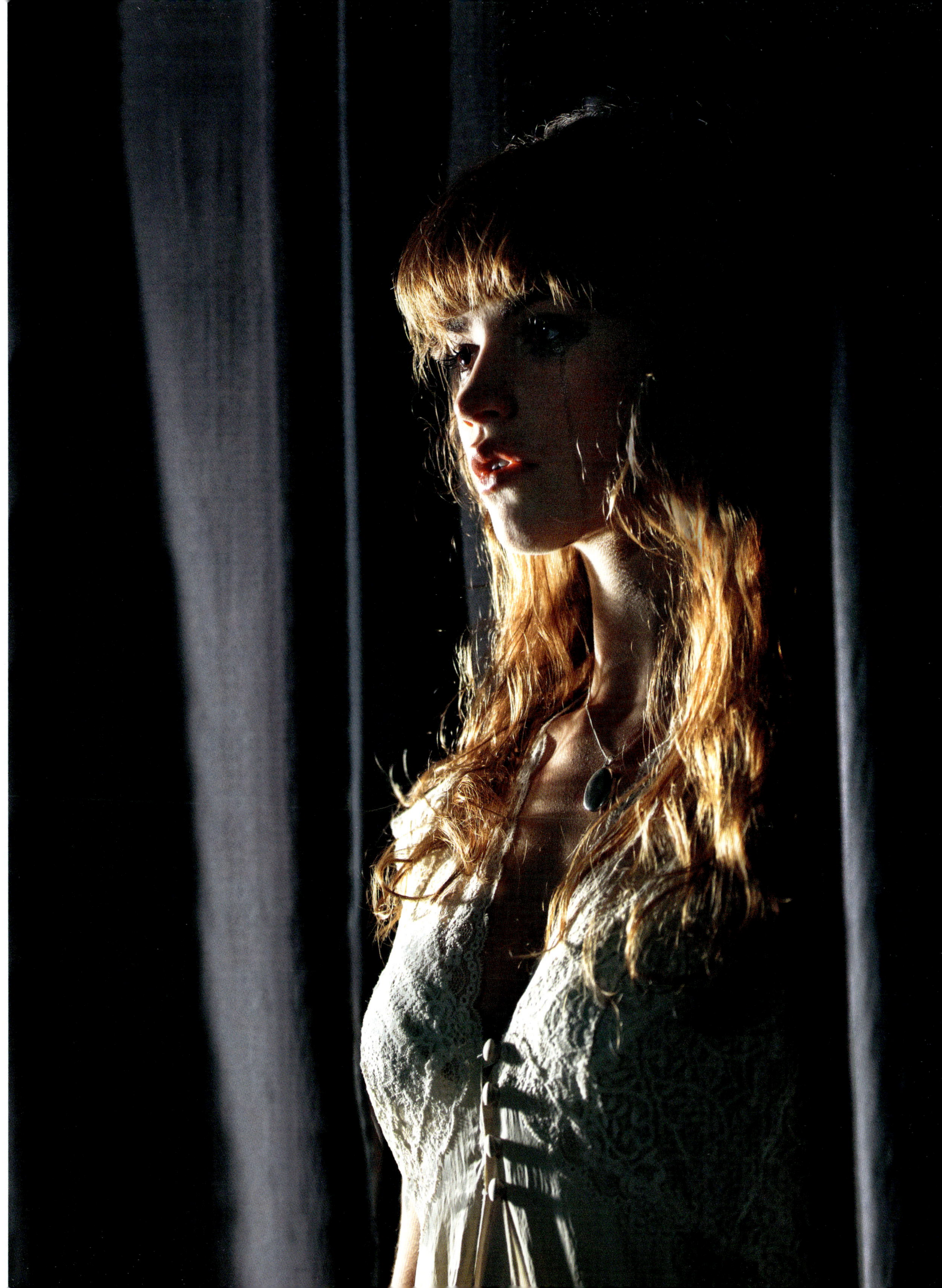

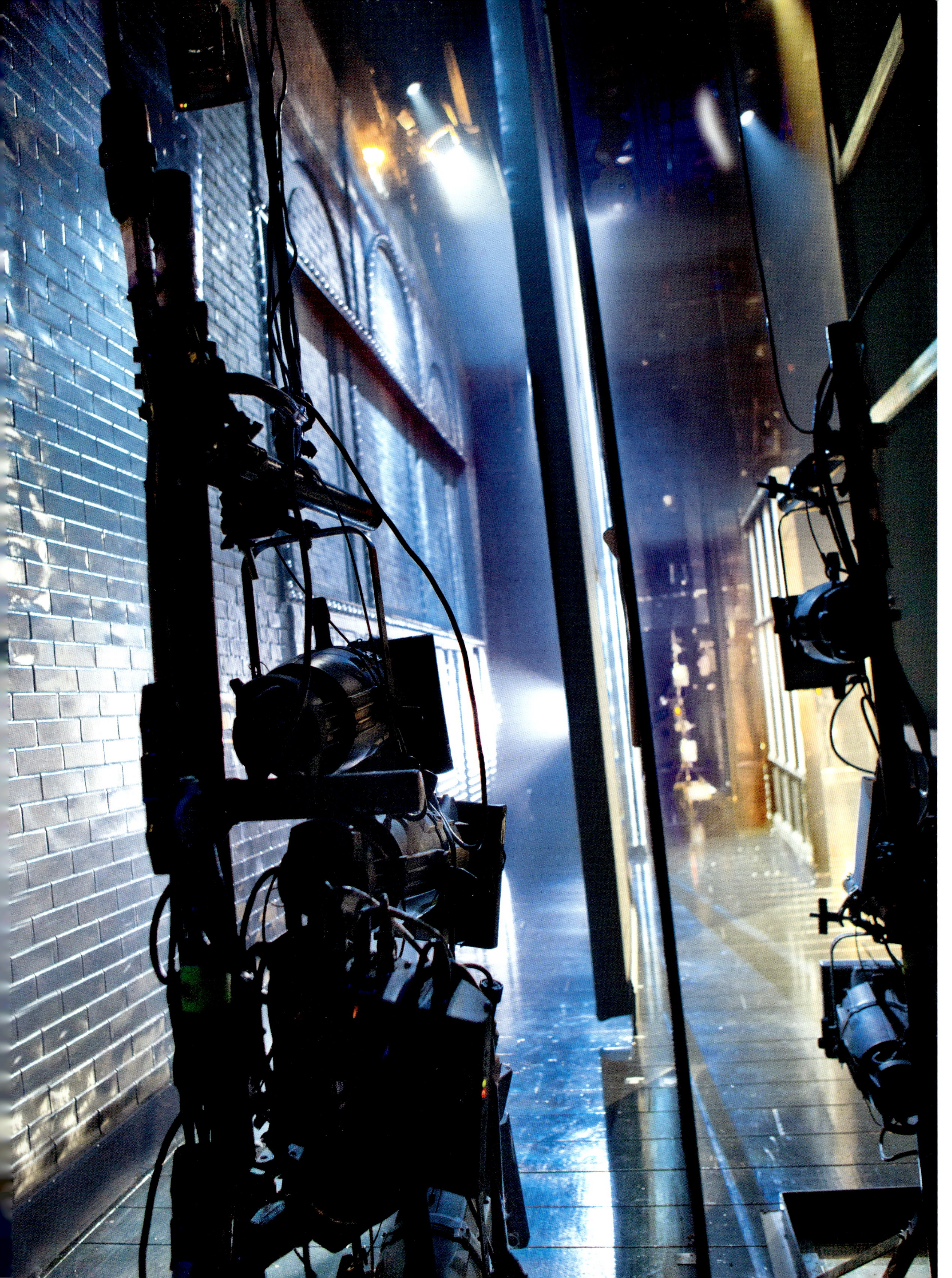

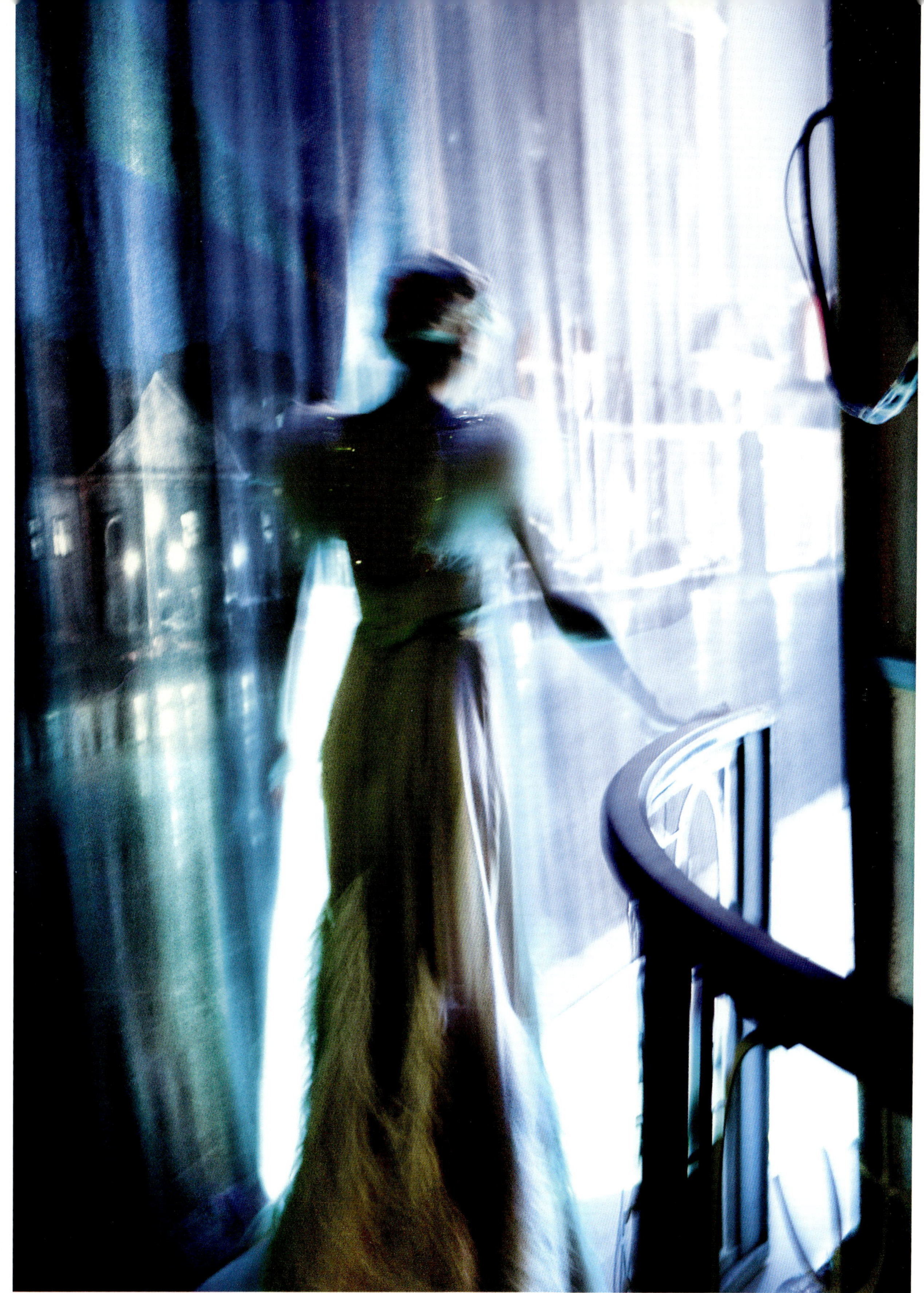

OPPOSITE: ***CABARET***,
SAVOY THEATRE, 2013
From the wings.

RIGHT: ***TOP HAT***,
ALDWYCH THEATRE, 2012
Backstage, the anticipation of a story about to unfold.

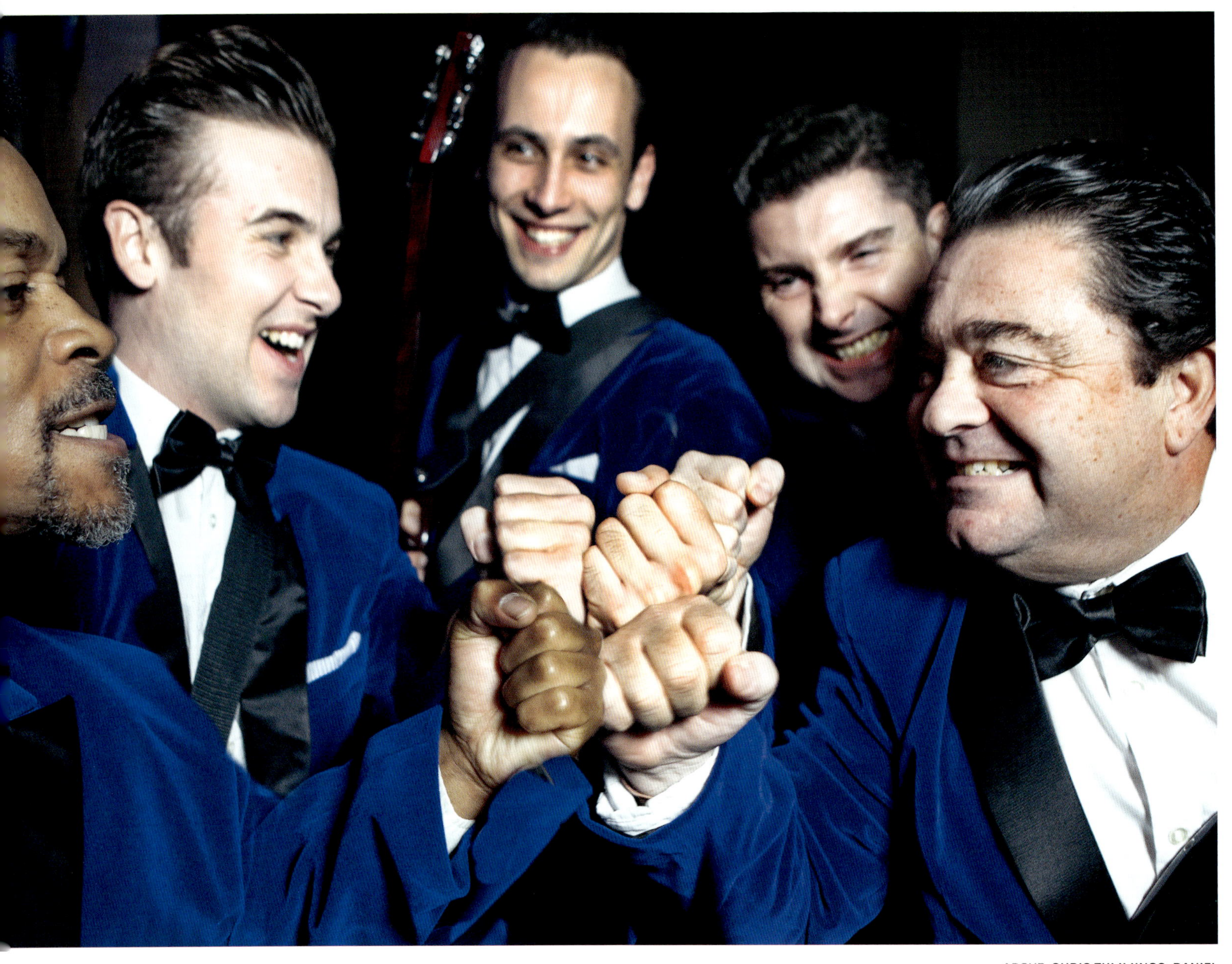

ABOVE: **CHRIS TUMMINGS, DANIEL MILES, JAMES LAWRENCE, LEE GILBERT, PHYLIP HARRIES, *ONE MAN, TWO GUVNORS*, WELSH TOUR, 2017**
Ramping up the energy, before bursting into action for a Welsh tour of the London hit.

OPPOSITE: **ANDREW RYAN, *CINDERELLA*, BIRMINGHAM HIPPODROME, 2016**
The skills for playing pantomime, with an unforgiving audience who demand to be entertained, are no less than for playing the classics. The timing and sense of the occasion have to be perfect.

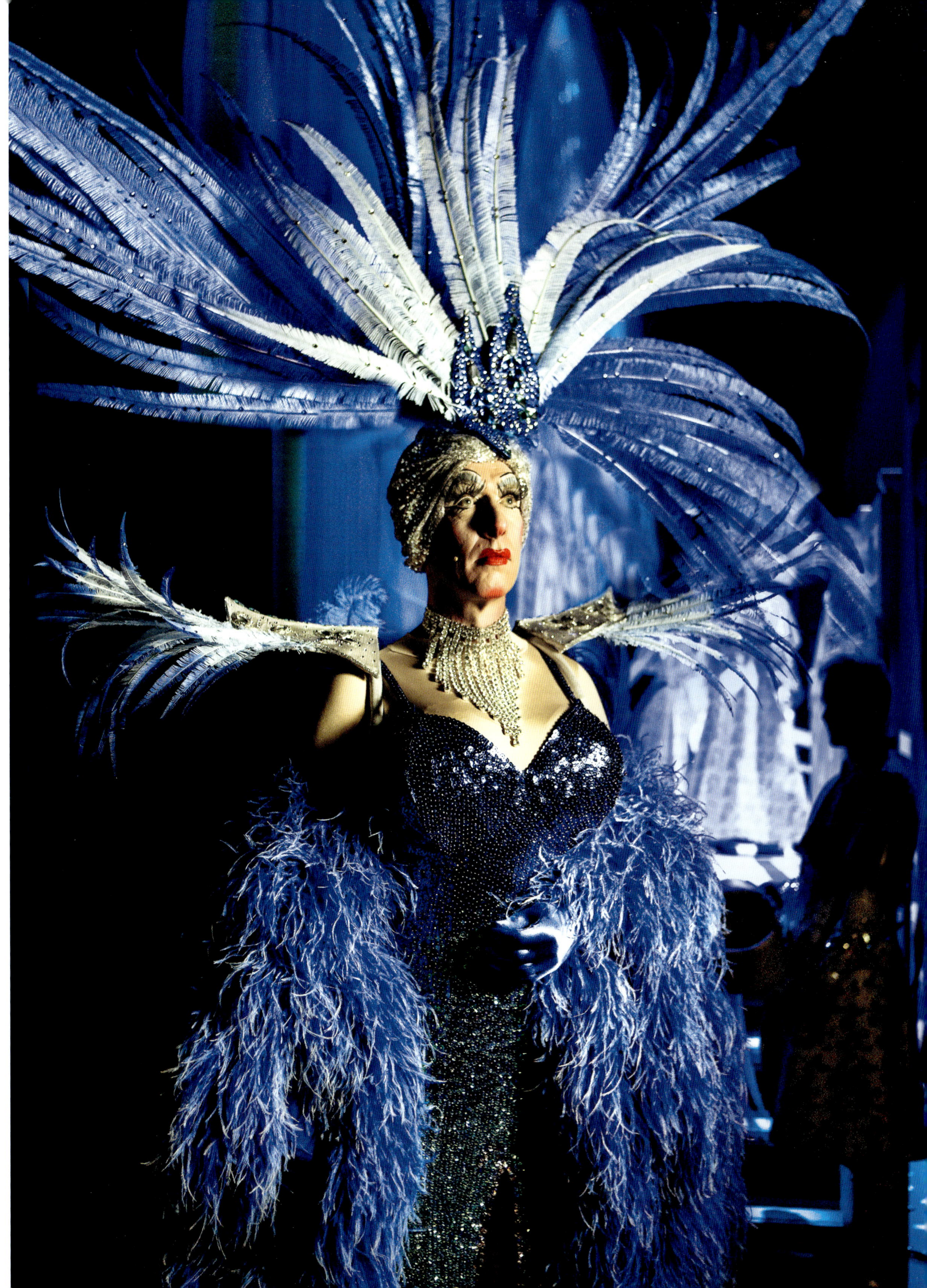

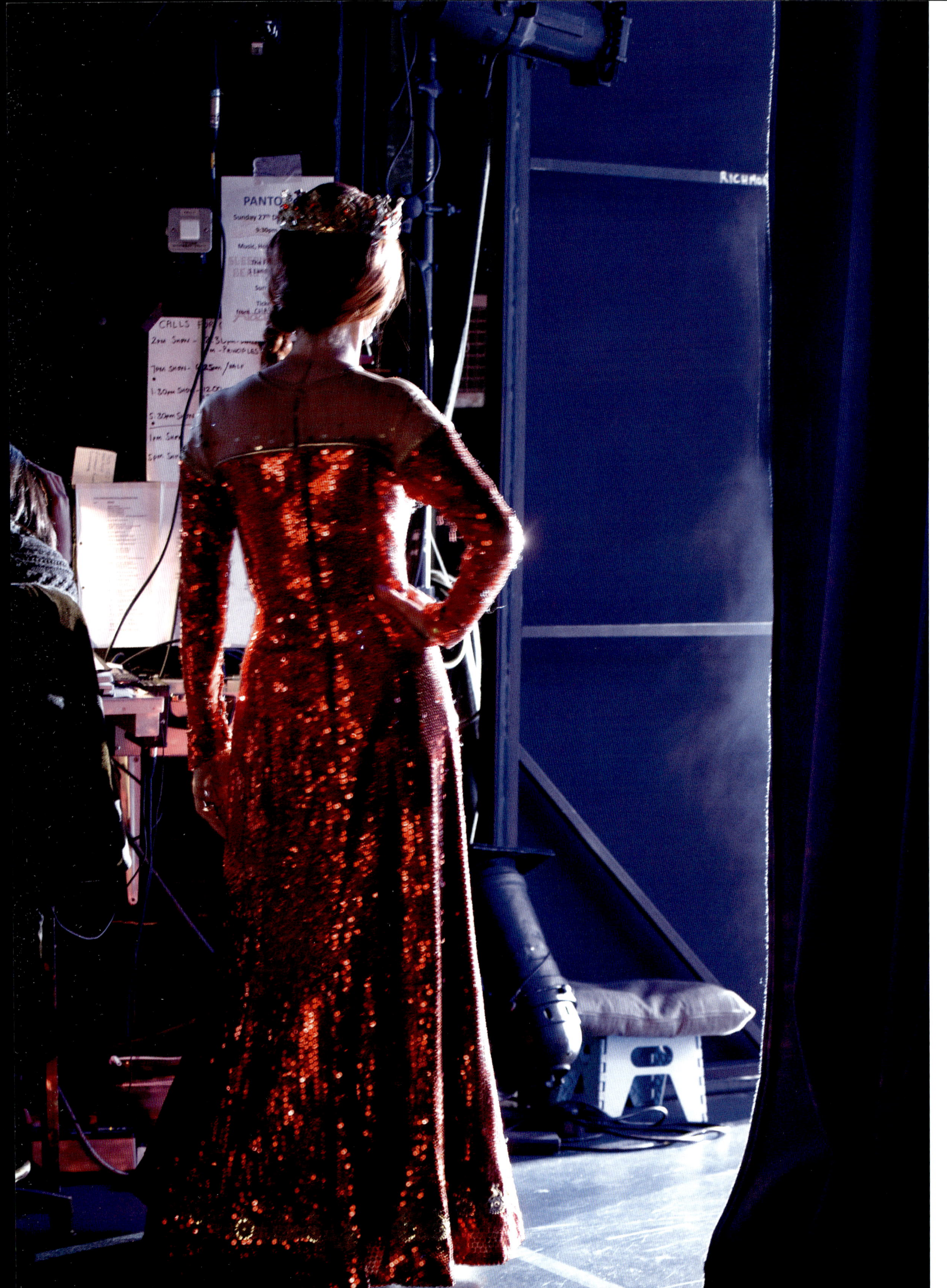

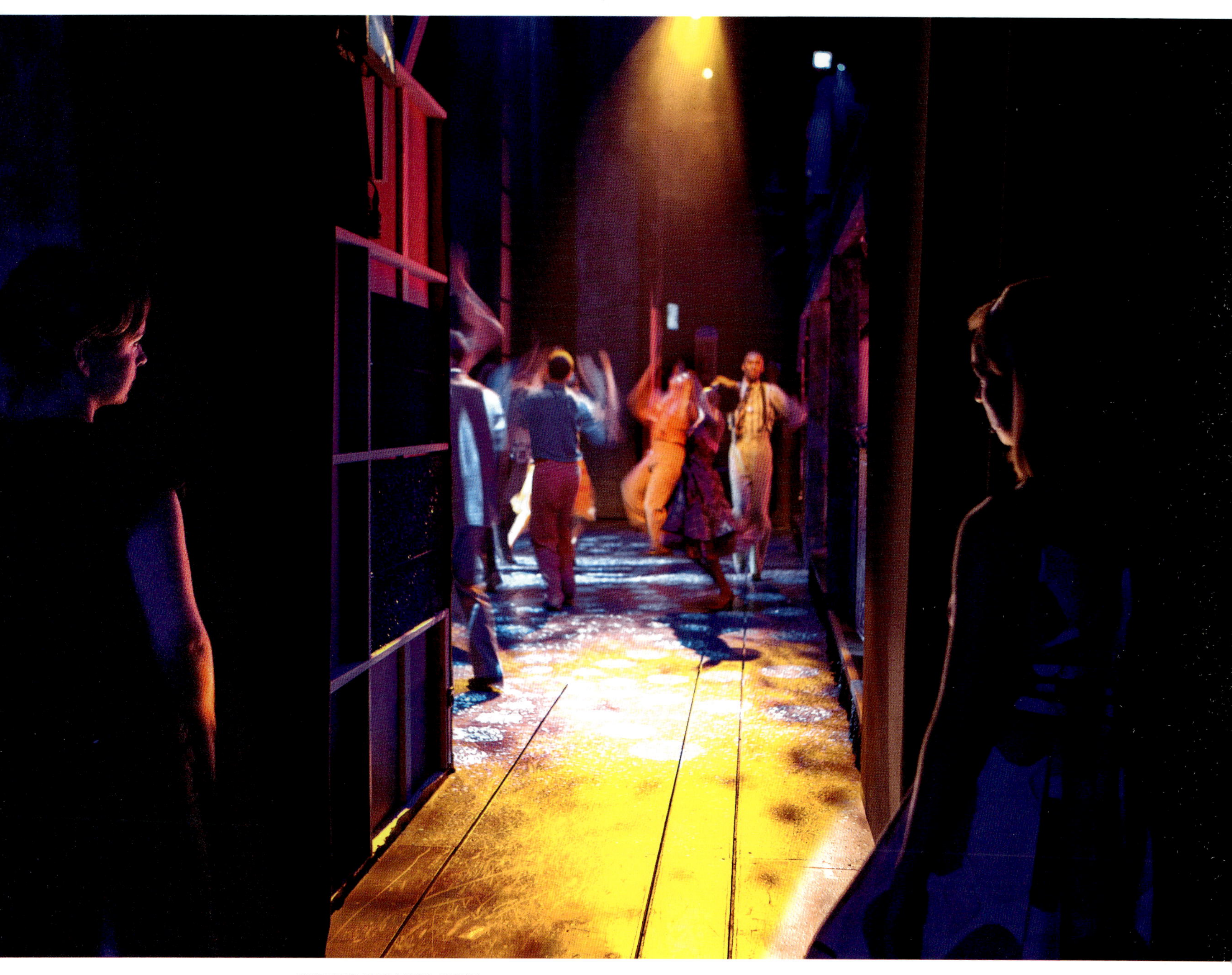

OPPOSITE: **JANE ASHER, *SNOW WHITE AND THE SEVEN DWARFS*, RICHMOND THEATRE, 2009**
Jane is about to take on a matinee audience, close to Christmas when expectations are high. She had them in the palm of her hand.

ABOVE: **MEMBERS OF THE CAST, *MEMPHIS*, SHAFTESBURY THEATRE, 2015**
Waiting to enter the scene.

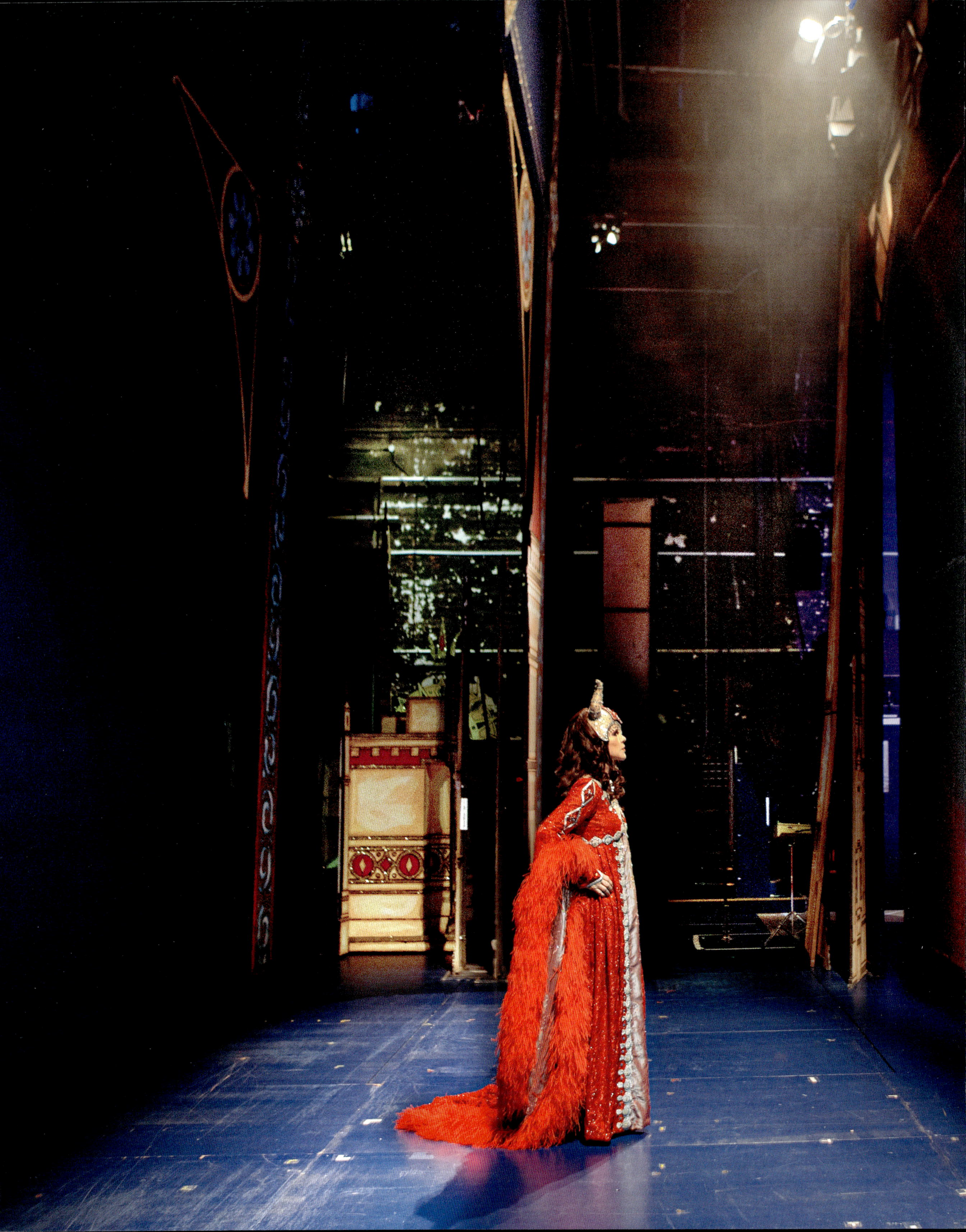

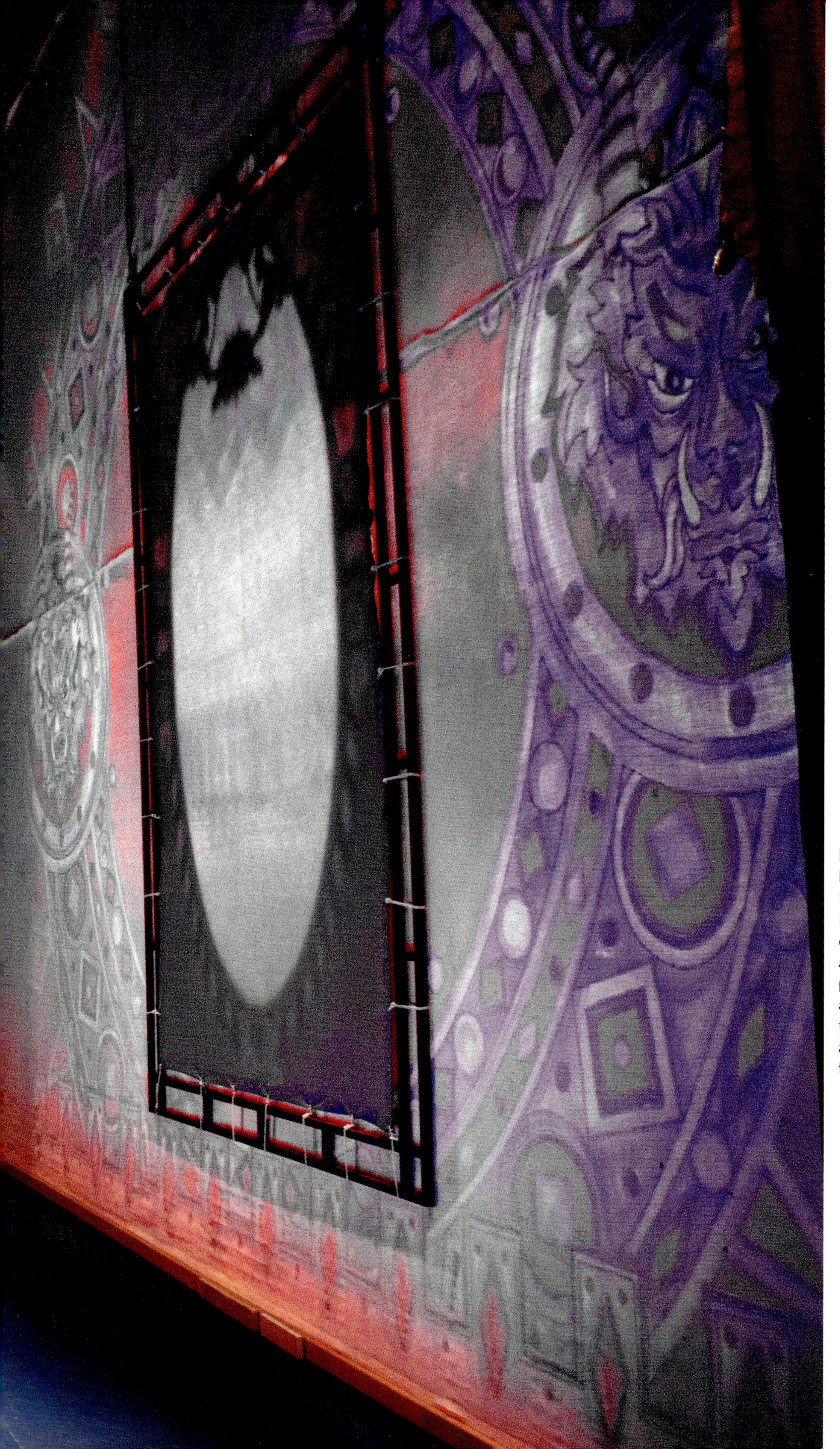

PRISCILLA PRESLEY, *SNOW WHITE*, NEW WIMBLEDON THEATRE, 2012
Being aware of her connection to Elvis, it was a relief to find Priscilla effortlessly charming. It took her a while to trust that in the English pantomime tradition, the more an audience boos the Lead Villainess the better her performance. She is about to open the show, just before the curtain rises.

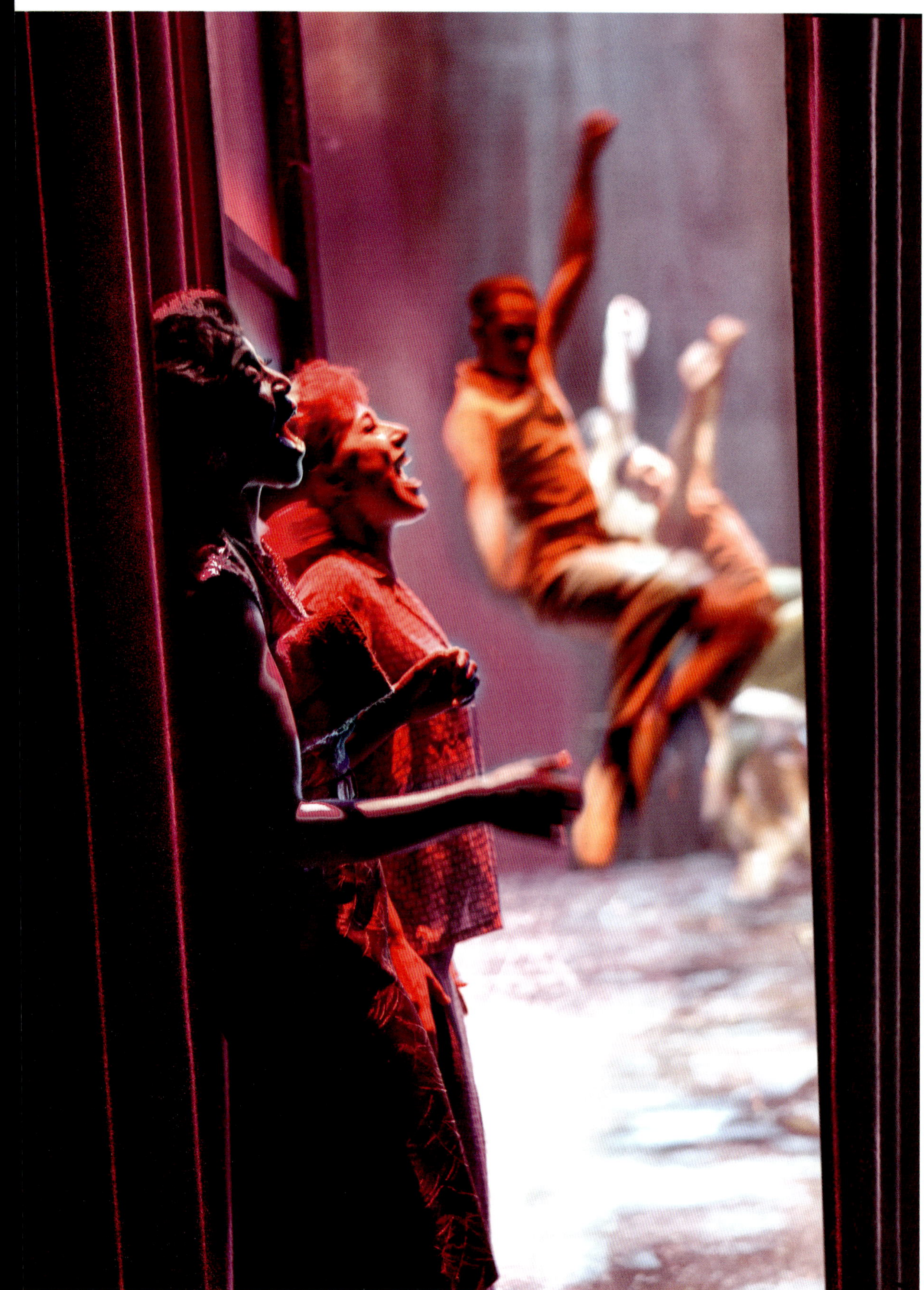

LEFT: **BEVERLEY KNIGHT AND CAST, *MEMPHIS*, SHAFTESBURY THEATRE, 2015**
Beverley is leading passionate vocals just off stage, to accentuate the harmony of the scene.

OPPOSITE: **GEORGE MacKAY, *THE CEMENT GARDEN*, VAULT FESTIVAL, 2014**
I was fortunate to see a young George before his rapid rise as one of the leading actors in demand.

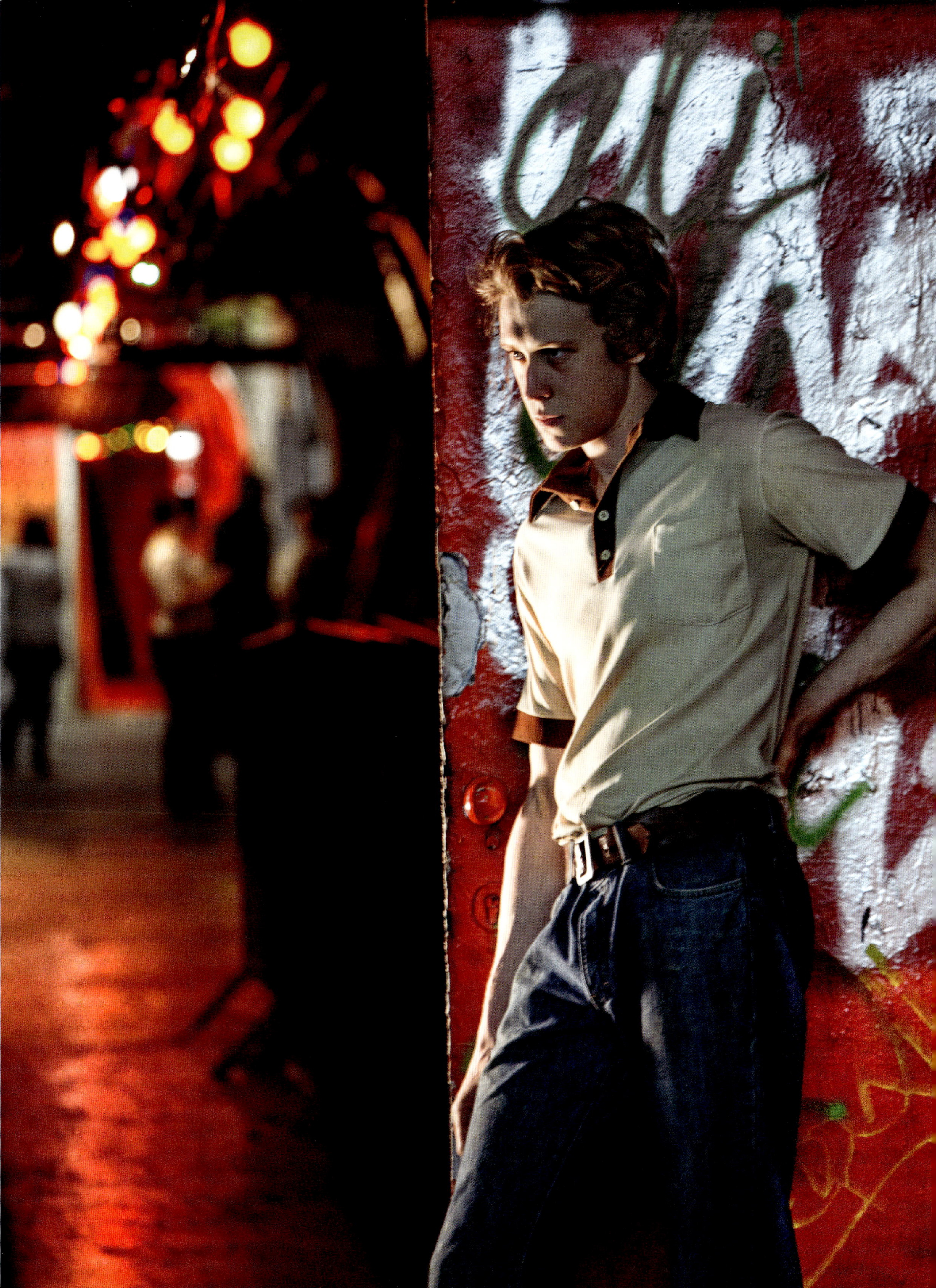

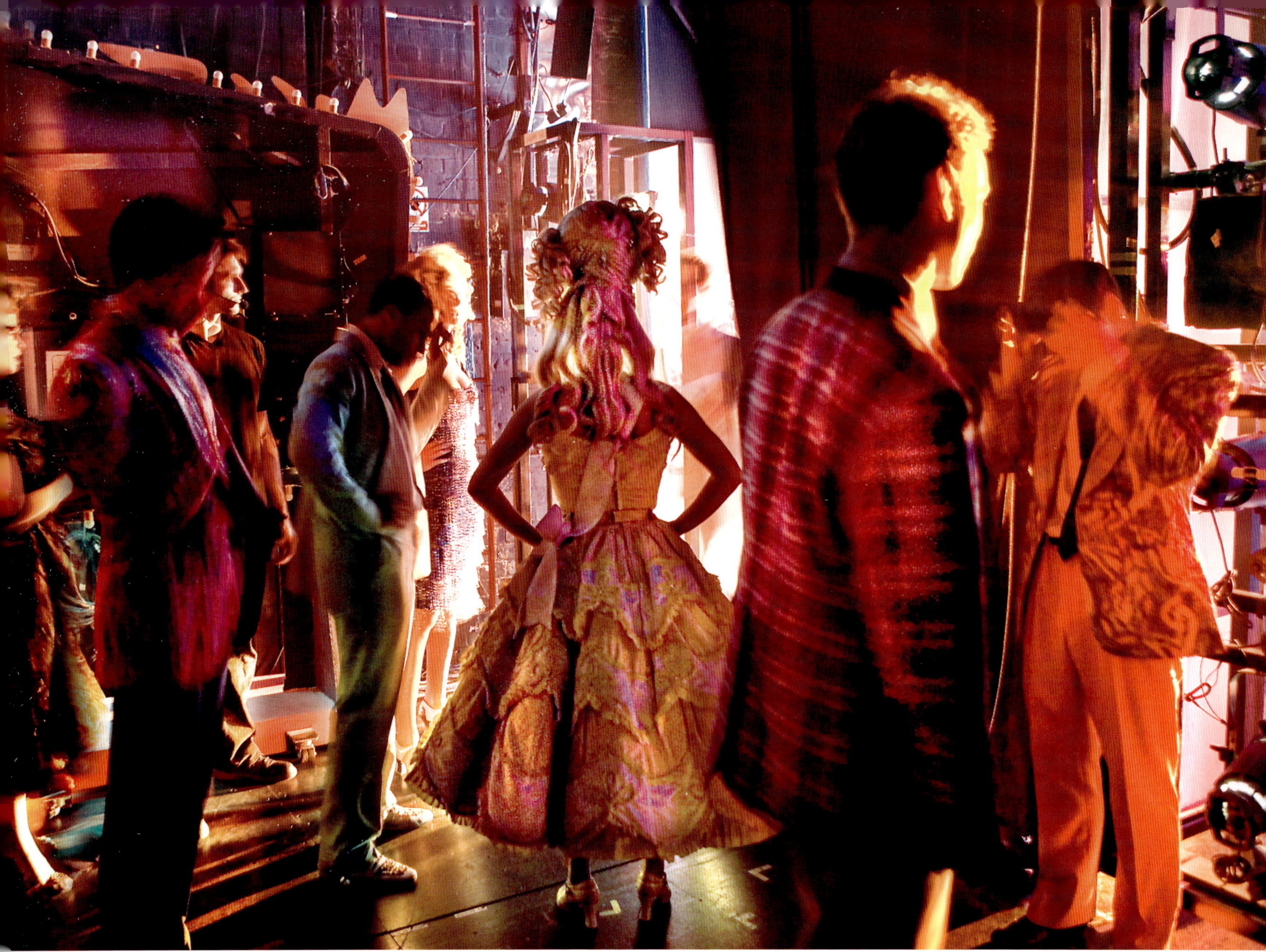

MEMBERS OF THE CAST, *HAIRSPRAY*, SHAFTESBURY THEATRE, 2009
Stage left, they are gathering for the next scene before entering the action.

MEMBERS OF THE CAST, *PRISCILLA QUEEN OF THE DESERT*, PALACE THEATRE, 2010
The actors have been given the green light to release a flurry of LGBT energy and colour onto the stage.

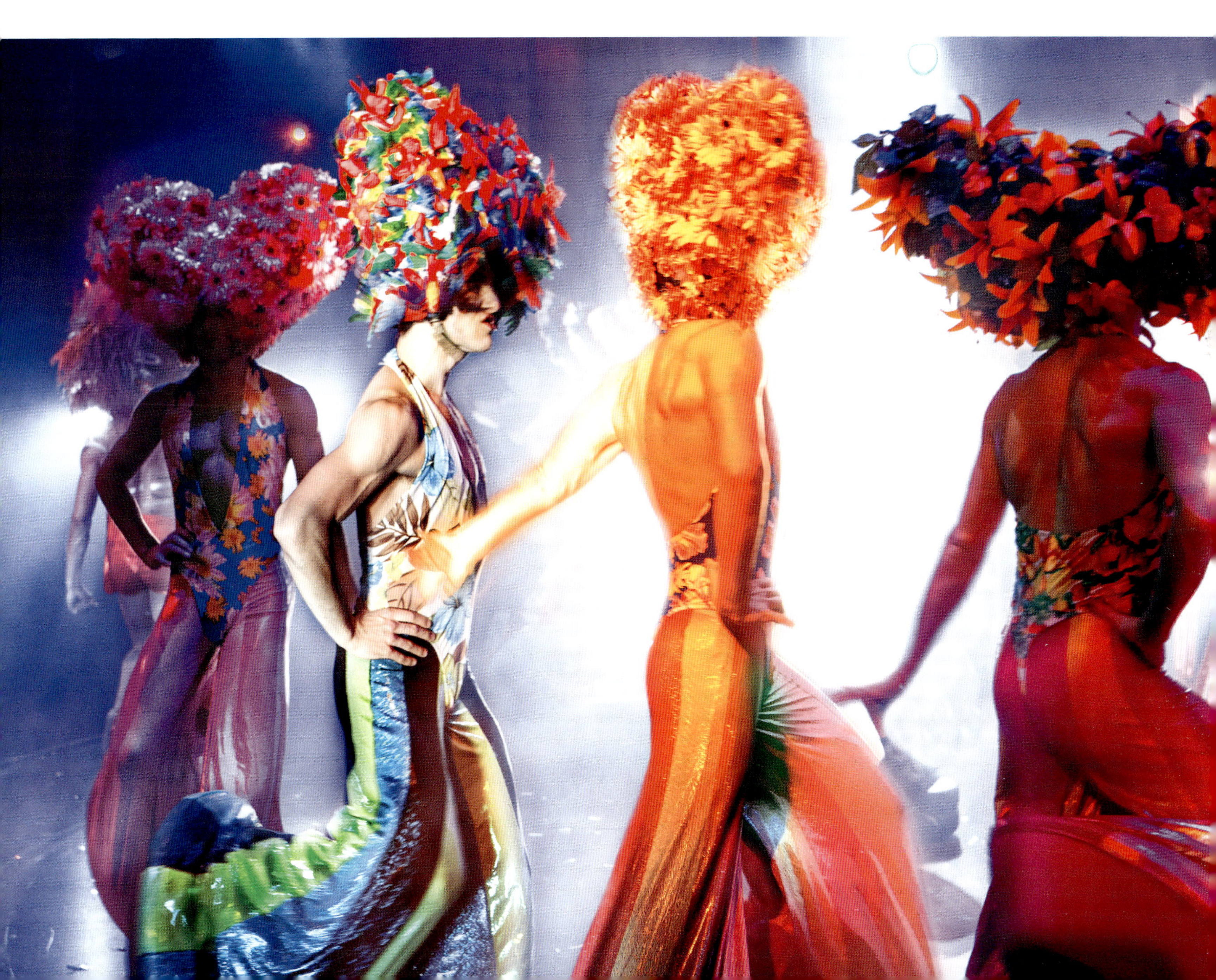

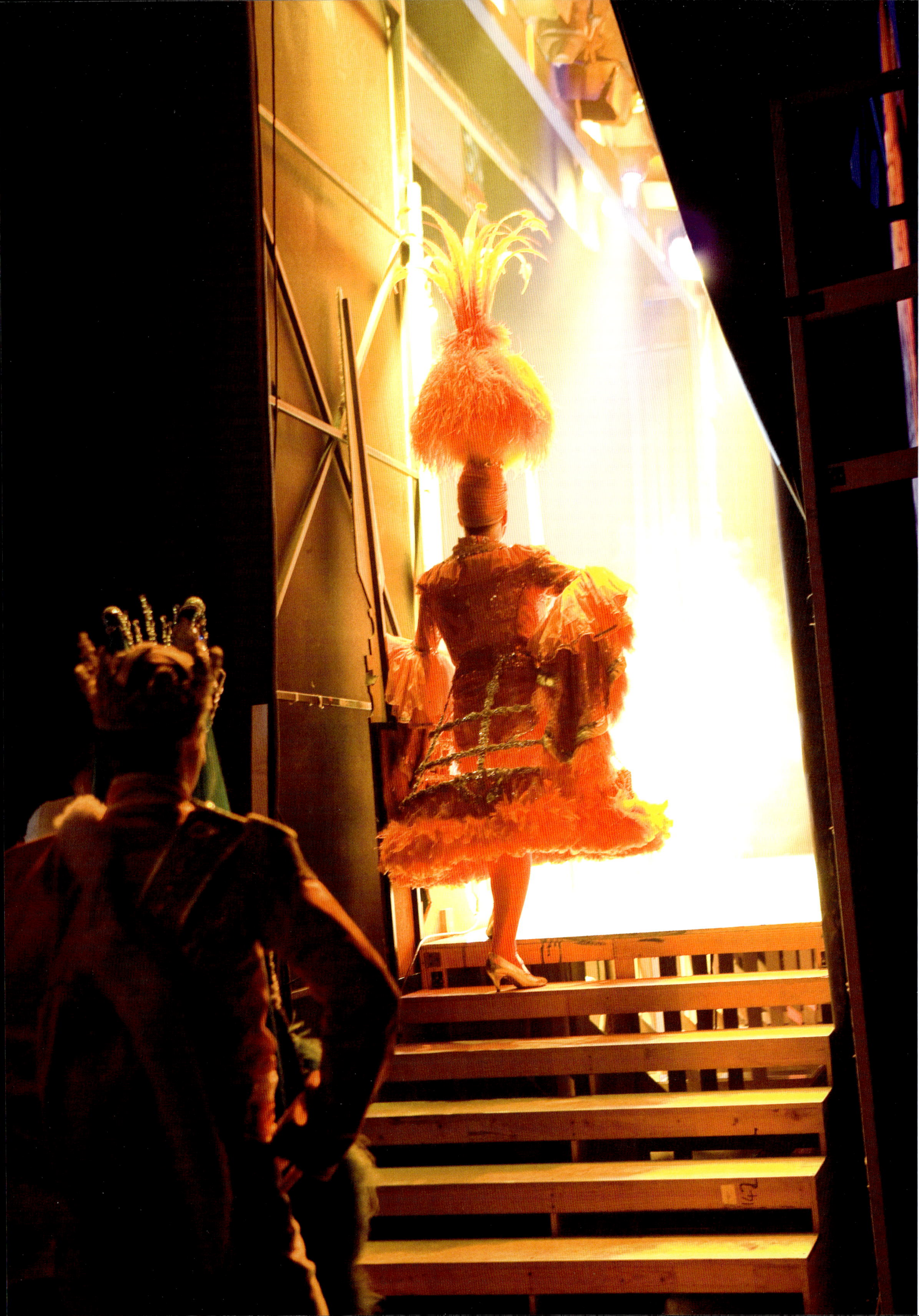

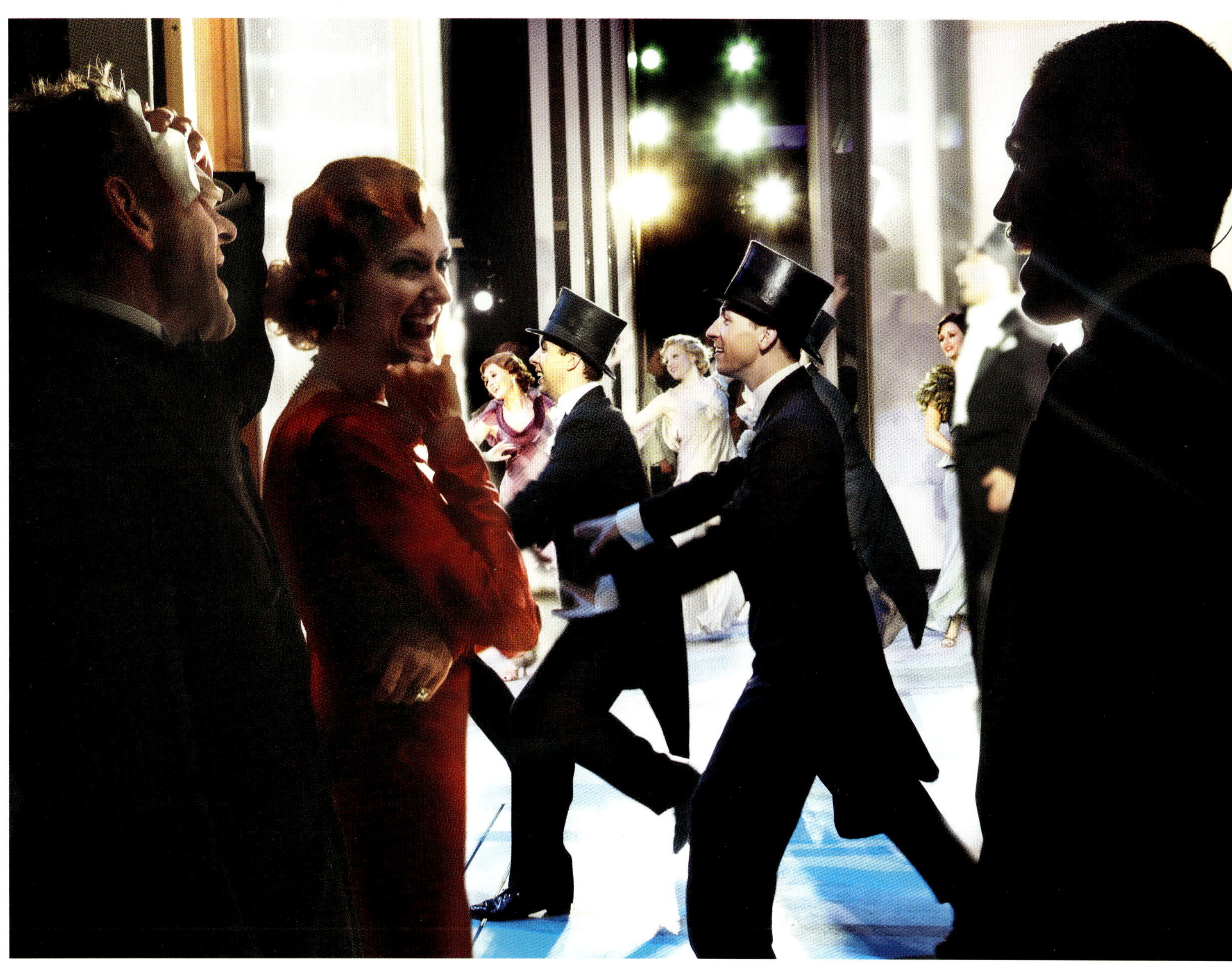

OPPOSITE: **MEMBERS OF THE CAST, *CINDERELLA*, LYRIC THEATRE HAMMERSMITH, 2012**
It is one step up, turn left and there are 1,000 more strangers to entertain. This could be Paris 1931 in black and white, the romanticism is all there.

ABOVE: **MEMBERS OF THE CAST, *TOP HAT*, ALDWYCH THEATRE, 2012**
It takes excitement, sweat and great skill to perform a top musical eight times a week. But for the audience it is sheer escapism.

FOLLOWING PAGES: **MEMBERS OF THE CAST, *CABARET*, SAVOY THEATRE, 2013**
The company taking a deserved curtain call after another physical and exhausting performance.

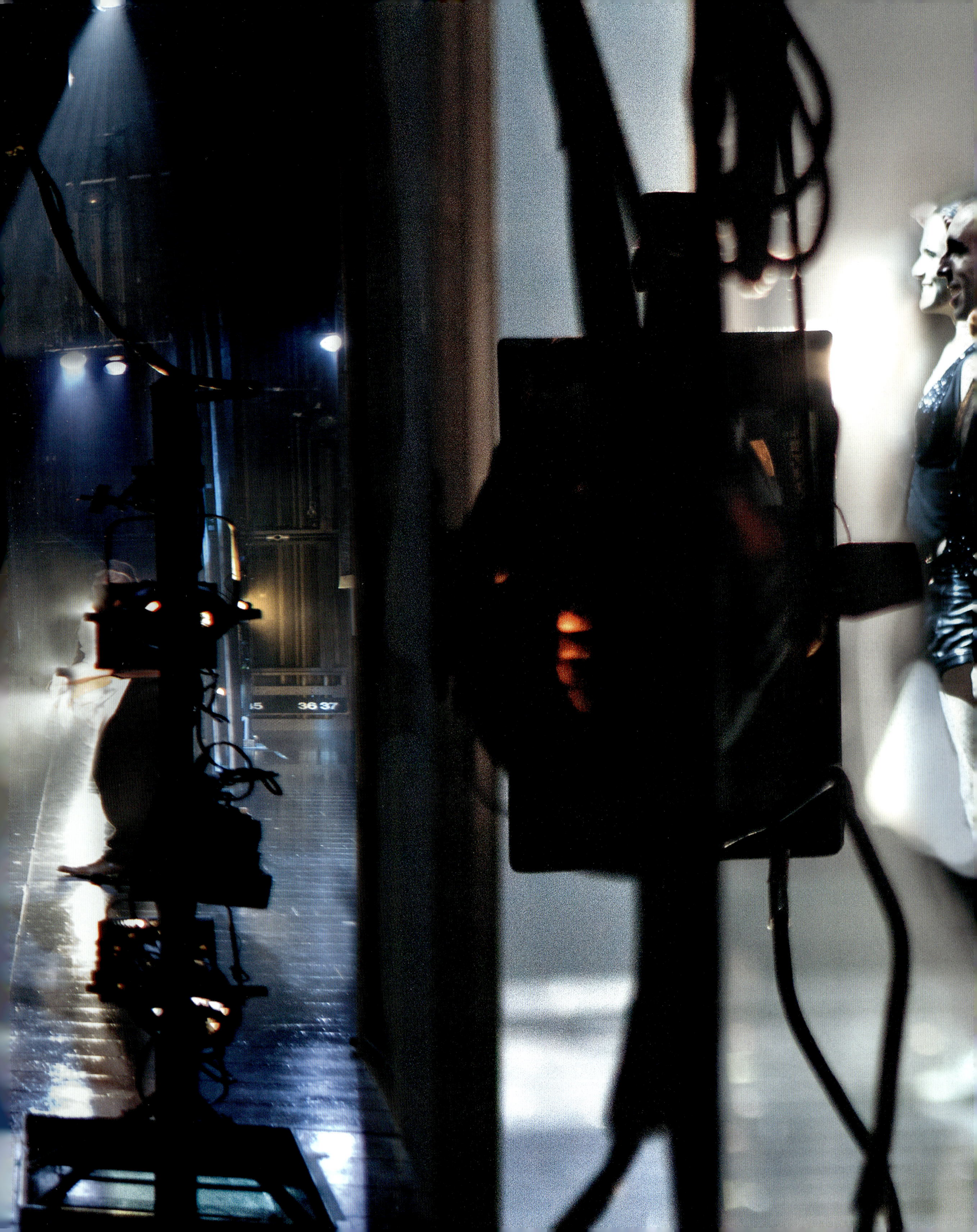
36 37

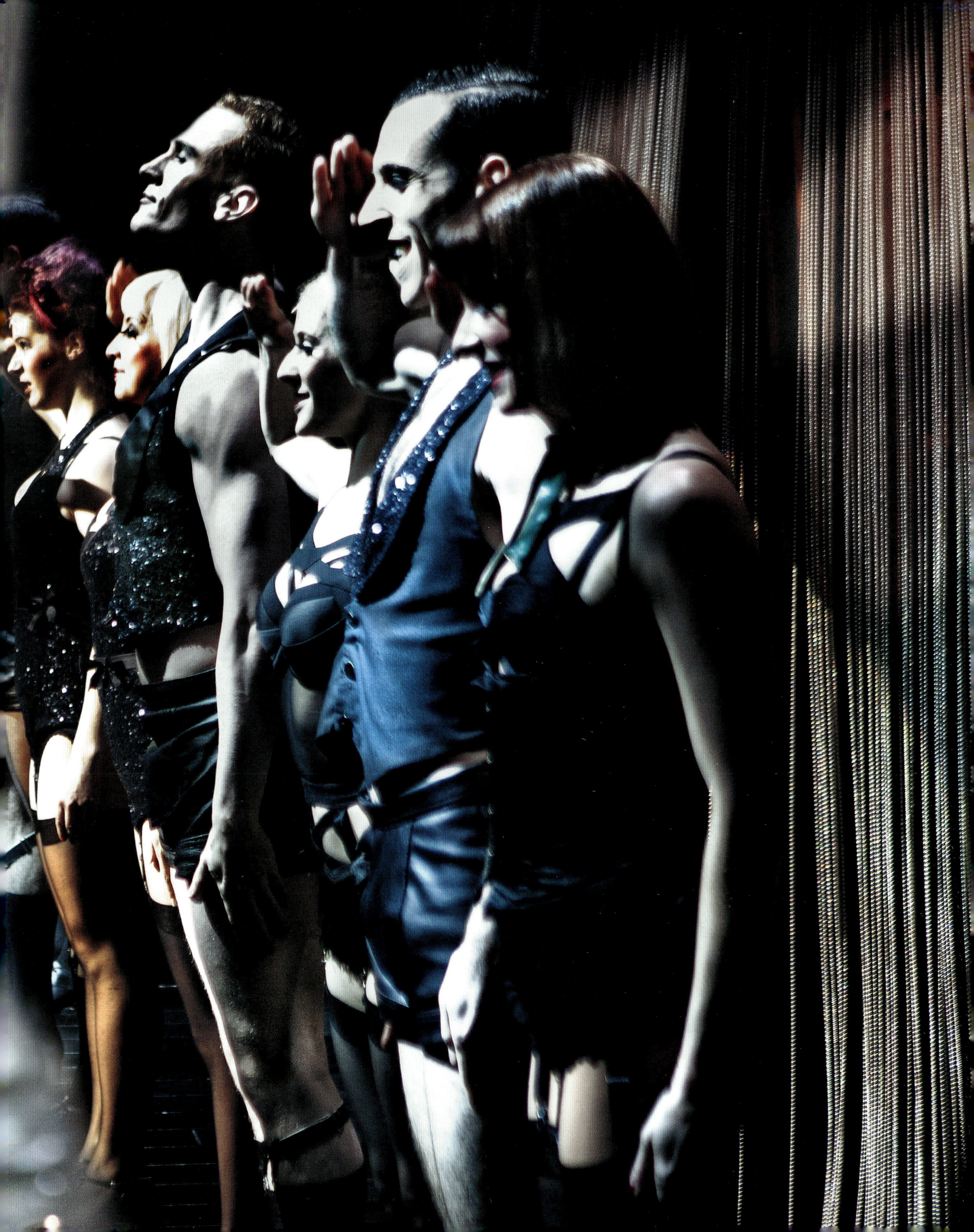

INDEX play titles are in italics, artists in roman

EXHIBITIONS

2019	The Half Lawrence Batley Theatre, Huddersfield
2018	Personal Theater Galerie Z22, Berlin
2017	The Half Schaezlerpalais, Augsburg
2014-15	The Half Bakhrushin Museum, Moscow
2014	I Kiss The World International Photography Festival, Amsterdam
2014	The Half Royal Shakespeare Company, Stratford
2013	The Half Theatre Royal, Plymouth
2013	Belarus Free Theatre Young Vic, London
2013	The Half Woodville Arts Centre, Gravesend
2012	The Half Northwall Arts Centre, Oxford
2012	The Making of *War Horse* National Theatre, London
2012	Simon Annand Photo 12, Paris
2012	The Half The Players, New York
2011	Simon Annand Idea Generation Gallery, London
2011	The Half Stephen Joseph Theatre, Scarborough
2010	The Half Focus Contemporary, Cape Town
2010	The Half V&A Museum, London
2009	The Half V&A Tour of UK, including The Lowry, Salford
2009	Cello Cadenza Kronberg Academy, Frankfurt
2009	The Half International Photography Festival, Arles
2008	The Half National Theatre, London
2005	The Dressing Room Theatre Museum, London (Exhibition of the Year Award)
1985	*The House of Bernarda Alba*/Núria Espert Lyric Theatre Hammersmith, London
1983	*Crime and Punishment*/Yuri Lyubimov Lyric Theatre Hammersmith, London

ACKNOWLEDGEMENTS

A photographer will only find what he or she is looking for. Here, it is the actors' discipline. *Time to Act* is on their side, supporting them. Its point of view is not predatory, and this trust has been rewarded by the actors.

A letter of intention, stating that images would be used to celebrate theatre as live performance, was sent prior to each backstage session. Letters were subsequently written to all the actors checking that they like their images. My gratitude to all the actors who have agreed to participate in *Time to Act*.

Sometimes the circumstances require an extra light, and therefore someone to hold it. It is not easy being an assistant and the role requires both empathy and reliability. The assistant needs to be fully aware of the action, in order to light it, but not engage with the subject unless the actor initiates an exchange, however tempting it might be to do so. Over the thirty-seven years of this monograph there have been a number of assistants who have helped to make it happen. Very grateful thanks are given to every one of them.

Also the company managers, floor managers, dressers, wig setters, stage-door keepers and anyone backstage who has supported this project. There are a special few who have gone way beyond the call of duty, many times, and they will know who they are.

This book could not have been realised without the input of Barney Wan, a legendary designer with impeccable credentials and talent. The photographers Barney has art directed include Helmut Newton, Eve Arnold, Cecil Beaton, Snowdon, Richard Avedon, Irving Penn, David Bailey, Bruce Webber, Guy Bourdin and William Klein. He led teams at British *Vogue* and *Queen*, and worked with French and Italian *Vogue*, *The Tatler* and *The Sunday Times*. Once a wizard, always a wizard.

Since 1983 many people have contributed to and supported this monograph of dressing-room photographs, whose aim is to celebrate theatre as live performance. Peter Wilson has encouraged and supported me from the very beginning. A true friend and colleague whose skill, wit and resources have steered this boat safely into harbour.

It is a special honour that two of my closest allies, Cate Blanchett and Victoria Broackes, agreed to write the foreword and the introduction.

I am particularly grateful to Christian Hutter and his wonderful team at Salz und Silber, including Andrea Wintermayr and Vanessa Magson, who have made this latest instalment a reality. Louise Brody designed the remarkable layout.

FRONT COVER: Phoebe Waller-Bridge, *Rope*, Almeida, 2009
BACK COVER Clockwise from top left: Paapa Essiedu, *Hamlet*, RSC, 2016; Lindsay Duncan, *Hay Fever*, Noël Coward Theatre, 2012; Ian McKellen, Patrick Stewart, *Waiting for Godot*, Theatre Royal Haymarket, 2009; Judi Dench, *Peter and Alice*, Noël Coward Theatre, 2013

Published in its Original Edition 2020 with the title:
Time to Act – An intimate photographic portrait of actors backstage
by Hutter und Donner GmbH, Salz und Silber, Gallery & Publisher

Salz und Silber
Annastraße 3
86150 Augsburg
Germany
www.salzundsilber.de

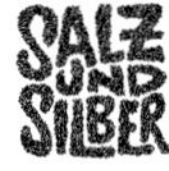

For the English edition:

Uitgeverij Terra is part of Uitgeverij TerraLannoo bv
P.O. Box 23202
1100 DS Amsterdam
The Netherlands
info@terralannoo.nl
www.terra-publishing.com

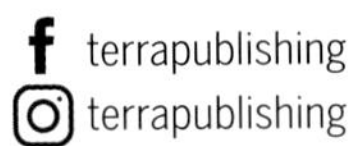
terrapublishing
terrapublishing

ISBN 978 90 8989 836 4
NUR 653

Publisher: Christian Hutter
Picture editing: Simon Annand, Barney Wan
Project Management: Vanessa Magson-Mann, Andrea Wintermayr
Index/Exhibitions texts: Laura Straub
Proofreading: Vanessa Magson-Mann

Design and picture selection: Louise Brody, lbdesign
Repro and pre-press: Gebhardt Reproduktion, Berlin

Printing and Binding: Printer Trento Italy
Paper: 150g Gardamatt Art